CompTIA Securit~
SYO-701 Cert Gu

T0073878

Companion Website and Pearson Test Prep Access Code

Access interactive study tools on this book's companion website, including practice test software, review exercises, Key Term flash card application, a study planner, and more!

To access the companion website, simply follow these steps:

1. Go to www.pearsonitcertification.com/register.
2. Enter the **print book ISBN**: 9780138293086.
3. Answer the security question to validate your purchase.
4. Go to your account page.
5. Click on the **Registered Products** tab.
6. Under the book listing, click on the **Access Bonus Content** link.

When you register your book, your Pearson Test Prep practice test access code will automatically be populated with the book listing under the Registered Products tab. You will need this code to access the practice test that comes with this book. You can redeem the code at **PearsonTestPrep.com**. Simply choose Pearson IT Certification as your product group and log into the site with the same credentials you used to register your book. Click the **Activate New Product** button and enter the access code. More detailed instructions on how to redeem your access code for both the online and desktop versions can be found on the companion website.

If you have any issues accessing the companion website or obtaining your Pearson Test Prep practice test access code, you can contact our support team by going to **pearsonitp.echelp.org**.

CompTIA® Security+ SY0-701 Cert Guide

Lewis Heuermann

Pearson

CompTIA® Security+ SY0-701 Cert Guide

Lewis Heuermann

Copyright © 2024 by Pearson Education, Inc.

Hoboken, New Jersey

All rights reserved. No part of this book shall be reproduced, stored in a retrieval system, or transmitted by any means, electronic, mechanical, photocopying, recording, or otherwise, without written permission from the publisher. No patent liability is assumed with respect to the use of the information contained herein. Although every precaution has been taken in the preparation of this book, the publisher and author assume no responsibility for errors or omissions. Nor is any liability assumed for damages resulting from the use of the information contained herein.

Please contact us with concerns about any potential bias at https://www.pearson.com/report-bias.html.

ISBN-13: 978-0-13-829308-6
ISBN-10: 0-13-829308-2

Library of Congress Cataloging-in-Publication Data: 2024931504

1 2024

Trademarks

All terms mentioned in this book that are known to be trademarks or service marks have been appropriately capitalized. Pearson IT Certification cannot attest to the accuracy of this information. Use of a term in this book should not be regarded as affecting the validity of any trademark or service mark.

Warning and Disclaimer

Every effort has been made to make this book as complete and as accurate as possible, but no warranty or fitness is implied. The information provided is on an "as is" basis. The author and the publisher shall have neither liability nor responsibility to any person or entity with respect to any loss or damages arising from the information contained in this book.

Special Sales

For information about buying this title in bulk quantities, or for special sales opportunities (which may include electronic versions; custom cover designs; and content particular to your business, training goals, marketing focus, or branding interests), please contact our corporate sales department at corpsales@pearsoned.com or (800) 382-3419.

For government sales inquiries, please contact governmentsales@pearsoned.com.

For questions about sales outside the U.S., please contact intlcs@pearson.com.

All terms mentioned in this book that are known to be trademarks or service marks have been appropriately capitalized. Pearson IT Certification cannot attest to the accuracy of this information. Use of a term in this book should not be regarded as affecting the validity of any trademark or service mark.

Microsoft and/or its respective suppliers make no representations about the suitability of the information contained in the documents and related graphics published as part of the services for any purpose. All such documents and related graphics are provided "as is" without warranty of any kind. Microsoft and/or its respective suppliers hereby disclaim all warranties and conditions with regard to this information, including all warranties and conditions of merchantability, whether express, implied or statutory, fitness for a particular purpose, title and non-infringement. In no event shall Microsoft and/or its respective suppliers be liable for any special, indirect or consequential damages or any damages whatsoever resulting from loss of use, data or profits, whether in an action of contract, negligence or other tortious action, arising out of or in connection with the use or performance of information available from the services.

The documents and related graphics contained herein could include technical inaccuracies or typographical errors. Changes are periodically added to the information herein. Microsoft and/or its respective suppliers may make improvements and/or changes in the product(s) and/or the program(s) described herein at any time. Partial screenshots may be viewed in full within the software version specified.

Microsoft® and Windows® are registered trademarks of the Microsoft Corporation in the U.S.A. and other countries. Screenshots and icons reprinted with permission from the Microsoft Corporation. This book is not sponsored or endorsed by or affiliated with the Microsoft Corporation.

GM K12, Early Career and Professional Learning
Soo Kang

Director, ITP Product Management
Brett Bartow

Executive Editor
Nancy Davis

Development Editor
Ellie C. Bru

Managing Editor
Sandra Schroeder

Senior Project Editor
Tonya Simpson

Copy Editor
Kitty Wilson

Indexer
Timothy Wright

Proofreader
Barbara Mack

Technical Editor
Chris Crayton

Publishing Coordinator
Cindy Teeters

Cover Designer
Chuti Prasertsith

Compositor
codeMantra

Contents at a Glance

Table of Contents

About the Author

Lewis Heuermann, CISSP, PMP, is a Navy submarine veteran and seasoned cybersecurity consultant who combines his extensive practical experience with deep academic insight to make cybersecurity accessible to all learners. His diverse background includes roles in systems and network engineering, network defense analysis, and cyber risk management. As a professor, he has developed and taught courses in cybersecurity and data analytics, utilizing tools like Python, SQL, Power BI, and Tableau. Lewis also holds several key IT certifications.

Dedication

To Katie, my loving wife, whose unwavering support and encouragement have been my constant. Your ability to keep me caffeinated and focused during those long-day and late-night writing sessions has been nothing short of miraculous. You were the one who finally convinced me to stop saying "One day…" when I talked about writing a book and instead say "Today…."

To Dominique, thank you for being a steadfast presence during all those early years of countless nights I spent on the phone troubleshooting network and server issues. Your patience, encouragement, and understanding during those challenging years played a significant role in my journey.

And to my wonderful children: When people tell you that you "can't," it just means they couldn't. Keep pushing and keep learning because "can't" never could do anything.

—Lewis

Acknowledgments

I extend my heartfelt thanks to the Pearson team, whose collective efforts have been instrumental in bringing this book to fruition. Ellie, your remarkable skill in making all the pieces of this complex puzzle fit seamlessly together is truly amazing. Chris, your meticulous attention to detail has elevated the quality of this work beyond my wildest imagination. Kitty, your sharp copyediting eye and expert grammar makes the pages sing!

Nancy, you have been the foundation of our team, guiding us with kindness, support, and an unwavering commitment to our collective goal. You saw something in me early and helped turn my dream into a reality. To all of my many mentors over the years, thank you for taking the time to slowly explain things to me when you didn't have the time to slow down. Each of you has contributed to this journey in unique and meaningful ways, and for that, I am eternally grateful.

About the Technical Reviewer

Chris Crayton is a technical consultant, trainer, author, and industry-leading technical editor. He has worked as a computer technology and networking instructor, information security director, network administrator, network engineer, and PC specialist. Chris has authored several print and online books on PC repair, CompTIA A+, CompTIA Security+, and Microsoft Windows. He has also served as technical editor and content contributor on numerous technical titles for several of the leading publishing companies. He holds numerous industry certifications, has been recognized with many professional and teaching awards, and has served as a state-level SkillsUSA final competition judge. Chris tech edited and contributed to this book to make it better for students and those wishing to better their lives.

We Want to Hear from You!

As the reader of this book, *you* are our most important critic and commentator. We value your opinion and want to know what we're doing right, what we could do better, what areas you'd like to see us publish in, and any other words of wisdom you're willing to pass our way.

We welcome your comments. You can email or write to let us know what you did or didn't like about this book—as well as what we can do to make our books better.

Please note that we cannot help you with technical problems related to the topic of this book.

When you write, please be sure to include this book's title and author as well as your name and email address. We will carefully review your comments and share them with the author and editors who worked on the book.

Email: community@informit.com

Reader Services

Register your copy of *CompTIA Security+ SY0-701 Cert Guide* for convenient access to downloads, updates, and corrections as they become available. To start the registration process, go to www.pearsonitcertification.com/register and log in or create an account*. Enter the product ISBN 9780138293086 and click Submit. When the process is complete, you will find any available bonus content under Registered Products.

*Be sure to check the box that you would like to hear from us to receive exclusive discounts on future editions of this product.

Introduction

Welcome to *CompTIA Security+ SY0-701 Cert Guide*. The CompTIA Security+ certification is widely accepted as one of the first security certifications you should attempt to attain in your information technology (IT) career. The CompTIA Security+ certification exam is designed to be a vendor-neutral exam that measures your knowledge of industry-standard technologies and methodologies. It acts as a great stepping stone to other vendor-specific certifications and careers. We developed this book to be something you can study from for the exam and keep on your bookshelf for later use as a security resource.

We would like to note that it would not be possible to cover all security concepts in depth in a single book. However, the Security+ exam objectives are looking for a basic level of computer, networking, and organizational security knowledge. Keep this in mind while reading through this text and remember that the main goal of this text is to help you pass the Security+ exam, not to have an encyclopedic knowledge of everything security—though you might get there someday!

As you read through this book, you will begin building your foundational knowledge, gaining hands-on familiarity and the know-how to pass the CompTIA Security+ exam. Good luck on the exam!

Goals and Methods

The number-one goal of this book is to help you pass the SY0-701 version of the CompTIA Security+ certification exam. To that effect, we have filled this book and practice exams with hundreds of questions/answers and explanations, including two full practice exams. The exams are located in Pearson Test Prep practice test software, in a custom test environment. These tests are meant to check your knowledge and prepare you for the real exam.

The CompTIA Security+ certification exam requires familiarity with computer security theory and hands-on knowledge. To aid you in understanding the Security+ certification objectives, this book uses the following methods:

- **Opening topics list:** This list defines the topics covered in the chapter.

- **Foundation Topics:** This is the heart of the chapter, explaining various topics from a theory-based standpoint as well as from a hands-on perspective. This section of each chapter includes in-depth descriptions, tables, and figures that are geared toward helping you build your knowledge so that you can pass the exam. Each chapter covers a full objective from the CompTIA Security+ exam blueprint.

- **Key Topics:** The Key Topic icons indicate important figures, tables, and lists of information that you should know for the exam. They are interspersed throughout the chapter and are listed in table format at the end of the chapter.

- **Key Terms:** Key terms without definitions are listed at the end of each chapter. See whether you can define them and then check your work against the definitions provided in the glossary.

- **Review Questions:** These questions and answers with explanations are meant to gauge your knowledge of the subjects covered in the chapter. If an answer to a question doesn't come readily to you, be sure to review the corresponding portion of the chapter.

- **Practice Exams:** Practice exams are included in the Pearson Test Prep practice test software. These exams test your knowledge and skills in a realistic testing environment. Take them after you have read through the entire book. Gain a thorough understanding of each one before moving on to the next one.

Who Should Read This Book?

This book is for anyone who wants to start or advance a career in computer security. Readers of this book may range from persons taking a Security+ course to individuals already in the field who want to keep their skills sharp or perhaps retain their job due to a company policy mandating that they take the Security+ exam. Some information assurance professionals who work for the Department of Defense (DoD) or have privileged access to DoD systems are required to become Security+ certified as per DoD directive 8570.01-Manual.

This book is also designed for people who plan on taking additional security-related certifications after the CompTIA Security+ exam. The book is designed in such a way to offer an easy transition to future certification studies.

Although not a prerequisite, it is recommended that CompTIA Security+ candidates have at least two years of IT administration experience, with an emphasis on hands-on and technical security concepts. The CompTIA Network+ certification is also recommended as a prerequisite. Before you begin your Security+ studies, you are expected to understand computer topics such as how to install operating systems and applications and networking topics such as how to configure IP addressing and what a VLAN is. This book shows you how to secure these technologies and protect against possible exploits and attacks. Generally, for people looking to enter the IT field, the CompTIA Security+ certification is attained after the A+ and Network+ certifications.

CompTIA Security+ Exam Topics

If you haven't downloaded the Security+ certification exam objectives from the CompTIA website (https://certification.comptia.org), do so now. Save the PDF file and print it out as well. It's a big document, and you should review it carefully. Use the blueprint's exam objectives list and acronyms list to aid in your studies while you use this book.

The following tables are excerpts from the exam objectives document. Table I-1 lists the CompTIA Security+ domains and each domain's percentage of the exam.

Table I-1 CompTIA Security+ Exam Domains

Domain	Exam Topic	% of Exam
1.0	General Security Concepts	12%
2.0	Threats, Vulnerabilities, and Mitigations	22%
3.0	Security Architecture	18%
4.0	Security Operations	28%
5.0	Security Program Management and Oversight	20%

The Security+ domains are further broken down into individual objectives. Table I-2 lists the CompTIA Security+ exam objectives and their related chapters in this book. It does not list the bullets and sub-bullets for each objective.

Table I-2 CompTIA Security+ Exam Objectives

Objective	Chapter(s)
1.1 Compare and contrast various types of security controls.	1
1.2 Summarize fundamental security concepts.	2
1.3 Explain the importance of change management processes and the impact to security.	3
1.4 Explain the importance of using appropriate cryptographic solutions.	4
2.1 Compare and contrast common threat actors and motivations.	5
2.2 Explain common threat vectors and attack surfaces.	6
2.3 Explain various types of vulnerabilities.	7
2.4 Given a scenario, analyze indicators of malicious activity.	8

Objective	Chapter(s)
2.5 Explain the purpose of mitigation techniques used to secure the enterprise.	9
3.1 Compare and contrast security implications of different architecture models.	10
3.2 Given a scenario, apply security principles to secure enterprise infrastructure.	11
3.3 Compare and contrast concepts and strategies to protect data.	12
3.4 Explain the importance of resilience and recovery in security architecture.	13
4.1 Given a scenario, apply common security techniques to computing resources.	14
4.2 Explain the security implications of proper hardware, software, and data asset management.	15
4.3 Explain various activities associated with vulnerability management.	16
4.4 Explain security alerting and monitoring concepts and tools.	17
4.5 Given a scenario, modify enterprise capabilities to enhance security.	18
4.6 Given a scenario, implement and maintain identity and access management.	19
4.7 Explain the importance of automation and orchestration related to secure operations.	20
4.8 Explain appropriate incident response activities.	21
4.9 Given a scenario, use data sources to support an investigation.	22
5.1 Summarize elements of effective security governance.	23
5.2 Explain elements of the risk management process.	24
5.3 Explain the processes associated with third-party risk assessment and management.	25
5.4 Summarize elements of effective security compliance.	26
5.5 Explain types and purposes of audits and assessments.	27
5.6 Given a scenario, implement security awareness practices.	28

Companion Website

Register this book to get access to the Pearson Test Prep practice test software and other study materials, as well as additional bonus content. Check this site regularly for new and updated postings written by the author that provide further insight into the more troublesome topics on the exam. Be sure to check the box indicting that you would like to hear from us to receive updates and exclusive discounts on future editions of this product or related products.

To access the companion website, follow these steps:

Step 1. Go to **www.pearsonitcertification.com/register** and log in or create a new account.

Step 2. On your Account page, tap or click the **Registered Products** tab and then tap or click the **Register Another Product** link.

Step 3. Enter this book's ISBN: **9780138293086**.

Step 4. Answer the challenge question to provide proof of book ownership.

Step 5. Tap or click the **Access Bonus Content** link for this book to go to the page where your downloadable content is available.

NOTE Please note that many of our companion content files can be very large, especially image and video files.

If you are unable to locate the files for this title by following the preceding steps, please visit http://www.pearsonitcertification.com/contact and select the Site Problems/Comments option. Our customer service representatives will assist you.

How to Access the Pearson Test Prep (PTP) App

You have two options for installing and using the Pearson Test Prep application: a web app and a desktop app. To use the Pearson Test Prep application, start by finding the registration code that comes with the book. You can find the code in these ways:

- You can get your access code by registering the print ISBN (9780138293086) on pearsonitcertification.com/register. Make sure to use the print book ISBN, regardless of whether you purchased an eBook or the print book. After you register the book, your access code will be populated on your account page under the Registered Products tab. Instructions for how to redeem the code are available on the book's companion website by clicking the Access Bonus Content link.

- Premium Edition: If you purchase the Premium Edition eBook and Practice Test directly from the Pearson IT Certification website, the code will be populated on your account page after purchase. Just log in at pearsonitcertification.com, click Account to see details of your account, and click the digital purchases tab.

NOTE After you register your book, your code can always be found in your account under the Registered Products tab.

Once you have the access code, to find instructions about both the PTP web app and the desktop app, follow these steps:

Step 1.   Open this book's companion website as shown earlier in this Introduction under the heading, "Companion Website."

Step 2.   Click the **Practice Test Software** button.

Step 3.   Follow the instructions listed there for both installing the desktop app and using the web app.

Note that if you want to use the web app only at this point, just navigate to pearsontestprep.com, log in using the same credentials used to register your book or purchase the Premium Edition, and register this book's practice tests using the registration code you just found. The process should take only a couple of minutes.

Customizing Your Exams

When you are in the exam settings screen, you can choose to take exams in one of three modes:

- Study mode
- Practice Exam mode
- Flash Card mode

Study mode enables you to fully customize an exam and review answers as you are taking the exam. This is typically the mode you use first to assess your knowledge and identify information gaps. Practice Exam mode locks certain customization options in order to present a realistic exam experience. Use this mode when you are preparing to test your exam readiness. Flash Card mode strips out the answers and presents you with only the question stem. This mode is great for late-stage preparation, when you really want to challenge yourself to provide answers without the benefit of seeing multiple-choice options. This mode does not provide the detailed score reports that the other two modes provide, so it is not the best mode for helping you identify knowledge gaps.

In addition to these three modes, you will be able to select the source of your questions. You can choose to take exams that cover all of the chapters, or you can narrow your selection to just a single chapter or the chapters that make up specific parts in the book. All chapters are selected by default. If you want to narrow your focus to individual chapters, simply deselect all the chapters and then select only those on which you wish to focus in the Objectives area.

There are several other customizations you can make to your exam from the exam settings screen, such as the time allowed for taking the exam, the number of questions served up, whether to randomize questions and answers, whether to show the number of correct answers for multiple-answer questions, and whether to serve up only specific types of questions. You can also create custom test banks by selecting only questions that you have marked or questions on which you have added notes.

Updating Your Exams

If you are using the online version of the Pearson Test Prep software, you should always have access to the latest version of the software as well as the exam data. If you are using the Windows desktop version, every time you launch the software, it will check to see if there are any updates to your exam data and automatically download any changes made since the last time you used the software. This requires that you be connected to the Internet at the time you launch the software.

Sometimes, due to a number of factors, the exam data might not fully download when you activate your exam. If you find that figures or exhibits are missing, you might need to manually update your exams.

To update a particular exam you have already activated and downloaded, simply select the **Tools** tab and click the **Update Products** button. Again, this is only an issue with the desktop Windows application.

If you wish to check for updates to the Windows desktop version of the Pearson Test Prep exam engine software, simply select the **Tools** tab and click the **Update Application** button. Doing so enables you to ensure that you are running the latest version of the software engine.

Figure Credits

Cover: greenbutterfly/Shutterstock

Figure 2-2: Kyryl Gorlov/123RF

Figure 2-3: Aliaksandr Karankevich/123RF

Figure 2-5: rewelda/Shutterstock

Figure 8-1: WannaCry ransomware

Figure 10-1: Amazon Web Services, Inc

Figures 11-2, 11-9, 19-2, 19-6, 19-9, 22-2–22-4: Microsoft Corporation

Figures 14-2, 14-3: Cisco Systems, Inc

Figure 19-7: Robert Koczera/123RF

Figure 22-1: MaxBelkov

Figure 22-5: Google LLC

Figure 22-6: Tenable®, Inc

Figure 22-7: LogRhythm, Inc

This chapter covers the following topics related to Objective 1.1 (Compare and contrast various types of security controls) of the CompTIA Security+ SY0-701 certification exam:

- Categories
- Control types

CHAPTER 1

Comparing and Contrasting the Various Types of Controls

In this chapter you'll learn about the various categories of controls, starting with an overview of technical, managerial, operational, and physical controls. Additionally, you learn the control types, including preventive, deterrent, detective, corrective, compensating, and directive controls.

"Do I Know This Already?" Quiz

The "Do I Know This Already?" quiz enables you to assess whether you should read this entire chapter thoroughly or jump to the "Chapter Review Activities" section. If you are in doubt about your answers to these questions or your own assessment of your knowledge of the topics, read the entire chapter. Table 1-1 lists the major headings in this chapter and their corresponding "Do I Know This Already?" quiz questions. You can find the answers in Appendix A, "Answers to the 'Do I Know This Already?' Quizzes and Review Questions."

Table 1-1 "Do I Know This Already?" Section-to-Question Mapping

Foundation Topics Section	Questions
Control Categories	1–5
Control Types	6–10

CAUTION The goal of self-assessment is to gauge your mastery of the topics in this chapter. If you do not know the answer to a question or are only partially sure of the answer, you should mark that question as wrong for purposes of self-assessment. Giving yourself credit for an answer you correctly guess skews your self-assessment results and might provide you with a false sense of security.

1. Which category of controls involves decisions and management of risk?

   a. Operational controls

   b. Managerial controls

   c. Technical controls

   d. Physical controls

2. The configuration and workings of firewalls and access control fall under which category of controls?

   a. Operational controls

   b. Technical controls

   c. Managerial controls

   d. Physical controls

3. Which control category involves securing physical access to an organization's building and equipment?

   a. Technical controls

   b. Managerial controls

   c. Operational controls

   d. Physical controls

4. Which category of controls is executed by people and involves user awareness and training?

   a. Operational controls

   b. Technical controls

   c. Managerial controls

   d. Physical controls

5. Security awareness training and formal change-management procedures are examples of which category of controls?

   a. Technical controls

   b. Operational controls

   c. Managerial controls

   d. Physical controls

6. Which type of controls are implemented to prevent incidents from happening, with examples such as access lists, passwords, and fences?

   a. Detective controls

   b. Corrective controls

   c. Deterrent controls

   d. Preventive controls

7. What type of controls are meant to deter threat actors from executing offensive assaults on an environment, thereby preventing incidents from occurring?

   a. Deterrent controls

   b. Corrective controls

   c. Preventive controls

   d. Detective controls

8. Detective controls are designed to do which of the following?

   a. Correct a problem during an incident

   b. Monitor and detect any unauthorized behavior or hazard

   c. Deter potential attackers

   d. Prevent incidents from happening

9. Corrective controls are used at which stage of an incident?

   a. Before the event

   b. During the event

   c. After the event

   d. They are not linked to a specific stage of an incident.

10. What is the main purpose of directive controls in an organization's security system?

    a. To provide physical protection against threats

    b. To guide the operation and use of systems within an organization

    c. To prevent incidents from happening

    d. To correct problems during an incident

Control Categories

Controls can be classified into four main categories—technical, managerial, operational, and physical—as described in the sections that follow.

Technical Controls

Technical controls are logical controls executed by a computer, or technical, system. Technical controls include authentication, access control, auditing, and cryptography. You might encounter these technical controls in places like a security system or logical access control. The configuration and workings of firewalls, session locks, RADIUS servers, and RAID 5 arrays fall into this category, as do concepts such as least-privilege implementation.

Managerial Controls

Managerial controls are techniques and concerns addressed by an organization's management (managers and executives). Generally, these controls focus on decisions and the management of risk. They also concentrate on procedures, legal and regulatory policies, the software development lifecycle (SDLC), the computer security lifecycle, information assurance, and vulnerability management/scanning. In short, these controls focus on how the security of data and systems is managed. Managerial, or administrative, controls include business and organizational processes and procedures, such as security policies and procedures, personnel background checks, security awareness training, and formal change-management procedures.

Operational Controls

Operational controls are controls executed by people that are designed to increase individual and group system security. They include user awareness and training, fault tolerance and disaster recovery plans, incident handling, computer support, baseline configuration development, and environmental security. The people who carry out the specific requirements of these controls must have technical expertise and understand how to implement what management desires of them. Operational controls include physical controls that form the outer line of defense against direct access to data, such as protecting backup media; securing output and mobile file storage devices; and paying attention to facility design details, including layout, doors, guards, locks, and surveillance systems.

Physical Controls

Physical controls can be considered the first line of defense in controlling access, as a firewall is the first line of defense for a network. Implementing physical access security methods should be a top priority for an organization. Unfortunately, securing physical access to an organization's building sometimes slumps to the bottom of the list. Or a system is employed, but it fails to mitigate risk properly. In some cases, the system is not maintained well. Proper building entrance access and secure access to physical equipment are vital. And anyone coming and going should be logged and surveilled.

Operational/physical controls include organizational culture and physical controls that form the outer line of defense against direct access to data, such as protecting backup media; securing output and mobile file storage devices; and paying attention to facility design details, including layout, doors, guards, locks, and surveillance systems. For more in-depth information, physical security is covered in detail in Chapter 2, "Summarizing Fundamental Security Concepts."

Summary of Control Categories

Table 1-2 provides a quick comparison view of the different control categories.

Key Topic

Table 1-2 Summary of Control Categories

Category	Description
Technical controls	Technical/logical controls are security controls put in place that are executed by technical systems. Technical controls include logical access control systems, security systems, encryption, and data classification solutions.
Managerial controls	Managerial, or administrative, controls include business and organizational processes and procedures, such as security policies and procedures, personnel background checks, security awareness training, and formal change-management procedures.
Operational controls	Operational controls encompass a range of procedures and actions carried out by personnel to enhance the security of individual and group systems. These controls include, but are not limited to, regular user training, implementation of fault tolerance measures, formulation of disaster recovery plans, and incident response coordination. Personnel responsible for these tasks must have the necessary technical skills and align their actions with the strategic security goals set by management.
Physical controls	Physical controls are a category of security measures designed to prevent unauthorized physical access to an organization's facilities and resources. They form a fundamental component of a layered defense strategy. Key elements include controlling entry points to buildings, securing access to sensitive equipment, and maintaining detailed logs of individuals' movements within the premises, alongside surveillance to monitor and record activities.

Control Types

The following sections focus on control types, including preventive controls, deterrent controls, detective controls, corrective controls, compensating controls, and directive controls.

Preventive Controls

Preventive controls are employed before an event occurs and are designed to prevent incidents from occurring. Examples include biometric systems designed to keep unauthorized persons out, network intrusion prevention systems (NIPSs) to prevent malicious activity, and RAID 1 to prevent loss of data. They are also sometimes referred to as deterrent controls. Preventive controls enforce security policy and are meant to prevent incidents from happening. The only way to bypass a preventive control is to find a flaw in its implementation or logic. These controls are usually not optional. Examples of preventive controls include access lists, passwords, and fences. Preventive controls include security awareness, separation of duties, access control, security policies, and intrusion prevention systems.

Deterrent Controls

An organization uses *deterrent controls* to try to deter threat actors from executing offensive assaults on its environment. The idea is that if potential threat actors see that this type of control is in place, they may decide to move on. An example of this type of control is an alarm system on a home. If a robber sees that the home clearly has an alarm system, they may decide to move on to the next house. Similarly, if threat actors on the Internet identify that an organization they are targeting is using a specific type of technology that would make it more difficult for them to carry out their attack, they may move on.

Deterrent controls are similar to preventive controls in the sense that the primary objective is to prevent an incident from occurring, but the rationale behind deterrent controls is to discourage attackers from proceeding just because of the fact that a control is in place. For example, a system banner warning that any unauthorized attempt to log in will be monitored and punished is a type of deterrent control. In fact, it would probably discourage casual users from attempting to access the system; however, it might not block determined attackers from trying to log in to the system. Deterrent controls are intended to discourage individuals from intentionally violating information security policies or procedures. Examples of deterrent controls include warnings indicating that systems are being monitored.

Detective Controls

Detective controls aim at monitoring and detecting unauthorized behavior or hazards. These types of controls are generally used to alert to failures in other types of controls, such as preventive, deterrent, and compensating controls. Detective controls are very powerful while an attack is taking place, and they are useful in postmortem analyses to understand what has happened. Audit logs, intrusion detection systems (IDSs), motion detection, and security information and event management (SIEM) systems are examples of detective controls.

Detective controls are used during an event to determine whether malicious activity is occurring or has occurred. Examples include CCTV/video surveillance, alarms, network intrusion detection systems (NIDSs), and auditing. Detective controls warn that physical security measures are being violated and attempt to identify unwanted events after they have occurred. Common technical detective controls include audit trails, intrusion detection systems, system monitoring, checksums, and anti-malware.

Corrective Controls

Corrective controls are used after an event has occurred. They limit the extent of damage and help the company recover from damage quickly. Tape backup, hot sites, and other fault tolerance and disaster recovery methods are also included in this category. Corrective controls, which are sometimes referred to as compensating controls, include all the controls used during an incident to correct a problem. Quarantining an infected computer, sending a guard to block an intruder, and terminating an employee for not having followed the security policy are all examples of corrective controls. Corrective controls are reactive and provide measures to lessen harmful effects or restore the system being impacted. Examples of corrective controls include operating system upgrades, data backup restores, vulnerability mitigation, and anti-malware.

Compensating Controls

Also known as alternative controls, *compensating controls* are mechanisms put in place to satisfy security requirements that are either impractical or too difficult to implement. For example, instead of using expensive hardware-based encryption modules, an organization might opt to use network access control (NAC), data loss prevention (DLP), and other security methods. Or, on the personnel side, instead of implementing separation of duties, an organization might opt to do additional logging and auditing. You should approach compensating controls with great caution. They do not give the same level of security as their replaced counterparts.

Of course, many security concepts can be placed in the category of physical as well as other categories listed in the sections that follow. For example, a locking door would be an example of a physical control as well as a preventive control.

Compensating controls are alternative controls that are intended to reduce the risk of an existing or potential control weakness. They can include audit trails and transaction logs that someone in a higher position reviews.

Directive Controls

Directive controls, also known as instructive controls, are strategies established to guide the operation and use of systems within an organization. These controls serve to instruct or direct individuals toward secure behavior. Examples of directive controls include standards, procedures, policy guidelines, and security awareness training programs.

For instance, standards define the approved use of hardware, software, security measures, and procedures within an organization. Procedures provide detailed instructions for executing certain tasks securely and effectively.

Policy guidelines, another form of directive controls, dictate how a specific policy should be executed, outlining the steps to be taken, roles and responsibilities, and expectations for adherence.

Security awareness training is a key directive control that educates staff about security policies and procedures, raising awareness about potential threats and how to avoid them. The primary goal is to influence employee behavior and cultivate a security-conscious work environment. You might see a security awareness control described as part of the "security culture." Culture can absolutely be an informal directive control.

Although directive controls may not provide the tangible physical or technical protection that other types of controls offer, they are crucial in establishing a security-minded culture within an organization. Directive controls act as a guiding light, leading individuals and companies toward secure practices and away from potential security risks. When encountering different policies, technologies, and procedures, it can be helpful to identify where they fall within control categories (such as directive controls) to enable better understanding of an organization's security infrastructure.

Summary of Control Types

When you see technologies, policies, and procedures in the future, attempt to place them within their proper control category. Semantics will vary from one organization to the next, but as long as you can categorize security features in a general fashion, such as by using the control types listed here, you should be able to define and understand just about any organization's security controls.

Table 1-3 provides a quick comparison view of the different control types.

Key Topic

Table 1-3 Summary of Control Types

Control type	Description
Preventive controls	Preventive controls include security awareness, separation of duties, access control, security policies, and intrusion prevention systems.
Deterrent controls	Deterrent controls are intended to discourage individuals from intentionally violating information security policies or procedures. Examples of deterrent controls include warnings indicating that systems are being monitored.
Detective controls	Detective controls warn that physical security measures are being violated. Detective controls attempt to identify unwanted events after they have occurred. Common technical detective controls include audit trails, intrusion detection systems, system monitoring, checksums, and anti-malware.
Corrective controls	Corrective controls are reactive and provide measures to lessen harmful effects or restore the system being impacted. Examples of corrective controls include operating system upgrades, data backup restores, vulnerability mitigation, and anti-malware.
Compensating controls	Compensating controls, also known as alternative controls, are intended to reduce the risk of an existing or potential control weakness. They include audit trails and transaction logs that someone in a higher position reviews.
Directive controls	Directive controls are security controls that provide guidance and set expectations to influence behavior within an organization. These controls, which can take the form of policies, procedures, or guidelines, dictate what actions should be taken to ensure security, and they establish rules for how specific situations should be handled.

Chapter Review Activities

Use the features in this section to study and review the topics in this chapter.

Review Key Topics

Review the most important topics in the chapter, noted with the Key Topic icon in the outer margin of the page. Table 1-4 lists these key topics and the page number on which each is found.

Key Topic

Table 1-4 Key Topics for Chapter 1

Key Topic Element	Description	Page Number
Table 1-2	Summary of Control Categories	7
Table 1-3	Summary of Control Types	11

Define Key Terms

Define the following key terms from this chapter and check your answers in the glossary:

technical controls, managerial controls, operational controls, physical controls, preventive controls, deterrent controls, detective controls, corrective controls, compensating controls, directive controls

Review Questions

Answer the following review questions. Check your answers with the answer key in Appendix A.

1. What control category is addressed by an organization's management?

2. What control category is designed to increase individual and group system security?

3. What control category includes firewalls?

4. What control type enforces security policy?

5. What control type is intended to discourage someone from violating policies?

6. What control type warns that physical security measures are being violated?

7. What control type includes all the controls used during an incident?

8. What control type is also known as an alternative control?

9. Which type of control would include something like door access?

10. Which type of control would you put in place to control access to a server room?

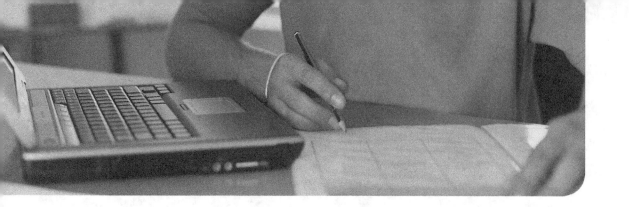

This chapter covers the following topics related to Objective 1.2 (Summarize fundamental security concepts) of the CompTIA Security+ SY0-701 certification exam:

- Confidentiality, integrity, and availability (CIA)

- Non-repudiation

- Authentication, authorization, and accounting (AAA)

- Gap analysis

- Zero Trust

- Physical security

- Deceptive and disruption technology

CHAPTER 2

Summarizing Fundamental Security Concepts

In this chapter, we'll look into fundamental security concepts in the physical and digital realms. It addresses key principles like confidentiality, integrity, availability (CIA) and advanced strategies like Zero Trust. The chapter also explores physical security measures, from bollards to sensors, emphasizing a multilayered approach to safeguarding assets. Finally, this chapter reviews some ways organizations can capture forensics and behavioral patterns of attackers who believe they are attacking an actual network when they are actually in a honeypot or honeynet.

"Do I Know This Already?" Quiz

The "Do I Know This Already?" quiz enables you to assess whether you should read this entire chapter thoroughly or jump to the "Chapter Review Activities" section. If you are in doubt about your answers to these questions or your own assessment of your knowledge of the topics, read the entire chapter. Table 2-1 lists the major headings in this chapter and their corresponding "Do I Know This Already?" quiz questions. You can find the answers in Appendix A, "Answers to the 'Do I Know This Already?' Quizzes and Review Questions."

Table 2-1 "Do I Know This Already?" Section-to-Question Mapping

Foundation Topics Section	Questions
Confidentiality, Integrity, and Availability (CIA)	1, 4
Non-repudiation	2
Authentication, Authorization, and Accounting (AAA)	3
Gap Analysis	5
Zero Trust	6, 7
Physical Security	8, 9
Deception and Disruption Technology	10

CAUTION   The goal of self-assessment is to gauge your mastery of the topics in this chapter. If you do not know the answer to a question or are only partially sure of the answer, you should mark that question as wrong for purposes of self-assessment. Giving yourself credit for an answer you correctly guess skews your self-assessment results and might provide you with a false sense of security.

1. The confidentiality component of the CIA triad is designed to:
   a. Ensure that data remains accurate and trustworthy over its lifecycle.
   b. Guarantee that systems and data are accessible when needed by authorized users.
   c. Protect information from unauthorized access and disclosure.
   d. Provide assurance that someone cannot deny the validity of something.

2. What is non-repudiation in the context of cybersecurity?
   a. The process of ensuring that systems are running correctly and efficiently
   b. The process of preventing unauthorized access to sensitive data
   c. The assurance that someone cannot deny the validity of something
   d. The process of ensuring that data is accurate, consistent, and trustworthy over its entire lifecycle

3. In the AAA framework, what does the authentication process do?
   a. It involves logging session statistics and usage information.
   b. It controls access to computer resources and enforces policies.
   c. It involves identifying a user, typically by having them enter a valid username and password.
   d. It enforces policies regarding what types of activities or resources a user is permitted to access.

4. In terms of the CIA triad, what does availability ensure?
   a. It protects data from unauthorized modification.
   b. It ensures that systems and data are accessible and usable when needed by authorized users.
   c. It protects information from unauthorized access.
   d. It provides a method to authenticate the sender of a message.

5. What is the primary goal of conducting a cybersecurity gap analysis?

   a. To compare an organization's existing security measures against an ideal state and identify areas of improvement

   b. To implement the latest cybersecurity technologies and software

   c. To authorize user access to network resources

   d. To deny the validity of a cybersecurity incident

6. In the Zero Trust model, which of the following best describes the role of adaptive identity?

   a. It provides a static method of verifying users or systems.

   b. It identifies users or systems based on context, such as behavior, location, or devices.

   c. It builds trust by allowing free access to all systems.

   d. It relies solely on passwords for user authentication.

7. In the Zero Trust security framework, the data plane is responsible for:

   a. Determining policies and security protocols.

   b. Making intelligent decisions based on policies.

   c. Enforcing policies determined by the control plane.

   d. Allowing all data packets to pass freely without inspection.

8. Which of the following best describes the function of an access control vestibule in a facility protection plan?

   a. It allows free access to anyone entering the facility.

   b. It ensures that both sets of entrance doors can be opened simultaneously.

   c. It creates a buffer zone at the entrance and provides an additional layer of access control.

   d. It prevents visibility into the entrance of the facility.

9. Which of the following types of sensors would be most effective for detecting movement due to changes in heat levels?

   a. Microwave sensors

   b. Ultrasonic sensors

   c. Pressure sensors

   d. Infrared sensors

10. What is the primary function of a honeytoken in a cybersecurity system?

    a. It serves as a backup for the system's data.

    b. It serves as an early warning system for unauthorized access or system breach.

    c. It enables an attacker to gain access to the system.

    d. It assists in decrypting encrypted data.

Foundation Topics

Confidentiality, Integrity, and Availability (CIA)

The CIA triad (see Figure 2-1) is a foundational concept in the field of cybersecurity and information security. CIA stands for *confidentiality*, *integrity*, *and availability*, and each of these principles is crucial to ensuring secure and reliable systems. We refer to it as a *triad* due to the inseparable and equally important elements of a comprehensive and balanced approach to cybersecurity. Let's explore each aspect of the CIA triad to fully understand their value to a cybersecurity program.

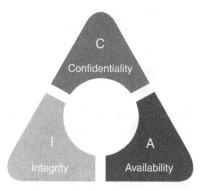

Figure 2-1   The CIA Triad

Confidentiality refers to protecting information from unauthorized access and disclosure. Techniques like encryption, access controls, and authentication processes are often used to ensure confidentiality. Only individuals with the necessary authorization and permissions should be able to access certain data. For example, a medical record should only be accessible to the patient and their healthcare provider. A breach of confidentiality might involve an unauthorized person reading an encrypted email or other sensitive communications.

Integrity is the part of the CIA triad that involves ensuring that data is accurate, consistent, and trustworthy over its entire lifecycle. It involves preventing unauthorized users from modifying data, whether in transit or storage. Techniques to ensure integrity include checksums, hashing algorithms, and digital signatures. Integrity is about making sure data has not been tampered with and remains in its original state unless changed by authorized individuals.

STUDY TIP   Confidentiality keeps secrets secret, and integrity keeps secrets from being changed/altered.

Availability is the part of the CIA triad that involves ensuring that systems and data are accessible and usable when needed by authorized users. This means ensuring that systems are running correctly and efficiently, that network infrastructure is robust and scalable, and that system failover mechanisms are in place to prevent downtime. Techniques to ensure availability include redundancy, failover, RAID, backups, and load balancing.

The application of the CIA triad in cybersecurity involves strategies and measures that ensure these three principles are upheld. Organizations use various methods and technologies to maintain the confidentiality, integrity, and availability of their data and systems, including firewalls, intrusion detection systems, anti-malware software, encryption protocols, data backups, and more. It's a guiding principle for designing, implementing, and managing an organization's security architecture. The CIA triad can be applied to measure and understand practically every aspect of cybersecurity throughout an organization.

Non-repudiation

Key Topic

Non-repudiation is the assurance that someone cannot deny the validity of something, such as a statement's author being unable to dispute the authorship of that statement. Non-repudiation is a legal concept that is widely used in information security to refer to a service that provides proof of the origin and integrity of the data. Non-repudiation makes it difficult to successfully deny who and where a message came from, and so it protects the authenticity and integrity of the message. Digital signatures can offer non-repudiation in online transactions, where it is crucial to ensure that a party to a contract or a communication can't deny the authenticity of the signature on a document or deny having sent the communication in the first place. In this context, non-repudiation refers to the ability to ensure that a party to a contract or a communication must accept the authenticity of their signature on a document or the sending of a message.

In forensics and digital security, non-repudiation means a service or system that provides proof of the integrity and origin of data. It refers to an authentication that can be said to be genuine with high confidence. Proof of data integrity is typically the easiest of these requirements to accomplish. A data hash such as SHA-2 usually ensures that the data will not be changed undetectably. Even with this safeguard, though, it is possible to tamper with data in transit, either through an on-path attack (formerly known as a man-in-the-middle attack) or phishing. As a result, data integrity is best asserted when the recipient already possesses the necessary verification information, such as after being mutually authenticated. The most common method of providing non-repudiation in the context of digital communications or storage is through digital signatures, which are powerful tools that provide non-repudiation in a publicly verifiable manner.

Authentication, Authorization, and Accounting (AAA)

Authentication, authorization, and accounting (AAA) is a framework for intelligently controlling access to computer resources, enforcing policies, auditing usage, and providing the information necessary for audits.

This process starts with identification, or proving you are who you are. *Authentication* processes provide a way of identifying a user, typically by having the user enter a valid username and valid password before access is granted. The AAA server compares a user's authentication credentials with other user credentials stored in a database, such as Active Directory. If the credentials match, the user is granted access to the network. If they do not match, the authentication fails, and access to the network is denied. Password reuse has been one of attackers' favorite methods for gaining access to systems controlled by AAA. If a user's credentials are exposed on one platform or even made public, attackers can add these passwords and usernames to their attack dictionary.

Authentication supposes that a user wants to gain *authorization* to a certain resource. After logging in to a system, for instance, a user may try to access a network drive share, printer, or gateway. The authorization process determines whether the user has the authority to issue such commands. In other words, authorization is the process of enforcing policies—determining what types or qualities of activities, resources, or services a user is permitted. Usually, authorization occurs in the context of authentication. After you have authenticated a user, that user may be authorized for different types of access or activity.

The final *A* of the AAA framework is *accounting*, which involves logging the resources a user consumes during access. This may include the amount of system time or the amount of data a user has sent or received during a session. Accounting is carried out by logging session statistics and usage information and is used for authorization control, compliance, billing, trend analysis, resource utilization, and capacity planning activities.

Say that you're going to the airport. You have your passport and plane ticket in hand and are ready to travel to a far-off tropical paradise. When you arrive at the security gate, the security guard asks for two things: your ID (passport) and your plane ticket. While you are standing there, an airport security dog sniffs around your luggage. The security agent and security dog are attempting to follow their authentication process to ensure that you are who you say you are (authenticating people), you aren't trying to sneak in items you should not have (authenticating systems), and you have authorization to be in the airport terminal (authentication models).

Authenticating people focuses on verifying the identity of a user who is trying to gain access to a network or system. You generally see this as a username and password or a passport/ID, which are then compared to stored user credentials in a database. ***Authenticating systems*** seeks to verify the identity of devices or systems that try to connect to a network or gain access to a sensitive area such as an airport terminal. Devices or systems can be a variety of devices, including a user's personal computer, servers, or Internet of Things (IoT) devices. The objective is to ensure that only trusted and authorized devices can access the network to reduce the risk of malicious activity.

Authorization models define the strategies and protocols used to verify the identity of users or systems. In the airport example, the security agent uses a defined process of checking your passport and plane ticket, and the security dog checks for unauthorized substances. Authorization models are critical in determining how authentication is implemented and what factors are considered during the authentication process. The most common authentication models include single-factor authentication (SFA), two-factor authentication (2FA), multifactor authentication (MFA), and risk-based authentication (RBA). We will explore these authentication models in greater detail in Chapter 19, "Implementing and Maintaining Identity and Access Management."

Gap Analysis

Gap analysis is a strategic planning tool used to evaluate the difference between the current state and an ideal or desired state. In the realm of cybersecurity, a gap analysis often involves assessing the existing security infrastructure, protocols, and policies against a predetermined standard or set of best practices. This evaluation helps identify areas where the organization's cybersecurity measures may be lacking or "gaps" where improvements are needed to reach the desired level of security. These gaps could relate to various aspects of security, from technology and software to personnel training and policy enforcement. Once these gaps are identified, the organization can devise a strategic plan to address and close these gaps, thereby enhancing the overall security posture. Performing regular gap analyses is critical to maintaining an up-to-date, effective security infrastructure that can adapt to evolving threats and vulnerabilities.

Zero Trust

Zero Trust is a network security concept that has been around for many years. The overall principle is to not trust anything by default but to allow access based on various known factors that build trust. The mechanisms for building trust revolve around authentication, authorization, and security posture validation. Before you allow any access, these factors must be addressed.

The ***control plane*** is a part of the network architecture that deals with routing and traffic control. In the Zero Trust model, the control plane plays a crucial role in making intelligent decisions based on policies and security protocols. The control plane features the following methods and strategies:

- *Adaptive identity* is a dynamic method of verifying and identifying users or systems based on context, such as behavior, location, or device. It's a crucial part of the Zero Trust model, as it ensures that trust is continually evaluated and adjusted based on changing conditions.

- *Threat scope reduction* involves strategies that limit the potential damage a threat can inflict on an organization. In the Zero Trust model, the scope of potential threats is reduced by limiting the privileges of users, systems, and processes in order to minimize the potential points of attack.

- *Policy-driven access control* is a system that grants or denies access to network resources based on predefined policies. These policies consider various factors, including the user's role, the type of data requested, and the security status of the device from which the request is made.

- In the Zero Trust architecture, a network is divided into **secured zones**, and each zone represents a portion of the network where resources of similar trust levels reside. By confining potential compromises to individual zones, the extent of potential breaches ("blast radius") is minimized.

- The *policy engine* is a central component in the data plane and the Zero Trust architecture as a whole. It is responsible for making real-time decisions about access requests based on the policies defined by the policy administrator, including determining which network resources a subject can access and under what conditions, as well as how that access should be monitored and logged.

- The *policy administrator* is responsible for defining and managing the policies that dictate how subjects can interact with network resources. They set conditions based on factors such as the identity of the subject, the nature of the requested resource, the security status of the device making the request, and other relevant context.

The *data plane*, sometimes referred to as the *forwarding plane*, deals with the transmission of user data within a network. In a Zero Trust security framework, the data plane is responsible for the enforcement of policies determined by the control plane and ensures that data packets are properly routed, inspected, and potentially blocked or modified based on the security protocols and policies in place. The data plane features the following methods and strategies:

- Within the data plane of the Zero Trust architecture, a *subject/system* refers to any entity, such as a user, device, or system process, that requests access to resources within the network. It's crucial to note that in the Zero Trust model, subjects are treated as potential threats, regardless of whether they originate from inside or outside the network. Their access permissions are always verified before being granted, and their interactions with the system are constantly monitored.

■ The *policy enforcement point (PEP)* is where the decisions of the policy engine come to life. It is the component of the network—such as a firewall, a router, or a switch—where access control policies are actively enforced. If a subject attempts to access a network resource, it is the PEP's job to allow or block that access based on the decisions of the policy engine and the rules set by the policy administrator.

■ *Implicit Trust Zones* within a Zero Trust architecture refer to segments of a network where devices and traffic are assumed to be safe and are granted certain privileges without continuous verification. These zones are typically legacy constructs where trust boundaries are predefined based on location or network segment. However, in Zero Trust, such zones are minimized or eliminated because the framework operates under the principle that trust is never assumed, regardless of location, necessitating constant verification of all devices and traffic.

Physical Security

Physical security is a crucial aspect of a comprehensive security strategy, aiming to protect physical assets such as buildings, equipment, and personnel from harm or unauthorized access. While we often focus on cyber threats in the digital age, the significance of physical security measures cannot be understated. Physical security involves a combination of technical tools such as security cameras and motion-detecting sensors and physical barriers such as bollards and access vestibules.

Bollards/Barricades

A *bollard* is a standalone post, typically made of steel, that is short, sturdy, and anchored in a hard surface such as concrete (see Figure 2-2). This low-profile, post-shaped deterrent is built with the purpose of blocking vehicle movement from certain directions while allowing for full pedestrian movement. Bollards are designed to withstand high impact and deflect potential blows away from the object or area they are in place to protect.

Figure 2-2   Bollards

Various bollard types offer different levels of protection. There is a rating system for the standards by which bollards and barriers are judged. The standards are based on perpendicular impact at a certain speed (K), with the highest rating indicating the strongest protection, such as a vehicle ramming the bollard/barrier at a higher speed.

Anti-ram bollards are security bollards that prevent vehicles from crashing through. There are different levels of anti-ram bollards. K4, K8, and K12 ratings offer various levels of protections against vehicles of different sizes.

Safety bollards give a warehouse or distribution center a path/road definition and divert traffic and intrusions. If traffic flow matters in your warehouse, the bollard type used matters. Bollards are also used inside warehouses to protect people, goods, and equipment.

Architectural and landscaping bollards offer a similar function, though they may be more focused on aesthetics than other types of bollards.

Barricades are barriers that are similar to guardrails (see Figure 2-3). Typically used as a material-handling solution, they offer more linear protection than bollards. Barriers prevent movement of both people and vehicles across a large area. They are typically constructed of steel or concrete and are designed with the goal of protection.

Figure 2-3   Barricade

Barriers are used to protect wide stretches of racking and walls in a facility. They are mounted to the floor, with a small amount of space between barriers and protected assets for protection in the event of impact. They are also used at the ends of racks and to protect utilities, around machines and conveyors, and anywhere it is important to designate and segregate a space. Guardrail barriers are typically painted a highly visible color such as yellow and used to define the working areas in a facility.

Access Control Vestibules

Access control vestibules are an excellent security addition to a facility protection plan. These purpose-built entries have panels built from prefabricated composite or metal and are used to control the traffic flow in facilities, providing security with a clear view of those entering (see Figure 2-4). An access control vestibule is configured to ensure that one of the doors to the entrance is always closed, which enhances security and also reduces the amount of hot/cold air escaping from the building. These vestibules are especially useful for companies or buildings with high traffic where doors are opened frequently.

An access control vestibule provides a buffer zone to the entrance of a facility, as well as an additional layer of physical security and access control. It uses interlocking doors, and both sets of doors cannot be opened at a single time; it thus creates a trap. With the vestibule entry being monitored and controlled at all times, the security team can ensure that the person attempting to enter the building has the clearance to do so. Security vestibules can also incorporate additional security measures into the design, such as PIN pads or badge scanners, depending on the facility's needs.

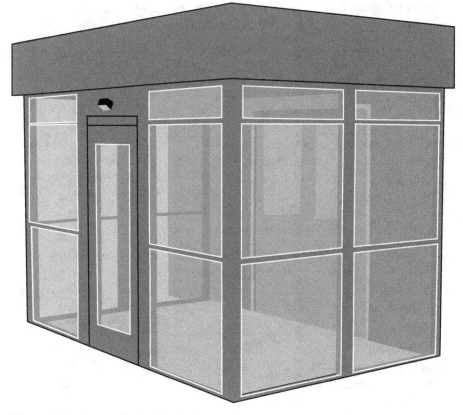

Figure 2-4   Access Control Vestibule

Fencing

Physical access controls consist of systems and techniques used to restrict access to a security perimeter and provide boundary protection. Major defenses include fencing and fence-monitoring systems. Fencing is usually the first line of defense at the perimeter of a property. Therefore, deploying the right fence for the right level of protection is important. Today's fences include crash barrier bollards and control lines to ensure that a rushing vehicle cannot pass. Fence-line trembler devices can alert the security desk to motion on the fence. When this approach is combined with other visible methods, such as CCTV, the threat is visible immediately, and the impact of the threat is reduced.

Pedestrian barriers should include controlled entry and exit points, locked gates, turnstiles, and electronic access control systems. Fencing can be as simple as wood or chain link, or it can be brick, steel, or wrought iron. Remember that the stronger the fence material, the less likely that it will be broken or traversed by criminals. Some safety fences are even made of vinyl and plastics to dissuade people from entering areas that are dangerous or under construction, but you need to ensure that signage is appropriate.

Video Surveillance

Closed-circuit television (CCTV) is mainly an older analog technology involving cameras connected to a coaxial cable network. All the cables lead back to a distribution system and then to a DVR and security monitors. One of the issues with CCTV is that it requires you to build a completely separate network, which might exist alongside your IP (data) network. In industrial plants, CCTV equipment may be used to observe parts of a process from a central control room—for example, when the environment is not suitable for humans. CCTV systems may operate continuously or only as required to monitor a particular event.

CCTV systems that use DVRs can provide recording for hours or even many years, and a variety of quality and performance options and extra features are available, such as motion detection. Most CCTV systems are being replaced today by IP camera networks with cloud storage options, although they are still being called CCTV.

CCTV is a surveillance tool. Cameras, whether they are real or dummy, tend to deter attackers, who fear being recorded and later prosecuted. Placing cameras at egress and ingress spots around facilities ensures that security guards are able to attend to issues that may be missed by the cameras, and they provide backup and evidence in solving crimes.

Security Guards

A *security guard* is a professional entrusted with protecting physical assets and spaces within an organization. Security guards play a pivotal role in enhancing cybersecurity by discouraging potential threats through their presence and preventing unauthorized access by diligently verifying identities at entry and exit points and curtailing tailgating, which is a common security breach. They regulate the movement of company property, deterring unauthorized removal of potentially sensitive materials. Through regular patrolling, security guards can identify and respond to suspicious activities swiftly, ensuring that any unauthorized individuals are promptly apprehended or removed.

Security guards are integral in emergency responses, often coordinating with law enforcement during incidents, and fostering a culture of security awareness within an organization. While their role might seem traditional, security guards form an essential layer of defense against physical and cyber threats, protecting the gateway to an organization's digital assets. Thus, they contribute significantly to a comprehensive and robust cybersecurity strategy.

Access Badges

An access badge is a credential used to gain entry to an area that has automated access control entry points. Entry points may be doors, turnstiles, parking gates, or other barriers. Various technologies are used to identify the holder of an access badge to an access control system. The most common technologies are proximity readers, barcodes, smart cards, and various biometric devices. Magnetic strip cards are fading from use. An access badge contains a number that is read by a card reader. This number is usually called the facility code, and it is sent to an access control system—a computer system that makes access control decisions based on information about the credential. If the credential is included in an access control list, the access control system unlocks the controlled access point. The transaction is stored in the system for later retrieval, and reports can be generated to show the dates and times cards were used to enter the controlled access point.

A reader radiates a 1- to 5-inch electrical field. When a card is presented to the reader, the reader's electrical field excites a coil in the card. The coil charges a capacitor and in turn powers an integrated circuit. The integrated circuit outputs the card number to the coil, which transmits it to the reader. The transmission of the card number happens in the clear; it is not encrypted. With basic understanding of radio technology and of card formats, proximity cards can be hacked.

A smart card or integrated circuit (IC) card is a physical electronic authorization device that is used to control access to a resource. It is typically a credit card–sized plastic card with an embedded IC chip, as illustrated in Figure 2-5. A smart card may include a pattern of metal contacts to electrically connect to the internal chip. Others are contactless, and some are both. Smart cards can provide personal identification, authentication, data storage, and application processing. Applications include identification, finances, mobile phones (SIM), public transit, computer security, schools, and healthcare. Modern credit cards have this IC built in for stronger protection. Smart cards may provide strong security authentication for single sign-on (SSO) within organizations.

Figure 2-5   Smart Card

Lighting

Lighting inside and outside a building can provide various levels of protection and safety for employees and the facility. Knowing there is lighting everywhere can also serve as a deterrent for potential attackers because it's possible for cameras to pick up any movement. Planning is required to design and deploy lighting appropriately to ensure that there are no dark spots and to provide safety for employees and the facility.

Building lighting and autosensing light switches can provide safety and visibility as well as reduce power requirements. Newer lighting is direct current (DC) based; because lights are now mostly LED based and do not require 110V, they can operate on 5V. As a result, entire DC power distribution systems have been developed.

Employee and visitor parking lot lighting is vital to the safety of employees and guests. It is important to ensure that lights in these areas overlap sufficiently to avoid dark spots or shadows. Having higher-power lighting at ingress and egress spots that are on separate controls and can be used during attacks or emergencies provides highly visible paths to certain spaces.

Sensors

The deployment of sensors is a cost-effective way to enhance and extend monitored areas. Sensors are capable of sensing and monitoring for everything from window and door openings, to water and gas leaks, to motion detection—and much more. Every organization deploys sensors in some manner. When used in conjunction with other deployed security measures, sensors can add an extra level of security in a reasonable manner. Many sensors enhance protection by providing notification/alerting for components. There are a variety of types of sensors, including the following:

Key Topic

- **Infrared:** Infrared sensors are designed to detect heat and motion, as every object emits some level of infrared radiation due to its temperature. These sensors emit or detect infrared radiation to sense their environment, and they are used in security systems to detect movement.

- **Pressure:** Pressure sensors, or pressure transducers, measure pressure levels. When strategically placed in certain areas, such as beneath floor mats or on doors and windows, they can alert security when pressure changes, indicating movement or an attempted breach.

- **Microwave:** Microwave sensors emit microwave radiation and measure reflections from objects to determine their distance, speed, or other characteristics. They are often used for motion detection, with any change in the reflection indicating movement.

- **Ultrasonic:** Ultrasonic sensors measure the distance to an object by using sound waves. They emit an ultrasonic wave and measure the time it takes for the wave to return after hitting an object. They can be used for detecting breaches, as a sudden change in the return time of the ultrasonic wave might indicate an intrusion.

Deception and Disruption Technology

Honeypots and honeynets attract and trap potential attackers to counteract any attempts at unauthorized access of the network. These solutions isolate the potential attacker in a monitored area and contain dummy resources that look to be of value to the perpetrator. While an attacker is trapped in one of these, the attacker's methods can be studied and analyzed, and the results of those analyses can be applied to the general security of the functional network.

Key Topic

A *honeypot* is generally a single computer but could also be a file, a group of files, or an area of unused IP address space, whereas a *honeynet* is one or more computers, servers, or an area of a network; a honeynet is used when a single honeypot is not sufficient. Either way, the individual computer or group of servers will usually not house any important company information. Various analysis tools are implemented to study the attacker; these tools, along with a centralized group of honeypots (or a honeynet), are known collectively as a honeyfarm.

One example of a honeypot in action is the spam honeypot. A spam honeypot can lure spammers in, enabling network administrators to study the spammers' techniques and habits, thus allowing the network admins to better protect their actual email servers, SMTP relays, SMTP proxies, and so on, over the long term. This solution might ultimately keep the spammers away from the real email addresses because the spammers are occupied elsewhere. Some of the information gained by studying spammers is shared with other network admins or organizations' websites dedicated to reducing spam. A spam honeypot could be as simple as a single email address or as complex as an entire email domain with multiple SMTP servers.

Of course, as with any other technology that studies attackers, honeypots also bear risks to the legitimate network. A honeypot or honeynet should be carefully fire-walled off from the legitimate network to ensure that attackers can't break through.

Honeyfiles can also be used as bait files to lure adversaries to access and then send alarms to security analysts for detection. They can also be used to potentially learn the tactics and techniques used by attackers. For instance, you could create a honey-file named credentials.txt to lure attackers who think they will have access to users' network credentials. Honeyfiles can be used to learn the attackers' tactics, tech-niques, and behavior without adversely affecting normal operations.

A *honeytoken* is a type of decoy used to detect, deflect, or deter attempts at unau-thorized use of information systems. It is essentially a piece of data, such as a dummy user account, that serves no legitimate purpose but is monitored for any access or usage. Any activity involving the honeytoken suggests malicious activity or a system breach, as there should be none under normal circumstances.

For example, a honeytoken could be a fictitious email account or user credentials planted within the database of a web service. These credentials would not be used by any legitimate user or administrator but would instead be designed to appear valuable to an attacker scanning for information. If an unauthorized user attempts to log in using these credentials, an alert notifies the system's administrators of the unauthorized access attempt. The honeytoken thus acts as an early warning system, helping detect breaches that might otherwise go unnoticed.

Chapter Review Activities

Use the features in this section to study and review the topics in this chapter.

Review Key Topics

Review the most important topics in the chapter, noted with the Key Topic icon in the outer margin of the page. Table 2-2 lists these key topics and the page number on which each is found.

Table 2-2   Key Topics for Chapter 2

Key Topic Element	Description	Page Number
Section	Confidentiality, Integrity, and Availability (CIA)	19
Section	Non-repudiation	20
Section	Authentication, Authorization, and Accounting (AAA)	21
Section	Gap Analysis	22
Section	Zero Trust	22
Section	Access Control Vestibules	26
List	Sensors	31
Paragraph	Honeypot	31
Paragraph	Honeyfile	32
Paragraph	Honeytoken	32

Define Key Terms

Define the following key terms from this chapter and check your answers in the glossary:

confidentiality; integrity; availability; non-repudiation; authentication, authorization, and accounting (AAA); authenticating people; authenticating systems; authorization model; gap analysis; Zero Trust; control plane; adaptive identity; threat scope reduction; policy-driven access control; secured zone; policy engine; policy administrator; data plane; subject/system; policy enforcement point (PEP); implicit trust zones; bollard; barricade; access control vestibule; closed-circuit television (CCTV); security guard; honeypot; honeynet; honeyfile; honeytoken

Review Questions

Answer the following review questions. Check your answers with the answer key in Appendix A.

1. What aspect of cybersecurity does non-repudiation address to maintain data integrity and assurance?

2. What role does authentication play in ensuring the legitimacy of people interacting with a system?

3. In what scenarios would authenticating systems increase overall system security?

4. What does a gap analysis identify to help an organization improve its cybersecurity practices?

5. How does the Zero Trust model enhance the security of an organization's systems and data?

6. What is the purpose of the control plane in a Zero Trust security framework?

7. How does the data plane in the Zero Trust model contribute to the enforcement of security policies?

8. What is the role of adaptive identity in a Zero Trust security architecture?

9. How does an access control vestibule aid in enhancing physical security measures in a facility?

10. What is the difference between a honeypot, a honeynet, and a honeytoken in the context of intrusion detection?

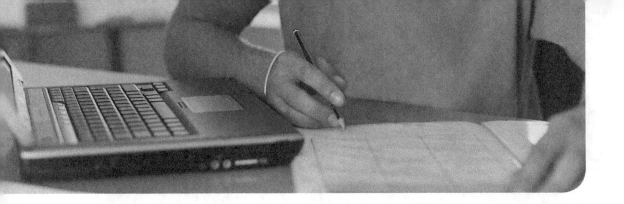

This chapter covers the following topics related to Objective 1.3 (Explain the importance of change management processes and the impact to security) of the CompTIA Security+ SY0-701 certification exam:

- Business processes impacting security operation

- Technical Implications

- Documentation

- Version control

CHAPTER 3

Understanding Change Management's Security Impact

This chapter examines the critical role of change management processes in fortifying an organization's cybersecurity posture. Change management is more than just an administrative task; it is a significant component of audit and compliance requirements, providing a structured approach for reviewing, approving, and implementing changes to information systems. Change management minimizes unplanned outages due to unauthorized alterations by helping to manage cybersecurity and operational risks. The process typically involves well-defined steps, such as requesting, reviewing, approving, or rejecting and testing, scheduling, implementing, and documenting changes. These steps can serve as a blueprint for standard operating procedures (SOPs) in change management, ensuring that each alteration is systematically vetted and executed. As you will see throughout this chapter, a structured approach is vital for maintaining the integrity and resilience of security mechanisms in the face of a constantly evolving threat landscape.

"Do I Know This Already?" Quiz

The "Do I Know This Already?" quiz enables you to assess whether you should read this entire chapter thoroughly or jump to the "Chapter Review Activities" section. If you are in doubt about your answers to these questions or your own assessment of your knowledge of the topics, read the entire chapter. Table 3-1 lists the major headings in this chapter and their corresponding "Do I Know This Already?" quiz questions. You can find the answers in Appendix A, "Answers to the 'Do I Know This Already?' Quizzes and Review Questions."

Table 3-1   "Do I Know This Already?" Section-to-Question Mapping

Foundation Topics Section	Questions
Business Processes Impacting Security Operations	1–4
Technical Implications	5–7
Documentation	8, 9
Version Control	10

CAUTION The goal of self-assessment is to gauge your mastery of the topics in this chapter. If you do not know the answer to a question or are only partially sure of the answer, you should mark that question as wrong for purposes of self-assessment. Giving yourself credit for an answer you correctly guess skews your self-assessment results and might provide you with a false sense of security.

1. Which of the following can be a consequence of an ineffective approval process?

    a. It can lead to poorly vetted changes being implemented, inadvertently introducing new system vulnerabilities.

    b. It can lead to a more comprehensive security solution.

    c. It can lead to failure of asset ownership protocols.

    d. It can cause communication problems between stakeholders.

2. Who is responsible for defining an asset's security requirements, managing its risk profile, and addressing any vulnerabilities in the system?

    a. Stakeholders

    b. Customers

    c. Owners

    d. Approvals

3. Who are stakeholders, in the context of security operations in an organization?

    a. Only the IT staff

    b. Only individuals or groups external to the business

    c. Only customers

    d. Any individual or group vested in the organization's security posture, which can include system users, IT staff, management, customers, investors, and any entity affected by a security breach or whose actions could impact the organization's security posture

4. What is the role of an approval process in an organization's security operations?

    a. To define the asset's security requirements

    b. To manage the risk profile of assets

    c. To dictate how changes impacting security are approved and who holds the authority to make such decisions

    d. To establish the accountability of asset owners

5. What is the primary purpose of an allow list in a system's security?

   a. To list all actions that are disallowed in the system

   b. To approve inputs a user or machine can perform in the system

   c. To list all the modifications to security protocols

   d. To identify the potential consequences or effects of a technology-related decision or event

6. What is the purpose of restricted activities in a computer or network system?

   a. To disrupt business operations and negatively impact employee productivity

   b. To list the potential consequences of a technology-related decision

   c. To uphold cybersecurity standards by limiting or prohibiting specific actions or operations

   d. To approve specific actions or operations

7. Why is understanding the technical implications of any new or existing system crucial in security operations?

   a. It is needed for the approval process.

   b. It helps in maintaining functionality and security for the system.

   c. It helps in defining the restricted activities.

   d. It assists in implementing deny lists.

8. Why is maintaining up-to-date documentation crucial in IT or cybersecurity operations?

   a. It is essential for updating policies and procedures.

   b. It ensures a clear understanding of system operations, facilitates staff training, and helps in troubleshooting issues.

   c. It helps in updating diagrams of systems or networks.

   d. It assists in managing network interfaces.

9. What is the significance of updating diagrams in IT and cybersecurity?

   a. It aids in creating user guides and technical specifications.

   b. It assists in understanding the rules governing how IT systems are used and secured.

         c. It ensures that everyone has an accurate and current picture of the systems, enhancing troubleshooting and system upgrades.

         d. It helps in updating policies and procedures.

10. Why is version control vital in IT and cybersecurity domains?

         a. It makes it possible to track changes to files, pinpoint when and by whom those changes were made, and, if necessary, revert to an earlier version.

         b. It helps to ensure the security of the data in the files.

         c. It allows the user to duplicate files for various purposes.

         d. It aids in the encryption of the files.

Foundation Topics

Business Processes Impacting Security Operations

Security operations in any organization are often heavily influenced by various business processes. A *business process* is a set of coordinated tasks and procedures that an organization uses to accomplish a specific organizational goal or to deliver a particular product or service. Each process—be it approval mechanisms, ownership protocols, stakeholder interactions, impact analysis, or test results evaluation—has the potential to shape the organization's security posture. For instance, an ineffective approval process could lead to poorly vetted changes being implemented and new system vulnerabilities inadvertently being introduced. It's important to note that the effectiveness of business processes is often gauged using performance baselines. A performance baseline serves as a standard measure to assess the impact of any changes on security, ensuring alignment with organizational security objectives.

On the other hand, a robust ownership protocol ensures that each asset, such as a data set or an application, has an assigned custodian, and ensures that its security requirements are regularly reviewed and addressed. Understanding the interaction between these business processes and security operations is crucial for maintaining a strong security stance and safeguarding an organization's assets.

Approval Process

The *approval process* is a crucial business procedure that dictates how changes impacting security are approved and who holds the authority to make such decisions. The approval process typically follows a step-by-step verification process to ensure that all necessary precautions are considered and the planned change will not introduce new vulnerabilities.

Ownership

In the context of security, *ownership* refers to the individual or team that is responsible for specific assets, such as databases or applications, and that is accountable for their security. Owners are typically responsible for defining an asset's security requirements, managing its risk profile, and addressing any vulnerabilities in the system. A crucial component of recognizing ownership is establishing accountability. Ownership ensures that each asset is consistently maintained, protected, and updated according to the security requirements of a specific system.

Stakeholders

Stakeholders are individuals or groups vested in an organization's security posture who can directly impact security procedures and policies. Stakeholders may include system users, IT staff, management, customers, investors, or any entity that would be affected by a security breach or whose actions could impact the security posture of an organization. Involving stakeholders in security decision-making processes can lead to more comprehensive security solutions, as diverse perspectives help in identifying potential threats and vulnerabilities. Remember that stakeholders can be internal or external to specific internal business departments or external to the business.

Impact Analysis

Impact analysis is a process that involves assessing the potential effects of changes on the organization's security landscape. You may encounter impact analysis in the form of a business impact analysis (BIA), which we will explore in depth in Chapter 24, "Understanding Elements of the Risk Management Process." An impact analysis also helps in proactively identifying possible security risks or issues to a system. Security analysts should conduct an impact analysis to better understand how to effectively allocate resources such as staff, budget, and tools.

Test Results

A *test result* is an outcome of a specific test, such as a penetration test, vulnerability assessment, or simulated attack. The test results of newly implemented security measures play a crucial role in determining the effectiveness of those measures and any adjustments needed.

Test results offer insights into the strengths and weaknesses of a system's security, informing decisions about necessary improvements or adjustments. Essentially, they serve as a report card for the organization's cybersecurity measures. It's crucial to note what type of test result you are reviewing and how the results were generated. A test result from a vulnerability scanner will show detailed technical insights specific to each system and will generally lack bias. A human-generated test result, such as a result in a cybersecurity risk assessment, might have subjective content and require additional context to be understood.

Backout Plan

Every change in an IT system or process needs a *backout plan*—a meticulously outlined procedure designed to revert any changes that negatively impact security or business operations. A backout plan is more than just a rollback strategy; it's a critical IT service management framework component. A backout plan adheres to a predefined action list and should be created before any software or system upgrade, installation, integration, or transformation occurs. This plan typically includes detailed steps and techniques for uninstalling a new system and reversing process changes to a pre-change working state. The objective is to ensure that automated system business operations continue smoothly, especially if post-implementation testing reveals that the new system fails to meet expectations. As a best practice, you should avoid making changes during peak business hours and always have a comprehensive backout plan.

Maintenance Window

A *maintenance window* is a designated time frame for performing system updates or changes that is strategically chosen to minimize disruptions. We used to say, "Maintenance on a Friday is guaranteed work on a Saturday." Choose your maintenance windows carefully to balance impacts on the business and plan for any unexpected operational impacts that result from your maintenance.

You might find that in a software as a service (SaaS) company, you need to do maintenance on the company's virtual private network (VPN). Engineers may use the VPN for secure remote access and use it frequently throughout the day to connect to development systems, but the usage levels may drop drastically after 6:00 p.m. You would therefore want to plan your maintenance window from 7:00 p.m. to minimize outages to any critical work happening at the company.

Standard Operating Procedure

A *standard operating procedure (SOP)* is a step-by-step instruction set to help workers carry out complex routine operations. SOPs are crucial for maintaining consistency, enhancing security, and ensuring that all team members follow best practices in daily operations. SOPs should be vetted all the way through the senior leadership team to ensure executive support for planned activities.

Key Topic Technical Implications

Technical implications refer to the potential consequences or effects of a technology-related decision or event in the cybersecurity landscape. Technical implications could involve alterations to network infrastructure, modifications to security protocols, or the need for additional server capacity following the implementation of new software or systems. It is important to ensure that you understand all technical implications of any new or existing system to ensure that you can maintain functionality and security for that system.

Allow Lists

Key
Topic

Allow lists, or whitelists, are lists of approved inputs a user or machine can enter on a system. Using an allow list is an easy and safe way to ensure well-defined inputs such as numbers, dates, or postal codes because it allows you to clearly specify permitted values and reject everything else. With HTML5 form validation, you get predefined allow list logic in the built-in data type definitions, so if you indicate that a field contains an email address, you have ready email validation. If only a handful of values are expected, you can use regular expressions to explicitly include them on an allow list.

Using an allow list gets tricky with free-form text fields, where you need some way to allow the vast majority of available characters, potentially in many different alphabets. Unicode character categories can be useful for allowing, for example, only letters and numbers in a variety of international scripts. You should also apply normalization to ensure that all input uses the same encoding, and no invalid characters are present. An allow list needs to be continuously updated as the company works with new applications and removes old ones, and a lot of resource time is required to maintain it. We will explore allow lists in greater detail in Chapter 9, "Understanding the Purpose of Mitigation Techniques Used to Secure the Enterprise."

Block Lists/Deny Lists

Key
Topic

In the context of input validation, a *deny list* is a list of specific elements, characters, or patterns that are disallowed from being entered into a system. When approaching input validation from a security perspective, you might be tempted to implement it by simply disallowing elements that might be used in an injection attack. For example, you might try to ban apostrophes and semicolons to prevent SQL injection (SQLi), parentheses to stop malicious users from inserting a JavaScript function, or angle brackets to eliminate the risk of someone entering HTML tags. Limiting or blocking specific inputs is called block listing or deny listing, and it's usually a bad idea because a developer can't possibly know or anticipate all possible inputs and attack vectors. Blocklist-based validation is hard to implement and maintain and very easy for an attacker to bypass.

Let's say you want to use deny lists despite their issues. These lists are an additional maintenance point, and you need to understand that these lists can potentially break things, and your upper layer programming should not depend on deny lists to stop attacks.

Restricted Activities

Restricted activities are specific actions or operations within a computer or network system that are limited or prohibited to maintain cybersecurity standards. These limitations are often defined through allow lists and deny lists, which, as you've just seen, explicitly outline what is permitted and what is not. For example, restricted activities may include accessing specific system components or downloading unapproved software.

Clearly defined restricted activities are crucial for upholding secure environments and effectively communicating IT systems' acceptable use to internal and external stakeholders. These restrictions are commonly introduced during the employee onboarding process through key documentation like acceptable use policies (AUPs). In change management, access to critical areas like the production environment and change management software is typically restricted to authorized personnel only to ensure that only qualified individuals can make or approve changes, reducing the risk of unauthorized or harmful modifications.

Downtime

Downtime is time during which a system, network, or software application is unavailable to end users or completely offline. Downtime can be scheduled, such as during maintenance windows, as discussed earlier, or it can be unplanned, sometimes due to technical problems or even cyberattacks. Acceptable downtime might be for critical system patching or planned upgrades. A common standard of availability is 99.999%, commonly referred to as "five 9s" availability. "Two 9s" would be a system that guarantees 99% availability in a one-year period, allowing up to 1% downtime, or 3.65 days of unavailability. You might find that if you leverage third-party services, you need to ensure that their systems match, or exceed, your published service-level agreements (SLAs). You may need to implement a change if there is a misalignment between the SLA you have with your clients and what any third-party services provide to you. Unplanned downtime can disrupt business operations, negatively impact employee productivity, and potentially result in data loss. IT professionals are often focused on reducing downtime, which is crucial in cybersecurity and IT management. It's essential to have strategies to address issues when they happen and minimize the duration and impact of unplanned downtime.

Planned downtime is needed to conduct IT maintenance activities, software installation or upgrades, and other activities requiring non-active systems. You might need to upgrade a firewall on the network, which would require turning off the current system. To prevent making the network and end users vulnerable, you would schedule downtime, typically in off-hours/non-peak time, to replace the network device.

Service Restart

In your role as an IT or security professional, one task you'll likely encounter is a *service restart*, which involves halting and then reactivating a system service to implement updates, patches, or configuration changes. This process is similar to turning off a car that's encountering a minor glitch and then restarting it.

The key aspect to note here is to understand the potential implications of a service restart, such as a momentary disruption of service. You need to ensure that potential users of the system are aware of any time impacts. You also need to thoroughly map the connections the service might have with other systems. You don't want to restart a service connected to a critical database that could make the organization or its data vulnerable to attackers. To minimize disruption to users, it is crucial to ensure that this action occurs during a predetermined maintenance window.

Application Restart

Software application restarts are sometimes necessary procedures. An ***application restart*** is like a service restart, but it is concentrated on a specific software application. An example you're no doubt familiar with is an app on your phone freezing and needing to be restarted to function correctly again.

Application restarts are common in IT and cybersecurity. You may often need to restart applications or systems to load patches and enforce updates. Again, communication and coordination with the stakeholders of the application are key.

Legacy Applications

In the course of your career, you will likely encounter older systems still running on a network for a variety of reasons. Handling ***legacy applications***, which are older software programs still serving a critical function in an organization, is a typical duty you might face.

Legacy applications allow you to leverage uncommon technology, and they can be fun, especially if the original engineers are still working on the system. However, dealing with legacy applications often requires understanding older technologies and the specific nuances associated with them, which can be especially challenging if the original engineers have moved on. It is important to understand any connection the legacy application requires to function. You might find limitations in the types of operating systems the organization must maintain if the legacy application requires a certain OS to run properly.

Dependencies

When working with software components, grasping dependencies is crucial. ***Dependencies*** refer to the relationships where one software component or service relies on another to function correctly. Think of the roof on a house. The roof may be supported by large beams of wood or stone columns. If you were to remove any of the beams or columns, you would jeopardize the integrity of the roof. Under-standing dependencies is critical when troubleshooting issues, managing updates, and implementing changes in the IT environment.

Services, newer applications, and legacy applications are all likely to have critical dependencies that you need to understand before you do any maintenance on them.

Documentation

An essential part of any IT or cybersecurity professional's role is the creation and maintenance of documentation. ***Documentation*** is written material that provides information about a system or process. It might include user guides, technical speci-fications, or system descriptions. Documentation may also be written for specific products (for example, product documentation, user guides) or for specific processes (for example, installation instructions, uninstallation guides, patching processes). Documentation can also include policies, procedures, standards, and guidelines. Many organizations have their own security policies that cover critical security top-ics such as change management and change control policies, information security policies, acceptable use policies (AUPs), and business continuity planning (BCP)/disaster recovery policies (DRPs).

Good documentation ensures a clear understanding of system operations, making it easier to train new staff and troubleshoot issues. It is often a good idea to begin with documentation when trying to ascertain any dependencies software or a system may require for operations and to map any dependencies.

Updating Diagrams

In the ever-evolving landscape of your IT environment, the process of updating diagrams plays a vital role. ***Updating diagrams*** is the process of editing current diagrams of systems or networks and inserting any changes that have occurred since the diagrams were originally created. As a best practice, you should ensure strong version control and put a version control number on every diagram. Diagrams can be visualized as maps or blueprints of your network or flowcharts of a process.

Updating diagrams ensures that everyone has an accurate and current picture of the systems. This clarity can significantly enhance troubleshooting and system upgrades. A good configuration management process helps to prevent small or large changes from going undocumented. Undocumented changes can lead to poor performance, inconsistencies, or noncompliance and can negatively impact business operations and security. Poorly documented changes add to instability and downtime. Having good network diagrams and well-written and up-to-date documentation is crucial and allows you to not only troubleshoot problems but also respond quickly to security incidents.

Updating Policies/Procedures

One crucial responsibility you will shoulder is updating policies and procedures. In the cybersecurity landscape, *policies* are the rules governing how IT systems are used and secured, whereas *procedures* are the specific steps required to implement these rules. It's worth noting that policies and procedures are directive controls and help communicate expectations to an organization. You must continuously revise policies and procedures to align with technological advancements, environmental shifts, or system modifications. Doing so ensures smooth, efficient, and secure operation of your IT infrastructure.

You should generally pay special attention to legacy applications that require unique user instructions. For instance, a legacy terminal application that is used to manage network interfaces could inadvertently expose privileged access if a policy changes but the corresponding procedures are not updated.

 ## Version Control

Understanding and effectively implementing version control is vital in IT and cybersecurity domains and extends into areas like documentation. *Version control* is a system that records changes to a file or set of files over time so that you can recall specific versions later. It allows you to track modifications, pinpoint when and by whom changes were made, and, if necessary, revert to an earlier version.

For example, in modern IT environments, code is often checked into a version control repository like GitLab or GitHub. Each change is integrated and tested with the rest of the software system. Organizations that lack proper version control face challenges in tracking bug fixes and security patches. Similarly, vendors and software providers that lack appropriate version control make it difficult for consumers to correlate, triage, and patch security vulnerabilities. Proper version control is a best practice and a necessity for maintaining a secure and efficient operational environment.

Failure to maintain version control can lead to confusion and potential problems. Consider, for instance, a potential issue when a team member says, "Aren't we on version 2.3?" only to discover that the system was updated to version 4.0 weeks ago. Effective version control not only aids in managing changes and troubleshooting issues in a collaborative environment but also plays a crucial role in communicating updates to policies and procedures throughout an organization. It's an essential component of any well-run organization.

Chapter Review Activities

Use the features in this section to study and review the topics in this chapter.

Review Key Topics

Review the most important topics in the chapter, noted with the Key Topic icon in the outer margin of the page. Table 3-2 lists these key topics and the page number on which each is found.

Table 3-2   Key Topics for Chapter 3

Key Topic Element	Description	Page Number
Section	Business Processes Impacting Security Operations	41
Section	Technical Implications	43
Paragraph	Allow lists	44
Paragraph	Deny list	44
Section	Documentation	47
Section	Version Control	48

Define Key Terms

Define the following key terms from this chapter and check your answers in the glossary:

business process, approval process, ownership, stakeholder, impact analysis, test result, backout plan, maintenance window, standard operating procedure (SOP), technical implications, allow list, deny list, restricted activity, downtime, service restart, application restart, legacy application, dependency, documentation, updating diagrams, policy, procedure, version control

Review Questions

Answer the following review questions. Check your answers with the answer key in Appendix A.

1. What is the primary purpose of patch management in an organization's security operations?

2. What is the role of business processes in security operations?

3. What is the significance of an approval process in an organization's security posture?

4. How does ownership of assets influence security operations in an organization?

5. Define the term *technical implications* in the context of cybersecurity.

6. What is an allow list, and what role does it play in system security?

7. What is the downside of relying solely on a block list, or deny list, for input validation?

8. What are restricted activities in the context of cybersecurity?

9. What is the importance of documentation in IT and cybersecurity operations?

10. Why is version control essential in IT and cybersecurity domains?

This chapter covers the following topics related to Objective 1.4 (Explain the importance of using appropriate cryptographic solutions) of the CompTIA Security+ SY0-701 certification exam:

- Public key infrastructure (PKI)
- Encryption
- Tools
- Obfuscation
- Hashing
- Salting
- Digital signatures
- Key stretching
- Blockchain
- Open public ledger
- Certificates

CHAPTER 4

Understanding the Importance of Using Appropriate Cryptographic Solutions

Safeguarding sensitive information in the digital world is just as important as protecting the workforce in a physical facility. To help achieve an appropriate level of security, you can leverage a toolbox of cryptographic measures and techniques that ensure comprehensive data protection of critical data and information transfers. This chapter explores essential cybersecurity concepts, beginning with public key infrastructure (PKI) and encryption, explaining the different keys, levels, and methods of securing data. The chapter then explores security tools that are needed for safeguarding digital assets, like Trusted Platform Module chips, hardware security modules, and key management systems. The chapter also covers obfuscation techniques such as steganography and tokenization, core security practices like hashing and salting, and the ins and outs of digital signatures and key stretching. Finally, the chapter examines blockchain technology and the critical role of certificates in establishing trust, including their management and various types. Let's get started!

"Do I Know This Already?" Quiz

The "Do I Know This Already?" quiz enables you to assess whether you should read this entire chapter thoroughly or jump to the "Chapter Review Activities" section. If you are in doubt about your answers to these questions or your own assessment of your knowledge of the topics, read the entire chapter. Table 4-1 lists the major headings in this chapter and their corresponding "Do I Know This Already?" quiz questions. You can find the answers in Appendix A, "Answers to the 'Do I Know This Already?' Quizzes and Review Questions."

Table 4-1   "Do I Know This Already?" Section-to-Question Mapping

Foundation Topics Section	Questions
Public Key Infrastructure (PKI)	1
Encryption	2–5
Tools	11
Obfuscation	12
Hashing	13
Salting	14
Digital Signatures	6
Key Stretching	15
Blockchain	7
Open public ledger	16
Certificates	8–10

CAUTION   The goal of self-assessment is to gauge your mastery of the topics in this chapter. If you do not know the answer to a question or are only partially sure of the answer, you should mark that question as wrong for purposes of self-assessment. Giving yourself credit for an answer you correctly guess skews your self-assessment results and might provide you with a false sense of security.

1. What is the primary function of public key infrastructure (PKI)?

   a. To distribute and store digital certificates

   b. To facilitate secure email transmissions only

   c. To bind public keys with user identities

   d. To generate public keys only

2. What is the main advantage of asymmetric encryption over symmetric encryption?

   a. It uses a pair of keys (public and private) for communication, which enhances security.

   b. It uses only one key for communication.

   c. It is less secure than symmetric encryption.

   d. It can only be used for large data sets.

3. What does full-disk encryption involve?

    a. It involves applying encryption only to certain partitions of a hard drive.

    b. It involves applying encryption to an entire hard drive, including data, files, the OS, and software programs.

    c. It involves encrypting only the OS of a hard drive.

    d. It involves encrypting only the data of a hard drive.

4. What does a cipher suite in Transport Layer Security (TLS) typically include?

    a. Only a key exchange algorithm

    b. Only a bulk encryption algorithm and message authentication code (MAC) algorithm

    c. Only an authentication algorithm

    d. A combination of key exchange algorithm, bulk encryption algorithm, message authentication code (MAC) algorithm, and potentially signatures and an authentication algorithm

5. What is the main difference between a stream cipher and a block cipher?

    a. A stream cipher encrypts plaintext digits one at a time, whereas a block cipher encrypts large blocks of digits.

    b. A block cipher always provides better security than a stream cipher.

    c. A block cipher always has higher speed and lower hardware complexity than a stream cipher.

    d. A stream cipher requires a longer key than a block cipher.

6. Which of the following best describes the purpose of a digital signature?

    a. To provide only authentication

    b. To ensure only data integrity

    c. To only generate public and private keys

    d. To verify the authenticity of digital messages and ensure that they were not altered in transit

7. What feature of a blockchain makes it difficult to cheat or change the system?

    a. Storage of data in blocks that are chained together

    b. Use as a ledger for transactions

    c. Duplicated digital ledger of transactions that is distributed across the network

    d. Storage of different types of information on a blockchain

8. Which of the following encoding formats is used for X.509 certificates and has restrictive rules for length, character strings, and how elements are sorted?

   a. Basic Encoding Rules (BER)

   b. Canonical Encoding Rules (CER)

   c. Distinguished Encoding Rules (DER)

   d. Privacy-Enhanced Mail (PEM)

9. What file format is used to store a server certificate, intermediate certificates, and a private key in one encryptable file?

   a. PEM

   b. DER

   c. P12/PFX

   d. X.509

10. If a certificate file uses the .der extension, what format is the certificate file in?

    a. ASCII

    b. Binary

    c. Text

    d. Unicode

11. Which of the following physical devices is specifically designed to secure digital keys and perform encryption and decryption tasks?

    a. Hardware Security Module (HSM)

    b. Trusted Platform Module (TPM)

    c. Key Management System (KMS)

    d. Secure Enclave

12. What is the primary purpose of obfuscation in data security?

    a. To encrypt data

    b. To alter or disguise data to make it less intelligible

    c. To store data in a secure location

    d. To transmit data securely

13. What is the primary use of hashing in cybersecurity?

    a. To encrypt data for secure transmission

    b. To add random data to passwords

    c. To verify the authenticity and integrity of data

    d. To convert passwords into longer keys

14. What is the purpose of adding a salt to a password before hashing?

    a. To safeguard the password in storage by adding randomness

    b. To make the password longer and easier to remember

    c. To encrypt the password

    d. To convert the password into a key for encryption

15. What is the primary objective of key stretching in cryptography?

    a. To reduce the size of the cryptographic key

    b. To make a key, typically a password, more secure against brute-force attacks

    c. To encrypt data using a longer key

    d. To store cryptographic keys securely

16. What role does the open public ledger play in blockchain transactions?

    a. It encrypts transaction data

    b. It verifies the authenticity of accounts and transaction availability

    c. It stores private keys for transaction security

    d. It directly transfers funds between accounts

Foundation Topics

Public Key Infrastructure (PKI)

This section highlights important public key infrastructure concepts, starting with key management. From there we dive into certificate authorities (CAs), intermediate CAs, and registration authorities (RAs). The discussion of PKI continues with coverage of certificate revocation lists (CRLs), certificate attributes, Online Certificate Status Protocol (OCSP), and certificate-signing requests (CSRs).

Public Key

A *key management system* is used for managing cryptographic keys throughout their lifecycle. *Public key infrastructure (PKI)* is a key management system of hardware and software, policies and procedures, and people. It is used to create, distribute, manage, store, and revoke digital certificates. If you have connected to a secure website in the past, you have used PKI. However, PKI can be used for other things as well, such as secure email transmissions and secure connections to remote computers and remote networks. PKI is all encompassing: It includes users, client computers, servers, services, and, most of all, encryption. Don't confuse PKI with public key encryption. Though they are related, PKI is a way of accomplishing public key encryption, but not all public key encryption schemes are PKI.

Private and Public Key

PKI creates asymmetric key pairs, each with a public key and a private key. The *private key* is kept secret, whereas the *public key* can be distributed. In some PKI implementations, a trusted third party, known as the escrow agent, securely stores private keys in a *key escrow*. This is done to ensure that under specific circumstances, such as when a private key is lost or a legal requirement applies, the key can be retrieved and used by authorized entities. While key escrow serves as a safety net, it also raises concerns about the potential misuse or unauthorized access to sensitive keys. If the key pair is generated at a server, it is considered to be centralized, and the public key is distributed as needed. If the key pair is generated at a local computer, it is considered to be decentralized, and the keys are not distributed; instead, they are used by that local system. An example of public key usage would be a certificate obtained by a web browser during an encrypted session with an e-commerce website. An example of private key usage would be a user needing to encrypt the digital signature of a private email. The difference is the level of confidentiality. The public key certificate obtained by the web browser is public and might be obtained by thousands of individuals. The private key used to encrypt the email is not to be shared with anyone.

In a nutshell, public key infrastructures are set up in such a way as to bind public keys with user identities. This is usually done with certificates distributed by a certificate authority. Less commonly, it is done by means of a root of trust.

Encryption

Encryption is the process of converting information into a coded format that is unreadable by unauthorized users. Encryption plays a crucial role in information security, serving as a critical defense against unauthorized data access. Several kinds and levels of encryption are designed to protect different types of data and meet various security needs. This section covers the wide-ranging topic of encryption, discussing its levels, its multiple uses, and various encryption techniques.

Level

You are likely to hear discussions of "levels of encryption." In the context of disk encryption, *level* refers to the extent or scope at which data is transformed into a secure format. Disk encryption protects information by converting it into unreadable code that cannot be deciphered easily by unauthorized people. Disk encryption involves using disk encryption software or hardware to encrypt every bit of data that goes on a disk or disk volume.

Full Disk

Full-disk encryption is a cryptographic method that involves applying encryption to an entire hard drive, including data, files, the operating system, and software programs. Full-disk encryption places an exterior guard on the internal contents of the device. Unlike past iterations of full-disk encryption, the process to encrypt hard drives has become quite simple and is supported by all the major vendors.

Under no circumstance should you store confidential files unencrypted (at rest) on your hard disks. You should use disk encryption when storing confidential or sensitive data. Disk encryption can mitigate risks of data exposure due to loss or theft of stored data. Full-disk encryption can provide "blanket" protection so users do not have to protect individually stored files, and it ensures that any remnants of data are secure. Such remnants can be temporary files, browser cache files, and application-specific automatic backups. All current operating systems provide disk encryption capability. All major operating systems support disk encryption, so there should be no reason not to use it.

Partition

A *partition* is a portion of a disk that the operating system treats as a separate unit. Different partitions can be useful for running different operating systems or even creating specific storage sections for system recovery. Users can also encrypt partitions independently of other portions of the operating system. This can be helpful when you need to store highly sensitive information alongside less-sensitive data.

File

Files are containers that hold data like text, images, audio, video, or a combination of them all. *File encryption* adds an even deeper granularity of security to data storage, allowing you to apply encryption at the file level. You might also find that encrypting specific files helps protect data in shared environments, such as in corporate computing environments.

Volume

A common way to secure large amounts of data on a disk is to encrypt the entire volume. A *volume* is a single accessible storage area that may include one or many physical drives. *Volume encryption* involves encrypting the entire volume, which might span multiple physical drives. By encrypting all the data on a specific volume, you can maintain the confidentiality of a large amount of data at once, enhancing overall security.

Database

One way to secure a database is through *database encryption*, which involves encrypting the database to protect sensitive information. Securing databases and applications that utilize those databases starts with five best practices:

- Separate the database from the web servers.

- Encrypt stored data, files, and backups of the database.

- Use a web application firewall (WAF), also called a database firewall. Remember to keep patches current and enable security controls.

- Ensure physical security. (This is usually a given, but don't leave anything to chance.) Ensure that your databases are in locked cabinets, follow hardening best practices for your specific database, manage access to the database, and tightly guard secrets.

- Make sure you have audit procedures and active monitoring of the database activity enabled. Also, ensure that alerts generate tickets and receive proper attention.

Record

A *record* is a collection of related data items that are treated as a unit, such as a row in a database or a spreadsheet. ***Record-level encryption*** involves securing these individual units of data, safeguarding the integrity and confidentiality of specific data entries in a larger data set.

Transport/Communication

Today, more than ever before, data security is essential, whether the data is stored on a disk, moving across a network, or being actively processed. ***Transport/communication*** refers to security measures applied to data in transit—that is, data as it moves across networks, from its origin to its destination. Encryption is critical for safeguarding this data from unauthorized access and potential breaches.

Encryption at Rest, in Transit/Motion, and in Processing

What do you need to encrypt? Without a doubt, you need to encrypt data. More specifically, you need to encrypt three types of data: data at rest, data in transit (or motion), and data in use (or processing). Understanding the unique requirements for securing these data states is essential for a robust cybersecurity strategy. Figure 4-1 provides a visual representation to help you grasp these concepts more effectively.

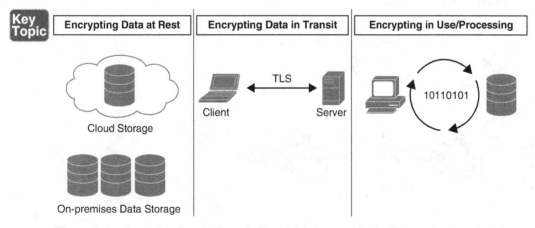

Figure 4-1 Encrypting Data at Rest, in Transit/Motion, and in Use/Processing

Data at rest is inactive data that is archived—that is, backed up or stored with a cloud storage service. Data in transit (also known as data in motion) is data that crosses a network or data that currently resides in computer memory. Data in use/processing can be described as actively used data undergoing constant change, such as data that's stored in databases or spreadsheets. We will explore these concepts of data states in greater detail in Chapter 12, "Comparing and Contrasting Concepts and Strategies to Protect Data."

Symmetric Versus Asymmetric Encryption

Symmetric and asymmetric encryption are key components in securing data and communications. *Symmetric encryption* employs a single key for both the encryption and decryption processes, making it more straightforward than asymmetric encryption but potentially less secure if the key is compromised. On the other hand, *asymmetric encryption* utilizes a pair of keys: a public key for encryption and a private key for decryption. This dual-key approach adds an extra layer of security but can be more complex to manage. The following sections delve deeper into the intricacies, advantages, and disadvantages of each method so you can understand their roles in data security.

Symmetric encryption, illustrated in Figure 4-2, is the simplest kind of encryption; it involves only one secret key to encrypt and decrypt information. Symmetric encryption is an old technique, and it's also the best-known technique. It involves using a secret key that can either be a number, word, or string of random letters. It is blended with the plaintext of a message to change the content in a particular way. The sender and recipient should know the secret key that is used to encrypt and decrypt all the messages.

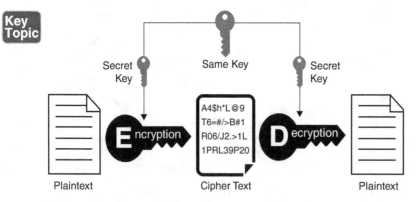

Figure 4-2 Symmetric Encryption

Examples of symmetric encryption algorithms include AES and RC4. AES (Advanced Encryption Standard) is the go-to symmetric block cipher in modern cryptography. Today's most widely used symmetric algorithms are AES-128, AES-192, and AES-256. The main disadvantage of symmetric key encryption is that all parties involved must exchange the key used to encrypt the data before they can decrypt it.

Multiple vulnerabilities have been discovered in RC4, rendering it obsolete. Older algorithms like Blowfish and DES were significant in advancing cryptography but have since been replaced due to their vulnerabilities and short key lengths. Today, AES is the most commonly deployed encryption standard, offering robust security and efficiency.

Whereas symmetric encryption uses the same key for encryption and decryption, asymmetric encryption uses two keys to encrypt plaintext. Secret keys are exchanged over the network. This type of encryption ensures that malicious persons do not misuse the keys. It is important to note that anyone who has a secret key can decrypt the message, and asymmetric encryption uses two related keys to boost security. A public key is made freely available to anyone who might want to send a message. The second key, which is private, is kept a secret so that only the recipient or the sender will know.

A message that is encrypted using a public key can only be decrypted using a private key, whereas a message encrypted using a private key can be decrypted using a public key. Security of the public key is not required because the key is publicly available and can be passed over the network or Internet. The asymmetric key has far better power in ensuring the security of information transmitted during communication.

Asymmetric encryption is mostly used in day-to-day communication channels, especially over the Internet. Asymmetric key encryption algorithms include ElGamal, RSA, DSA, elliptic-curve techniques, and PKCS.

Figure 4-3 illustrates asymmetric encryption.

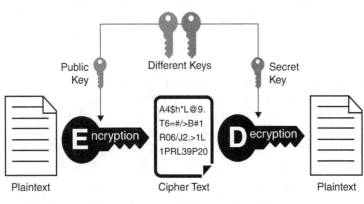

Figure 4-3 Asymmetric Encryption

To use asymmetric encryption, you must have a way of discovering public keys. One commonly used technique is to use digital certificates in a client/server model of communication. A certificate is a package of information that identifies a user and a server. It contains information such as an organization's name, the organization that issued the certificate, the user's email address and country, and the user's public key. When a server and client require a secure encrypted communication, they send a query over the network to the other party, which sends back a copy of the certificate. The other party's public key can be extracted from the certificate. A certificate can also be used to uniquely identify the holder.

In an asymmetric key system, each user has a pair of keys: a private key and a public key. To send an encrypted message, you must encrypt the message with the recipient's public key. The recipient then decrypts the message with their private key. Remember that public keys encrypt, and private keys decrypt.

Table 4-2 highlights the differences between symmetric and asymmetric encryption.

Key Topic

Table 4-2 Symmetric Versus Asymmetric Encryption

Symmetric Encryption	Asymmetric Encryption
Uses a single key that needs to be shared among the people who need to receive the message.	Uses a pair of public keys and a private key to encrypt and decrypt messages when communicating.
Is an older technique than asymmetric encryption.	Is a newer technique than symmetric encryption, which was introduced to complement the inherent problem of the need to share the key in the symmetric encryption model.
Takes relatively less time than asymmetric encryption	Takes relatively more time than symmetric encryption

Key Exchange

Key exchange, also known as key establishment, is a method in cryptography by which cryptographic keys are exchanged between two parties, allowing use of a cryptographic algorithm. If the sender and receiver wish to exchange encrypted messages, each must be equipped to encrypt messages to be sent and to decrypt messages received. The nature of the equipping they require depends on the encryption technique they might use. If they use a code, both require a copy of the same source code. If they use a cipher, they need appropriate keys. If the cipher is a symmetric key cipher, both need a copy of the same key. If it is an asymmetric key cipher with the public/private key property, each needs the other's public key. Figure 4-4 illustrates the key exchange process.

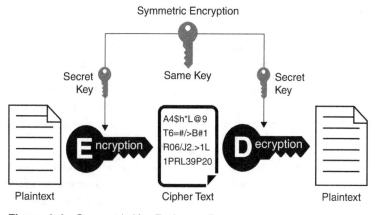

Figure 4-4 Symmetric Key Exchange Process

Algorithms

An *algorithm* is a mathematical formula used in cryptographic processes. A *cipher suite* is a set of algorithms that help secure a network connection that uses Transport Layer Security (TLS). A cipher suite usually contains a set of algorithms that include a key exchange algorithm, bulk encryption algorithm, and message authentication code (MAC) algorithm.

The key exchange algorithm is used to exchange a key between two devices. This key is used to encrypt and decrypt the messages being sent between two machines. The bulk encryption algorithm is used to encrypt the data being sent. The MAC algorithm provides data integrity checks to ensure that the data sent does not change in transit. In addition, cipher suites can include signatures and an authentication algorithm to help authenticate the server and/or client. Hundreds of different cipher suites contain different combinations of these algorithms. Some cipher suites offer better security than others.

The structure and use of the cipher suite concept are defined in the TLS standard document. TLS 1.2 was the most prevalent version of TLS. The newer version of TLS (TLS 1.3) includes additional security requirements for cipher suites. Cipher suites defined for TLS 1.2 cannot be used in TLS 1.3 and vice versa unless otherwise stated in their definition. TLS 1.2 was defined in RFC 5246 and was in use after 2008 by the majority of all web browsers. TLS 1.3 was finalized on March 21, 2018, and the final version was published in August of that year in RFC 8446. The major benefits of TLS 1.3 over TLS 1.2 are improved security and faster speed.

A stream cipher is a symmetric key cipher in which plaintext digits are combined with a pseudorandom cipher digit stream known as a keystream. In a stream cipher, the plaintext digits are encrypted one at a time, each with the corresponding digit of the keystream, to give a digit of the ciphertext stream. Because encryption of each digit is dependent on the current state of the cipher, it is also known as a state cipher. A digit is typically a bit, and the combining operation is an exclusive OR (XOR).

The pseudorandom keystream is typically generated serially from a random seed value using digital shift registers. The seed value serves as the cryptographic key for decrypting the ciphertext stream. Stream ciphers represent a different approach to symmetric encryption from block ciphers.

Stream ciphers typically execute at a higher speed than block ciphers and have lower hardware complexity. However, stream ciphers can be susceptible to serious security problems if used incorrectly; in particular, the same starting state seed must never be used twice.

A block cipher is an encryption method that applies a deterministic algorithm along with a symmetric key to encrypt a block of text instead of encrypting one bit at a time, as occurs with stream ciphers. For example, a common block cipher, AES, encrypts 128-bit blocks with a key of predetermined length: 128, 192, or 256 bits. Block ciphers operate on large blocks of digits with a fixed, unvarying transformation. This distinction is not always clear-cut. In some modes of operation, a block cipher primitive is used in such a way that it effectively acts as a stream cipher.

Key Length

Key length is the number of bits in an encryption algorithm's key. A short key length means poor security. However, a long key length does not necessarily mean good security. The key length determines the maximum number of combinations required to break an encryption algorithm.

The strength of encryption is related to the difficulty of discovering the key, which in turn depends on both the cipher used and the length of the key.

Encryption strength is often described in terms of the size of the keys used to perform the encryption: Longer keys may provide stronger encryption. Key length is measured in bits. The 128-bit keys for use with the RC4 symmetric key cipher supported by SSL provide significantly better cryptographic protection than 40-bit keys for use with the same cipher. 128-bit RC4 encryption is 3×1026 times stronger than 40-bit RC4 encryption.

Different ciphers require different key lengths to achieve the same level of encryption strength. The RSA cipher used for public key encryption, for example, can use only a subset of all possible values for a key of a given length, due to the nature of the mathematical problem on which it is based. Other ciphers, such as those used for symmetric key encryption, can use all possible values for a key of a given length rather than a subset of those values.

Thus, a 128-bit key for use with a symmetric key encryption cipher would provide stronger encryption than a 128-bit key for use with the RSA public key encryption cipher. This difference explains why the RSA public key encryption cipher must use a 512-bit key (or longer) to be considered cryptographically strong, whereas symmetric key ciphers can achieve approximately the same level of strength with a 64-bit key.

NOTE   Many cryptographic implementations are broken before the encryption itself is broken.

Tools

An array of *tools*—specialized technologies and protocols—are designed to secure and manage digital information. These tools include Trusted Platform Module (TPM) chips, which safeguard information on computer systems; hardware security modules (HSMs), which secure digital keys and perform encryption and decryption; key management systems (KMSs), which handle the administration of cryptographic keys throughout their lifecycle; and secure enclaves, which are protected spaces within processors to keep sensitive data safe. Each of these tools plays a critical role in the encryption and safekeeping of digital communications and data, ensuring that they remain secure at rest, in transit, and during processing. Understanding how to effectively use these tools is essential to enforcing robust security protocols in any digital environment.

Trusted Platform Module

Trusted Platform Module (TPM) technology is designed to provide hardware-based, security-related functions. A TPM chip is a secure cryptoprocessor that is designed to carry out cryptographic operations. The chip includes multiple physical security mechanisms to make it tamper resistant, and malicious software is unable to tamper with the security functions of the TPM chip. Some of the key advantages of using TPM technology are that you can do the following:

Key Topic

- Generate, store, and limit the use of cryptographic keys.

- Carry out platform device authentication by using the TPM chip's unique RSA key, which is burned into the chip.

- Ensure platform integrity by taking and storing security measurements.

TPM technology is used for system integrity measurements and for key creation and use. During a system's boot process, the boot code that is loaded can be measured and recorded in the TPM chip. The integrity measurements can be used as evidence of how a system started and to make sure that a TPM-based key was used only when the correct software was used to boot the system.

In more modern Windows versions, such as Windows 10 and Windows 11, the operating system automatically initializes and takes ownership of the TPM chip. This means that in most cases, you should avoid configuring a TPM chip through the TPM management console (**tpm.msc**).

NOTE   Trusted Platform Module (TPM) chips and hardware security modules (HSMs) provide strong hardware-based cryptographic solutions across a number of use cases, including password protection and device identification and authentication.

Hardware Security Module

Hardware security modules (HSMs) are physical devices that act as secure cryptoprocessors. This means they are used for encryption during secure login/ authentication processes, during digital signings of data, and for payment security systems. The beauty of a hardware-based encryption device such as an HSM (or a Trusted Platform Module chip) is that it is faster than software encryption.

HSMs can be found in adapter card form, as devices that plug into a computer via USB, and as network-attached devices. They are generally tamper-proof, providing a high level of physical security. They can also be used in high-availability clustered environments because they work independently of other computer systems and are used solely to calculate the data required for encryption keys. However, many of these devices require some kind of management software to be installed on the computer they are connected to. Some manufacturers offer this software as part of the purchase, but others do not, forcing the purchaser to build the management software themselves. Due to this lack of management software and the cost involved in general, HSMs have seen slower deployment with some organizations. This concept also holds true for hardware-based drive encryption solutions.

Often, HSMs are involved in the generation, storage, and archiving of encrypted key pairs such as the ones used in SSL/TLS sessions online, public key cryptography, and PKI.

Key Management System

When safeguarding digital data, a *key management system (KMS)* is indispensable. It's the backbone of managing cryptographic keys—the secret codes that lock and unlock your data. When data breaches seem almost routine, a robust KMS can be a game changer. These are the central functions of a KMS:

- **Generation of cryptographic keys:** A KMS is responsible for creating strong and secure keys. These keys are the first line of defense in protecting your data. The strength of a cryptographic key lies in its randomness and complexity, which a KMS ensures.

- **Secure storage of keys:** Just as you wouldn't leave the keys to your house under the doormat, cryptographic keys need to be stored securely. A KMS stores cryptographic keys in a protected environment, shielded from unauthorized access and potential threats.

- **Key exchange:** Sharing cryptographic keys securely is essential, especially in environments where data needs to be shared across networks or between users. A KMS facilitates the secure exchange of these keys, ensuring that they don't fall into the wrong hands during transmission.

- **Key use and access control:** It's not enough to just create and store keys; a KMS also manages who can use them and for what purpose. This means setting policies and permissions for key access, ensuring that only authorized users and applications can use the keys.

- **Key replacement and rotation:** Over time, cryptographic keys can become vulnerable, or their integrity can be compromised. A KMS manages the lifecycle of keys, replacing and rotating them as needed. This is a critical aspect of maintaining long-term data security.

A KMS is clearly a vital component in your security toolbox, serving as a secure vault for cryptographic keys. It reduces data breach risks by ensuring only authorized access to sensitive information. A KMS upholds data integrity and meets regulatory compliance requirements while also streamlining operations by automating key management.

Secure Enclave

The secure enclave is a crucial element of advanced security systems, providing additional protection for sensitive data on a device. The *secure enclave* is a hardware-based feature in certain devices, such as iPhones, that securely handles encryption and decryption tasks. This microprocessor within a larger chip uses its boot process and runs a distinct operating system from the primary device, effectively segregating it. It's designed to resist tampering and prevent its data from being accessed by any means other than using its strict protocol. Unlocking specific data requires keys such as biometric information (for example, fingerprints or facial recognition data), ensuring that this sensitive data remains secure even if the primary device is compromised.

The entire secure enclave is designed to resist software and hardware attacks. Its unique hardware and firmware are inextricably tied together, meaning a breach in one does not lead to a vulnerability in the other. Its ability to ensure data integrity in the face of threats, including sophisticated physical attacks, makes the secure enclave a key tool in secure data management and transmission.

Obfuscation

Obfuscation is a critical technique for protecting sensitive information by making it less obvious to unauthorized users. Obfuscation involves altering or disguising the original data to prevent it from being easily understood or accessed. While encryption is a commonly used method for securing data, obfuscation adds an extra layer of security by further complicating the data, making it challenging to decipher without the proper tools or knowledge.

The objective of obfuscation is not just to encrypt the data but to make it confusing, unclear, or unintelligible. This is particularly useful in scenarios where encryption alone may not suffice or where the data needs to be used in a specific way that encryption would hinder.

This section explores various obfuscation methods and the unique approach and application of each of them.

Steganography

Steganography is the practice of hiding a secret message inside or even on top of something that is not secret. That something can be just about anything you want. These days, steganography may involve embedding a secret piece of text inside a picture or hiding a secret message or script inside a Microsoft Word or Excel document.

The purpose of steganography is to conceal and deceive. It is a form of covert communication and can involve the use of any medium to hide messages. Steganography is not a form of cryptography because it doesn't involve scrambling data or using a key. Instead, it is a form of data hiding and can be executed in unique ways.

Steganography has been used for centuries, but these days, hackers and IT pros use it. The word *steganography* is composed of the Greek roots *steganos*, for "hidden" or "covered" and *graph*, for "to write." Put these words together, and you have something close to "hidden writing" or "secret writing." A number of apps can be used for steganography, including Steghide, Foremost, Xiao, Stegais, and Concealment.

TIP   The Kali Linux distribution includes a number of steganography tools that can be useful in not only hiding data but detecting and uncovering steganography data.

Audio Steganography

You not only can hide secret information in images and documents but also can hide data and files in audio files. *Audio steganography* is a technique used to transmit hidden information by modifying an audio signal in an imperceptible manner. It is the science of hiding some secret text or audio information in a host message.

The host message before steganography and the steganography message after steganography have the same characteristics. Tools like DeepSound allow you to hide and extract secret data or files directly from audio files. Newer tools also support encrypting secret files using AES-256 to improve data protection.

Embedding secret messages in digital sound is a more difficult process. Various techniques for embedding information in digital audio have been established. Audio steganography consists of a carrier or audio file, a message, and a password. The carrier, also known as a *cover file*, conceals the secret information. With steganography, the sender wants the secret message they send to remain secret. The secret message can be any source: file, text, image, or another audio file. The file is encoded (*steg*) with the secret key, which is provided to the receiver, who can decode the message and the corresponding file. The cover file combined with the secret information is known as a *stego-file*. Figure 4-5 shows the audio steganography process.

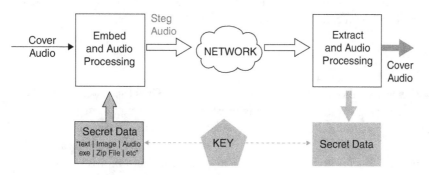

Figure 4-5   Audio Steganography Model

Video Steganography

Video steganography is a technique used to hide any kind of file in a cover video file. The use of video-based steganography can be more secure than steganography with other multimedia files because of the size and complexity. A video is a collection of frames, and each frame is an image. So if you pull out all the frames from a video, you can use this method to store the data using least significant bit (LSB) steganography and stitch those frames back into a video with the secret message. You can use tools like OpenCv to extract frames from a video, and to extract audio, you could use FFmpeg, which is free and open source. After you have mixed in the steg, you can use FFmpeg to stitch it all together with the hidden message to form a video. How many videos have you watched streamed from the Internet? Now imagine that at least 5% of them have included some hidden data.

Image Steganography

Image steganography is a technique used to hide any kind of file in an image file. There are currently three effective methods for applying image steganography:

- **Least significant bit (LSB) substitution:** This method works by iterating through the pixels of an image and extracting the alpha, red, green, and blue (ARGB) hexadecimal values. It then separates the color channels and gets the least significant bit. Meanwhile, it also iterates through the characters of the message, setting the bit to its corresponding binary value.

- **Blocking:** This method works by breaking up an image into blocks and using Discrete Cosine Transforms (DCT). Each block is broken into 64 DCT coefficients that approximate luminance and color—the values of which are modified for hiding messages.

- **Palette modification:** This method replaces the unused colors in an image's color palette with colors that represent the hidden message.

Tokenization

Tokenization is used mostly when protecting data at rest. It is the process of randomly generating a token value for plaintext data and storing the mapping in a database. Tokenization is difficult to scale securely due to the performance and size of the underlying database. Tokenized data is difficult to exchange because it requires direct access to the database (or token vault). Encryption provides a better way to scale and exchange sensitive data in a secure manner.

Database tokenization is the process of turning sensitive data into nonsensitive data called *tokens* that can be used in a database or an internal system without bringing it into scope. The tokens are sent to an organization's internal systems for use, and the original data is stored in a secure token vault. There is no key, or algorithm, that can be used to derive the original data for a token; instead, tokens are sent to a token vault. Figure 4-6 illustrates the tokenization process.

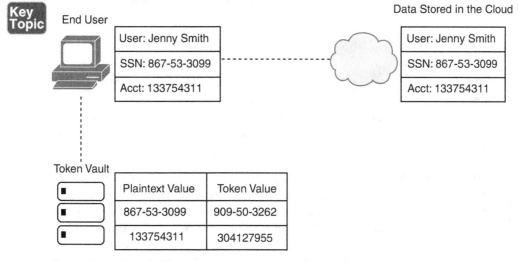

Figure 4-6 Tokenization

The token value can be used in applications as a substitute for the real data. If and when the real data needs to be retrieved, the token is submitted to the vault, and the index is used to cross-reference and fetch the real value for use in the authorization process. To the end user, this operation is performed seamlessly and nearly instantaneously by the browser or application. Users are likely not aware that the data is stored in the cloud in a different format.

The advantage of tokens is that there is no mathematical relationship to the real data they represent. If they are breached, there is no problem because they have no meaning. No key can reverse them back to the real data values. Consideration can also be given to the design of a token to make it more useful. Apple Pay uses a similar technology; for example, the last four digits of a payment card number can be preserved in the token so that the tokenized number (or a portion of it) can be printed on the customer's receipt so they can see a reference to their actual credit card number. The printed characters might be all asterisks plus those last four digits. In this case, the merchant has only a token, not a real card number, for security purposes.

NOTE   Remember that tokenization assigns a random surrogate value with no mathematical relationship and can still be reversed by linking the token back to the original data. Outside of the system, a token has no value; it is just meaningless data.

Data Masking

Data masking (also known as data obfuscation) is the act of hiding sensitive information/data with specific characters or other data in order to protect it. For example, data masking (and obfuscation) has been used to protect personally identifiable information (PII) or commercially sensitive data from unauthorized users and attackers.

Substitution is a technique that has been used for data masking and obfuscation. Using this technique, you substitute the original data with another authentic-looking value. For instance, you may replace a Social Security number or credit card number with a fake number. Figure 4-7 shows a basic example of substitution.

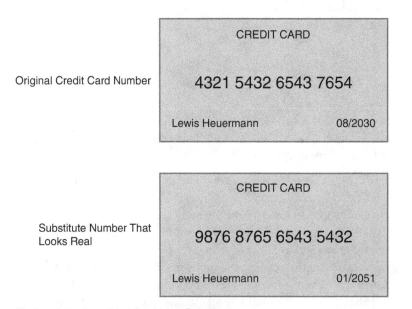

Figure 4-7   Data Masking Using Substitution

Figure 4-8 shows another example of masking that involves revealing only the last four digits of the credit card number.

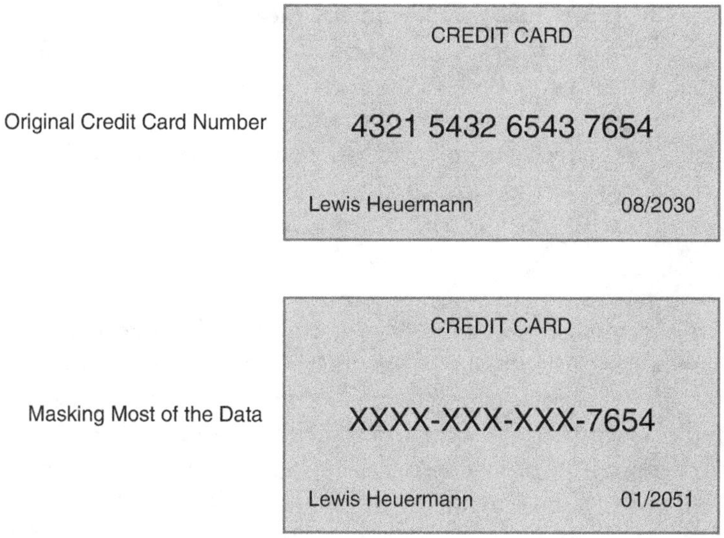

Original Credit Card Number

CREDIT CARD

4321 5432 6543 7654

Lewis Heuermann   08/2030

Masking Most of the Data

CREDIT CARD

XXXX-XXX-XXX-7654

Lewis Heuermann   01/2051

Figure 4-8   Additional Data Masking Example

Hashing

Hashing is a one-way function in which data is mapped to a fixed-length value. Hashing is primarily used for authentication. As described in the next section, salting is an additional step that can be added during hashing (typically in association with hashed passwords); it adds an additional value to the end of the password to change the hash value produced. Whereas encryption is meant to protect data in transit, hashing is meant to verify that a file or piece of data hasn't been altered—that is, to ensure that it is authentic. In other words, it serves as a checksum.

Here's how hashing works. Each hashing algorithm outputs at a fixed length. For instance, SHA-256 outputs a hash value that is 256 bits, usually represented by a 64-character hexadecimal string. The size of the data block differs from one algorithm to another, but it remains the same for a particular algorithm. For example, SHA-1 takes in the message/data in blocks of 512 bits only. So, if a message is exactly 512 bits long, the hash function runs only once, which is 80 rounds in the case of SHA-1. Similarly, if the message is 1024 bits, it's divided into two blocks of 512 bits, and the hash function is run twice. Because there is nearly no chance of a message being exactly the same size as the block, a technique called *padding* is used. Padding takes the entire message and divides it into fixed-size data blocks. The hash function is repeated multiple times—one time for each data block. The output of the first data block is fed as input along with the second data block. If you change a bit anywhere in the message, the entire hash value changes; this is called the avalanche effect.

Every hash value is unique. If two different files produce the same unique hash value, this is called a collision, and it makes the algorithm essentially useless. Let's say you want to digitally sign a piece of software and make it available for download on your website. To do this, you create a hash of the script or executable you're signing. Then, after adding your digital signature, you hash that, too. Next, the whole thing is encrypted so that it can be downloaded.

Salting

In cryptography, a *salt* is random data that is used as an additional input to a one-way function that hashes data, a password, or a passphrase. *Salting* is the addition of random data to a password before hashing. Salts are used to safeguard passwords in storage. Historically, a password was stored in plaintext on a system, but over time, additional safeguards were developed to protect a user's password against being read from the system. A salt is one of those methods.

Salts can help defend against precomputed hash attacks (for example, rainbow tables). Because salts do not have to be memorized by humans, they can make the size of the hash table required for a successful attack prohibitively large without placing a burden on the users. Because salts are different in each case, they also protect commonly used passwords or users who use the same password on several sites by making all salted hash instances for the same password different from each other.

Digital Signatures

A *digital signature* is a mathematical scheme for verifying the authenticity of a digital message or document. A valid digital signature, where the prerequisites are satisfied, gives a recipient very strong reason to believe that the message was created by a known sender (authentication) and that the message was not altered in transit (integrity).

Digital signatures are a standard element of most cryptographic protocol suites and are commonly used for software distribution, in financial transactions, with contract management software, and in other cases where it is important to detect forgery or tampering. Digital signatures are often used to implement electronic signatures, including any electronic data that carries the intent of a signature.

Digital signatures employ asymmetric cryptography. In many instances, they provide a layer of validation and security to messages sent through a nonsecure channel. Properly implemented, a digital signature gives the receiver reason to believe the message was sent by the claimed sender. Properly implemented digital signatures are difficult to forge. Digital signature schemes, in the sense used here, are cryptographically based and must be implemented properly to be effective. Digital signatures can also provide non-repudiation, meaning that the signer cannot successfully claim they did not sign a message while also claiming that their private key remains secret. Some non-repudiation schemes offer a timestamp for the digital signature so that even if the private key is exposed, the signature is valid.

A digital signature scheme typically consists of three algorithms:

- A key generation algorithm that selects a private key uniformly at random from a set of possible private keys. The algorithm outputs the private key and a corresponding public key.

- A signing algorithm that, given a message and a private key, produces a signature.

- A signature verifying algorithm that, given the message, public key, and signature, either accepts or rejects the message's claim to authenticity.

Two main properties are required for a digital signature:

- The authenticity of a signature generated from a fixed message and fixed private key can be verified by using the corresponding public key.

- Generating a valid signature for a party without knowing that party's private key should be computationally infeasible.

A digital signature is an authentication mechanism that enables the creator of the message to attach a code that acts as a signature. The Digital Signature Algorithm (DSA), developed by the National Institute of Standards and Technology (NIST), is one of many examples of a signing algorithm.

> **NOTE** As organizations move away from paper documents with ink signatures, digital signatures can provide added assurance of the provenance, identity, and status of an electronic document and can also be used to acknowledge informed consent and approval by a signatory.

Key Stretching

Key stretching techniques are used to make a possibly weak key, typically a password or passphrase, more secure against a brute-force attack by increasing the resources (time and possibly space) needed to test each possible key. Key stretching is a cryptographic process that involves converting a password to a longer and more random key for cryptographic purposes. The process of converting a password into a key is accomplished by using a type of algorithm known as a key derivation function, which may include a salt and also pepper with the password to make the key more difficult to guess:

- **Salt:** Randomly generated data that is used as an additional input to a one-way function that hashes data.

- **Pepper:** A randomly generated value that is added to a password hash and should be kept secret. Also referred to as a secret salt.

Key stretching can also be applied to the top level key rather than to a password. If a password is extremely long, key stretching can result in a shorter and less secure key.

Blockchain

A *blockchain* records information in a way that makes it difficult or impossible to change, hack, or cheat the system. A blockchain is a specific type of database. It differs from a typical database in the way it stores information: A blockchain stores data in blocks that are then chained together. As new data comes in, it is entered into a fresh block. When a block is filled with data, it is chained onto the previous block, and so the data is chained together in chronological order. Different types of information can be stored on a blockchain, but the most common use so far has been as a ledger for transactions.

A blockchain is essentially a digital ledger of transactions that is duplicated and distributed across the entire network of computer systems on the blockchain. Each block in the chain contains a number of transactions, and every time a new transaction occurs on the blockchain, a record of that transaction is added to every participant's ledger. The decentralized database managed by multiple participants is known as distributed ledger technology (DLT).

Open Public Ledger

The *open public ledger* organizes blocks of information into a long chain. When a buyer and seller engage in a transaction, the blockchain verifies the authenticity of their accounts. This is done by using the public ledger and by checking whether the funds are available to proceed with the transactions. However, if the funds are not available in the buyer's account or if they are promised to another party, the sale is prevented, effectively making double buying impossible. The public ledger is not maintained and monitored by a central authority, as occurs with banks or governments; rather, the public ledger is stored on the personal computers or electronic devices of the individuals and businesses who use the blockchain. To use a blockchain, you must donate to the collective. In this way, the need for a central authority is eliminated because every member of the blockchain has access to the ledger. Further, the ledger itself cannot be falsified. If one individual tampers with their ledger, the blockchain verifies that ledger against the other ledgers owned by the rest of the community and rejects it quickly.

Certificates

A *certificate* functions as a digital passport for establishing trust between entities in online communications. It's an electronic document issued by a certificate authority (CA) that verifies the identity of the certificate holder and provides proof of their legitimacy. When you connect to a secure website, your browser validates the site's certificate, issued by an entity such as DigiCert, to confirm the security of your connection. The CA serves as a neutral third party, vouching for the identities involved in the digital exchange.

Certificate Authorities

A *certificate authority (CA)* is an entity (usually a server) that issues certificates to users. In a PKI system that uses a CA, the CA is known as a trusted third party. Most PKI systems use a CA. The CA is also responsible for verifying the identity of the recipient of the certificate. An example of a technology that uses certificates is a secure website. If you open your browser and connect to a secure site, the browser first checks the certificate that comes from DigiCert or another similar company; in this way, it *validates* the certificate. You (the user) and the website are the two parties attempting to communicate. The CA is a third party that negotiates the security of the connection between you and the website.

For a user to obtain a digital identity certificate from a CA, the user's computer must initiate a certificate signing request (CSR) and present two items of information: proof of the user's identity and a public key. This public key is then compared to the CA's private key and, if the match is successful, the certificate is granted to the user.

As a basic example, say that you connect to www.paypal.com. When you connect to this website, it automatically redirects you to https://www.paypal.com, which is secured by way of a DigiCert-issued certificate. You know you have been redirected to a secure site because the browser provides various indicators. For instance, the web browser will probably show a padlock in the locked position, as shown in Figure 4-9.

Figure 4-9 A Secure Connection, Shown in Firefox

If you were to click on the padlock icon area of the address field in Firefox, you could get to the certificate details. Figure 4-10 shows some of the certificate details associated with the paypal.com domain.

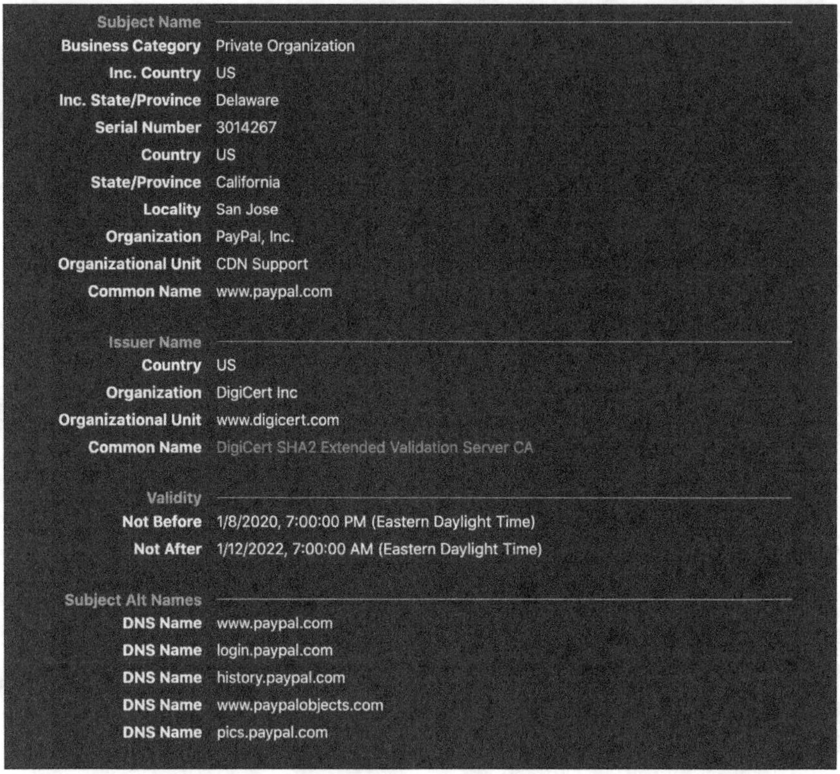

Subject Name
Business Category   Private Organization
Inc. Country   US
Inc. State/Province   Delaware
Serial Number   3014267
Country   US
State/Province   California
Locality   San Jose
Organization   PayPal, Inc.
Organizational Unit   CDN Support
Common Name   www.paypal.com

Issuer Name
Country   US
Organization   DigiCert Inc
Organizational Unit   www.digicert.com
Common Name   DigiCert SHA2 Extended Validation Server CA

Validity
Not Before   1/8/2020, 7:00:00 PM (Eastern Daylight Time)
Not After   1/12/2022, 7:00:00 AM (Eastern Daylight Time)

Subject Alt Names
DNS Name   www.paypal.com
DNS Name   login.paypal.com
DNS Name   history.paypal.com
DNS Name   www.paypalobjects.com
DNS Name   pics.paypal.com

Figure 4-10   Details of a DigiCert Certificate

The certificate shows when the certificate was originally issued and when it will expire, among other information. You can also see in Figure 4-10 that the certificate has been fingerprinted with SHA-256 (a variant of SHA-2), which enables you or the website (or issuer) to verify the integrity of the certificate. If for some reason the certificate cannot be verified by any of the parties, and the issuer confirms this, the issuer needs to revoke it and place it in the certificate revocation list (CRL), as discussed shortly. The Details tab gives advanced and more complete information about the certificate used.

TIP   Look at a few more websites that use SSL/TLS certificates and peruse the General and Details tabs. Compare the certificates with each other to learn more about the different levels of encryption, different levels of fingerprinting, and different issuing companies.

Recipients can use one or more certificates. Certificate mapping defines how many certificates are associated with a particular recipient. If an individual certificate is mapped to a recipient, it is known as one-to-one mapping. If multiple certificates are mapped to a recipient, it is known as many-to-one mapping. Multiple certificates might be used if the recipient requires multiple secure (and separate) communications channels.

In some cases, a registration authority (RA) is used to verify requests for certificates. If a request is deemed valid, the RA informs the CA to issue the certificate. An RA might also be used if the organization deals with several CAs. In this case, the RA is at the top of a hierarchical structure and verifies the identity of the user. An RA isn't necessary in PKI, but if you are centrally storing certificates, a CA is necessary.

Certificate authorities aren't just for the rich and famous. You can have a CA, too! If you are running a Windows server, you can install your own CA—for example, one that utilizes L2TP or possibly SSL/TLS. Of course, a server's built-in certificates are not necessarily secure. If you were to implement this technology in a secure environment in your organization, you would probably want to obtain proper certificates from a trusted source to use with the Windows server. When implementing certificates in the Windows Server operating system, you would use the Active Directory Certificate Services (AD CS) utility to define object identifiers (OIDs), which are built into AD CS for either low, medium, or high assurance. Or, you could have Windows randomly assign them. For security purposes, it is a good idea to obtain the OID before completing the configuration of the CA.

Certificate authorities can be subverted through the use of social engineering. If a person posing as a legitimate company managed to obtain certificates from a trusted source, those certificates would appear to be valid certificates and could cause widespread damage due to connections made by unsuspecting users—at least until the certificates were revoked. This happens sometimes, but the CA issuer usually finds out quickly and takes steps to mitigate the problem, such as by revoking the certificate(s) and notifying any involved parties of the incident.

Certificate Revocation Lists

A *certificate revocation list (CRL)* is a list of certificates that are no longer valid or that have been revoked by the issuer. There are two possible states of revocation: revoked, which means a certificate has been irreversibly revoked and cannot be used again, and hold, which means a certificate is temporarily invalid. Reasons for revoking a certificate include the compromise or theft of a certificate or an entire CA, unspecified certificates, superseded certificates, held certificates, and key or encryption compromise. The CRL is published periodically—usually every 24 hours. This list enables users of an issuer's certificates to find out whether a certificate is valid.

CRLs, like the certificates themselves, carry digital signatures to prevent denial-of-service and spoofing attacks; a CRL is digitally signed by the CA.

Online Certificate Status Protocol (OCSP)

An alternative to using a CRL is to use *Online Certificate Status Protocol (OCSP)*. It contains less information than a CRL does, and the client side of the communication is less complex. However, OCSP does not require encryption, making it less secure than a CRL.

The attributes in a certificate are essentially the various fields that define things like who issued the certificate and whom it is issued to. In addition, these attributes include information about what the certificate user intended, when it was issued, and when it will expire. These are just a few of the various attributes used in digital certificates. These attributes can then be used for authentication and validation purposes. Table 4-3 summarizes some of the most commonly used attributes and what they are used for.

Key Topic

Table 4-3   Certificate Attributes

Attribute	Description
Common name (CN)	The common name is the fully qualified domain name (FQDN) of the entity that the certificate is issued to. The CN field is very often submitted incorrectly with certificate-signing requests. The CN should be the same FQDN as the DNS name you are using in the web address you are using to access the site. If it is different from what is in the certificate, you will receive an error.
Organization (O)	This is the legal name of the organization that owns the site that the certificate will be used on.
Locality (L)	The Locality field is used to specify the city where the legal organization is located. This should always be the full name (such as North Carolina instead of NC).
Organizational unit (OU)	The OU is typically the department within the organization that will be utilizing the certificate.
Country name (C)	The country name is simply the two-letter country code where the legal organization is located. For instance, US would be used for United States.
Serial number	This is the number issued and tracked by the CA that issued the certificate.
Issuer	This is the CA that issued this certificate. (Even root certificates need to have their certificates issued from someone—perhaps even themselves.)

Attribute	Description
Validity dates	These dates are shown in the time window during which the certificate is considered valid. If a local computer believes the date to be off by a few years, that same PC may consider the certificate invalid due to its own error about the time. Using the Network Time Protocol (NTP) helps prevent this problem.
Public key	The contents of the public key and the length of the key are often shown. After all, the public key is public.
Thumbprint algorithm and thumbprint	This is the hash for the certificate. On a new root certificate, you could use a phone to call and ask for the hash value and compare it to the hash value you see on the certificate. If it matches, you have just performed out-of-band verification (using the telephone) of the digital certificate.
Certificate-signing request (CSR)	A CSR is a message sent from an applicant to a certificate authority in order to apply for a digital identity certificate. It usually contains the public key for which the certificate should be issued, along with some additional attributes.

Self-Signed

A *self-signed certificate* acts as both the creator and the endorser of its own identity, using its private key for the signature. Unlike certificates authenticated by a public CA, which are widely recognized for their authenticity, a self-signed certificate lacks this broader trust. For instance, when you visit a website with a self-signed certificate, your browser flags it with a warning, indicating that the certificate hasn't been verified by a trusted external party. Think of this in terms of getting something notarized; the notary acts as a trusted third party. A self-signed certificate is much like an individual who notarizes their own document rather than having it signed by an official notary public: This is acceptable in certain internal or testing scenarios but not for widespread public interaction where trust is needed the most.

The Subject Alternative Name field (or fields) in PKI certificates allows an organization to specify additional hostnames, domain names, email addresses, or URIs for use with a single certificate. The idea of using a Subject Alternative Name field in a certificate is to provide flexibility to system administrators. Figure 4-11 shows a Subject Alternative Name field used for a Gmail server. Two DNS names are listed here: mail.google.com and inbox.google.com. The single certificate can therefore be used for both of these domain names.

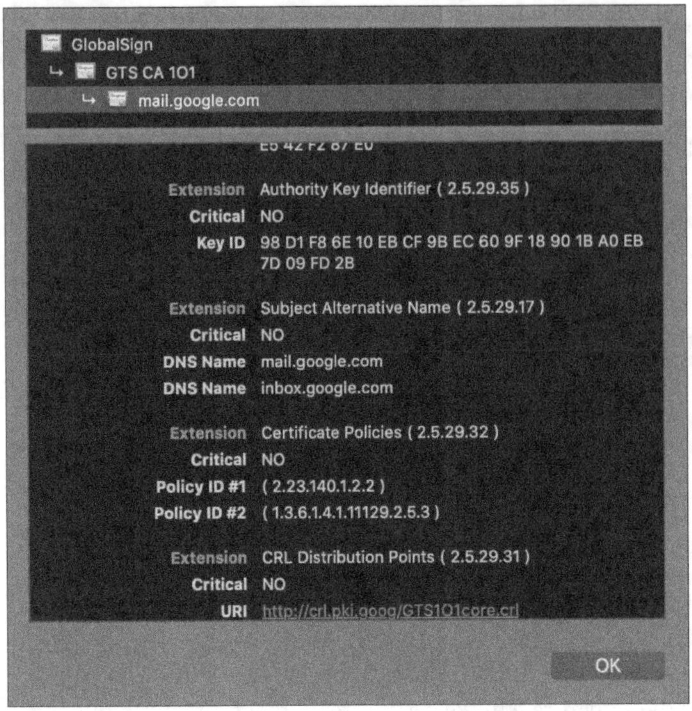

Figure 4-11   Subject Alternative Name

A certificate is issued with a valid *from* date and valid *to* date. This is the period of time that the certificate should be considered valid. If the certificate is encountered any time before or after those dates, the application that is validating the certificate (such as a web browser) should produce an error message stating that the certificate is not valid. It is important when issuing a certificate to issue it for a sufficient period of time. For instance, if a certificate is meant for long-term use and the application or device utilizing the certificate is not easily updated, you might want to extend the certificate validation period. This way, the certificate will not unexpectedly expire and break the application.

A certificate is a digitally signed electronic document that binds a public key with a user identity. The identity information might include a person's name and organization, or it may include other details relevant to the user to whom the certificate is to be issued. Most certificates are based on the X.509 standard, which is a common PKI standard developed by the ITU-T that often incorporates the single sign-on (SSO) authentication method. This way, a recipient of a single X.509 certificate has access to multiple resources, possibly in multiple locations. Although it is difficult to compromise X.509 certificates that use MD5 and SHA1 hashes, it can be done. A more powerful hashing algorithm such as SHA-2 should be implemented with a certificate. X.509 is the core of the Public Key Infrastructure Exchange (PKIX), which is the IETF's public key infrastructure (X.509) working group. Components of an X.509 certificate include the following:

- Owner (user) information, including public key

- Certificate authority information, including name, digital signature, serial number, issue and expiration dates, and version

Certificates can be used for connections to websites, for email, and for many other things in the Internet world, as well as for encryption done locally. For example, a user working in a Windows environment might want to use Encrypting File System (EFS) to encrypt data locally. The Windows domain can be configured to allow for user certificates governing and enhancing this encryption process. So, certificates can be used internally or externally, but most people are more familiar with certificates used to make secure HTTP connections, usually with SSL/TLS-based certificates. We focus mostly on that type of certificate as we move forward.

It's a good idea to classify certificates the way companies that sell them do: as domain, organizational, and extended validation certificates. In domain validation (DV) certificates, the certificate authority checks the rights of the applicant to use a specific domain name. With organizational validation (OV) certificates, the CA goes beyond this and also conducts some vetting of the organization involved and displays the results to customers. With extended validation (EV) certificates, the CA goes even further, conducting a thorough vetting of the organization. The process of issuing these certificates is strictly defined.

Many companies have subdomains for their websites. For example, h4cker.org might have subdomains such as tools.h4cker.org and software.h4cker.org. Generally, if you connect to a secure website that uses subdomains, a single certificate allows for connections to the main website and the subdomains. This is known as a wildcard certificate; for example, *. h4cker.org would apply to all subdomains of h4cker.org. Your organization might allow this or, for additional security, might use a different certificate for each subdomain (possibly using certificates from different providers), but this approach can become expensive. For small businesses and organizations, a single certificate is usually enough. In fact, if the provider allows it, a small organization can use a multidomain certificate. By modifying the Subject Alternative Name (SAN) field, an organization can specify additional hostnames, domain names, IP addresses, and so on. Table 4-4 provides a summary of the various certificate types and how they are used.

Key Topic

Table 4-4   Certificate Types

Type	Description
Wildcard	A single certificate allows for connections to the main website and its subdomains.
Code signing	Software developers often use code signing certificates to sign the code they have created, whether it is a software driver, an application, or an executable program. The intent is to provide the end user with the ability to verify that the code has not been tampered with.
Self-signed	A self-signed certificate is created and used on a system that not only creates the certificate but also signs it, using its own private key. This type of certificate does not offer the same authentication assurance as a publicly signed certificate because it is not signed by a trusted certificate authority.
Machine/computer	A machine certificate, also known as a computer certificate, is typically used when authenticating a computer or user connecting to a network via a VPN or 802.1x.
Email	An email certificate is meant to be used for signing and encrypting email communications.
User	A user certificate is typically used when authenticating a computer or user connecting to a network via a VPN or 802.1x. With a user certificate, the Subject Alternative Name field in the certificate contains the user principal name (UPN), which is used in the authentication process.
Root	A root certificate contains the public key of the CA server and other details about the CA server.
Domain validation	A domain validation certificate ensures that the holder has the right to use a specific domain name.
Extended validation	An extended validation certificate is issued to an organization that has undergone a thorough vetting.

A certificate chain is a list of certificates that utilizes the chain of trust concept. Each component of the system is validated from the bottom up. In a certificate chain, also known as a certification path, the anchor for this trust is the root certificate authority. At the bottom of the chain is the end-entity certificate for a machine/ computer certificate. That's the certificate that you see if you look at the details of a secure HTTPS session in your web browser. It then handshakes with an intermediate certificate belonging to an intermediate CA. This certificate signs the end-entity certificate. It then handshakes with the root certificate, which represents the root certificate authority. It signs the intermediate certificate and is self-signing, which means that it not only creates the certificate but also signs it with its own private key. The root CA employs code signing, digitally signing and timestamping the certificate to provide integrity and authenticity. However, even this can be defeated, so as a security administrator, you always have to be on the lookout for common vulnerabilities and exposures (CVEs) detailing revoked certificates and even entire issuing certificate companies that may have been compromised.

You should know several certificate formats for the Security+ SY0-701 exam. They can be identified in part by their file extension or the encoding type used. First, let's look at the ITU-T X.690 encoding formats:

- **Basic Encoding Rules (BER):** This is the original rule set governing the encoding of the ASN.1 data structure. Any data created is encoded with a type identifier, a length description, and the content's value. BER can use one of several encoding methods.

- **Canonical Encoding Rules (CER):** This is a restricted version of BER that allows the use of only one encoding type; all others are restricted.

- **Distinguished Encoding Rules (DER):** Another restricted variant of BER, this allows for only one type of encoding and has restrictive rules for length, character strings, and how elements are sorted. It is widely used for X.509 certificates. For example, certificate enrollment in Windows servers uses DER exclusively.

Now, let's briefly examine the certificate formats and extensions you might encounter. PEM is a common format that uses base64-encoded ASCII files. PEM stands for Privacy-Enhanced Mail and can be identified with the .pem file extension, though the format might also use the .crt, .cer, or .key extensions. This format uses the DER encoding method. If the certificate uses a file extension different from .pem, you can determine whether it is a PEM certificate by opening the file with a text editor and looking for the Begin Certificate and End Certificate statements. However, if the certificate uses the .der extension, then the certificate file is in binary form instead of ASCII. Because it is in binary, you will not see the Begin Certificate and End Certificate statements that are displayed in a .pem file.

P12/PFX is a binary format based on PKCS#12 that is used to store a server certificate, intermediate certificates, and the private key, in one encryptable file. It is typically used to import and export certificates and private keys. You may see the .pfx and .p12 extensions associated with PKCS#12-based files. .pfx stands for Personal Information Exchange, and Microsoft uses this format for release signing. The certificate and its private and public keys are stored in the .pfx file. A .pfx file can also be developed by combining a private key with a PKCS#7 (.p7b) file, as might be done in Windows Internet Information Services (IIS). .p7b format certificates can be used by themselves in IIS as the basis for S/MIME and single sign-on.

NOTE   Some of these extensions are also used for different types of data, such as private keys, and not only for certificates. It is also possible to convert from one format to another by using tools such as OpenSSL.

A web of trust is a decentralized trust model that addresses issues associated with the public authentication of public keys common to CA-based PKIs. It is considered peer-to-peer in that there is no root CA; instead, self-signed certificates that have been attested to by the creator are created and used. Users can decide what certificates they want to trust and can share those trusted certificates with others, causing the web of trust to grow. Of course, one of the most common reasons that a certificate issuer is not recognized by a web browser is due to unknown self-signed certificates. This model can also interoperate with standard CA architectures inherent to PKI. The more people who show trust in a certificate, the higher the chance that it is legitimate. This model is used by PGP, which enables users to start their own web of trust, self-publishing their own public key information.

One way to add security to the certificate validation process is to use certificate pinning, also known as SSL pinning or public key pinning. It can help detect and block many types of on-path attacks by adding an extra step beyond normal X.509 certificate validation. Essentially, a client obtains a certificate from a CA in the normal way but also checks the public key in the server's certificate against a hashed public key used for the server name. This functionality must be incorporated into the client side, so it is important to use a secure and up-to-date web browser on each client in order to take advantage of certificate pinning.

An alternative to OCSP is OCSP stapling (previously known as TLS Certificate Status Request), which allows the presenter of the certificate to bear the cost involved when providing OCSP responses.

Certificate keys can also be held in escrow. In key escrow, a secure copy of a user's private key is held in case the key is lost. This may be necessary so that third parties such as government or other organizations can ultimately gain access to communications and data encrypted with that key. If data loss is unacceptable, you should implement key escrow in your PKI.

When installing a certificate authority to a Windows server, you can set up a recovery agent for lost or corrupted keys. To do this, you need to use the Windows Server operating system and need to set up an enterprise-level CA. In this configuration, the certificates (or private keys) are archived at the CA. If a key recovery agent has been configured, lost, or corrupted, keys can be restored. It's important to use some type of software that can archive and restore keys in case of an incident or disaster.

Another way to avoid single points of failure, such as a single CA, is to organize certificate authorities in a hierarchical manner. At the top of the tree is a root CA; underneath are subordinate, or intermediate, CAs that offer redundancy and can sign certificates on behalf of the root CA. Though CA exclusivity is common, it is not the only type of architecture used to bind public keys to users. In some cases, a centralized model for certificates is not required or desired.

If a root CA is compromised, all of its certificates are then also compromised, which could affect an entire organization and beyond. The entire certificate *chain of trust* can be affected. One way to add a layer of security to prevent root CA compromise is to set up an offline root CA. Because it is offline, it will not be able to communicate over the network with the subordinate CAs—or any other computers for that matter. Certificates are transported to the subordinate CAs *physically* using USB flash drives or other removable media. Of course, you would need to have secure policies regarding the use and transport of media and would need to incorporate data loss prevention (DLP), among other things. But the offline root CA has some obvious security advantages compared to an online root CA. You should consider this *offline* mindset when dealing with critical data and encryption methods.

NOTE One thing to take away from this discussion of certificates is that there have been many certificate exploits in the past, and lots of vulnerabilities still exist. Be very careful when planning for the use of certificates.

Third-Party

A third-party CA is entrusted with the responsibility of verifying the identity of entities and issuing them digital certificates. A ***third-party certificate*** serves as digital ID cards, underlining the entity's authenticity to all other parties on the Internet.

Root of Trust

Earlier we discussed web of trust as it applies to PKI in general. In this section, we discuss ***root of trust*** as a source that can be implicitly trusted within a cryptographic system. It is the foundational element in a system, from which all security measures are derived. As discussed earlier in this chapter, a well-implemented root of trust, often a hardware-based module, can protect against tampering and ensure that software operations are secure from inception.

In certificate management, the root CA forms the root of trust. It is the topmost authority in the certificate chain and is inherently trusted by the system to validate and sign certificates. This trust extends downstream to all issued certificates, forming the basis of the certificate hierarchy.

Implementing a robust third-party CA and a reliable root of trust is essential in establishing and maintaining a secure PKI system. It ensures secure, authenticated communication and data protection in a network, building trust for the users and applications involved.

Certificate-Signing Request

A certificate-signing request (CSR) is basically an application for a digital identity certificate. It's what an entity sends to a CA when it needs to secure its online communications. The CSR includes the public key that will be included in the certificate and other identifying information. Think of it as a formal request, in which a company or an individual says, "This is my public key, and these are my credentials; please issue a certificate that proves it's really me." The CA then verifies the credentials, and if everything checks out, it issues a certificate that browsers and other entities trust, confirming the entity's authenticity.

Wildcard

As mentioned earlier in this chapter, *wildcard* certificates provide a cost-effective and efficient solution for organizations managing multiple subdomains. Consider a company with various services, like mail.example.com and shop.example.com. Rather than securing each subdomain with an individual certificate, a single wildcard certificate, denoted as *.example.com, can be used to secure all current and future subdomains. This streamlines the process and reduces costs, especially for small businesses. However, some organizations requiring a higher security level might opt for a separate certificate for each subdomain, with the certificates potentially coming from different providers, despite the additional expense. The choice between a wildcard certificate and individual certificates depends on the organization's size, security needs, and budgetary considerations.

Chapter Review Activities

Use the features in this section to study and review the topics in this chapter.

Review Key Topics

Review the most important topics in the chapter, noted with the Key Topic icon in the outer margin of the page. Table 4-5 lists these key topics and the page number on which each is found.

Key Topic

Table 4-5 Key Topics for Chapter 4

Key Topic Element	Description	Page Number
Figure 4-1	Encrypting Data at Rest, in Transit/Motion, and in Use/Processing	61
Figure 4-2	Symmetric Encryption	62

Key Topic Element	Description	Page Number
Table 4-2	Symmetric Versus Asymmetric Encryption	64
List	Key advantages of using TPM technology	67
Figure 4-6	Tokenization	73
Section	Key Stretching	77
Table 4-3	Certificate Attributes	82
Table 4-4	Certificate Types	86

Define Key Terms

Define the following key terms from this chapter, and check your answers in the glossary:

public key infrastructure (PKI), private key, public key, key escrow, encryption, level, full-disk encryption, partition, file encryption, volume encryption, database encryption, record-level encryption, transport/communication, symmetric encryption, asymmetric encryption, key exchange, algorithm, key length, tools, Trusted Platform Module (TPM), hardware security module (HSM), key management system (KMS), secure enclave, obfuscation, steganography, tokenization, data masking, hashing, salting, digital signature, key stretching, blockchain, open public ledger, certificate, certificate authority (CA), certificate revocation list (CRL), Online Certificate Status Protocol (OCSP), self-signed certificate, certificate-signing request (CSR), third-party certificate, root of trust, wildcard

Review Questions

Answer the following review questions. Check your answers with the answer key in Appendix A.

1. How does public key infrastructure (PKI) contribute to an organization's security operations?

2. How does public key infrastructure (PKI) ensure the secure exchange of digital certificates?

3. What is the role of disk encryption in ensuring data security, and how does it differ across disk, partition, and file levels?

4. How does hashing ensure the authenticity of a file or piece of data, and what is the role of salting in this process?

5. What is the function of padding in the process of hashing, and how does it contribute to the avalanche effect?

6. How do digital signatures verify the authenticity of digital messages or documents, and what are the key properties required for a digital signature?

7. How does a blockchain differ from a typical database, and what type of data is most commonly stored on a blockchain?

8. What is the role of the open public ledger in a blockchain transaction, and how does it help eliminate the need for a central authority?

9. How does a certificate authority (CA) contribute to the security of digital communications, and what is the process for a user to obtain a digital identity certificate from a CA?

10. What is the concept of the root of trust in PKI, and how does it differ from the web of trust model?

This chapter covers the following topics related to Objective 2.1 (Compare and contrast common threat actors and motivations) of the CompTIA Security+ SY0-701 certification exam:

- Threat actors

- Attributes of actors

- Motivations

CHAPTER 5

Comparing and Contrasting Common Threat Actors and Motivations

This chapter reviews threat actors, including nation-state actors, unskilled attackers, hacktivists, insider threats, organized crime, and shadow IT. It investigates the attributes of threat actors, such as internal/external nature, resources/funding, and level of sophistication/capability, and reviews a wide range of their motivations.

"Do I Know This Already?" Quiz

The "Do I Know This Already?" quiz enables you to assess whether you should read this entire chapter thoroughly or jump to the "Chapter Review Activities" section. If you are in doubt about your answers to these questions or your own assessment of your knowledge of the topics, read the entire chapter. Table 5-1 lists the major headings in this chapter and their corresponding "Do I Know This Already?" quiz questions. You can find the answers in Appendix A, "Answers to the 'Do I Know This Already?' Quizzes and Review Questions."

Table 5-1 "Do I Know This Already?" Section-to-Question Mapping

Foundation Topics Section	Questions
Threat Actors	1–4
Attributes of Actors	4–7
Motivations	8–10

CAUTION The goal of self-assessment is to gauge your mastery of the topics in this chapter. If you do not know the answer to a question or are only partially sure of the answer, you should mark that question as wrong for purposes of self-assessment. Giving yourself credit for an answer you correctly guess skews your self-assessment results and might provide you with a false sense of security.

1. Which type of threat actor is often associated a juvenile and typically has a limited amount of resources?

   a. Unskilled attacker

   b. Hacktivist

   c. Cybercriminal

   d. Insider threat

2. What term describes an entity, often tied to a nation-state actor, that has the highest level of resources, including intelligence, and poses a significant threat?

   a. Script kiddie

   b. Advanced persistent threat (APT)

   c. Shadow IT

   d. Hacktivist

3. What does shadow IT refer to in the context of an organization?

   a. Threat actors operating in the shadows

   b. The use of IT systems and services without the approval of the corporate IT department

   c. Cyberattacks carried out during the night

   d. Covert operations conducted by insider threats

4. Which motivation is typically associated with hacktivists?

   a. Financial gain

   b. Protesting against something they disagree with

   c. Revenge

   d. Increasing their reputation in the hacking world

5. Hacktivists conduct cyberattacks in order to:

   a. cause disruptions and protest against things they disagree with.

   b. gain financial benefits.

   c. steal intellectual property.

   d. cause disruptions for personal satisfaction.

6. Which type of threat actor is likely to have the most resources and funding at their disposal?

    a. Hacktivist

    b. Unskilled attacker

    c. Nation-state actor

    d. Disgruntled employee

7. What is the primary intent of criminals in the context of cyber threats?

    a. To protest against a certain cause

    b. To steal intellectual property

    c. To make money

    d. To disrupt services for personal satisfaction

8. What action typically initiates an active intrusion in a cybersecurity context?

    a. The victim identifying an intrusion attempt

    b. The victim attacking an adversary

    c. The adversary launching an attack against the victim

    d. The adversary leaving a backdoor for future access

9. Which motivation for hacking involves the unauthorized transfer of data from a computer?

    a. Espionage

    b. Data exfiltration

    c. Service disruption

    d. Disruption chaos

10. What motivation could be driven by deeply held political ideologies or philosophical concepts?

    a. Revenge

    b. Ethical

    c. Financial gain

    d. Philosophical/political beliefs

Foundation Topics

Key Topic

Threat Actors

It's important to understand the types of attackers that you might encounter and their characteristics and personality traits. Keep in mind that these threat actors can find ways to access systems and networks just by searching the Internet. Some attacks can be perpetrated by people with little knowledge of computers and technology. *Threat actors* typically have the intent to compromise the confidentiality, integrity, or availability of a system, often for personal, financial, or political gain. However, other actors have increased knowledge, and with knowledge comes power—the type of power you want to be ready to handle. However, all levels of attackers can be dangerous. Let's look at several of the actors now.

An *unskilled attacker* has little or no technology skills and uses code that was written by others and is freely available on the Internet. For example, an unskilled attacker might copy a malicious PHP script directly from one website to another; only the knowledge of how to copy and paste is required. Unskilled individuals are often referred to as *script kiddies*. This derogatory term is often associated with juveniles. Though the processes they use are simple, unskilled attackers can knowingly (and even unwittingly) inflict incredible amounts of damage on insecure systems. These people almost never have internal knowledge of a system and typically have a limited amount of resources, so the amount, sophistication, and extent of their attacks are constrained. They are often thrill seekers and are motivated by a need to increase their reputation in the hacking world.

A *hacktivist* gets their name from a combination of the terms *hack* and *activist*. As with the term *hacker*, the name *hacktivist* is often applied to different kinds of activities—from hacking for social change, to hacking to promote political agendas, to full-blown cyberterrorism. Due to the ambiguity of the term, a hacktivist could be inside a company or could attack from the outside, and hacktivists have varying amounts of resources and funding. However, a hacktivist is usually far more competent than an unskilled attacker.

Cybercriminals might work on their own, or they might be part of *criminal syndicates* and *organized crime*—a centralized enterprise run by people motivated mainly by money. Individuals who are part of an organized crime group are often well funded and may have a high level of sophistication.

Individuals might also carry out cyberattacks for governments and nation-states. In such cases, the government is known as an advanced persistent threat (APT). A set of computer-attacking processes can also be an APT. Often, an APT entity has the highest level of resources, including open-source intelligence (OSINT) *and* covert sources of intelligence. This, coupled with extreme motivation, makes an APT one of the most dangerous foes.

In many cases, APTs are tied to nation-state actors. It is no longer taboo for governments to use cyber techniques as a method of warfare. **Nation-state actors** are often government supported and can use adversarial techniques to steal intellectual property, cause disruption, and potentially compromise critical infrastructure.

Companies should be prepared for insiders and competitors as well. In fact, insiders and competitors might be one and the same. An **insider threat** refers to an individual within an organization who has authorized access to the organization's resources and information systems, which might enable them to exploit vulnerabilities or misuse data for malicious purposes. An insider threat can be one of the deadliest threats to servers and networks, especially if the person making the threat is a system administrator or has security clearance at the organization. However, not all insiders are malicious.

Think about the risks that shadow IT may introduce in a company. In **shadow IT**, an employee or a group of employees use IT systems, network devices, software, applications, and services without the approval of the corporate IT department. For example, an engineer might deploy a physical or virtual server and host their own application in it. The engineer might not often patch or monitor that system for security vulnerabilities. Consequently, threat actors may be able to compromise the vulnerable system or application. This problem has grown exponentially in recent years because more companies and individuals are adopting cloud-based applications and services. It is very easy to "spin off" a new virtual machine (VM), container, or storage element in the cloud. Employees often put sensitive corporate information in cloud services that are often not closely monitored, and this introduces significant risk to the organization.

You should know these actors and their motivations, but in the end, it doesn't matter too much what you call particular attackers. You need to be ready to prevent basic attacks as well as advanced attacks and treat them all with respect.

Attributes of Actors

Now that you have learned about the different types of threat actors, let's talk about their attributes, intent, and motivation. The intent and motivation, in most cases, depend on the type of attacker. For example, the motivation for hacktivists is typically related to protesting against something that they do not agree with (such as a political or religious belief or human rights). Hacktivists tend to use disruption techniques, perform denial-of-service (DoS) attacks, or deface websites. The intent of criminals is typically to make money. Nation-state actors can also have different motivations and intents. Some nation-state actors just want to steal intellectual property from another nation or government or a corporation; others want to cause disruption and bring down critical infrastructure. Another example is an internal actor (insider) who might be motivated by money offered by an external actor (either to steal information or to cause disruption). The internal actor could also be a disgruntled employee who leaves a backdoor either to later access confidential information or to trigger a DoS condition on critical systems and applications.

Another difference between the different types of threat actors is the level of sophistication/capability and the resources and funding. A disgruntled employee, a hacktivist, and an amateur unskilled attacker will not likely have the resources and funding that nation-state actors may have at their disposal. Criminal organizations in some cases may have more resources, money, and access to sophisticated exploits than hacktivists.

Resources and funding refers to the tangible and intangible assets that a threat actor has at their disposal to conduct cyberattacks. *Resources* generally refer to the tools, technology, people, and information at the disposal of a threat actor. *Funding* is more specific to financial means that a threat actor can leverage to support their activities. Resources and funding can be limitations for unskilled attackers. However, an advanced nation-state likely will have access to money that threat actors can use to finance their operations by purchasing advanced hacking tools, hiring skilled individuals, or paying for servers and other infrastructure.

An active intrusion starts with an adversary targeting a victim. The adversary may use various capabilities along with some form of infrastructure to launch an attack against the victim. Capabilities can be various forms of tools, techniques, and procedures, and the infrastructure is what connects the adversary and the victim.

Motivations

Motivation is the underlying reasons or drives that inspire an individual or a group to act in a certain way. These reasons can be varied and complex, often extending beyond mere financial gain to include elements such as ideology, revenge, or the desire for recognition. The array of possible motivations, each presenting unique challenges, necessitates a nuanced understanding of cybersecurity threats. Table 5-2 describes various motivations frequently observed with hacking and cyberattacks.

Table 5-2 Threat Actor Motivations

Motivation	Definition
Data exfiltration	The unauthorized transfer of data from a computer
Espionage	Spying, typically to obtain secret or confidential information

Motivation	Definition
Service disruption	An intentional act to bring services or operations to a halt
Blackmail	The act of threatening to reveal embarrassing, disgraceful, or damaging information unless a demand (usually for money) is met
Financial gain	The intention to increase one's wealth
Philosophical/political beliefs	Deeply held views relating to political ideologies or philosophical concepts
Ethical	Actions that conform to accepted standards of behavior
Revenge	The act of retaliation against perceived wrongs
Disruption/chaos	The act of creating disorder or confusion through disruptive activities

War

In cybersecurity, *war*, which is often referred to as cyber warfare, encapsulates state-sponsored, politically motivated attacks on an adversary's information systems. These attacks can be part of larger national security and defense strategies or stand-alone actions intended to cause disruption, gather intelligence, or sabotage critical infrastructure. Security engineers must always consider the possibility of such sophisticated, state-backed cyber threats, which might involve advanced persistent threats (APTs), potentially demanding heightened security measures and advanced threat-detection capabilities. Understanding the landscape of cyber warfare, its tactics, and potential implications is paramount for security engineers to defend their networks and sensitive data adequately.

Cyberattacks during wartime, like the ones witnessed in Ukraine, are an example of how the digital landscape can be used as a battlefield. In such cases, cyber warfare takes on a literal meaning, with attacks happening alongside or in lieu of traditional physical combat. Such cyberattacks can target critical infrastructure like power grids, communication networks, and government systems to cause disruption, create chaos, and impair the ability of a nation to defend itself or carry out its normal functions.

The Ukraine example shows the disruptive power of cyber warfare. In 2015, a cyberattack on Ukraine's power grid left hundreds of thousands without electricity. This is considered one of the first successful cyberattacks on a power grid. Security engineers studying such incidents understand that they must prepare for data breaches and attacks that aim to control, sabotage, or disrupt critical infrastructure.

Chapter Review Activities

Use the features in this section to study and review the topics in this chapter.

Review Key Topics

Review the most important topics in the chapter, noted with the Key Topic icon in the outer margin of the page. Table 5-3 lists these key topics and the page number on which each is found.

Table 5-3 Key Topics for Chapter 5

Key Topic Element	Description	Page Number
Section	Threat Actors	98
Section	Attributes of Actors	99
Table 5-2	Threat Actor Motivations	100
Section	War	101

Define Key Terms

Define the following key terms from this chapter and check your answers in the glossary:

threat actor, unskilled attacker, hacktivist, organized crime, nation-state actor, insider threat, shadow IT, resource, funding, motivation, data exfiltration, espionage, service disruption, blackmail, financial gain, philosophical/political beliefs, ethical, revenge, disruption/chaos, war

Review Questions

Answer the following review questions. Check your answers with the answer key in Appendix A.

1. What term is commonly used to describe an unskilled attacker who uses code written by others that is freely available on the Internet?

2. How would you differentiate a hacktivist from an unskilled attacker in terms of their competencies?

3. What characterizes an advanced persistent threat (APT) in terms of resources and motivation?

4. What does the term shadow IT refer to, and what risks does it pose to an organization?

5. How do the motivations of hacktivists typically differ from those of cybercriminals?

6. What could be the motivation behind an internal threat actor's actions?

7. How do resources and funding influence the level of sophistication and capability in cyberattacks?

8. What does the term active intrusions refer to in the context of cyber threats?

9. What is data exfiltration in the context of cybersecurity threats?

10. How do philosophical/political beliefs as motivation influence the actions of a threat actor?

This chapter covers the following topics related to Objective 2.2 (Explain common threat vectors and attack surfaces) of the CompTIA Security+ SY0-701 certification exam:

- Message-based
- Image-based
- File-based
- Voice call
- Removable device
- Vulnerable software
- Unsupported systems and applications
- Unsecure networks
- Open service ports
- Default credentials
- Supply chain
- Human vectors/social engineering

CHAPTER 6

Understanding Common Threat Vectors and Attack Surfaces

This chapter explores the diverse landscape of threat vectors and attack surfaces, from technical aspects like open service ports and unsecured networks to human vectors such as social engineering and impersonation. You'll gain insights into common methods attackers use, which will enable you to identify and mitigate risks and equip you to strengthen your organization's cybersecurity defenses.

The potential avenues for cyber threats and attacks have grown exponentially due to the interconnectedness of the world today. This chapter focuses on enhancing your understanding of various threat vectors and attack surfaces. It covers a broad spectrum of topics, each serving as a potential entry point for cyber threats. You'll learn about the vulnerabilities associated with different forms of communication, such as emails, instant messages, and voice calls. This chapter also discusses how files and images can be weaponized to compromise security.

The chapter discusses the intricacies of device vulnerabilities, including the risks tied to removable devices and software susceptibilities. It examines wired and wireless network vulnerabilities, along with the risks posed by open service ports and default credentials.

This chapter also explores the often-overlooked vulnerabilities in the supply chain, including those introduced by managed service providers, vendors, and suppliers. Finally, this chapter addresses the human element, detailing the psychology behind various social engineering attacks, such as phishing and business email compromise.

"Do I Know This Already?" Quiz

The "Do I Know This Already?" quiz enables you to assess whether you should read this entire chapter thoroughly or jump to the "Chapter Review Activities" section. If you are in doubt about your answers to these questions or your own assessment of your knowledge of the topics, read the entire chapter. Table 6-1 lists the major headings in this chapter and their corresponding "Do I Know

This Already?" quiz questions. You can find the answers in Appendix A, "Answers to the 'Do I Know This Already?' Quizzes and Review Questions."

Table 6-1   "Do I Know This Already?" Section-to-Question Mapping

Foundation Topics Section	Questions
Message-Based	1, 2
Image-Based	3
Vulnerable Software	4
Unsupported Systems and Applications	5
Unsecure Networks	6, 7
Supply Chain	8
Human Vectors/Social Engineering	9, 10

CAUTION   The goal of self-assessment is to gauge your mastery of the topics in this chapter. If you do not know the answer to a question or are only partially sure of the answer, you should mark that question as wrong for purposes of self-assessment. Giving yourself credit for an answer you correctly guess skews your self-assessment results and might provide you with a false sense of security.

1. What is the term used to describe the cyber threat involving the use of SMS messages to trick recipients into downloading malicious software or divulging personal information?

   a. Spear-phishing

   b. Spam

   c. Smishing

   d. Malware

2. Which of the following methods is described as a less-secure form of strong authentication that is vulnerable to on-path attacks and sends a question to the user's phone via SMS to ask if the authorization attempt is approved?

   a. Email authentication

   b. SMS OTP

   c. SMS challenge/response

   d. IM authentication

3. What is one of the methods attackers can use to spread malware through digital images?

    a. Deleting metadata

    b. Embedding destructive code within an image

    c. Increasing image resolution

    d. Compressing the image

4. Which security approach requires installation on individual client devices and can provide more granular control and customization but may be more resource intensive?

    a. Agentless security

    b. Client-based security

    c. Unsupported security

    d. Patched security

5. What does the term unsupported systems and applications refer to?

    a. Systems with extensive technical support

    b. Systems that have reached end-of-life (EOL) and no longer receive regular updates

    c. Systems supported by multiple vendors

    d. Systems that are newly launched

6. Which of the following wireless network security protocols is considered outdated and susceptible to exploitation if used in modern networks?

    a. WPA3

    b. WEP

    c. WPA2

    d. WPA2-Enterprise

7. What technique involves scanning a list of telephone numbers and dialing them to search for computer systems and fax machines, sifting out phone numbers associated with voice lines?

    a. Vishing

    b. Smishing

    c. War-dialing

    d. Typosquatting

8. Which approach is critical in the context of supply chain cybersecurity for identifying and addressing security gaps in vendors?

   a. Regular product quality assessment

   b. Continuous monitoring and vendor risk management

   c. Strictly focusing on the cost-efficiency of vendors

   d. Emphasizing only raw material quality

9. What term refers to phishing attacks accomplished through telephone conversations, where attackers might impersonate legitimate institutions to steal sensitive information?

   a. War-dialing

   b. Typosquatting

   c. Vishing

   d. Smishing

10. In which social engineering technique does an attacker register a domain that is a common typo of a legitimate site to host malware or impersonate the real website and leverage human error when typing a URL?

   a. Smishing

   b. War-dialing

   c. Typosquatting

   d. Vishing

Foundation Topics

Message-Based

Message-based communication, like email, SMS, and instant messaging (IM), has become essential to interpersonal and professional interactions in today's digitally connected world. These platforms are quick and convenient, but they also provide a sizable surface for online threats. These messaging techniques are widely used, which makes them a desirable target for attackers, who use a variety of strategies to take advantage of users. Message-based threat vectors take advantage of the trust and immediate nature of these forms of communication for everything from phishing and smishing to the spread of malware.

Email

One of the most prevalent threat vectors in cybersecurity is email. Attackers frequently use email to spread malicious links or attachments that can cause a user's system to download malware. Phishing emails are common. They may pretend to be from reliable sources to trick users into disclosing personal or financial information. A more specific variation of phishing, known as spear-phishing, targets particular people or organizations and is frequently conducted using information pertinent to the target. Combining technological safeguards like spam filters and secure email gateways with ongoing user training to spot and avoid suspicious emails is necessary to protect against email threats.

Short Message Service (SMS)

Also known as text messaging, SMS is a threat vector that cybercriminals frequently use. *Short Message Service (SMS)* is a method used to provide one-time passwords to different types of one-time password (OTP) services. Attackers may use SMS messages to trick recipients into downloading malicious software or divulging personal information by including links to phony websites. This is called *smishing* (a combination of "SMS" and "phishing"). Smishing attacks frequently pretend to be from a bank and say that the recipient's account has been compromised to convey a sense of urgency. We will cover smishing in greater detail later in this chapter. Users may be more likely to fall for these scams than for other attacks because SMS messages are considered more private and less vulnerable to security risks. It is crucial to inform users about these potential risks.

Mobile devices with SMS text capability can be used for authentication via OTP and challenge/response. With authentication via OTP, a one-time password is sent to the user's phone via SMS, and the user enters the OTP into the login authentication and is approved.

With one form of challenge/response, a user receives a text asking them to tap Yes or No. This is a less-secure form of strong authentication because it is vulnerable to on-path attacks (previously known as man-in-the-middle, or MITM, attacks). With another form of challenge/response, the user receives a text asking them for a reply via SMS. If the user texts back "Yes," authentication is completed, and the user is logged in. If the user texts back "No," authentication fails, and the user is not logged in. SMS is susceptible to SIM takeover, brute-force attacks, keyboard logging, on-path attacks, phishing, and common computer access attacks because, after all, most cell phones are computers.

Instant Messaging (IM)

Instant messaging (IM) platforms are widely used for personal and business communication, which means they are also targeted by cyberattackers. Attackers may use instant messaging to spread malware via nefarious links or attachments, take advantage of holes in the IM software, or carry out phishing scams. In contrast to email, instant messaging frequently conveys a sense of immediacy and trust, mainly if the attacker has gained access to a known contact's account. People may therefore be more likely to click on harmful links or heed misleading instructions. The use of current software with security patches, proper authentication techniques, and user education on spotting and reporting suspicious activity are all examples of security measures for instant messaging.

Spam and Spam over Internet Messaging (SPIM)

Spam has traditionally been the term used to describe unwanted and unsolicited email messages. However, email messages are not the only way that attackers or malicious users send spam. Users may also receive spam (numerous messages) via social media sites and instant/Internet messaging applications. For instance, you might be talking to other security professionals over a Discord server and have someone hop on the server and send dozens of unwanted messages, perhaps protesting against something. Or you may receive unwanted messages and scam offers via Facebook Messenger, WhatsApp, Keybase, Signal, WeChat, Telegram, or any other instant messaging application.

TIP   Several free services enable you to obtain DNS-based blocking lists of spammers, as well as ways that you can report spam events. An example is SpamCop (www.spamcop.net).

Image-Based

Digital images are an essential part of today's online content but can also be used as a vector for threats. *Image-based* threats refer to the malicious manipulation or exploitation of digital images to hide or deliver malware, engage in phishing activities, or execute other harmful actions. Attackers can embed destructive code within an image or manipulate its metadata to spread malware through email, social media, or other online platforms. The hidden code may be executed when the image is opened, leading to system compromise. Safeguards such as updated antivirus/anti-malware software and cautious downloading from untrusted sources can help mitigate this risk.

File-Based

File-based threats use common files, such as documents, spreadsheets, or PDFs, to carry harmful scripts. These threats occur when malicious code is embedded within or attached to these files, which are transmitted or shared to infect systems or networks. This type of threat is common in attachments sent via email, downloaded from websites, or transferred through file-sharing services. Opening such files can trigger malicious code, leading to unauthorized access or other adverse effects. Awareness and training, scanning of attachments with security tools, and strict file permissions can minimize the risk.

Voice Call

Voice call threats encompass a range of malicious activities conducted via phone calls, including deceptive practices such as vishing (voice phishing), unauthorized call interception, and fraudulent caller ID spoofing. These threats aim to deceive or manipulate individuals through telephone communication. Often, an attacker impersonates a legitimate entity to solicit personal or financial information or manipulates caller ID information to appear trustworthy. Secure call authentication methods, awareness and user training, and reporting of suspicious calls are critical defenses against voice call threats.

Removable Device

Using portable storage devices like USB drives, external hard drives, or memory cards can inadvertently introduce *removable device* threats, which are risks associated with transmitting or carrying malware via these devices. When an infected removable device is connected to a computer, the infected machine may execute the malicious code, leading to data theft, system compromise, or spread of malware to other connected systems. Implementing policies restricting the use of removable devices, scanning them with up-to-date antivirus/anti-malware software, and educating users about safe handling practices can help mitigate these risks.

Vulnerable Software

Vulnerable software is software that has flaws or weaknesses in its code or design. Attackers can exploit vulnerable software to gain unauthorized access, disrupt operations, or cause other malicious activities. To avoid vulnerable software, it's essential to understand the concepts of client-based and agentless security solutions:

- **Client-based security:** *Client-based security* requires installation of software (an agent) on a client device itself, whether it's a computer, mobile device, or network appliance. The agent actively monitors and protects against malicious activities, such as exploiting software vulnerabilities. It can provide more granular control and customization but may be more resource intensive.

- **Agentless security:** *Agentless security* doesn't require installation on individual client devices. Instead, it involves centrally monitoring and enforcing security policies, often through network devices or virtual appliances. An agentless approach can offer a lighter footprint and easier management, especially in diverse environments with various devices and operating systems.

Both approaches aim to protect against the risks associated with vulnerable software, but they do so in different ways. Client-based solutions may provide deeper insights and control at the device level, whereas agentless options might offer more extensive coverage with a reduced maintenance burden. Choosing the right method depends on organizational needs, the complexity of the environment, and specific security requirements.

Unsupported Systems and Applications

Unsupported systems and applications are software tools or platforms that do not receive regular updates, security patches, or technical support from the developer or vendor. This situation often arises when a software version reaches its official end-of-life (EOL) or the company that developed the software goes out of business or discontinues support for particular products. We will cover EOL in greater detail in Chapter 7, "Understanding Various Types of Vulnerabilities."

The security risks associated with unsupported systems and applications can be high, particularly when known vulnerabilities remain unaddressed. Without updates, systems become prime targets for cybercriminals, who may exploit unpatched flaws to gain unauthorized access, manipulate data, or launch broader attacks in an organization.

For businesses operating in regulated industries, using unsupported software can also lead to noncompliance with legal and industry standards, resulting in fines or other penalties. To mitigate these risks, organizations must upgrade to supported software versions or implement specific security controls that adequately safeguard unsupported systems. A detailed inventory of all software and a regular review of support status is essential to an effective cybersecurity strategy, ensuring that unsupported systems do not become a weak link in the organization's security posture.

Key Topic Unsecure Networks

Unsecure networks need to have appropriate security measures to safeguard the data transmitted. They can be categorized into different types, such as wireless, wired, and Bluetooth, each with distinct characteristics and potential vulnerabilities. This section provides a general overview of these types of networks:

> **NOTE**   We explore more concrete ways to harden these systems—including wireless networks, network devices, and mobile devices—in Chapter 14, "Applying Common Security Techniques to Computing Resources."

- **Wireless networks:** A *wireless network* is a network in which devices are connected without physical cables. Wireless networks that are improperly configured or that lack robust encryption protocols can be susceptible to unauthorized access and eavesdropping. Attackers might exploit weak Wi-Fi passwords or outdated security standards like WEP to intercept data or create rogue access points to mislead users.

- **Wired networks:** *Wired networks*, where devices are interconnected using physical cables, are generally considered more secure than their wireless counterparts. Wired networks can still be vulnerable if proper segmentation and access controls are not implemented. Attackers with physical access to the network cabling or ports might intercept data or introduce malicious devices such as network taps.

- **Bluetooth networks:** *Bluetooth networks* allow short-range communication between devices. However, they can be exploited if devices are set to "discoverable" mode or if known Bluetooth protocol vulnerabilities are not patched. Attackers may launch attacks such as BlueBorne to spread malware or gain control of devices.

An unsecured network exposes an organization or individual to potential cyber threats like data theft, on-path attacks, or unauthorized control over networked devices. Proper security measures such as robust encryption (for example, WPA3 for

Wi-Fi), network segmentation, firewalls, and continuous monitoring can mitigate these risks. Also, educating users about the dangers of connecting to untrusted or open networks and enforcing policies to guide safe network usage are essential strategies for enhancing network security.

Open Service Ports

Open service ports are network communication endpoints that are left accessible and unguarded on a computer system. Applications use these ports to communicate with other devices over a network. Open service ports can present a significant security risk when not adequately secured.

An open service port can be compared to an unlocked door in a building. Just as an unlocked door allows anyone to enter, an open service port can allow unauthorized access to an application or even the underlying operating system. Attackers can exploit open ports to conduct activities such as information gathering, service disruption, or remote control of the system.

TIP: Scanning Your Computer Ports   If you want to identify open ports on your computer, you can run a simple test using the Windows command prompt. Open the command prompt and enter the following command:

```
Netstat -ano
```

This command will display all currently existing network connections via open ports and open listening ports that are not immediately establishing connections. You can refer to the Microsoft documentation on the **netstat** command for more information.

The risk associated with open service ports can be mitigated through proper security measures such as the following:

- **Port scanning:** Regular port scanning is an essential practice for maintaining a secure network environment. Among the most widely used tools for this purpose is Nmap, also known as Network Mapper. Nmap is a versatile and powerful open-source tool that is capable of discovering hosts and services on a computer network. Another tool is Masscan, which is known for its speed and serves a similar purpose to Nmap. Netcat is more straightforward than Nmap and offers excellent functionality, including port scanning, file transfer, and setup of backdoors. These tools are covered in greater detail in Chapter 17, "Understanding Security Alerting and Monitoring Concepts and Tools," which focuses on network security monitoring techniques. By regularly employing port scanning tools like Nmap, Masscan, and Netcat, you can identify which ports are open and take appropriate action to close or secure unnecessary ports.

- **Firewall configuration:** By using a firewall to control the traffic allowed to enter or exit through specific ports, you can block unnecessary ports, thus limiting exposure.

- **Monitoring and logging:** It is a good idea to implement continuous monitoring and logging to detect suspicious activities on open ports and take corrective actions if needed.

- **Patching and upkeep:** One way to secure a network is to ensure that the services running on open ports are up to date with the latest security patches and configurations.

By understanding the necessity of each open port and applying appropriate security controls, organizations can significantly reduce the risks associated with open service ports and enhance the overall security posture of their systems.

Default Credentials

Default credentials pose a significant security risk, especially when it comes to default device or operating system credentials. Routers, switches, and other network device manufacturers often ship their products with simple default passwords, expecting the end user to change these credentials during initial setup. However, many organizations leave these default credentials in place. This lax approach to security is akin to leaving the front door of your house unlocked; it invites unauthorized access and potential compromise. Websites like defaultpassword.com and search engines like Shodan (www.shodan.io) make it easy for attackers to identify devices using default credentials that are exposed to the Internet.

The issue extends beyond hardware. Software developers and administrators sometimes leave hardcoded or default credentials in place, exposing individual devices and entire cloud environments to various forms of attack. The security adage "Why do you need hackers if you have default passwords?" rings true here. Changing default credentials and restricting network access to critical systems is crucial. Some manufacturers now require users to change default passwords during initial setup, but compliance is inconsistent.

The common practice of credential harvesting exacerbates the problem of default credentials. Attackers dump harvested usernames and passwords on platforms like Pastebin or GitHub, making it even easier to compromise systems where users have reused their credentials. It's not just about changing the defaults; it's also about ensuring that credentials are unique, complex, and confidential to reduce the risk of unauthorized access.

Supply Chain

The term *supply chain* refers to the interconnected network of organizations, resources, and processes involved in creating, producing, and delivering a product or service. The supply chain presents unique challenges and risks, particularly to managed service providers (MSPs), vendors, and suppliers.

Managed service providers (MSPs) are organizations that manage IT services for other companies. While they offer efficiency and expertise, they can also introduce risks if not properly secured. An insecure MSP can provide a pathway for attackers to access their clients' networks. Ensuring that MSPs follow stringent security protocols and regularly undergo security assessments is crucial in mitigating this type of risk.

Vendors are companies that provide products or services to other businesses. Like MSPs, vendors with inadequate cybersecurity measures can become a weak link in the security chain. Vendor risk management, including regular security assessments, contractual obligations, and continuous monitoring, can help identify and address security gaps.

Suppliers provide raw materials or components that are used in the manufacturing of products. In the context of cybersecurity, the integration of compromised components or the use of insecure logistics networks can lead to vulnerabilities in the end product. Regular audits, certifications, and robust cybersecurity requirements can mitigate these risks.

The overall security of the supply chain is only as strong as its weakest link. The interconnected nature of the supply chain means that a security breach in any one part can have far-reaching consequences across multiple organizations. Therefore, an integrated approach that involves thorough risk assessment, continuous monitoring, and collaboration among all parties in the supply chain is essential for mitigating risks and ensuring robust cybersecurity across the entire chain.

Human Vectors/Social Engineering

In cybersecurity, the human element often emerges as the most unpredictable and vulnerable attack surface. Human vectors, or social engineering, refer to the psychological manipulation of individuals to gain unauthorized access to information or systems. While firewalls, encryption, and other technical measures can provide robust security, they can be rendered ineffective if an individual in the organization falls prey to manipulation—especially if that individual has elevated privileges. Human vectors or social engineering attacks exploit the innate human tendencies of trust and curiosity to bypass even the most fortified security systems.

Social engineering is not just a single tactic but a broad category of manipulative techniques aimed at the human psyche. From phishing emails that mimic trusted sources to pretexting scenarios that involve elaborate false narratives, social engineering attacks are as diverse as they are deceptive. These attacks don't just target uninformed or naïve users; they are often sophisticated enough to deceive even the most security-conscious individuals.

The key to defending against social engineering lies in technical safeguards and a holistic approach that combines technology, regular training, and a culture of security awareness. This section explores the various forms of social engineering, including phishing, vishing, smishing, and more, to equip you with the knowledge to recognize and counter these insidious attempts to manipulate human behavior in order to gain unauthorized access.

Phishing

Phishing is the attempt to fraudulently obtain private information. A phisher usually masquerades as someone else, perhaps another entity. For example, an attacker could impersonate an employee of a company or a business partner to attempt to steal sensitive data from the victim. Phishing is usually done by electronic communication rather than in person. For a phishing attack to succeed, little information about the target is necessary. A phisher might target thousands of individuals without much concern as to their background. An example of phishing would be an email that requests verification of private information. The email might have links to a malicious website designed to lure people into a false sense of security in order to fraudulently obtain information. The website is likely to look like a legitimate website. A common phishing technique is to pose as a vendor (such as an online retailer or domain registrar) and send email confirmations of orders that targets supposedly placed.

This is a triple-whammy. First, the orders are obviously fake; a person might say, "Hey, wait! I didn't place these orders!" and may click the link(s) in the email and land on the false web page. Second, if a person thinks it's a legitimate order (perhaps the person places many orders, and the fraudulent one looks like another legitimate one), the person might click a link to track the order, again landing on the bogus web page. Third, once at the web page, the person is asked to enter credentials for an account (which then leads to credit card fraud and identity theft). In addition, the page might include Trojans and other malicious scripts that are delivered to the unsuspecting person on exit. Sheesh, talk about cyberbullying!

Generally, an attacker needs no information about the target to conduct a phishing attack. However, some phishers actually target specific groups of people or even specific individuals. This is known as spear phishing. And when an attacker targets key stakeholders and senior executives (CEOs, CFOs, and so on), it is known as whaling. Whaling attacks are much more detailed and require that the attacker know a good deal of information about the target (much of which is freely available on the Internet).

Many different types of social engineering are often lumped into the phishing category, but actual phishing for private information is normally limited to email and websites.

Several open-source tools can help automate or accelerate social engineering attacks (including sending phishing and spear phishing emails). An example of these tools (and one of the most popular) is the Social Engineering Toolkit (SET). Example 1-1 demonstrates how attackers can use SET to send spear phishing emails to a victim and either select existing payloads or create their own.

Example 1-1   The Social Engineering Toolkit

```
[---] The Social-Engineer Toolkit (SET) [---]


[---] Created by: David Kennedy (ReL1K) [---]


[---] Development Team: JR DePre (pr1me) [---]


[---] Development Team: Joey Furr (j0fer) [---]


[---] Development Team: Thomas Werth [---]


[---] Development Team: Garland [---]


[---] Report bugs: davek@trustedsec.com [---]


[---] Follow me on Twitter: dave_rel1k [---]


[---] Homepage: https://www.trustedsec.com [---]
 Welcome to the Social-Engineer Toolkit (SET). Your one
 stop shop for all of your social-engineering needs..


 Join us on irc.freenode.net in channel #setoolkit


 The Social-Engineer Toolkit is a product of TrustedSec.
 Visit: https://www.trustedsec.com
```

```
 Select from the menu:
   1) Spear-Phishing Attack Vectors
   2) Website Attack Vectors
   3) Infectious Media Generator
   4) Create a Payload and Listener
   5) Mass Mailer Attack
   6) Arduino-Based Attack Vector
   7) SMS Spoofing Attack Vector
   8) Wireless Access Point Attack Vector
   9) QRCode Generator Attack Vector
  10) Powershell Attack Vectors
  11) Third Party Modules
  99) Return back to the main menu.
set> 1


Welcome to the SET E-Mail attack method. This module allows you to
specially craft email messages and send them to a large (or small)
number of people with attached fileformat malicious payloads. If you
want to spoof your email address, be sure "Sendmail" is installed (it
is installed in BT4) and change the config/set_config SENDMAIL=OFF
flag to SENDMAIL=ON.


There are two options, one is getting your feet wet and letting SET
do everything for you (option 1), the second is to create your own
FileFormat payload and use it in your own attack. Either way, good
luck and enjoy!


   1) Perform a Mass Email Attack
   2) Create a FileFormat Payload
   3) Create a Social-Engineering Template
  99) Return to Main Menu

set:phishing>1
/usr/share/metasploit-framework/
 Select the file format exploit you want.
 The default is the PDF embedded EXE.
              ********** PAYLOADS **********
1) SET Custom Written DLL Hijacking Attack Vector (RAR, ZIP)
  2) SET Custom Written Document UNC LM SMB Capture Attack
  3) Microsoft Windows CreateSizedDIBSECTION Stack Buffer Overflow
  4) Microsoft Word RTF pFragments Stack Buffer Overflow (MS10-087)
  5) Adobe Flash Player "Button" Remote Code Execution
  6) Adobe CoolType SING Table "uniqueName" Overflow
```

```
 7) Adobe Flash Player "newfunction" Invalid Pointer Use
 8) Adobe Collab.collectEmailInfo Buffer Overflow
 9) Adobe Collab.getIcon Buffer Overflow
10) Adobe JBIG2Decode Memory Corruption Exploit
11) Adobe PDF Embedded EXE Social Engineering
12) Adobe util.printf() Buffer Overflow
13) Custom EXE to VBA (sent via RAR) (RAR required)
14) Adobe U3D CLODProgressiveMeshDeclaration Array Overrun
15) Adobe PDF Embedded EXE Social Engineering (NOJS)
16) Foxit PDF Reader v4.1.1 Title Stack Buffer Overflow
17) Apple QuickTime PICT PnSize Buffer Overflow
18) Nuance PDF Reader v6.0 Launch Stack Buffer Overflow
19) Adobe Reader u3D Memory Corruption Vulnerability
20) MSCOMCTL ActiveX Buffer Overflow (ms12-027)

set:payloads>
```

NOTE SET and other penetration testing tools are not covered on the Security+ SY0-701 exam. Example 1-1 is provided for your reference only. SET and similar tools can be installed in different Linux distributions. Some of the most popular Linux distributions for security penetration testing are Kali Linux, Parrot Security, and Black Arch.

To defend against such attacks, users should install a phishing filter or add-on and enable it on the web browser. Also, all users should be trained to realize that institutions will *not* call or email requesting private information. If people are not sure, they should hang up the phone or simply delete the email. A quick way to find out whether an email is phishing for information is to hover over a link. You will see a URL domain name that is far different from that of the institution that the phisher is claiming to be; it is likely to be a URL of a site located in a distant country. Many phishers are also probably engaging in spy-phishing: a combination of spyware and phishing that effectively makes use of spyware applications. A spyware application of this sort is downloaded to the target, which then enables additional phishing attempts that go beyond the initial phishing website.

Vishing

Phishing attacks can also be accomplished through telephone conversations. Phone or voice phishing, known as *vishing*, works in the same manner as phishing but is initiated using a phone call (often over a VoIP system). Vishing is typically used to steal sensitive information such as Social Security numbers, credit card numbers, or other information used in identity theft schemes. Attackers might impersonate and spoof caller ID to hide themselves when performing vishing attacks.

In many vishing attacks, the phone call often sounds like a prerecorded message from a legitimate institution (bank, online retailer, donation collector, and so on). The message asks the unsuspecting person for confidential information such as their name, bank account number, code, and so on—under the guise of needing to verify information for the person's protection. It's really the opposite, of course, and many people are caught unaware by these types of scams every day. Through the use of automated systems (such as the ones telemarketers use), vishing can be perpetuated on large groups of people with little effort.

> **NOTE**   A similar technique using automated systems is known as *war-dialing*. This type of attack occurs when a device (modem or other system) is used to scan a list of telephone numbers and dial them in search of computer systems and fax machines. The technique sifts out the phone numbers associated with voice lines and the numbers associated with computers. The result is a list that can later be used by other attackers for various purposes.

Smishing

Because phishing has been an effective tactic for threat actors, they have found ways other than using email to fool their victims into following malicious links or activating malware from emails. A number of phishing campaigns have used SMS to send malware or malicious links to mobile devices. This social engineering technique is also known as *smishing* (short for "SMS phishing").

One example of smishing is the Bitcoin-related SMS scams that have surfaced in recent years. Numerous victims have received messages instructing them to click links to confirm their accounts and claim Bitcoin. A user who clicks such a link might be fooled into entering sensitive information on the attacker's site.

Misinformation/Disinformation

Misinformation is false or misleading information that is spread without malicious intent, whereas *disinformation* is intentionally deceptive. In cybersecurity, these tactics can create confusion or hide malicious activities. Educating employees on how to critically evaluate information and verify sources can help prevent these threats.

Impersonation

Impersonation involves pretending to be someone else to gain trust or access. An attacker might impersonate a colleague, a boss, or even a family member to trick an individual into divulging sensitive information. Training employees to verify identities through multiple channels can mitigate this risk.

Business Email Compromise (BEC)

Business email compromise (BEC) is a sophisticated scam that targets businesses by compromising legitimate business email accounts. It often involves impersonation and is used to conduct unauthorized transfers of funds. Implementing multifactor authentication and continuous monitoring of email activities can provide layers of defense against BEC.

Pretexting

Pretexting is a type of social engineering attack in which a person invents a scenario, or pretext, in the hope of persuading a victim to divulge information. Preparation and some prior information are often needed before pretexting can be attempted; impersonation is often a key element. By impersonating the appropriate personnel or third-party entities, a person performing pretexting hopes to obtain records about an organization, its data, and its personnel. IT and other employees should always be on the lookout for impersonators and should always ask for identification when someone is trying to obtain information. If there is any doubt, the issue should be escalated to a supervisor and/or a call should be made to the authorities.

Watering Hole Attack

A *watering hole attack* is a strategy that targets users based on the websites they frequent. An attacker loads malware beforehand on one or more websites in the hopes that the user will access those sites and activate the malware, with the goal of infecting the user's system and possibly their whole network. To figure out users' browsing habits, an attacker might guess or use direct observation. So, this type of attack may also build on other social engineering methods, such as eavesdropping, pretexting, and phishing.

Popular websites such as Google and Microsoft would be difficult to infect with malware. Attackers go after smaller websites. For example, let's consider a company that manufactures widgets. Chances are that the company will need to purchase plastic and other resources to build the widgets. Users will connect to suppliers' websites, often via the Internet or possibly an intranet. Suppliers' websites are known for lacking security, and they make excellent targets. If many users in the company go to these same websites often, it's just a matter of time before someone clicks on the wrong website element or gets tricked in another manner. Then malware gets installed on the client computer and possibly spreads throughout the company. An attacker might also redirect users to other websites, where more hardcore malware (such as ransomware) or other scams are located.

The problem is that you, as a security administrator, can't actively prevent the malware on the targeted websites. You can suggest prevention methods to those companies—such as software patches and secure coding—but can't force them into action. So, you should focus on localized prevention methods, including training users, reducing web browser functionality, blocking known malicious websites based on threat intelligence, and monitoring in the form of antimalware software and IDSs/IPSs.

Brand Impersonation

Brand impersonation is a tactic in which attackers pretend to represent a trusted brand, such as a well-known bank or technology company. This impersonation can be used in phishing emails or fake websites to deceive victims into providing personal or financial information. Regular education, awareness training, and technical controls like email filtering can help individuals recognize and avoid these impersonation attempts.

Typosquatting

Typosquatting is a technique that takes advantage of human error. Knowing that users often type in URLs incorrectly, a typosquatter registers a domain that is a common typo of a legitimate site to impersonate the real website and host malware or perform other malicious techniques to compromise users' systems. For example, an attacker might register the domain gogle.com to impersonate the website google.com and host malware or perform any other malicious technique to compromise users' systems.

Chapter Review Activities

Use the features in this section to study and review the topics in this chapter.

Review Key Topics

Review the most important topics in the chapter, noted with the Key Topic icon in the outer margin of the page. Table 6-2 lists these key topics and the page number on which each is found.

Table 6-2 Key Topics for Chapter 6

Key Topic Element	Description	Page Number
Section	Message-Based	109
Section	Vulnerable Software	112
Section	Unsecure Networks	113
Section	Supply Chain	116
Section	Human Vectors/Social Engineering	116

Define Key Terms

Define the following key terms from this chapter and check your answers in the glossary:

Short Message Service (SMS), spam, image-based, file-based, voice call, removable device, vulnerable software, client-based security, agentless security, unsupported systems and applications, wireless network, wired network, Bluetooth network, open service ports, supply chain, phishing, vishing, smishing, misinformation, disinformation, pretexting, watering hole attack, brand impersonation, typosquatting

Review Questions

Answer the following review questions. Check your answers with the answer key in Appendix A.

1. What risks are associated with image-based threats, and what measures can be used to mitigate these risks?

2. Describe the differences between client-based and agentless security in the context of vulnerable software.

3. How can organizations handle the risks associated with unsupported systems and applications?

4. What vulnerabilities can arise from wireless networks, and how can they be addressed?

5. How can wired networks become vulnerable, and what preventive measures can be taken?

6. What are the risks associated with Bluetooth networks, and how can they be reduced?

7. What is the role of managed service providers (MSPs) in the supply chain, and how can their risks be mitigated?

8. How can vendors introduce risks into the supply chain, and what actions can be taken to address these risks?

9. Explain the concept of vishing and how individuals can protect themselves from such attacks.

10. What is typosquatting, and how can attackers use it as a tactic?

This chapter covers the following topics related to Objective 2.3 (Explain various types of vulnerabilities) of the CompTIA Security+ SY0-701 certification exam:

- Application
- Operating system (OS)-based
- Web-based
- Hardware
- Virtualization
- Cloud-specific
- Supply chain
- Cryptographic
- Misconfiguration
- Mobile device
- Zero-day

CHAPTER 7

Understanding Various Types of Vulnerabilities

This chapter delves into the multifaceted world of vulnerabilities that may be present in various technologies and platforms, including applications, operating systems, web-based systems, hardware, virtualization, cloud computing, supply chain, and mobile devices. You'll learn about specific vulnerabilities, such as memory injection, buffer overflow, race conditions, malicious updates, and the risks associated with obsolete technologies, and this information will equip you to identify, understand, and combat these various types of vulnerabilities.

"Do I Know This Already?" Quiz

The "Do I Know This Already?" quiz enables you to assess whether you should read this entire chapter thoroughly or jump to the "Chapter Review Activities" section. If you are in doubt about your answers to these questions or your own assessment of your knowledge of the topics, read the entire chapter. Table 7-1 lists the major headings in this chapter and their corresponding "Do I Know This Already?" quiz questions. You can find the answers in Appendix A, "Answers to the 'Do I Know This Already?' Quizzes and Review Questions."

Table 7-1 "Do I Know This Already?" Section-to-Question Mapping

Foundation Topics Section	Questions
Application	1, 2
Operating System (OS)–Based	3
Web-Based	4, 5
Hardware	6
Virtualization	7
Cloud Specific	8
Supply Chain	9
Mobile Device	10

CAUTION The goal of self-assessment is to gauge your mastery of the topics in this chapter. If you do not know the answer to a question or are only partially sure of the answer, you should mark that question as wrong for purposes of self-assessment. Giving yourself credit for an answer you correctly guess skews your self-assessment results and might provide you with a false sense of security.

1. Which vulnerability enables an attacker to introduce malicious code into a system's memory, making detection challenging?

   a. Zero-day

   b. Malicious update

   c. Memory injection

   d. Race condition

2. What is one of the primary measures for preventing buffer overflow?

   a. Using secure channels for updates

   b. Implementing stack protection

   c. Educating users about updates

   d. Monitoring time of use

3. What is a key strategy for mitigating operating system–based vulnerabilities?

   a. Parameterized queries

   b. Least-privilege principle

   c. Time-of-check synchronization

   d. Content security policy

4. What is a common mitigation strategy for both SQL vulnerabilities and cross-site scripting (XSS) vulnerabilities?

   a. Implementing a content security policy (CSP)

   b. Proper input validation

   c. Regular updates to firmware

   d. Both a and b

5. What are the three main types of cross-site scripting (XSS) vulnerabilities?

   a. Stored XSS, buffer overflow XSS, DOM-based XSS

   b. Stored XSS, reflected XSS, DOM-based XSS

    c. Memory injection XSS, reflected XSS, TOC-based XSS

    d. Stored XSS, malicious update XSS, TOU-based XSS

6. Which vulnerability occurs when hardware products no longer receive essential security updates from the manufacturer?

    a. Buffer overflow

    b. Vulnerability scanning

    c. End-of-life (EOL) hardware vulnerability

    d. Race condition

7. Which vulnerability in virtualization might allow one virtual machine to access data remnants from another virtual machine?

    a. Virtual machine (VM) escape

    b. Buffer overflow

    c. Resource reuse

    d. Malicious update

8. Which of the following types of clouds is involved when a service provider offers applications and storage space to the general public over the Internet?

    a. Private cloud

    b. Community cloud

    c. Public cloud

    d. Hybrid cloud

9. Which of the following strategies is essential for maintaining the security of software products in the context of supply chain vulnerabilities?

    a. Side loading restriction

    b. Internal personnel audits

    c. Patch management

    d. Jailbreaking restrictions

10. What does the term side loading refer to in the context of mobile device vulnerabilities?

    a. Installing applications from official app stores

    b. Implementing additional security controls

    c. Installing applications from sources outside the official app store

    d. Regularly updating the mobile operating system

Foundation Topics

Application

The application layer is often a prime target for attackers because it is a gateway to user interactions and data. Vulnerabilities at this level can be especially detrimental, providing multiple avenues for malicious intrusion. This section delves into specific application vulnerabilities, including memory injection, buffer overflow, race conditions, and malicious updates. Understanding these vulnerabilities is essential for both software developers and security professionals, as it guides the development of secure code, robust defenses, and the implementation of proper risk management. These vulnerabilities—whether arising from coding errors, design flaws, or other factors—can be mitigated through careful design, thorough testing, and continuous monitoring and updating of the application environment.

Memory Injection

Memory injection is a technique in which an attacker introduces (injects) malicious code into a system's memory. Rather than executing malicious code directly on a host system, the attacker exploits a vulnerability in a legitimate process running on the system, allowing the injected code to run within the security context of the legitimate process. This can make detection more challenging, as the malicious code appears to be part of a trusted operation.

Memory injection attacks can be particularly disastrous because they exploit legitimate processes to execute malicious code, making them difficult to detect. However, several mitigation strategies can be employed to protect against such an attack. One practical approach is to use endpoint detection and response (EDR) solutions, which monitor for unusual behavior in system processes. These solutions can flag anomalies, such as a process suddenly allocating a large amount of memory, which could indicate an injection attempt.

Another strategy is application whitelisting, which involves allowing only preapproved applications to run on the system. This can prevent malicious code from being executed, even if that code is injected into a legitimate process. Regularly patching and updating software is a way to fix known vulnerabilities that might be exploited for memory injection.

Data Execution Prevention (DEP) is another helpful feature that can be enabled on Windows systems. DEP prevents code from being run from data pages, which can block many types of memory injection attacks. Similarly, Address Space Layout Randomization (ASLR) can make it more difficult for an attacker to predict the location where the injected code will execute, adding another layer of defense.

Finally, user education and awareness training can play a crucial role in protecting against a memory injection attack. Users should be trained to recognize phishing attempts and other social engineering tactics that attackers might use to initially compromise a system and then conduct a memory injection attack.

Buffer Overflow

Buffer overflow is a common security flaw that occurs when a program writes more data to a buffer (temporary data storage area) than it can hold. An attacker can cause erratic program behavior, crashes, and incorrect data, and they may even execute arbitrary code by overrunning the buffer's boundary and overwriting adjacent memory. This could potentially lead to a complete system compromise if exploited effectively. Buffer overflows have historically been associated with many high-profile security breaches, and understanding this vulnerability is essential for securing both legacy and modern software applications.

Buffer overflow vulnerabilities can have severe consequences, but there are multiple strategies to mitigate the risks. One of the key mechanisms for preventing buffer overflow is stack protection, also known as stack canaries. Stack protection involves placing a small, random value (the "canary") between the buffer and control data on the stack. When a buffer overflow occurs, the canary value is likely to be overwritten. Regularly checking the integrity of the canary during program execution allows the system to detect a buffer overflow before it leads to code execution, thereby preventing potential exploitation. This process is usually handled automatically by the compiler or the operating system, so developers may not need to manually implement canary checking.

In addition to implementing stack protection, you can take several other preventive measures:

- **Code auditing:** It is important to regularly review and audit your code to identify potential buffer overflow vulnerabilities. Automated tools can assist in this process.

- **Developer training:** It is also important to educate developers on secure coding practices, emphasizing the importance of bounds checking and input validation.

- **Compiler tools:** When possible, use compiler-based protections like DEP and ASLR to make exploitation more difficult.

- **Safe functions:** It is a good idea to replace unsafe standard library functions that do not perform bounds checking (like **strcpy** and **sprintf** in C/C++) with safer alternatives (like **strncpy** and **snprintf**).

- **Patching:** It is important to keep web and application servers up to date with the latest security patches to fix known vulnerabilities.

- **Application scanning:** It is a good idea to use application security testing tools to scan for vulnerabilities in custom-built and third-party applications.

Race Conditions

A *race condition* is a situation in which the behavior of a software system depends on the relative timing of events, such as the order in which threads are scheduled to run. When multiple processes access shared resources concurrently and at least one of them modifies the resource, a race condition can lead to unpredictable results. Here are some specific examples of race conditions:

- **Time-of-check (TOC):** This refers to the moment when a system checks the state or condition of an object or resource. A change in state between the TOC and the time the resource is used can lead to incorrect behavior or security vulnerabilities.

- **Time-of-use (TOU):** TOU refers to the time a resource is accessed or used. A change in state between the checking of the resource and its use is referred to as a TOCTOU (time-of-check to time-of-use) race condition. Attackers can exploit such a condition to gain unauthorized access or escalate privileges.

Understanding race conditions, especially in a multithreading environment, is crucial in software development and cybersecurity. It requires careful synchronization and control to ensure that operations are carried out in the correct order and that shared resources are accessed safely.

Malicious Update

A *malicious update* occurs when legitimate software or firmware is altered or replaced with a version containing harmful code through an update mechanism. Attackers may exploit the normal update process, disguising their destructive code as a routine update. Users, believing they are simply updating their software or system, may unknowingly install the malicious version, leading to potential theft of sensitive information, unauthorized system access, or other damage. Prevention measures include the following:

- Using secure channels for updates

- Verifying updates with digital signatures

- Educating users about the risks of updates from untrusted sources

For example, if an attacker gains control of the update server or can manipulate the update process through an on-path attack, they can provide the malicious update to unsuspecting users. Thinking they are receiving an official update from the software provider, users may install it without suspicion. Once it is installed, the malicious update may execute harmful actions such as stealing sensitive information, providing backdoor access, or damaging the system.

To mitigate the risk of malicious updates, organizations should use secure and authenticated channels for delivering updates, apply digital signatures to verify the integrity of updates, and educate users to be cautious with update prompts from untrusted sources. Regular monitoring and security assessment of the update mechanism can also help in detecting and preventing potential malicious updates.

Operating System (OS)–Based

Operating system–based vulnerabilities are weaknesses in the system software that manages hardware resources and provides various services for computer programs. These vulnerabilities can arise from improper configuration, outdated components, or inherent design flaws. Effective strategies for mitigating such vulnerabilities include adhering to regular OS update and patch management schedules, applying the least-privilege principle, and implementing robust monitoring and logging systems.

Web-Based

Web-based vulnerabilities include weaknesses in web applications and services that can allow unauthorized actions to be performed within those systems. This section discusses several specific types of web-based vulnerabilities.

Structured Query Language Injection (SQLi) Vulnerabilities

Structured Query Language injection (SQLi) vulnerabilities are related to flaws that enable an attacker to manipulate SQL queries in web applications. SQL, a domain-specific language used in programming for managing data held in relational database management systems, can be exploited through improperly validated user inputs. This exploitation is commonly known as SQLi. Mitigating this vulnerability involves proper input validation, use of parameterized queries, and application of the least-privilege access principle to database accounts.

Cross-Site Scripting (XSS) Vulnerabilities

A *cross-site scripting (XSS) vulnerability* enables an attacker to inject malicious scripts into web pages viewed by other users. These vulnerabilities are categorized into three main types:

- **Stored XSS:** The malicious script is permanently stored on the target server.

- **Reflected XSS:** A malicious script is embedded in a URL, affecting users who click the manipulated link.

- **DOM-based XSS:** This vulnerability occurs within the Document Object Model (DOM), the programming interface for web documents, allowing manipulation of web page elements.

Mitigation strategies for XSS vulnerabilities include use of input validation to sanitize user inputs and implementation of a content security policy (CSP) to prevent unauthorized script execution.

Hardware

Hardware vulnerabilities relate to the susceptibility of physical devices and components within a computer system. They can lead to unauthorized access, data corruption, or system failure.

Firmware

Firmware vulnerabilities pertain to weaknesses in the specific class of computer software that provides low-level control over a device's hardware functions. An attacker exploiting these vulnerabilities might alter or replace the firmware, thereby gaining control over the entire system or device. Security measures for addressing firmware vulnerabilities often include regular updates to the latest versions, validation of firmware signatures to ensure authenticity, and use of hardware-based security features, which may provide additional protection against unauthorized alterations.

End-of-Life (EOL)

End-of-life (EOL) hardware is hardware that has reached the stage in its lifecycle when the manufacturer no longer supports it. This lack of support often means that the hardware does not receive essential security updates or patches, and so it is especially susceptible to exploitation. The most effective way to mitigate EOL hardware vulnerabilities is through a proactive replacement or upgrading process to ensure that hardware components remain current and supported.

By comprehending the nature of firmware and EOL vulnerabilities in hardware, professionals in the field of cybersecurity can develop targeted strategies to secure physical devices within a technology infrastructure. Recognizing the specific challenges posed by these vulnerabilities makes it possible to implement precise measures to prevent unauthorized access and maintain the integrity of hardware systems.

Legacy

You might be surprised at the number of small, medium, and large organizations that are still using *legacy platforms and devices* that have passed the vendor's last day of software and hardware support. These legacy devices often are core infrastructure devices, such as routers and switches. If you run devices that have passed the last day that a vendor will provide software and hardware fixes, it is almost guaranteed that you will be running vulnerable devices because when devices are past the last day of support, vendors will not investigate or patch security vulnerabilities in those devices. Companies and service providers that run these devices are at great risk. When possible, you should try to keep these systems on a segmented network or air-gapped and separated from critical function systems.

Key Topic Virtualization

Virtualization is a technology that allows the creation of virtual instances of physical hardware and is often used to optimize resource utilization within computer systems. Vulnerabilities in virtualization can lead to unauthorized access or control over these virtual resources.

Virtual Machine (VM) Escape

A *virtual machine (VM) escape* occurs when an attacker can break out of the confines of a virtual machine and gain access to the host system. This breach can expose all other VMs on that host, making it a severe security concern. Proper configuration of the virtual environment, regular updates to virtualization software, and use of security tools designed for virtualized systems are essential in preventing VM escape. Following the principle of least privilege in granting access rights can further reduce the risk of this vulnerability.

Resource Reuse

In virtualization, *resource reuse* involves sharing physical resources, such as memory and processing power, among multiple virtual instances. A vulnerability in this area might allow one virtual machine to access data remnants from another, leading to potential data leakage between different virtual environments. Implementing secure data-clearing techniques and ensuring proper isolation of resources is fundamental to mitigating this risk. Careful monitoring for suspicious behavior within the virtual environment and adherence to best practices in virtual resource management can further enhance security against resource reuse vulnerabilities.

Cloud Specific

Key Topic

Cloud computing is a way of offering on-demand services that extend the capabilities of a person's computer or an organization's network. Cloud computing services might be free services, such as personal browser-based email from various providers, or they may be offered on a pay-per-use basis, such as services that offer data access, data storage, infrastructure, and online gaming. A network connection of some sort is required to make the connection to the cloud and gain access to these services in real time.

Some of the benefits an organization can realize by using cloud-based services include lowered cost, less administration and maintenance, more reliability, increased scalability, and possibly increased performance. For example, a small business with a few employees definitely needs email, but it likely can't afford the costs of an email server and perhaps does not want to have its own hosted domain and the costs and work that go along with that. By connecting to a free web browser–based service, a small business can obtain nearly unlimited email, contacts, and calendar solutions. However, the company has no administrative control, and there are some security concerns, as discussed shortly.

Cloud computing services are generally broken down into several categories of services:

Key Topic

- **Software as a service (SaaS):** This is the most commonly used and recognized of the service categories. With SaaS, a complete packaged software solution is rented to the user. The service is usually provided through some type of front end or web portal. While the end user is free to use the service from anywhere, the company pays a per-use fee. Examples of SaaS offerings are Office 365, Gmail, Webex, Zoom, Dropbox, and Google Drive.

NOTE Often compared to SaaS is the application service provider (ASP) model. SaaS typically offers a generalized service to many users. However, an ASP typically delivers a service (perhaps a single application) to a small number of users.

- **Infrastructure as a service (IaaS):** This service offers computer networking, storage, load balancing, routing, and VM hosting. More and more organizations are seeing the benefits of offloading some of their networking infrastructure to the cloud through the use of IaaS.

- **Platform as a service (PaaS):** This service provides various software solutions to organizations, especially the ability to develop applications in a virtual environment without the cost or administration of a physical platform. PaaS is used for easy-to-configure operating systems and on-demand computing. Often, it involves IaaS as well for an underlying infrastructure to the platform. Cloud-based virtual desktop environments (VDEs) and virtual desktop infrastructures (VDIs) are often considered to be part of this service but also can be part of IaaS.

- **Security as a service (SECaaS):** In this service, a large service provider integrates its security services into the company's or customer's existing infrastructure. The concept is that the service provider can provide the security more efficiently and more cost-effectively than a company can, especially if it has a limited IT staff or budget. The Cloud Security Alliance (CSA) defines various categories to help businesses implement and understand SECaaS, including encryption, data loss prevention (DLP), continuous monitoring, business continuity and disaster recovery (BCDR), and vulnerability scanning.

NOTE New services periodically arrive, such as monitoring as a service (MaaS), which is a framework that facilitates the deployment of monitoring within the cloud in a continuous fashion. There are many types of cloud-based services. If they don't fall into the preceding list, then they often fall under the category "anything as a service" (XaaS).

A cloud service provider (CSP) might offer one or more of these services. The National Institute of Standards and Technology (NIST) provides a great resource that explains the different cloud service models: Special Publication (SP) 800-145: The NIST Definition of Cloud Computing. We summarize these cloud service models here:

- **Public cloud:** In this type, a service provider offers applications and storage space to the general public over the Internet. Examples include free, web-based email services and pay-as-you-go business-class services. The main benefits of this type of cloud include low (or zero) cost and scalability. Providers of public cloud space include Google Cloud Platform (GCP), Microsoft Azure, and Amazon Web Services (AWS).

- **Private cloud:** This type is designed with a particular organization in mind. With a private cloud, a security administrator has more control over the data and infrastructure. A limited number of people have access to the cloud, and they are usually located behind a firewall of some sort. Resources might be provided by a third party or could come from the server room or data center.

- **Hybrid cloud:** This is a mixture of public and private clouds. Dedicated servers located within the organization and cloud servers from a third party are used together to form the collective network. In hybrid scenarios, confidential data is usually kept in-house.

- **Community cloud:** This is another mix of public and private but one where multiple organizations can share the public portion. Community clouds appeal to organizations that usually have a common form of computing and data storage.

The type of cloud an organization uses is usually dictated by its budget, the level of security it requires, and the human resources (or lack thereof) it has to administer its resources. While a private cloud can be very appealing, it is often beyond the means of an organization, which must instead seek a public or community-based cloud. However, it doesn't matter what type of cloud is used: Resources still have to be secured by someone, and you'll have a hand in that security one way or another.

Cloud security hinges on the level of control you retain and the types of security controls you implement. When an organization makes a decision to use cloud computing, probably the most important security control concern to administrators is the loss of physical control of the organization's data. A more in-depth list of cloud computing security concerns includes lack of privacy, lack of accountability, improper authentication, lack of administrative control, data sensitivity and integrity problems, data segregation issues, location of data and data recovery problems, malicious insider attacks, bug exploitation, lack of investigative support when there is a problem, and finally, questionable long-term viability—basically everything you worry about for your local network and computers! Keep in mind that cloud service providers can be abused as well: Attackers often attempt to use providers' infrastructure to launch powerful attacks.

Solutions to these security issues include the following:

- **Complex passwords:** Strong passwords are beyond important; they are critical, as mentioned many times in this text. As of the writing of this book, accepted password schemes include the following:

  - **For general security:** A minimum of 10 characters, including at least 1 capital letter, 1 number, and 1 special character

  - **For confidential data:** A minimum of 15 characters, including a minimum of 2 capital letters, 2 numbers, and 2 special characters

When it comes to the cloud, you might just opt to use the second password option for every type of cloud. Public clouds can be insecure, and private clouds are likely to house the most confidential data. To enforce the type of password you want your users to choose, a strong server-based policy is recommended.

However, passwords will not protect your data and systems. Passwords can be stolen and often are reused. This is why multifactor authentication is so important!

■ **Powerful authentication methods:** Multifactor authentication can offer a certain amount of defense in depth. If one form of authentication is compromised, the other works as a backup. For example, in addition to providing a password, a person might be asked to provide biometric confirmation, such as a thumbprint or voice authorization, for an additional PIN, or to swipe a smart card. Multifactor authentication may or may not be physically possible, depending on the cloud environment being used, but if at all possible, it should be considered. An example of a multifactor authentication solution is DUO (https://duo.com), which provides a way to integrate multifactor authentication with many different types of deployments; DUO enables users to use a phone app to confirm their identity and authenticate to specific resources or an application.

■ **Strong cloud data access policies:** We're talking the who, what, and when. When it comes to public clouds especially, you should specifically define which users have access, exactly which resources they have access to, and when they are allowed to access those resources. Configure strong passwords and consider two-factor authentication. Configure policies from servers that govern the users; for example, use Group Policy objects on a Windows Server domain controller. Audit any and all connected devices and apps. Consider storing different types of data with different services. Some services do better than others with media files, for example. Remember that cloud storage is not backup. Approach the backing up of data as a separate procedure.

■ **Encryption:** Encryption of individual data files, whole disk encryption, digitally signed virtual machine files,...the list goes on. Because many users will access data through a web browser, perhaps the most important factor is a robust public key infrastructure (PKI), as discussed further in Chapter 4, "Understanding the Importance of Using Appropriate Cryptographic Solutions."

■ **Standardization of programming:** The way applications are planned, designed, programmed, and run on the cloud should all be standardized from one platform to the next and from one programmer to the next. Most important is standardized testing in the form of input validation, fuzzing, and known environment, unknown environment, or partially known environment testing.

■ **Protection of all the data:** This includes storage-area networks (SANs), general cloud storage, and the handling of big data (for example, astronomical data). When data is stored in multiple locations, it is easy for some of it to slip through the cracks. Detailed documentation of what is stored where (and how it is secured) should be kept and updated periodically. As a top-notch security administrator, you don't want your data to be tampered with. There-fore, implementing some cloud-based security controls can be very helpful. For example, consider deterrent controls (to prevent tampering with data), preventive controls (to increase the security strength of a system that houses data), corrective controls (to reduce the effect of any data tampering that has occurred), and detective controls (to detect attacks in real time and have a defense plan that can be immediately carried out).

What else are you, as administrator, trying to protect here? You're concerned with protecting the identity and privacy of your users (especially executives because they are high-profile targets). You need to secure the privacy of credit card numbers and other super-confidential information. You want to secure physical servers that are part of the server room or data center because they might be part of your private cloud. You want to protect your applications with testing and acceptance procedures. (Keep in mind that these things all need to be done within contractual obligations with any third-party cloud providers.) Finally, you're interested in promoting the availability of your data. After all of your security controls and methods have been implemented, you might find that you have locked out more people than first intended. So, your design plan should contain details that will allow for available data but in a secure manner.

Customers considering using cloud computing services should ask for transparency—or detailed information about the provider's security. The provider must be in com-pliance with the organization's security policies; otherwise, the data and software in the cloud become far less secure than the data and software within the customer's own network. This concept, and most of the concepts in the first half of this chapter, should be considered when planning whether to have data, systems, and infrastructure contained on premises, in a hosted environment, in the cloud, or in a mix of these. If there is a mix of on-premises infrastructure and cloud provider infrastructure, a com-pany might consider using a cloud access security broker (CASB)—a software tool or service that acts as a gatekeeper, allowing a company to extend the reach of its security policies beyond its internal infrastructure.

Other "Cloud"-Based Concerns

Other technologies to watch out for are loosely connected with what can be called "cloud technologies." One example is social media. Social media environments can include websites as well as special applications that are loaded directly on to com-puters (mobile or desktop), among other ways to connect, both legitimate and ille-gitimate. People share the darndest things on social media websites and can easily compromise the security of employees and data. The point? There are several ways to access social media platforms, and it can be difficult for a security administrator to find every website, application, service, and port that is used by social media. In cases such as these, you might consider implementing more allow lists and block/deny lists to safeguard applications so that users are better locked down.

Another thing to watch for is P2P networks. File sharing, gaming, media streaming, and all the world is apparently available to a user—if the user knows where to look. However, P2P often comes with a price: malware and potential system infiltration. That is, computers can become unwilling participants in the sharing of data on a P2P network. This is one example in which the cloud invades client computers, often without the user's consent. For access to file sharing, Peer-to-Peer (P2P), and torrents, you need a permanent "padlock."

Then there's the Dark Web, which is another type of P2P (often referred to as an F2F, for "friends to friends") system that creates connections between trusted peers (unlike most other P2Ps) but uses nonstandard ports and protocols. This makes it a bit more difficult to detect. The Dark Web is a safe haven for illegal activities that are designed specifically to resist surveillance. Computers that are part of an administrator's network and, more often, virtual machines in the admin's cloud, can be part of the Dark Web and can easily go undetected by the admin. In some cases, an employee of the organization (or an employee of the cloud provider) might have configured some cloud-based resources to join the Dark Web. You might face devastating legal consequences if illegal activities are traced to your organization. Thorough checks of cloud-based resources can help prevent such a situation. Also, screening of employees, careful inspection of service-level agreements with cloud providers, and the use of third-party IT auditors can help you avoid the possibility of Dark Web connectivity, P2P links, and improper use of social media.

Supply Chain

Supply chain vulnerabilities include weaknesses in the interconnected networks that deliver products or services from initial creation to final delivery.

Service Provider

Service providers are third-party vendors that deliver specific services. A breach or weakness with a service provider can impact the overall security posture of an organization. Regular assessments of service providers can highlight potential risks, and having clearly defined roles and responsibilities in contracts ensures alignment with required security practices.

Hardware Provider

Hardware providers provide the physical equipment for a computing environment. With hardware providers, flaws or compromises within the physical components supplied by hardware manufacturers are of concern. Issues could include counterfeit components, compromised firmware, or physical tampering. Implementing regular supply chain audits can ensure the integrity and authenticity of the products, and secure sourcing from trusted suppliers can minimize the risk of compromised hardware.

Software Provider

Software provider vulnerabilities refer to potential weaknesses in vendor software products or services. These vulnerabilities may vary widely, including unintentional coding errors or intentional malicious insertions. Understanding the composition of software and conducting regular security assessments can uncover potential vulnerabilities. Patch management, where the provider offers regular updates and patches for known issues, is essential for maintaining the security of software products.

These aspects of supply chain vulnerabilities offer insights into the interconnected risks within the complex ecosystem of providers, manufacturers, and vendors. Careful management and oversight of each element in the supply chain are critical in defending against potential breaches and ensuring the overall security of products and services.

Cryptographic

Cryptographic vulnerabilities arise from weaknesses in the methods used to encrypt and decrypt information, safeguarding data integrity and confidentiality. They can result from outdated algorithms, weak keys, or flawed implementations. Properly selecting cryptographic standards, regularly updating encryption algorithms, and adhering to industry best practices are ways you can mitigate these vulnerabilities. As discussed in Chapter 4, understanding the importance of using appropriate cryptographic solutions is key to securing your environment.

Misconfiguration

Misconfiguration, which is often due to incorrect setup or configuration of software, hardware, or networks, can lead to unauthorized access or exposure to sensitive information. Regularly conducting system audits, following documented configuration standards, and employing automated configuration management tools can help in identifying and correcting misconfigurations.

Mobile Device

Mobile device vulnerabilities encompass security weaknesses within smartphones, tablets, and other portable devices. They may include insecure data storage, weak authentication mechanisms, or outdated operating systems. Employing strong access controls, regular software updates, and mobile device management (MDM) solutions can protect against such vulnerabilities.

Side Loading

Side loading refers to installing applications on a mobile device from sources outside the official app store. This practice can introduce vulnerabilities, as side-loaded applications may contain malicious code or may bypass security controls. Restricting side loading through device policies and educating users about the risks associated with unofficial app sources can mitigate this threat.

Jailbreaking

Jailbreaking involves removing restrictions imposed by the device manufacturer or carrier to allow the user greater control over the system and the ability to install unauthorized applications. While jailbreaking may offer increased customization, it also exposes the device to potential security threats. Ensuring adherence to device usage policies and employing security measures that detect or prevent jailbreaking can help maintain the security of mobile devices.

Key Topic Zero-Day Vulnerabilities

A *zero-day vulnerability* is a type of vulnerability that is disclosed by an individual or exploited by an attacker before the creator of the software can create a patch to fix the underlying issue. Attacks leveraging zero-day vulnerabilities can cause great damage even after the creator knows of the vulnerability because it may take time to release a patch to prevent the attacks and fix damage caused by them.

Zero-day attacks can be prevented by using newer operating systems that have protection mechanisms and by updating those operating systems. They can also be prevented by using multiple layers of firewalls and by using lists of approved applications, which allow only known good applications to run. Collectively, these preventive methods are referred to as *zero-day protection*.

Table 7-2 summarizes the vulnerabilities and attacks covered so far.

Key Topic

Table 7-2 Vulnerabilities and Attacks

Vulnerability	Description
Memory injection	An attack that injects malicious code into a running application, altering its execution
Buffer overflow	A vulnerability in which a process stores data outside the memory that the developer intended, often leading to code execution

Vulnerability	Description
Race conditions (TOC/TOU)	Vulnerabilities that occur when the timing of actions impacts the behavior of a system, leading to unintended access or information disclosure
Malicious update	An unauthorized update that introduces malicious code or behavior into an existing system
SQL injection (SQLi)	An attack that manipulates SQL queries, often via web forms, to gain unauthorized access to a database
Cross-site scripting (XSS)	A vulnerability that exploits the trust a user's browser has in a website, often through code injection in web forms
Firmware vulnerability	A security weakness in firmware that can be exploited to gain unauthorized access or control
End-of-life hardware	Hardware that is no longer supported and that is therefore susceptible to unpatched vulnerabilities
Legacy systems	Older systems that may not be compatible with current security measures
VM escape	A vulnerability that allows an attacker to break out of a virtual machine and interact with the host system
Resource reuse	In virtualization, insecure reuse of resources that can lead to data leakage
Cloud-specific vulnerabilities	Security weaknesses that are unique to cloud-based systems
Supply chain risks	Risks associated with third-party service, hardware, and software providers
Cryptographic vulnerabilities	Weaknesses in encryption methods that can be exploited to gain unauthorized access or data
Misconfiguration	Incorrect configuration of software or hardware that leaves a system vulnerable
Mobile device risks	Vulnerabilities related to side-loading apps or jailbreaking devices
Zero-day attack	An attack executed on a vulnerability in software before that vulnerability is known to the software creator

The CompTIA Security+ SY0-701 exam is a comprehensive test that evaluates your understanding of various facets of cybersecurity—not just programming and applications. While having a foundational grasp of programming languages like Visual Basic, C++, C#, PowerShell, Java, Python, HTML, JavaScript, PHP, and SQL is essential, the exam also covers a wide array of vulnerabilities that you need to be familiar with. These include hardware-related vulnerabilities such as firmware issues, end-of-life hardware, and legacy systems. You should know about risks like virtual machine (VM) escape and resource reuse in virtualization. Cloud-specific vulnerabilities are also part of the exam objectives, as are supply chain risks involving service, hardware, and software providers. Cryptographic vulnerabilities, misconfigurations, and mobile device risks like side loading and jailbreaking are also covered. Last but not least, you'll need to understand zero-day vulnerabilities. This broad knowledge base will equip you for the exam as well as for real-world scenarios where you might need to liaise with different departments, from programming to operations.

Chapter Review Activities

Use the features in this section to study and review the topics in this chapter.

Review Key Topics

Review the most important topics in the chapter, noted with the Key Topic icon in the outer margin of the page. Table 7-3 lists these key topics and the page number on which each is found.

Table 7-3 Key Topics for Chapter 7

Key Topic Element	Description	Page Number
Section	Memory Injection	130
Section	Race Conditions	132
Section	Web-Based	133
Section	Virtualization	135
Paragraph	Cloud computing	136
Paragraph	Software-as-a-service (SaaS)	136
Section	Service Provider	141
Section	Software Provider	142
Section	Zero-Day Vulnerabilities	143
Table 7-2	Vulnerabilities and Attacks	143

Define Key Terms

Define the following key terms from this chapter and check your answers in the glossary:

memory injection, buffer overflow, race condition, malicious update, operating system–based vulnerability, Structured Query Language injection (SQLi) vulnerability, cross-site scripting (XSS) vulnerability, firmware vulnerability, end-of-life (EOL), legacy platform or device, virtual machine (VM) escape, resource reuse, service provider, hardware provider, software provider, cryptographic vulnerability, misconfiguration, side loading, jailbreaking, zero-day vulnerability

Review Questions

Answer the following review questions. Check your answers with the answer key in Appendix A.

1. What are the critical vulnerabilities in the application layer, and how can these vulnerabilities be mitigated?

2. How can a race condition in a software system lead to security vulnerabilities, and what are the ways to prevent such conditions?

3. What are the common vulnerabilities in an operating system, and what strategies can be used to mitigate those weaknesses?

4. How can SQL and cross-site scripting (XSS) vulnerabilities be exploited in web applications, and what strategies can be used to mitigate these risks?

5. What is side loading, and what are the security implications of this practice on mobile devices?

6. What risks are associated with firmware and end-of-life (EOL) hardware vulnerabilities, and how can they be mitigated?

7. What vulnerabilities are associated with virtualization, and how can they be addressed?

8. Discuss the security vulnerabilities associated with public, private, and community clouds.

9. Explain how the interconnected risks within the complex ecosystem of providers, manufacturers, and vendors in the supply chain can impact the overall security posture of an organization. What strategies can be employed to defend against potential breaches?

10. Discuss the vulnerabilities associated with side loading and jailbreaking in mobile devices. How can organizations mitigate these threats through device policies and user education?

This chapter covers the following topics related to Objective 2.4 (Given a scenario, analyze indicators of malicious activity) of the CompTIA Security+ SY0-701 certification exam:

- Malware attacks

- Physical attacks

- Network attacks

- Application attacks

- Cryptographic attacks

- Password attacks

- Indicators

CHAPTER 8

Understanding Indicators of Malicious Activity

Threats and attacks come in various forms, each requiring a distinct detection, prevention, and mitigation approach. This chapter explores a comprehensive range of topics, including different types of malware, such as ransomware, Trojans, worms, and spyware; various attack methodologies, such as physical attacks, brute-force attacks, and RFID cloning; diverse network and application attacks; specific cryptographic and password attacks; and indicators that signal potential malicious activities.

"Do I Know This Already?" Quiz

The "Do I Know This Already?" quiz enables you to assess whether you should read this entire chapter thoroughly or jump to the "Chapter Review Activities" section. If you are in doubt about your answers to these questions or your own assessment of your knowledge of the topics, read the entire chapter. Table 8-1 lists the major headings in this chapter and their corresponding "Do I Know This Already?" quiz questions. You can find the answers in Appendix A, "Answers to the 'Do I Know This Already?' Quizzes and Review Questions."

Table 8-1 "Do I Know This Already?" Section-to-Question Mapping

Foundation Topics Section	Questions
Malware Attacks	1, 2
Physical Attacks	3
Network Attacks	4, 5
Application Attacks	6
Cryptographic Attacks	7
Password Attacks	8
Indicators	9

CAUTION   The goal of self-assessment is to gauge your mastery of the topics in this chapter. If you do not know the answer to a question or are only partially sure of the answer, you should mark that question as wrong for purposes of self-assessment. Giving yourself credit for an answer you correctly guess skews your self-assessment results and might provide you with a false sense of security.

1. What is ransomware?

   a. A type of antivirus software

   b. A type of malware that restricts access to a computer system and demands payment to regain access

   c. A physical attack on a computer system

   d. A systematic method of trying all possible passwords

2. Which method is commonly used to infect a system with ransomware?

   a. Amplified DDoS attack

   b. DNS attack

   c. Phishing or spear phishing attack

   d. Brute-force attack

3. Which is the best description of a physical attack?

   a. An attack that targets network services

   b. An attack on the tangible components of an information system

   c. A type of malware

   d. A method used to crack passwords

4. What is the main difference between amplified and reflected DDoS attacks?

   a. Amplified attacks use network protocols that respond with more data, whereas reflected attacks forge the victim's IP address as the source.

   b. Amplified attacks forge the victim's IP address, whereas reflected attacks use network protocols that respond with more data.

   c. Amplified attacks target DNS, whereas reflected attacks target Wi-Fi networks.

   d. Amplified attacks are a type of ransomware, whereas reflected attacks are a type of virus.

5. What kind of application attack exploits a flaw in an application's memory handling, allowing for the execution of arbitrary code or causing the application to crash?

    a. Injection

    b. Replay

    c. Buffer overflow

    d. Privilege escalation

6. Which cryptographic attack involves forcing the rollback of a strong algorithm in favor of an older, weaker algorithm, possibly in combination with an on-path attack?

    a. Downgrade

    b. Birthday

    c. Collision

    d. Upgrade

7. What type of password attack attempts to compromise a system by using a large number of usernames with a few commonly used passwords, avoiding rapid account lockouts?

    a. Brute-force attack

    b. Password hashing

    c. Password spraying

    d. Dictionary attack

8. What indicator might suggest an active brute-force attempt to access an account, requiring further investigation?

    a. Blocked content

    b. Account lockout

    c. Concurrent session usage

    d. Secure connection

9. Which indicator may signify unauthorized access or sharing of credentials when detected within a system?

    a. Secure connection

    b. Account lockout

    c. Blocked content

    d. Concurrent session usage

Foundation Topics

Malware Attacks

Malicious software, or malware, is software designed to infiltrate a computer system and possibly damage it without the user's knowledge or consent. Malware is a broad term used by computer professionals to include viruses, worms, Trojan horses, spyware, rootkits, adware, and other types of undesirable software.

Of course, as a security professional, you don't want malware to infect your systems, but to defend against it, you first need to define it and categorize it. Then you can put preventive measures into place. It's also important to locate and remove or quarantine malware from a computer system in the case that it does manifest itself.

For the Security+ SY0-701 exam, you need to know about several types of malware attacks. *Malware* is malicious software designed to infiltrate, damage, or gather information from a system without the user's consent. Over the past several years, an emphasis shift from viruses to other types of malware, such as spyware and ransomware, has occurred. Most people know about viruses and have some kind of antivirus software running. However, many people are still confused about the various other types of malware, how they occur, and how to protect against them. As a result, computer professionals spend a lot of time fixing malware issues that are not virus related and training users on how to protect against them in the future.

Ransomware

Some less-than-reputable persons use a particularly devious type of malware known as *ransomware*, which restricts access to a computer system and demands that a ransom be paid. Ransomware informs the user that in order to decrypt the files or unlock the computer to regain access to the files, a payment must be made to one of several banking services (typically using crypto currency, such as Bitcoin). It often propagates as a Trojan or worm, and it usually makes use of encryption to cause the user's files to be inaccessible. This use of encryption is also known as *cryptoviral extortion*. Examples of ransomware include WannaCry, NotPetya, Nyetya, SamSam, and BadRabbit. One of the most common ransomware infection methods is via phishing and spear-phishing attacks. You learned about phishing and spear-phishing in Chapter 6, "Understanding Common Threat Actors and Attack Surfaces."

Figure 8-1 shows a message displayed to the victim of a ransomware attack. The ransomware illustrated in this figure is the well-known ransomware WannaCry.

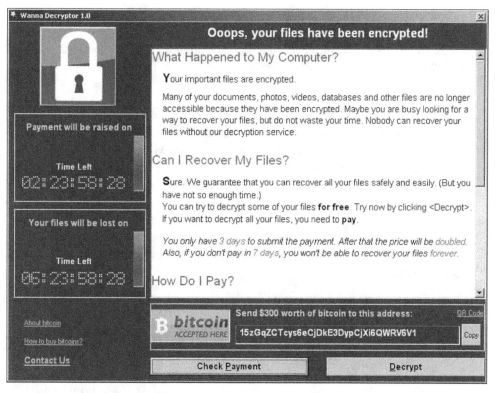

Figure 8-1 A Ransomware Attack

NOTE Sometimes a user will inadvertently access a fraudulent website (or pop-up site) which says that all of the user's files have been encrypted, and payment is required to decrypt them; some imposing government-like logo typically accompanies the statement. But many of these sites don't actually encrypt the user's files. This is plain old extortion, and no real damage is done to the computer or files. These types of sites can be blocked by pop-up blockers, phishing filters, and the user's common sense when clicking searched-for links.

Trojans

Trojan horses, or simply *Trojans*, appear to perform desirable functions but are actually performing malicious functions behind the scenes. They are not technically viruses and can easily be downloaded without being noticed. They can also be transferred to a computer by way of removable media, especially USB flash drives. One example of a Trojan is a file that is contained within a downloaded program such as a key generator—known as a keygen and used with pirated software—or another executable. If a user complains about slow system performance and numerous antivirus alerts, and they recently installed a questionable program from the Internet or from a USB flash drive, their computer could be infected by a Trojan.

Worms

A *worm* is much like a virus except that it self-replicates, whereas a virus does not. It does this in an attempt to spread to other computers. Worms take advantage of security holes in operating systems and applications, including backdoors. They look for other systems on the network or through the Internet that are running the same applications and replicate to those other systems. With a worm, the user doesn't need to access and execute the malware. A virus needs some sort of carrier to get it to the next victim, and it needs explicit instructions to be executed, or it must be executed by the user. A worm does not need a carrier or explicit instructions in order to be executed.

A well-known example of a worm is Nimda (*admin* backward), which propagated automatically through the Internet in 22 minutes in 2001, causing widespread damage. It spread through network shares, mass emailing, and operating system vulnerabilities.

Sometimes a worm does not carry a payload, meaning that in and of itself, it does not contain code that can harm a computer. It may or may not include other malware, but even if it doesn't, it can cause general disruption of network traffic and computer operations because of its self-replicating ability.

In the late 2010s, different types of ransomware (including WannaCry) propagated like worms by scanning and infecting vulnerable systems, leveraging a known Windows SMB vulnerability.

Spyware

Spyware is malware that secretly monitors and collects user activity, including keystrokes, browsing habits, and personal information. Indicators of spyware might include the following:

- Unexpected system behavior, such as slow performance
- Unusual network traffic patterns, potentially indicating that data is being sent to remote servers
- The presence of unknown software or processes running on the system

Mitigating spyware involves using anti-malware tools, keeping software up to date, and practicing safe browsing habits.

Bloatware

Bloatware is software that consumes excessive system resources and often comes preinstalled on devices. Though not always malicious in intent, bloatware can hinder system performance. Indicators of bloatware include the following:

- Decreased system performance or slow startup

- The presence of unfamiliar applications that are challenging to remove

- Consumption of significant memory or disk space by unknown applications

Bloatware removal typically involves specialized uninstallation tools or manual removal by knowledgeable technicians.

Virus

A computer *virus* is code that runs on a computer without the user's knowledge; it infects the computer when the code is accessed and executed. For viruses to do their dirty work, they first need to be executed by the user in some way. A virus also has reproductive capability and can spread copies of itself throughout the computer after it is first executed—by the user or otherwise. By infecting files accessed by other computers, a virus can spread to those other systems as well. The problem is that computers can't call in sick on Monday; they need to be up and running as much as possible—more than the average human.

A virus may replicate itself by modifying other computer programs and inserting its code.

Indicators of a virus include the following:

- Unusual system crashes or errors

- The creation of unknown files or modification of existing ones

- Antivirus/anti-malware software alerts or disabled security tools

Combatting viruses requires robust antivirus/anti-malware solutions, regular system scanning, and adherence to safe downloading and email practices.

Keylogger

An attacker may use a *keylogger* to capture every keystroke of a user in a system and steal sensitive data (including credentials). There are two main types of keyloggers: keylogging hardware devices and keylogging software. A hardware (physical) keylogger is usually a small device that can be placed between a user's keyboard and the main system. Software keyloggers are dedicated programs designed to track and log user keystrokes.

TIP   Keyloggers are legal in some countries and designed to allow employers to oversee the use of their computers. However, recent regulations like the General Data Protection Regulation (GDPR) in the European Union (EU) have made keyloggers a very sensitive and controversial topic. Threat actors use keyloggers for the purpose of stealing passwords and other confidential information.

There are several categories of software-based keyloggers:

- **Kernel-based keylogger:** With this type of keylogger, a program on the machine obtains root access to hide itself in the operating system and intercepts keystrokes that pass through the kernel. This method is difficult both to write and to combat. Such keyloggers reside at the kernel level, which makes them difficult to detect, especially for user-mode applications that don't have root access. They are frequently implemented as rootkits that subvert the operating system kernel to gain unauthorized access to the hardware. This makes them very powerful. A keylogger using this method can act as a keyboard device driver, for example, and thus gain access to any information typed on the keyboard as it goes to the operating system.

- **API-based keylogger:** With this type of keylogger, compromising APIs reside inside a running application. Different types of malware have taken advantage of Windows APIs, such as **GetAsyncKeyState()** and **GetForegroundWindow()**, to perform keylogging activities.

- **Hypervisor-based keylogger:** This type of keylogger is effective in virtual environments, where a hypervisor could be compromised to capture sensitive information.

- **Web form–grabbing keylogger:** Keyloggers can steal data from web form submissions by recording the web browsing on submit events.

- **JavaScript-based keylogger:** Malicious JavaScript tags can be injected into a web application to capture key events (such as the **onKeyUp()** JavaScript function).

- **Memory-injection-based keylogger:** This type of keylogger tampers with the memory tables associated with a browser and other system functions.

You Can't Save Every Computer from Malware!

On a sad note, sometimes computers become so infected with malware that they cannot be saved. In this case, the data should be backed up (by removing the hard drive and slaving it to another system, if necessary), and the operating system and applications should be reinstalled. The UEFI/BIOS of the computer should also be flashed. After the reinstallation, the system should be thoroughly checked to make sure there are no residual effects, and the system's hard drive performs properly.

Logic Bomb

A *logic bomb* is code that has in some way been inserted into software; it is meant to initiate one of many types of malicious functions when specific criteria are met. Logic bombs blur the line between malware and a malware delivery system. They are indeed unwanted software, but they are intended to activate viruses, worms, or Trojans at a specific time. Trojans set off on a certain date are also referred to as *time bombs*. The logic bomb ticks away until the correct time, date, and other parameters have been met. Some of the worst bombs do not incorporate any explosion whatsoever. A logic bomb could be contained within a virus or loaded separately. Logic bombs are more common in movies than they are in real life, but they are sometimes used—and with grave consequences. But more often than not, they are detected before they are set off. If you, as a security administrator, suspect that you have found a logic bomb or a portion of the code of a logic bomb, you should notify your superior immediately and check your organization's policies to see if you should take any other action. Action could include placing network disaster recovery processes on standby, notifying the software vendor, and closely managing usage of the software, including, perhaps, withdrawing it from service until the threat is mitigated. A logic bomb is the evil cousin of an Easter egg.

Easter eggs historically have been platonic extras added to an OS or application as a sort of joke; often, they were missed by quality control and subsequently released by the manufacturer of the software. Easter eggs are not normally documented (as they are tossed in at the last minute by humorous programmers), and they are meant to be harmless, but today they are not allowed by responsible software companies and are thoroughly scanned for. Because an Easter egg (and who knows what else) can possibly slip past quality control, and because of the growing concerns about malware in general, many companies have adopted the idea of *trustworthy computing*, which is a newer concept that sets standards for how software is designed, coded, and checked for quality control. Sadly, as far as software goes, the Easter egg's day has passed.

Rootkit

A *rootkit* is a type of software designed to gain administrator-level control over a computer system without being detected. The term is a combination of the words *root* (referring to the root user in a UNIX/Linux system or administrator in a Windows system) and *kit* (referring to a software kit). The purpose of a rootkit is usually to perform malicious operations on a target computer at a later date without the knowledge of the administrators or users of that computer. A rootkit is a variation of a virus that attempts to dig in to the lower levels of the operating system—components of the OS that start up before any anti-malware services come into play. Rootkits can target the UEFI/BIOS, boot loader, kernel, and more. An example of a boot loader rootkit is the Evil Maid Attack, which can extract the encryption keys of a full disk encryption system. Another (more current) example is the Alureon rootkit, which affects the master boot record (MBR) and low-level system drivers (such as atapi.sys). This particular rootkit was distributed by a botnet and affected more than 200,000 (known) computers running Microsoft operating systems.

Rootkits are difficult to detect because they are activated before the operating system has fully booted. A rootkit might install hidden files, hidden processes, and hidden user accounts. Because rootkits can be installed in hardware or software, they can intercept data from network connections, keyboards, and so on.

A successfully installed rootkit enables unauthorized users to gain access to a system and act as the root or administrator user. A rootkit is copied to a computer as a binary file. This binary file can be detected by signature-based and heuristic-based antivirus programs; however, after the rootkit is executed, it can be difficult to detect because most rootkits are collections of programs working together that can make many modifications to the system. When subversion of the operating system takes place, the OS can't be trusted, and it is difficult to tell whether an antivirus program is running properly or whether any other efforts to combat malware are having any effect. Although security software manufacturers attempt to detect running rootkits, they are unlikely to be successful. The best way to identify a rootkit is to use removable media (a USB flash drive or a special rescue disc) to boot the computer. This way, the operating system is not running, and therefore, the rootkit is not running, making it much easier to detect using the external media.

Sometimes rootkits will hide in the MBR. Often, operating system manufacturers recommend scrubbing the MBR (rewriting it, for example, within System Recovery Options or another recovery environment) and then scanning with antivirus software. This solution depends on the type of rootkit. The use of GPT in lieu of MBR helps to discourage rootkits. I suggest using GPT whenever possible.

Unfortunately, because of the difficulty involved in removing a rootkit, the best way to combat rootkits is to reinstall all software (or reimage the system). Generally, an IT technician, upon detecting a rootkit, will do just that because reinstalling usually takes less time than attempting to fix all the rootkit issues; plus, it is a way to verify that the rootkit has been removed completely.

Physical Attacks

Physical attacks focus on the tangible components of information systems, including hardware devices, data storage mediums, or entire physical locations. These attacks might manifest through visible damage to hardware, unauthorized physical access to secure facilities, or tampering with cables and connectors. Implementing secure facilities, surveillance, and regular monitoring of physical access can deter these types of attacks.

Brute-Force Attacks

In a ***brute-force attack***, the attacker systematically tries all possible passwords or encryption keys to gain unauthorized access. Offline brute-force attacks occur when an attacker gains a hashed file of passwords and attempts to crack them using specialized tools. Strong password hashing, salts, and monitoring for unauthorized access to sensitive files are essential in defending against such attacks. Online brute-force attacks involve repeated direct login attempts on the target system. Multiple failed login attempts from the same IP address or rapid successive login attempts are indicators. Common mitigation strategies include account lockout policies, CAPTCHA challenges, and monitoring of login activities.

Another form of physical attack is a physical brute-force attack, in which an attacker may literally break down a door or otherwise force their way into a secure location to gain unauthorized access. Implementing secure facilities, surveillance, and regular monitoring of physical access points can serve as effective deterrents against these types of attacks.

Radio Frequency Identification (RFID) Cloning

Radio frequency identification (RFID) cloning involves duplicating information from an RFID tag, such as the tag found in an access card or payment system. Unauthorized access to RFID-enabled areas or unusual patterns in RFID transactions might signal this type of attack. Employing encrypted RFID communication, secondary authentication methods, and vigilant monitoring of RFID access logs can protect against RFID cloning.

Environmental

Environmental threats are natural or human-caused disruptions affecting the physical environment where systems operate, such as floods, fires, or power surges. Indicators of these threats include abnormal temperature or humidity levels or alarms from environmental monitoring systems. Having disaster recovery plans in place, using environmental controls, and regularly inspecting physical infrastructure are essential practices to mitigate environmental threats.

Network Attacks

Network attacks target network services and data availability, integrity, and confidentiality. These attacks use various tactics, including distributed denial-of-service (DDoS) attacks, Domain Name System (DNS) attacks, wireless attacks, on-path attacks, credential replay, and malicious code.

Distributed Denial-of-Service (DDoS) Attacks

A *distributed denial-of-service (DDoS)* overwhelms a target system with traffic, rendering it unresponsive. There are two specialized types of DDoS attacks:

- **Amplified DDoS attacks:** An *amplified DDoS attack* uses network protocols that respond with more data than they receive. The attacker can flood the victim's system with substantial traffic by spoofing the victim's IP address and sending small requests to servers that reply with larger responses.

- **Reflected DDoS attacks:** In a *reflected DDoS attack*, an attacker sends requests to various servers, forging the victim's IP address as the source. The servers then send the response to the victim, leading to an influx of unwanted traffic.

Mitigating DDoS attacks often involves traffic filtering, rate limiting, and coordination with upstream Internet service providers.

Domain Name System (DNS) Attacks

A *Domain Name System (DNS) attack* targets the system that translates human-readable domain names into IP addresses. By disrupting this service, an attacker can redirect users to malicious sites or make legitimate sites unavailable. Techniques to prevent DNS attacks include implementing DNSSEC (Domain Name System Security Extensions) and regularly monitoring DNS requests and responses.

Wireless Attacks

Wireless attacks exploit vulnerabilities in Wi-Fi networks. Understanding the various types of wireless attacks can help in implementing effective countermeasures. Here are some specific attacks to be aware of:

- **Packet sniffing:** Attackers capture and analyze network traffic to gather information or find vulnerabilities. Countermeasure: Use strong encryption protocols like WPA3.

- **Rogue access points:** Unauthorized Wi-Fi access points are added to a network, often to bypass security measures. Countermeasure: Regularly audit the network for unauthorized devices.

- **Wi-Fi phishing and evil twin:** Attackers mimic a legitimate access point to deceive users into connecting, often to steal credentials. Countermeasure: Employ network authentication and alert users to only connect to known networks.

- **Spoofing attack:** An attacker impersonates another device by falsifying data, often to gain unauthorized access. Countermeasure: Implement MAC address filtering and always use strong authentication.

- **Encryption cracking:** An attacker decrypts secure traffic to eavesdrop on communications. Countermeasure: Use the latest encryption standards and regularly update keys.

- **On-path attack:** An attacker intercepts and possibly alters communication between two parties without their knowledge. Countermeasure: Use VPNs for secure communication.

- **Denial-of-service (DoS) attack:** An attacker disrupts network services by overwhelming them with traffic. Countermeasure: Implement rate limiting and IP filtering.

- **Wi-Fi jamming:** An attacker floods a network with excessive traffic to disrupt service. Countermeasure: Use intrusion detection systems to identify and block jamming attacks.

Employing robust encryption, secure authentication protocols, and network monitoring can counteract these threats.

On-Path Attacks

An *on-path attack* occurs when an attacker intercepts and possibly alters communication between two parties without their knowledge. Implementing end-to-end encryption, employing secure communication protocols, and validating certificates are common defenses against on-path attacks.

Credential Replay

Credential replay involves capturing valid user credentials and reusing them to gain unauthorized access. Strong authentication mechanisms, such as multifactor authentication and time-based one-time passwords, can prevent credential replay.

Malicious Code

Malicious code refers to software that performs unauthorized actions on a network, such as viruses, worms, or Trojan horses. Detection and prevention strategies include deploying anti-malware tools, regularly updating software, and employing network intrusion detection systems.

Application Attacks

An *application attack* exploits software application weaknesses, potentially leading to unauthorized access, data theft, or system disruption. Understanding the nuances of different types of application attacks is vital for prevention and response.

Injection

An *injection attack* occurs when malicious data is inserted into a query or command, which the application then mistakenly executes. This can lead to unauthorized access to data, modification of data, or remote command execution. Prevention techniques include using prepared statements, using proper input validation, and employing security controls like web application firewalls (WAFs).

Buffer Overflow

A *buffer overflow attack* exploits flaws in an application's memory handling, specifically when more data is written to a buffer than the buffer can handle. This can cause the application to crash or execute arbitrary code. Countermeasures include utilizing programming languages and compilers that manage memory safely, employing runtime protections, and regularly reviewing code to detect potential vulnerabilities. For more information, see Chapter 7, "Understanding Various Types of Vulnerabilities."

Replay

Replay attacks involve the unauthorized capture and retransmission of valid authentication data, such as tokens or credentials. Time-based restrictions, encryption, and use of single-use or expiring authentication tokens are common strategies for mitigating replay attacks.

Privilege Escalation

Privilege escalation is the act of exploiting a bug or design flaw in an application to gain elevated access to resources that are usually restricted. This can occur through exploiting user permissions or system vulnerabilities. Adhering to the principle of least privilege, regularly patching systems, and monitoring user activities are essential in preventing privilege escalation.

Forgery

Forgery attacks, such as cross-site request forgery (CSRF), trick users into performing actions they didn't intend to, typically without their knowledge or consent. Using anti-forgery tokens, implementing proper authentication controls, and employing same-origin policies are strategies to counteract forgery attacks.

Directory Traversal

Directory traversal, or path traversal, allows an attacker to access files and directories stored outside the application's intended folder structure. This can lead to unauthorized viewing, deletion, or modification of files. Implementing proper access controls, validating user input, and using a secure method for file handling are critical defenses against directory traversal.

Cryptographic Attacks

Attackers can launch different *cryptographic attacks*, which are attacks against weak cryptography (crypto) implementations. The following sections describe three common crypto attacks: downgrade, collision, and birthday attacks.

Downgrade

A *downgrade attack* is a type of cryptographic attack that forces the rollback of a strong algorithm in favor of an older, lower-quality algorithm or mode of operation. Attackers leverage systems that have legacy crypto algorithms typically enabled for backward compatibility with older systems. Attackers may perform a downgrade attack in combination with an on-path attack.

Downgrade attacks can take many forms. They can even target the crypto algorithm itself (such as downgrading from AES to DES or RC4) or the version of an algorithm (such as downgrading from TLS 1.3 to 1.0).

Collision

A *collision* occurs when two different files end up using the same hash. Message Digest Algorithm 5 (MD5) is a legacy hashing algorithm that is used to attempt to provide data integrity. By checking the hash produced by the downloaded file against the original hash, you can verify the file's integrity with a level of certainty. However, MD5 hashes are susceptible to collisions. Due to their low collision resistance, MD5 is considered to be harmful today. MD5 is also vulnerable to threats such as rainbow tables and preimage attacks. The best way to protect against these attacks is to use a stronger type of hashing function, such as SHA-2 or higher.

The Secure Hash Algorithm (SHA) is one of a number of hash functions designed by the U.S. National Security Agency (NSA) and published by NIST. These functions are used widely in the U.S. government. Because MD5 and SHA-1 have vulnerabilities, government agencies and the private sector started using SHA-2 and newer implementations.

NOTE   For more on hashing algorithms, see Chapter 4, "Understanding the Importance of Using Appropriate Cryptographic Solutions."

It is important that a hashing algorithm be collision resistant. If it has the capability to avoid the same output from two guessed inputs (by an attacker attempting a collision attack), a hashing algorithm is collision resistant. When it comes to cryptography, "perfect hashing" is not possible because usually unknowns are involved, such as the data to be used to create the hash and what hash values have been created in the past. Though perfect is not possible, it is possible to increase collision resistance by using a more powerful hashing algorithm.

Birthday

A *birthday attack* is an attack on a hashing system that involves attempting to send two different messages with the same hash function, causing a collision. It is based on the birthday problem in probability theory (also known as the birthday paradox). It can be summed up simply as follows: A randomly chosen group of people will have a pair of persons with the same calendar date birthday. Given a standard calendar year of 365 days, the probability of this occurring with 366 people is 100% (367 people on a leap year). So far, this makes sense and sounds logical.

The paradox (thoughtfully and mathematically) comes into play when fewer people are involved. With only 57 people, there is a 99% probability of a match (a much higher percentage than one would think), and with only 23 people, there is a 50% probability. Imagine that and blow out your candles—and by this I mean use hashing functions with strong collision resistance. Because if attackers can find any two messages that digest the same way (that is, use the same hash value), they can deceive a user into receiving the wrong message. To protect against a birthday attack, you should use a secure transmission medium, such as SSH, or encrypt the entire message that has been hashed.

Password Attacks

A *password attack* is an attack focused on exploiting weak passwords. There are many different ways that attackers can steal passwords, crack passwords, and perform other credential-based (password-based) attacks. The following sections describe the most common password-based attacks.

Password Spraying

Password spraying is a type of attack in which an attacker attempts to compromise a system by using a large number of usernames with a few commonly used passwords. Traditional brute-force attacks involve attempting to gain unauthorized access to a single account by guessing the password. This can quickly result in the targeted account getting locked out because commonly used account-lockout policies allow for a limited number of failed attempts (typically three to five) during a set period of time. During a password-spraying attack (also known as the "low-and-slow" method), the malicious actor attempts a single commonly used password (such as *Password1*, *COVID19*, or *asdasd*) against many accounts before moving on to attempt a second password, and so on. This technique allows the actor to remain undetected by avoiding rapid or frequent account lockouts.

Brute-Force Attacks

In a brute-force attack, an attacker uses random numbers and characters to crack a user's password. A brute-force attack on an encrypted password can take hours, days, months, or years, depending on the complexity and length of the password. The speed of success depends on the speed of the CPU's power. A brute-force attack attempts every combination of letters, numbers, and characters.

> **TIP** Tools such as 0phtCrack, LCP, Cain and Abel, and John the Ripper can all perform dictionary, hybrid, and brute-force password cracking.

Indicators

Indicators of potential malicious activity within a system or network serve as vital signals or warnings that something may be amiss. *Indicators* encompass a wide array of behaviors, patterns, or anomalies that, when detected, could point to unauthorized access, malware infection, or other types of cyber threats. The careful observation and analysis of these indicators form an essential part of an organization's security posture, allowing for early detection and prompt response to emerging threats. By understanding the different indicators and their significance, security professionals can craft more robust defense mechanisms and be better prepared to act when something falls outside expected norms.

Account Lockout

An *account lockout* is often a response to repeated failed login attempts and prevents the user from accessing the system for a specific period of time or requires manual administrator intervention. While it serves as a security measure, account lockout might also indicate a brute-force attempt to access an account. By monitoring account lockouts and investigating their causes, you can unveil possible unauthorized access attempts.

Concurrent Session Usage

Concurrent session usage refers to detecting multiple simultaneous sessions from a single user account that may signify unauthorized access or sharing of credentials. Analyzing the nature and source of concurrent sessions helps determine whether user activity is genuine or a potential security compromise.

Blocked Content

Blocked content typically arises from security measures that prevent access to malicious or unauthorized websites, files, or emails. Increased blocked content might signify an active threat or increased risk exposure, necessitating further investigation.

Impossible Travel

Impossible travel refers to login attempts from geographically distant locations in a time frame that makes physical travel impossible. Say that the same user logs in from New York and from Tokyo within a single hour. Since it's highly improbable that the user could travel from New York to Tokyo in one hour (at least for the moment), this login pattern is a strong indication of compromised credentials.

Resource Consumption

An abnormal increase in resource consumption, such as CPU, memory, or network bandwidth, might signal a malware infection or an ongoing attack, such as a DDoS attack. Monitoring system resources and identifying anomalies allow for timely intervention.

Resource Inaccessibility

Sudden inaccessibility of essential resources such as files, databases, or network services might indicate a ransomware attack, hardware failure, or other malicious activity. A swift investigation is crucial to determine the cause and restore access.

Out-of-Cycle Logging

Unexpected or irregular logging activities outside normal patterns can signal a potential intrusion or unauthorized access. Analyzing these logs and correlating them with other system activities help identify threats.

Published/Documented Indicators

Some threat indicators are publicly documented or shared within threat intelligence communities. Leveraging these known indicators to compare against internal system behaviors can aid in early threat detection.

Missing Logs

The sudden disappearance or alteration of log files might indicate an attacker's attempt to cover their tracks. Regular log monitoring and integrity checks are essential to detect and respond to such manipulations.

In understanding and monitoring these varied indicators, organizations are empowered to detect suspicious or malicious activities early in the attack cycle. Combining these indicators with proactive security measures and an informed response strategy enhances the overall resilience and safety of the system or network.

Chapter Review Activities

Use the features in this section to study and review the topics in this chapter.

Review Key Topics

Review the most important topics in the chapter, noted with the Key Topic icon in the outer margin of the page. Table 8-2 lists these key topics and the page number on which each is found.

Table 8-2 Key Topics for Chapter 8

Key Topic Element	Description	Page Number
Paragraph	Malware attacks	152
Section	Ransomware	152
Section	Trojans	153
Section	Worms	154
Section	Logic Bomb	157

Key Topic Element	Description	Page Number
Section	Rootkit	157
Section	Network Attacks	160
Section	Downgrade	163
Section	Birthday	164
Section	Password Spraying	165
Section	Brute-Force Attacks	165

Define Key Terms

Define the following key terms from this chapter and check your answers in the glossary:

malware, ransomware, Trojan, worm, spyware, bloatware, virus, keylogger, logic bomb, rootkit, brute-force attack, radio frequency identification (RFID) cloning, environmental threat, network attack, distributed denial-of-service (DDoS) attack, amplified DDoS attack, reflected DDoS attack, Domain Name System (DNS) attack, wireless attack, on-path attack, credential replay, malicious code, application attack, injection attack, buffer overflow attack, replay attack, privilege escalation, forgery attack, directory traversal, cryptographic attack, downgrade attack, collision, birthday attack, password attack, indicator, account lockout, concurrent session usage

Review Questions

Answer the following review questions. Check your answers with the answer key in Appendix A.

1. What are the key components of malicious software (malware), such as viruses, worms, and Trojan horses, and how do they differ from one another?

2. Discuss the two specialized types of distributed denial-of-service (DDoS) attacks: amplified and reflected DDoS attacks. How do they operate, and what makes them distinct?

3. Describe the nature of ransomware and its common methods of infection. What are some well-known examples, and how does ransomware employ encryption?

4. What measures can be taken to defend against brute-force attacks, both offline and online? Explain the importance of strong password hashing, use of salts, and monitoring of unauthorized access.

5. How do physical attacks impact information systems? What are some of the ways in which physical security can be implemented to deter these types of attacks?

6. Explain how a buffer overflow attack works, what its potential consequences are, and how it can be prevented.

7. What is a replay attack, in the context of application attacks, and how can an organization mitigate its risks?

8. Among the indicators of potential malicious activity, discuss the significance of blocked content and the actions that security professionals might take upon observing an increase in blocked content in a system or network.

This chapter covers the following topics related to Objective 2.5 (Explain the purpose of mitigation techniques used to secure the enterprise) of the CompTIA Security+ SY0-701 certification exam:

- Segmentation
- Access control
- Application allow list
- Isolation
- Patching
- Encryption
- Monitoring
- Least privilege
- Configuration enforcement
- Decommissioning
- Hardening techniques

Understanding the Purpose of Mitigation Techniques Used to Secure the Enterprise

This chapter explores various mitigation techniques for securing the enterprise. It focuses on the implementation and understanding of practices like segmentation, access control (including ACLs and permissions), application allow listing, isolation, patching, encryption, monitoring, least privilege, configuration enforcement, decommissioning, and hardening techniques such as encryption, endpoint protection, host-based firewalling, use of HIPS, disabling of ports/protocols, default password changes, and the removal of unnecessary software. Together, these measures create a multilayered defense strategy, enhancing the overall security posture of an organization by minimizing vulnerabilities and ensuring that the essential security principles of confidentiality, integrity, and availability are upheld.

"Do I Know This Already?" Quiz

The "Do I Know This Already?" quiz enables you to assess whether you should read this entire chapter thoroughly or jump to the "Chapter Review Activities" section. If you are in doubt about your answers to these questions or your own assessment of your knowledge of the topics, read the entire chapter. Table 9-1 lists the major headings in this chapter and their corresponding "Do I Know This Already?" quiz questions. You can find the answers in Appendix A, "Answers to the 'Do I Know This Already?' Quizzes and Review Questions."

Table 9-1 "Do I Know This Already?" Section-to-Question Mapping

Foundation Topics Section	Questions
Segmentation	1
Access Control	2
Application Allow List	8
Isolation	9

Foundation Topics Section	Questions
Patching	3, 4
Encryption	10
Monitoring	11
Least Privilege	5
Configuration Enforcement	12
Decommissioning	13
Hardening Techniques	6, 7

CAUTION   The goal of self-assessment is to gauge your mastery of the topics in this chapter. If you do not know the answer to a question or are only partially sure of the answer, you should mark that question as wrong for purposes of self-assessment. Giving yourself credit for an answer you correctly guess skews your self-assessment results and might provide you with a false sense of security.

1. What is the primary purpose of network segmentation in computer networks?

   a. Increasing storage capacity

   b. Isolating groups of hosts and enhancing security

   a. Enhancing user interface

   d. Allowing unlimited access to information

2. What is the main function of access control lists (ACLs) in a network?

   a. Increasing network speed

   b. Granting or denying permissions to specific IP addresses, protocols, or ports

   c. Providing email access

   d. Analyzing financial data

3. Why is patching considered essential in the healthcare industry?

   a. It improves the efficiency of medical devices.

   b. It protects patient confidentiality by fixing vulnerabilities.

   c. It increases patient capacity.

   d. It enables integration with financial systems.

4. Which of the following challenges is specific to patching in the manufacturing industry?

    a. Disrupting patient care

    b. Compliance with PCI DSS

    c. Affecting production schedules due to downtime

    d. Slowing down bureaucratic processes

5. What does the principle of least privilege primarily aim to minimize?

    a. Access to new features

    b. Cost of software maintenance

    c. Potential damage from accidental mishaps or intentional malicious activities

    d. Complexity of user interfaces

6. What is the primary function of encryption as a hardening technique?

    a. Increasing data accessibility

    b. Transforming data into a coded form to protect it

    c. Speeding up data transmission

    d. Enabling multi-user access

7. What does a host-based intrusion prevention system (HIPS) primarily provide?

    a. Increased network speed

    b. Storage solutions for user data

    c. Real-time protection against known and unknown threats by monitoring host behavior and blocking malicious traffic from the network layer up through the application layer

    d. Improved user interface

8. What is the primary benefit of implementing a centrally managed application allow list in cybersecurity?

    a. To increase the speed of application performance

    b. To provide more granular control over which applications are permitted to run

    c. To automatically update applications

    d. To reduce the cost of software licensing

9. What is the purpose of isolating a compromised endpoint in a network environment?

   a. To improve its performance

   b. To separate it from the rest of the network to prevent further infection

   c. To increase its storage capacity

   d. To prepare it for a software update

10. What is the main objective of encryption in data security?

   a. To speed up data transmission

   b. To compress data for storage

   c. To convert information into a coded form for confidentiality and integrity

   d. To categorize data for easier access

11. Which of these best represents the primary focus of monitoring in cybersecurity?

   a. Improving system efficiency

   b. Observing and analyzing system activities for potential security incidents

   c. Managing user accounts

   d. Conducting system backups

12. What is the main purpose of configuration enforcement in an IT environment?

   a. Standardizing and consistently applying system settings and policies across the network

   b. Streamlining software installation processes

   c. Enhancing the user interface of systems

   d. Reducing the energy consumption of devices

13. Which of these best describes the decommissioning process in IT lifecycle management?

   a. Upgrading hardware or software to the latest version

   b. Expanding the capacity of IT systems

   c. Taking hardware, software, or subsystems out of active service

   d. Merging multiple IT systems into a single platform

Foundation Topics

Segmentation

Segmentation is the process of dividing a computer network into subnetworks, each of which is a network segment or layer. This helps improve performance and enhances security by isolating groups of hosts together, limiting access to sensitive information. When a network is divided into segments, the potential impact of a breach can be confined, preventing a compromised system from accessing the entire network. Implementing network segmentation appropriately requires understanding of data flows and business needs and adherence to proper policies and protocols to ensure that the divisions serve functional and security purposes.

Access Control

Access control is the selective restriction of access to a place or resource. It is an essential aspect of security management that ensures only authorized users have access to specific resources, and it's achieved through various means, discussed in the following sections.

Key Topic

Access Control Lists (ACLs)

Access control lists (ACLs) are vital tools in network security that allow administrators to define rules that control the traffic into and out of a network. ACL rules can be configured to grant or deny permissions to specific IP addresses, protocols, or ports, thereby enhancing control over network access.

Consider an enterprise with different departments, such as Human Resources, Finance, and Development. Each of these departments requires access to different resources within the network, and some information should remain confined within specific departments. In this scenario, an ACL might be applied to the Finance department's subnet to ensure that only authorized personnel within Finance can access sensitive financial data. The ACL rules could be configured as follows:

- *Allow* access to the Finance department's subnet from IP addresses belonging to authorized Finance department workstations.

- *Deny* access to the Finance department's subnet from IP addresses belonging to the Human Resources or Development departments.

- *Allow* necessary general access to shared resources like email and intranet but continue to restrict access to the financial data.

Specific ACL configurations ensure that only the intended users within the Finance department can access the sensitive financial information, thereby maintaining confidentiality and integrity. Other departments are restricted from accessing this data but can still reach common shared resources within the enterprise.

Network ACLs can be implemented at various levels of the OSI model:

- A Layer 2 ACL operates at the data link layer and implements filters based on Layer 2 information. An example of this type of access list is a MAC access list, which uses information about the MAC address to create the filter.

- A Layer 3 ACL operates at the networking layer. Cisco devices usually allow Layer 3 ACLs for different Layer 3 protocols, including the ones that are most commonly used today: IPv4 and IPv6. In addition to selecting the Layer 3 protocol, a Layer 3 ACL allows the configuration of filtering for a protocol using raw IP, such as OSPF or ESP.

- A Layer 4 ACL operates at the transport layer. An example of a Layer 4 ACL is a TCP- or UDP-based ACL. Typically, a Layer 4 ACL includes the source and destination. This allows filtering of specific upper-layer packets.

Permissions

Permissions are defined rights to perform actions on a system. They are typically associated with files, directories, or processes and determine who (or what) can read, write, or execute them. Implementing permissions helps ensure that users and systems interact with only the resources necessary for their roles, thus limiting potential abuse or mistakes that could lead to security incidents.

Windows Permissions

In Windows, permissions are an integral part of the access control model, which includes permissions, ownership of objects, inheritance of permissions, user rights, and object auditing. The operating system uses security identifiers (SIDs) to represent users and groups, also known as security principals. These SIDs are assigned rights and permissions that dictate their actions on various objects, such as files, folders, printers, and registry keys.

Access control lists (ACLs) are used to manage permissions, allowing resource managers to take actions such as the following:

- Deny access to unauthorized users and groups
- Set well-defined limits on access for authorized users and groups

Permissions can be set for various objects, including files, Active Directory objects, and system objects such as processes. Common permissions include read, modify, change owner, and delete. Object owners often set permissions at the container level to make it easier to manage access control.

Windows also supports a feature called inheritance, where child objects automatically inherit the permissions of their parent container. This simplifies the management of permissions across a hierarchy of objects.

Linux Permissions

Linux employs a relatively simple but effective model for file permissions, which are crucial for system security. Permissions in Linux are displayed using the **ls -l** command and can be modified using the **chmod** command. Files and directories in Linux have three sets of permissions:

- Owner permissions
- Group permissions
- Others

These permissions are represented symbolically (**r** for read, **w** for write, **x** for execute) or numerically using octal values (**4** for read, **2** for write, **1** for execute).

For directories, permissions work slightly differently:

- Read (**r**) allows the user to view the contents of the directory.
- Write (**w**) allows the user to modify the directory's contents, including adding or removing files.
- Execute (**x**) allows the user to access the directory and its metadata.

Linux also supports special permissions, such as SUID and SGID, and the "sticky bit," which provide additional privileges over the standard permission sets.

Best Practices

In Windows, granting permissions to security groups rather than to individual users is safer and generally results in easier management and better system performance.

In Linux, using the **chown** and **chgrp** commands can help you change a file's user and group ownership, providing an extra layer of control.

Application Allow List

Antivirus/anti-malware, firewall, and endpoint security management systems generally have ***application allow lists***, sometimes called application whitelists. If you are currently using a block list, you might consider also implementing a centrally managed application allow list, which gives you more granular control. With an application allow list, you spend time up front building an allow list of approved applications on your network. Then, using your central management or endpoint security solution, you roll out the allow list enterprisewide. After an incident, you should spend the time building or updating an application allow list and then enable and enforce it. This way, you can keep users from installing unauthorized applications that could lead to breaches.

Let's consider a large financial organization as an example. Say that this organization handles sensitive financial data of thousands of clients, and the IT department is tasked with ensuring the confidentiality, integrity, and availability of the data. One of the major concerns is that unauthorized applications might contain malware or lead to security vulnerabilities.

To tackle this challenge, the organization implements an application allow list that is centrally managed within the organization's existing antivirus/anti-malware, firewall, and endpoint security management systems. Let's look at how the organization can approach figuring out what to place on the application allow list:

1. **Identify approved applications:** First, the IT security team identifies all legitimate and necessary applications required for various functions in the organization, including banking software, client management systems, office productivity tools, and specialized financial analysis applications.

2. **Build the allow list:** The team spends substantial time building a comprehensive allow list of approved applications. This list is meticulously curated to ensure that only verified and trusted applications are included. (Note that it is important to regularly audit this list to ensure that all applications on the list should still have access and to ensure that unauthorized applications have not made it onto the list.)

3. **Deploy and centrally manage the solution:** The allow list is integrated into the organization's central management or endpoint security solution, allowing for unified control and consistent application across all devices and departments within the enterprise.

4. **Respond to an incident and update the list:** If a security incident occurs, such as an unauthorized application being discovered or a breach, the allow list needs to be promptly reviewed and updated. This iterative process ensures that

the list remains up-to-date with the organization's evolving needs and threat landscape.

5. **Assess user impact:** With the allow list enforced throughout the enterprise, users are prevented from installing unauthorized applications that could lead to breaches. The centralized control ensures consistent policy enforcement without hindering legitimate business operations.

The use of an application allow list by the financial institution illustrates how a sophisticated approach to managing authorized applications can bolster security in an environment where the stakes are high and the data is of critical value. It's an example of proactive security management that aligns with the business.

Isolation

Once an endpoint has been compromised because of malware, a virus, or a Trojan, or when it is part of a wider attack, it needs to be automatically quarantined and isolated or manually isolated. *Isolation* is the process of separating a suspected infected device from the rest of the computing environment. With a compromised endpoint, you should consider three things:

■ Is there something on this host (private or personal data or critical evidence) that cannot be obtained from some other source?

■ Can you safely reimage the device? In other words, can you trust underlying systems, BIOS/UEFI, drivers, firmware, or other operating systems after the reimage?

■ Can you wait until the investigation is completed before attempting any action?

The answers to these questions and corporate policy will help you determine the right course of action. Isolated hosts are good sources of evidence either on the disk/media or in memory, so investigators often want them intact. Investigators can build a list of what was done and how. That list then can be used to help protect these systems in the future. There are ways to isolate a host from the rest of the systems and network so that it can only operate in a sandbox to be observed by analysts and investigators during an incident; this approach allows for greater evidence collection.

TIP   NIST SP 800-123 and SP 800-83 are general guides to server and host security best practices, including isolation of compromised devices. See https://nvlpubs.nist.gov/nistpubs/specialpublications/nist.sp.800-83r1.pdf and https://nvlpubs.nist.gov/nistpubs/legacy/sp/nistspecialpublication800-123.pdf.

Key Topic

Patching

Patching refers to updating or fixing a system, including software applications, drivers, and operating systems, by applying patches or updates. These updates often contain fixes for known security vulnerabilities, improvements to performance, or new features. For example, if a vulnerability is discovered in an enterprise's web server software, a patch can be applied to correct the issue, thereby closing the potential entry point for attackers. Regular patching is essential to maintaining the security of systems and protecting against known threats, as outdated systems can be more easily exploited.

Patching is a universal cybersecurity practice, but industries tend to approach the process differently, based on the impacts in their environment. Here are some examples of how different industries might approach patching and some special challenges they encounter when balancing security with meeting operational demands:

- **Healthcare:**
  - **Importance:** Because personal health information (PHI) is highly sensitive, regular patching in healthcare is vital to protect patient confidentiality.
  - **Challenges:** Patching medical devices and legacy systems without disrupting patient care services can be complex.
  - **Solutions:** Implementing a patch management policy that includes testing of patches in isolated environments before deployment can reduce potential risks to critical systems.

- **Financial services:**
  - **Importance:** Financial institutions handle large volumes of sensitive data related to banking details and finances. Timely patching is essential to protect against fraud and data breaches.
  - **Challenges:** Compliance with regulatory requirements, such as PCI DSS, adds complexity to the patching process.

- **Solutions:** A well-structured patch management process that is aligned with regulatory requirements helps ensure consistent security while maintaining compliance.

- **Manufacturing:**

  - **Importance:** In manufacturing, securing industrial control systems (ICSs) and Internet of Things (IoT) devices is critical. Patching helps protect these systems against vulnerabilities that could lead to production disruptions.

  - **Challenges:** Downtime for patching can affect production schedules, and some embedded systems may be difficult to update.

  - **Solutions:** Scheduled patching during non-peak hours and robust testing prior to deployment can mitigate potential disruptions.

- **Education sector:**

  - **Importance:** Educational institutions manage a diverse array of devices and user roles. Patching is key to protecting student and staff information.

  - **Challenges:** The wide variety of systems and decentralized nature of some educational networks can complicate patch management.

  - **Solutions:** Centralized patch management solutions that are tailored to the unique environment of an educational institution can streamline the process and ensure timely updates.

- **Government and public sector:**

  - **Importance:** Patching in government systems is critical for national security and the protection of citizens' data.

  - **Challenges:** Bureaucratic processes and complex, interconnected systems can slow down the patching process.

  - **Solutions:** Implementing clear guidelines, automating patch deployment where possible, and establishing a dedicated security team can enhance the efficiency and effectiveness of patching.

Encryption

Encryption is the process of converting information into a coded form, making it unreadable without the correct decryption key or algorithm. It protects the confidentiality and integrity of data, both in transit and at rest. For instance, an enterprise might encrypt sensitive customer data stored in a database or use Secure Sockets Layer (SSL)/Transport Layer Security (TLS) encryption for secure communication over the Internet. Encrypting this data prevents unauthorized parties from accessing or altering it, ensuring that only those with the proper credentials can view or modify the information.

Monitoring

Monitoring involves continuous observation and analysis of system activities and behaviors to detect and respond to potential security incidents. It can include monitoring network traffic, user activity, system performance, and logs. For example, an enterprise's security information and event management (SIEM) system might alert administrators if suspicious login patterns are detected, such as numerous failed login attempts from a foreign IP address. Monitoring provides real-time insights into what's happening within the systems and networks, enabling prompt detection of suspicious or anomalous activity and facilitating swift response to mitigate potential threats.

Least Privilege

Key Topic

The *principle of least privilege* dictates that individuals or systems should have only the minimal levels of access—or permissions—needed to accomplish their tasks. This minimizes the potential damage from accidental mishaps or intentional malicious activities.

In a hospital setting, for example, nurses might have access to patient medical records but not to the financial information of the hospital. Similarly, an IT technician may have the right to update system software but not to access confidential HR records.

Implementing the least-privilege principle effectively limits the risk of unauthorized access and minimizes the potential impact of compromised credentials.

Configuration Enforcement

Configuration enforcement involves the standardized and consistent application of system settings, policies, and controls across an organization's network, systems, and devices. It ensures that all elements of the IT environment adhere to defined security policies and best practices, thereby reducing vulnerabilities.

For example, an enterprise might enforce strong password policies across all user accounts, requiring a mix of characters and regular password changes. This configuration enforcement can be implemented through Group Policy or other centralized management tools. By standardizing and enforcing these security configurations, the organization ensures that all users comply with the best practices, reducing the risk of weak passwords that attackers could exploit.

Decommissioning

Decommissioning refers to the planned process of taking hardware, software, or subsystems out of active service. It is often essential to lifecycle management as systems end their usable life or become obsolete.

Consider, for example, a server hosting an application that is no longer needed. Simply unplugging the server without proper decommissioning may leave residual data, configurations, or connections that could be exploited later. An appropriate decommissioning process includes carefully reviewing the system, removing sensitive data, uninstalling software, and ensuring that network connections are terminated. In some cases, physical destruction of the hardware may be required.

By following a structured decommissioning process, an organization mitigates potential security risks associated with obsolete or unused systems. The system is safely retired without leaving lingering vulnerabilities that malicious actors might exploit.

Hardening Techniques

Key Topic

One essential strategy to safeguard enterprise systems and data is the hardening process. *Hardening techniques* consist of systematic measures taken to minimize the attack surface of systems and reduce vulnerabilities. By eliminating unnecessary functions, restricting access, employing protective tools, and setting stringent configurations, an organization can make it considerably more challenging for potential intruders to exploit weaknesses. These practices are not limited to any particular type of hardware or software; they can be applied to servers, workstations, network devices, applications, and more.

The following sections delve into specific hardening techniques, each aimed at strengthening an organization's security posture and fortifying its defenses against potential threats.

Encryption

As mentioned earlier, *encryption* is the process of transforming data into a coded form, making it unreadable without the correct decryption key. Encryption can be used to harden and protect data stored on disks (full disk encryption) or specific files and folders and data transmitted over networks. Encryption ensures that the data remains unintelligible without the proper keys, even if an unauthorized person gains access to it.

Installation of Endpoint Protection

Installation of endpoint protection refers to implementation of security solutions designed to secure endpoints or user devices such as computers, smartphones, and tablets. By installing endpoint protection software, an organization can protect against malware, phishing attacks, and other threats that target user devices. These solutions often include antivirus, anti-malware, and other security features tailored to defend the individual endpoints.

Host-Based Firewall

A *host-based firewall* is a software firewall installed on individual devices. Unlike a network firewall that protects an entire network, a host-based firewall controls incoming and outgoing traffic for the specific host on which it is installed. This type of firewall can be configured to allow or deny traffic based on rules set by the administrator, providing an additional layer of protection for individual systems.

Host-Based Intrusion Prevention System (HIPS)

A *host-based intrusion prevention system (HIPS)* provides real-time protection against known and unknown threats by monitoring the behavior of the host system. A HIPS can block or alert administrators to potential attacks if suspicious activity is detected. For example, if an application tries to modify a critical system file, the HIPS might block the action and notify the security team.

Disabling Ports/Protocols

Specific ports and protocols on systems may be unnecessary for an organization's operations and can pose security risks if left open. Identifying and *disabling unused or unnecessary ports and protocols* reduces the attack surface, limiting potential entry points for attackers. However, it's vital to approach this task with caution and awareness.

A thorough examination of all open ports must be conducted before they are closed. Security engineers typically build a list of ports and protocols to exclude in much the same way the IT team assesses, researches, and builds an approve list, as discussed earlier in this chapter. Closing ports without understanding their functions can severely impact services that use the ports, potentially causing system outages. With each port/service, an organization can implement a tailored approach to port and protocol management, strengthening their defense against potential breaches without compromising essential functionalities.

Default Password Changes

Many devices and systems have default usernames and passwords, which are often well known and easily exploited. *Default usernames and passwords* are credentials automatically installed or programmed into a device or software system.

Changing default credentials to solid and unique usernames and passwords is a simple yet effective hardening technique that prevents unauthorized access through commonly exploited credentials.

Removal of Unnecessary Software

Unnecessary software includes programs on a system that are no longer in use or that were replaced by an updated design. You may hear this also referred to as "tech debt" if there is an obscure reason to keep the software on a system. Unnecessary software can introduce vulnerabilities, especially if it needs to be updated or better maintained. An organization can reduce potential weak points that attackers might exploit by identifying and removing software that is not required for business operations.

Chapter Review Activities

Use the features in this section to study and review the topics in this chapter.

Review Key Topics

Review the most important topics in the chapter, noted with the Key Topic icon in the outer margin of the page. Table 9-2 lists these key topics and the page number on which each is found.

Table 9-2 Key Topics for Chapter 9

Key Topic Element	Description	Page Number
Section	Access Control Lists (ACLs)	175
Section	Isolation	179
Section	Patching	180
Section	Least Privilege	182
Paragraph	Hardening techniques	183

Define Key Terms

Define the following key terms from this chapter and check your answers in the glossary:

segmentation, access control, access control list (ACL), permissions, application allow list, isolation, patching, encryption, monitoring, principle of least privilege, configuration enforcement, decommissioning, hardening techniques, installation of endpoint protection, host-based firewall, host-based intrusion prevention system (HIPS), disabling unused or unnecessary ports and protocols, default usernames and passwords, unnecessary software

Review Questions

Answer the following review questions. Check your answers with the answer key in Appendix A.

1. How does network segmentation contribute to both the improvement of performance and the enhancement of security within an organization's network?

2. Describe the role of access control lists (ACLs) in a multi-department enterprise and how they might be applied to ensure that only authorized personnel can access sensitive information.

3. Why is patching considered a universal cybersecurity practice, and how do different industries, such as healthcare, financial services, and manufacturing, approach it differently?

4. Explain the principle of least privilege and give examples of how it might be implemented in a hospital setting.

5. What are some common hardening techniques used to safeguard enterprise systems, and how does each of these techniques contribute to reducing the attack surface of systems?

6. Discuss the importance of encryption as a hardening technique and how it can be used to protect data stored on disks, specific files, folders, and data transmitted over networks.

This chapter covers the following topics related to Objective 3.1 (Compare and contrast security implications of different architecture models) of the CompTIA Security+ SY0-701 certification exam:

- Architecture and infrastructure concepts
- Considerations

Comparing and Contrasting Security Implications of Different Architecture Models

Understanding the security implications across various architectural models becomes critical as the modern technology landscapes evolve. This chapter explores a broad array of topics, including traditional and cloud-based infrastructures; cutting-edge concepts like infrastructure as code (IaC), serverless computing, and microservices; and considerations related to network isolation, containerization, virtualization, and industrial control systems (ICS). It also explores essential topics related to system availability, such as resilience, cost, scalability, and risk factors that impact an organization's overall security posture.

"Do I Know This Already?" Quiz

The "Do I Know This Already?" quiz enables you to assess whether you should read this entire chapter thoroughly or jump to the "Chapter Review Activities" section. If you are in doubt about your answers to these questions or your own assessment of your knowledge of the topics, read the entire chapter. Table 10-1 lists the major headings in this chapter and their corresponding "Do I Know This Already?" quiz questions. You can find the answers in Appendix A, "Answers to the 'Do I Know This Already?' Quizzes and Review Questions."

Table 10-1 "Do I Know This Already?" Section-to-Question Mapping

Foundation Topics Section	Questions
Architecture and Infrastructure Concepts	1–7
Considerations	8, 9

CAUTION The goal of self-assessment is to gauge your mastery of the topics in this chapter. If you do not know the answer to a question or are only partially sure of the answer, you should mark that question as wrong for purposes of self-assessment. Giving yourself credit for an answer you correctly guess skews your self-assessment results and might provide you with a false sense of security.

1. Which of the following accurately describes a responsibility matrix in cloud computing?

    a. A detailed report of all the virtual machines within a cloud environment

    b. A marketing tool used by cloud service providers (CSPs) to promote their services

    c. A guideline that defines the sole responsibilities of the customer within the cloud environment

    d. An outline that divides responsibilities between a cloud service provider (CSP) and a customer and defines who is responsible for security, compliance, operations, and management in the cloud environment

2. What are the primary benefits of utilizing a hybrid cloud architecture?

    a. Increased complexity and limited scalability

    b. Flexibility, scalability, and diverse deployment options with considerations in data integration, network connectivity, security, compliance, and cost

    c. Sole focus on reducing the costs of maintaining private infrastructure

    d. Unified security policies without considerations for compliance or data integration

3. Software-defined networking (SDN) was originally created for what purpose?

    a. To increase the complexity of network configuration

    b. To allow network devices to operate without any control mechanisms

    c. To decouple control from the forwarding functions in networking equipment

    d. To reduce the security features in network devices

4. Which of the following accurately describes the concept of an air gap in network infrastructure?

    a. It's a gap filled with a special type of gas that boosts network signals.

    b. It refers to a network that can be remotely accessed by any device.

    c. It refers to a computer system that has no physical connection to other networks to reduce the likelihood of network attacks.

    d. It's a logical segmentation method that uses software configuration.

5. What is a container image in the context of containerization?

   a. A physical storage device that contains essential documents.

   b. A visual diagram that outlines the structure of a network.

   c. A bundle that contains a program and its dependencies under a root file system.

   d. A software tool for optimizing network performance.

6. What is the primary purpose of virtualization in cloud and networking architectures?

   a. To create physical hardware systems

   b. To create multiple simulated environments or dedicated resources from a single physical hardware system

   c. To reduce the efficiency of resource utilization

   d. To limit the deployment of applications

7. What are PLCs and RTUs in the context of SCADA systems, and how do they function?

   a. Software packages for data processing

   b. Microcomputers that communicate with objects like turbines, machines, and gauges and that route information to SCADA software

   c. Network cables used for connectivity

   d. Security measures to protect data

8. What is the main risk associated with the inability to patch effectively across all architectures?

   a. Increased flexibility in system design

   b. Reduction in vulnerabilities

   c. The possibility of vulnerabilities, data breaches, and system downtime

   d. Improvement in overall system performance

9. In the context of risk transference in system architecture, which of the following statements accurately describes the strategic approach to managing uncertainty?

a. Risk transference shifts all accountability and ownership of a risk to another party, completely absolving the original organization of responsibility.

b. Risk transference involves shifting specific risks to another party, such as through outsourcing or insurance, but does not remove accountability if a vulnerability is leveraged in that risk.

c. Risk transference primarily focuses on eliminating all technological risks by relying solely on external parties.

d. Risk transference is an ad hoc method that does not consider core competencies, potential liabilities, or specialized expertise.

Foundation Topics

Architecture and Infrastructure Concepts

Cloud

Cloud computing is a way of offering on-demand services that extends the capabilities of a computer or a network. These might be free services, such as personal browser-based email from various providers, or they could be offered on a pay-per-use basis, such as services that offer data access, data storage, infrastructure, or online gaming. A network connection of some sort is required to make the connection to the cloud and gain access to these services in real time.

Some of the benefits of using cloud-based services include lowered cost, less administration and maintenance, more reliability, increased scalability, and possibly increased performance. A basic example of a cloud-based service is browser-based email. A small business with few employees definitely needs email, but it might not be able to afford an email server and perhaps does not want to have its own hosted domain and deal with the costs and work that go along with that. By connecting to a free web browser–based service, the small business can obtain nearly unlimited email, contacts, and calendar solutions. However, this model offers the business no administrative control, and there are some security concerns.

Key Topic

Responsibility Matrix

A *responsibility matrix* in cloud computing outlines the division of responsibilities between a cloud service provider (CSP) and a customer. This matrix, often called a shared responsibility model, defines who is responsible for security, compliance, operations, and management in a cloud environment. Unlike in traditional on-premises environments, where the organization handles every aspect, in the cloud, responsibilities shift between the CSP and the customer, depending on the service model (such as IaaS, PaaS, or SaaS).

Under typical circumstances, the CSP is responsible for the underlying infrastructure, including the physical hardware, networking components, and data center facilities. It manages the core cloud computing resources, such as virtual machines, databases, and storage, ensuring their availability, scalability, and security at the infrastructure level. For higher-level services, such as platform as a service (PaaS) or software as a service (SaaS), the CSP might also be responsible for application hosting, runtime environments, and underlying operating systems. You must carefully read all agreements to understand what the CSP is responsible for in your situation.

The customer's responsibility varies based on the cloud service model. With IaaS, the customer is typically responsible for operating systems, applications, and data, while the CSP takes care of the underlying infrastructure. With PaaS, the customer's responsibility shifts to managing the applications and data, and the CSP handles everything else. The customer's responsibility in SaaS mainly involves working data and user access, and the CSP takes care of almost everything else. It is important for a customer to understand their responsibility in maintaining security, compliance, and data integrity, as outlined in the service agreement with the CSP. Understanding this division ensures that security controls are implemented correctly and compliance requirements are satisfied.

Hybrid Considerations

A *hybrid cloud* is an architecture that integrates private and public cloud services, facilitating data and application sharing between them. A hybrid cloud provides flexibility, scalability, and diverse deployment options but demands careful consideration of data integration, network connectivity, security, compliance, and cost. A well-architected hybrid cloud offers the control of a private cloud combined with the efficiency of a public cloud. However, it may present challenges in managing multiple environments and ensuring smooth integration.

The following are some special considerations in a hybrid environment:

- **Data integration:** Hybrid clouds allow seamless data sharing between private and public cloud environments, which can create complexities in data synchronization, consistency, and governance. Proper data integration techniques are essential to ensure seamless data flow and accessibility.

- **Network connectivity:** A hybrid cloud demands robust network connectivity to enable seamless communication between private and public environments. Challenges include maintaining secure and fast connections, minimizing latency, and implementing consistent networking policies.

- **Security:** Security considerations in a hybrid cloud can be complex as data and applications may reside in different environments, each with unique security protocols. Unified security policies, encryption, and identity management are essential to safeguard data across all domains.

- **Compliance:** Regulatory compliance can be challenging due to differing legal requirements in public and private environments. Careful alignment of privacy policies and compliance controls across the hybrid infrastructure is crucial.

- **Cost:** While a hybrid cloud provides flexibility, managing multiple environments can increase complexity and cost. Effective cost management requires understanding of the pricing structure of public cloud services and the overhead of maintaining private infrastructure.

Third-Party Vendors

Third-party vendors are external organizations or service providers that offer specialized services or applications that integrate with the cloud provider's offerings. Third-party vendors may provide specialized security tools, analytics platforms, or industry-specific applications, enhancing the cloud environment's functionality. Engaging third-party vendors brings added capabilities but also introduces risks, including potential security vulnerabilities or compliance issues. A significant risk of leveraging third-party vendors is the increased exposure of the organization to vulnerabilities it might not be able to manage.

> **TIP**   NIST's Special Publication (SP) 800-145 provides a great overview of the definitions of cloud computing concepts. You can access this document at https://csrc.nist.gov/publications/detail/sp/800-145/final.

Infrastructure as Code (IaC)

Modern applications and deployments (on-premises and in the cloud) require scalability and integration with numerous systems, APIs, and network components. This complexity introduces risks, including network configuration errors that can cause significant downtime and network security challenges. Consequently, networking functions such as routing, optimization, and security have also changed. The next generation of hardware and software components in enterprise networks must support both the rapid introduction and rapid evolution of new technologies and solutions. Network infrastructure solutions must keep pace with the business environment and support modern capabilities that help drive simplification within the network. These elements have fueled the creation of software-defined networking (SDN).

SDN was originally created to decouple control from the forwarding functions in networking equipment. This is done to use software to centrally manage and "program" the hardware and virtual networking appliances to perform forwarding. We will dig into SDN in more depth later in the chapter.

Organizations are adopting a framework often referred to as *infrastructure as code (IaC)*, which involves managing and provisioning computer data centers through machine-readable definition files rather than physical hardware configuration or interactive configuration tools.

Serverless

Another popular architecture is the serverless architecture. Be aware that *serverless* does not mean that you do not need a server somewhere. Instead, ***serverless architecture*** involves using cloud platforms to host and/or to develop code. For example, you might have a serverless app that is distributed in a cloud provider like Amazon Web Services (AWS), Microsoft Azure, or Google Cloud Platform (GCP).

Serverless is a cloud computing execution model in which the cloud provider (AWS, Azure, Google Cloud, and so on) dynamically manages the allocation and provisioning of servers. Serverless applications run in stateless containers that are ephemeral and event triggered (fully managed by the cloud provider). AWS Lambda is one of the most popular serverless architectures in the industry. Figure 10-1 shows a "function," or application, in AWS Lambda.

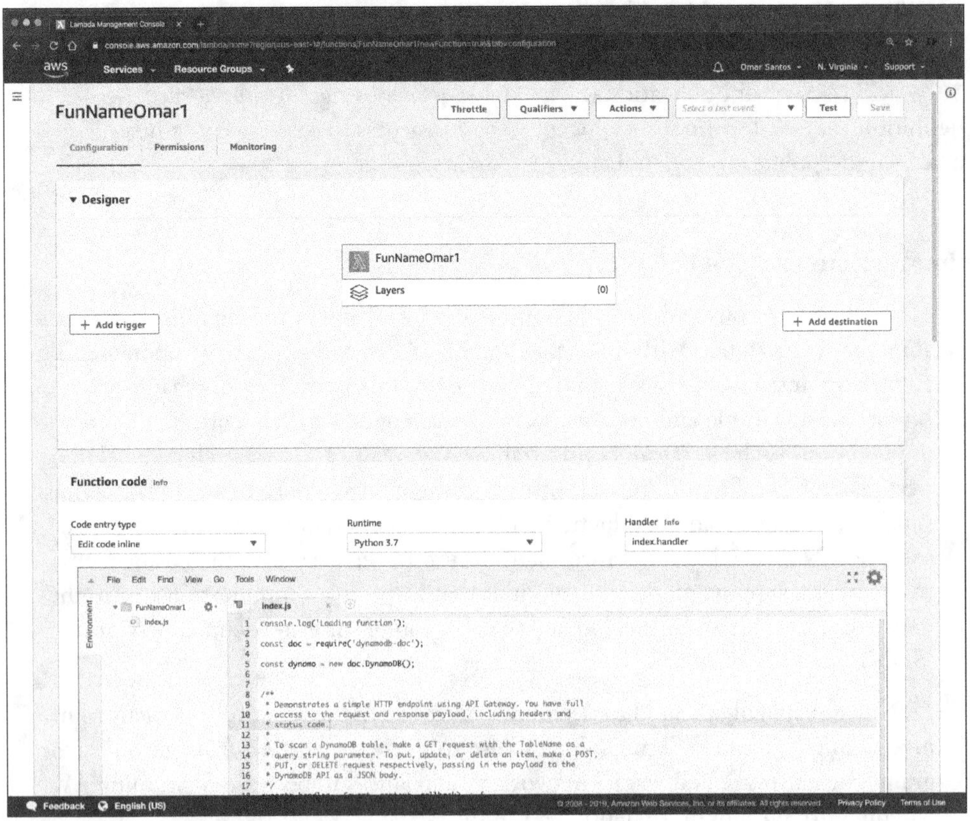

Figure 10-1   AWS Lambda

In AWS Lambda, you run code without provisioning or managing servers, and you pay only for the compute time you consume. When you upload your code, Lambda takes care of everything required to run and scale your application (offering high availability and redundancy).

Figure 10-2 summarizes the evolution of computing from physical servers to virtual machines, containers, and serverless solutions. Virtual machines and containers may be deployed on premises or in the cloud.

Microservices

Key Topic

The term *microservices* describes how an application can be deployed as a collection of services that are highly maintainable and testable and independently deployable. Microservices are organized around business capabilities and enable the rapid, frequent, and reliable delivery of large, complex applications. Most microservices developed and deployed by organizations are based on containers.

Application programming interfaces (APIs), such as RESTful APIs, are the frameworks through which developers can interact with an application. Microservices use APIs to communicate with each other, and APIs can also be used to expose data and application functionality to third-party systems.

Microservices and APIs need to be secured. Traditional segmentation strategies do not work well in these virtual and containerized environments. The ability to enforce network segmentation in container and VM environments is called *microsegmentation*. Microsegmentation occurs at the VM level or between containers in either a VLAN or a subnet. Microsegmentation solutions need to be "application aware," which means the segmentation process starts and ends with the application itself.

Most microsegmentation environments apply a zero trust model, which dictates that users cannot talk to applications, and applications cannot talk to other applications unless a defined set of policies permits them to do so.

Network Infrastructure

Network infrastructure refers to hardware and software resources that facilitate network connectivity, communication, operations, and management of an enterprise network. It provides a communication path and services between users, processes, applications, and external networks, enabling various devices and components to connect and communicate within an internal and external environment.

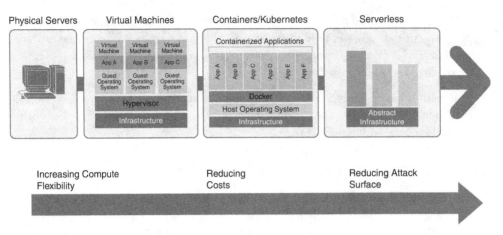

Figure 10-2 The Evolution of Computing from Physical Servers to Serverless

Physical Isolation

Physical isolation is the separation of different network parts through distinct physical components, such as cables, switches, or dedicated hardware firewalls. Creating barriers that restrict physical access to specific areas of the network enhances security and minimizes potential risks. An organization might physically isolate its sensitive data servers by placing them in a secured room with restricted access, connected through separate network switches, and protected by a hardware firewall. You might hear this type of sensitive isolation referred to as an "enclave." This strategy helps in preventing unauthorized access and potential interference with critical systems.

Air-Gapped

Air gapping is the practice of ensuring that there is a gap of air or a lack of connection between a computer and a network. An air-gapped computer system has no physical connection to other computers, networks, or unsecured systems. If a computer isn't directly connected to a network, it can't be attacked through the network. So, to compromise this type of computer, hackers have to "cross the air gap," which means they need to be physically sitting down in front of the computer. As security administrator, you should consider disabling ports and enforcing a policy of not using USB thumb drives to reduce the likelihood of viruses and data theft.

Logical Segmentation

In contrast to physical isolation, logical segmentation is achieved through software and configuration rather than physical components. *Logical segmentation* involves dividing a network into separate segments or subnets based on factors like functionality, security requirements, or departmental boundaries. An enterprise might divide its internal network into different VLANs for multiple departments like HR, Finance, and R&D. Each VLAN operates as a separate logical network, restricting communication and enhancing security. Even though data and resources share the same physical infrastructure, logical segmentation ensures that data and resources are isolated based on specific criteria, adding a layer of control and protection.

Software-Defined Network (SDN)

Software-defined networking (SDN) is an innovative approach to network management that separates the control plane from the data plane within network devices. This decoupling allows the network's control logic (the control plane) to be centralized and directly programmable, independent of the underlying hardware that forwards packets (the data plane).

In traditional networking, three different "planes," or elements, allow network devices to operate: the management, control, and data planes. (Refer to Chapter 2, "Summarizing Fundamental Security Concepts," which covers the data plane and control plane in greater detail.) The control plane has always been separated from the data plane. There was no central brain (or controller) that controlled the configuration and forwarding. Routers, switches, and firewalls were managed by using the command-line interface (CLI), graphical user interfaces (GUIs), and custom Tcl scripts.

NOTE Tcl is a high-level, general-purpose, interpreted dynamic programming language. It was designed with the goal of being very simple but powerful. Tcl casts everything into the mold of a command—even programming constructs like variable assignment and procedure definition.

Originally, firewall management was conducted through individual web portals, while router configurations were handled using command-line interface (CLI) methods. The advent of software-defined networking (SDN) brought about the concept of a centralized control mechanism. This centralized SDN controller offers a comprehensive overview of the entire network, using a uniform protocol to manage and configure various network infrastructure components.

As show in Figure 10-3's network layout, an SDN controller in a data center setting is responsible for overseeing the network infrastructure.

The SDN controller is proficient at calculating network paths and reachability across numerous devices within the network. It then transmits flow instructions to network switches, which use the instructions for data routing. This innovation marks a significant shift from the previous distributed control model to a more centralized and intelligent network management system. You might see documentation referring to this shift from a "semi-intelligent" approach to a "central and intelligent" one.

TIP Projects like Open vSwitch (OVS) stand out in open-source SDN controllers. OVS leverages the OVS Database (OVSDB) management protocol and the Open-Flow protocol for network management. Similarly, the Cisco Application Policy Infrastructure Controller (Cisco APIC) is a central component in the Cisco Application Centric Infrastructure (ACI) framework. Another notable open-source project is OpenDaylight (ODL), which aims to advance SDN controllers for interoperability across various vendors. OpenDaylight also collaborates with the OpenStack Neutron project, addressing network inefficiencies through a northbound interface while managing several southbound interfaces, including OVSDB and OpenFlow.

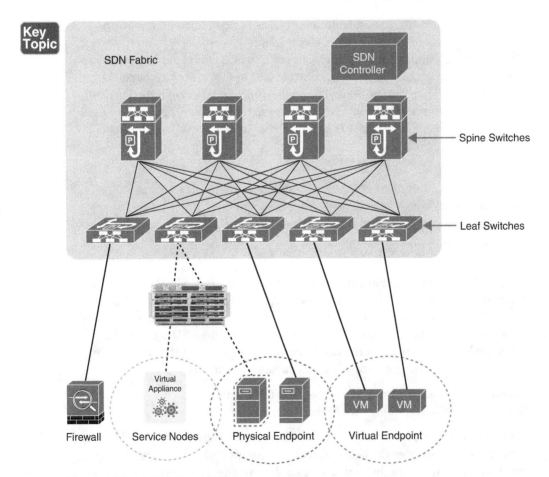

Figure 10-3 A High-Level SDN Implementation

SDN has brought about transformative changes, especially in software-based network devices' control and data planes, including virtual switches in hypervisors. Projects like Open vSwitch have been instrumental in driving these industry-wide changes.

The impact of SDN extends to both the physical and virtual switches within the management plane, gaining widespread adoption in data center environments.

A more recent development in this field is software-defined visibility (SDV). Although similar to SDN, SDV is tailored explicitly for delivering detailed insights into network activities, whether on-premises or in the cloud. In SDV environments, RESTful APIs are commonly utilized to orchestrate and automate various security and monitoring operations across an organization's network infrastructure.

On-premises

Given the availability of cloud-based systems, a relatively uncommon setup is an on-premises build. An *on-premises* computing architecture has hardware, software, servers, and network resources housed and managed within the organization's physical location. Unlike cloud-based solutions, where third-party providers host resources, an on-premises solution gives an organization complete control of and responsibility for its IT infrastructure—including the management, maintenance, and security of the systems. Often abbreviated as "on-prem," this approach allows for more direct oversight of the technology and data, potentially offering higher levels of customization and compliance with specific regulatory requirements. However, it may also come with increased costs and complexity, requiring dedicated personnel and equipment to manage and maintain the environment effectively.

Key Topic: Centralized Versus Decentralized

In general, access control can be centralized or decentralized. Centralized access control means that one entity is responsible for administering access to resources. Decentralized access control means that more than one entity is responsible, and those entities are closer to the actual resources than the entity would be in a centralized access control scenario.

Centralized and decentralized systems refer to two contrasting approaches to data management and processing in an organizational network or architecture.

Centralized Systems

A *centralized system* is characterized by consolidating control, data storage, and processing in a single location or server. With a centralized system, only the IT department can add a user to a system, and HR is solely responsible for onboarding new employees. This approach provides uniformity and consistency in decision making and offers a single point for monitoring and control. In enterprise architectures, centralized systems simplify management. Remember, though, that they can pose challenges such as a single point of failure, scalability issues, and potentially longer data access times for remote users.

Decentralized Systems

Decentralized systems distribute data and control across multiple locations, servers, or nodes. A decentralized approach offers higher resilience and flexibility, allowing for independent operations, greater autonomy, and faster access times. However, decentralized systems may bring complexity in management, potential inconsistency, and the need for more robust coordination mechanisms. The choice between centralized and decentralized systems must consider factors like organizational size, geographical spread, scalability, and specific performance requirements.

Containerization

Key Topic

Before you can even think of building a distributed system, you must first understand how the container images that contain your applications make up all the underlying pieces of such a distributed system. An application is normally composed of a language runtime, libraries, and source code. For instance, an application may use third-party or open-source shared libraries such as the Linux Kernel (www.kernel.org), nginx (https://nginx.org), or OpenSSL (www.openssl.org). These shared libraries are typically shipped as shared components in the operating system that you installed on a system. The dependencies on these libraries introduce difficulties when an application developed on your desktop, laptop, or any other development machine (or "dev system") has a dependency on a shared library that isn't available when the program is deployed out to the production system. Even when the dev and production systems share exactly the same version of the operating system, bugs can occur when programmers forget to include dependent asset files inside a package that they deploy to production.

The good news is that you can package applications in a way that makes it easy to share them with others. In such a case, containerization becomes very useful. Docker, one of the most popular container runtime engines, makes it easy to package an executable and push it to a remote registry, from which it can later be pulled by others.

Container registries are available in all of the major public cloud providers (for example, AWS, Google Cloud Platform, and Microsoft Azure) as well as services to build images. You can also run your own registry using open-source or commercial systems. These registries make it easy for developers to manage and deploy private images, and image-builder services provide easy integration with continuous delivery systems.

A *container image* bundles a program and its dependencies into a single artifact under a root file system. A container is made up of a series of file system layers. Each layer adds, removes, or modifies files from the preceding layer in the file system. The overlay system is used both when packaging up the image and when the image is actually being used. During runtime, there are various different concrete implementations of such file systems, including aufs, overlay, and overlay2.

Let's look at an example of how container images work. Figure 10-4 shows three container images: A, B, and C. Container Image B is "forked" from Container Image A. Then, in Container Image B, Python version 3 is added. Furthermore, Container Image C is built on Container Image B, and the programmer adds OpenSSL and nginx to develop a web server and enable TLS.

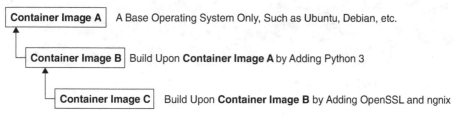

Figure 10-4 How Container Images Work

Abstractly, each container image layer builds on the previous one. Each parent reference is a pointer. The example in Figure 10-4 includes a simple set of containers; in many environments, you will encounter a much larger directed acyclic graph.

Before we jump into the many details of Docker commands and their outputs, let's take a moment to understand what Docker is. Docker is a platform designed to facilitate containerized applications' development, distribution, and running. It handles complex setup, allowing you to focus on coding. A container is a lightweight, standalone package that contains everything needed to run a piece of software, including the code, runtime, libraries, and system tools. This ensures that the software runs the same way regardless of where it is deployed. For more information, you can visit Docker's official website: www.docker.com.

Even though the Security+ SY0-701 exam does not cover Docker in detail, it is still good to see a few examples of Docker containers, images, and related commands. Figure 10-5 shows the output of the **docker images** command.

The Docker images shown in Figure 10-5 are intentionally vulnerable applications that you can use to practice your skills. These Docker images and containers are included in a VM called WebSploit (websploit.org) by Omar Santos. This VM is built on top of Kali Linux and includes several additional tools, along with the aforementioned Docker containers. This can be a good tool for familiarizing yourself with Docker and also learning and practicing offensive and defensive security skills.

```
┌─[omar@websploit]─[~]
└──── $sudo docker images
REPOSITORY                    TAG        IMAGE ID       CREATED          SIZE
santosomar/yascon-hackme      latest     d778e2d4c6c2   2 weeks ago      1.03GB
santosomar/grayhat-mmxx       latest     0e3e47fb167f   3 weeks ago      532MB
santosomar/rtv-safemode       latest     ba39d0ae6ff3   3 months ago     705MB
santosomar/webgoat            latest     cd4f5cf4ef0c   5 months ago     477MB
santosomar/mayhem             latest     bc85735e7bc1   6 months ago     312MB
santosomar/juice-shop         latest     5f05adef2b06   7 months ago     308MB
santosomar/webgoat            <none>     d7867884fb69   10 months ago    380MB
santosomar/hackme-rtov        latest     2e9fe51489a0   15 months ago    265MB
santosomar/bwapp              latest     35d0ed4da0ae   16 months ago    441MB
santosomar/hackazon           latest     ac1ccdb947ab   19 months ago    767MB
santosomar/dvwa               latest     105011d6abeb   19 months ago    393MB
santosomar/mutillidae_2       latest     7c041505981b   19 months ago    800MB
santosomar/dvna               latest     4d74d852a9aa   2 years ago      270MB
┌─[omar@websploit]─[~]
└──── $
```

Figure 10-5 Displaying Docker Images

Figure 10-6 shows the output of the **docker ps** command, which you can use to see all the running Docker containers in a system.

```
┌─[omar@websploit]─[~]
└──── $sudo docker ps --format "table {{.Names}}\t{{.Ports}}\t{{.Status}}"
NAMES            PORTS                                              STATUS
yascon-hackme    0.0.0.0:9002->80/tcp                               Up 22 hours
grayhat-mmxx     0.0.0.0:9001->8000/tcp                             Up 22 hours
rtv-safemode     0.0.0.0:3306->3306/tcp, 0.0.0.0:9000->80/tcp       Up 22 hours
mayhem           0.0.0.0:88->22/tcp, 0.0.0.0:8889->80/tcp           Up 22 hours
hackme-rtov      0.0.0.0:8888->80/tcp                               Up 22 hours
hackazon         0.0.0.0:8887->80/tcp                               Up 22 hours
dvna             0.0.0.0:8886->9090/tcp                             Up 22 hours
bwapp2           3306/tcp, 0.0.0.0:8885->80/tcp                     Up 22 hours
mutillidae_2     3306/tcp, 0.0.0.0:8884->80/tcp                     Up 22 hours
dvwa             0.0.0.0:8883->80/tcp                               Up 22 hours
juice-shop       0.0.0.0:8882->3000/tcp                             Up 22 hours
webgoat          0.0.0.0:9090->9090/tcp, 0.0.0.0:8881->8080/tcp     Up 22 hours
┌─[omar@websploit]─[~]
└──── $
```

Figure 10-6 Output of the **docker ps** Command

You can use a public, cloud provider, or private Docker image repository. Docker's public image repository is called Docker Hub. You can find images by going to the Docker Hub website (https://hub.docker.com) or by using the **docker search** command, as demonstrated in Figure 10-7.

In Figure 10-7, the user is searching for a container image that matches the **ubuntu** keyword.

TIP   You can practice and deploy your first container by using Katacoda, which is an interactive system that allows you to learn many different technologies, including Docker, Kubernetes, Git, TensorFlow, and many others.

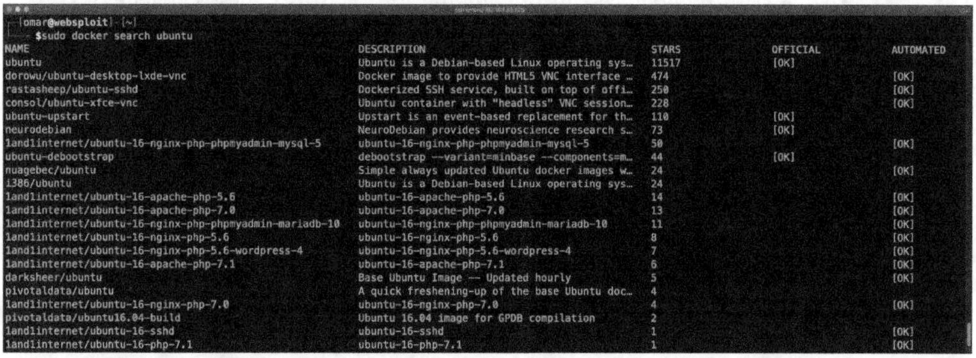

Figure 10-7   Output of the **docker search** Command

In larger environments, you are not likely to deploy and orchestrate Docker containers manually but instead want to automate as much as possible. This is where Kubernetes comes into play. Kubernetes (often referred to as k8s) automates the distribution, scheduling, and orchestration of application containers across a cluster.

Kubernetes consists of the following components:

- **Control plane:** This component coordinates all the activities in a cluster (scheduling, scaling, and deploying applications).

- **Node:** This VM or physical server acts as a worker machine in a Kubernetes cluster.

- **Pod:** This group of one or more containers provides shared storage and networking, including a specification for how to run the containers. Each pod has an IP address, and it is expected to be able to reach all other pods within the environment.

Multiple technologies and solutions are available to manage, deploy, and orchestrate containers. The following are the most popular examples:

- **Kubernetes:** One of the most popular container orchestration and management frameworks, originally developed by Google, Kubernetes is a platform for creating, deploying, and managing distributed applications. You can download Kubernetes and access its documentation at https://kubernetes.io.

- **Nomad:** This container management and orchestration platform is from HashCorp. You can download and obtain detailed information about it at www.nomadproject.io.

- **Apache Mesos:** This distributed Linux kernel provides native support for launching containers with Docker and AppC images. You can download Apache Mesos and access its documentation at https://mesos.apache.org.

- **Docker Swarm:** This container cluster management and orchestration system is integrated with the Docker Engine. You can access the Docker Swarm documentation at https://docs.docker.com/engine/swarm.

Virtualization

Virtualization technology has fundamentally changed the way organizations manage and allocate hardware resources. *Virtualization* technology creates multiple simulated environments or dedicated resources from a single physical hardware system. While there are many benefits to virtualization—including cost reduction, resource optimization, and scalability—it's crucial to understand that these advantages don't come without security trade-offs. Let's look into the specific security implications of deploying virtualization environments. Understanding these challenges is key to ensuring a robust security posture, a concept that aligns closely with the Security+ certification.

Security Implications

The security of a virtualized environment is complex, and the risks are multifaceted. Each aspect requires careful consideration, from the potential for isolation failure to the challenges posed by VM sprawl. Here are some of the most pressing security concerns you should be aware of:

- **Isolation failure:** One of the cornerstones of virtualization is the isolation of VMs from each other. However, this isolation is not foolproof. For example, vulnerabilities in the hypervisor—the software layer that enables virtualization—can be exploited to break this isolation, allowing unauthorized access to sensitive data on other VMs.

- **VM sprawl:** The ease of deploying VMs can lead to "VM sprawl," a situation in which an organization loses track of the number and state of its VMs. This increases the attack surface, and each unmonitored VM becomes a potential entry point for attackers. Imagine an outdated VM running a legacy application; it could be easily compromised and become a launchpad for attacks on more critical systems.

- **Resource exhaustion:** VMs share the resources of the host machine. An attacker could deliberately overload a VM, causing resource exhaustion that affects all VMs on the host. For instance, a DDoS attack targeting a single VM could inadvertently bring down other critical services running on the same host.

- **Insecure interfaces and APIs:** Virtualization platforms often provide various management interfaces, which, if not properly secured, can be a weak link in the security chain. An attacker accessing these interfaces could manipulate VM settings, allocate resources, or even delete VMs.

- **Data leakage:** In multi-tenant environments, where multiple parties use the same physical hardware, misconfigurations can lead to data leakage between VMs. For example, if a financial institution and a retail store share the same physical server, a misconfiguration could expose sensitive financial data to unauthorized parties.

Now that we have discussed the security concerns around virtualization, it's clear that while virtualization offers numerous advantages, it also introduces unique vulnerabilities that can be exploited if not properly managed. However, these risks shouldn't deter you from leveraging the benefits of virtualization. Instead, they should encourage you to implement best practices to mitigate these vulnerabilities. Let's review some practical strategies for safeguarding your virtualized environments. Here are some mitigation strategies you should be aware of:

- **Regular patching:** Consistently updating the hypervisor and the operating systems running on VMs is crucial. This ensures that known vulnerabilities are patched, reducing the risk of exploitation.

- **Resource allocation:** Implementing resource quotas for VMs can prevent resource exhaustion attacks. For example, setting a CPU usage limit for each VM ensures that no single VM can monopolize the host's resources.

- **Access control and monitoring:** It is important to implement robust access control mechanisms, such as multifactor authentication for hypervisor access. In addition, continuous monitoring can help detect unauthorized activities in real time. For instance, setting up alerts for unusual CPU or network activity can help in the early detection of an attack.

- **Encryption and network segmentation:** Data should be encrypted at rest and in transit. Network segmentation can further isolate VMs handling sensitive data, making it harder for attackers to move laterally across the network.

- **Policy and governance:** Establishing a governance policy for the lifecycle management of VMs can prevent VM sprawl. This involves setting guidelines for when VMs should be created, maintained, and decommissioned.

IoT

The ***Internet of Things (IoT)*** is the interconnected network of physical devices that communicate and exchange data with each other through the Internet or other networking technologies. These devices can range from everyday household items such as smart refrigerators and thermostats to industrial machinery, medical equipment, and vehicles.

IoT devices have embedded sensors, software, and other technologies that allow them to collect and transmit data, receive instructions, and even operate autonomously in some cases. By connecting these devices to centralized systems, the IoT enables more efficient data sharing and automation of tasks, providing enhanced control, monitoring, and insights.

The benefits of the IoT are undeniable; however, high-profile attacks combined with uncertainty about security best practices and their associated costs are keeping many businesses from adopting the technology. In addition, end users are wary of the consequences of IoT security breaches. Recent research indicates that 90% of consumers lack confidence in IoT device security.

NOTE IoT manufacturers should do thorough security risk assessments that examine vulnerabilities in devices and network systems as well as in user and customer back-end systems. Risk must be mitigated for the entire IoT lifecycle of a deployment, especially as it scales.

TIP You should change default manufacturer usernames and passwords.

Cybersecurity must be designed into IoT devices from the ground up and at all points in the ecosystem to prevent vulnerabilities in one part from jeopardizing the security of the entire system. Today's IoT ecosystems are complex; devices in virtually every industry—from cellular networks to cloud applications to back ends—can be connected and configured to send data. Hackers are constantly looking for ways to exploit IoT system vulnerabilities. Because IoT devices are so diverse, there is no "one size fits all" cybersecurity solution that can protect an IoT deployment.

The following components are associated with the IoT:

Key
Topic

- **Sensors:** Sensor cybersecurity implications go well beyond the voice-controlled devices you talk to at home, such as your lights and TV. Sensors are part of the critical infrastructure used to monitor and manage power plants, refineries, ships, and air traffic. Because sensors are small and versatile, functionality is crucial, but security is usually secondary and largely dependent on outside security systems. To protect sensors from attacks, you should use a layered and air-gapped approach when designing and deploying supporting networks.

- **Smart devices:** Smart devices are everywhere, from wired and wireless networks that control lighting to A/C, garage doors, security systems, and curtains; they are embedded in TVs, toasters, and even barbecue grills. To protect smart devices, you should disable features that you are not using and enable them only when required, use strong encryption methods, and employ complex passwords. You should turn privacy settings to their highest levels and select to not share data and, where possible, change the default manufacturer usernames and passwords.

- **Wearables:** Wearables include smart watches, pedometers, glasses, 3D headsets, smart clothing, health and fitness devices, heart and chemical and gas sensors, and more. Security for these devices has been improving thanks to high-performing processors but is still lacking in many aspects. We have seen breaches of smart watches that disclose running patterns. To protect wearables, you should change all default settings, disable features and functions you're not using, set privacy settings to their highest level, and turn off location tracking where possible.

- **Facility automation:** An unprotected building automation system can quickly become a high risk with potential life-threatening damage to its occupants and the building itself; therefore, securing these systems is a necessity. Even the most severe data breach in a traditional organization is unlikely to have a direct physical impact on the life of occupants of the building. However, a malicious attack on a building automation system can very easily pose a significant threat to the health and safety of the occupants. Protecting these systems typically starts with a network that is separate and isolated from the corporate network, separate firewalls and monitoring, and a strict zero trust approach to any connections made to this network.

- **Weak defaults:** From the implementation of weak protocols to default usernames and passwords, many of today's IoT devices are shipped with weak defaults. There are countless IoT devices and applications in your home and business; using weak or default passwords places devices at greater risk of exposing personal information or being used as pivot devices to gain a strong foothold inside. Pending legislation would require IoT device manufacturers to use strong encryption methods and require complex passwords during setup. However, until that happens, you must change default passwords and utilize the strongest encryption method a device supports. If you are unable to get past this, consider changing the device to something that has stronger capabilities. Don't use Admin as a username because it's the most common username used in attacks. Also, be sure to change default passwords to complex nondictionary types. In addition, you should run regular audits and scans on all IoT devices (possibly using one of the several open-source IoT scanners that are available), check for new and/or unknown devices on your network, and check the logs of those devices for password lockouts and strange activity. Another option is to check Shodan (a repository of Internet-accessible devices), which is where attackers go to find insecure devices to attack. Ideally, your devices are not listed there, but if they are, plug them in behind a firewall, turn off unused features, and use secure complex passwords.

Key Topic Industrial Control Systems (ICS)/Supervisory Control and Data Acquisition (SCADA)

Supervisory control and data acquisition (SCADA) systems and industrial control systems (ICSs) are made up of a combination of specialized software and hardware elements that allow organizations to do the following:

- Monitor equipment processes and performance

- Perform data monitoring and collection

- Facilitate data analysis and storage of analyzed data

- Perform remote control of equipment, devices, components, and processes

- Trigger alerts and alarms when performance or deviation aberrations are detected

- Report generators for scheduled and automated variance reporting and comparison, as well as production efficiency and status code statistics

SCADA systems are crucial for industrial organizations because they help to maintain efficiency, process data for smarter decisions, and communicate system issues to help mitigate downtime.

The basic SCADA architecture starts with a series of configurable devices called programmable logic controllers (PLCs) or remote terminal units (RTUs). PLCs and RTUs are microcomputers that communicate with an array of objects such as turbines, machines, gauges, sensors, and end devices, and then route the information from those objects to computers with SCADA software. The SCADA software processes, distributes, and displays the data, helping operators and other employees analyze the data and make important decisions.

For example, a SCADA system may quickly notify an operator that a batch of products shows a high incidence of errors. The operator can pause the operation and view the SCADA system data via a human–machine interface (HMI) to determine the cause of the issue. The operator can then review the data to determine whether a specific machine in the process was malfunctioning. The SCADA system's capability to notify the operator of an issue helps that person resolve it and prevent further loss.

To defend against cyberattacks, a firewall can act as a security buffer between a SCADA network and a corporate network. SCADA systems should never be connected to the Internet, even with firewalls in place. You should configure internal firewalls that include virtual private networks (VPNs) for internal administration of remote SCADA systems as an added layer of protection. To address authentication and authorization security concerns, you need to configure the authentication process in the software to identify authorized users for access to the SCADA system, enable logging to track users' activity and alerting to warn of deviations to critical controls, and ensure least-privilege access. Depending on the perceived risk of cyberattack on the SCADA system, you should deploy intrusion detection and off-site redundancy, as part of a defense-in-depth strategy:

- **Facilities:** Using facility controls like HVAC, elevator, lighting, room temperature, occupancy, parking, and device usage sensors, facility managers are able to monitor and control whether a building is operating optimally. A SCADA system can help an organization reduce its carbon footprint through energy management by automatically turning off lights and air conditioning to sections of the building that are unoccupied.

- **Industrial:** ICS and SCADA systems monitor, control, sense, and warn engineers of all aspects of the processes in industrial plants. SCADA systems can control the flow of crude oil being turned into gasoline, asphalt, and chemicals like cleaning supplies. Such complex processes have many controls that could be dangerous if inappropriately configured.

- **Manufacturing:** Control systems in the manufacturing process depend heavily on data, performance monitoring, and capabilities to control remote equipment, which are among the most-discussed concerns in manufacturing. These components are frequently mentioned as the backbones of "Industry 4.0," which is the current trend of automation and data exchange in manufacturing technologies. It includes cyber-physical systems, the Internet of Things, and cloud computing. Industry 4.0 creates what has been called the "smart factory."

Monitoring, data capture and analysis, and equipment control from anywhere are recognized as highly effective ways to improve facility and equipment productivity, performance, and efficiency. The benefits of using SCADA control systems in the manufacturing process include reducing product errors and discards (thanks to earlier problem detection and remedies), improving productivity, and maximizing the effectiveness of machine uptime. Maintenance benefits of the use of data and sensors include more accurate diagnostics, more efficient maintenance processes, and the enablement of predictive maintenance. Data-driven insights into equipment performance can facilitate more accurate calibration, operation, and decision-making processes.

- **Energy:** The global need for cost-effective electrical power is on the rise, and SCADA systems aid in energy management. Thanks to factory automation productivity and accuracy and ever-expanding data centers, there is increasing demand on electrical power utilities. An organization can integrate alternative energy sources, such as solar and wind, in its overall facility power source planning to obtain efficiency, stability, and safety. For power distribution system generators, operators, and manufacturers alike, unplanned downtime is extremely costly, risky, and inconvenient. For operators, a stable, sustainable load flow across all components of a system is key for uninterrupted, safe operation. For manufacturers, any unplanned downtime can mean delays in production and missed deadlines. Predictive and proactive maintenance strategies can maximize uptime by alerting operators and manufacturers to potential issues early. In addition, transit authorities use SCADA technology to regulate electricity to subways, trams, and trolley buses.

- **Logistics:** SCADA systems are capable of managing parts inventories for just-in-time manufacturing, regulating industrial automation and robots, and monitoring processes and quality control. Transit authorities use SCADA technology to automate traffic signals for rail systems; to track and locate trains, trucks, and buses; and to control railroad crossing gates. Continuous communication for trucks, locomotives, and transport vehicles provides valuable information, such as location and status, and is especially important for autonomous vehicles. SCADA systems can regulate traffic lights, control traffic flow, and detect out-of-order signals. Other specialized systems extend GPS and cargo tracking systems; knowing where ships, trains, trucks, and inventory are located anywhere in the world is critical to meet today's demand for products. These systems require special security considerations, and regulators have long insisted that these systems be air-gapped to reduce threats. A key mitigation against attacks on SCADA systems and ICS is to reduce the attack surface by segregating the SCADA network from the corporate LAN with a firewall. An ICS is managed via a SCADA system. SCADA systems drive HMIs for operators to monitor the status of a system while in the field. Other ICS components include industrial automation and control systems (IACSs), distributed control systems (DCSs), programmable logic controllers (PLCs), and remote terminal units (RTUs).

Figure 10-8 shows a basic SCADA diagram.

Sensors
Sends Data to PLCs or RTUs

PLCs or RTUs
Feeds Data to the SCADA System

HMI/SCADA Panel View
Supervise and Control from
an Operational Terminal

Manual Inputs
Sends Data to PLCs or RTUs

PLCs or RTUs
Feeds Data to the SCADA System

HMI/SCADA Computer
Supervise and Control
from a Workstation

Figure 10-8   SCADA Diagram

Real-Time Operating System (RTOS)

A *real-time operating system (RTOS)* is a software component that rapidly switches between tasks, giving the impression that multiple programs are being executed at the same time on a single processing core. In fact, the processing core can execute only one program at any one time, and the RTOS is actually rapidly switching between individual programming threads or tasks to give the impression that multiple programs are executing simultaneously.

An RTOS differs from a typical operating system in that it normally provides hard real-time responses, with fast, highly deterministic reactions to external events.

When switching between tasks, an RTOS has to choose the most appropriate task to load next. Several scheduling algorithms are available, including round robin, cooperative, and hybrid scheduling. However, to provide a responsive system, most RTOSs use a preemptive scheduling algorithm, such as VxWorks.

Securing an RTOS starts with minimizing the attack surface by turning off features, services, and access that are not necessary. You should assume that external systems are insecure. Do not make assumptions about what other devices a system is connected to. It is safest to assume that external devices are insecure and approach securing them from this perspective.

Key Topic

Embedded Systems

Embedded systems are specialized computer systems designed to perform dedicated functions or tasks within a larger system. Many embedded systems have substantial design constraints compared to desktop computing applications. The combination of cost pressure, long lifecycle, real-time requirements, reliability requirements, and lack of design culture standards can make it difficult to successfully apply traditional computer design methodologies and tools to embedded applications. Embedded systems in many cases must be optimized for lifecycle and business-driven factors rather than for security and maximum computing throughput. Knowing the strengths and weaknesses of current approaches can help set expectations appropriately, identify risk areas, and suggest ways to build and meet industrial needs.

High Availability

High availability (HA) is a characteristic of a system that aims to ensure an agreed-upon level of operational performance—usually uptime—for a higher-than-normal period. Modernization has resulted in increased reliance on these systems, which need to be available at all times. Availability refers to the ability of users to obtain a service or good or to access a system—whether to submit new work, update or alter existing work, or collect the results of previous work. Three principles of system design in reliability engineering can help achieve high availability:

- **Elimination of single points of failure:** This means adding or building redundancy into a system so that failure of a component does not mean failure of the entire system.

- **Reliable crossover:** In redundant systems, the crossover point tends to become a single point of failure. Reliable systems must provide for reliable crossover.

- **Detection of failures as they occur:** If the preceding two principles are observed, a user may never see a failure, but the maintenance activity is a must.

High availability is measured as the time a system is reachable. Assuming that 100% is never failing, HA is the widely held but difficult-to-achieve standard of availability of a system or service known as "five nines," or 99.999% available. Availability percentage is measured as follows:

Availability = (Minutes in a month – Minutes of downtime) × 100/minutes in a month

For example, if there is a service-level agreement (SLA) for five nines, the end user can expect that the service will be unavailable for 26.3 seconds per month and 5 minutes 15 seconds per year.

 # Considerations

System architectures require special considerations, including planning, design, implementation, and evaluation of a given environment. Considerations in system architecture involve comprehensive assessment of various factors, including technical specifications, organizational goals, regulatory compliance, security needs, and user requirements that influence the design and implementation of a system. Both cloud-based and on-premises architectures require a multidimensional approach that balances technical specifications with organizational goals, regulatory requirements, security policies, and user needs. Architects can address these unique requirements and create efficient, functional environments aligned with broader strategic objectives. Let's explore some of the considerations you must evaluate when reviewing architectures.

Availability

Availability in the architectural environment is essential for sustaining continuous business operations. *Availability* is the assurance that a system or component will be accessible and ready for use when required, reflecting its ability to operate continuously without failure. Ensuring high availability requires redundant components, load balancing, and failover mechanisms. In today's connected world, where businesses and users expect round-the-clock access to services, designing for availability is crucial in building user trust and competitive advantage. Ensure that you review any SLA that requires a specific percentage of uptime or response time in the event of an incident.

Resilience

Building resilience in the architectural environment requires a comprehensive approach, including preventive measures and recovery strategies. From redundant hardware and network pathways to robust incident response plans, resilience ensures that a system can withstand failures and attacks without significantly impacting functionality. *Resilience* in system architecture is the ability of a system to recover and continue functioning even after adverse events such as hardware failures, cyberattacks, or other disruptions occur. Strong resilience reflects an organization's readiness to adapt and respond to unexpected challenges, enhancing stability and reliability.

Cost

Cost considerations are fundamental to the architectural design process, encompassing initial investments in hardware and software and ongoing operational costs. We often hope for an unlimited budget, but rarely is that a reality. Cost in an architectural environment refers to the total expenses incurred in a system's acquisition, implementation, operation, and maintenance and encompasses both capital and operational expenditures. Architects can create a cost-effective environment that supports growth and innovation without compromising quality or performance by optimizing resource utilization, employing scalable solutions, and aligning with budgetary constraints. Security engineers can and should get involved early in the engineering process to help identify early cost savings through secure design.

Responsiveness

Responsiveness in architecture refers to how efficiently a system responds to user demands and adapts to changing conditions. Responsiveness involves optimizing performance, automating routine tasks, and proactively addressing issues. In an increasingly dynamic technological landscape, responsiveness is critical to staying agile and meeting evolving user expectations. We have all experienced essential systems responding sluggishly or giving the "spinning hourglass of death." Users and clients tend to quickly report poor system responsiveness!

Scalability

Scalability is integral to future-proofing the architectural environment. If you cannot expand on an architecture, your system quickly becomes "tech debt" and a high risk for the organization. *Scalability* refers to a system's capability to grow or shrink in response to changes in demand. By employing modular, flexible designs and embracing cloud and virtualization technologies, architects can build scalable environments that can expand to accommodate business growth and contract during periods of low demand, ensuring optimal resource utilization.

Ease of Deployment

Ease of deployment indicates the simplicity and efficiency with which a system can be rolled out and integrated into existing infrastructure—that is, its readiness for quick implementation. Ease of deployment involves standardizing configurations, automating processes, and ensuring compatibility with existing infrastructure. Simplifying deployment reduces time to market and minimizes potential errors and complications, facilitating a smoother transition to the new environment. As with cost, you can quickly help other IT and engineering teams identify easy deployment by getting involved early in the development process.

Risk Transference

Risk transference in system architecture involves shifting specific risks or potential losses to another party, such as through outsourcing or insurance, as part of a strategic approach to risk management. By strategically transferring risks, an organization can focus on its core competencies, reduce potential liabilities, and harness specialized expertise when needed. It represents a calculated approach to managing uncertainty in the increasingly complex technological landscape. However, remember that risk transference does not equate to lack of ownership. Just because you transfer a risk does not remove your accountability if a threat actor finds a vulnerability to leverage in that risk.

Ease of Recovery

Ease of recovery in architecture means having robust disaster recovery and business continuity plans. You can test the ease of recovery by simply considering how much time/energy/resources it would take to build a particular critical system from the ground up. Recovery includes regular backups, redundancy, and clear recovery procedures. When systems are designed with recovery in mind, organizations are better prepared to handle failures or disasters. Easy recovery minimizes downtime and reduces long-term impacts.

Patch Availability

Patch availability typically applies to the accessibility of software updates and fixes provided by software vendors to address vulnerabilities, enhance functionality, or improve system performance. In cloud and networking architectures, the availability of timely and relevant patches is crucial to maintaining security and operational efficiency. The architecture must accommodate regular updates, including real-time monitoring for new patches, compatibility testing, and seamless integration with existing systems. A process that aligns with the software's development lifecycle ensures that patches are applied promptly, without causing disruptions.

In many cases, to understand what systems need to be patched, you need to work closely with engineering departments to fully understand what vendors exist in the environment. Organizations must consider potential delays in vendor patch releases and develop strategies to mitigate risks through temporary fixes, controls, or configurations. In a distributed and complex environment, patch availability is a central concern that requires robust management and strategic alignment with the overall security and operational goals.

Inability to Patch

Patch management involves applying software updates, known as patches, to fix vulnerabilities, improve functionality, or enhance security. The *inability to patch* prevents a system from effectively receiving critical security updates and can be critical across all architectures, leading to vulnerabilities, data breaches, and system downtime. An architecture must be designed with patch management in mind, enabling seamless updates without disturbing existing functionalities. Designing an architecture should include building a system that can automatically test and validate patches across network components, including embedded systems and cloud infrastructure. Centralized patch management strategies and robust testing protocols can reduce the risk of incorrect or faulty fixes. You can either invest the time up front to build a resilient system or pay the cost of remediation after a system is deployed.

Power

Power consumption describes the amount of electrical energy consumed by a device, system, or network during operation. In cloud and networking architectures, power consumption considerations involve energy efficiency across the entire network, from end-user devices to massive data centers. Architectural considerations must include optimizing power use in processing, storage, and transmission and consider alternative energy sources and cooling techniques. Also, an architecture must be resilient in the face of power-based attacks. It is important to ensure that critical systems can maintain operation even under adverse conditions.

Compute

Compute resources are the hardware and software components that enable data processing and computation, including CPUs, memory, storage, and the underlying algorithms and programs. In cloud and networking architectures, compute resources must be effectively distributed and optimized across various components, including embedded devices, servers, and virtualized environments. Architectural decisions must consider scalability, performance, cost, integration with existing systems, and compatibility with various platforms and technologies. This might involve leveraging containerization, virtualization, or other modern architectural patterns for flexibility and efficiency. The physical location and constraints of computing resources should be aligned with the specific requirements and security considerations of an organization's network and cloud infrastructure.

Chapter Review Activities

Use the features in this section to study and review the topics in this chapter.

Review Key Topics

Review the most important topics in the chapter, noted with the Key Topic icon in the outer margin of the page. Table 10-2 lists these key topics and the page number on which each is found.

Table 10-2   Key Topics for Chapter 10

Key Topic Element	Description	Page Number
Section	Responsibility Matrix	193
Section	Infrastructure as Code (IaC)	195
Section	Serverless	196
Section	Microservices	197
Figure 10-3	A High-Level SDN Implementation	200
Section	Centralized Versus Decentralized	201
Paragraph	Containerization	202
List	Understanding IoT devices	209
Section	Industrial Control Systems (ICS)/Supervisory Control and Data Acquisition (SCADA)	210
Section	Embedded Systems	214
Section	Considerations	215

Define Key Terms

Define the following key terms from this chapter and check your answers in the glossary:

cloud computing, responsibility matrix, hybrid cloud, third-party vendor, infrastructure as code (IaC), serverless architecture, microservices, network infrastructure, physical isolation, air gapping, logical segmentation, software-defined networking (SDN), on-premises, centralized system, decentralized system, container image, virtualization, Internet of Things (IoT), supervisory control and data acquisition (SCADA) systems and industrial control systems (ICSs), real-time operating system (RTOS), embedded system, high availability (HA), availability, resilience, cost, responsiveness, scalability, ease of deployment, risk transference, ease of recovery, patch availability, inability to patch, power consumption, compute resources

Review Questions

Answer the following review questions. Check your answers with the answer key in Appendix A.

1. What was the original purpose of software-defined networking (SDN) in the context of infrastructure as code (IaC)?

2. How does an air-gapped system contribute to network security within network infrastructure?

3. In the context of containerization, what is the composition of a container image, and how are container images utilized?

4. What benefits does virtualization bring to cloud and networking architectures?

5. Why are SCADA systems crucial for industrial organizations?

6. Why is it essential to design architecture with patch management in mind, and what strategies can be employed?

This chapter covers the following topics related to Objective 3.2 (Given a scenario, apply security principles to secure enterprise infrastructure) of the CompTIA Security+ SY0-701 certification exam:

- Infrastructure considerations
- Secure communication/access
- Selection of effective controls

CHAPTER 11

Applying Security Principles to Secure Enterprise Infrastructure

This chapter explores key infrastructure considerations, ranging from infrastructure design, device placement, security zones, and attack surfaces to specific technologies such as firewalls, intrusion prevention systems, and secure communication protocols, as well as advanced concepts like Software-Defined Wide Area Network and secure access service edge. Through this chapter's comprehensive exploration of these elements, you will understand how to optimize network security, balance failure modes, and select effective controls while maintaining seamless connectivity and alignment with organizational goals.

"Do I Know This Already?" Quiz

The "Do I Know This Already?" quiz enables you to assess whether you should read this entire chapter thoroughly or jump to the "Chapter Review Activities" section. If you are in doubt about your answers to these questions or your own assessment of your knowledge of the topics, read the entire chapter. Table 11-1 lists the major headings in this chapter and their corresponding "Do I Know This Already?" quiz questions. You can find the answers in Appendix A, "Answers to the 'Do I Know This Already?' Quizzes and Review Questions."

Table 11-1 "Do I Know This Already?" Section-to-Question Mapping

Foundation Topics Section	Questions
Infrastructure Considerations	1–7
Secure Communication/Access	8
Selection of Effective Controls	9

CAUTION   The goal of self-assessment is to gauge your mastery of the topics in this chapter. If you do not know the answer to a question or are only partially sure of the answer, you should mark that question as wrong for purposes of self-assessment. Giving yourself credit for an answer you correctly guess skews your self-assessment results and might provide you with a false sense of security.

1. Which of the following best describes the importance of device placement in a network architecture?

   a. Only for aesthetic purposes

   b. To randomly distribute hardware devices

   c. To strategically position devices considering security, efficiency, and accessibility

   d. To minimize the need for network cables

2. What does it mean when a system is configured to fail closed?

   a. The system remains accessible if a part of it fails.

   b. The system becomes inaccessible if a part of it fails.

   c. The system becomes more efficient if a part of it fails.

   d. None of the above

3. What is the significance of understanding a device's attributes, such as active versus passive monitoring in a network environment?

   a. To increase the device's market value

   b. To select and configure devices based on specific requirements

   c. To make the device look appealing

   d. None of the above

4. In an active/passive scenario, what happens when the active device goes offline?

   a. The passive device becomes active.

   b. Both devices become passive.

   c. The entire system shuts down.

   d. The passive device also goes offline.

5. What is the primary purpose of a jump server in a network?

   a. To increase network speed

   b. To access other devices on the network

   c. To detect and prevent intrusions

   d. To distribute network traffic

6. Which of the following components are commonly implemented within the broader umbrella of port security?

   a. 802.1X and Extensible Authentication Protocol (EAP)

   b. Jump servers and proxy servers

   c. VPN and UTM

   d. Active and passive monitoring

7. Unified threat management (UTM) is often associated with what kind of firewall?

   a. Traditional firewall

   b. Next-generation firewall (NGFW)

   c. Stateless firewall

   d. All of the above

8. What is one of the primary purposes of a virtual private network (VPN)?

   a. To slow down network connections

   b. To connect two or more computers or devices that are not on the same private network

   c. To monitor network traffic for potential threats

   d. To limit access to network devices

9. Why is the process of selecting effective controls crucial in managing risks?

   a. To increase operational costs

   b. To mitigate risks to an acceptable level based on comprehensive risk assessment

   c. To ignore potential risks

   d. To complicate the risk management process

Infrastructure Considerations

Infrastructure considerations play a critical role in shaping the security and functionality of an enterprise's IT landscape. They encompass the strategies and tactics for aligning systems and components, ensuring optimal performance, availability, and protection against threats. Careful planning and assessment are vital to creating a cohesive environment that meets organizational needs while adhering to security principles. You will need to spend a significant amount of time gathering the requirements of the enterprise before making any decisions about the issue discussed in this section. As with so many other things in IT, investing the time up front will save you a lot of pain.

Device Placement

Device placement involves the thoughtful positioning of hardware devices within a network. It involves considering security requirements, network efficiency, and accessibility. For instance, placing a firewall close to a network's perimeter can prevent unauthorized access, whereas placing a server containing sensitive data in a secure location can minimize exposure to potential threats. You also need to consider the organization's crown jewels. Security engineers sometimes consider only where sensitive information is stored, but it's important to also consider how sensitive information travels to storage, which we will discuss later in this chapter. The way devices are placed can significantly influence the security and functionality of a network.

Security Zones

Security zones are segregated areas in a network that are under specific security policies and controls. Creating different zones that segregate varying levels of trust can prevent unauthorized access to sensitive information. For example, a public-facing web server may be placed in a screened subnet separate from an internal network that contains confidential data. Zoning enhances security by adding layers of protection and controlling access between different parts of the network.

You might encounter different approaches to creating security zones. Here are a few to keep in mind.

- **Internal zones:** Often referred to as trusted zones, internal zones include segments where sensitive or internal data is processed. Internal zones often have more relaxed security policies than do external, or untrusted, zones, but access is limited to authorized personnel.

- **External, or untrusted, zones:** External zones are areas where connections from the public Internet or other untrusted networks are allowed. Rigorous security measures are usually implemented in these zones to prevent unauthorized access to internal resources.

- **Screened subnet:** A screened subnet is a specialized external zone where public-facing services like web or mail servers are placed. A screened subnet is isolated from the Internet and the internal trusted zones to provide additional protection for the internal network.

- **Specialized zones:** In some environments, there may be a need for specialized zones to meet regulatory compliance requirements (for example, a PCI zone for handling credit card data) or to isolate environments with different security requirements (for example, a development zone separated from a production zone).

As you can see, there are several options when creating security zones, and they play a vital role in a defense-in-depth strategy by containing potential breaches within a zone and providing different levels of protection tailored to the specific requirements of each part of the organization.

Attack Surface

The *attack surface* of a system refers to the totality of the vulnerabilities and potential points through which an unauthorized user might breach security. It includes all the interfaces, services, protocols, and code that expose the system to the outside world. The larger and more complex the attack surface, the greater the potential risk. Managing the attack surface requires an understanding of all these entry points and a strategic approach to minimize unnecessary exposure. Techniques to reduce the attack surface include turning off or disabling unnecessary services, closing open ports, applying patches and updates, using firewalls to restrict incoming and outgoing traffic, and implementing strong authentication mechanisms. Understanding and minimizing the attack surface is integral to a robust cybersecurity posture, as it enables an organization to reduce the potential vectors an attacker might exploit.

For example, in a basic web application environment, the attack surface includes all the points where an unauthorized user could access the underlying sensitive data. Suppose the web application uses APIs, an insecure back-end connection to a database, or an unprotected user input field. An attacker could leverage these weak points, and so this is an attack surface for the organization.

Connectivity

Connectivity in the context of infrastructure refers to how different parts of the network, systems, or applications connect and communicate with each other and with external entities. It involves various protocols, devices, channels, and technologies that enable data to flow between different system parts. Connectivity considerations are vital for efficiency, functionality, and security because digital systems are useless if the data or information cannot safely arrive at its destination. Security considerations related to connectivity involve encrypting data in transit, securing connection endpoints, employing secure protocols, and using security measures like VPNs or firewalls to protect the connections. A strong connectivity strategy considers not only the functional requirements for data exchange but also the potential risks and includes measures to ensure that connections are secure, reliable, and in line with organizational security policies and regulatory requirements. Remember connectivity when working with engineering or any other department on a new system design!

Failure Modes

In a *fail-open* configuration, if a portion of the system fails, the rest of the system will still be available, or "open." In a *fail-closed* configuration, if a portion of a system fails, the entire system will become inaccessible or simply shut down.

Depending on the level of security your organization requires, you might have a mixture of fail-open and fail-closed systems. Let's say that the DNS server forwards information to several different zones and that one of those zones fails for one reason or another. You might decide that it is more beneficial to the network to have the rest of the DNS server continue to operate and service the rest of the zones instead of shutting down completely, so you would want the DNS server to fail open. However, the database server might have confidential information that you cannot afford to lose, so if one service or component of the database server fails, you might opt to have the database server stop servicing requests altogether—that is, to fail closed. Another example would be a firewall/router. If the firewall portion of the device failed, you would probably want the device to fail closed. Even though the network connectivity could still function, you probably wouldn't want it to because there would be no firewall protection.

The solution you implement depends on the level of security you require and the risk that can be associated with devices that fail open. It also depends on whether the server or device has a redundancy associated with it. If the DNS server mentioned previously has a secondary redundant DNS server that is always up and running and ready to take requests at a moment's notice, you might opt to instead configure the first DNS server to fail closed and let the secondary DNS server take over entirely.

Device Attribute

Device attributes are specific characteristics and functionalities that determine how a security device operates in a network environment. These attributes, such as active versus passive monitoring or inline versus tap/monitor configurations, play a crucial role in defining a device's behavior, capabilities, and impact on network traffic. We will discuss how each attribute should be considered in an environment. Network administrators and security engineers need to understand these distinctions when selecting and configuring devices to meet specific security, performance, and reliability requirements.

Key Topic

Active vs. Passive

In an *active/active* scenario, the devices perform work simultaneously, sharing the load. In this type of implementation, two devices typically run the same software or service. This is an important aspect of the implementation of any type of failover or load balancing. If one device has a different version—even if it is slightly different—this can cause issues with the failover or load-balancing process.

In an *active/passive* scenario, one device actively performs work while the other works in a standby capacity. The passive device becomes active only when the active device goes offline or is manually switched to be the secondary.

Inline vs. Tap/Monitor

Inline monitoring involves positioning a security device (firewall, IPS, IDS, and so on) directly in the network traffic flow. With this configuration, all traffic must pass through the device and can actively intervene, block, or modify the traffic based on the device's capabilities. Inline monitoring provides real-time, active monitoring and the ability to take immediate actions based on predefined rules or detected threats. The potential downside to this approach is that if the device fails, it could disrupt the entire network traffic flow, creating a single point of failure. As discussed earlier in this chapter, it is important to ensure that you do not accidentally create a point of failure that could quickly become an attack surface. In addition, a device's processing capacity may become a bottleneck if the device cannot handle the traffic volume.

Unlike with the inline approach, devices configured in tap, or monitor, mode are not placed directly in the flow of traffic but are connected to the network in a way that allows them to observe, or "tap into," the traffic without actively interfering with it. This passive monitoring approach can be used to analyze and log network behavior without the risk of disrupting traffic if the device fails. In *tap (or monitor) mode*, a hardware or software component enables the observation and capture of network data as it travels between points. Tap, or monitor, mode is often used for intrusion detection, network troubleshooting, and performance monitoring. While it allows for detailed analysis and visibility, it doesn't offer the same real-time intervention capabilities as an inline configuration, as it can observe but not actively block or alter traffic.

Network Appliances

Network appliances, also known as network devices or hardware, play a vital role in ensuring a network's smooth functioning, security, and efficiency. Specialized network devices include a wide range of components such as jump servers, proxy servers, intrusion prevention systems (IPSs)/intrusion detection systems (IDSs), load balancers, and sensors, each of which serves a specific purpose within the network infrastructure. As we explore each of these items in this section, consider how you could efficiently and effectively secure each one of them. When properly secured, these network appliances contribute to a robust and resilient architecture, promoting enhanced security, performance, and scalability.

Jump Servers

A *jump server*, also known as a *jump box*, is a device on a network that is typically used to access other devices on the network. For instance, you might have direct access to a Windows system via Remote Desktop Protocol from outside your network or on a secure enclave. Gaining access to that machine allows you to access devices that you do not have direct access to. For example, a jump server might be installed on a screened subnet for managing the servers within the screened subnet.

Proxy Servers

A *proxy server* acts as an intermediary for clients, which are usually located on a LAN, and the servers that they want to access, which are usually located on the Internet. *Proxy* means "go-between," or "mediator," and a proxy server acts as a mediator in between a private network and a public network. The proxy server evaluates requests from clients and, if they meet certain criteria, forwards the requests to the appropriate server. There are several types of proxies, including a couple you should be familiar with:

- **IP proxy:** This type of proxy secures a network by keeping machines behind it anonymous; it does this through the use of NAT. For example, a basic four-port router can act as an IP proxy for the clients on the LAN it protects. An IP proxy can be a victim in many types of network attacks, especially DoS attacks. Regardless of whether an IP proxy is an appliance or a computer, it should be updated regularly, and its log files should be monitored periodically and audited according to organization policies.

■ **Caching proxy:** This type of proxy attempts to serve client requests without actually contacting the remote server. Although there are FTP and SMTP proxies, among others, the most common caching proxy is the HTTP proxy, also known as a web proxy, which caches web pages from servers on the Internet for a set amount of time. Examples of caching proxies include WinGate (for Windows systems) and SquidProxies (commonly used on Linux-based systems). Figure 11-1 shows a caching proxy in action.

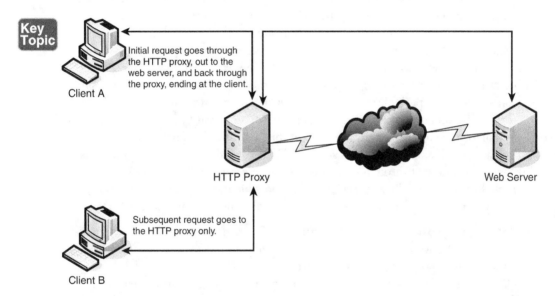

Figure 11-1 An HTTP Proxy in Action

For example, let's say your coworker (Client A) accesses www.google.com and is the first person to do so on the network. This client request goes through the HTTP proxy and is redirected to Google's web server. As the data for Google's home page comes in, the HTTP proxy stores, or caches, that information. When another person on your network (Client B) makes a subsequent request for www.google.com, the bulk of that information comes from the HTTP proxy instead of from Google's web server. This saves bandwidth on the company's Internet connection and increases the speed at which client requests are carried out.

Most HTTP proxies check websites to verify that nothing has changed since the last request. Because information on the Internet changes quickly, a time limit of

24 hours is common for storing cached information before it is deleted. Web browsers make use of a proxy autoconfiguration (PAC) file, which defines how the browser can automatically choose a proxy server. The file itself and the embedded JavaScript function pose a security risk in that the file can be exploited and modified, ultimately redirecting the user to unwanted (and potentially malicious) websites. You should consider disabling PAC files and autoconfiguration in general in client web browsers.

Other types of proxies are available to apply policies, block undesirable websites, audit employee usage, and scan for malware. Depending on the software used or appliance installed, one device or computer might do all these things or just one or two of them. Reverse proxies can also be implemented to protect a screened subnet server's identity or to provide authentication and other secure tasks. This is done when users on the Internet are accessing server resources on your network. Generally, a proxy server has more than one network adapter so that it can connect to the various networks for which it is acting as a mediator. The network adapters in a proxy should be periodically monitored for improper traffic and for possible network attacks and other vulnerabilities. A proxy server might be the same device as a firewall, or it could be separate. Because of this, a multitude of network configurations are possible. Proxy servers, especially HTTP proxies, can be used maliciously to record traffic sent through them; because most of the traffic is sent in unencrypted form, this could be a security risk. A possible mitigation would be to chain multiple proxies together in an attempt to confuse onlookers and potential attackers.

Most often, a proxy server is implemented as a forward proxy. This means that clients looking for websites or files via an FTP connection pass their requests through to the proxy. However, there is also a reverse proxy, where multiple HTTP or FTP servers use a proxy server and send out content to one or more clients. These HTTP and FTP servers could be located in a server farm or similar grouping, and the reverse proxy might also undertake the role of load balancer in this situation. A reverse proxy can act as another layer of defense for an organization's FTP or HTTP servers. An application proxy might be used as a reverse proxy; an example is Microsoft's Web Application Proxy, which enables remote users to connect to the organization's internal network to access multiple servers. Reverse proxies are often multipurpose by design, allowing HTTP, FTP, email, and other types of data connections. However, it is also possible to have a single application stored on several servers and configure those servers to work together using clustering technology. The clustering might be controlled by the servers themselves, or, more commonly, a load balancer may be installed in front of the servers to distribute the network load among them. That load balancer in effect acts as a reverse proxy.

Regardless of the type, a proxy often modifies the requests of the "client computer"—whatever that client is—providing for a level of anonymity. But in some cases, you might need a proxy that does not modify requests. This is known as a transparent proxy. Although a transparent proxy allows for increased efficiency, it provides less protection for the client system.

Intrusion Prevention System (IPS)/Intrusion Detection System (IDS)

In network security, two essential components are *intrusion detection systems (IDSs)* and *intrusion prevention systems (IPSs)*. Both IDSs and IPSs are critical in monitoring and protecting networks from malicious activities. An IDS is an observer, passively scanning network traffic for suspicious patterns and alerting administrators to potential breaches. An IPS goes a step further, actively intervening to block or mitigate identified threats. IDSs and IPSs have unique functionalities, and together they help you defend against cyberattacks.

The value of an IDS lies in its continuous monitoring and detection capabilities, which enable you to identify potential security threats promptly. By generating alerts, an IDS provides crucial insights that can lead to further investigation and action. On the other hand, an IPS is more proactive, working in real time to neutralize threats as they occur. It can alter, drop, or reroute malicious traffic, preventing a threat from causing harm. The synergy between these two systems allows for comprehensive network protection, combining observation and action.

Although IDSs and IPSs are similar, they are distinct in their approaches to network security. An IDS primarily focuses on detection, acting as a sentinel that watches and warns. It relies on human intervention to respond to alerts. An IPS, on the other hand, is an automated guard that takes immediate measures to thwart potential attacks. Whereas an IDS offers a deep analysis of potential threats, an IPS emphasizes rapid responses to known threats. Understanding these differences is vital for implementing the right balance of detection and prevention in a security framework.

We can use the example of a home security system to examine the distinct roles and collaboration between IDSs and IPSs:

- **IDSs:** Think of an IDS as a security camera mounted at the entrance of a home. Its primary task is to continually monitor the surroundings and detect any unusual activities, such as a stranger approaching the door. Once it recognizes something unusual, the IDS sends an alert to the homeowner. However, the camera doesn't take any action to prevent the intrusion. It provides information and leaves the homeowner responsible for evaluating the situation and deciding on the appropriate action, such as calling the authorities or ignoring it as a false alarm.

- **IPSs:** Think of an IPS as an advanced alarm system that's integrated within the same home as the security camera (representing an IDS) just discussed. Unlike the security camera, this alarm system does more than detect an intrusion. If a window is broken or a door is forced open, the alarm system automatically triggers preventive measures, like locking other doors or even notifying the local police. Similarly, an IPS takes immediate action based on predefined rules and doesn't rely on human intervention to respond to the threat.

■ **Combining IDSs and IPSs:** By integrating both the security camera (IDS) and an advanced alarm system (IPS), a home can achieve a layered approach to security. Similarly, whereas an IDS offers the visibility and awareness needed to recognize potential threats, an IPS ensures an immediate and automated response to confirmed intrusions. Together, they provide a comprehensive security solution, with the IDS as the watchful eye and the IPS as the protective shield.

Whereas an IDS is more about monitoring and detection, an IPS emphasizes prevention and immediate action. Both systems play vital roles, and their effective combination can significantly enhance an organization's overall security posture.

Load Balancer

Load balancing is often used with redundant servers. A load-balancing cluster is a group of computers connected together for the purpose of sharing resources, such as CPU, RAM, and hard disks. The cluster can share CPU power and other resources, and it can balance the CPU load among all the servers. Microsoft Cluster Server can provide load balancing (although it can also act in failover mode), enabling parallel, high-performance computing. Several third-party vendors offer clustering software for operating systems and virtual operating systems as well. It is a common technique in web and FTP server farms, as well as in IRC servers, DNS servers, and NTP servers.

There are several types of load balancers. Network load balancers automatically distribute incoming traffic across multiple network paths. This capability increases the availability of the network during component outages, misconfigurations, attacks, and hardware failures. Most network load balancers utilize routing protocols to help make path decisions during a network overload or network failure. A load balancer spreads out the network load to various switches, routers, and servers. Server load balancers distribute the traffic load based on specific selected algorithms to each of the servers in a group. A load balancer is typically placed in front of a group of servers to evenly distribute the load among them.

In network load balancing, when a router learns multiple routes to a specific network via routing protocols such as RIP, EIGRP, and OSPF, it installs the route with the lowest administrative distance in the routing table. If the router receives and installs multiple paths with the same administrative distance and cost to a destination, load balancing of network traffic will occur.

To mitigate risks associated with failures of load balancers, you can deploy two servers in an active/active or active/passive configuration. With active/active configuration, traffic is split between the two servers, typically in a round-robin fashion. With active/passive configuration, all traffic is sent to the active server, and the passive server is automatically promoted to active status if the current active server fails or is taken down for maintenance.

Sensors

The *sensors* in a network are devices, such as IPS or IDS devices, that inspect the traffic. In today's networks, they can also come in the form of next-generation firewalls (NGFWs). These devices also have the capability to provide intrusion detection and prevention protection and work as sensors on a network. In addition, with the use of NetFlow Version 9, also known as IPFIX, the network itself can become a sensor.

The following sections discuss collectors and aggregators, which are used to provide this function via NetFlow. For instance, it is very difficult (and expensive) to deploy hundreds of sensor appliances in the network of a large organization. When a security incident or breach is detected, the incident responders need answers fast! They do not have time to go over terabytes of packet captures, and they definitely cannot analyze every computer on the network to find the root cause and source of the breach. You can use NetFlow to obtain a high-level view of what is happening on a network, and then the incident responder can perform a deep-dive investigation with packet captures and other tools later in the investigation. Sniffers can be deployed as needed in key locations where suspicious activity is suspected. The beauty of NetFlow is that you can deploy it anywhere you have a supported router, switch, firewall, or endpoint.

Port Security

Port security plays a pivotal role in safeguarding network access and ensuring that unauthorized devices are not allowed to communicate through network ports. *Port security* protection mechanisms act as gatekeepers, managing the connection process based on defined policies and standards. I have personally experienced times when port security blocked legitimate traffic, causing extended network outages, which is why security engineers should be intimately involved in the network configuration process.

Within the broader umbrella of port security, two essential components are commonly implemented: 802.1X and Extensible Authentication Protocol (EAP). The 802.1X standard is a framework that provides port-based network access control, while EAP is a universal authentication framework that's frequently used in conjunction with 802.1X. Together, they facilitate secure authentication and streamline network access control, forming an integral part of contemporary network security strategies.

802.1X and EAP

802.1X is an IEEE standard that defines port-based network access control (PNAC). Not to be confused with 802.1X WLAN standards, IEEE 802.1X is a data link layer authentication technology used to connect hosts to a LAN or WLAN. 802.1X allows you to apply a security control that ties physical ports to end-device MAC addresses and prevents additional devices from being connected to the network. It is a good way of implementing port security—much better than simply setting up MAC filtering.

NOTE   Many vendors, such as Intel and Cisco, refer to 802.1X with a lowercase *x*; however, the IEEE displays this on its website with an uppercase *X*, as does the IETF. The protocol was originally defined in 2001 (802.1X-2001) and was then redefined in 2004 and 2010 (802.1X-2004 and 802.1X-2010, respectively).

Setting up security control starts with the central connecting device, such as a switch or wireless access point. Such a device must enable 802.1X connections and must have the 802.1X protocol (and supporting protocols) installed. Vendors that offer 802.1X-compliant devices (for example, switches and wireless access points) include Cisco, Symbol Technologies, and Intel. Next, the client computer needs to have an operating system, or additional software, that supports 802.1X. The client computer is known as the supplicant. All recent Windows versions support 802.1X. macOS offers support as well, and Linux computers can use Open1X to enable client access to networks that require 802.1X authentication.

802.1X encapsulates the *Extensible Authentication Protocol (EAP)* over wired or wireless connections. EAP is not itself an authentication mechanism; rather, it defines message formats. 802.1X is an authentication mechanism and defines how EAP is encapsulated within messages. Figure 11-2 shows an 802.1X-enabled network adapter. In the figure, you can see that the box for enabling 802.1X has been checked and that the type of network authentication method for 802.1X is EAP—specifically, Protected Extensible Authentication Protocol (PEAP).

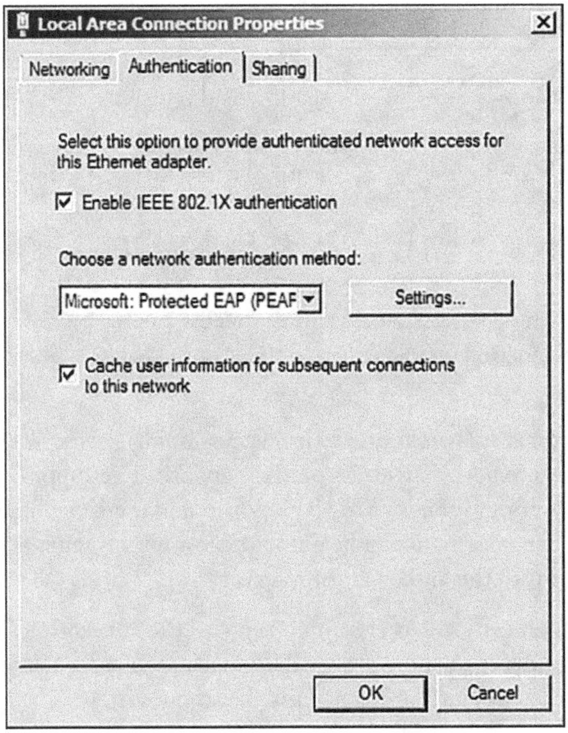

Figure 11-2   An 802.1X-Enabled Network Adapter in Windows

NOTE   To enable 802.1X in Windows, you access the Local Area Connection Properties page.

These are the three components of an 802.1X connection:

- **Supplicant:** A software client running on a workstation. This is also known as an authentication agent.

- **Authenticator:** A wireless access point or switch.

- **Authentication server:** An authentication database, most likely a RADIUS server.

The typical 802.1X authentication procedure has four steps (see Figure 11-3):

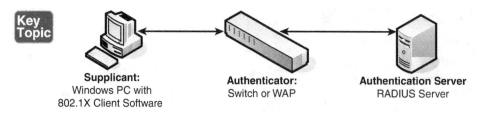

Supplicant:
Windows PC with
802.1X Client Software

Authenticator:
Switch or WAP

Authentication Server
RADIUS Server

Figure 11-3   Components of a Typical 802.1X Authentication Procedure

Step 1.   **Initialization:** If a switch or wireless access point detects a new supplicant, the port connection enables port 802.1X traffic; other types of traffic are dropped.

Step 2.   **Initiation:** The authenticator (switch or wireless access point) periodically sends EAP requests to a MAC address on the network. The supplicant listens for this address and sends an EAP response that might include a user ID or other similar information. The authenticator encapsulates this response and sends it to the authentication server.

Step 3.   **Negotiation:** The authentication server sends a reply to the authenticator. The authentication server specifies which EAP method to use. (These are listed next.) Then the authenticator transmits that request to the supplicant.

Step 4.   **Authentication:** If the supplicant and authentication server agree on an EAP method, the two transmit until there is either success or failure to authenticate the supplicant computer.

Following are several types of EAP authentication:

- **EAP-MD5:** This challenge-based form of authentication provides basic EAP support. It enables only one-way authentication and not mutual authentication.

- **EAP-TLS:** This version uses Transport Layer Security, which is a certificate-based system that enables mutual authentication. It does not work well in enterprise scenarios because certificates must be configured or managed on the client side and server side.

- **EAP-TTLS:** This version uses Tunneled Transport Layer Security and is basically the same as EAP-TLS except that it is done through an encrypted channel, and it requires only server-side certificates.

- **EAP-FAST:** Flexible Authentication via Secure Tunneling (FAST) uses a protected access credential instead of a certificate to achieve mutual authentication.

■ **PEAP:** Protected Extensible Authentication Protocol (PEAP) uses MS-CHAPv2, which supports authentication via Microsoft Active Directory databases. It competes with EAP-TTLS and includes legacy password-based protocols. It creates a TLS tunnel by acquiring a public key infrastructure (PKI) certificate from a server known as a certificate authority (CA). The TLS tunnel protects user authentication much as EAP-TTLS does.

IEEE 802.1X

Although 802.1X is often used for port-based network access control on LANs, especially VLANs, it can also be used with VPNs for remote authentication. Central connecting devices such as switches and wireless access points remain the same, but on the client side, 802.1X needs to be configured on a VPN adapter instead of a network adapter.

Firewall Types

Firewalls are everywhere today. Businesses large and small use them, and many households have simpler versions of these protective devices as well. You need to be aware of several types of firewalls, and you definitely want to spend some time configuring hardware and software firewalls. There are many free software-based firewalls and firmware-based emulators that you can download. A quick Internet search provides several options.

A firewall is used to protect an entire network, but other tools are often implemented as well, such as proxy servers that help protect users and computers by keeping them anonymous, honeypots that are meant to attract hackers and other types of attackers into a false computer or network, and data loss prevention (DLP) devices that keep confidential data from leaving the network. But by far the most important element in a network is the firewall, so let's begin with that.

Network-based firewalls are primarily used to section off and protect one network from another. They are a primary line of defense and are extremely important in network security. There are several types of firewalls; some run as software on server computers, some run as standalone dedicated appliances, and some work as just one function of many on a single device. They are commonly represented as a sort of "brick wall" between a LAN and the Internet, as shown in Figure 11-4.

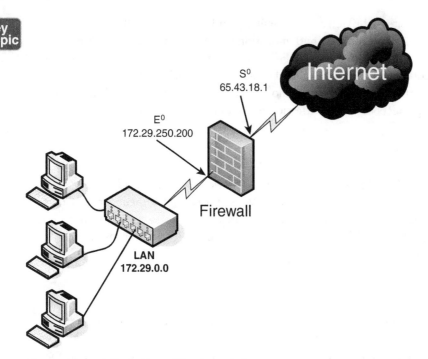

Figure 11-4   A Basic Firewall Implementation

Just as a firewall in a physical building is there to slow the spread of a fire and contain it until the fire department arrives, a firewall in a computer network is there to keep malicious attacks at bay. Often, a firewall (or the device the firewall resides on) has NAT in operation as well. In Figure 11-4, note that the firewall has the local address 172.29.250.200; this connects it to the LAN. It also has the Internet address 65.43.18.1, which enables connectivity for the entire LAN to the Internet while hiding the LAN's IP addresses. By default, the IP address 65.43.18.1 is completely shielded. This means that all inbound ports are effectively closed and do not enable incoming traffic unless a LAN computer initiates a session with another system on the Internet. However, a good security administrator always checks this to make sure. First, you should access the firewall's firmware (or software application, as the case may be) and verify that the firewall is on. Next, you scan the firewall with third-party applications such as Nmap (https://nmap.org) or with a web-based port scanning utility. If any ports are open or unshielded, you should deal with them immediately. Then you should rescan the firewall for vulnerabilities.

Important point: Firewalls should be used only as they were intended to be used. A company firewall should not handle any other extraneous services—for example, acting as a web server or as an SMTP server. Using a firewall as it was intended to be used reduces its vulnerability.

Generally, a firewall inspects traffic that passes through it and permits or denies traffic based on rules set by an administrator. These rules are stored within access control lists (ACLs). With regard to firewalls, an ACL is a set of rules that apply to a list of network names, IP addresses, and port numbers. These rules can be configured to control inbound and outbound traffic. This is a bit different from ACLs with respect to operating systems, but the same basic principles apply: Basically, one entity is granted or denied permission to another entity. If you decide that a specific type of traffic should be granted access to your network, you *explicitly allow* that traffic as a rule within an ACL. If, on the other hand, you decide that a specific type of traffic should *not* be granted access, you *explicitly deny* that traffic within an ACL. And finally, if a type of network traffic is not defined in the firewall's rule set, it should be stopped by default. This is the concept of *implicit deny* and is usually a default rule in a firewall's ACL. It is often added automatically to the end of a firewall's rule set (ACLs) and is also known as "block all."

Firewall rules should be specific. Here's an example of a firewall rule:

```
deny TCP any any port 53
```

This rule can be used to restrict DNS zone transfers (as they run on top of TCP and use port 53), but other DNS traffic still functions properly. The rule is specific: It gives the transport layer protocol to be filtered and the exact port, and it also states that it applies to *any* computer's IP address on the inbound and outbound sides. Be careful with firewall rules and ACLs; they need to be written very carefully so as not to filter required traffic.

NOTE Traffic can also be passed to other computers and servers or to specific ports.

A lot of firewalls today have SPI and NAT built in, and you also should be aware of a few other types of firewall methodologies:

- **Packet filtering:** Packet filtering is used to inspect each packet that is passing through the firewall and accept or reject it based on rules. However, there are two types: *stateless packet inspection* and *stateful packet inspection* (also known as SPI, or a stateful firewall). A *stateless* packet filter, also known as pure packet filtering, does not retain memory of packets that have passed through the firewall; a *stateless* packet filter can therefore be vulnerable to IP spoofing attacks. But a firewall running stateful packet inspection is normally not vulnerable to this because it keeps track of the state of network connections by examining the header in each packet. It can distinguish between legitimate and illegitimate packets. This function operates at the network layer of the OSI model.

- **NAT gateway:** Also known as NAT endpoint filtering, NAT gateway filters traffic according to ports (TCP or UDP). This can be done in three ways: by way of basic endpoint connections, by matching incoming traffic to the corresponding outbound IP address connection, or by matching incoming traffic to the corresponding IP address and port.

- **Application-level gateway (ALG):** An ALG applies security mechanisms to specific applications, such as FTP or BitTorrent. It supports address and port translation and checks whether the type of application traffic is allowed. For example, your company might allow FTP traffic through the firewall but might decide to disable Telnet traffic (which is probably a wise choice). The ALG checks each type of packet coming in and discards Telnet packets. Although this adds a powerful layer of security, it is resource intensive, which could lead to performance degradation.

- **Circuit-level gateway:** A circuit-level gateway works at the session layer of the OSI model and applies security mechanisms when a TCP or UDP connection is established; it acts as a go-between for the transport and application layers in TCP/IP. After a connection has been made, packets can flow between the hosts without further checking. Circuit-level gateways hide information about the private network, but they do not filter individual packets.

A firewall can be set up in several different physical configurations. For example, it could be set up in a back-to-back configuration (with two firewalls surrounding the screened subnet), as shown in Figure 11-5, or as a three-leg perimeter configuration.

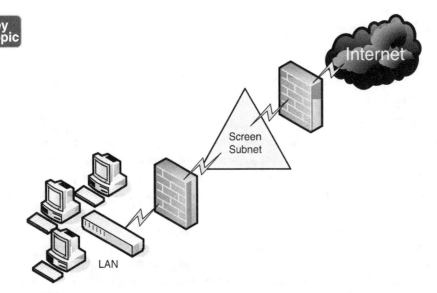

Figure 11-5   Back-to-Back Firewall (Screened Subnet) Configuration

Generally, there is one firewall, and the network and all devices and computers reside "behind" it.

NOTE   If a device is "behind" a firewall, it is also considered to be "after" the firewall, and if a device is "in front of" a firewall, it is also known as being "before" the firewall. Think of the firewall as the drawbridge of a castle. When you are trying to gain admittance to the castle, the drawbridge is probably closed. You would be in front of the drawbridge, and the people inside the castle would be behind the drawbridge. This basic analogy should help you understand the whole "in front of" and "behind" business as it relates to data attempting to enter the network and devices that reside on your network.

Logging is also important when it comes to a firewall. Firewall logs should be the first thing you check when an intrusion has been detected. You should know how to access the logs and how to read them. For example, Figure 11-6 shows two screen captures: The first displays the Internet sessions on a basic small office/home office (SOHO) router/firewall, and the second shows log events such as blocked packets. Look at the blocked Gnutella packet that is pointed out. You know it is a Gnutella packet because the inbound port on the firewall that the external computer is trying to connect to shows as port 6346, which is associated with Gnutella. Gnutella is an older P2P file-sharing network. None of the computers on this particular network use or are in any way connected to the Gnutella service. These external computers are just random clients of the Gnutella P2P network trying to connect to anyone possible.

It's good that these packets have been blocked, but maybe you don't want the IP address shown (24.253.3.20) to have any capability to connect to your network at all. To eliminate that IP address, you could add it to an inbound filter or to an ACL.

Web Application Firewall (WAF)

So far, we have discussed host-based and network-based firewalls. However, both of these types of firewalls can also fall into the application firewall category. If either type runs protocols that operate on the application layer of the OSI model, it can be classified as an application firewall. A *web application firewall (WAF)* is a specialized firewall that secures web applications by monitoring and filtering HTTP/HTTPS traffic between a web application and the Internet. It operates at the application layer and is designed to detect and prevent attacks such as SQL injection, cross-site scripting (XSS), and other vulnerabilities specific to web applications. This level of granularity allows it to provide more nuanced security measures tailored to web-based applications, as opposed to traditional firewalls that operate at the network layer. This is something a stateful network firewall cannot do because this function operates at the application layer of the OSI model. Many host-based firewalls fall into this category, but when it comes to network-based firewalls, it varies.

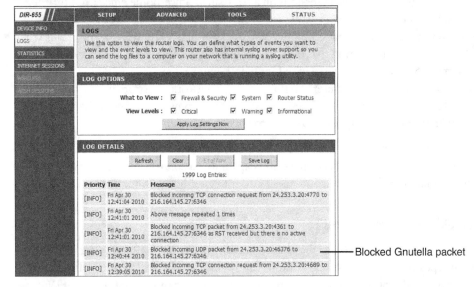

Figure 11-6   SOHO Router/Firewall Internet Sessions

A basic SOHO router with built-in firewalling capabilities would usually not fall into the application firewall category. However, more advanced network appliances from companies such as Barracuda, Citrix, Fortinet, and Smoothwall do fall into this category; they allow for more in-depth monitoring of the network by controlling the input, output, and access to applications and services all the way up through the application layer of the OSI model. These appliances might also be referred to as network-based application layer firewalls. Now that's a mouthful. For the Security+ SY0-701 exam, just be ready for multiple terms used by companies and technicians.

Going a step further, some of the aforementioned network appliances have tools that are designed to specifically protect HTTP sessions from XSS attacks and SQL injection. These types of tools are WAFs and can help protect the servers in the environment.

> **NOTE**   A firewall appliance needs more than one network adapter so that it can connect to more than one network; this is known as a *multihomed connection*. It might be dual-homed (two adapters), or perhaps it has more network adapters—maybe three—in case you want to implement a screened subnet or another perimeter security technique.

Firewalls are often considered to be all-in-one devices, but actually they provide specific functionality, as discussed in this section. Still, it is common to hear people refer to a firewall when they are really talking about another technology or even another device. For example, many SOHO users have an all-in-one multifunction network device. This device has four ports for wired connections, plus a wireless antenna; it connects all the computers to the Internet and also has a firewall built in. Because some users consider this to be simply a firewall, you should teach them about the benefits of disabling service set identifier (SSID) broadcasting and enabling MAC filtering. By disabling SSID broadcasting, the average user cannot connect to the device wirelessly. An attacker knows how to bypass this setting, but it is an important element of security that you should implement after all trusted computers have been connected wirelessly. MAC filtering denies access to any computer that does not have one of the MAC addresses listed.

To make matters a bit more confusing, a firewall can also act as or in combination with a proxy server, as discussed in the following section.

Unified Threat Management (UTM)

A relatively new concept, *unified threat management (UTM)* is the culmination of everything we have discussed in this chapter so far. As early as the year 2000, it was realized that a firewall was no longer enough to protect an organization's network. Other devices and technologies such as NIDSs/NIPSs, content filters, anti-malware gateways, data leak prevention, and virtual private networks were added to networks to better protect them. However, with all these extra devices and technologies come added cost and more administration. UTM providers simplify the whole situation by offering all-in-one devices that combine the various levels of defense into one solution. A UTM device is an integrated security solution that consolidates multiple security functions into a single device. The all-in-one device might also be referred to as a next-generation firewall (NGFW). However, UTM devices and NGFWs differ in significant ways, which we will discuss later. Companies such as Cisco,

Fortinet, and Sophos (to name a few) offer UTM solutions; often such a solution is a single device that sits last on the network before the Internet connection. A UTM device typically has a straightforward web-based GUI, which is good news for a beleaguered security administrator like you who might be burning the midnight oil researching the latest attacks and prevention methods. A UTM device centralizes setup for antivirus, anti-malware, intrusion prevention, VPN, and firewall functions, saving even more time between opening the box and protecting the network. For this reason, UTM devices tends to be a good option for smaller businesses.

There's a caveat to all this, and it is a common theme in network security: A single point of defense is a single point of failure. If an attacker can get past the UTM, their job is done. Secondary and backup UTM devices, as well as server-based HIDSs, strike a balance and create a certain level of defense in depth, while still retaining some simplicity. Another consideration is that UTM devices should be quick. If a UTM device is to take the place of several other devices, its data processing and traffic flow requirements are steep. As a smart network or security administrator, you will consider implementing a device that exceeds your current needs and then some.

Next-Generation Firewall (NGFW)

Next-generation firewalls (NGFWs) are an evolution of traditional firewalls, designed to go beyond port and protocol inspection by adding application-level inspection, intrusion prevention, and intelligence from outside the firewall. Unlike UTM systems that offer broad security capabilities, NGFWs focus on deep packet inspection, application-level control, and user identity management.

NGFWs offer granular control over network traffic, enabling the implementation of detailed security policies and providing advanced security features such as threat intelligence feeds and integration with other security technologies. This results in a more robust security posture. NGFWs also offer enhanced logging and reporting features that provide a clearer network view, making identifying and responding to threats easier. However, the advanced features of NGFWs can make them more challenging to manage, requiring specialized knowledge and training. They are also often more expensive than traditional firewalls or UTM devices in terms of initial investment and ongoing maintenance.

Companies like Cisco, Fortinet, and Palo Alto Networks offer NGFW solutions that are particularly beneficial for organizations with complex network architectures, multiple branches, or under strict regulatory compliance requirements. Such organizations often have the in-house expertise to manage the advanced features of NGFWs.

Another example of a proxy in action is Internet content/URL filtering. An Internet content/URL filter, or simply a content filter, is usually applied as software at the application layer and can filter out various types of Internet activities, such as websites accessed, email, instant messaging, and more. A content filter often functions as a content inspection device and disallows access to inappropriate web material (which is estimated to be a big percentage of the Internet!) and websites that take up far too much of an organization's Internet bandwidth. Internet content filters can be installed on individual clients, but by far the more efficient implementation is as an individual proxy that acts as a mediator between all the clients and the Internet. These proxy versions of content filters secure the network in two ways:

- By forbidding access to potentially malicious websites

- By blocking access to objectionable material that employees might feel is offensive

They can also act as URL filters so that even if an employee inadvertently types an incorrect URL, they can rest assured that any objectionable material will not show up on their display.

Internet filtering appliances analyze just about all the data that comes through them, including Internet content, URLs, HTML tags, metadata, and security certificates such as the kind you would automatically receive when going to a secure site that starts with https. However, revoked certificates and certificate revocation lists (CRLs) are not filtered because they are published only periodically. Some of these appliances are even capable of malware inspection.

Another similar appliance is a web security gateway. Web security gateways (such as Forcepoint, previously known as Websense) act as go-between devices that scan for viruses, filter content, and act as data loss prevention (DLP) devices. This type of content inspection/content filtering is accomplished by actively monitoring the users' data streams in search of malicious code, bad behavior, or confidential data that should not be leaked outside the network.

Next, we compare hardware and software firewalls and appliance versus host-based versus virtual firewalls.

Hardware vs. Software

Firewall devices can come in many forms and flavors and can include a variety of different features. Most organizations have at least one hardware firewall—a traditional firewall. This purpose-built device runs proprietary software to provide the firewall functions discussed in previous sections. Hardware-based firewalls are normally sold and differentiated based on throughput capacity as well as the number and type of physical ports available. For instance, a lower-end firewall might support only 100 Mbps of throughput, and a higher-end service provider–grade hardware firewall might support 300 Gbps throughput. The throughput depends on the memory and CPU as well as other proprietary hardware that makes up the device. On the other hand, a software-based firewall is a piece of software that can run on a specific platform to provide the firewall functions discussed previously. For instance, a software firewall may be able to run on a supported Linux distribution, utilizing whatever hardware that platform is installed on. Typically today, a hardware-based firewall is best for higher performance.

Layer 4/Layer 7

An appliance is essentially the same thing as a hardware-based firewall. It is purpose built to run a specific piece of software or firmware that provides firewall functions. All of the same assertions mentioned for software-based firewalls also apply to an appliance-based firewall.

Firewalls can be grouped into two main categories that exist at Layer 4 and Layer 7 of the OSI model. A *Layer 4 firewall* focuses on basic transport-level attributes such as IP addresses and port numbers, and a *Layer 7 firewall* provides more nuanced, content-based filtering. Host-based firewalls, often referred to as personal firewalls, are software applications that you can install on end-user machines or servers to protect them from external security threats and intrusions. The term *personal firewall* typically applies to basic software that can control Layer 3 and Layer 4 access to client machines. Most modern operating systems have host-based firewalls built in and enabled by default. It is important to implement an on-by-default firewall for your user devices as well as servers.

A virtual firewall is typically used in a virtual environment for the purpose of controlling access between virtual machines. It can also come in the form of a container that enables you to integrate into a containerized environment and control traffic within. Figure 11-7 illustrates a virtual firewall implementation.

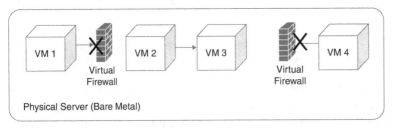

Figure 11-7   A Virtual Firewall Implementation

> **NOTE** We discuss various tools and technologies separately in this chapter so that you understand how to work with each of them. But you should keep in mind that many of these technologies are often consolidated into a single solution, and this trend will likely continue as we move forward.

Secure Communication/Access

Secure communication/access is not just a requirement but a necessity in safeguarding the integrity, availability, and confidentiality of information as it traverses the digital landscape. This section explores some of the innovative technologies and methodologies designed to reinforce secure channels of communication and access.

Virtual Private Network (VPN)

A *virtual private network (VPN)* is a connection between two or more computers or devices that are not on the same private network. Generally, VPNs use the Internet to connect one host to another. It is desirable for only proper users and data sessions to make their way to a VPN device, and so data encapsulation and encryption are used. A tunnel is created through any LANs and WANs that might intervene; this tunnel connects the two VPN devices to each other. Every time a new session is initiated, a new tunnel is created, which makes the connection secure.

Point-to-Point Tunneling Protocol (PPTP) and Layer 2 Tunneling Protocol (L2TP) are common VPN connections that can cause a lot of havoc if the security settings are not configured properly on the client side and server side.

Figure 11-8 shows a virtual private network. Note that the VPN server is on one side of the cloud, and the VPN client is on the other. The VPN client has a standard IP address to connect to its own LAN. However, it receives a second IP address from the VPN server or a DHCP device. This second IP address works "inside" the original IP address. So, the client computer has two IP addresses; in essence, the VPN address is encapsulated within the logical IP address. VPN adapters, regardless of the Internet connection used, can use MS-CHAP, as shown in Figure 11-8. To further increase the security of the authentication, you can use a separate RADIUS server with the VPN server.

Figure 11-8   A VPN

Figure 11-8 shows a single computer connecting to a VPN server at an office; this is a typical setup known as VPN remote access. However, organizations sometimes need to connect multiple offices to each other. This is done with a site-to-site configuration, where each site has a VPN device (SOHO router, concentrator, or server) that takes care of VPN connections for each network of computers. Site-to-site VPNs are generally more secure because you, as administrator, can specify that only specific networks can connect—and can do it in a private intranet fashion. If a company is growing, site-to-site is the way to go, whether the company is geographically expansive or is simply inhabiting separate spaces of the same building. When separate networks are connected in the same building, it is often wise to use a VPN because the physical wiring might pass through a public area.

In a Windows Server environment, you can set up remote access using one of three role services: Direct Access and VPN (RAS) Service, Routing Service, and Web Application Proxy Service. The Direct Access and VPN (RAS) Service offers traditional VPN and Direct Access options for remote connectivity. Microsoft recommends using Always On VPN for clients running Windows 10 or later. Routing Service enables network traffic routing between LAN subnets and supports various routing technologies. Web Application Proxy Service provides reverse proxy capabilities for internal web applications, allowing external access while pre-authenticating via Active Directory Federation Services (AD FS). These role services can be installed using the Add Roles and Features Wizard in Server Manager or specific Windows PowerShell commands.

You don't have to use a server for incoming VPN sessions. Several vendors offer hardware appliances. Larger organizations that need hundreds of simultaneous connections should opt for a VPN concentrator as their solution. A hardware appliance might be part of your unified threat management (UTM) solution.

Older VPNs use either PPTP (port 1723) or L2TP (port 1701) with IPsec. They can also incorporate CHAP on the client side and RADIUS servers for authentication. As discussed earlier in this chapter, newer VPNs protect traffic by using TLS.

For example, OpenVPN uses this type of encryption (see https://openvpn.net). TLS solutions for VPN improve on endpoint security and enable always-on VPN functionality so that a user can always have access via the VPN without the need to periodically disconnect and reconnect.

Watch out for split tunneling, which occurs when a client system (for example, a mobile device) can access a public network and LAN at the same time using one or more network connections. For example, a remote user might connect to the Internet through a hotel's Wi-Fi network. If the user needs to access resources on the company LAN, the VPN software takes control. But if the user needs to connect to websites on the Internet, the hotel's gateway provides those sessions. While this capability can enable conservation of bandwidth and increase efficiency, it can also bypass upper-layer security that is in place in the company infrastructure. Before allowing split tunneling, you should test it thoroughly. For example, you should simulate the split tunnel from a remote location and then perform vulnerability scans and capture packets. Then you can analyze the session in depth and log your findings. The converse of a split tunnel configuration would be a full tunnel. With a full tunnel configuration, all traffic is sent through the VPN tunnel back to the head end and out through the corporate network.

Remote Access

Remote access refers to the ability of an authorized user to connect to a network, a system, or an application from a location outside the organization's physical premises. Even more important than authenticating local users is authenticating remote users. The chances of illegitimate connections increase when you allow remote users to connect to your network. Examples of remote authentication technologies include RAS, VPN, TACACS+, and CHAP.

Remote Access Service (RAS) began as a service that enabled dial-up connections from remote clients. Today, more and more remote connections are made with high-speed Internet technologies such as cable Internet and fiber-optic connections. But you can't discount dial-up connections, which are still used in certain areas where other Internet connections are not available as well as in many network operation centers and server rooms that need fail-safes to take control of networking equipment.

One of the best things you can do to secure an RAS server is to deny access to individuals who don't require it. Even if a user or user group is set to "not configured," it is wise to specifically deny them access. You should allow access to only those users who need it and on a daily basis monitor the logs that list who connected. If there are any unknowns, you should investigate immediately. Also, be sure to update the permissions list often to account for remote users being terminated or otherwise leaving the organization.

Another important security precaution is to set up RAS authentication. One secure way is to use the Challenge-Handshake Authentication Protocol (CHAP), which is an authentication scheme used by the Point-to-Point Protocol (PPP), which is the standard for dial-up connections. CHAP uses a challenge-response mechanism with one-way encryption. Therefore, it is not capable of mutual authentication in the way that Kerberos is. Microsoft developed its own version of CHAP, known as MS-CHAP; an example is shown in Figure 11-9. The figure shows the Advanced Security Settings dialog box for a dial-up connection. In this particular configuration, notice that encryption is required and that the only protocol allowed is MS-CHAPv2. It's important to use Version 2 of MS-CHAP because it provides for mutual authentication between the client and the authenticator. Of course, the RAS server has to be configured to accept MS-CHAP connections as well. You also have the option to enable EAP for the dial-up connection. Other RAS authentication protocols include Shiva Password Authentication Protocol (SPAP), which is less secure, and Password Authentication Protocol (PAP), which sends usernames and passwords in plaintext—which is obviously insecure and should be avoided. Therefore, PAP should not be used in networks today.

NOTE   MS-CHAP uses the MD5 hashing algorithm, which is known to be insecure.

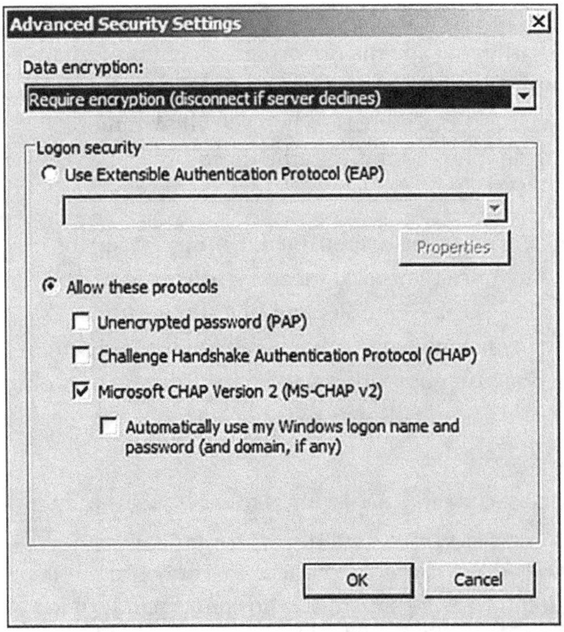

Figure 11-9   MS-CHAP Enabled on a Dial-up Connection

NOTE   You should use CHAP, MS-CHAP, or EAP for dial-up connections. Also, you should verify that the protocol you choose among these options is configured properly on the RAS server and dial-up client to ensure a proper handshake.

The CHAP authentication scheme consists of several steps. It authenticates a user or network host to entities such as Internet access providers. CHAP periodically verifies the identity of a client by using a three-way handshake. The verification is based on a shared secret. After the link has been established, the authenticator sends a challenge message to the peer. The encrypted results are compared, and the client is either authorized or denied access.

The actual data transmitted in these RAS connections is encrypted as well. By default, Microsoft RAS connections are encrypted by the RSA RC4 algorithm.

NOTE   You might wonder why dial-up connections are still relevant. Well, they are important for two reasons. First, the supporting protocols, authentication types, and encryption types are used in other technologies; dial-up is the basis for those systems. Second, as previously mentioned, some organizations still use dial-up connections for remote users or for administrative purposes. And hey, don't downplay dial-up connections. Old-school dial-up guys used to tweak connections to the point where they were as fast and reliable as some DSL versions. There may still be some dial-up die-hards out there as well. Plus, some areas of the United States and the rest of the world have no other option than dial-up.

However, RAS has morphed into something that goes beyond just dial-up. VPN connections that use dial-up, cable Internet, fiber, and so on are all considered remote access.

Terminal Access Controller Access Control System (TACACS) is another remote authentication protocol that was often used in UNIX networks. In UNIX, the TACACS service is known as the TACACS daemon. The newer and more commonly used implementation of TACACS is called Terminal Access Controller Access Control System Plus (TACACS+). It is not backward compatible with TACACS, however. TACACS+ and its predecessor, XTACACS, were developed by Cisco. TACACS+ uses inbound port 49, as its forerunners do; however, it uses TCP instead of UDP as the transport mechanism. The older TACACS and XTACACS technologies are not commonly seen anymore. The two common protocols for remote authentication used today are RADIUS and TACACS+. We will explore RADIUS in greater depth in Chapter 15, "Understanding the Security Implications of Proper Hardware, Software, and Data Asset Management."

Table 11-2 summarizes the local and remote authentication technologies covered thus far.

Table 11-2 Authentication Technologies

Authentication Type	Description
802.1X	An IEEE standard that defines port-based network access control (PNAC). 802.1X is a data link layer authentication technology used to connect devices to a LAN or WLAN. It defines EAP.
Kerberos	An authentication protocol designed at MIT that enables computers to prove their identity to each other in a secure manner. It is used most often in client/server environments; the client and server verify each other's identity.
CHAP	An authentication scheme used by Point-to-Point Protocol (PPP), which is the standard for dial-up connections. CHAP uses a challenge-response mechanism with one-way encryption. Derivatives include MS-CHAP and MS-CHAPv2.
RADIUS	A protocol used to provide centralized administration of dial-up, VPN, and wireless authentication. It can be used with EAP and 802.1X. It uses ports 1812 and 1813, or 1645 and 1646, over a UDP transport.
TACACS+	Remote authentication developed by Cisco, which is similar to RADIUS but separates authentication and authorization into two separate processes. It uses port 49 over a TCP transport.

Tunneling

Key Topic

Tunneling refers to creating a virtual and private pathway to transmit data across a network securely. Think of it as building a protected channel that encapsulates data to shield it from potential unauthorized access as it traverses from origin to destination. This encapsulation method provides a solid foundation for robust communication by crafting a secure connection over a publicly accessible network like the Internet. Using protocols such as Transport Layer Security (TLS) and Internet Protocol Security (IPsec) reinforces the integrity and confidentiality of data, making tunneling a cornerstone in the design and operation of safe network environments.

Transport Layer Security (TLS)

Transport Layer Security (TLS) is an encryption protocol for data transfers and is the modern successor to the SSL protocol that is now widely used for secure communication over the Internet. While the term SSL is still commonly used, it's important to note that all versions of SSL are now deprecated. TLS is the standard that has been adopted for secure communications, including VPNs.

One of the most popular features of a TLS VPN is the capability to launch a browser such as Google Chrome, Microsoft Edge, or Firefox and simply connect to the address of the VPN device, as opposed to running a separate VPN client program to establish an IPsec VPN connection. In most implementations, a clientless solution is possible. Users can access corporate intranet sites, portals, and email from almost anywhere. Even airport kiosks can establish clientless TLS VPN tunnels to access required resources.

One of the most popular features of a TLS-based VPN is its clientless nature, which we will discuss in greater depth in a moment. Users can launch a web browser, connect to the VPN device's address, and gain secure access to corporate resources. This eliminates the need for a separate VPN client program, making it a cost-effective and user-friendly solution. Because TLS operates over TCP port 443, which is commonly allowed through firewalls, opening additional ports is usually unnecessary.

The wide-ranging availability of TLS in remote-access VPN provides some appealing properties:

- **Secure communication using cryptographic algorithms:** HTTPS/TLS offers confidentiality, integrity, and authentication.

- **Ubiquity:** The ubiquity of TLS makes it possible for VPN users to remotely access corporate resources from anywhere, using any PC, without having to preinstall a remote-access VPN client.

- **Low management cost:** The clientless access makes this type of remote-access VPN free of deployment costs and free of maintenance problems at the end-user side. This is a huge benefit for IT management personnel, who would otherwise spend considerable resources to deploy and maintain their remote-access VPN solutions.

- **Effective operation with a firewall and NAT:** A TLS VPN operates on the same port as HTTPS (TCP/443). Most Internet firewalls, proxy servers, and NAT devices have been configured to correctly handle TCP/443 traffic. Consequently, there is no need for any special consideration to transport TLS VPN traffic over the networks. This has been viewed as a significant advantage over native IPsec VPNs, which operate over IP protocol 50 (ESP) or 51 (AH), which in many cases requires special configuration on the firewall or NAT devices to let traffic pass through.

As TLS VPN evolves to fulfill another important requirement of remote-access VPNs (namely, the requirement of supporting any application), some of these properties are no longer applicable, depending on which TLS VPN technology the VPN users choose. But overall, these properties have been the main drivers for the popularity of TLS VPNs in recent years and are heavily marketed by TLS VPN vendors as the main reasons for IPsec replacement.

NOTE   OpenVPN is an example of a TLS-based VPN open-source implementation. You can download and obtain detailed information about OpenVPN at https://openvpn.net.

Today's TLS VPN technology uses TLS for secure transport and employs a heterogeneous collection of remote-access technologies, such as reverse proxy, tunneling, and terminal services, to provide users with different types of access methods that fit different environments. Subsequent chapters examine some commonly used TLS VPN technologies, such as the following:

- Reverse proxy technology
- Port-forwarding technology and smart tunnels
- AnyConnect Secure Mobility Client (a TLS VPN tunnel client)
- Integrated terminal services

HTTPS provides secure web communication between a browser and a web server that supports the HTTPS protocol. TLS VPN extends this model to allow VPN users to access corporate internal web applications and other corporate application servers that might or might not support HTTPS—or even HTTP. TLS VPN does this by using several techniques that are collectively called reverse proxy technology.

A reverse proxy is a proxy server that resides in front of the application servers (normally web servers) and functions as an entry point for Internet users who want to access the corporate internal web application resources. To external clients, a reverse proxy server appears to be the true web server. Upon receiving the user's web request, a reverse proxy relays the user request to the internal web server to fetch the content on behalf of the user and then relays the web content to the user with or without presenting additional modifications to the data.

Many web server implementations support reverse proxy. One example is the mod_proxy module in Apache. With so many implementations, you might wonder why you need a TLS VPN solution to have this functionality. The answer is that TLS VPN offers much more functionality than traditional reverse proxy technologies:

- TLS VPN can transform complicated web and some non-web applications that simple reverse proxy servers cannot handle. The content transformation process is sometimes called webification. For example, TLS VPN solutions enable users to access Windows or Linux file systems. The TLS VPN gateway must be able to communicate with internal Windows or Linux servers and "webify" the file access in a web browser–presentable format for the VPN users.

- TLS VPN supports a wide range of business applications. For applications that cannot be webified, TLS VPN can use other resource access methods to support them. For users who demand ultimate access, TLS VPN provides network-layer access to directly connect a remote system to the corporate network, in the same manner as an IPsec VPN.

- TLS VPN provides a true remote-access VPN package, including user authentication, resource access privilege management, logging and accounting, endpoint security, and user experience.

The reverse proxy mode in TLS VPN is also known as clientless web access or just clientless access because it does not require any client-side applications to be installed on the client machine.

Internet Protocol Security (IPsec)

Internet Protocol Security (IPsec) is a suite of protocols that provides a secure means of transmitting data over an IP network through cryptographic security services. It operates at the network layer of the OSI model and is commonly used to establish secure VPN tunnels. IPsec uses the Internet Key Exchange (IKE) protocol to negotiate and establish secured site-to-site or remote-access VPN tunnels. IKE is a framework provided by the Internet Security Association and Key Management Protocol (ISAKMP) and parts of two other key management protocols: Oakley and Secure Key Exchange Mechanism (SKEME). IKE is defined in RFC 2409, and IKE Version 2 (IKEv2) is defined in RFC 5996.

IKE has two phases. Phase 1 is used to create a secure bidirectional communication channel between the IPsec peers. This channel is known as the ISAKMP security association (SA). Phase 2 is used to negotiate the IPsec SAs.

IKEv1 Phase 1

In IKEv1 Phase 1 negotiation, several attributes are exchanged:

- Encryption algorithms
- Hashing algorithms
- Diffie-Hellman groups
- Authentication method
- Vendor-specific attributes

The following typical encryption algorithms are used in IPsec:

- **Advanced Encryption Standard (AES):** 128 bits long
- **AES 192:** 192 bits long
- **AES 256:** 256 bits long

TIP   AES-GCM (supported only in IKEv2 implementations) stands for Advanced Encryption Standard (AES) in Galois/Counter Mode (GCM). AES-GCM is a block cipher that provides confidentiality and data-origin authentication; it is more secure than traditional AES. AES-GCM supports three different key strengths: 128-, 192-, and 256-bit keys. The longer the key length, the more secure the implementation; however, a longer key length increases the compute resources needed for its mathematical crypto calculations. GCM is a mode of AES that is required to support the National Security Agency (NSA) Suite B, which is a set of cryptographic algorithms that devices must support to meet federal standards for cryptographic strength. AES-GMAC (supported only in IKEv2 IPsec proposals), which stands for Advanced Encryption Standard Galois Message Authentication Code, is a block cipher mode that provides only data-origin authentication. It is a variant of AES-GCM that allows data authentication without encrypting the data. AES-GMAC also offers the three different key strengths provided by AES-GCM (128-, 192-, and 256-bit keys).

The hashing algorithms used in IPsec include the following:

- Secure Hash Algorithm (SHA-1)
- Message Digest Algorithm 5 (MD5)

TIP   Cisco has an excellent resource that provides an overview of all cryptographic algorithms. The same document outlines the algorithms that should be avoided and the ones that are recommended (at press time). You can access this document at https://tools.cisco.com/security/center/resources/next_generation_cryptography.

The common authentication methods are preshared keys (where peers use a shared secret to authenticate each other) and digital certificates with the use of public key infrastructure (PKI).

Small- and medium-sized organizations use preshared keys as their authentication mechanism. Many large organizations use digital certificates for scalability, centralized management, and additional security mechanisms.

You can establish a Phase 1 SA in main mode or aggressive mode. In main mode, the IPsec peers complete a six-packet exchange in three round trips to negotiate the ISAKMP SA, whereas aggressive mode completes the SA negotiation in three packet exchanges. Main mode provides identity protection if preshared keys are used. Aggressive mode offers identity protection only if digital certificates are employed.

NOTE   Cisco products that support IPsec typically use main mode for site-to-site tunnels and use aggressive mode for remote-access VPN tunnels. This is the default behavior when preshared keys are used as the authentication method.

Figure 11-10 illustrates the six-packet exchange in main mode negotiation.

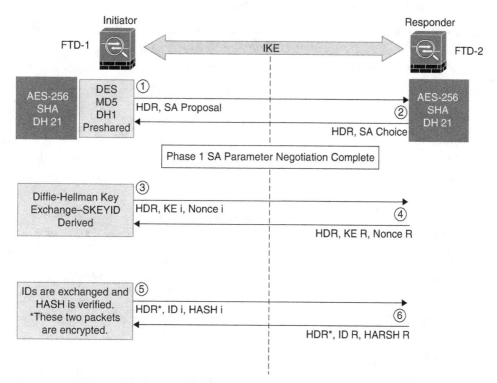

Figure 11-10   IPsec Phase 1 Main Mode Negotiation

In Figure 11-10, two firewall devices are configured to terminate a site-to-site VPN tunnel between them. The firewall labeled FTD-1 is the initiator, and FTD -2 is the responder. The following steps are illustrated in Figure 11-10:

Step 1.   FTD-1 (the initiator) has two ISAKMP proposals configured. In the first packet, FTD-1 sends its configured proposals to FTD-2.

Step 2. FTD-2 evaluates the received proposal. Because it has a proposal that matches the offer of the initiator, FTD-2 sends the accepted proposal back to FTD-1 in the second packet.

Step 3. The Diffie-Hellman exchange and calculation process is started. Diffie-Hellman is a key agreement protocol that enables two users or devices to authenticate each other's preshared keys without actually sending the keys over the unsecured medium. FTD-1 sends the key exchange payload and a randomly generated value called a nonce.

Step 4. FTD-2 receives the information and reverses the equation, using the proposed Diffie-Hellman group/exchange to generate the SKEYID. The SKEYID is a string derived from secret material that is known only to the active participants in the exchange.

Step 5. FTD-1 sends its identity information. The fifth packet is encrypted with the keying material derived from the SKEYID. The asterisk in Figure 11-10 indicates that this packet is encrypted.

Step 6. FTD-2 validates the identity of FTD-1, and FTD-2 sends its own identity information to FTD-1. This packet is also encrypted.

TIP IKE uses UDP port 500 for communication. UDP port 500 is used to send all the packets described in the previous steps.

For IKEv2, you can configure multiple groups. The system orders the settings from the most secure to the least secure and negotiates with the peer using that order. For IKEv1, you can select a single option only:

- **Diffie-Hellman Group 1:** 768-bit modulus. DH group 1 is considered insecure, so please do not use it.

- **Diffie-Hellman Group 2:** 1024-bit modulus. This option is no longer considered good protection.

- **Diffie-Hellman Group 5:** 1536-bit modulus. Formerly considered good protection for 128-bit keys, this option is no longer considered good protection.

- **Diffie-Hellman Group 14:** 2048-bit modulus. Considered good protection for 192-bit keys.

- **Diffie-Hellman Group 19:** 256-bit elliptic curve.

- **Diffie-Hellman Group 20:** 384-bit elliptic curve.

- **Diffie-Hellman Group 21:** 521-bit elliptic curve.

- **Diffie-Hellman Group 24:** 2048-bit modulus and 256-bit prime order subgroup. This option is no longer recommended.

IKEv1 Phase 2

IKEv1 Phase 2 is used to negotiate IPsec SAs. This phase is also known as *quick mode*. The ISAKMP SA protects the IPsec SAs because all payloads are encrypted except the ISAKMP header.

A single IPsec SA negotiation always creates two security associations—one inbound and one outbound. Each SA is assigned a unique security parameter index (SPI) value: one by the initiator and the other by the responder.

TIP   The security protocols AH and ESP are Layer 3 protocols and do not have Layer 4 port information. If an IPsec peer is behind a PAT device, the ESP or AH packets are typically dropped because there is no Layer 4 port to be used for translation. To work around this, many vendors, including Cisco Systems, use a feature called *IPsec passthrough*. The PAT device that is capable of IPsec passthrough builds the Layer 4 translation table by looking at the SPI values on the packets. Many industry vendors, including Cisco Systems, implement another feature called NAT Traversal (NAT-T). With NAT-T, the VPN peers dynamically discover whether an address translation device exists between them. If they detect a NAT/PAT device, they use UDP port 4500 to encapsulate the data packets, consequently allowing the NAT device to successfully translate and forward the packets. IKEv2 enhances the IPsec interoperability between vendors by offering built-in technologies such as Dead Peer Detection (DPD), NAT Traversal (NAT-T), and Initial Contact.

Another interesting point is that if the VPN router needs to connect multiple networks over the tunnel, it must negotiate twice as many IPsec SAs. Remember that each IPsec SA is unidirectional, so if three local subnets need to go over the VPN tunnel to talk to the remote network, six IPsec SAs are negotiated. IPsec can use quick mode to negotiate these multiple Phase 2 SAs, using the single preestablished ISAKMP (IKEv1 Phase 1) SA. The number of IPsec SAs can be reduced, however, if source and/or destination networks are summarized.

Many different IPsec attributes are negotiated in quick mode, as shown in Table 11-3.

Table 11-3   IPsec Attributes

Attribute	Possible Values
Encryption	None, AES-128, AES-192, AES-256. AES is recommended. The higher the key length of the AES implementation, the more secure it is.
Hashing	MD5, SHA-1, null (SHA-1 is recommended).
Identity information	Network, protocol, port number.
Lifetime	120–2,147,483,647 seconds.
	10–2,147,483,647 kilobytes.
Mode	Tunnel or transport.
Perfect Forward Secrecy (PFS) group	None, 1, 2, or 5.

In addition to generating the keying material, quick mode also negotiates identity information. The Phase 2 identity information specifies which network, protocol, and/or port number to encrypt. Hence, the identities can vary anywhere from an entire network to a single host address, allowing a specific protocol and port.

Figure 11-11 illustrates the Phase 2 negotiation between the two routers that just completed Phase 1.

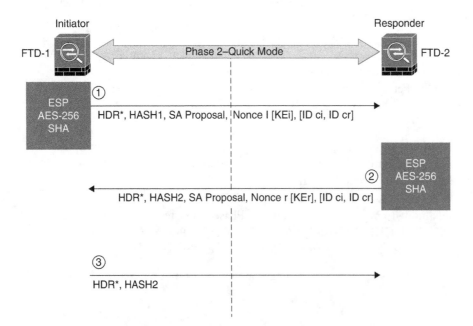

Figure 11-11   IPsec Phase 2 Negotiation

The following steps are illustrated in Figure 11-11:

Step 1. FTD-1 sends the identity information, IPsec SA proposal, nonce payload, and (optionally) the key exchange payload if Perfect Forward Secrecy (PFS) is used. PFS is used to provide additional Diffie-Hellman calculations.

Step 2. FTD-2 evaluates the received proposal against its configured proposal and sends the accepted proposal back to FTD-1, along with its identity information, nonce payload, and the optional key exchange payload.

Step 3. FTD-1 evaluates the FTD-2 proposal and sends a confirmation that the IPsec SAs have been successfully negotiated. This starts the data encryption process.

IPsec uses two different protocols to encapsulate the data over a VPN tunnel:

- **Encapsulation Security Payload (ESP):** IP Protocol 50
- **Authentication Header (AH):** IP Protocol 51

NOTE ESP is defined in RFC 4303, and AH is defined in RFC 4302.

IPsec can use two modes with either AH or ESP:

- **Transport mode:** Protects upper-layer protocols, such as UDP and TCP
- **Tunnel mode:** Protects the entire IP packet

Transport mode is used to encrypt and authenticate the data packets between the peers. A typical example is the use of GRE over an IPsec tunnel. Tunnel mode is used to encrypt and authenticate the IP packets when they are originated by the hosts connected behind the VPN device. Tunnel mode adds an additional IP header to the packet, as illustrated in Figure 11-12.

Figure 11-12 demonstrates the major difference between transport mode and tunnel mode. It includes an example of an IP packet encapsulated in GRE and the difference when it is encrypted in transport mode versus tunnel mode. As demonstrated in Figure 11-12, the overall size of the packet is larger in tunnel mode than in transport mode.

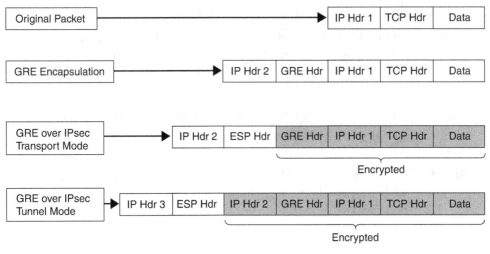

Figure 11-12   Transport Mode Versus Tunnel Mode in IPsec

IKEv2

IKE Version 2 (IKEv2), which is defined in RFC 5996, enhances the performance of dynamic key exchange and peer authentication. IKEv2 simplifies the key exchange flows and introduces measures to fix vulnerabilities that are present in IKEv1. Both IKEv1 and IKEv2 protocols operate in two phases. IKEv2 provides a simpler and more efficient exchange.

Phase 1 in IKEv2 is IKE_SA, consisting of the message pair IKE_SA_INIT. IKE_SA is comparable to IKEv1 Phase 1. The attributes of the IKE_SA phase are defined in the key exchange policy. Phase 2 in IKEv2 is CHILD_SA. The first CHILD_SA is the IKE_AUTH message pair. This phase is comparable to IKEv1 Phase 2. Additional CHILD_SA message pairs can be sent for rekey and informational messages. The CHILD_SA attributes are defined in the data policy.

The following differences exist between IKEv1 and IKEv2:

- IKEv1 Phase 1 has two possible exchanges: main mode and aggressive mode. There is a single exchange of a message pair for IKEv2 IKE_SA.

- IKEv2 has a simple exchange of two message pairs for the CHILD_SA. IKEv1 uses an exchange of at least three message pairs for Phase 2. In short, IKEv2 is designed to be more efficient than IKEv1, with fewer packets exchanged and less bandwidth needed.

- IKEv2 supports the use of next-generation encryption protocols and anti-DoS capabilities.

- Despite the fact that IKEv1 supports some of the authentication methods used in IKEv2, IKEv1 does not allow the use of EAP. EAP enables IKEv2 to provide a solution for remote-access VPN, as well.

TIP   IKEv1 and IKEv2 are incompatible protocols; consequently, you cannot configure an IKEv1 device to establish a VPN tunnel with an IKEv2 device.

Many technologies have been used for site-to-site VPN and have evolved through the years—from static traditional crypto maps to DMVPN, GETVPN, and FlexVPN.

Software-Defined Wide Area Network (SD-WAN)

Software-Defined Wide Area Network (SD-WAN) is a networking architecture that uses software-based controls to optimize and manage data traffic across a wide-area network (WAN). By leveraging software to decouple the control mechanism from the network hardware, SD-WAN enables more responsive and flexible network management.

We can draw an analogy between SD-WAN and a modern, intelligent traffic management system in a bustling city. In a traditional traffic system, fixed traffic lights and signs dictate traffic flow, leading to possible congestion and inefficiency. Traditional traffic can be likened to a conventional WAN, where rigid hardware and manual configuration constrain the network's adaptability. Conversely, SD-WAN acts as an intelligent traffic management system that dynamically adjusts traffic lights and reroutes vehicles based on real-time conditions, traffic flow, and other variables. The centralized control allows for the efficient redirection of traffic, minimizing congestion and optimizing the use of available roads.

This adaptability in SD-WAN translates into real-world advantages for network management. Automated control, increased visibility, and the ability to adapt to changing network conditions on the fly make SD-WAN an essential tool for modern businesses that rely on robust and responsive connectivity. Just as an intelligent traffic system leverages technology to improve transportation within the city, SD-WAN utilizes software to enhance and simplify the management of wide-area networks, ushering in a new era of network performance and reliability.

Secure Access Service Edge (SASE)

Secure access service edge (SASE) is a cloud-native architecture that combines network security functions with WAN capabilities to support organizations' dynamic, secure access needs. Essentially, SASE integrates network and security services into a single, unified platform, providing secure and seamless access to resources regardless of where users are located. It employs strategies like zero trust network architecture to offer granular control over network access, enhancing the overall security posture for data exchange and remote connectivity.

Selection of Effective Controls

In any organization or system, controls act as mechanisms to manage and mitigate risks, ensuring that objectives are achieved with minimal disruption. These controls can be technical, procedural, or managerial, and they play a vital role in safeguarding assets and maintaining integrity. Selecting effective controls is not a one-size-fits-all process; it requires an in-depth understanding of the particular environment, risks, regulations, and organizational goals.

Selecting effective controls begins with identifying and assessing the risks that must be managed. Selecting effective controls involves a comprehensive risk assessment, understanding the potential impact of those risks, and aligning them with organizational priorities. Once risks are identified and prioritized, appropriate controls can be selected to mitigate the risks to acceptable levels. The controls must be tailored to fit the specific scenario, balancing the need for security with the potential cost and operational impact.

The selection of controls is not a static process. Once implemented, controls must be regularly evaluated to ensure that they continue functioning as intended. Regular evaluation of controls involves monitoring their performance, reviewing their alignment with evolving risks, and making adjustments as necessary. Regular audits, reviews, and feedback mechanisms are critical to maintain the effectiveness of controls. The continuous monitoring of controls ensures that they remain suitable for the environment in which they are deployed and adapt to changes in technology, regulations, and business needs.

Chapter Review Activities

Use the features in this section to study and review the topics in this chapter.

Review Key Topics

Review the most important topics in the chapter, noted with the Key Topic icon in the outer margin of the page. Table 11-4 lists these key topics and the page number on which each is found.

Key Topic

Table 11-4 Key Topics for Chapter 11

Key Topic Element	Description	Page Number
Section	Active vs. Passive	229
Figure 11-1	An HTTP Proxy in Action	231
List	IDS and IPS descriptions and examples	233
Section	Load Balancer	234
Figure 11-3	Components of a Typical 802.1X Authentication Procedure	238
Figure 11-4	A Basic Firewall Implementation	240
List	Types of firewall methodologies beyond SPI and NAT	241
Figure 11-5	Back-to-Back Firewall (Screened Subnet) Configuration	242
Section	Unified Threat Management (UTM)	245
Figure 11-8	A VPN	250
Paragraph	Tunneling definition and example	254

Define Key Terms

Define the following key terms from this chapter and check your answers in the glossary:

device placement, security zones, attack surface, connectivity, fail-open, fail-closed, device attributes, active/active, active/passive, inline monitoring, tap (or monitor) mode, jump server, proxy server, intrusion detection system (IDS), intrusion prevention system (IPS), load balancing, sensor, port security, 802.1X, Extensible Authentication Protocol (EAP), web application firewall (WAF), unified threat management (UTM), next-generation firewall (NGFW), Layer 4 firewall, Layer 7 firewall, virtual private network (VPN), remote access, Transport Layer Security (TLS), Internet Protocol Security (IPsec), Software-Defined Wide Area Network (SD-WAN), secure access service edge (SASE), selecting effective controls

Review Questions

Answer the following review questions. Check your answers with the answer key in Appendix A.

1. Explain how device placement can significantly influence the security and functionality of a network and provide an example of placing a specific device for optimal security.

2. Discuss the considerations involved in deciding whether a system should fail open or fail closed and provide examples of when each might be appropriate

3. Describe how device attributes like inline versus tap/monitor configurations play a role in defining a security device's behavior and impact on network traffic.

4. Explain the difference between active/active and active/passive scenarios and discuss how each impacts failover or load balancing in a network.

5. Discuss the role and functions of various network appliances, such as jump servers, proxy servers, intrusion prevention systems (IPSs)/intrusion detection systems (IDSs), load balancers, and sensors.

6. Explain the significance of port security and how mechanisms like 802.1X and Extensible Authentication Protocol (EAP) facilitate secure authentication and streamline network access control.

7. Describe the concept of unified threat management (UTM) and how it relates to next-generation firewalls (NGFWs) in modern network security.

8. Discuss the functionality of a virtual private network (VPN), including how data encapsulation and encryption are used to create secure connections.

9. Explain the process of selecting effective controls, including identifying and assessing risks, understanding potential impacts, and tailoring controls to specific scenarios.

This chapter covers the following topics related to Objective 3.3 (Compare and contrast concepts and strategies to protect data) of the CompTIA Security+ SY0-701 certification exam:

- Data types
- Data classifications
- General data considerations
- Methods to secure data

CHAPTER 12

Comparing and Contrasting Concepts and Strategies to Protect Data

This chapter takes an in-depth look at data security and discusses various types of data, such as regulated, trade secret, and intellectual property, to underscore the need for understanding what is being protected. It covers the practice of classifying data based on sensitivity and impact, discusses the different states in which data exists, and addresses specialized concerns like data sovereignty and geolocation. This chapter also explores a range of methods for securing data, from encryption to permission settings, providing a comprehensive resource for enhancing data security in organizations.

"Do I Know This Already?" Quiz

The "Do I Know This Already?" quiz enables you to assess whether you should read this entire chapter thoroughly or jump to the "Chapter Review Activities" section. If you are in doubt about your answers to these questions or your own assessment of your knowledge of the topics, read the entire chapter. Table 12-1 lists the major headings in this chapter and their corresponding "Do I Know This Already?" quiz questions. You can find the answers in Appendix A, "Answers to the 'Do I Know This Already?' Quizzes and Review Questions."

Table 12-1 "Do I Know This Already?" Section-to-Question Mapping

Foundation Topics Section	Questions
Data Types	1
Data Classifications	2
General Data Considerations	3, 5, 6
Methods to Secure Data	4, 7–10

CAUTION   The goal of self-assessment is to gauge your mastery of the topics in this chapter. If you do not know the answer to a question or are only partially sure of the answer, you should mark that question as wrong for purposes of self-assessment. Giving yourself credit for an answer you correctly guess skews your self-assessment results and might provide you with a false sense of security.

1. Which data type is subject to laws and regulations due to its sensitivity?

    a. Trade secret

    b. Regulated data

    c. Intellectual property

    d. Legal information

2. What kind of data classification label would be applied to source code in a commercial setting?

    a. Sensitive

    b. Public

    c. Confidential or proprietary

    d. Restricted

3. What type of data is stored in databases, file systems, or storage media?

    a. Data in transit

    b. Data in use

    c. Data at rest

    d. Data sovereignty

4. What is the primary method of securing data that is moving from one location to another?

    a. Hashing

    b. Masking

    c. Emailing

    d. Transport Layer Security (TLS)

5. What type of data is being accessed, processed, or manipulated?

    a. Data at rest

    b. Data in use

    c. Data in transit

    d. Data sovereignty

6. What does GDPR regulate?

    a. How U.S.-based companies store data

    b. How European citizens' data is stored

    c. Countries in the Asia-Pacific (APAC) region

    d. Public data in the European Union

7. Which method replaces specific data within a database with fictitious but structurally similar data?

    a. Obfuscation

    b. Hashing

    c. Masking

    d. Tokenization

8. What does segmentation involve in terms of network management?

    a. Encrypting the entire network

    b. Dividing a network into various segments

    c. Assigning geographic restrictions

    d. Replacing data with tokens

9. You need to restrict access to certain folders on a company server that contain sensitive company data. What type of method could you use to secure the data?

    a. Hash the data

    b. Mark the file as a trade secret

    c. Permission restriction

    d. Mark the file as regulated

10. What best describes geotagging?

    a. Identifying real-world data transfer rates based on digital access

    b. Embedding geographic information into digital media

    c. Storing geographic data in a database

    d. Limiting access to data based on roles in an organization

Foundation Topics

Data Types

In data security, understanding the variety of data types is crucial for effective protection and compliance. I will take the poetic liberty of modifying a common phrase in business for our purposes here and say, "You can't protect what you don't understand." Different types of data have varying sensitivity levels and are subject to unique regulatory guidelines that you need to identify in your organization. Knowing these distinctions aids in implementing appropriate security measures:

Key Topic

- **Regulated data:** *Regulated data* is subject to laws and regulations, often due to its sensitivity. For instance, medical records are regulated by the Health Insurance Portability and Accountability Act (HIPAA) in the United States, which mandates strict controls over storage and transmission of such data.

- **Trade secret:** A *trade secret* is confidential information that gives a business a competitive advantage over others in the industry. A proprietary algorithm used for data analysis could be viewed as a trade secret, and its unauthorized disclosure could severely harm the business.

- **Intellectual property:** *Intellectual property (IP)* includes creative works, inventions, and designs protected by legal rights such as patents, copyrights, or trademarks. If a software engineer develops unique code for a company, that source code could be considered copyrighted, along with the software application.

- **Legal information:** Data directly related to legal processes or obligations falls in the *legal information* category. For example, signed contracts or employee agreements are legal documents that require specific handling and storage procedures.

- **Financial information:** Financial information includes all data on an organization's financial operations and performance, such as balance sheets, income statements, cash flow reports, tax records, and transaction histories. In many jurisdictions, financial information is subject to stringent regulations such as the Sarbanes-Oxley Act (SOX) in the United States, which mandates strict controls over the integrity and confidentiality of financial data. The Gramm-Leach-Bliley Act (GLBA) requires financial institutions to explain their information-sharing practices to their customers and to safeguard sensitive data. Compliance with the Payment Card Industry Data Security Standard (PCI DSS) is also essential for organizations that handle credit card transactions. Unauthorized access to or disclosure of financial information can lead to legal repercussions and severely damage an organization's reputation and stakeholder trust.

- **Human- and non-human-readable data:** *Human-readable data* is easily understood without the help of a machine (for example, a text document or a book). *Non-human-readable data*, on the other hand, can be understood only with the help of specific software or hardware (for example, machine code or encrypted files).

Data Classifications

Data classification is the practice of categorizing data into various types based on its sensitivity level, accessibility requirements, and the impact that *unauthorized access* could have on an organization or individuals. Proper classification aids in effective data management and application of security controls, ensuring that each data type is treated appropriately based on its importance and risk profile.

To protect an asset, an organization first needs to understand how important that asset is. For example, the unauthorized disclosure of the source code of a product might have a greater impact on an organization than the disclosure of a public configuration guide. The first step in implementing an access control process is to classify assets or data based on the potential damage a breach to the confidentiality, integrity, or availability of that asset or data could cause.

The commercial sector has some variety in the way data classification is done. Here are some commonly used classification labels in the commercial sector:

- **Confidential or proprietary:** Unauthorized access to confidential or proprietary information could cause grave damage to an organization. Examples of information or assets that could receive this type of classification include source code and trade secrets.

- **Sensitive:** Unauthorized access to *sensitive data* could cause some damage to an organization. Examples of information or assets that could receive this type of classification are internal team email and financial information.

- **Public:** *Public data* is openly available information that can be freely accessed without causing harm or presenting risks if exposed. It doesn't require the same level of stringent security controls as sensitive or restricted data. For example, a government agency's public press releases are categorized as public data. These documents are intended for widespread distribution, and unauthorized access to or dissemination of this information would not result in any significant negative impact.

■ **Restricted:** *Restricted data* requires the highest level of security measures to protect its integrity, confidentiality, and availability. Due to its sensitive nature or its stringent legal obligations, restricted data demands specific controls to mitigate the risk of unauthorized access and consequent financial, legal, or reputational harm. For instance, medical professionals and select administrative staff are often the only individuals permitted to access patient medical records in a hospital setting. Encrypting these records adds an extra layer of security, and unauthorized disclosure could result in legal consequences and violate patient privacy. Therefore, restricted data typically undergoes encryption and is accessible only to a select group of authorized individuals within an organization.

■ **Private:** Unauthorized access to *private data* could cause severe damage to an organization. Examples of information or assets that could receive this type of classification are human resource information (for example, employee salaries) and medical records.

■ **Critical:** *Critical data* is essential to the continued function of a business. Loss of this type of data would result in significant monetary loss for an organization.

Classification schema will differ from one company to another, but it is important that all departments within a company use the same schema consistently. For each label, there should be a clear definition identifying when that label should be applied and what damage would be caused by unauthorized access. Because the classification of data may also be related to specific times or other contextual factors, the asset-classification process should include information on how to change data classification.

General Data Considerations

General data considerations encompass the broader aspects of data management and security that apply across different types of data and classifications. Data considerations often include but are not limited to data states, handling procedures, and security measures. Grasping these fundamental aspects ensures that an organization can effectively protect its data assets.

Data States

Understanding the different states in which data can exist—specifically, data at rest, data in transit, and data in use—is crucial for implementing appropriate security measures. For instance, the strategies for protecting a company's archived employee records, considered data at rest, will differ significantly from the strategies for securing an email containing sensitive project information, characterized as data in transit. Figure 12-1 illustrates a basic multi-location network that includes common network components such as computers, printers, a data storage network, and routers that link to the Internet. Let's take a look at each data state in Figure 12-1 and review some examples of each of them.

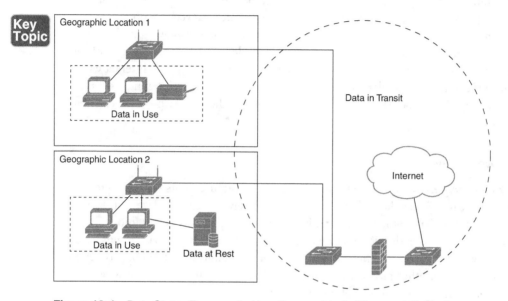

Figure 12-1 Data States Represented in a Geographically Dispersed Network

Data at Rest

Data at rest isn't merely idle; it's information stored in databases, file systems, or storage media. USB thumb drive on your desk? Data at rest. External hard drive used to back up files? Data at rest. An organization's archived financial reports stored on a secure server? Also data at rest. While data at rest is not actively being used, it still requires security measures such as strong encryption algorithms to mitigate risks like unauthorized access or data theft. Figure 12-1 shows that data at rest may reside on a storage server in an office or in a cloud instance.

Data in Transit

Data in transit refers to data moving from one location to another, such as across the Internet or private networks. When an employee sends an email containing confidential client details to another department, that email is considered data in transit. During this active movement, the data is vulnerable to unauthorized interception. Therefore, securing it with methods like Transport Layer Security (TLS) is vital.

Figure 12-1 shows that data in transit covers all the connectivity between geographic locations and even includes the movement of data in each geographic location.

Data in Use

When data is being accessed, processed, or manipulated, it is classified as *data in use*. Suppose a healthcare provider views a patient's medical records on their system. The data is susceptible to real-time threats like unauthorized viewing in this state. Effective countermeasures in this case might include role-based access controls or real-time monitoring to ensure that only authorized individuals can interact with the data. Figure 12-1 shows data in use at all user terminals and peripheral devices such as printers. Remember that data must be in transit to the printer before it can be used by the printer.

Data Sovereignty

Data sovereignty refers to the legal and regulatory requirements that apply to data based on where it is collected or processed. These laws often mandate that data must remain within that country's borders. For example, in the European Union (EU), the General Data Protection Regulation (GDPR) stipulates that companies must store European citizens' data within EU borders unless an equivalent level of protection is guaranteed in another jurisdiction. Noncompliance with these regulations can result in severe penalties, including substantial fines.

Geolocation

Geolocation is the process of identifying or estimating the real-world geographic location of an object or a person based on digital information, such as GPS coordinates. This concept extends beyond the conventional Global Positioning System (GPS) to include other technologies and methods, such as GPS tagging, geofencing, and IP-based location services.

The deployment of geolocation services should be approached with caution, given the trade-offs between utility and security vulnerabilities. Particularly in work settings, where many employees use personal mobile devices—commonly referred to as bring your own device (BYOD) settings—geolocation raises multiple security concerns.

Disabling geolocation features, including GPS, whenever possible is advisable for privacy and security. For example, geotagging is a form of geolocation that involves embedding geographic identification information, such as latitude and longitude coordinates, into various digital media, like photographs, websites, or SMS messages. While popular in social media, geotagging could inadvertently reveal the location of high-profile executives or other key organizational members, making them targets for attacks.

Methods to Secure Data

The landscape of cybersecurity demands a multifaceted approach to safeguard data. The various methods often intersect and overlap, complementing one another to create a robust, multilayered security posture. These methods are essential components of a modern cybersecurity framework, from advanced encryption to geographic-based restrictions. Their proper understanding and implementation are pivotal for contemporary data protection. Let's explore some of the key methods of securing data.

Key Topic
Geographic Restrictions

Geographic restrictions limit access to data based on a user's geographic location. These restrictions serve multiple purposes, such as complying with local laws, reducing the risk of cyberattacks, and protecting sensitive information. For instance, a U.S.-based financial institution may block access to its servers from countries where it doesn't operate to minimize the risk of international cyberattacks. As another example, streaming services often use geographic restrictions to comply with licensing agreements to ensure that content is available only in specific regions. Government agencies also employ geographic restrictions to safeguard sensitive data. For example, they may restrict access to servers containing classified information to IP addresses originating within the country, ensuring that the data remains secure and within national borders. In healthcare, geographic restrictions can be used to comply with regulations like HIPAA in the United States, which may require that medical data be stored and accessed only within the country.

Encryption

Encryption is the process of transforming readable data into an encoded format that can be reverted to readable form only with a decryption key. If an unauthorized user intercepts an encrypted email, they would be unable to understand its contents without the correct decryption key, ensuring that sensitive information remains secure during transmission. See Chapter 9 for a deeper dive into encryption.

Hashing

Hashing is the process of converting data into a fixed-length string of characters and is commonly used for verifying data integrity. In the context of password storage, hashing algorithms produce hash values that are saved instead of the actual passwords. When a user attempts to log in, the system compares the hash value of the entered password against the stored hash, safeguarding the original password from direct exposure.

Hashing protects the integrity of a file or other data by showing if something was altered from its original state. For example, let's use the beloved "Hello, World!" as an example.

Suppose you have a document containing the text "Hello, World!" and you want to ensure its integrity. You could use the SHA-256 hashing algorithm to generate a hash value for this document. The hash might look something like this:

A591A6D40BF420404A011733CFB7B190D62C65BF
0BCDA32B57B277D9AD9F146E

If even a single character in the document changes, the hash will change dramatically. For example, changing the text to "hello, World!" (note the lowercase *h*) might produce a hash like this:

8E1EDB6A0F0E422D5D4C634F28EBCACEA08A7F2A8CB8E757B-
5D7A48E46B57E2A

As you can see, even a small change results in a completely different hash, which allows you to quickly verify the document's integrity.

Going back to our password hashing discussion, let's see what that would look like in a hash. Let's say a user chooses the password Secure123. Instead of storing this password in plaintext, the system would store the hash of the password. Using SHA-256, the hash might look like this:

D2D2D2D2D2D2D2D2D2D2D2D2D2D2D2D2D2D2D2D2D2D2D2D2D2D2D2
D2D2D2D2D2

Now, to add an extra layer of security, you decide to salt the hash. (We explored salting in Chapter 4, and here you can see its application in a password hash.) You generate a random salt, say abc123, and append it to the password before hashing:

Password: Secure123 Salt: abc123 Combined: Secure123abc123

The new hash might look like this:

3C218FC9B3759285BC4F0F8424A82A5F002312C240A1A0A4650E7E9D4665
205B

Even if another user has the same password, the salt ensures that the stored hash values will be different.

Masking

Data masking involves replacing specific data in a database with fictitious but structurally similar data. For instance, the last four digits of a Social Security number might be visible, with asterisks replacing the rest. Data masking is commonly used in customer service scenarios where personnel need limited access to customer data.

Tokenization

Tokenization is a strong method for protecting sensitive information like financial data or personal identifiers. Rather than storing your credit card number, a tokenization system replaces it with a placeholder, or "decoy" value, such as ABCD-EFGH-IJKL-MNOP. This decoy, called a *token*, is devoid of meaningful information when viewed independently, significantly reducing the risk if a data breach occurs. When a future transaction needs to be processed, this token is then securely converted back to the original credit card number through a separate, secure system, ensuring the confidentiality and integrity of the original data.

The original credit card number and its corresponding token are mapped in a secure, isolated database in a tokenization system. This mapping is done through a tokenization service, ensuring that only authorized systems or entities can convert the token to its original value. When a transaction is initiated, the system calls upon this secure tokenization service to retrieve the original credit card number associated with the token. This service is isolated and heavily protected, significantly reducing the risk that the original data will be compromised.

Obfuscation

Obfuscation involves making data unintelligible and harder to understand without affecting its functionality. Source code obfuscation, for example, transforms the original programming code into a version that's difficult to reverse engineer, providing an additional layer of security against unauthorized tampering. If you could see the source code, you likely would not be able to read the plaintext version but would encounter jumbled text instead.

Segmentation

Segmentation involves dividing a network into various segments to isolate data or resources. This can be particularly effective in a corporate setting, where sensitive HR records are kept on a separate network segment from the general office network, limiting cross-segment data access and reducing the risk of internal breaches.

The following are some common departmental segmentations you might encounter in a corporate setting:

- **Finance:** The finance segment of the network is a highly secure area of the network designed to protect sensitive financial information, including payroll data, budget spreadsheets, tax records, and financial statements. Access to this segment is usually restricted to authorized finance and accounting personnel. Security measures may include multifactor authentication, encrypted data transmission, and rigorous audit trails to monitor who has accessed what data and when.

- **Firewall:** Public-facing servers are placed in the firewall segment, also known as a screened subnet. The firewall segment acts as a buffer zone between the external network (the Internet) and the internal network. It's designed to provide an additional layer of security and reduce the risk of external attacks reaching the internal network. Security appliances like intrusion detection systems (IDSs) and intrusion prevention systems (IPSs) are commonly deployed here to monitor and control incoming and outgoing traffic.

- **Engineering:** The engineering segment is typically isolated to ensure that the development and testing environments are secure and stable. This segment may contain code repositories, development servers, and other technical resources that are crucial for product development. Access is generally restricted to engineers, developers, and QA testers. Security protocols might include version control systems to track changes to code and virtual LANs (VLANs) to isolate development from testing environments further.

- **Sales:** The sales segment typically contains customer relationship management (CRM) systems, sales records, and other customer-related data. This segment is crucial for the sales team to manage leads, track customer interactions, and finalize sales. Given the sensitive nature of customer data, this segment often employs strict access controls, data encryption, and periodic security audits to ensure compliance with data protection regulations.

Permission Restrictions

Permission restrictions specify who can do what within a system or network. For instance, in a hospital setting, doctors may have full access to patient records, while administrative staff might only have permission to view contact details. Permission restrictions limit the potential for unauthorized access or modification of sensitive data.

You might see some variation in how permission restrictions are implemented in different environments. You might see role-based access control (RBAC) used in one case and attribute-based access control (ABAC) used in another. With RBAC, access permissions are assigned to specific organizational roles rather than to individual users. For instance, in a hospital setting, doctors might have different access permissions than nurses or administrative staff. A doctor might be able to access and modify patient medical records, whereas a nurse might only have read access to these records. With ABAC, access is granted based on additional attributes such as location, time, and even the type of device being used. For instance, a remote employee may only be able to access certain sensitive files if they connect from a company-issued laptop during regular working hours.

You can also include least privilege as a way to restrict permissions to systems. We explored least privilege in Chapter 9, "Understanding the Purpose of Mitigation Techniques Used to Secure the Enterprise," and will dig even deeper into it in Chapter 19, "Implementing and Maintaining Identity and Access Management."

Chapter Review Activities

Use the features in this section to study and review the topics in this chapter.

Review Key Topics

Review the most important topics in the chapter, noted with the Key Topic icon in the outer margin of the page. Table 12-2 lists these key topics and the page number on which each is found.

Table 12-2 Key Topics for Chapter 12

Key Topic Element	Description	Page Number
List	Data types commonly used for effective data protection and compliance	274
List	Data classifications used to categorize data	275
Figure 12-1	Data States Represented in a Geographically Dispersed Network	277
Section	Data at Rest	277
Section	Data in Transit	277
Section	Data in Use	278
Section	Geographic Restrictions	279
Paragraph	Hashing example of a "Hello, World!" file and a password hash	280

Define Key Terms

Define the following key terms from this chapter and check your answers in the glossary:

regulated data, trade secret, intellectual property (IP), legal information, human-readable data, non-human-readable data, data classification, unauthorized access, sensitive data, public data, restricted data, private data, critical data, data at rest, data in transit, data in use, data sovereignty, geolocation, geographic restriction, encryption, hashing, data masking, tokenization, obfuscation, segmentation, permission restrictions

Review Questions

Answer the following review questions. Check your answers with the answer key in Appendix A.

1. What is the key distinction between regulated data and intellectual property in terms of data types?

2. What is the first step an organization should take to protect an asset, according to the data classification process?

3. How does data in transit differ from data at rest?

4. What does the GDPR mandate about data storage for European citizens?

5. What are some of the security concerns that arise from geolocation in a BYOD setting?

6. How does hashing protect stored passwords?

7. What is the primary purpose of data masking?

8. How does tokenization protect sensitive information like financial data?

9. What is the main objective of segmentation in a corporate setting?

10. How do role-based access control and attribute-based access control differ in terms of implementation of permission restrictions?

This chapter covers the following topics related to Objective 3.4 (Explain the importance of resilience and recovery in security architecture) of the CompTIA Security+ SY0-701 certification exam:

- High availability
- Site considerations
- Platform diversity
- Multi-cloud systems
- Continuity of operations
- Capacity planning
- Testing
- Backups
- Power

Understanding the Importance of Resilience and Recovery in Security Architecture

This chapter delves into the critical aspects of ensuring organizational resilience against a variety of challenges, including system failures and security incidents. It covers the fundamentals of continuity of operations planning (COOP), with a focus on high availability, capacity planning, and incident response planning. It also explores methods for testing the efficacy of these plans, such as with tabletop exercises, simulations, and failover tests. The chapter provides insights into parallel processing as a technique for validating system reliability and extensively covers backup strategies, detailing their benefits and drawbacks. In addition, it discusses the importance of power management in maintaining high availability, including the roles of uninterruptible power supplies (UPSs) and generators in emergency scenarios.

"Do I Know This Already?" Quiz

The "Do I Know This Already?" quiz enables you to assess whether you should read this entire chapter thoroughly or jump to the "Chapter Review Activities" section. If you are in doubt about your answers to these questions or your own assessment of your knowledge of the topics, read the entire chapter. Table 13-1 lists the major headings in this chapter and their corresponding "Do I Know This Already?" quiz questions. You can find the answers in Appendix A, "Answers to the 'Do I Know This Already?' Quizzes and Review Questions."

Table 13-1 "Do I Know This Already?" Section-to-Question Mapping

Foundation Topics Section	Questions
High Availability	9
Site Considerations	5, 6
Platform Diversity	10

Foundation Topics Section	Questions
Mutli-Cloud System	1
Continuity of Operations	2
Capacity Planning	3
Testing	4
Backups	7
Power	8

CAUTION   The goal of self-assessment is to gauge your mastery of the topics in this chapter. If you do not know the answer to a question or are only partially sure of the answer, you should mark that question as wrong for purposes of self-assessment. Giving yourself credit for an answer you correctly guess skews your self-assessment results and might provide you with a false sense of security.

1. What is a key benefit of using a multi-cloud system?

    a. Lower costs

    b. Faster data retrieval

    c. Reduced dependency on a single cloud service provider

    d. Easier management

2. What does COOP address?

    a. Natural disasters only

    b. Cybersecurity attacks only

    c. An all-hazards approach to emergencies

    d. Only alternate facility setup

3. What is the focus of technology in capacity planning?

    a. People and staffing only

    b. Computational power, software, and hardware

    c. Infrastructure planning only

    d. Future cloud storage needs

4. What do tabletop exercises aim to validate and improve?

    a. Incident response plan

    b. Software code quality

    c. Infrastructure resilience

    d. Staffing efficiency

5. Which type of redundant site is a near duplicate of the original site and can be up and running within minutes?

    a. Hot site

    b. Warm site

    c. Cold site

    d. Tape-based backup site

6. What type of redundant site do organizations commonly choose because it offers a balance between configuration and cost?

    a. Hot site

    b. Warm site

    c. Cold site

    d. Tabletop exercise

7. What does an onsite backup strategy offer as a benefit?

    a. Protection against local disasters

    b. Fast access to backups for quick recovery

    c. Encryption

    d. Real-time data availability

8. What is the purpose of an uninterruptible power supply (UPS)?

    a. To provide a permanent solution for power failures

    b. To convert mechanical energy into electrical energy

    c. To provide near-instantaneous protection from input power interruptions

    d. To replace the main power source

9. What is the primary difference between load balancing and clustering in the context of high availability?

    a. Load balancing distributes traffic, whereas clustering combines multiple servers into one.

    b. Load balancing is for planned outages, whereas clustering is for unplanned outages.

     c. Load balancing is used in cloud computing, whereas clustering is used in on-premises environments.

     d. Load balancing enhances system availability, whereas clustering focuses on business continuity.

10. What is the primary reason for implementing platform diversity in an organization's IT environment?

     a. To reduce costs by using multiple vendors

     b. To reduce systemic risks associated with a single point of failure

     c. To improve performance by using specialized hardware and software from only a single vendor

     d. To simplify management by using a variety of platforms

Foundation Topics

High Availability

High availability (HA) is a design approach that ensures that a system or an application remains accessible and operational over an extended period. This uptime is often quantified as a percentage, such as "five nines" (99.999%) availability. HA is crucial for organizations as it is the first layer of resilience against planned and unplanned outages. To set up an HA system, you must first understand the components required. Let's review some of the key components of an HA system.

Key Components

The key components of HA are as follows:

Key Topic

- **Redundant hardware:** HA uses multiple instances of critical hardware components like servers, switches, and routers to eliminate single points of failure.

- **Automated backups:** Regularly scheduled backups are automated to ensure that the most recent data is always available for recovery.

- **Failover mechanisms:** A system or network is configured to switch to a standby system or network automatically if the primary one fails, ensuring uninterrupted service.

Cloud Environments

In cloud computing, the level of HA is often determined by the storage class selected and the associated costs. Cloud vendors offer various storage classes with different availability and durability metrics. The choice should be based on a thorough risk analysis during the integration process. As discussed earlier, the decision is based on the risk tolerance and what needs to be protected. For mission-critical applications supported by back-end databases, opting for greater storage availability is usually advised.

Load balancing involves distributing incoming network or application traffic across multiple servers, which enhances the availability and reliability of applications. You have likely encountered load balancing in your daily life without realizing what was happening behind the scenes. Here are a few ways you might encounter load balancing:

- **E-commerce websites:** During high-traffic events like Black Friday, e-commerce platforms use load balancers to distribute incoming user requests across multiple servers. This ensures that no single server is overwhelmed and provides a smooth shopping experience for users.

- **Streaming services:** Companies like Netflix use load balancing to distribute streaming requests among a pool of servers. This ensures that high numbers of simultaneous viewers can watch content without experiencing lags or downtime.

- **Financial institutions:** Banks often employ load balancers to manage the high volume of transactions, especially during peak business hours, to ensure that customer requests for account balances, transfers, and other services are processed efficiently.

Clustering involves connecting multiple servers to function as a single system. The use of clustering might not be as obvious as the use of load balancing, but you might be able to guess how this approach could impact your daily life. Here are some ways you might see clustering in action:

- **Database systems:** In industries that require high data availability, such as healthcare, database clusters are used. If one database server fails, another can take over. This can be implemented, for example, to ensure that patient records are always accessible.

- **High-performance computing (HPC):** Research institutions and meteorological departments often use clusters to perform complex calculations. The workload is distributed across multiple computers to speed up computational tasks.

- **Telecommunications:** Telecom companies use clustering for their billing systems, customer databases, and service applications to ensure high availability and fault tolerance. If one node in a cluster fails, the other nodes can continue to handle calls and data traffic without interruption.

While load balancing and clustering aim for optimum resource utilization, they serve different aspects of resilience and recovery. Load balancing efficiently allocates tasks to avoid server overload, enhancing system availability. Clustering contributes to recovery by allowing for seamless failover, ensuring that services continue running even if one cluster server fails.

Site Considerations

In the confidentiality, integrity, and availability (CIA) triad, redundant sites fall into the category *availability*. In the case of a disaster, a redundant site can act as a safe haven for data and users. Redundant sites are sort of a gray area between redundancy and a disaster recovery method. If you have a redundant site and need to use it, a disaster of some sort has probably occurred. The better the redundant site, the less time the organization loses, and the less it seems like a disaster and more like a failure that you have prepared for. Of course, the outcome depends on the type of redundant site your organization decides on.

Regarding the types of redundant sites, I like to refer to the story of Goldilocks and the three bears. One bowl of porridge was too hot, one was too cold, and one was just right. Whereas all the bowls of porridge were in the same house, one type of recovery site doesn't live in the same forest as the primary site. Most organizations opt for a warm redundant site as opposed to a hot, cold, or geographically distant site. Let's look at the various options now:

Key Topic

- **Hot site:** A *hot site* is a near duplicate of the organization's original site that can be up and running within minutes (or maybe a little longer). Computers and phones are installed and ready to go, a simulated version of the server room stands ready, and the vast majority of the data is replicated to the site on a regular basis in the event that the original site is not accessible to users for some reason. Hot sites are used by companies that would face financial ruin if a disaster made their main site inaccessible for a few days or even a few hours. This is the only type of redundant site that can facilitate a full recovery.

- **Warm site:** A *warm site* has computers, phones, and servers, but they might require some configuration before users can start working on them. A warm site might also need to have backups of data restored, and the backups are likely to be several days old. Organizations most often choose this type of site because it has a good amount of configuration yet is less expensive than a hot site.

- **Cold site:** A *cold site* has tables, chairs, bathrooms, and possibly some technical setup, such as basic phone, data, and electric lines. Otherwise, a lot of computer configuration and data restoration is necessary before the site can be properly utilized. This type of site is used only if a company can handle the stress of being nonproductive for a week or more.

- **Geographically distant site:** A company may use *geographic dispersion* for compute resources, which involves setting up a computing environment, such as a data center or resource center, in another location at least 50 miles away from the main compute campus data center. We live in a connected world, with employees, contractors, servers, data, and connected resources dispersed throughout the world. This dispersal is essential for a company with a global presence, and it also contributes to resilience. Local issues are likely to be isolated, allowing the rest of the workforce to continue operating as normal. Companies that have workforces dispersed in remote locations throughout the world have adopted and learned to utilize technology to connect people and resources. To implement geographic dispersal within your company for compute resources, you can set up a computing environment, such as a data center or resource center, in another location at least 50 miles away from the main compute campus data center. You should also consider placing resources closer to groups of users who might be in another city or country. By way of a wide-area network, you can configure resources that are local to the users to respond first, thereby providing resilience and resource dispersal.

Although they are redundant, these types of sites are generally known as backup sites because if they are required, a disaster has probably occurred. A good network security administrator tries to plan for and rely on redundancy and fault tolerance as much as possible before having to resort to disaster recovery methods.

Platform Diversity

Platform diversity refers to implementation of different hardware or software platforms within an organization's IT environment. The rationale behind this approach is to reduce systemic risks resulting from having a single point of failure. For example, if an organization relies solely on one vendor's product and that product becomes compromised, the entire organization can be at risk.

By diversifying platforms, an organization increases its resilience and enhances its ability to recover from security incidents and technical failures.

Multi-Cloud System

A *multi-cloud system* involves multiple cloud service platforms, such as AWS, Azure, and Google Cloud, which fulfill different computational and storage needs. This arrangement reduces dependency on a single cloud service provider, mitigating the risks associated with downtime or security issues tied to a single vendor. In the event of an outage or compromise in one cloud service, the operations can continue on another, ensuring high availability and robust disaster recovery options.

You might be noticing by now that a major principle of resilience is giving yourself options, such as options to default to another server, site, or cloud provider. Let's dive deeper into what happens when multiple problems occur at once.

Continuity of Operations

Continuity of operations planning (COOP) is a federal initiative to encourage people and departments to plan to address how critical operations will continue under a broad range of circumstances. COOP is important as a good business practice and because it leads to recovery and survival in and after emergency situations. A continuity of operations plan addresses emergencies from an all-hazards approach. A continuity of operations plan establishes policy and guidance, ensuring that critical functions continue and that personnel and resources are relocated to an alternate facility in the event of an emergency. Such a plan should develop procedures for the following:

- Alerting, activating, notifying, and deploying employees

- Identifying critical business functions

- Establishing an alternate facility or work-from-home process

- Creating a roster of personnel with authority and knowledge of business operational functions

Creating a continuity of business operations plan is a guided process and a team effort that draws on the team's understanding of department operations and emergency management's expertise in preparing for contingencies.

A continuity of operations plan could be activated in response to a wide range of events or situations—from a fire in a building to a natural disaster to the threat or occurrence of a terrorist attack. Any event that makes it impossible for employees to work in their regular facility could result in the activation of the continuity of operations plan.

NOTE   Continuity planning is simply the good business practice of ensuring the execution of essential functions and a fundamental duty of public and private entities that are responsible to their stakeholders.

Capacity Planning

Capacity planning involves determining the resources—people, technology, and infrastructure—that an organization will require in the future. By anticipating these needs, the organization can make informed decisions to ensure optimal performance and availability of people, technology, and infrastructure.

In capacity planning, *people* refers to the staffing requirements needed to maintain and operate systems efficiently. Insufficient staffing or lack of specialized skills can be bottlenecks that compromise an organization's resilience and ability to recover from incidents. Effective capacity planning assesses the number of employees needed and the skill sets required to sustain operations and manage contingencies.

Technology capacity planning involves evaluating the computational power, software, and hardware needed to meet future organizational demands. It entails meticulously analyzing technology usage patterns and forecasting future needs based on business growth, seasonal fluctuations, and other variables. Strategic technology capacity planning ensures that an organization is neither overprovisioned, which would result in unnecessary costs, nor underprovisioned, which could lead to performance issues and potential downtime.

Infrastructure refers to physical or virtual resources that support the technology and people within an organization. This includes everything from server racks to network cables, cloud storage solutions, and data centers. Effective infrastructure planning is critical for ensuring that an organization can scale its operations smoothly and maintain high levels of availability and resilience.

Testing

Testing is critical to validating an organization's resilience and recovery strategies within its security architecture. The objective is to evaluate whether the existing processes and technologies can meet defined recovery time objectives (RTOs) and recovery point objectives (RPOs). (We will cover RTOs and RPOs in greater depth in Chapter 25, "Understanding the Processes Associated with Third-Party Risk Assessment and Management.") Testing can be carried out through various methods, such as tabletop exercises, failover tests, simulations, and parallel processing.

Key Topic

Tabletop Exercises

A *tabletop exercise* is used to validate and improve an organization's incident response plan (IRP). Real-life scenarios are used to put the response plan to the test, highlighting areas where the team excels and areas to be addressed. A tabletop exercise also ensures that everyone on the team knows their roles and responsibilities in the event of an attack. A tabletop exercise aligns everyone's understanding of the process, helps assign roles to team members, and provides participants with knowledge through hands-on experience. The exercise begins with the IRP in a classroom-type setting and gauges team performance against the following questions: What happens when you encounter a breach? Who does what, when, how, and why? What roles will HR, legal, IT, corporate communication, and company officers play? Who is assigned to spearhead the effort, and what specific authority will they have? What resources are available to them when they need them?

Consider a scenario where a major natural disaster, such as an earthquake, has struck near a data center that houses critical infrastructure for a financial institution. The discussion would include steps to assess the immediate damage to physical infrastructure and cyber assets. Participants might be asked questions like:

- What is the first action you would take to ensure staff safety?

- How quickly can you shift our operations to a backup site?

- What steps should be taken to communicate with stakeholders, including customers and regulatory bodies?

- Are data encryption and secure data transfer mechanisms in place to protect data during the transition?

- What are the measures to validate that the backup systems are operational and data integrity is maintained?

Through this mock scenario, team members will examine their incident response plans in detail, evaluate the viability of their continuity of operations plan, and determine if they can meet the stipulated RTOs and RPOs. This offers a valuable opportunity for team members to mentally rehearse their roles and responsibilities, ensuring a higher level of preparedness for actual incidents.

Failover

Failover testing involves switching operational functions from a primary system to a secondary system to evaluate the organization's ability to continue operations when a critical system fails. In the context of high availability and disaster recovery, a successful failover process should be seamless, with minimal impact on users and operations. Failover tests are essential for verifying that redundancy mechanisms and contingency plans are functional.

Before diving into the specifics of conducting failover tests and understanding different failover configurations, it's crucial to understand the overarching considerations that guide these processes. These considerations include the timing of the tests, who should be involved, and the configurations that best suit the organization's needs. In determining when and how to conduct failover testing, you need to consider the following:

- **Timing:** Failover tests are best conducted during off-peak hours to minimize the impact on operations. Remember that you also need to ensure that you have access to outside support if something goes wrong outside of your department.

- **Notification:** Key stakeholders, including IT staff and management, should be notified in advance.

- **Who performs the test:** Network administrators and engineers typically conduct the test, often in coordination with a disaster recovery team. The disaster recovery team should be on standby in case something doesn't go as planned and the system is not recovering normally.

Types of failover configurations include the following:

- **Active/active:** In an active/active scenario, all the devices perform work simultaneously, sharing the load. This approach is commonly used with web server farms and DNS servers. Both systems should run the same software or services.

- **Active/passive:** In an active/passive scenario, one device performs work while the other is in standby mode, becoming active only when the primary device goes offline or is manually switched to the secondary.

Microsoft's Cluster service is a great example of a system that can act in both active/active and active/passive modes, enabling parallel, high-performance computing. It is commonly used in web and FTP server farms, as well as in IRC servers, DNS servers, and Network Time Protocol (NTP) servers. A significant consideration is to ensure that both devices in a failover configuration are running the same software version to avoid compatibility issues during the failover process. It is important to read the latest Microsoft releases before setting up an entire Cluster service.

Simulations

A *simulation*, sometimes referred to as a security incident response simulation (SIRS), is an internal event that provides a structured exercise to practice a team's incident response procedures and plan in a simulated realistic scenario, where components such as deadlines and external injects increase the realism of the event. *Injects* are scenario-based actions that help add a realistic element to an event. SIRS events are about preparing team members with realistic simulations and helping them improve response capabilities. The value in these exercises is what is obtained, retained, and fed back into the plan, including the following:

- Validating the readiness of both the team and the plan

- Identifying and documenting deficiencies to facilitate constructive feedback

- Helping develop team member confidence

- Providing evidence of compliance, depending on the industry

The value and benefit derived from team members participating in SIRS include increases in the organization's effectiveness during stressful live events.

Whereas a tabletop exercise is primarily a theoretical discussion aimed at strategizing and understanding individual roles, a simulation exercise immerses participants in a dynamic environment that mimics real-life conditions. In a tabletop exercise, the focus may be on what should be done; in a simulation, the focus is on actually doing it. The key differences lie in the depth of engagement and the level of practical skill testing involved. Tabletops help identify gaps in plans and understanding, while simulations test the organization's operational capabilities to react to and recover from incidents.

Parallel Processing

Parallel processing involves running the same tasks concurrently in both the primary and secondary systems. It helps verify that the backup system will produce the same output as the primary system under the same conditions. It offers a way to ensure that the failover system is operational and also accurate and reliable.

Backups

In any resilient and recoverable security architecture, backups serve as a critical component to ensure business continuity and data integrity. A *backup* is a copy of data and system configurations that is stored separately from the original. Various methods and considerations exist for implementing backups, each with its own set of benefits and drawbacks. Table 13-2 offers a comparative analysis of key elements in backup strategies that are aimed at helping you understand the nuances of each approach. You can design a backup regimen that best suits your organization's specific needs once you identify the approach needed.

Table 13-2 Backup Element Benefits and Drawbacks

Backup Element	How It Works	Benefits	Drawbacks
Onsite backup	Local storage provides immediate data retrieval without Internet latency	Fast access to backups for quick recovery	Vulnerable to onsite disasters such as fire or theft
Offsite backup	Data is stored in a geographically separate location	Protection against local disasters	Can be slow to recover due to distance and potential bandwidth limitations
Backup frequency	Regularly scheduled backups capture recent changes	Minimizes data loss	High-frequency backups can consume considerable resources
Encryption algorithm	Encryption algorithms obscure data, making it unreadable without a decryption key	Enhances data security	Requires computational overhead and may slow the backup and recovery process
Snapshot	Takes a "picture" of the data at a given time, allowing rollback to specific states	Quick data recovery for specific moments in time	Consumes storage space, especially if snapshots are frequently taken

Backup Element	How It Works	Benefits	Drawbacks
Recovery	Utilizes backup copies to restore lost or compromised data	Ensures data integrity and availability after a disaster	Can be time-consuming, depending on the backup type and size
Replication	Continuously copies data to a secondary location, enabling instant switchover in the event of a failure	Real-time data availability	Consumes additional storage and network resources
Journaling	Keeps a record of changes to the data, enabling point-in-time recovery	Allows for detailed recovery options	Can require considerable storage and computational resources

As you can see in the table, no single backup strategy is universally optimal or preferred; rather, the best approach is often a composite of multiple methods tailored to an organization's unique requirements and risk profile. Hybrid environments are also possible, with critical systems in the cloud and a mix of endpoint systems rooted in a physical architecture. In such an environment, the backup solution needs to meet the needs of each of these different user profiles.

Table 13-3 lists common backup types you will encounter in most enterprise environments.

Key Topic

Table 13-3 Common Backup Types

Backup Type	Description
Full backup	This is the most complete type of backup, where all selected data is copied. While it provides the highest level of protection, it also takes the most time and storage space.
Incremental backup	Only the data that has changed since the last backup (full or incremental) is copied. Incremental backups save time and storage space but require a full backup for data recovery.
Differential backup	This backs up all the data that has changed since the last full backup. It requires more space than an incremental backup but less space than a full backup. You'll need the last full backup and the last differential backup for recovery.
Mirror backup	This real-time backup immediately copies any changed data. It's useful for critical systems but can be resource intensive.
Continuous data protection (CDP)	This is an advanced backup method that saves a copy of every change made to the data, essentially capturing every version of the data at every point in time.

Backup Type	Description
Cloud backup	Data is backed up to a remote cloud-based server. It's an offsite backup option that's increasingly popular but requires a reliable Internet connection for both backup and recovery.
Virtual backup	This involves backing up virtual machines, capturing the state and data of each virtual system.
Bare-metal backup	This is a backup of an entire system, including the operating system and all applications. It allows for the recovery of a complete system in the event of failure.

Power

Power management refers to the provisioning, control, and effective use of electricity to ensure the uninterrupted operation of a facility, particularly a data center in an IT environment. A well-designed power management strategy is pivotal in maintaining high availability and ensuring that systems remain operational even during electrical failures.

Key Topic

Uninterruptible Power Supply (UPS)

An *uninterruptible power supply (UPS)*, sometimes called an uninterruptible power source, is an electrical device that provides emergency power to a load when the input power source or main power fails. A UPS differs from an auxiliary or emergency power system or standby generator in that it provides near-instantaneous protection from input power interruptions by supplying energy stored in batteries or supercapacitors. A UPS allows you enough time to properly and safely power down equipment until power is fully restored. A UPS has a limited runtime due to the storage capability of batteries and is meant to be a temporary solution; in most cases, it provides enough time to properly shut down resources. Some newer UPSs and servers are aware of each other, and when power fails, a signal is sent to the server, asking it to properly shut down.

NOTE UPSs are used to protect electronic equipment and provide immediate emergency power in the event of a complete or temporary power failure.

Key Topic

Generators

A *generator* provides power to spaces and devices during complete power loss or may be used in an area where standard electrical service isn't available. Generators range from 800 watts to over 500,000 watts, and there are different types of generators for different deployment requirements. Generators convert mechanical or chemical energy into electrical energy. They do this by capturing the power of motion and turning it into electrical energy by forcing electrons from the external source through an electrical circuit. The formula to figure out the generator size you need is (Running wattage × 3) + Starting wattage = Total wattage needed. Implementing a corporate generator strategy requires preplanning, sizing and capacity planning, and ensuring a sufficient platform to house the generators, fuel supply, and power transfer equipment.

Chapter Review Activities

Use the features in this section to study and review the topics in this chapter.

Review Key Topics

Review the most important topics in the chapter, noted with the Key Topic icon in the outer margin of the page. Table 13-4 lists these key topics and the page number on which each is found.

Table 13-4   Key Topics for Chapter 13

Key Topic Element	Description	Page Number
List	High availability key components	291
Paragraph	Clustering examples	292
List	Site considerations	293
Section	Capacity Planning	295
Section	Tabletop Exercises	296
Table 13-2	Backup Element Benefits and Drawbacks	299
Table 13-3	Common Backup Types	300
Section	Uninterruptible Power Supply (UPS)	301
Section	Generators	301

Define Key Terms

Define the following key terms from this chapter and check your answers in the glossary:

high availability (HA), load balancing, clustering, hot site, warm site, cold site, geographic dispersion, platform diversity, multi-cloud system, continuity of operations planning (COOP), capacity planning, technology capacity planning, infrastructure, testing, tabletop exercise, failover testing, simulation, parallel processing, backup, onsite backup, offsite backup, backup frequency, encryption algorithm, snapshot, recovery, replication, journaling, power management, uninterruptible power supply (UPS), generator

Review Questions

Answer the following review questions. Check your answers with the answer key in Appendix A.

1. Explain the concept of high availability and its significance in COOP. What components are generally included in a high availability architecture?

2. What is capacity planning, and why is it important for an organization's long-term strategy? Discuss its role in the context of resources like CPU, memory, storage, and network bandwidth.

3. Describe the purpose and methods involved in testing the effectiveness of an incident response plan. Why is this process critical?

4. How does parallel processing contribute to system resilience, and what does it aim to verify in backup systems?

5. Discuss the different elements of backup strategies, as laid out in Table 13-2. What are the benefits and drawbacks of each, and why is it often beneficial to use a composite of multiple methods for backups?

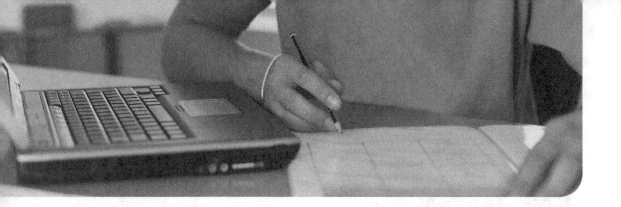

This chapter covers the following topics related to Objective 4.1 (Given a scenario, apply common security techniques to computing resources) of the CompTIA Security+ SY0-701 certification exam:

- Secure baselines
- Hardening targets
- Wireless devices
- Mobile solutions
- Wireless security settings
- Application security
- Sandboxing
- Monitoring

CHAPTER 14

Applying Common Security Techniques to Computing Resources

This chapter comprehensively examines application security measures for protecting data and code. It highlights the significance of input validations in web applications, explaining their role in mitigating vulnerabilities like cross-site scripting and SQL injection. The chapter then discusses the importance of secure cookies and the technology behind setting secure flags to prevent session hijacking. It provides an in-depth analysis of static code analysis (SAST) and details the steps for effective implementation. The chapter also discusses code signing, explaining its role in ensuring software authenticity and integrity through cryptographic hashing. The chapter also touches on the concept of sandboxing as a mechanism for testing untrusted code in a controlled environment and delves into the crucial role of monitoring in proactively identifying and mitigating security risks. Finally, the chapter offers a holistic understanding of the layered strategies and techniques that constitute modern cybersecurity measures.

"Do I Know This Already?" Quiz

The "Do I Know This Already?" quiz enables you to assess whether you should read this entire chapter thoroughly or jump to the "Chapter Review Activities" section. If you are in doubt about your answers to these questions or your own assessment of your knowledge of the topics, read the entire chapter. Table 14-1 lists the major headings in this chapter and their corresponding "Do I Know This Already?" quiz questions. You can find the answers in Appendix A, "Answers to the 'Do I Know This Already?' Quizzes and Review Questions."

Table 14-1 "Do I Know This Already?" Section-to-Question Mapping

Foundation Topics Section	Questions
Secure Baselines	2
Hardening Targets	4
Wireless Devices	5

Foundation Topics Section	Questions
Mobile Solutions	6
Wireless Security Settings	7
Application Security	1, 3
Sandboxing	8
Monitoring	9, 10

CAUTION   The goal of self-assessment is to gauge your mastery of the topics in this chapter. If you do not know the answer to a question or are only partially sure of the answer, you should mark that question as wrong for purposes of self-assessment. Giving yourself credit for an answer you correctly guess skews your self-assessment results and might provide you with a false sense of security.

1. What is the primary goal of application security?

   a. Improving application speed

   b. Increasing application features

   c. Preventing data or code within an app from being stolen or intercepted

   d. Aiding in application deployment

2. When capturing a baseline configuration for a network, what is the primary purpose of conducting an inventory assessment?

   a. To enforce strong password policies

   b. To list all hardware and software components

   c. To identify potential vulnerabilities

   d. To centrally manage security settings

3. Where is the secure cookie attribute set?

   a. On the client side

   b. In the browser's cookie jar

   c. By the application server in an HTTP response

   d. In the HTTP request

4. What is an advanced technique for hardening mobile devices?

   a. Applying geofencing

   b. Understanding the current wireless environment for planning

    c. Identifying potential vulnerabilities

    d. Running scheduled scans

5. What is the main goal of a site survey for wireless equipment?

    a. To enforce strong password guidelines

    b. To plan and optimize a Wi-Fi network

    c. To identify potential vulnerabilities

    d. To list all hardware and software components

6. What is crucial for a successful bring your own device (BYOD) implementation?

    a. Geofencing

    b. Storage segmentation

    c. Asset tagging

    d. Version control

7. What is a key feature of WPA3-Personal in wireless security settings?

    a. Use of preshared key (PSK)

    b. Optional use of 192-bit AES encryption

    c. Backward compatibility with WEP

    d. Requirement for manual reauthentication

8. What does sandboxing help prevent?

    a. Code duplication

    b. Code refactoring

    c. Unauthorized or malicious code from affecting the system

    d. Code compilation errors

9. What is one of the primary roles of monitoring in cybersecurity?

    a. Software updates

    b. Continuous surveillance of systems

    c. Application deployment

    d. System backups

10. What could the monitoring system in a financial institution be programmed to do upon detecting fraudulent activities?

   a. Log the user out

   b. Notify the bank manager

   c. Temporarily freeze the account

   d. Complete the transaction

Foundation Topics

Secure Baselines

A *secure baseline* is a standardized minimum set of configurations and security controls for systems and software. Establishing, deploying, and maintaining secure baselines are critical steps to ensure that computing resources adhere to a consistent and secure operational state. These baselines are not just checklists but strategic guidelines that serve as a starting point for system configuration, reducing the likelihood of vulnerabilities that could be exploited.

When establishing a secure baseline, you begin by identifying the minimal functional requirements for a system or an application to operate. To do so, you thoroughly analyze software settings, user access controls, and network configurations. By identifying what is necessary and sufficient, you minimize the attack surface, which is the totality of potential vulnerabilities in a given system.

 The following sections discuss a number of details to consider when you are establishing a secure baseline.

Inventory Assessment

Before you can secure assets, you need to know what those assets are. An inventory assessment involves creating a comprehensive list of all hardware and software components within an organization's network. It should include servers, workstations, network devices, and other connected systems.

Key points:

- **Asset tagging:** Assign unique identifiers to each asset for easier tracking.

- **Version control:** Note the version of each software in your organization to identify outdated or unsupported versions that may pose security risks.

Vulnerability Scanning

Once you know what you're working with, the next step is to identify potential vulnerabilities. Automated vulnerability scanning tools can scan systems to find known security issues, such as open ports, outdated software, or insecure default configurations.

Key points:

- **Scheduled scans:** Regularly schedule vulnerability scans to catch new vulnerabilities and review the results.

- **Manual review:** Automated tools can miss context; a manual review can help prioritize vulnerabilities based on actual organizational risk.

Minimum Configuration Standards

The goal is to define the least-permissive settings that allow the system or application to function as required. This is the essence of the principle of least privilege discussed in previous chapters as a form of access control, and it also applies in this context.

Key points:

- **Disable unnecessary services:** Turn off services and features not required for the system's primary function.

- **User access control:** Limit user permissions to only what is necessary for their roles.

Documentation

Documenting your secure baseline is crucial for accountability and future reference. This documentation should include all configurations and settings and the rationale behind them. Your documentation can also serve as confirmation that key stakeholders were involved in agreeing to the minimum configuration standards just discussed.

Key points:

- **Change log:** Maintain a record of any changes made to the baseline, who made them, and why. Establish a governance process to approve changes before they are implemented.

- **Audit trail:** Ensure that the documentation is in a format that can be easily audited for compliance purposes.

Deployment

After establishing and documenting your secure baseline, it's time to implement it. Always start by deploying the configurations in a test environment or sandbox to validate their effectiveness. (We discuss sandbox environments later in this chapter.)

Key points:

- **Validation testing:** Confirm that the baseline settings do not disrupt necessary functions.

- **Rollback plan:** Have a plan to revert changes in the event of unforeseen issues during deployment.

Ongoing Maintenance

Security is not a one-time task but an ongoing process. Your secure baseline will need regular updates to adapt to new security challenges, changes in configurations, and just the natural evolution of business.

Key points:

- **Patch management:** Regularly update software and systems to patch known vulnerabilities.

- **Review and update:** Periodically review the secure baseline to ensure that it aligns with current security best practices.

Deployment of a secure baseline involves applying the predetermined configurations to the computing resources in the operational environment. This could be done manually, but automated configuration management tools are often used for efficiency and accuracy. The deployment process should be well documented to maintain accountability and to provide a foundation for audits or reviews.

Maintaining a secure baseline is an ongoing process. With the ever-changing landscape of threats and vulnerabilities, periodic reviews and updates to the baseline are essential. Maintenance activities can include patch management, which involves updating system components and reassessing access controls to ensure that they align with the baseline. Regularly auditing the system against the baseline ensures that deviations are identified and corrected promptly.

By diligently establishing, deploying, and maintaining secure baselines, you can help organizations protect their computing resources and adapt to emerging security challenges. As with most of what we do in cybersecurity, you will find that this is an ongoing process that requires consistent and constant review.

Hardening Targets

Hardening targets refers to the process of strengthening the security defenses of various types of computing resources to resist attacks. You will likely encounter several types of devices with unique requirements and vulnerabilities, including mobile devices, workstations, switches, routers, cloud infrastructure, and other critical assets. Let's explore some of the specific use cases where hardening the system is critical.

Mobile devices are handheld computing gadgets like smartphones and tablets. Hardening these devices involves implementing security measures such as multifactor authentication (MFA) and data encryption. Different manufacturers also have certain features enabled by default, like location tracking services or marking messages as having been read in a text message. Sometimes hardening a mobile device is as simple as requiring a PIN or a fingerprint to unlock the device.

As you can see, hardening mobile devices is a multifaceted approach that goes beyond basic security measures. For instance, mobile device management (MDM) solutions can be deployed to centrally manage various security settings. (We will discuss MDM in greater depth later in this chapter.) Hardening mobile devices includes enforcing strong password policies, controlling application installations, and even remotely locking or wiping a device if it's compromised. As discussed in Chapter 12, "Comparing and Contrasting Concepts and Strategies to Protect Data," geofencing is an advanced technique that enables you to set geographic boundaries within which a device must operate. Specific security protocols can be triggered if the device moves outside these boundaries, such as locking the device or sending alerts to administrators. You will need to research all the allowed mobile devices at a specific organization and research any default settings that might violate your security requirements.

Workstations are high-performance computers used for specialized applications. Historically, a workstation might have been a large tower sitting below a desk with a monitor connected. Today, a workstation may also be a mobile device like a laptop, tablet, or cloud-based account. The hardening process for workstations can include disabling unnecessary services, restricting user permissions, and using strong antivirus programs.

Hardening often involves disabling unnecessary services and ports to minimize the attack surface when it comes to workstations. Software allow listing can also ensure that only approved applications can run on the system.

Firmware, the low-level software that controls the hardware, should also be securely updated as manufacturers release patches. This is crucial because vulnerabilities at the firmware level can be particularly damaging and may bypass other security measures that are in place. Make sure to follow the manufacturer's guidelines for secure firmware updates, which often include verifying the source and integrity of the update files.

Anti-malware software is another factor to consider in workstation hardening. This software must be kept up-to-date, and regular scans should be scheduled to catch any threats that may have slipped through other layers of defense. Real-time scanning features can provide additional protection by examining files as they are accessed or downloaded.

Switches are network devices that efficiently manage data traffic by sending packets to specific devices rather than broadcasting to all network devices. Hardening a switch can involve actions like disabling unused ports and applying port security. For instance, if a switch is configured to only recognize devices with preregistered MAC addresses, that's a case of switch hardening.

A *router* serves as a gateway between a local network and the broader Internet. Hardening a router means enhancing its security through methods such as changing default login credentials, enabling firewall settings, or disabling remote management. An example would be setting up a home router with a unique username and password and customized firewall rules. Routers are complex and offer several ways to harden the system to provide better security for an organization's network.

Cloud infrastructure refers to the hardware and software components, such as servers and storage, that enable cloud computing. Hardening the cloud infrastructure includes setting up strict access controls and encrypting data at rest and in transit. A cloud storage account that only permits access from specific IP addresses while encrypting the stored data is a good example of cloud infrastructure hardening. Each vendor has specific settings and recommendations for hardening cloud accounts on their infrastructure. You should always research any best practices a vendor offers.

Servers are computer systems or software that manage access to centralized resources or services in a network. Hardening might involve limiting service access, restricting permissions, and regularly updating software. For instance, a web server that disables FTP service and limits HTTP access to certain IP addresses has undergone server hardening. Server hardening may depend on the operating system in use. Remember that Linux and Microsoft operating systems vary greatly on what services and systems require attention to ensure that unnecessary ports or services are not left open.

Supervisory control and data acquisition (SCADA) systems and industrial control systems (ICSs) are essential control systems that oversee complex industrial operations. Hardening these systems is a critical security measure and involves tactics such as deploying specialized firewalls and enacting stringent access controls.

For instance, a hardened SCADA system at a power plant might be configured to accept command inputs only from specific authenticated computers in order to reduce the attack surface. A common but risky feature in some older or less secure ICS/SCADA systems is burned-in passwords—that is, passwords that are hard-coded into the system and cannot be easily changed. While they may offer some level of initial security, the unchangeable nature of these passwords makes them vulnerable targets for attackers who can exploit them for unauthorized access once they are discovered. Modern hardening practices strongly advise against using burned-in passwords and recommend regular password rotation and multifactor authentication as more secure alternatives, but you will still encounter these insecure practices that require hardening.

Hardening these systems is a critical security priority and includes tactics like deploying specialized firewalls and enacting stringent access controls. Additional measures include scheduling regular firmware updates and patches during non-critical operational hours. Network segmentation is also crucial; separating SCADA systems from business networks is advisable to prevent cross-contamination. Virtual local area networks (VLANs) can isolate different types of traffic, such as administrative and operational traffic. For susceptible systems, consider complete physical isolation from all other networks, known as air-gapping.

Embedded systems are computing devices specifically designed to perform dedicated functions or tasks within a more extensive system. Hardening an embedded system means disabling unnecessary features and services. A smart TV that has non-essential ports and Internet services disabled is an example of embedded system hardening. A recent addition to the smart home landscape is light bulbs. The embedded systems that make these lightbulbs change colors might also open up the home network to potential vulnerabilities. Ensure that smart appliances like refrigerators automatically update their firmware to protect against known vulnerabilities.

A *real-time operating system (RTOS)* is a specialized operating system that is designed to process data within strict time constraints. RTOSs are likely to be in medical devices, automotive controls, and industrial automation. Hardening an RTOS includes a variety of strategies, such as real-time monitoring to identify and flag irregular activities that could indicate security breaches. For example, you could harden a medical device using an RTOS by configuring it to encrypt patient data before it transmits the data to a central server. This encryption ensures that even if the data is intercepted during transmission, it remains unintelligible to unauthorized parties, thereby safeguarding patient confidentiality and the integrity of the medical system. You might also employ network segmentation to isolate an RTOS from other less secure systems, reducing the risk of lateral movement attacks.

Internet of Things (IoT) devices are physical objects connected to the Internet to collect and exchange data. They often integrate physical and digital systems. Hardening these devices involves several security measures, such as changing default passwords to stronger, unique credentials and ensuring that the firmware is up-to-date to protect against known vulnerabilities. For instance, a smart doorbell configured to communicate only with a secure, encrypted home network is an example of effective hardening of an IoT device. This setting ensures that the doorbell isn't an easy entry point into your home network for would-be attackers. It is a good idea to keep smart home devices on a separate VLAN from the main computing devices. This ensures that if an IoT device is compromised, the attacker can't easily move on to more critical systems. An even more complex hardening approach would employ device behavior analytics to monitor for any unusual activities that could indicate compromise.

Table 14-2 summarizes some of the key hardening techniques you might encounter in each of these categories.

Table 14-2 Summary of Hardening Techniques

Key Topic

Category	Hardening Techniques	Examples
ICS/SCADA	Firmware updates, network segmentation, VLANs, air-gapping	Update firmware quarterly, isolate control systems from the corporate network, use VLANs to segregate traffic, physically isolate highly sensitive systems
Embedded systems	Disable unnecessary features, apply firmware updates	Turn off non-essential smart TV apps, disable unused ports, update smart light bulb firmware
RTOS	Real-time monitoring, data encryption	Implement intrusion detection systems, encrypt patient data in medical devices
IoT devices	Change default passwords, apply firmware updates, ensure network-level security	Use strong, unique passwords for smart doorbells, update firmware for smart thermostats, ensure that smart cameras connect only to encrypted networks

Wireless Devices

Wireless devices have become ubiquitous in today's fast-paced, interconnected world. These devices operate without physical wired connections, relying instead on methods such as Wi-Fi, Bluetooth, or cellular networks to communicate. While the lack of cords offers greater mobility and flexibility, it also introduces unique installation considerations. Two key aspects integral to effectively installing and operating wireless devices are site surveys and heat maps.

Strategic wireless access point (WAP) placement is vital, and it is essential to perform a site survey before deploying wireless equipment. A *site survey* is a comprehensive assessment conducted to understand the current wireless environment and to plan and optimize a Wi-Fi network. Utilizing Wi-Fi analysis tools, the survey produces a heat map that visualizes wireless activity in a specific area. This information is crucial for determining the optimal locations for placing access points to ensure effective coverage and performance. Usually, the best place for a WAP is in the center of a building so that equal access can be given to everyone on the perimeter of the organization's property, and there is the least chance of the signal bleeding over to other organizations. If needed, you can attempt to reduce the transmission power level of the antenna, which can reduce the broadcast range of the WAP. Also, to avoid interference in the form of EMI or RFI, you should keep WAPs away from any electrical panels, cables, devices, motors, or other equipment that might give off an electromagnetic field. If necessary, you can shield a device creating an electromagnetic field or shield the access point itself.

To really know how to best arrange and secure your wireless connections, you need to understand the different wireless systems and antenna types available.

The most common wireless system, a point-to-multipoint system, is commonly used in WLANs where a single central device (such as a SOHO wireless router) connects to multiple other wireless devices that could be located in any direction. Specifically, it makes use of omnidirectional antennas such as vertical omnidirectional antennas and ceiling domes. A typical wireless router might have two, three, four, or more vertical omnidirectional antennas. For example, with the introduction of 802.11ax, otherwise known as Wi-Fi 6, wireless access points and routers are utilizing up to eight antennas. This is due in part to the fact that 802.11ax works on both 2.4-GHz and 5-GHz frequency bands.

With the constant innovation in wireless technology, we also see the introduction of technologies such as multi-user multiple-input and multiple-output (MU-MIMO), which uses a mechanism called *beamforming* for transmitting and receiving signals. This helps to greatly increase the efficiency of the range. Although the technology is continuing to evolve, the placement of the WAPs and deployment of the antennas remains similar. Antennas can be rotated so that they are parallel to each other or at an angle to each other; for example, 180 degrees is often a good configuration to, in essence, "sweep" the area for wireless transmissions. However, you might choose a different method. For example, you might have 100 computers on one floor and two WAPs to work with. The best method might be to position them at vertical angles from each other. One would be in the building's northeast corner and the other in the southwest corner. Then, each set of three antennas could be positioned in a 90-degree sweep, as shown in Figure 14-1. As long as the building isn't larger than the range of the antennas, this setup should allow for excellent wireless coverage.

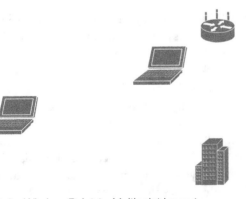

Figure 14-1   Wireless Point-to-Multipoint Layout

Addressing channel overlap through channel selection and channel width selection can impact performance and security as well. In this case, 5-GHz frequency bands usually offer better performance than 2.4-GHz bands, but attackers can monitor both bands over the air. Some WAPs can be set to autoconfigure, in which they can seek the least-used wireless frequencies/channels; this can be great for performance but might be a security risk. Consider using less common channel numbers and perhaps a narrower channel—for example, 40 MHz instead of 80 MHz for 802.11ac. And remember to reduce antenna power levels as much as possible. Once again, you must test carefully and then balance performance and security for optimal organization efficiency.

In some more simplistic point-to-point wireless systems, only two points need to be connected; these points are usually fixed in location. In such a case, you would use a directional antenna—for example, a parabolic antenna (dish) or a Yagi antenna.

Whatever you implement, it's a good idea to perform a wireless site survey. There are three kinds of wireless surveys you might perform, each with its own purpose, and all of which are usually based on software that collects WLAN data and signal information (though hardware can also be used to measure radio frequencies):

- A passive site survey listens to WLAN traffic and measures signal strength.

- An active survey actually sends and receives data to measure data transfer rate, packet loss, and so on.

- A predictive survey is a simulated survey based on real data such as the WAP to be used, the distance between the average computer and WAP, and so on.

Surveys can be instrumental in uncovering nonaggressive interference such as neighboring radio waves and electrical equipment (RFI and EMI, mentioned earlier).

One of the tools used most commonly in site surveys is a Wi-Fi analyzer. Wi-Fi analyzers come in many forms. Some are hardware devices that are created specifically to analyze the wireless signals in an area. A Wi-Fi analyzer may be a piece of software that runs on a laptop and works in conjunction with either the wireless adapter that is built into the laptop or a third-party adapter that connects via USB. The main purpose of a Wi-Fi analyzer is to create a picture of the signal and channel saturation in the area surveyed. From a security perspective, you can also use a Wi-Fi analyzer to create a heat map of how far your Wi-Fi network signals are able to reach.

Surveys can also be used to locate aggressive jamming techniques, which may be caused by wireless signal jammers. A signal jammer, which can easily be purchased online, can be used to initiate a denial-of-service attack against a wireless network. Such an attack is made by creating random noise on the channel used by the WAP or by attempting to short out the device with powerful radio signals. You can use wireless software (such as inSSIDer Paessler PRTG) to locate signal jammers in or around a building so that you can remove them. You can also use wireless software to identify potential wireless replay attacks that might exist within the network infrastructure.

A *heat map* serves as a visual representation displaying the distribution of wireless signal strength across a specific area. A heat map is typically color-coded, with warm colors denoting strong signal areas and cool colors indicating weaker zones. For example, after deploying a wireless network in an office, a heat map could reveal that the Wi-Fi signal in a distant conference room is weak, prompting the need for additional access points or repositioning of existing ones.

Mobile Solutions

Mobile solutions have become essential for individual and organizational success in the modern digital landscape. These solutions involve a range of technologies and strategies designed to facilitate mobile usage and management, making it easier than ever before to work, connect, and secure information while on the go. This section explores various facets of mobile solutions, including mobile device management (MDM), deployment models (including BYOD, COPE, and CYOD), and connection methods (including cellular, Wi-Fi, and Bluetooth).

Mobile Device Management

Key Topic

The key to a successful *bring your own device (BYOD)* implementation—where employees use their personal devices for work tasks—is to ensure storage segmentation, which means a clear separation of organizational and personal information, applications, and other content. Where the data ownership line occurs must be unmistakable. For networks with a lot of users, you should consider third-party offerings from companies that make use of *mobile device management (MDM)* platforms. These centralized software solutions allow you to control, configure, update, and secure remote mobile devices such as Android, iOS, and other devices from an administrative console. MDM software can be run from a server within an organization or administered within the cloud. MDM can make your job as a mobile IT security administrator more manageable. From a central location, you can carry out application management, content management, and patch management tasks. You can also set up more secure levels of mobile device access control.

Access control is the methodology used to allow access to computer systems. For larger organizations, MDM software makes it easy for you to view inventory control, such as how many devices are active for each of the mobile operating systems used. It also makes it simpler to track assets, such as devices themselves, and the types of data each device contains.

In addition, MDM software makes it less complicated to disable unused features on multiple devices at once, thereby increasing the efficiency of the devices, reducing their footprint, and ultimately making them more secure. For instance, an employee who happens to have both a smartphone and a tablet capable of making cellular calls doesn't necessarily need the latter. As administrator, you could disable the tablet's cellular capability, which would increase battery efficiency as well as security for that device.

Users have mixed reactions to BYOD policies. Some employees like the idea of using their own devices (which they might not have been allowed to use at work previously) and not having to train on a separate work computer. However, some employees believe that BYOD is just a way to move computing costs from the company to the user, and their level of trust is low. This brings up a variety of legal concerns, such as the right to privacy. Companies that offer BYOD MDM solutions counter this perception by drawing a clear line, defining exactly what employers can see (for example, corporate email) and what they can't see (such as personal texts). In general, these companies try to protect the privacy of individuals. Many organizations write clear privacy policies that define, if necessary, selective wipes of secure corporate data while protecting personal data.

Part of the debate over BYOD includes some additional concerns; for example, additional legal concerns exist about employee misconduct and fraud. Anything that could possibly implicate an employee of wrongdoing would have to be found in the organizational portion of the data. From a forensics point of view, however, and because a device can't be split in two, if any potential wrongdoing is investigated, the device would need to be confiscated for analysis.

Most employees (of all age groups) are concerned with how onboard devices (such as onboard cameras) can be used against them with or without their knowledge. Companies that offer BYOD solutions tend to refer to the camera (and photos/video taken) as part of the personal area of the device. However, those same companies include GPS location as something they can see, but this can be linked to a corporate login, with GPS tracking users only when they are logged in. Onboarding and offboarding in general are additional concerns. Essentially, *onboarding* means that you, as security administrator, take control of the device temporarily to configure it, update it, and perhaps monitor it, and *offboarding* means that you relinquish control of the device when finished with it. This control brings up some questions for employees: When does it happen? How long does it last? How will my device be affected? Are there any architectural/infrastructural concerns? For example, will the BYOD solution change the core files of my device? Will an update done by a person when at home render the device inactive the next day at work? This is just the tip of the iceberg when it comes to questions and concerns about BYOD. The best course of action is for an organization to set firm policies about all of these topics.

Policies that need to be instituted include an acceptable use policy, a data ownership policy, and a support ownership policy. In essence, these policies define what users are allowed to do with their devices (during work hours), who owns what data and how that data is separated, and under what scenarios the organization as opposed to the user takes care of technical support for a device.

To help secure the mobile devices in a BYOD enterprise environment, some third-party providers offer an embedded certificate authority for managing devices and user identity, sophisticated posture monitoring and automated policy workflow so that noncompliant devices do not get enterprise access, and certificate-based security to secure email and reduce the chance of data loss.

Unfortunately, smartphones and tablets (and other mobile devices) can be victims of attacks. Attackers might choose to abuse your service or use devices as part of a larger-scale attack and possibly to gain access to account information. Though mobile devices can be considered computers, there are some other factors to consider specifically for mobile devices.

Users of mobile devices should be careful about giving their phone number to others and should avoid listing their phone number on any websites, especially when purchasing products. You should train your users not to follow any links sent by email or by text message if they are unsolicited. (If there is any doubt in a user's mind, then it is best to ignore a communication.) Explain to your users the issues with downloadable software such as games and ringtones. Also, use a locking code/password/gesture that's hard to guess and ensure that the mobile device locks after a specific amount of time has elapsed. In addition, use complex passwords when necessary—for example, if required by company policy.

In general, mobile operating system software must be updated just like desktop computer software. If you keep mobile devices up-to-date, there will be less chance that they will be affected by viruses and other malware. You can encrypt data in several ways, and some organizations even have policies that specify how data will be encrypted. More good general tips are available at the following Cybersecurity & Infrastructure Security Agency (CISA) websites:

> https://www.cisa.gov/sites/default/files/publications/Mobile%2520Security%2520One%2520Pager.pdf
>
> https://www.cisa.gov/sites/default/files/publications/Mobile%20Security%20Tip%20Card_0.pdf
>
> https://www.cisa.gov/sites/default/files/publications/cyber_threats_to_mobile_phones.pdf

MDM Security Feature Concerns: Application and Content Management

We've already talked about how applications should usually be updated to the latest version and discussed the importance of proper user interaction. Now let's delve a bit deeper and talk about ways to encrypt data that is transferred through applications.

Encryption is one of the best ways to ensure that data is secured and that applications work properly, without interference from potential attackers. However, you should consider whole device encryption, which involves encrypting the internal memory and any removable (SD) cards. Sometimes you might forget about one or the other of these. Don't forget about encrypting data in transit—data that is on the move between a client and a server. Most applications for mobile devices communicate with a server of some sort; for example, when a person uses a web browser, an email client, a contacts database, or apps that work independently of a browser but operate in a similar manner, meaning that they ultimately connect to a server. Weather apps, games, social media apps, and so on all fall into this category.

Let's consider a web browser, for instance. Web browsers on mobile devices connect to websites much as they do on desktop computers. While it was once common for basic websites to use Hypertext Transfer Protocol (HTTP), the modern standard has shifted toward using HTTP Secure (HTTPS) for most websites, not just those requiring personally identifiable information (PII). HTTPS employs encryption protocols like Transport Layer Security (TLS) to secure the transmitted data, offering a more secure communication channel. This shift toward the use of HTTPS aims to enhance website authenticity, secure user accounts, and maintain the privacy of user communications on the Internet.

Whatever the security protocol, the important point here is that the server you are connected to makes use of a database that stores encryption keys. The key (or a portion thereof) is sent to the client device and is agreed upon (that is, handshaking occurs) so that the transfer of data, especially private information, is encrypted and protected. Often, HTTPS pages are used to aid in the process of authentication—the confirmation of a person's (or computer's) identity, typically with the help of a username/password combination. Examples include when you log in to your account with a bank or with a shopping portal.

One of the important roles for the server is key management—the creation, storage, usage, and retirement of encryption keys. Proper key management (and the regular updating of keys) is your primary concern as a security administrator. Generally, an organization purchases a key algorithm from a third-party company such as Veri-Sign. That company informs the organization if a key has become compromised and needs to be revoked. These third parties might also take part in credential management (management of usernames, passwords, PINs, and other passcodes, which are usually stored within a secure database) to make things a bit easier for you. Whether this is the case depends on the size of the organization and its budget. Key management gets quite in depth, as you can imagine. For now, realize that a mobile device is an easy target. It is important to scrutinize applications (especially third-party apps) to make sure they are using a solid encryption plan when personal information is transferred back and forth.

Authentication to servers and other networks (and all their applications) can get even more complicated when the concept of transitive trust is implemented. Effectively, transitive trust occurs when two networks (or more) have a relationship such that users logging in to one network get access to data on the other. In days gone by, these types of trusts were created automatically between different sections of networks; however, it was quickly realized that this type of transitivity was insecure, allowing users (and potential attackers) access to other networks that they shouldn't have had access to. There's a larger looming threat here as well. Transitive trust is based on the transitive property in mathematics, which states that if A is equal to B, and B is equal to C, then A is automatically equal to C. Put into computer terms: If the New York network trusts the California network, and the California network trusts the Hong Kong network, then the New York network automatically trusts the Hong Kong network. You can imagine the security concerns here, as well as the domino effect that could occur. So, organizations usually prefer nontransitive trust, where users need to be authenticated to each network separately and therefore are limited in terms of the applications (and data) they have access to on a per-network basis.

To further restrict users and increase application security, allow lists are often used. With application allow listing, you, as the administrator, create a list of approved applications, and users can work with only those applications—and no others. This is often done within a computer policy and can be made more manageable by using a mobile device management system (as described earlier in this chapter). Users often need access to several apps, such as phone, email, contacts, and web browser apps. These applications would be on the allow list, and if a user tried to use other apps, they would be denied or, at the very least, prompted for additional user credentials. If a user needed access to another app, such as the camera, you would weigh the security concerns (GPS, links to social media, and so on) and decide whether to add the app to the allow list. Allow listing can also be helpful when dealing with apps that utilize OAuth—a common mechanism used by social media companies to permit users to share account information with third-party applications and websites.

Contrast the use of allow lists with the use of block lists/deny lists, which deny access to individual applications. Deny lists are commonly used when working with email and by antivirus/anti-malware and hardware-based intrusion detection system (HIDS) programs.

MDM Security Feature Concerns: Remote Wipe, Geofencing, Geolocation, Screen Locks, Passwords and PINs, and Full Device Encryption

More than 100 mobile devices end up missing (often stolen) every minute. Yes—every minute! You can imagine the variety of reasons these thefts occur. The worst attack that can be perpetuated on a smartphone or tablet is theft. The theft of a mobile device means the possible loss of important data and personal information. There are a few ways to protect against this loss of data and to recover from the theft of a mobile device if it does happen.

First, mobile devices in an organization should utilize data encryption. The stronger the encryption, the more difficult it is for a thief to decode and use the data on the device. If at all possible, you should use full device encryption. Most modern mobile device operating systems such as Apple iOS and Android have this capability built in. So there really is no reason not to have it enabled on devices. The conversations on phones can also be encrypted. Voice encryption can protect the confidentiality of spoken conversations and can be implemented with a special microSD chip (preferably) or with software.

Mobile devices should also be set up for GPS tracking so that they can be tracked if they are lost or stolen. The more quickly a device can be located, the less risk of data loss, especially if it is encrypted. However, GPS tracking can also be a security vulnerability for a device and possibly a user if an attacker knows how to track the phone.

The beauty of mobile devices is in their inherent portability—that and the ability to track SIM cards. If you are an administrator for mobile devices, you should consider using remote lockout programs. If a device is lost or stolen, you can lock the device, disallowing access to a would-be attacker. In addition, you can configure a device to use the "three strikes and you're out" rule, meaning that if a user tries to be authenticated to the device and is unsuccessful, they are locked out after three attempts.

Of course, we all know that password authentication is not the strongest authentication method. Using multifactor authentication is a way to enhance the strength of authentication security—for instance, using biometrics as one of the authentication factors, alongside password/PIN authentication. Most modern mobile devices and even tablets have some sort of biometrics capability, such as fingerprint or facial recognition. For data that is extremely sensitive, you might want to take it to the next level and consider a remote wipe program. If the mobile device is reported as lost or stolen, such a program can remove all data from the phone in a bit-by-bit process, making it difficult (or impossible) to recover. This process is known as *sanitizing* the phone remotely. Of course, a solid backup strategy should be in place before a remote wipe solution is implemented.

Screen locks, complex passwords, and care when connecting to wireless networks are also important. Although a screen lock won't deter knowledgeable attackers, it will usually deter the average person who, for example, finds a stray phone sitting in a coffee shop, mall, or other public location. Users should receive training when they first receive their devices. Although many organizations don't take the time for training, it is a great way to show users how to secure their devices and also to ensure that their encryption, GPS tracking, and other features are working properly. Users can also be trained on how to inform your organization and local law enforcement in the event that a device is lost or stolen, effectively reducing the risk of data loss by allowing you to find the device faster or mitigate the problem in other ways.

Another important function of an MDM solution is providing context-aware authentication by limiting or preventing access to organization resources based on the device profile and security posture; for example, a device that is rooted should not be able to access certain resources.

NOTE In the case of theft, the two best ways to protect against the loss of confidential or sensitive information are encryption and a remote wipe program.

Table 14-3 summarizes some of the mobile security concerns that are addressed by implementing mobile device management. With a mixture of user adherence to corporate policies, the workplace respecting the user's right to privacy, and a strong security plan, BYOD can be a success.

Key Topic

Table 14-3 Mobile Device Security Concerns and Countermeasures

Mobile Device Security Topic	Countermeasure
Malware	Update device to latest version (or point release for the current version).
	Use security suites and AV software. Enable them if preloaded on the device and update regularly.
	Train users to carefully screen email and selectively access websites.
	Be careful of social networks and third-party apps.
Botnets and DDoS attacks	Download apps from a legitimate source. If BYOD is in place, use company-approved apps.
	Refrain from rooting or jailbreaking the device.
	Have data backed up in case the device becomes part of a botnet and has to be wiped.
SIM cloning	Use V2 and newer cards with strong encryption algorithms.
Wireless attacks	Use a strong password for the wireless network.
	Turn off unnecessary wireless features such as mobile hotspots and tethering.
	Disable Bluetooth if not in use for long periods of time (for security and also to conserve the battery).
	Set the device to undiscoverable.

Mobile Device Security Topic	Countermeasure
Theft	Use data and voice encryption (especially in BYOD implementations).
	Implement lockout, remote locator, and remote wipe programs.
	Limit the amount of confidential information stored on the device.
	Use screen locks and complex passwords.
Application security	Use encryption from reputable providers.
	Use anti-malware endpoint protection platforms.
	Utilize nontransitive trusts between networks and apps.
	Allow list applications.
	Disable geotagging.
BYOD concerns	Implement storage segmentation.
	Use an MDM solution.
	Create and implement clear policies that the organization and users must adhere to.
	Consider CYOD or COPE as opposed to BYOD.

Deployment Models

Around 2011, organizations began to allow employees to bring their own mobile devices into work and connect them to the organization's network (for work purposes only, of course). This BYOD concept has since grown into a more popular method of computing for many organizations. BYOD is enticing from a budgeting standpoint but can be very difficult on you, as security administrator, and possibly on the users as well.

A computer is a computer. It doesn't matter if it's a PC from 1986 or a mobile device from this year. All computers need to be secured using the same principles and policies; however, mobile devices have historically tended to fall through the cracks. So, companies have really started gearing up the security for these devices. In most organizations, it is not feasible to stop people from bringing their smartphones to work. Some organizations have decided to embrace this practice and benefit from it with BYOD policies. Companies may implement similar strategies, such as *choose your own device (CYOD)*, where employees select a device from a company-approved list, or *corporate-owned, personally enabled (COPE)*, where the company supplies employees with phones that can also be used for personal activities.

Although these policies create a whole slew of new security considerations, some organizations are implementing BYOD and CYOD successfully by creating a well-defined demarcation point between a user's data and the organization's. When a company institutes this concept, along with an MDM solution and strong policies related to theft, wireless attacks, and application security, mobile devices can survive and thrive in the enterprise or small office yet remain safe and accessible for personal use.

NOTE   Some organizations utilize a virtual desktop infrastructure (VDI) to address BYOD challenges. This way, users can use their own hardware or corporate-owned hardware but connect to a VDI environment to access all the applications and data needed to do their work.

Secure Implementation of BYOD, CYOD, and COPE

Implementations of BYOD, CYOD, and COPE are all similar. For simplicity in this section, we refer to these collectively as BYOD unless CYOD or COPE needs to be addressed specifically.

An organization's BYOD implementation should be driven by its policies. As a security administrator, you should at least have a mobile device and acceptable use policy for connecting to your corporate network. The specifics of this policy should be ironed out before you begin your implementation. One of the primary concerns that should be addressed in the policy is what kind of devices you will allow on your network. Identifying these devices helps determine which is the best solution for implementing BYOD in your organization. Another determination you need to make is what kind of access you are planning to offer users of the BYOD system. For instance, if you are in a corporate environment, you may or may not allow BYOD-registered devices to access corporate data. You might decide to only allow them to access the Internet on a segmented network. If you are only allowing access to the Internet and the traffic is utilizing a segmented network that cannot interact with corporate data, your risk is much lower, and you will not need to do as much valida-tion of the device when connecting to the network. However, if the device is going to be connecting to your corporate network, where it will have access to corporate data and mission-critical applications, you will want to implement your BYOD system in a much stricter manner. For example, a device connecting to a corporate network should be required to go through a multifactor authentication process. You should then evaluate the device's security posture to determine if it meets the mini-mum requirements set in your policies for mobile devices. This includes minimum operating system level, up-to-date and clean antivirus/anti-malware software state, validation that the device is not jailbroken, and so on.

Of course, when you are securely implementing a BYOD program, your primary goal should be to keep corporate and personal data safe. In some cases, this can and should require the devices connecting to meet some stringent requirements.

However, for a BYOD program to be successful, the experience should be as easy as possible for the end user as well as for you, as administrator. This is where picking the right tools to implement comes in. A number of software vendors offer BYOD solutions. It is best for you to evaluate these solutions against your policies and requirements to determine which one is best for your organization. One example is Cisco Identity Services Engine (ISE). Figure 14-2 shows the dashboard for ISE.

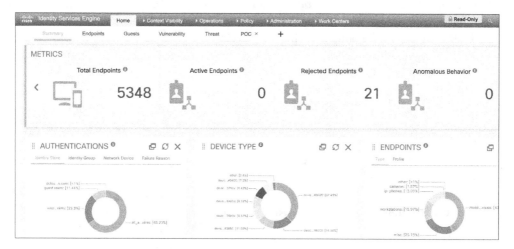

Figure 14-2   Cisco Identity Services Engine Dashboard View

Most BYOD platforms include a capability for implementing policy, monitoring, and onboarding devices, just to name a few. Figure 14-3 shows the BYOD work center in Cisco ISE. As you can see, it is essentially a step-by-step guide or wizard for getting started with implementing BYOD in an organization.

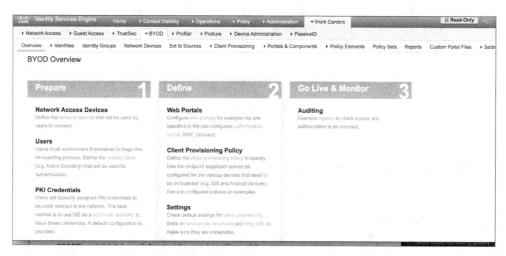

Figure 14-3   Cisco Identity Services Engine BYOD Work Center

Connection Methods

Bluetooth, radio frequency identification (RFID), and near-field communication (NFC) are not wireless networking technologies in the general sense, the way Wi-Fi is. But anything that has two or more wireless devices that communicate with each other could technically be considered a wireless network.

Like any wireless technology, **Bluetooth** is vulnerable to attack. Bluejacking and Bluesnarfing are two types of vulnerabilities to Bluetooth-enabled devices. Bluetooth is also vulnerable to conflicts with other wireless technologies. For example, some WLAN (or Wi-Fi) standards use the 2.4-GHz frequency range, as does Bluetooth, and even though Bluetooth uses frequency hopping, conflicts can occur between 802.11g or 802.11b networks and Bluetooth personal area networks (PANs). To avoid this, you should use Bluetooth version 1.2 devices or greater, which employ adaptive frequency hopping, improving resistance to radio interference. Also, you should consider placing Bluetooth access points (if they are used) and WLAN access points in different areas of the building. Some companies have policies governing Bluetooth usage; in some cases, it is not allowed if 802.11 standards are in place, and in some cases, a company may enforce rules that say Bluetooth can be used only outside the building. In other cases, a company may put its 802.11 devices on specific channels or use WLAN standards that use the 5-GHz range.

Bluetooth-equipped devices can use NFC, which allows two mobile devices (or a mobile device and a stationary computer) to be automatically paired and transmit data. NFC is not limited to Bluetooth, but Bluetooth is probably the technology most commonly used to transmit data wirelessly over short distances. Of course, even though the distance is short, attackers can still eavesdrop on NFC. In addition, NFC is a data transmission protocol, but it is not necessarily secure. Data can be destroyed by use of a jammer, and users are also at risk of replay attacks. As of this writing, NFC does not offer preventive security in this respect, but users can prevent these attacks by using only applications that offer SSL/TLS or other secure channels during an NFC session.

Any time a cell phone or smartphone connects, it uses some type of wireless service. Whether it's 5G, 4G, 3G, GSM, Wi-Fi, infrared, RFID, or Bluetooth, security implications exist. To minimize risks, the best solution is to turn off the particular service when not in use, use airplane mode, or simply turn off the mobile device altogether when it is not being used.

Bluetooth is especially vulnerable to virus attacks, as well as Bluejacking and Bluesnarfing. Bluejacking involves sending unsolicited messages to Bluetooth-enabled devices such as mobile phones. You can stop Bluejacking by setting the affected Bluetooth device to undiscoverable or by turning off Bluetooth altogether.

Bluesnarfing is unauthorized access of information from a wireless device through a Bluetooth connection. Generally, Bluesnarfing involves theft of data (calendar information, phone book contacts, and so on). Ways of discouraging Bluesnarfing include using a pairing key that is not easy to guess. (Stay away from 0000 and similar default Bluetooth pairing keys!) Otherwise, you should set Bluetooth devices to undiscoverable (only after setting up legitimate Bluetooth devices, of course) or turn off Bluetooth altogether.

Wi-Fi, a technology that allows devices to exchange data wirelessly over a computer network, has many vulnerabilities as well. Not only should mobile devices connect in a secure, encrypted fashion, but also you, as security administrator, need to keep a sharp eye on the current Common Vulnerabilities and Exposures (CVEs) list and the available updates and patches for those vulnerabilities. For example, there was a flaw in the programming of a well-known Wi-Fi System on Chip (SoC). The firmware had a vulnerability that could result in buffer overflows, which could then be exploited by attackers—connecting remotely via Wi-Fi—ultimately enabling them to execute their own code. Sometimes SoCs are not properly vetted for vulnerabilities, so you must be ready to patch at a moment's notice. This approach applies not only to smartphones and other typical mobile devices but to just about all devices in the Internet of Things (IoT) that have built-in Wi-Fi connections.

Let's not forget about *cellular connections*, which use mobile network technologies like 2G, 3G, 4G, and 5G for data and voice communication. Many companies don't allow cellular access on company premises, instead relying on Wi-Fi methods, such as Wi-Fi calling. This is common in CYOD and COPE environments. But if cellular is necessary in a BYOD environment, security can be increased by using newer devices, updating the devices' operating systems, updating the preferred roaming list (PRL), updating identification technologies (such as IMEI and IMSI), and using a VPN for data connections over cellular. You should use these methods for employees who must be on the road as well. And if there are foreseeable instances where cellular is not available for mobile employees, you should be sure they understand the risks of open Wi-Fi networks and know that they should avoid them as much as possible.

When it comes down to it, the use of the Global Positioning System (GPS) in general—and GPS derivatives such as GPS tagging, geofencing, and geolocation—should be examined carefully, weighing the benefits against the possible vulnerabilities. Many executives and other employees use their mobile devices at work, which brings up many security concerns besides GPS, collectively known as BYOD concerns and described in the following sections.

For the purposes of privacy, it is best to disable GPS whenever possible. Also, you should consider disabling other GPS and geolocation-related technologies. For example, with geotagging, geographic identification information, such as latitude and longitude coordinates, is added to photographs, websites, SMS messages, and more. Geotagging is common in social media and can be a great tool, but it can also be an easy way for attackers to zero in on high-profile executives and other employees of an organization. In these cases, you should consider implementing a *geofence*—a virtual fence that defines the boundaries of an actual geographic area. Geofencing is an excellent way to be alerted to users entering and exiting an organization's physical premises and can provide security for wireless networks by defining the physical borders and allowing or disallowing access based on the physical location of users or, more accurately, the users' computers or mobile devices.

Some organizations rely on satellite communications (SATCOM)—sometimes for long-distance communications and sometimes for communication between buildings in a campus in a point-to-point or point-to-multipoint deployment. Either way, it is important to understand that SATCOM devices can be at risk if their firmware is not updated. Exploits could include the installation of malicious firmware and the execution of arbitrary code. Updating may require physical access to the parabolic antenna using a laptop or terminal device. But remember that the easier it is to access these antennas, the more likely they are to be hacked by malicious individuals. Of course, in some cases these antennas can be hacked remotely as well. Secure planning is necessary when it comes to physical access, firewalling (if possible), and especially updating.

A wireless connection method that is often overlooked when it comes to security is infrared. It is employed in many technologies that we use every day, including mobile phones. Consequently, it is often not secured properly. Of course, many wireless receivers can be added to a device by simply plugging in a USB adapter. This capability is also often overlooked.

Remember that wireless technologies are always evolving, and anything is hackable, given time and ingenuity. When it comes to over-the-air (OTA) technology, you should be ever vigilant: Know the latest exploits and prepare a worthy defense.

Secure Implementation Best Practices

The best practices for secure implementation of communication methods and receivers are all similar, and the same controls can apply in most situations. Some of the biggest security issues with mobile device connection methods and receivers are vulnerabilities in the actual firmware and/or the software that runs on the device to interface with these technologies. These vulnerabilities can be used to interrupt or capture the communications between devices. The way to address this type of concern is to always verify that you are using the latest software version available for the device or radio. When it comes to mobile devices, typically these types of software updates are packaged into a larger update for the device that includes other fixes and features. However, sometimes a vulnerability is so severe that it requires a hotfix or patch to quickly address the vulnerability. Either way, keeping a device up to date is a solid approach to this concern.

There is software on a device that interacts with the hardware radio. That access can be controlled through the operating system permissions. By limiting access to the use of these communication mechanisms, you are essentially reducing the attack surface. Doing so helps mitigate the impact of software vulnerabilities as they come up. Keep in mind that if you are not using a specific connection method, you can simply turn it off. This again reduces your attack surface. Of course, turning off a connection is not always possible, so it is always a decision you need to make based on the environment you are in. For instance, if you're at a large security conference such as DEFCON, turning off all unnecessary connection methods is a very good idea. If you are just sitting around your house, however, there is obviously less of a concern that someone might be acting in a malicious way to attack your device.

Wireless Security Settings

Wireless networks are omnipresent in our daily lives, offering unparalleled convenience and accessibility. However, this convenience often comes at the cost of potential security vulnerabilities. This section aims to address these concerns by providing a comprehensive guide to securing wireless networks. It delves into various protocols and measures, such as Wi-Fi Protected Access 3 (WPA3), AAA/RADIUS authentication, cryptographic protocols, and other authentication methods. Understanding these settings is crucial for anyone involved in network administration, cybersecurity, or personal wireless network management. Keep reading to gain valuable insights into tightening the security of your wireless networks.

Weak encryption or no encryption can significantly compromise the security of a wireless network. This shortfall often happens if someone connects an older or outdated device that supports only weaker, older types of encryption. Imagine that you're a network administrator for a small business that has upgraded its wireless infrastructure. Your task is to ensure the highest level of security for the new network. One of your primary considerations will be the type of encryption and authentication to use. In this situation, Wi-Fi Protected Access 3 (WPA3) should be your go-to standard. Unlike its predecessor, WPA2, WPA3 employs Simultaneous Authentication of Equals (SAE). SAE replaces the older preshared key (PSK) system, which was susceptible to brute-force and offline dictionary attacks. How does SAE make a difference? In a brute-force attack, an attacker tries to gain access by repeatedly attempting different passwords. SAE counters this by initiating a live handshake process between the connecting device and the network. This handshake requires both parties to be present during authentication, making offline dictionary attacks ineffective. In addition, SAE's handshake process employs forward secrecy, meaning that even if an attacker intercepts the handshake, they can't use it to decrypt past sessions.

Wi-Fi Protected Access 3 (WPA3)

Key Topic

Wi-Fi Protected Access 3 (WPA3) is a security protocol designed to enhance wireless network security. WPA3-Personal improves upon WPA2 by using SAE, which, as just discussed, replaces the older PSK method and the optional use of 192-bit AES. Setting up WPA3-Personal involves a series of steps that are generally carried out through the wireless router's administrative interface. Log in to your router and look for the advanced settings. In ASUS routers the WPA-3 setting is located under Authentication Method. In a Cisco router, the settings are found under Access Control > Security.

Note that Cisco routers have two possible settings for WPA-3 Personal: WPA3 Only and WPA3 Transition Mode. The main difference is that WPA3 Only will only transmit and accept connections using WPA3 SAE. WPA Transition Mode will transmit out using WPA2 and WPA3 to allow devices to connect using either encryption mode.

For WPA3-Enterprise, the minimum encryption standard is 192-bit AES, but it also supports more advanced encryption methods like 256-bit Galois/Counter Mode Protocol (GCMP-256) and 384-bit Hashed Message Authentication Code with Secure Hash Algorithm (HMAC-SHA-384). These are cryptographic protocols that provide even more robust data protection, making it extremely difficult for unauthorized parties to decipher intercepted data. In the Cisco world, WPA3 has two operating modes: WPA3 Only and WPA3 192-bit. In WPA3 Only connecting devices are required to have 802.11w (PMF) active. WPA3 192-bit uses 192-bit encryption and leverages 802.1X for stronger security. (Refer to Chapter 11, "Applying Security Principles to Secure Enterprise Infrastructure," for a discussion of 802.1X.) We explore the specific cryptographic protocols for WPA3-Personal and WPA3-Enterprise later in this chapter.

WPA3-Personal is accessible for smaller setups because it doesn't require an extensive authentication server setup, unlike the Enterprise version. It still offers robust security features like SAE, which protects against common attacks. This means that even home users or small businesses can benefit from strong security without needing the infrastructure a larger organization might require.

Remote Authentication Dial-In User Service (RADIUS) Federation

Remote Authentication Dial-In User Service (RADIUS) federation serves a crucial role when an organization operates multiple RADIUS servers, which may even be located on different networks. RADIUS federation enables these servers to communicate securely by establishing trust relationships and creating a centralized management core to oversee these relationships and route authentication requests. The use of RADIUS federation is commonly paired with the 802.1X authentication standard.

This federated approach to network authentication is flexible enough to be extended across multiple organizations, allowing for seamless, secure communication among disparate systems.

Let's take a look at a scenario that might play out at a multi-site university where Wi-Fi is needed on all campuses. Imagine that you're a student at that university. Each campus has a Wi-Fi network, and you find it frustrating to enter your login credentials every time you move from one campus to another. The university's IT department faces the challenge of making this process more seamless without compromising security.

The solution is to implement RADIUS federation for wireless networks. RADIUS, which stands for Remote Authentication Dial-In User Service, is a protocol that provides centralized authentication, authorization, and accounting (AAA) management for users who connect and use a network service.

Here's a step-by-step guide to how RADIUS federation solves this problem:

Key Topic

1. **Set up the primary RADIUS server:** The university sets up a central RADIUS server that holds the primary list of usernames and passwords. This server is the ultimate reference that says "yes" or "no" when a user tries to connect to Wi-Fi.

2. **Set up the local RADIUS servers:** Each campus sets up its own local RADIUS server that is responsible for handling Wi-Fi connections at that location.

3. **Establish trust:** The local RADIUS servers are configured to trust the primary RADIUS server. They exchange cryptographic keys or certificates with each other.

4. **Authenticate:** When you first connect to the Wi-Fi at your home campus, your login credentials (usually your university username and password) are sent from the local RADIUS server to the primary RADIUS server for verification.

5. **Create a token:** Upon successful verification, the primary RADIUS server creates an "authentication token," which is sort of a digital hall pass.

6. **Store the token:** The token is sent back and stored on the local RADIUS server you initially connected to.

7. **Move between campuses:** Now, let's say you go to a different campus. Your device will try to connect to the Wi-Fi there.

8. **Verify the token:** The local RADIUS server at the new campus contacts the primary RADIUS server to see if you have a valid authentication token.

9. **Connect automatically:** If a valid token is found, the new local RADIUS server allows you to connect to the Wi-Fi without asking for your username and password again.

These tokens are time sensitive. They expire after a certain period, requiring you to reenter your credentials, which provides an added layer of security.

RADIUS offers a number of advantages:

- **User convenience:** You don't have to enter your credentials when you change locations.

- **Enhanced security:** All authentication is funneled through a central server, making it easier to monitor for suspicious activity.

- **Ease of management:** Managing one central RADIUS server is simpler for the IT department than managing multiple separate ones.

The university enhances the security of its wireless networks across all campuses by implementing a RADIUS federation setup, making life much easier for its roaming students like you and the staff.

Cryptographic Protocols

Cryptographic protocols are the backbone of secure wireless communications. While older standards like WEP and WPA have been deprecated, WPA3 has emerged as the current benchmark for wireless security. It offers a comprehensive suite of features to bolster authentication and encryption.

WPA3-Personal, for instance, allows users to select passwords that are easier to remember without sacrificing security. This is achieved through a technology that is resistant to offline dictionary attacks, where an attacker tries to guess the network password without further network interaction. The protocol also ensures forward secrecy, meaning that even if a password is compromised later, previously transmitted data remains secure.

WPA3-Enterprise takes security further by mandating Protected Management Frames (PMF) across all connections. It supports multiple Extensible Authentication Protocol (EAP) methods and requires a minimum of 128-bit AES-CCMP for authenticated encryption. It employs a minimum 256-bit HMAC with SHA-256 for key derivation and confirmation. In addition, it offers robust management frame protection through a minimum 128-bit BIP-CMAC-128.

For organizations that require heightened security, WPA3-Enterprise offers a 192-bit security mode. This mode employs EAP-TLS using a 384-bit elliptic curve for authentication and 256-bit GCMP for authenticated encryption. Key derivation and confirmation are performed using a 384-bit HMAC with SHA-384, and management frame protection is enhanced to 256-bit BIP-GMAC-256.

Let's look at a few scenarios where you might have to decide between WPA3-Enterprise and WPA3-Personal.

Imagine that you're a network administrator for a small business. You're tasked with upgrading the wireless network to ensure maximum security. WPA3-Personal would be an ideal choice over a more complex WPA3-Enterprise implementation. WPA3-Personal's resistance to offline dictionary attacks allows employees to use easier-to-remember passwords without compromising security. This means even if an attacker tries to guess the network password, the technology behind WPA3-Personal thwarts such attempts. Moreover, it ensures forward secrecy, so even if a password is compromised later, previously transmitted data remains secure.

In a corporate setting where sensitive data is frequently transmitted over the network, WPA3-Enterprise is the go-to standard. It mandates the use of PMF across all connections, offering an additional layer of security. This is crucial for protecting against potential on-path attacks that could compromise data integrity.

For a financial institution that requires the highest level of security, WPA3-Enterprise with 192-bit security mode is the best option. This mode employs advanced cryptographic tools like 384-bit elliptic curve for authentication and 256-bit GCMP for authenticated encryption. This ensures that financial transactions and customer data are protected with the highest level of security available.

In a healthcare facility where patient data is of utmost importance, WPA3-Enterprise can offer more robust security than WPA3-Personal offers. WPA3-Enterprise employs a minimum 256-bit HMAC with SHA-256 for key derivation and confirmation, ensuring that patient records are securely transmitted and stored.

Authentication Protocols

Authentication protocols serve as rules defining how users or systems prove their identity to gain access to a network. These protocols can vary widely based on several factors, such as the type of network, the level of security needed, and whether the authentication process is local or remote.

In a corporate environment, Lightweight Directory Access Protocol (LDAP) is often the go-to choice for wireless network authentication. Imagine that you're an IT administrator tasked with securing a corporate Wi-Fi network. You could configure the network to use LDAP, validating employees' credentials against a centralized directory. When an employee attempts to connect to the Wi-Fi network, the LDAP protocol cross-references the entered username and password with the central directory. If the credentials match, the employee gains access to the network. This setup allows centralized management of credentials and seamless integration with existing corporate directories, enhancing security and administrative efficiency.

Now consider a high-security government facility where the stakes for network security are even higher. In such a setting, Kerberos is often employed to add an extra layer of security. As the person responsible for the facility's wireless network, you would set up Kerberos to generate a time-sensitive "ticket" when a user attempts to connect. This ticket is then used for authentication, effectively reducing the window of opportunity for potential attackers. The key advantage here is the use of time-sensitive tickets and mutual authentication between the user and the network, which significantly elevates the security posture of the wireless network.

In educational settings like university campuses, 802.1X might be used for wireless network authentication. As a network administrator at a university, you might implement 802.1X on wireless access points across various departments. When a student or faculty member tries to connect to the Wi-Fi, the 802.1X protocol initially places the port in an "unauthorized" state. The port only transitions to an "authorized" state after the user's credentials have been successfully verified. This approach offers granular control over network access at the port level and can be combined with other authentication protocols, such as LDAP or Kerberos, for multilayered security.

Finally, it's worth mentioning that LDAP and Kerberos aren't limited to localized scenarios. For instance, a multinational corporation could employ federated LDAP to allow employees from different countries to access a unified wireless network. A coalition of government agencies could also use federated Kerberos authentication to enable secure, time-sensitive access across multiple secure wireless networks.

Application Security

Application security refers to security measures at the application level, the goal of which is to prevent data or code within an app from being stolen, intercepted, or hijacked. It encompasses the security considerations that are made during application development and design, and it also involves systems and approaches to protect apps after they are deployed.

Application security can include hardware, software, and procedures that identify or minimize security vulnerabilities. A router that prevents anyone from viewing a computer's IP address from the Internet is a form of hardware application security. But security measures at the application level are also typically built into the software, such as an application firewall that strictly defines what activities are allowed and prohibited. Procedures can entail things like an application security routine that includes protocols such as regular testing.

Input Validations

Input validation is the first step in checking the type and content of data supplied by a user or an application. Improper input validation is a major factor in many web security vulnerabilities, including cross-site scripting (XSS) and SQL injection (SQLi).

What is input validation? Any system or application that processes input data needs to ensure that it is valid. This applies both to information provided directly by the user and data received from other systems. Validation can be done on many levels, from simply checking the input types and lengths (syntactic validation) to ensuring that supplied values are valid in the application context (semantic validation).

In web applications, input validation typically means checking the values of web form input fields to ensure that a date field contains a valid date, an email field contains a valid email address, and so on. This initial client-side validation is performed directly in the browser, but submitted values also need to be checked on the server side.

> **NOTE**   While we generally talk about *user input* or *user-controlled input*, a good practice is to check all inputs to an application and treat them as untrusted until validated.

Let's see how to ensure proper input validation in web applications. Traditionally, form fields and other inputs were validated in JavaScript, either manually or using a dedicated library. Implementing validation is a tedious and error-prone process, so it's a good idea to check for existing validation features before you go the DIY route. Many languages and frameworks come with built-in validators that make form validation much easier and more reliable. For input data that should match a specific JSON or XML schema, you should validate input against that schema.

Secure Cookies

The *secure cookie* attribute is an option that can be set by the application server when sending a new cookie to the user within an HTTP response. The purpose of the secure attribute is to prevent cookies from being observed by unauthorized parties due to the transmission of the cookies in plaintext.

Cookies may contain sensitive information that shouldn't be accessible to an attacker eavesdropping on a channel. To ensure that cookies aren't transmitted in plaintext, you can send them with the secure flag.

Web browsers that support the secure flag only send cookies having the secure flag when the request uses HTTPS. This means that setting the secure flag of a cookie prevents browsers from sending it over an unencrypted channel. The unsecure cookies issue is commonly raised in penetration test reports performed by pen testers if the environment they are running on is missing the correct credentials.

Secure session cookies store information about a user session after the user logs in to an application. This information can be highly sensitive because an attacker can use a session cookie to impersonate a victim in *session hijacking* or *cookie hijacking*. The goal of this hijacking is to steal a valid and authorized cookie from real users.

Static Code Analysis

Static application security testing (SAST), or ***static code analysis***, is a testing methodology that involves analyzing source code to find security vulnerabilities that make an organization's applications susceptible to attack. SAST involves scanning an application in the known environment, before the code is compiled. Static code analysis takes place very early in the software development lifecycle because it does not require a working application and can take place without code being executed. It helps developers identify vulnerabilities in the initial stages of development and quickly resolve issues without breaking builds or passing on vulnerabilities to the final release of the application.

Static code analysis tools give developers real-time feedback while they code and can help them fix issues before they pass the code to the next phase of the Software Development Lifecycle (SDLC). This analysis prevents costly security-related issues from being afterthoughts. SAST tools also provide graphical representations of the issues found, from source to sink. They help navigate the code more easily. Some tools point out the exact locations of vulnerabilities and highlight risky code. Tools can also provide in-depth guidance on how to fix issues and the best place in the code to fix them, without requiring deep security domain expertise.

Developers can also create the customized reports they need with SAST tools; these reports can be exported offline and tracked using dashboards. Tracking all the security issues reported by a tool in an organized way can help developers remediate these issues promptly and release applications with minimal problems. This process contributes to the creation of a secure SDLC.

> **NOTE** It's important to note that SAST tools must be run on an application on a regular basis, such as during daily/monthly builds, every time code is checked in, or during a code release.

Effectively running a static code analysis involves six steps:

Step 1.   Select a static analysis tool that can perform the specific code review. The tool should be able to understand the underlying framework of the software.

Step 2. Create the scanning infrastructure and deploy the tool.

Step 3. Customize the tool to suit the needs of the analysis.

Step 4. Prioritize and onboard applications. Scan high-risk applications first.

Step 5. Analyze scan results, remove all false positives, and track each result. The team should be apprised of each defect and should schedule appropriate and timely remediation.

Step 6. Provide governance and training. Proper governance ensures that your development team employs the tools properly and consistently.

Code Signing

Code signing is the process of digitally signing executables and scripts to confirm that the software author can guarantee that the code has not been altered or corrupted since it was signed. The process employs the use of a cryptographic hash to validate authenticity and integrity. Digitally signing code provides both data integrity to prove that the code was not modified and source authentication to identify who signed the code. Furthermore, digitally signing code defines code signing use cases and can help identify security problems that arise when applying code signing solutions to those use cases. Code signing allows you to be sure you are downloading the right file from the right author/publisher instead of from an attacker who wants to steal your data.

Before developers can sign their work, they need to generate a public/private key pair. This is often done locally through software tools such as OpenSSL. Developers then give the public key and the organization's identity information to a trustworthy certificate authority (CA). The CA verifies the authenticity of identity information and then issues the certificate to the developer. This is the code signing certificate that was signed by the CA's private key and contains the developer organization's identity and the developer's public key.

When developers are ready to sign their work to establish authorship, they hash all the code they wrote. The value that is spit out is then encoded using a private key (usually generated by the author), along with the code signing certificate that contains the public key and identity of the author (proving the authorship). The output of this process is then added to the software to be shipped out.

This process constitutes a code signing operation. The public key of the CA is preinstalled in most browsers and operating system trust stores. When a user tries to download the software, that user uses the CA's public key to verify the authenticity of the code signing certificate embedded in the software to confirm that it's from a trustworthy CA. The developer's public key is then extracted from the certificate and used to decrypt the encrypted hash. Then the software is hashed again, and the new value is compared to the decrypted one. If the user's hash value and developer's hash value match, the software hasn't been corrupted or tampered with during transmission. The result is your assurance that you can run the code safely.

Sandboxing

Sandboxing is a critical security technique that involves creating a confined execution environment where untrusted or suspicious code can run without posing a risk to the system. This isolated sandbox serves as a tightly controlled set of resources for guest programs, limiting their scope and potential impact.

Imagine a corporate setting where employees frequently receive email attachments that could come from various sources. Some attachments might be essential for business operations, while others could potentially contain malicious code. In this scenario, sandboxing can be utilized as part of the organization's email filtering solution.

When an employee receives an email attachment, instead of directly opening the file, the attachment is first sent to a sandbox environment. In the sandbox, the attachment is automatically opened and executed. The code's behavior is then observed in real time: Does it try to access the file system? Does it make any unauthorized network calls? Is it attempting to encrypt files for a ransomware attack?

If the code shows malicious behavior within the sandbox, it is flagged, and the email can be automatically quarantined to prevent it from reaching the intended recipient. The attachment is deemed safe if no malicious actions are observed and the email is delivered to the employee's inbox.

By leveraging this sandboxing technique, the organization adds an extra layer of security, effectively minimizing the risk of a malware infection through email attachments without impeding the workflow of its employees.

Key Topic — Monitoring

Monitoring is the backbone of proactive cybersecurity, allowing for the continuous surveillance of systems, networks, and applications. By detecting, logging, and responding to specific activities or conditions, monitoring identifies current issues and anticipates future vulnerabilities. This is essential for maintaining the operational health of any digital environment and is a cornerstone of security measures in modern enterprises.

Consider the example of a financial institution that manages many transactions every second. While some transactions are routine and legitimate, the organization must be vigilant about fraud that could compromise the institution and its customers. In this setting, advanced monitoring tools could be deployed that are equipped with machine learning algorithms trained to recognize patterns indicative of fraudulent behavior.

For example, the monitoring system could flag unusual account activities like sudden large withdrawals, frequent international transactions within a short time frame, or simultaneous login attempts from multiple locations. The monitoring system could automatically alert the cybersecurity team for immediate investigation when any suspicious pattern is detected. In addition, if the system identifies what it deems a fraudulent transaction, it could be programmed to temporarily freeze the account, pending verification from the account holder.

However, the utility of monitoring in this context continues beyond just detecting fraudulent activities. It also logs all the data related to the suspicious event, creating an audit trail that can be used for future analysis, regulatory compliance, and legal proceedings, if necessary.

Through continuous monitoring, the financial institution minimizes the risk of fraudulent transactions, thereby safeguarding its assets and its customers' financial security.

Chapter Review Activities

Use the features in this section to study and review the topics in this chapter.

Review Key Topics

Review the most important topics in the chapter, noted with the Key Topic icon in the outer margin of the page. Table 14-4 lists these key topics and the page number on which each is found.

Table 14-4 Key Topics for Chapter 14

Key Topic Element	Description	Page Number
Paragraph	Secure baseline process details	309
Table 14-2	Summary of Hardening Techniques	315
Section	Mobile Device Management	318
Table 14-3	Mobile Device Security Concerns and Countermeasures	324
Section	Wi-Fi Protected Access 3 (WPA3)	332

Key Topic Element	Description	Page Number
List	Step-by-step process for RADIUS federation	333
Paragraph	LDAP scenario for authenticating users in a corporate environment	335
List	Six steps for running a static code analysis effectively	338
Section	Monitoring	340

Define Key Terms

Define the following key terms from this chapter and check your answers in the glossary:

secure baseline; deployment; hardening targets; mobile device; workstation; switch; router; cloud infrastructure; server; supervisory control and data acquisition (SCADA) systems and industrial control systems (ICSs); embedded system; real-time operating system (RTOS); Internet of Things (IoT) device; site survey; heat map; bring your own device (BYOD); mobile device management (MDM); choose your own device (CYOD); corporate-owned, personally enabled (COPE); Bluetooth; Wi-Fi; cellular connection; Wi-Fi Protected Access 3 (WPA3); authentication protocol; application security; input validation; secure cookie; static code analysis; code signing; sandboxing; monitoring

Review Questions

Answer the following review questions. Check your answers with the answer key in Appendix A.

1. What kind of security is provided by a router that prevents anyone from viewing a computer's IP address from the Internet?

2. What are some common web security vulnerabilities that improper input validation can lead to?

3. How can secure session cookies be exploited in an attack?

4. What kind of feedback do SAST tools provide developers?

5. List the six steps involved in effectively running a static code analysis.

6. What is required from a developer before they can sign their work in code signing?

7. What happens to an email attachment when sandboxing is used in a corporate setting?

8. What additional feature does monitoring provide besides detecting current issues in cybersecurity?

This chapter covers the following topics related to Objective 4.2 (Explain the security implications of proper hardware, software, and data asset management) of the CompTIA Security+ SY0-701 certification exam:

- Acquisition/procurement process
- Assignment/accounting
- Monitoring/asset tracking
- Disposal/decommissioning

CHAPTER 15

Understanding the Security Implications of Hardware, Software, and Data Asset Management

This chapter provides an overview of asset management with a focus on cyber-security. It covers acquisition and third-party risk assessment, emphasizes the role of asset assignment and accountability, and concludes with asset disposal and decommissioning guidelines. Monitoring and classification strategies are also briefly explored, tying together the asset management lifecycle.

"Do I Know This Already?" Quiz

The "Do I Know This Already?" quiz enables you to assess whether you should read this entire chapter thoroughly or jump to the "Chapter Review Activities" section. If you are in doubt about your answers to these questions or your own assessment of your knowledge of the topics, read the entire chapter. Table 15-1 lists the major headings in this chapter and their corresponding "Do I Know This Already?" quiz questions. You can find the answers in Appendix A, "Answers to the 'Do I Know This Already?' Quizzes and Review Questions."

Table 15-1 "Do I Know This Already?" Section-to-Question Mapping

Foundation Topics Section	Questions
Acquisition/Procurement Process	1, 2
Assignment/Accounting	3
Monitoring/Asset Tracking	4
Disposal/Decommissioning	5, 6

CAUTION   The goal of self-assessment is to gauge your mastery of the topics in this chapter. If you do not know the answer to a question or are only partially sure of the answer, you should mark that question as wrong for purposes of self-assessment. Giving yourself credit for an answer you correctly guess skews your self-assessment results and might provide you with a false sense of security.

1. What is the primary objective of vendor assessment in the procurement process?

   a. Cost evaluation

   b. Feature evaluation

   c. Security evaluation

   d. Usability evaluation

2. In the context of third-party risk management (TPRM), what should be a continuous activity?

   a. Legal documentation

   b. Risk assessments

   c. Contract negotiation

   d. Vendor replacement

3. What does the assignment/accounting process help establish within an organization?

   a. Business goals

   b. Lines of responsibility and accountability

   c. Sales strategies

   d. Asset pricing

4. Why are monitoring and asset tracking important?

   a. To make informed marketing decisions

   b. To make informed decisions related to security and budgeting

   c. To maintain vendor relationships

   d. To accelerate product development

5. In the disposal/decommissioning phase, what does sanitization primarily aim to achieve?

   a. Data retrieval

   b. Data retention

   c. Data deletion

   d. Data encryption

6. What does data retention primarily involve?

   a. Keeping data for a specific period, as mandated by law or policy

   b. Deleting data immediately after use

   c. Randomly destroying data

   d. Constantly updating data

Foundation Topics

Acquisition/Procurement Process

The acquisition or procurement process is the initial asset management phase and sets the stage for securely handling hardware, software, and data assets. The *acquisition process* is far more than merely purchasing the required resources; it involves a comprehensive strategy to ensure that what is being procured meets the organization's security policies, standards, and compliance requirements.

A prosperous and secure procurement process also requires teamwork and is built on solid internal relationships. You must include leaders from the supply department, the engineering department for software engineering procurements, and any leaders who can offer insights into details of the asset under review. Just as one person cannot know everything, one security analyst cannot assess everything alone.

Here are a few key points to consider when conducting a procurement review:

- **Vendor assessment:** Assess the credibility and security measures of vendors. Ensure that they comply with industry standards and legal requirements. Ask for documents on the products you will use and request copies of any external assessments done on the organization and its products.

- **Security standards:** Choose products that adhere to recognized security standards and best practices. Ensure that the standards the product was assessed against align with your organization's requirements. For example, you might have a product that went through a NIST 800-53 assessment for a non-healthcare environment, but you need to use the product in a hospital. A NIST 800-53 assessment is not the same as a HIPAA assessment. In this example, you would need to request that the vendor assess the product from a HIPAA perspective.

- **Licensing and support:** Ensure that products have proper licensing and support to facilitate long-term security management. Many service-based organizations rely on the details of a service-level agreement (SLA), and you should, too. Read the vendor's licensing documents (Does the vendor leverage third-party plug-ins? Do these plug-ins require any sort of licensing limitations for the vendor your organization might inherit?) and confirm your understanding of any support post-purchase.

- **Budget and costing:** Financial planning must incorporate the costs of securing the assets, such as firewalls, anti-malware software, or encryption tools. If a purchase requires you to add more defenses to your network or software, that should factor into your purchasing decision.

Check out Table 15-2 for examples of questions you might ask to ensure a thorough review of the procurement process.

Key Topic

Table 15-2 Example Questions for Procurement Process Review

Procurement Review Topic	Questions a Security Analyst Might Ask
Vendor assessment	■ Have we checked the vendor against a validated industry-standard checklist (for example, ISO 27001, CSA STAR)?
	■ Did we request copies of the vendor's most recent third-party security assessments?
Security standards	■ Does the product or service align with our organizational security policies and compliance requirements (for example, NIST, HIPAA)?
	■ Have we conducted a gap analysis between the product's security standards and our own?
Licensing and support	■ Have we reviewed the vendor's end user license agreement (EULA) to identify any potential security concerns (for example, third-party data sharing)?
	■ Is there a dedicated support team for the product that can promptly assist with security concerns?
Budget and costing	■ Have we factored the additional security costs, such as for additional firewalls or security training, into the overall budget for this asset?
	■ Have we considered the long-term cost implications of maintaining and upgrading this asset's security features?

A vital but often-overlooked aspect of the acquisition and procurement process is third-party risk management (TPRM). TPRM involves evaluating and managing the risks associated with outsourcing services or buying products from third-party vendors. As organizations increasingly rely on external vendors for various services and products—from cloud storage to software solutions—it is imperative to scrutinize the security posture of these third parties.

Before entering into any contractual relationship, it is important to perform due diligence on a third party's security policies, track record, and compliance with industry standards. You should ensure that security expectations and requirements are clearly outlined in contracts or SLAs. This might include data protection, compliance, and incident response clauses. Risk assessments are not a one-time activity. Continuous monitoring of the third party's security measures is essential to adapt to evolving risks and vulnerabilities. You should conduct risk assessments and require them from your vendors as well.

Assignment/Accounting

The ***assignment and accounting process*** is indispensable for maintaining a secure and organized environment in asset management. It lays the groundwork for ensuring that each asset—hardware, software, or data—is accounted for and has a designated owner. This aspect of asset management is pivotal because it establishes lines of responsibility and accountability, thus affecting an organization's overall security posture.

Ownership is the designation of the individual or department within the organization that is responsible for an asset, from acquisition to decommissioning. For example, in many organizations, the IT department could be considered the owner of all network routers. If a vulnerability is detected in a specific software application, pinpointing the owner expedites the mobilization of the appropriate team to resolve the issue. Ownership typically extends to tasks such as updates, maintenance, and asset decommissioning. Software development teams could be considered owners of plug-ins or modules used in software products. If a vulnerability is detected there, they would be the ones to resolve the issues.

Once ownership is established, each asset must be classified based on its sensitivity, importance, and criticality to the organization. This is known as classification. Assets could be classified into various categories, such as public, internal, or confidential. For instance, a public-facing website might require basic security measures and might be classified as public. In contrast, a database that contains customer financial information would require advanced encryption and restricted access and would thereby be classified as confidential.

As another example, within a sales department, quarterly sales data might be classified as sensitive, with access limited to senior management. In contrast, daily sales metrics could be classified as internal, with accessibility granted to the entire sales team.

The importance of proper assignment/accounting practices must be balanced. It involves determining who is responsible for each asset (ownership) and informs what level of security and oversight each asset will require (classification). Going back to the point we discussed earlier, you must build bridges internally in an organization to ensure that assets are appropriately classified based on the information they will handle.

Monitoring/Asset Tracking

Monitoring and asset tracking are central pillars of effective asset management and are vital for maintaining an organization's cybersecurity hygiene. They provide continuous visibility into the status, location, and condition of all assets within an organization. Tracking this information ensures that the company can make informed decisions related to security, budgeting, and overall operations.

Inventory

Inventory refers to maintaining a detailed record of all organizational assets, including what assets exist and pertinent details such as make, model, software version, and patch level. For instance, in an enterprise scenario, knowing the software versions running on different workstations helps to ensure that any security updates are deployed uniformly, thus preventing potential vulnerabilities.

For example, a healthcare provider may have a variety of assets to monitor, from hospital bed sensors to database servers containing patient records. By keeping a well-maintained inventory, the organization can quickly identify which devices must be updated when a security patch is released for a particular software product.

Enumeration

Enumeration takes inventory management a step further. It involves actively identifying the assets within an environment and mapping them in a way that details their relationships and dependencies. This could be particularly beneficial during penetration testing or when mapping the surface of an attack vector. For instance, understanding that a specific server is central to multiple business operations will help in prioritizing its security.

Imagine an organization running an e-commerce website. Enumeration would involve detailing not just the web servers but also databases, back-end services, and even third-party APIs that the platform interacts with. Knowing each asset's role provides a fuller picture of potential security risks and allows for more effective incident response planning.

Disposal/Decommissioning

The lifecycle of any hardware, software, or data asset within an organization doesn't cease at the end of its useful tenure; it extends to how these assets are appropriately disposed of, or *decommissioned*. This phase is crucial for several reasons. First, improper disposal can lead to unauthorized data retrieval and subsequent data breaches. Second, environmental concerns dictate the responsible disposal of electronic waste. Third, regulatory compliance often mandates specific procedures for asset disposal and data retention.

In some instances, the asset in question may contain sensitive or proprietary information, the leaking of which could place the organization at significant legal and reputational risk. In other cases, the asset might still have financial value and could be resold or donated, but only after it has been adequately sanitized to prevent unauthorized data access. In addition, specific industries like healthcare and finance have stringent regulations like HIPAA and SOX, which mandate particular procedures and documentation for asset disposal and decommissioning.

Given these considerations, disposal and decommissioning are hardly trivial tasks; they require detailed planning, secure processes, and, often, specialized third-party services to ensure that they are executed correctly. It involves the same amount of review that went into the purchase, only in reverse. Whether dealing with data sanitization, physical destruction, certification, or long-term data retention, each subprocess within asset disposal and decommissioning comes with its own set of best practices, challenges, and legal obligations. This is another opportunity to work with others internally in the organization to ensure that assets are destroyed in ways that are appropriate to their classification.

Sanitization

Sanitization refers to removing data from a storage device so that it cannot be recovered, even with advanced data recovery tools. This is usually achieved by overwriting existing data with random information. For example, when decommissioning a hard drive used in a healthcare setting, thorough sanitization should be executed to make sure no residual patient data is accessible.

There are different levels of sanitization based on the data classification and associated risks. For highly sensitive data, multiple passes of overwriting might be implemented, sometimes coupled with physical destruction techniques like degaussing, where the magnetic field of the storage device is disrupted.

Destruction

Destruction is the physical disassembly or obliteration of hardware assets. In the case of a hard drive, this could mean shredding the drive into small fragments. This method is generally employed when the device is no longer functional or useful and contains data that, if leaked, could pose a serious security risk. An organization dealing with national security might shred or incinerate old hard drives rather than risk data leakage. Table 15-3 provides a few examples of physical destruction methods.

Key Topic

Table 15-3   Physical Destruction Methods

Method of Destruction	Applicable Hardware	Process Description	Considerations
Shredding	Hard drives, SSDs	Physical shredding into small fragments	Ensures complete data destruction; loud and messy operation
Degaussing	Magnetic media	Applying a magnetic field to disrupt stored data	Effective only for magnetic storage; not useful for SSDs
Incineration	All types	Burning hardware in a controlled environment	Effective but poses environmental concerns; may require special facilities
Crushing	Hard drives, SSDs	Using a hydraulic press to deform the device	Less thorough than shredding; manual removal of data may still be required
Drilling	Hard drives	Drilling holes through the platters	Cost-effective but labor intensive; may not destroy data on undrilled portions
Acid bath	Chips, PCBs	Immersion in corrosive liquid to dissolve parts	Hazardous and requires special handling; environmental concerns

Certification

Certification in the context of disposal and decommissioning refers to the documentation and validation that the decommissioning process has been executed according to company policy and applicable laws or regulations. For example, a business in the financial sector might need to comply with specific standards or laws, such as the Sarbanes-Oxley Act. A certificate of destruction often serves as a legally binding document that confirms that the asset has been disposed of securely and responsibly.

Data Retention

Data retention is keeping certain types of information for a specified period, as mandated by either company policy or regulatory requirements. For instance, tax-related documents need to be stored securely for seven years before they can be deleted or destroyed. Patient records might have a different retention period in a medical setting, as dictated by laws like HIPAA. During this time, the data must remain secure and accessible only to authorized personnel. Once the data retention period expires, these files should be sanitized or destroyed according to company and legal guidelines.

Chapter Review Activities

Use the features in this section to study and review the topics in this chapter.

Review Key Topics

Review the most important topics in the chapter, noted with the Key Topic icon in the outer margin of the page. Table 15-4 lists these key topics and the page number on which each is found.

Table 15-4   Key Topics for Chapter 15

Key Topic Element	Description	Page Number
List	Key points to consider when conducting procurement review	348
Table 15-2	Example Questions to Consider During the Procurement Process	349
Section	Assignment/Accounting	350
Table 15-3	Physical Destruction Methods	353

Define Key Terms

Define the following key terms from this chapter and check your answers in the glossary:

acquisition process, assignment and accounting process, ownership, monitoring and asset tracking, inventory, enumeration, decommissioned, sanitization, destruction, certification, data retention

Review Questions

Answer the following review questions. Check your answers with the answer key in Appendix A.

1. What key departments should be involved in a secure and prosperous procurement process?

2. How does third-party risk management (TPRM) contribute to the acquisition and procurement process?

3. What are the two main aspects of the assignment and accounting process in asset management?

4. What are the subprocesses involved in the disposal and decommissioning phase of asset management?

This chapter covers the following topics related to Objective 4.3 (Explain various activities associated with vulnerability management) of the CompTIA Security+ SY0-701 certification exam:

- Identification methods
- Analysis
- Vulnerability response and remediation
- Validation of remediation
- Reporting

CHAPTER 16

Understanding Various Activities Associated with Vulnerability Management

This chapter provides a comprehensive guide to vulnerability and risk management in cybersecurity. Beginning with various identification methods like vulnerability scanning and application security, it explores real-time threat feeds and the secretive corners of the dark web. This chapter also looks at penetration testing, responsible disclosure programs, and bug bounty initiatives as part of an intricate auditing process. The focus then shifts to analysis, encompassing concepts like confirmation, CVSS, CVE, and risk tolerance. The chapter also addresses vulnerability response and remediation strategies, from patching to insurance and segmentation, before discussing the importance of validation through rescanning, audits, and verification. Finally, the chapter explores the critical role of reporting and turning data into actionable insights for both technical teams and decision makers.

"Do I Know This Already?" Quiz

The "Do I Know This Already?" quiz enables you to assess whether you should read this entire chapter thoroughly or jump to the "Chapter Review Activities" section. If you are in doubt about your answers to these questions or your own assessment of your knowledge of the topics, read the entire chapter. Table 16-1 lists the major headings in this chapter and their corresponding "Do I Know This Already?" quiz questions. You can find the answers in Appendix A, "Answers to the 'Do I Know This Already?' Quizzes and Review Questions."

Table 16-1 "Do I Know This Already?" Section-to-Question Mapping

Foundation Topics Section	Questions
Identification Methods	1–3
Analysis	4–6
Vulnerability Response and Remediation	7, 8
Validation of Remediation	9
Reporting	10

CAUTION   The goal of self-assessment is to gauge your mastery of the topics in this chapter. If you do not know the answer to a question or are only partially sure of the answer, you should mark that question as wrong for purposes of self-assessment. Giving yourself credit for an answer you correctly guess skews your self-assessment results and might provide you with a false sense of security.

1. What is the primary focus of static analysis?

   a. Evaluating a program while it's running

   b. Analyzing an application's source code before execution

   c. Real-time threat evaluation

   d. Manual review of system documentation

2. What does dynamic analysis examine?

   a. An application in its running state

   b. Source code before a program is run

   c. Encrypted email channels

   d. Third-party audits

3. What is the primary objective of a responsible disclosure program?

   a. To offer financial incentives to hackers

   b. To encourage the ethical reporting of security vulnerabilities

   c. To perform both static and dynamic analyses

   d. To examine the source code

4. What is the impact of a false positive in cybersecurity?

   a. Increases overall security

   b. Signals an activity as a threat when it is not

   c. Indicates a flaw in dynamic analysis

   d. Always leads to immediate rectification of issues

5. What does the Common Vulnerability Scoring System (CVSS) help with?

   a. Encouraging ethical hacking

   b. Automated rescanning of vulnerabilities

   c. Assessing vulnerabilities in a standardized way

   d. Providing a financial cushion against potential loss

6. What is the focus of vulnerability classification?

    a. Identifying issues during runtime

    b. Organized categorization of identified vulnerabilities

    c. Offering monetary rewards for discovering vulnerabilities

    d. Serving as an organizational memory for cybersecurity

7. What is a common challenge with patching?

    a. Ethical reporting of vulnerabilities

    b. Scheduling issues due to system downtime

    c. Exposing subtle flaws or vulnerabilities

    d. Encouraging ethical hacking

8. What should an analyst consider regarding cybersecurity insurance?

    a. Types of incidents covered

    b. The synergistic relationship between static and dynamic testing

    c. The deadline for resolving vulnerabilities

    d. The nature and severity of software vulnerabilities

9. What distinguishes an audit from an automated scan in cybersecurity?

    a. It is always automated.

    b. It involves a thorough manual review.

    c. It involves real-time threat evaluation.

    d. It only focuses on vulnerabilities during runtime.

10. What is a key consideration in cybersecurity reporting?

    a. The type of audience for a report

    b. The type of vulnerability

    c. The financial incentives offered for discovering vulnerabilities

    d. The type of incidents covered by insurance

Foundation Topics

Identification Methods

Identification methods are foundational techniques in vulnerability management that are explicitly designed to locate, identify, and document security flaws in an organization's digital ecosystem. Without these methods, attempting to analyze or remediate vulnerabilities would be like searching for a needle in a haystack.

Vulnerability Scan

Several tools and methods are employed to identify, categorize, and mitigate security vulnerabilities. These typically include, but are not limited to, the following:

- Static application security testing (SAST) tools analyze source code or binaries without executing the program.

- Dynamic application security testing (DAST) tools test applications while running to find vulnerabilities that might not be visible in the code.

- Interactive application security testing (IAST) tools combine aspects of both SAST and DAST for more comprehensive analysis.

- Threat intelligence platforms (TIPs) gather data from various sources to provide insights about potential vulnerabilities.

- Security information and event management (SIEM) systems provide real-time analysis of security alerts generated by network hardware and applications.

Within this suite of tools, vulnerability scanners and software composition analysis (SCA) tools play a crucial role:

- **Vulnerability scanners:** These are automated tools that scan systems, networks, or applications for known vulnerabilities. A vulnerability scanner runs a *vulnerability scan* to look for known vulnerabilities in a system. It works by comparing information about the software running on a system (such as version numbers and configurations) against databases of known vulnerabilities. Figure 16-1 illustrates the workflow of a typical automated vulnerability scanner, showcasing how it can detect weaknesses by scanning the targeted assets, correlating the findings with a vulnerability database, and generating a report of identified vulnerabilities.

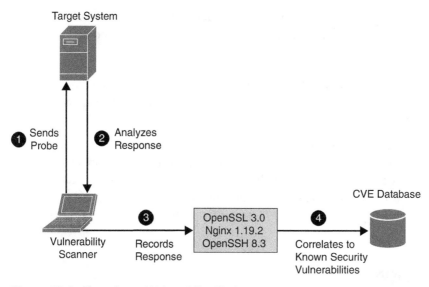

Figure 16-1   Coordinated Vulnerability Disclosures

■ **Software composition analysis (SCA):** These tools specialize in identifying open-source components within codebases. They help in detecting known vulnerabilities within these components, licensing issues, and out-of-date libraries that might impact the security posture of an application.

Together, these tools help a vulnerability management team get a broad and deep view of the security stance of their applications and systems, ensuring that they can respond effectively to threats.

Vulnerability scanners are all different, but most follow a process like this (refer to Figure 16-1):

Step 1.   In the discovery phase, the scanner uses a tool such as Nmap to perform host and port enumeration. Using the results of the host and port enumeration, the scanner begins to probe open ports for more information.

Step 2.   When the scanner has enough information about the open port to determine what software and version are running on that port, it records that information in a database for further analysis. The scanner can use various methods to make this determination, including banner information.

Step 3.   The scanner tries to determine if the software that is listening on the target system is susceptible to any known vulnerabilities. It does this by correlating a database of known vulnerabilities against the information recorded in the database about the target services.

Step 4.   The scanner produces a report on what it suspects could be vulnerable. Keep in mind that these results are often false positives and need to be validated.

One of the main challenges with automated vulnerability scanners is the number of false positives and false negatives. We will explore false positives and false negatives in great depth later in this chapter.

Vulnerability scanners sometimes can send numerous IP packets to the target system at a very fast pace. This can be intrusive, and the IP packets can potentially cause negative effects and even crash the application or system. Some scanners can be configured in such a way that it is possible to throttle the probes and IP packets that it sends to the target system in order to be nonintrusive and to not cause any negative effects in the system.

Application Security

Application security is a specialized realm within the broader landscape of identification methods that focuses on the vulnerabilities in software applications. In the modern business environment, where software is increasingly the interface of interaction with customers, vendors, and even within the organization itself, application security cannot be an afterthought. For example, a financial institution heavily relies on various software applications for transactions, customer data storage, and inter-departmental communications. A single vulnerability in these applications can lead to unauthorized fund transfers, data breaches, or even regulatory fines. Hence, methods like static analysis, dynamic analysis, and package monitoring are pivotal in safeguarding these software assets. Let's dig into some of the finer points of application security through static analysis, dynamic analysis, and package monitoring in the application security process.

Key Topic

Static analysis, also known as static application security testing (SAST), is a security testing method that examines the source code, bytecode, or binaries of an application for potential security vulnerabilities. This examination occurs without executing the program, enabling developers to identify and address issues during the initial stages of software development.

The strategic advantage of employing SAST is its ability to provide early and thorough code evaluation. SAST tools perform in-depth analyses to uncover security weaknesses that, if left undetected, could lead to serious vulnerabilities once the application is in operation. This proactive measure is key in developing a secure coding framework to effectively minimize the risk of future breaches.

Take, for instance, an electronic health records (EHR) system employed by a network of hospitals. With SAST, developers can identify areas in the source code that may lead to vulnerabilities, such as hardcoded passwords, which could be exploited if the code went into production unchecked. Specifically, if a portion of the EHR system's code handles sensitive patient information like Social Security numbers, SAST could reveal whether this data is being held and stored securely. It can detect issues such as whether sensitive information is stored in plaintext or whether the code is susceptible to buffer overflows—both of which could have serious implications for data security.

As you can see, SAST is more than just a debugging tool; it is a critical part of the secure software development lifecycle. SAST is a thorough approach to bug detection in the early stages of program development, and it promotes a preventive approach to security rather than a reactive one. An organization can ensure a more robust, secure software release by identifying and fixing security issues early, keeping user data safe, and maintaining trust.

Key Topic

Dynamic analysis takes the opposite approach from static code analysis: It is executed while a program is in operation. Dynamic application security testing (DAST) looks at an application from the outside in, examining it in its running state and trying to manipulate it to discover security vulnerabilities. A dynamic test simulates an attack against a web application and analyzes the application's reactions to determine whether it is vulnerable. Dynamic analysis is capable of exposing a subtle flaw or vulnerability that is too complicated for static analysis alone to reveal. Used wisely, automated tools can dramatically improve the return on testing investment. Automated testing tools are an ideal option in certain situations. Automating tests that are run on a regular basis during the software development lifecycle (SDLC) are also helpful.

As an enterprise strives to secure the SDLC, it must be noted that there is no panacea. Neither static nor dynamic testing alone can offer blanket protection. Ideally, an enterprise will perform both static and dynamic analyses, taking advantage of the synergistic relationship that exists between static and dynamic testing.

Package monitoring involves continually surveilling third-party software packages and libraries that an application incorporates. Complexity arises because some organizations use many of these packages without understanding the security ramifications. Take, for instance, an e-commerce platform developed by a web development agency using a content management system (CMS) like WordPress. The CMS platform would likely use third-party plug-ins for payment gateways, inventory management, and customer relationship management.

Let's get more specific. Imagine that one of the third-party payment gateway plug-ins used by the CMS has a vulnerability that allows for unauthorized fund transfers. With effective package monitoring, this vulnerability could be identified as soon as it is publicly disclosed—or even sooner, if the monitoring taps into private vulnerability databases. The web development agency could immediately patch the plug-in or replace it with a secure alternative, thereby averting financial loss and reputational damage on the e-commerce website.

Threat Feed

A *threat feed* can be a real-time repository and transmission channel for data points or indicators that could signify cyber threats. A threat feed can be tailored to the specific needs of an organization. For instance, a threat feed at a multinational corporation might ingest data on new phishing attacks and disseminate the information across all corporate endpoints to block similar incoming emails.

Open-Source Intelligence (OSINT)

Open-source intelligence (OSINT) involves scouring publicly available databases, online forums, and code repositories to assemble a nuanced view of the current threat landscape. A cybersecurity analyst at a retail company might set up web scrapers to continuously pull data from GitHub repositories that disclose vulnerabilities affecting point-of-sale (POS) systems. These alerts could be automatically integrated into a threat feed, which can prompt immediate action, such as applying patches or tightening firewall rules specific to POS systems. A challenge with OSINT sources is in the nature of their openness. You need to fact-check all data and ensure that your threat feed only pulls from reliable sources.

Proprietary/Third-Party

A *proprietary threat feed* is a specialized channel that may require a subscription. Unlike OSINT, these feeds are curated and may include analysis of a threat's impact. For instance, a bank could subscribe to a service like Recorded Future or FireEye to get tailored data on threats aimed explicitly at financial institutions. These services might provide decrypted payloads of banking Trojans in circulation, allowing the bank's cybersecurity team to fortify their defense mechanisms specifically against these Trojans.

Information-Sharing Organization

Information-sharing organizations and groups such as information sharing and analysis centers (ISACs) serve as hubs where companies can contribute and receive threat information. Suppose you are an executive at a pharmaceutical company that is part of a healthcare ISAC. This ISAC may have a threat feed that immediately informs you when a new vulnerability is discovered in a commonly used EHR program, allowing your IT team to assess the risk and take appropriate countermeasures before exploitation occurs.

ISACs exist for different industry sectors. Examples include automotive, aviation, communications, IT, natural gas, elections, electricity, financial services, and healthcare ISACs. You can learn more about ISACs at www.nationalisacs.org.

Dark Web

Dark web is a term that often conjures images of clandestine online activities—and rightfully so. The **dark web** is a part of the Internet, also often known as the deep web, that encompasses all web pages not indexed by standard search engines like Google or Bing. However, the dark web is actually a specific segment of the deep web, distinguished by its requirement for special software access. The special software access is often where you will find attackers looking to take advantage of novice users and where illicit activities occur.

It's important to understand that the dark web is not readily accessible through conventional means. Accessing it typically requires the use of tools such as Tor (The Onion Router), which routes web traffic through multiple layers of encryption and network relays, concealing users' identities and activities. This level of secrecy makes the dark web a hotbed of illegal operations, including the trade of stolen data and various illicit services.

For cybersecurity professionals, it is important to recognize the dark web as a significant factor in the threat landscape. While individuals can access the dark web, specialized third-party services provide the most insightful dark web monitoring and intelligence. These services play a critical role in cybersecurity, offering early detection of stolen data or credentials and alerting organizations to potential breaches or compromises.

By leveraging these third-party monitoring services, businesses can gain advanced warning of data being sold or shared on the dark web, potentially preventing full-scale breaches. However, such services come at a cost and require careful consideration and understanding of what they can realistically deliver.

In some cases, security professionals go to the dark web to research and find different threats and exploits that could affect their organization. This task is easier said than done. This is why several companies sell "dark web monitoring" and threat intelligence services. For instance, a cybersecurity team in a technology company may find a dark web forum where a user claims to have found an exploit for a popular brand of network routers. The team could purchase this exploit for analysis (assuming that ethical and legal guidelines are followed) and, if it proves legitimate, could add this information to their threat feed and quickly act to secure their network infrastructure against this newly discovered exploit.

Penetration Testing

Penetration testing mimics real-world attacks to identify potential vulnerabilities in a system, a network, or an application. Unlike automated vulnerability scans, it's a hands-on approach that provides a deeper understanding of various security loopholes. Tools commonly used in penetration testing include Metasploit for payload crafting and Burp Suite for web vulnerability scanning. A real-world scenario might involve testing a company's email system to determine its susceptibility to phishing attacks.

You will learn more about penetration testing in Chapter 27, "Understanding Types and Purposes of Audits and Assessments." For now, here is a high-level review of what a legal penetration test might look like:

Step 1.   **Planning and scope definition:** Outline the objectives, target systems, and boundaries. Obtain legal permissions for the test.

Step 2.   **Reconnaissance:** Collect as much information as possible about the target system. This might include identifying IP addresses, network services, and potential entry points.

Step 3.   **Exploitation:** Execute the planned attacks in a controlled environment. This can range from SQL injections to social engineering tactics.

Step 4.   **Post-exploitation:** Assess the impact of the exploitation. What data could an attacker access? Can they escalate their privileges or move laterally within the network?

Step 5.   **Reporting:** Document findings, methodologies, and recommendations. It is critical for stakeholders to understand the vulnerabilities, their impacts, and the steps needed for remediation.

Responsible Disclosure Program

A *responsible disclosure program* is a framework that encourages the ethical reporting of security vulnerabilities. It outlines the procedures for external security researchers to report vulnerabilities they have discovered in a company's software or systems. The program specifies a secure reporting mechanism, often an encrypted email or a dedicated online portal, and may offer monetary rewards or public recognition incentives. By establishing a clear reporting channel and expectations, the program helps companies patch vulnerabilities before they can be exploited maliciously.

In a responsible disclosure program, timing and coordination are paramount. After ethical hackers discover a vulnerability, they contact the company through a predefined channel that may be encrypted for security. The company then acknowledges the submission and begins its internal assessment. One key aspect is setting a deadline for resolving the issue. Depending on the severity of the vulnerability, this can range from a few days to a few months. Critical issues, such as those that could lead to unauthorized access to sensitive data, often have shorter deadlines for remediation.

Bug Bounty Program

A *bug bounty program* is a specialized type of responsible disclosure program that offers financial incentives to security researchers for discovering and reporting software vulnerabilities. Organizations host these programs to crowd source the identification of security flaws in their software, systems, or online services. The compensation offered in a bug bounty program can range from nominal to thousands of dollars, depending on the severity and impact of the vulnerability discovered. Beyond just the reward, ethical hackers often receive public recognition, which can be valuable for career progression. It's crucial to understand that not all vulnerabilities fetch the same bounty. The reward value usually corresponds to the severity and impact of the discovered issue. Aspiring cybersecurity professionals should be proficient in documenting their findings clearly and concisely, as this is required in almost all bug bounty programs.

System/Process Audit

An audit is not merely a compliance checkbox but an opportunity for an organization to critically evaluate its internal processes and controls. During a *system or process audit*, each component of the system or process and its associated policies is reviewed. System or process audits range from analyzing user access controls to data backup strategies. Specialized tools like Nessus or Wireshark might be used to examine network traffic and configurations. In healthcare, audits commonly ensure compliance with regulations like HIPAA, scrutinizing the encryption methods used for patient records and the training employees receive on safeguarding this data.

Analysis

Key Topic

Analysis is a central component in cybersecurity that balances data collection and actionable decision making. *Analysis* transforms raw data about vulnerabilities and threats into comprehensive insights. This helps cybersecurity experts assess the severity of risks, confirm the validity of vulnerabilities, and make data-driven decisions to bolster an organization's defense mechanisms.

Confirmation

Confirmation isn't just an administrative checkbox but a rigorous validation process that either affirms or negates the existence of a suspected vulnerability. In this phase, analysts grapple with false positives and false negatives, which reflect the accuracy of prior vulnerability assessments. A *false positive*, which signals an activity as a threat when it is not, isn't merely an inconvenience. It can act as a smokescreen, hiding a real issue by overwhelming a security team with false alarms. On the other end, a *false negative*, a real threat that goes unnoticed, can be even more damaging. It could be the ticking time bomb that allows unauthorized access to critical systems. Confirmation often involves cross-referencing findings with known vulnerability databases and possibly retesting to ensure that the risk is accurately stated.

Prioritize

Beyond identifying vulnerabilities, analysts must prioritize them—a step that matches the technicalities of cybersecurity with the practicalities of business operations. *Prioritization* is not as straightforward as first addressing the vulnerability with the highest potential impact. Analysts often have to factor in the asset's value to the organization, the nature of the data that could be compromised, and the broader impact on the user experience and business continuity. It's a complex juggling act that requires a deep understanding of cybersecurity principles and the organization's operational intricacies.

Common Vulnerability Scoring System (CVSS)

When it comes to evaluating the gravity and urgency of a system vulnerability, the *Common Vulnerability Scoring System (CVSS)* stands as an industry pillar. The CVSS is a multifaceted tool that provides a robust mechanism for assessing vulnerabilities in a standardized way. It quantifies the nature and severity of software vulnerabilities, aiding security professionals and organizations in making informed decisions about risk mitigation.

What sets CVSS apart is its multifaceted approach, broken down into three core groups: the base group, the temporal group, and the environmental group. Each of these groups scrutinizes a different facet of a vulnerability, providing a rounded view of the risk involved:

- **Base group:** This foundation layer contains immutable vulnerability characteristics that are constant over time and in environments.

  - **Exploitability metrics:** These metrics encapsulate various aspects of exploiting a vulnerability. They include the following:

  - **Attack vector (AV):** AV categorizes the required proximity between an attacker and a target. Values range from network (N) to physical (P).

- **Attack complexity (AC):** AC gauges the conditions that must be met to exploit the vulnerability.

- **Privileges required (PR):** PR assesses the level of privileges an attacker needs.

- **User interaction (UI):** UI indicates whether user interaction is necessary for exploitation.

- **Scope (S):** S reflects the reach of a vulnerability's impact beyond the initial target.

- **Impact metrics:** These metrics are measures of the consequences of a vulnerability. They include the following:

  - **Confidentiality impact (C):** Gauges the level of impact on confidentiality.

  - **Integrity impact (I):** Gauges the level of impact on data integrity.

  - **Availability impact (A):** Measures the level of impact on system availability.

- **Temporal group:** This layer examines the attributes of a vulnerability that may change over time, including exploit code maturity, remediation level, and report confidence.

- **Environmental group:** This layer allows an organization to tailor CVSS scores based on specific environmental characteristics, providing a customized risk assessment.

CVSS generates scores that range from 0 to 10, with a higher score indicating greater severity. These scores are accompanied by a vector string, a concise textual representation that shows how the score was calculated. Each metric within the three core groups contributes to this overall score. The formula for the score considers the potential damage if the vulnerability is exploited and how accessible the vulnerable component is to an attacker.

CVSS provides a qualitative interpretation for the quantitative base score:

- **None:** 0.0
- **Low:** 0.1–3.9
- **Medium:** 4.0–6.9
- **High:** 7.0–8.9
- **Critical:** 9.0–10.0

Practical Utility

Beyond merely calculating vulnerability severity, CVSS scores are frequently integrated into broader organizational risk management frameworks. These scores help organizations determine the urgency of vulnerabilities and the order in which they should be patched or mitigated.

For example, consider a scenario in which a vulnerability allows an external attacker to disable a firewall by sending a specially crafted packet. The attack vector (AV) would be network (N), the attack complexity (AC) would be low (L), and the availability impact (A) would be high (H). Based on these and other metrics, a CVSS score can be calculated to help prioritize this vulnerability in relation to others.

Common Vulnerability Enumeration (CVE)

The *Common Vulnerability Enumeration (CVE)* system, sometimes referred to by either Common Weakness Enumeration (CWE) or Common Vulnerabilities and Exposures (CVE), isn't just a list but a vital tool that brings standardization to the otherwise convoluted world of vulnerability management. Every entry in the CVE database provides a wealth of information beyond simply describing the vulnerability. The CVE database helps analysts contextualize a threat, offering historical data about how similar vulnerabilities have been exploited. The provided metadata and references act as guides for both understanding the issue and determining effective remediation strategies.

Common Weakness Enumeration is a MITRE project that tracks some of the top software weaknesses. To learn more about the CWE see the MITRE website: https://cwe.mitre.org/.

Common Vulnerabilities and Exposures (CVEs) is a list of publicly available security flaws that you should be familiar with for the security field and the Security+ SY0-701 exam. See https://cve.mitre.org to learn more.

Vulnerability Classification

Vulnerability classification refers to the organized categorization of identified vulnerabilities within a system or application, usually based on criteria such as the nature of a vulnerability, the level of risk it poses, the component affected, or the potential impact. Vulnerability classification is an exercise in knowledge management that brings more than order to the chaos. By categorizing vulnerabilities into types like SQL injection or buffer overflow, analysts can identify recurring issues and establish patterns. These patterns then serve as a roadmap for solution development. Moreover, a well-organized classification system can serve as a lingua franca that enables more effective communication between departments or organizations, making the collective cybersecurity ecosystem more robust.

Exposure Factor

Quantitative risk assessment is a systematic approach used in cybersecurity to measure the potential impact of risks in monetary terms. Central to this approach is the exposure factor (EF), which plays a pivotal role in determining the single loss expectancy (SLE), a figure representing the cost of a single instance of a risk occurring.

The *exposure factor* is the percentage of loss a company would incur if a specific asset were compromised. This figure is essential in the risk calculation process because it directly influences the financial assessment of risks. You will learn about calculating SLE and ALE in more depth in Chapter 24, "Understanding Elements of the Risk Management Process," but this section takes a quick look so you can see how EF fits into the equation.

For instance, consider a business asset such as a server or a database. If a vulnerability in this asset is exploited, the EF estimates what percentage of the asset's value would be lost. It is, therefore, a reflection of the severity of a potential security incident.

To calculate the single loss expectancy (SLE), you would use the EF as follows:

$$SLE = Asset\ Value \times EF$$

Let's apply this with unique values. Imagine that a retail company's online transaction system processes $200,000 in sales daily. If a vulnerability in the system were to be exploited, leading to transaction interruptions, the EF would represent the expected financial loss from such an incident.

If the risk assessment identifies that a security breach would result in losing 30% of the daily transactions, the EF would be 0.30 (or 30%).

Here's how the company would use the SLE formula in this case:

$$SLE = Asset\ Value \times EF$$
$$= \$200,000 \times 0.30$$
$$= \$60,000$$

This calculation means that for each day the transaction system is compromised, the expected monetary loss would be $60,000. Understanding and applying this calculation allows an organization to prioritize risks and focus its cybersecurity measures more effectively.

Incorporating the EF into risk management overall enables decision makers to quantify the potential losses from risks and make informed decisions about where to invest in security controls. An organization can allocate resources by identifying the most significant potential losses to protect the most vulnerable and valuable assets first.

Environmental Variables

Environmental variables in cybersecurity refer to specific conditions or factors within an organization's operating context that can influence the impact of a vulnerability. Environmental variables pull the focus from the general to the specific, underlining that no vulnerability exists in a vacuum. An analyst needs to consider how the organization's unique environment—from its network topology to existing security measures and user behavior—might affect the vulnerability's impact and exploitability. It's a process of contextualizing vulnerabilities, acknowledging that while two organizations might face the same threat, their risks could differ dramatically due to these environmental variables.

Industry/Organizational Impact

Industry/organizational impact refers to the potential consequences that a security vulnerability might have beyond the immediate boundaries of the entity where it was discovered, potentially influencing the wider sector or market in which the organization operates. A vulnerability's ripple effects often transcend an organization's confines, affecting entire industries. Understanding the industry-specific impact enables an analyst to foresee how a single vulnerability could cascade into a sector-wide crisis. This broad view can guide the organization's and the industry's risk mitigation strategies.

Risk Tolerance

Risk tolerance weaves together the threads of financial strategy and cybersecurity. *Risk tolerance* defines the extent to which an organization is willing to allow exposure to threats. An analyst must align their recommendations and actions with the organization's financial ability and willingness to accept risks. It becomes a framework to determine whether the cost of mitigating a vulnerability is justified by the reduction in risk.

Imagine that FinServ Corp, a financial services firm, operates in a highly regulated environment. FinServ Corp has access to vast amounts of sensitive client data, conducts millions of transactions daily, and is subject to stringent compliance requirements. Because the stakes are incredibly high—any breach could result in financial loss, severe reputational damage, and potential legal penalties—FinServ Corp's risk tolerance is extremely low.

To align its cybersecurity practices with its low-risk tolerance, the company may take the following steps:

Step 1. **Prioritization of critical assets:** The organization identifies its most valuable and sensitive data, like client financial records and proprietary trading algorithms. These assets are given the highest level of protection.

Step 2. **Multifactor authentication:** FinServ Corp mandates multifactor authentication (MFA) across all its systems to minimize the risk of unauthorized access.

Step 3. **Regular audits and penetration testing:** The organization invests heavily in periodic security audits and ethical hacking to simulate potential breaches, thus identifying vulnerabilities before malicious actors do.

Step 4. **Data encryption:** As a further layer of security, the company employs end-to-end encryption for data in transit and at rest.

Step 5. **Incident response planning:** FinServ Corp has a robust incident response plan that can be activated within minutes of detecting a security breach to limit the potential damage.

Step 6. **Employee training:** Recognizing that many breaches result from internal errors or ignorance, FinServ Corp makes rigorous cybersecurity training programs mandatory for all employees, not just the IT staff.

Step 7. **Compliance management:** The organization has a dedicated compliance team that works with the cybersecurity team to ensure that all protocols meet or exceed government and industry standards.

Step 8. **Insurance:** FinServ Corp's comprehensive cyber liability insurance policy covers any potential financial losses due to cyber incidents, reinforcing its low tolerance for risk.

Step 9. **Continuous monitoring and adaptation:** In the highly dynamic cybersecurity landscape, the company employs state-of-the-art monitoring tools and regularly revisits its risk assessments, tweaking its strategy as needed.

Step 10. **Board-level oversight:** In line with its low tolerance for risk, the company ensures that cybersecurity discussions are not just confined to the IT department but are also a routine part of board meetings.

FinServ Corp aligns its cybersecurity posture with its low tolerance for risk, thus effectively mitigating the impact of potential threats.

You can see how a simple matter of assessing risk tolerance has significant downstream impacts that guide processes beyond just cybersecurity or IT.

Vulnerability Response and Remediation

Vulnerability response and remediation is the systematic process of addressing and fixing identified vulnerabilities in an organization's technology environment. Vulnerability response and remediation is a multifaceted endeavor that requires a coordinated strategy that accounts for immediate and long-term concerns. Whether you're applying patches, opting for insurance, or employing advanced segmentation techniques, the goal is to manage and mitigate risks effectively. Let's dive into the individual components that come together to create a robust vulnerability response and remediation strategy.

Patching

Patching is more than just updating software; it's a complex process with challenges. *Patching* involves applying updates to software components to fix known vulnerabilities. Analysts often grapple with scheduling issues, as patches may require system downtime that disrupts business operations. Compatibility is another concern; sometimes a patch to fix one issue breaks other functionalities. It's essential to perform a rigorous impact analysis and coordinate with other departments to ensure that patching occurs with minimal disruption.

Insurance

In the realm of risk tolerance, cybersecurity insurance offers financial risk transference. *Cybersecurity insurance* is a financial cushion against the potential loss or compromise of data. It doesn't eliminate the vulnerabilities but mitigates the financial fallout of a cyber incident. However, insurance policies can be complicated. An analyst should be familiar with the fine print, such as the types of incidents covered and the conditions under which a claim can be filed. A policy might cover ransom payments but could be void if basic security protocols were not followed, like meeting minimum patching requirements or conducting regular third-party audits.

Segmentation

Network segmentation is generally the responsibility of network engineers, although security analysts may offer input based on vulnerability assessments. *Segmentation* involves dividing a network into smaller segments to contain potential breaches and minimize damage. Segmenting a network could include setting up physical barriers or air-gapped systems in more hardware-centric contexts. When performed effectively, segmentation can prevent a vulnerability in one segment from compromising the integrity of another.

In a healthcare setting with multiple departments, the administrative network should be segmented from the patient records network. This way, if an attacker gains access to the administrative network, the segmentation acts as a buffer, making it harder to compromise sensitive medical data.

Compensating Controls

Compensating controls are alternate controls intended to reduce the risk of an existing or potential control weakness. They can include audit trails and transaction logs that someone in a higher position reviews. In situations where immediate remediation isn't feasible, compensating controls come into play. This is usually a collaborative effort involving security analysts, network administrators, and sometimes legal and compliance teams. While these controls can be effective stopgaps, they can also add to an organization's technical debt if not managed properly. Overreliance on compensating controls may lead to a patchwork security posture that becomes difficult to manage in the long run. Take, for example, an outdated but critical piece of hardware in a manufacturing plant that can't be patched. A compensating control might involve creating an isolated network for that hardware, thereby preventing it from being an entry point into the more extensive corporate network and adding complexity to the network.

Exceptions and Exemptions

Exceptions and exemptions are created when certain vulnerabilities are accepted due to business needs or technical constraints—but this is not a decision to make lightly. Suppose a publishing company uses a legacy content management system that has known vulnerabilities. The company might opt for an exception due to the high system replacement cost and the low risk of exploitation. However, that would likely involve additional monitoring and other controls to mitigate potential risks.

Tracking exceptions and exemptions is often the duty of governance, risk management, and compliance (GRC) teams. These exceptions are typically documented and monitored closely to evaluate ongoing risk. Failure to properly track these can lead to security gaps going unnoticed, posing a significant risk of exploitation. Without a robust tracking mechanism, an organization may grapple with undetected vulnerabilities that could have severe consequences.

As you navigate the maze of vulnerability response and remediation, it becomes clear that this is not just a technical endeavor but also an exercise in risk management, collaboration, and continuous monitoring.

Validation of Remediation

Validation of remediation is the keystone that completes the arch of the vulnerability management process. It's not enough to just patch a hole; you must ensure that the patch holds. *Validation of remediation* ensures that vulnerabilities have been adequately addressed and that controls effectively mitigate risks. Now, how does one confirm that vulnerabilities have been completely closed? The following sections explain.

Rescanning

Rescanning involves running vulnerability scans again after applying patches or making other changes. It's a way of proving that remediation efforts have worked. Keep in mind that this isn't as straightforward as pressing a Scan button again. Timing is crucial. Conducting a rescan too soon might yield false positives because some patches require system reboots or specific conditions in order to take effect fully. Conversely, waiting too long can expose the system to additional risks. Imagine deploying a patch to close an SQL injection (SQLi) vulnerability, only to discover that it's still exploitable during a rescan. The ramifications could range from unauthorized data access to full system compromise.

Audit

Audits offer a different flavor of validation. Unlike a rescan, which is more automated in nature, an *audit* involves a thorough manual review, often conducted by an independent third party or an internal audit team. The process involves scrutinizing not only the effectiveness of the patches but also the documentation, change management protocols, and compliance with legal requirements. For instance, if your organization is subject to the GDPR, an audit will assess how well your remediation efforts align with data protection mandates. It's a multidimensional review that evaluates your remediation strategies in the broader context of organizational policies and regulatory landscapes.

Verification

Verification involves synthesizing insights from rescanning and auditing activities to affirm the success or failure of remediation efforts. This is where the rubber meets the road in terms of actionable intelligence. Verification pinpoints the efficacy of remedial actions using various techniques, such as reviewing logs or conducting penetration tests. Let's say you've implemented rate limiting to mitigate a DDoS attack. A verification process might involve artificially generating high traffic to the server to see if the rate-limiting measures kick in as expected. It's a stress test of your remedial measures under controlled conditions.

Navigating through these layers of validation helps solidify an organization's security posture. While each layer has unique characteristics, they are interconnected, complementing each other to provide a comprehensive review of your remediation strategies. As you move from one stage to another, the focus shifts from immediate technical verification to long-term sustainability and compliance, painting a holistic picture of an organization's resilience against cyber threats.

Reporting

Finally, we arrive at an often-overlooked component of the vulnerability management process: reporting. Often relegated to a clerical chore, reporting is far from mere paperwork—it's the foundational layer upon which future strategies are built. *Reporting* involves turning scanning, patching, verification, and validation into actionable insights and serves as the organizational memory for cybersecurity efforts. But what makes a report more than a heap of raw data, and what should you look for when distilling these complex narratives?

The heart of effective reporting lies in the audience. Crafting a report for a technical team will be drastically different than creating a report for senior management or a regulatory body. Each audience has its own set of key performance indicators (KPIs) and concerns. Whereas an IT manager might be deeply interested in the minutiae of attack vectors, the C-suite will likely focus on big-picture implications such as overall risk posture and potential business impact.

Imagine a scenario where an intrusion detection system identifies suspicious activity from an internal network to a high-risk external IP address. A report for the IT team would delve into the technical specifics: ports used, data packets transferred, and protocols exploited. On the other hand, a report tailored for the board of directors might translate those details into business language, such as potential data compromise, reputational damage, or compliance risks.

Substantive reporting also involves trend analysis, which is often overlooked but crucial for proactive security measures. Are brute-force attacks increasing after a recent organizational change? Did a new software implementation introduce unanticipated vulnerabilities? Trend analysis can offer foresight that helps an organization pivot its strategies to preempt future threats.

In addition to internal considerations, reporting often extends to external entities like regulatory bodies or information-sharing organizations. Timeliness and accuracy here are more than good practices; they're often legally mandated. Late or inaccurate reports can result in steep fines or even sanctions, not to mention erosive effects on stakeholder trust.

As you integrate data, always remember the principle of least privilege and include only information that the audience absolutely needs to know. This isn't just about clarity; it's a security measure. You wouldn't want an internal report that's brimming with sensitive details to end up in the wrong hands.

Reporting is not the end but a feedback loop that circles back to inform all the previous stages in the vulnerability and risk management chain covered in this chapter. It consolidates the efforts and findings into a format that can be used for decision making, compliance, and continual improvement. As a cybersecurity professional, you need to become proficient at the art of reporting not just to be a chronicler of past events but to be a visionary who shapes future security landscapes. A well-formed report often encourages others to begin again at the first topic of this chapter and restart those scans to continue closing gaps!

Chapter Review Activities

Use the features in this section to study and review the topics in this chapter.

Review Key Topics

Review the most important topics in the chapter, noted with the Key Topic icon in the outer margin of the page. Table 16-2 lists these key topics and the page number on which each is found.

Key Topic

Table 16-2   Key Topics for Chapter 16

Key Topic Element	Description	Page Number
Paragraph	Identification methods	360
Paragraph	Static analysis	362
Paragraph	Dynamic analysis	363
Section	Responsible Disclosure Program	366
Paragraph	Analysis	367
Section	Exposure Factor	371
Section	Patching	374

Key Topic Element	Description	Page Number
Section	Insurance	374
Section	Validation of Remediation	376
Section	Reporting	377

Define Key Terms

Define the following key terms from this chapter and check your answers in the glossary:

identification method, vulnerability scan, application security, static analysis, dynamic analysis, package monitoring, threat feed, open-source intelligence (OSINT), proprietary threat feed, information-sharing organization, dark web, penetration testing, responsible disclosure program, bug bounty program, system or process audit, analysis, confirmation, false positive, false negative, prioritization, Common Vulnerability Scoring System (CVSS), Common Vulnerability Enumeration (CVE), vulnerability classification, exposure factor, environmental variable, industry/organizational impact, risk tolerance, vulnerability response and remediation, patching, cybersecurity insurance, segmentation, compensating control, exception or exemption, validation of remediation, rescanning, audit, verification, reporting

Review Questions

Answer the following review questions. Check your answers with the answer key in Appendix A.

1. What kind of analysis focuses on examining an application's source code before the application is run?

2. In the realm of cybersecurity, what does a false positive incorrectly flag?

3. What is the main goal of a responsible disclosure program in cybersecurity?

4. What does CVSS stand for, and what is its primary function?

5. What is one challenge often associated with the patching process?

6. What should be considered when crafting a cybersecurity report?

This chapter covers the following topics related to Objective 4.4 (Explain security alerting and monitoring concepts and tools) of the CompTIA Security+ SY0-701 certification exam:

- Monitoring computing resources
- Activities
- Tools

CHAPTER 17

Understanding Security Alerting and Monitoring Concepts and Tools

This chapter focuses on the essentials of security alerting and monitoring. It explores how to monitor computing systems, applications, and infrastructure and discusses key activities such as log aggregation, alerting, and scanning. This chapter also delves into tools like Security Content Automation Protocol (SCAP) and security information and event management (SIEM) systems.

"Do I Know This Already?" Quiz

The "Do I Know This Already?" quiz enables you to assess whether you should read this entire chapter thoroughly or jump to the "Chapter Review Activities" section. If you are in doubt about your answers to these questions or your own assessment of your knowledge of the topics, read the entire chapter. Table 17-1 lists the major headings in this chapter and their corresponding "Do I Know This Already?" quiz questions. You can find the answers in Appendix A, "Answers to the 'Do I Know This Already?' Quizzes and Review Questions."

Table 17-1 "Do I Know This Already?" Section-to-Question Mapping

Foundation Topics Section	Questions
Monitoring Computing Resources	1
Activities	2, 3
Tools	4–6

CAUTION The goal of self-assessment is to gauge your mastery of the topics in this chapter. If you do not know the answer to a question or are only partially sure of the answer, you should mark that question as wrong for purposes of the self-assessment. Giving yourself credit for an answer you correctly guess skews your self-assessment results and might provide you with a false sense of security.

1. What is the primary function of monitoring systems in computing resources?

   a. Generating real-time reports

   b. Issuing alerts for unauthorized login attempts

   c. Ensuring optimal system functioning

   d. All of the above

2. Which tool is commonly used in the realm of log aggregation to sift through large volumes of data and identify security threats?

   a. Firewall

   b. Antivirus software

   c. Security information and event management (SIEM) system

   d. Password manager

3. What is the main purpose of reporting in cybersecurity?

   a. To store raw data

   b. To translate technical language into digestible formats for decision making

   c. To issue real-time alerts

   d. To scan for vulnerabilities

4. Which of the following languages is not part of the current SCAP specifications?

   a. Open Vulnerability and Assessment Language (OVAL)

   b. Extensible Configuration Checklist Description Format (XCCDF)

   c. Hypertext Markup Language (HTML)

   d. Open Checklist Interactive Language (OCIL)

5. What is the main advantage of agent-based solutions for system monitoring?

   a. Simplicity

   b. Reduced system load

   c. More in-depth data and control

   d. Leverage of existing protocols

6. What types of data does data loss prevention (DLP) software classify? (Choose all that apply.)

   a. Regulated data

   b. Confidential data

   c. Business-critical data

   d. Open Vulnerability and Assessment Language (OVAL)

Foundation Topics

Monitoring and Computing Resources

In the dynamic world of cybersecurity, the adage "knowledge is power" couldn't be more accurate. Whether you're safeguarding a small startup or a large enterprise, awareness is the first step in any robust cybersecurity strategy. The need for awareness is where the concept of monitoring computing resources comes into play. By continuously keeping tabs on various aspects of your computing environment, from system performance to network traffic, you're not only preventing potential issues but also gathering invaluable data that can help refine your security measures.

Monitoring computing resources refers to continuously overseeing an organization's information technology assets to ensure that they operate within expected parameters and performance levels. Monitoring computing resources is akin to having a 24/7 security guard who watches over your property and understands its inner workings, regular visitors, and potential weaknesses. This complex task is generally broken down into monitoring systems, applications, and the overarching infrastructure. Each of these aspects has its own set of challenges and solutions, practical considerations, and essential metrics to watch.

The sections that follow explore each of these layers, shedding light on what to monitor, why it matters, and how best to navigate the hurdles you're likely to encounter along the way. The goal is to give you a nuanced understanding of this critical area. By understanding security alerting and monitoring concepts, you'll be better prepared to identify vulnerabilities, protect assets, and contribute to your organization's overall cybersecurity health.

Monitoring computing resources begins with keeping a close eye on systems— including servers, workstations, and network devices. The goal of *monitoring systems* is to ensure that the systems are running optimally and free of vulnerabilities and to ensure that they are not unintentionally participating in any unauthorized activities. One way you can achieve this is through the use of monitoring software, which can generate real-time reports and issue alerts based on certain events or conditions, such as CPU overuse or unauthorized login attempts.

System monitoring involves deciding what metrics to track. You might be interested in CPU and memory utilization to predict when you'll need to scale resources or as indicators of compromise. As discussed in Chapter 16, "Understanding Various Activities Associated with Vulnerability Management," one challenge is false positives—alerts that might indicate a problem but that are actually normal activities. A potential solution to this challenge is alert tuning, which involves refining the monitoring parameters to reduce false alerts while not missing out on genuine issues. For instance, you might set thresholds for when an alert should be triggered based on historical data and observed behavior so that you're not notified every time CPU usage spikes momentarily during a nightly backup. You will learn more about alert tuning later in this chapter.

Application monitoring involves overseeing the performance and health of software applications. It's not just about ensuring that an application is up and running; it's also about ensuring that it's secure and responsive and that it delivers optimal performance. Tools for application monitoring often check metrics like response times, error rates, and transaction volumes.

Practical considerations with application monitoring are related to making sure the monitoring doesn't impact the application's performance. Challenges often arise when applications are updated or modified. New versions can introduce new metrics to monitor or make old metrics obsolete. Security engineers sometimes serve as the central point of contact for application updates. It is important for software engineers to consider some of the hardware requirements that systems engineers manage.

It is important to develop a robust deployment pipeline that includes monitoring configurations as a key part of any update. For example, consider a financial trading platform that needs to implement monitoring. This monitoring could be geared to alert administrators to performance issues and unusual trading patterns that might indicate security vulnerabilities being exploited. Catching mistakes early can save millions of dollars in damages.

Infrastructure monitoring is a broader practice that encompasses systems, applications, networking equipment, and even the data centers or cloud services where resources reside.

Infrastructure monitoring is a critical practice that ensures the cohesive and secure operation of all technological components within an organization. It involves close observation of systems, applications, and networking hardware, as well as the physical or virtual environments they inhabit.

One of the primary methods for monitoring infrastructure is through the collection and analysis of logs, which are detailed records of events and changes in a system or in network devices. Logs can indicate normal operation or flag issues such as security breaches, system failures, or performance bottlenecks.

Syslog is a widely adopted protocol for tracking and diagnosing issues in network devices, servers, and other IT infrastructure. As a standard for message logging, Syslog can handle a variety of device logs, offering administrators the ability to consolidate logging data from different types of equipment in a centralized repository. This protocol is crucial for Security+ candidates to understand because it provides the structure through which log data can be uniformly analyzed and audited.

Simple Network Management Protocol (SNMP) is another vital tool for infrastructure monitoring. SNMP is used to manage network-connected devices by collecting information about their operation. The information collected can include performance metrics, error rates, and the status of various device components. SNMP managers poll agents in devices to retrieve this data, allowing for real-time monitoring and the ability to alert administrators to issues that may impact business operations or security.

In addition to Syslog and SNMP, numerous third-party tools specialize in infrastructure monitoring. These tools often offer advanced features such as automated alerting, trend analysis, and visualization capabilities that help condense complex data into actionable insights. Gartner listed the following tools as the top five for the North American region in 2023 for infrastructure monitoring:

- Paessler PRTG

- Datadog

- OpManager

- SolarWinds Server & Application Monitor

- Dynatrace

You can find the full list at https://www.gartner.com/reviews/market/infrastructure-monitoring-tools.

In practice, infrastructure monitoring often involves a complex set of metrics across various types of hardware and software. The challenge lies in the diversity of these resources and the sheer volume of data generated. False negatives—results that fail to detect actual issues—are also a significant concern. If you have ever heard the adage "Eat an elephant one bite at a time," that's what you do here as well. If your infrastructure is large, you need to work with other stakeholders in the business to figure out where the most valuable assets (the "crown jewels") exist and start mapping out the infrastructure from there.

Another approach to this challenge is leveraging a security information and event management (SIEM) system that aggregates data from various sources for a unified view. For instance, monitoring tools can be set to flag an unusually high data transfer rate between a data storage server and an external IP address, which might indicate a data exfiltration attempt. We will explore the value of SIEM systems later in this chapter.

Activities

Navigating the labyrinthine world of cybersecurity isn't just about setting up firewalls and installing antivirus software. To ensure a truly resilient defense, you need to take a continuous and proactive approach that involves a series of well-coordinated activities. *Cybersecurity activities* help identify risks and understand their nature, prioritize them, and ultimately mitigate or eliminate them. From collecting logs from various sources to creating alerts, scanning for vulnerabilities, and generating insightful reports, these actions are the heartbeat of a cybersecurity program.

The sections that follow delve into a number of cybersecurity activities, explaining the purpose and utility of each of them. You'll gain insights into challenges often encountered, practical considerations to keep in mind, and solutions to common problems.

Key Topic

Log Aggregation

Log aggregation is the critical process of gathering disparate log data from various sources, such as servers, applications, databases, and network devices, and bringing the data into a single, centralized repository for examination. This consolidation is pivotal, as it helps turn isolated data points into a coherent story, much as a detective pieces together clues to form a complete picture of a case.

Log aggregation is not just about collecting data; it's also about making sense of it. The volume of log data generated by IT environments can be staggering, and without the right tools, important security signals could be lost in the noise. Specialized tools like syslog-ng and rsyslog are designed to manage and process log data, allowing for real-time analysis and the generation of comprehensive reports. By parsing, filtering, and classifying log messages, they facilitate quicker identification of patterns or anomalies that could signify potential security incidents. SIEM systems further enhance this capability. SIEM systems take the process to the next level by providing more sophisticated data analysis, event correlation, and alerting mechanisms. They can be configured to focus on the most relevant security data, enabling security professionals to swiftly detect, prioritize, and respond to the threats most significant to an organization's cyber health.

syslog-ng is widely recognized for its versatile configuration options. For instance, you can set up syslog-ng to route logs from different servers into separate files or databases, making it easier to track issues by server. It can also filter logs based on content, storing only messages that match certain criteria, which is especially useful for pinpointing security-related events. For example, you can configure syslog-ng to collect only logs that indicate failed login attempts, which assists in detecting potential brute-force attacks.

syslog-ng can be integrated with various database systems, such as MySQL or MongoDB, allowing logs to be stored in a structured format conducive to more complex queries and analyses. An organization could set up syslog-ng to parse logs and extract specific fields, which can then be inserted into a database table. This structured approach enhances the ability to perform sophisticated analytics, such as identifying trends over time or detecting anomalous sequences of events that could indicate security breaches.

rsyslog, on the other hand, excels in high-performance log processing and is often used in environments that generate massive volumes of log data. It can work with various transport protocols, such as TCP (Transmission Control Protocol) for reliable log transmission and RELP (Reliable Event Logging Protocol) for ensuring that no log data is lost during transit.

rsyslog can be used to implement rate limiting. It is critical to avoid log overflow and potential loss of important security messages during a distributed denial-of-service (DDoS) attack. In such scenarios, rsyslog can be configured to preserve system stability by discarding less-critical logs when a certain threshold is exceeded.

rsyslog's modular design allows for high customizability. It can be coupled with advanced message queues like Kafka for log message buffering, which is particularly useful in ensuring log integrity and preventing data loss during peak loads or network issues.

When combined with a SIEM system, syslog-ng and rsyslog can be configured to forward logs in a structured format that the SIEM system can easily interpret, allowing for real-time security alerting and rapid response. This unified view is indispensable for helping organizations monitor their security landscape and react immediately to potential threats.

Let's say you're the cybersecurity specialist for a midsized company. You have various systems logging data: web servers, database servers, and employee workstations, among others. One Monday, you notice that some unusual activity triggered several low-level alerts over the weekend. Rather than viewing these logs separately, you use a log aggregation tool to centralize the information. Your morning might look something like this:

Step 1.   **Configure sources:** First, you ensure that all your logging sources are correctly configured to send logs to your log aggregation tool. In this case, let's say you're using ELK Stack for log aggregation. You're also using Elasticsearch (acts as a search and analytics engine), Logstash (used for processing and aggregating the logs), and Kibana (used for visualizing and querying the data stored in Elasticsearch).

Step 2.   **Centralize logs:** Your logs start flowing into Elasticsearch, where they are indexed and stored. Instead of checking logs from multiple places, you have a unified view in Kibana, the visualization layer of ELK Stack.

Step 3.   **Set filters:** You apply filters to pinpoint the events that triggered the alerts. For example, you may set a filter to view only logs where the HTTP response code was 404 (not found) or 403 (forbidden).

Step 4.   **Identify patterns:** When you start filtering, you notice a pattern: Numerous 403 errors originated from a single IP address over the weekend. Since these were low-level alerts on their own, they didn't trigger any immediate concern, but the aggregated view reveals a potential threat.

Step 5.   **Investigate:** Now that you've identified a pattern, you look into other activities from the same IP address. You notice multiple failed login attempts on a company web application, which raises further suspicion.

Step 6.   **Take action:** Based on your aggregated logs and the detected pattern, you decide that this behavior warrants immediate attention. You temporarily block the IP address and begin an internal investigation.

Step 7.   **Update alert mechanism:** You update your alerting mechanisms to prevent similar incidents from slipping through the cracks. For example, you might set an alert to trigger if an IP address generates multiple 403 errors within a short time frame.

Step 8.   **Documentation and reporting:** Finally, you document the entire event, from detection to resolution, and create a report to serve as your team's learning point and improve future response mechanisms.

Of course, not every log aggregation event will go this clearly or excitedly, but you can see the power of log aggregation in identifying and responding to security threats that might otherwise go unnoticed.

Alerting

Alerting functions as the early warning system for your security infrastructure. The *alerting* mechanisms identifies activities that may be of concern based on rules you have predefined. Once these rules are triggered, an alert signals the need for immediate attention.

However, achieving the right balance in alert sensitivity is a significant challenge. You can expect to spend a considerable amount of time on alert tuning. If your alerts are too sensitive, your team may be bombarded with false positives. False positives can lead to alert fatigue—a state where analysts become desensitized to the alerts because so many of them turn out to be irrelevant or non-critical. When this happens, there's a risk that a real threat could go unnoticed, getting lost in the noise of incessant low-priority alerts.

On the other hand, if the alerting system is too lenient, it runs the risk of letting genuine threats slip through the net, endangering the system it's meant to protect.

This is where alert tuning comes into play. Alert tuning is a continuous process of refining the alerting rules and mechanisms to ensure that they are neither too stringent nor too lax. Effective alert tuning can reduce the occurrence of false positives, thereby lessening the strain on the cybersecurity team and minimizing the risk of alert fatigue. This delicate balance allows a team to focus on the alerts that truly matter, providing an opportunity to act swiftly and decisively when a genuine security threat is detected.

Scanning

Scanning serves as a proactive measure to identify potential weaknesses within systems, applications, and networks. While the basic definition captures the essence of scanning, there is far more to the activity than just running an automated tool. Think of scanning as not just a regular health checkup but a comprehensive diagnostic test that examines multiple aspects of digital health.

Scanning can identify many issues, ranging from outdated software and insecure settings to weak passwords and open ports that could serve as entry points for attackers. Automated tools like Nessus, OpenVAS, and Qualys are often employed to perform these scans. However, these tools are only as good as the expertise of the people using them. Therefore, it's crucial to not just rely on a tool's output but to interpret the results through a nuanced understanding of your specific environment and needs.

Scanning isn't a "set it and forget it" task. The landscape of potential vulnerabilities is continually evolving, as are the tools designed to exploit those vulnerabilities. Therefore, periodic scanning is essential, but so is keeping scanning tools themselves to detect the latest vulnerabilities.

After scanning, the raw data must often be filtered and analyzed to determine its severity and potential impact. Not all vulnerabilities are created equal; some may pose immediate and severe risks, requiring rapid remediation, while others might be less urgent. Effective scanning, therefore, involves not just the identification but also the prioritization of vulnerabilities. Prioritizing scan findings aids in allocating resources efficiently—whether the resources are the attention of your security team or computational resources for patches and fixes.

A single scan is seldom enough to ensure security. Vulnerabilities often have dependencies on each other, and fixing one could expose another. Once you have completed any sort of patching or modification to a system, running a post-remediation scan is advisable to ensure that the fixes have been effective and haven't opened up new avenues for attack.

Key Topic

Reporting

Reporting is the connective tissue that links raw data to strategic action. While logs, alerts, and scans are essential for monitoring, their real value is only unlocked when they are synthesized into reports that stakeholders can act upon. *Reporting* translates the often technical language of cybersecurity into a digestible format that everyone from the technical team to senior management can understand and use for decision making.

For instance, an effective report for the technical team might include a breakdown of all detected vulnerabilities, the systems they affect, and recommended courses of action for each. A technical report like this would go into the nitty-gritty, offering details about the nature of the vulnerabilities, their Common Vulnerability Scoring System (CVSS) ratings, and so forth.

For senior management, the same data might be rolled into a higher-level report that addresses the potential business impact of these vulnerabilities. An executive report could include projected financial costs in the case of a breach, potential reputational damage, and strategic recommendations for risk mitigation. Thus, reporting serves an informational purpose and acts as a guide for decision making, resource allocation, and strategic planning.

Remember that a report typically isn't binary. You might find that a report is meant to serve both a technical need and an executive need. In this case, you would provide an executive summary that summarizes the main findings of the report and then drills down into the details. Say that you work for a company called CyberCorp, and you create the following report:

- CyberCorp Report
- Cybersecurity Monthly Report—July 2024
- Executive Summary
    - 35 potential vulnerabilities detected
    - 10 high-risk vulnerabilities successfully remediated
    - Average risk score reduced by 15% from last month

- Technical Analysis

  - Vulnerability 1: SQL Injection on Web Portal

    — Affected Systems: Web servers
    — CVSS Rating: 9.1
    — Status: Remediated
    — Action taken: Patch applied and re-tested

  - Vulnerability 2: Outdated SSL certificates

    — Affected Systems: E-commerce website
    — CVSS Rating: 5.3
    — Status: Pending
    — Recommended action: Update certificates by July 15

- Management Overview

  - Business impact

    — Projected financial loss if SQL injection was exploited: $2M
    — Reputational damage: High

  - Strategic recommendations

    — Replace SSL with TLS certificates to avoid potential loss of customer trust.
    — Allocate more resources for real-time monitoring to catch vulnerabilities as they occur.

The report in this theoretical example serves as an analytical and decision-making tool. While it offers in-depth details for the technical team to act upon, it also gives senior management a clear picture of the risk landscape and actionable strategic recommendations.

Archiving

The past can often inform the present and future in the digital realm. *Archiving* involves securely storing historical data, including logs and reports, for long-term retrieval and analysis. It's the equivalent of using a well-organized filing cabinet where you can quickly find documents when you need to revisit an old case or validate compliance during an audit. The challenge is determining what to archive and for how long, considering legal requirements and potential future analysis. Archiving solutions often employ strong encryption and are designed to ensure data integrity, safeguarding the information from tampering or accidental deletion.

Key Topic

Alert Response and Remediation/Validation

The real test of your security capabilities occurs after an alert is generated. The *alert response process* involves validating whether an alert indicates a genuine security threat or a false positive. This is where the concepts of quarantining and alert tuning come into play. Once an alert triggers, it's crucial to act swiftly to minimize potential damage.

Quarantining involves isolating a suspect file or problematic system activity in a secure environment away from the network. For instance, if an email attachment is flagged as suspicious, the email can be moved to a quarantine area. Quarantining prevents the email from interacting with other network elements and possibly spreading malware. After the quarantine, analysts assess whether the item is genuinely harmful or benign. The quarantined items can be deleted or restored, depending on the outcome of this validation process.

After the validation phase, the next step often involves refining your monitoring alert mechanisms, a process commonly known as *alert tuning*. It's not uncommon for security systems to generate false positives, which can clutter your workflow and divert attention from real threats. For example, let's say you've set your SIEM system to alert you after three failed login attempts within a minute, as this might indicate a brute-force attack. However, you find that this sensitive setting results in multiple alerts being triggered by employees mistyping passwords. To improve the system's accuracy, you might adjust the rules to trigger an alert only after five failed attempts, and you might also introduce additional parameters like geographic location. Alert tuning is, therefore, a continuous process of fine-tuning to strike a balance between alert sensitivity and specificity.

Quarantine and alert tuning are essential cogs in the alert response and remediation wheel. Together, they form a feedback loop of detection, validation, and tuning that serves as a learning process. Each iteration of this loop further refines your security measures and alert systems, making them more robust and responsive to the ever-evolving threat landscape.

Tools

In cybersecurity, having the right set of tools in your toolkit can make the difference between a well-secured environment and a vulnerable one. *Cybersecurity tools* can range from specialized protocols for automating security checks to real-time monitoring and management solutions. This section gives you a comprehensive overview of essential cybersecurity tools. It delves into various types of tools used for enhancing and maintaining cybersecurity posture, including Security Content Automation Protocol (SCAP), antivirus software, and data loss prevention (DLP) mechanisms. While the idea of a "perfect" toolset might vary from organization to organization, being familiar with these different types of solutions will help you make informed decisions when building or refining your cybersecurity architecture.

Security Content Automation Protocol (SCAP)

Security Content Automation Protocol (SCAP) was created to provide a standardized solution for security automation. The goal with SCAP is to maintain system security by ensuring that security configuration best practices are implemented in the enterprise network, verifying the presence of patches, and maintaining complete visibility of the security posture of systems and the organization at all times.

The current SCAP specifications include the following:

- **Languages:**

    - **Open Vulnerability and Assessment Language (OVAL):** OVAL is an international community standard to promote open and publicly available security content and to standardize the transfer of this information in security tools and services. More information about OVAL is available at https://oval.mitre.org.

    - **Extensible Configuration Checklist Description Format (XCCDF):** XCCDF is a specification for a structured collection of security checklists and benchmarks. More information about XCCDF is available at https://scap.nist.gov/specifications/xccdf.

    - **Open Checklist Interactive Language (OCIL):** OCIL is a framework for collecting and interpreting responses from questions offered to users. More information about OCIL is available at https://scap.nist.gov/specifications/ocil.

    - **Asset Identification (AI):** AI is a specification designed to quickly correlate different sets of information about enterprise computing assets. More information about AI is available at https://scap.nist.gov/specifications/ai.

    - **Asset Reporting Format (ARF):** ARF is a specification that defines the transport format of information about enterprise assets and provides a standardized data model to streamline the reporting of such information. More information about ARF is available at https://scap.nist.gov/specifications/arf.

- **Enumerations:**

    - **Common Vulnerabilities and Exposures (CVE):** CVE assigns identifiers to publicly known system vulnerabilities. Cisco assigns CVE identifiers to security vulnerabilities according to the Cisco public vulnerability policy at https://sec.cloudapps.cisco.com/security/center/publicationListing.x. More information about CVE is available at https://cve.mitre.org.

- **Common Platform Enumeration (CPE):** CPE is a standardized method of naming and identifying classes of applications, operating systems, and hardware devices. More information about CPE is available at https://nvd.nist.gov/cpe.cfm.

- **Common Configuration Enumeration (CCE):** CCE provides unique identifiers for configuration guidance documents and best practices. The main goal of CCE is to enable organizations to perform fast and accurate correlation of configuration issues in enterprise systems. More information about CCE is available at https://nvd.nist.gov/cce/index.cfm.

NOTE   Other community-developed enumerators, such as Common Weakness Enumeration (CWE), are currently being expanded and further developed. CWE is a dictionary of common software architecture, design, code, and implementation weaknesses that can lead to security vulnerabilities. More information about CWE is available at http://cwe.mitre.org. Another emerging enumerator is Common Remediation Enumeration (CRE). More information about CRE is available at http://scap.nist.gov/specifications/cre.

- **Metrics:**
  - **Common Vulnerability Scoring System (CVSS):** CVSS is a standards-based scoring method that conveys vulnerability severity and helps determine the urgency and priority of response. You can obtain the latest CVSS specification documentation, examples of scored vulnerabilities, and a calculator at first.org/cvss.

  - **Common Configuration Scoring System (CCSS):** More information about CCSS is available at https://csrc.nist.gov/publications/nistir/ir7502/nistir-7502_CCSS.pdf.

NOTE   Two emerging metrics specifications are the Common Weakness Scoring System (CWSS) and the Common Misuse Scoring System (CMSS). CWSS is a methodology for scoring software weaknesses, and it is part of CWE. More information about CWSS is available at https://cwe.mitre.org/cwss. CMSS is a standardized way to measure software feature misuse vulnerabilities. More information about CMSS is available at https://scap.nist.gov/emerging-specs/listing.html#cmss.

■ **Integrity:** Integrity is provided by the Trust Model for Security Automation Data (TMSAD), which is a trust model for maintaining integrity, authentication, and traceability of security automation data. More information about TMSAD is available at https://csrc.nist.gov/publications/nistir/ir7802/NISTIR-7802.pdf.

Figure 17-1 summarizes the components of SCAP.

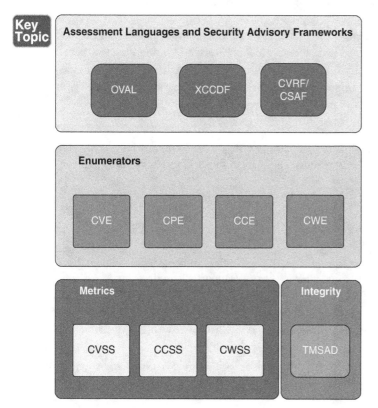

Figure 17-1 SCAP Components

Benchmarks

Security ***benchmarks*** are standard points of reference designed to facilitate the assessment of a system's security level. These benchmarks provide a set of guidelines for configuring systems to an established security baseline, which industry experts generally recognize as a good practice. Benchmarks are critical because they provide the following benefits:

■ **A baseline for security posture:** They help an organization understand its current security state and how it can be improved.

- **Consistency across systems:** By applying the same benchmarks, organizations ensure a consistent level of security across all their systems.

- **Measurements for improvement:** They allow organizations to track improvements over time and evaluate the effectiveness of their security measures.

- **Industry comparisons:** Benchmarks make it possible to compare the security of an organization against peers and competitors.

One notable source for cybersecurity benchmarks is the Center for Internet Security (CIS). CIS benchmarks are widely respected, consensus-based guidelines that are developed by a community of cybersecurity experts. These benchmarks provide recommendations for hardening various systems, including operating systems, web servers, application servers, and network infrastructure devices. You can learn more about CIS Benchmarks at https://www.cisecurity.org/cis-benchmarks.

Table 17-2 summarizes benchmarks and secure configuration guides for platforms/vendors, web servers, operating systems, application servers, and network infrastructure devices.

Table 17-2   Benchmarks/Secure Configuration Guides

Framework	Description	Examples
Platform/vendor-specific guides	Some guides are specific to vendor products, and many times they are documented and provided by the vendors themselves.	Cisco configuration guides: www.cisco.com/c/en/us/support/all-products.html Red Hat Enterprise Linux Security Guide: https://access.redhat.com/documentation/en-us/red_hat_enterprise_linux/7/html/security_guide/index
Web server guides	Web server security hardening guides are available from organizations like the Center for Internet Security and DISA.	Center for Internet Security (CIS) Apache Benchmark: www.cisecurity.org/benchmark/apache_http_server/ DISA Apache Server Security Technical Implementation Guide: www.stigviewer.com/stig/apache_server_2.4_unix_site/
Operating system guides	Operating system security hardening guides are available from organizations like the Center for Internet Security and DISA, as well as specific OS vendors.	Center for Internet Security (CIS) Windows Server Benchmark: www.cisecurity.org/benchmark/microsoft_windows_server/ DISA Technical Implementation Guides: https://public.cyber.mil/stigs/

Framework	Description	Examples
Application server guides	Application server security hardening guides are available from organizations like the Center for Internet Security and DISA.	Oracle Hardening Guide: https://docs.oracle.com/cd/E25178_01/fusionapps.1111/e16690/F371476AN1062D.htm DISA Technical Implementation Guides: https://public.cyber.mil/stigs/
Network infrastructure device guides	Network infrastructure device hardening guides are available from organizations like the Center for Internet Security and DISA, as well as specific device vendors.	VMware Security Hardening Guides: www.vmware.com/security/hardening-guides.html Cisco CIS Benchmark: www.cisecurity.org/benchmark/cisco/ Cisco Security Hardening Guide: www.cisco.com/c/en/us/support/docs/ip/access-lists/13608-21.html

Agents/Agentless

Tools, monitoring, and management can be conducted through agents or can be agentless. An *agent-based solution* requires the installation of a software agent on each system that is being monitored. A software agent collects data and sends it back to a centralized management system. For example, software like McAfee ePO or Microsoft's System Center uses agents to carry out tasks on individual systems. The advantage is that you often get more in-depth data and control. However, deployment of agents can be complex, and there is a risk that they might consume too many system resources.

On the other hand, an *agentless solution* monitors and manages systems without requiring a software agent on each system. Tools like SolarWinds and Nagios typically use existing protocols to perform their tasks remotely. The benefits of an agentless solution are simplicity and reduced system load, but you might sacrifice some depth of monitoring or control.

Security Information and Event Management (SIEM)

A *security information and event management (SIEM) system* is a specialized device or software that is used for security monitoring; it collects, correlates, and helps security analysts analyze logs from multiple systems. SIEM systems typically allow for the following functions:

- **Log collection:** This includes receiving information from devices with multiple protocols and formats, storing the logs, and providing historical reporting and log filtering. A log collector is software that is able to receive logs from multiple sources (data input) and in some cases offers storage capabilities and log analysis functionality.

■ **Log normalization:** This function extracts relevant attributes from logs received in different formats and stores them in a common data model or template. This allows for faster event classification and operation. Non-normalized logs are usually kept for archival, historical, and forensic purposes.

■ **Log aggregation:** This function aggregates information based on common information and reduces duplicates.

■ **Log correlation:** This is probably one of the most important SIEM functions. It refers to the capability of a system to associate events gathered by various systems—in different formats and at different times—and create a single actionable event for the security analyst or investigator. Often the quality of a SIEM system is related to the quality of its correlation engine.

■ **Reporting:** Event visibility is also a key functionality of a SIEM system. Reporting capabilities usually include real-time monitoring and historical base reports.

Most modern SIEM systems integrate with other information systems to gather additional contextual information to feed the correlation engine. For example, they can integrate with an identity management system to get contextual information about users or with NetFlow collectors to get additional flow-based information.

Figure 17-2 shows how a SIEM system can collect and process logs from routers, network switches, firewalls, intrusion detection, and other security products that may be in an organization's infrastructure. Such a system can also collect and process logs from applications, antivirus, anti-malware, and other host-based security solutions.

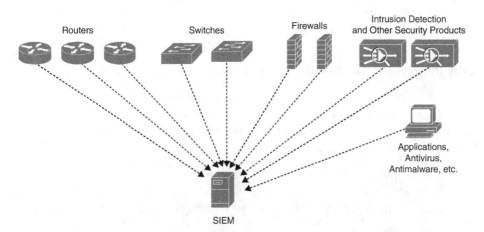

Figure 17-2 SIEM System Collecting and Processing Logs from Disparate Systems

Security operation center analysts and security engineers often collect packet captures as part of their investigation of a security incident. Packet captures provide the greatest detail about each transaction happening in the network. Full packet capture has been used for digital forensics for many years; however, most malware and attackers use encryption to bypass and obfuscate their transactions. IP packet metadata can still be used to potentially detect an attack and determine the attacker's tactics and techniques.

Key Topic NetFlow

NetFlow, originally developed by Cisco, is a protocol used for collecting and monitoring network traffic data. It enables network administrators to understand the source, destination, volume, and paths of traffic flow across their networks. This understanding is vital for several security tasks, such as anomaly detection, traffic profiling, and network performance monitoring.

While Cisco initiated NetFlow, it has been standardized in the form of IPFIX by the Internet Engineering Task Force (IETF), as documented in RFC 7011 through RFC 7015 and RFC 5103. Although IPFIX introduces some terminology changes, it retains the core principles laid out by NetFlow version 9, establishing a universal protocol for flow information exchange.

> **NOTE**   IPFIX was designed to create a common, universal standard of export for flow information from routers, switches, firewalls, and other infrastructure devices. IPFIX defines how flow information should be formatted and transferred from an exporter to a collector. IPFIX is documented in RFC 7011 through RFC 7015 and RFC 5103.

SIEM systems, such as Micro Focus ArcSight, LogRhythm, IBM QRadar, and Splunk, use NetFlow data to aggregate and correlate information, offering a panoramic view of network activity essential for security analysts. This correlation helps identify anomalies and potential threats, mainly when dealing with encrypted traffic, where content analysis is limited.

NetFlow captures provide an efficient alternative to packet captures by focusing on traffic metadata. This efficiency is important as full packet capture requires extensive storage, particularly in high-traffic environments. By contrast, NetFlow data, which includes source and destination IP addresses, port numbers, protocol types, and class of service, can be stored and analyzed over extended periods, allowing for trend analysis and proactive threat detection.

To leverage NetFlow, administrators typically enable it on network devices, specifying which interfaces to monitor and where to send the data. The configured

NetFlow collector then aggregates this data, which can be analyzed to establish a baseline of normal network behavior, making it easier to detect deviations that may indicate security threats.

The use of NetFlow in security extends beyond threat detection. It is a strategic tool for maintaining network reliability and performance—a key aspect of a robust security posture. By examining metadata, organizations can detect irregularities that could signify security incidents, enabling proactive defense measures before a breach occurs.

NetFlow data contributes to the identification of unusual patterns that could indicate insider threats through user behavior analysis. It's not only about recognizing the signs of a compromise but also about understanding the baseline of regular network activity to spot deviations.

One of the drawbacks of collecting full packet captures in every corner of your network is the requirement for storage because packet captures in busy networks can require a significant amount of disk space. This is why numerous organizations often collect network metadata with NetFlow and store such data longer than when collecting packet captures.

Organizations can also deploy sentiment analysis tools and solutions to help monitor customer sentiment and brand reputation. Often these tools can reveal the intent and tone behind social media posts, as well as keep track of positive or negative opinions. Threat actors may try to damage a company's reputation by creating fake accounts and bots on social media platforms like X, Facebook, or Instagram. Attackers can use these fake accounts and bots to provide negative public comments against the targeted organization.

Antivirus Software

Antivirus software, also known as anti-malware, is a computer program used to prevent, detect, and remove malware. Antivirus software was originally developed to detect and remove computer viruses, hence the name. Just how destructive are viruses? According to a report published by Cybersecurity Ventures in May 2019, the damages from ransomware cost businesses an astonishing $11 billion in lost productivity and remediation. Numerous viruses and Trojans have damaged networks and cost companies billions of dollars.

Antivirus software is an integral part of most corporate computing environments and policies. The process of selecting antivirus software varies greatly from organization to organization, but in any case, it's important to implement and monitor the solution after it's in place. Every endpoint device, workstation, tablet, and phone should have antivirus software installed. Newer firewalls, routers, and switches implement and integrate antivirus software and should be enabled where possible. Your entire server environment should have antivirus protection installed.

Data Loss Prevention (DLP)

Data loss prevention (DLP) is a data protection strategy. It is a set of tools used to detect potential data breaches and data exfiltration transmissions. It has capabilities to prevent them by monitoring, detecting, and blocking sensitive data while in use/processing, in motion/transit, and at rest.

DLP software classifies regulated, confidential, and business-critical data and identifies violations of policies defined by organizations or within a predefined policy pack, typically driven by regulatory compliance such as the Health Insurance Portability and Accountability Act of 1996 (HIPAA), Payment Card Industry Data Security Standard (PCI DSS), or General Data Protection Regulation (GDPR). When those violations are identified, DLP software enforces remediation with alerts, encryption, and other protective actions to prevent end users from accidentally or maliciously sharing data that could put the organization at risk.

Data loss prevention software and tools monitor and control endpoint activities, filter data streams on corporate networks, and monitor data in the cloud to protect data at rest, in motion/transit, and in use/processing. DLP software also provides reporting to meet compliance and auditing requirements and identify areas of weakness and anomalies for forensics and incident response.

Simple Network Management Protocol (SNMP) Traps

Simple Network Management Protocol version 3 (SNMPv3) represents the evolution of SNMP with an emphasis on enhancing security measures for network management. SNMPv3 introduces mechanisms to ensure message integrity, source authenticity, and confidentiality of data packets traversing the network.

A key feature within SNMPv3's suite of capabilities is the use of "traps." *Simple Network Management Protocol (SNMP) traps* are alert messages sent from an SNMP-enabled device to a management station or system to indicate a significant event or a change in the device's status. Unlike a polling mechanism, where an SNMP manager periodically requests information from devices, traps are initiated by the devices themselves and provide immediate notification without the delay of a polling cycle. This feature is important for timely response to potential issues impacting network performance or security.

The security features provided in SNMPv3 are integral to the operation of SNMP traps:

- **Message integrity:** By including a checksum within a trap message, SNMPv3 ensures that the data has not been altered during transmission, providing confidence that the information is accurate and uncorrupted.

- **Authentication:** SNMPv3 implements authentication protocols, such as HMAC-MD5 or HMAC-SHA, to confirm that a trap originates from a legitimate source. This helps prevent unauthorized devices from sending false alerts to the management system.

■ **Encryption:** To maintain the confidentiality of the content of a trap, SNMPv3 can encrypt messages using protocols like DES or AES. Encryption protects sensitive information in the traps from being read by unauthorized parties that intercepted them.

Configuring SNMPv3 involves setting up users and defining their roles within a security model, as well as establishing the level of security to apply. For instance, when configuring traps, you might choose between different security levels:

■ **No authentication and no privacy (noAuthNoPriv):** This level employs no authentication or encryption and is suitable for basic monitoring purposes where information sensitivity is low.

■ **Authentication without privacy (authNoPriv):** At this level, traps are authenticated to ensure that they come from a legitimate source, which can be appropriate for control messages.

■ **Authentication with privacy (authPriv):** The highest level of security for SNMPv3, which combines authentication and encryption, is suitable for traps containing sensitive data.

Each level of security determines how SNMPv3 will handle trap messages. To set these configurations on networking devices such as Cisco devices, you typically use commands that define the SNMP group, user, and level of security, as demonstrated in Examples 17-1 and 17-2.

Example 17-1 shows the configuration of Cisco IOS XE and Cisco ASA firewall samples.

Example 17-1   Configuring SNMPv3

```
Cisco IOS, IOS-XE, IOS-XR and OS-NX
snmp-server community <your-community> RO


Cisco ASA
snmp-server community <your-community> snmp-server contact
<your-contact>
snmp-server location <your-location> snmp-server host <interface>
<NMS-IP>
 poll community <your-community> version 2c
```

To verify that your devices have been properly configured, you can use an open-source tool called SNMPWALK. Using tools such as SNMPWALK is beneficial for verifying the correct setup of SNMP on devices, allowing administrators to simulate the reception of SNMP messages, including traps.

Example 17-2 shows the **snmpwalk -v3** command help and options available when using the tool.

Example 17-2   snmpwalk -v3 Command Help

```
snmpwalk -v3 -l <noAuthNoPriv|authNoPriv|authPriv> -u <username>
[-a <MD5|SHA>] [-A <authphrase>] [-x <DES|AES>] [-X <privaphrase>]
<ipaddress>[:<dest_port>] [oid]


# snmpwalk v3 example with authentication and encryption
snmpwalk -v3 -l authPriv -u UserMe -a SHA -A AuthPass1 -x AES -X
PrivPass2 192.168.10.1:161 1.3.6.1.2.1.1
```

To use SNMPWALK on most Debian-based operating systems, you install Net-SNMP by using the **apt-get install snmp snmpwalk** command.

Management Information Bases (MIBs) play a vital role in SNMP traps. MIBs are databases that define the structure of the management data on a device, including the hierarchy of all SNMP-manageable elements. When an SNMP trap is triggered, it refers to specific MIB entries to indicate what event has occurred. Understanding how to read and interpret MIBs is crucial for diagnosing the issues signaled by SNMP traps.

Key Topic

Vulnerability Scanners

Identifying vulnerabilities before attackers do is crucial. *Vulnerability scanners* are tools designed to automate the identification of weaknesses in systems and networks. Vulnerability scanners are the digital equivalents of sentinels, constantly looking for weaknesses in the fabric of an organization's network. These automated sentries, such as Nessus and OpenVAS, play a pivotal role in the proactive defense strategy by scanning systems and networks against extensive databases of known vulnerabilities. Their function aligns perfectly with the Security+ exam's emphasis on proactive threat identification and response.

Vulnerability scanners operate through several stages:

1. **Pre-assessment:** Before scanning begins, it's important to define the scope of the assessment and configure the scanner with appropriate credentials and settings to ensure thorough and accurate scanning.

2. **Scanning:** The scanners probe systems, applications, and networks to identify known vulnerabilities, such as unpatched software, misconfigurations, and insecure protocols. They do this by using a combination of checks that include network and port scanning, protocol analysis, and application-level testing.

3. **Post-scan analysis:** Once a scan is complete, the tools provide detailed reports categorizing vulnerabilities by their severity levels (critical, high, medium, and low). This prioritization aids cybersecurity professionals in resource allocation and remediation planning, enabling them to address the most dangerous vulnerabilities first.

4. **Remediation and verification:** Security teams use the information from vulnerability scanners to remediate identified issues. It is crucial to verify that remediation efforts have been successful by rerunning scans and ensuring that no vulnerabilities remain unaddressed.

5. **Continuous monitoring:** Regular scans are necessary as part of an ongoing vulnerability management program to discover new vulnerabilities as they emerge.

Vulnerability scanners are not infallible and do have limitations; they can generate false positives (benign items mistakenly reported as risks) and false negatives (where real vulnerabilities go undetected). They might not always understand the context of a vulnerability and its actual impact in a specific environment.

When setting up vulnerability scanners, consider the following configurations:

- Ensure that scanners have the credentials for authenticated scans, providing deeper inspections than unauthenticated scans.

- Define specific targets within the network, such as IP address ranges or particular devices, to maintain focus and avoid unauthorized scanning.

- Schedule scans during periods of low network traffic to minimize disruption of daily operations.

- Keep the scanner's database current to detect the newest vulnerabilities.

Several notable software vendors offer robust vulnerability scanning solutions:

- **Tenable Nessus:** This tool is known for having extensive vulnerability management capabilities and providing detailed reports that assist in remediating identified issues.

- **Greenbone OpenVAS:** As an open-source option, this tool provides a cost-effective solution with community support and regular updates.

- **Rapid7 InsightVM:** This tool offers live monitoring and integrates with cloud services for real-time insights into network risks.

- **Qualys VM:** This cloud-based solution ensures continuous monitoring with automated updates, accommodating many IT infrastructures.

- **Tripwire IP360:** This tool features advanced scoring and prioritization, which helps concentrate efforts on the most significant vulnerabilities first.

For integration and broader security context, consider the following when using vulnerability scanners:

- Align vulnerability scanning with SIEM systems to synthesize vulnerability data with other security insights for a well-rounded threat analysis.

- Pair with patch management systems to streamline the remediation process by automatically applying required patches to systems identified as vulnerable.

These tools usually have compliance reporting features to help adhere to regulatory standards. You still need to ensure the configuration of reports to meet specific compliance requirements, utilizing filters and segmentation as necessary. Finally, it is important to set up alerting mechanisms to notify the cybersecurity team promptly when critical vulnerabilities are found and ensure swift action to mitigate potential threats.

Vulnerability scanners are clearly important in identifying system and network vulnerabilities; however, they must complement other security reviews, like manual penetration testing and code reviews. Human expertise is invaluable for interpreting scanner output, reducing false positives, and performing tests beyond the scope of automated tools.

Chapter Review Activities

Use the features in this section to study and review the topics in this chapter.

Review Key Topics

Review the most important topics in the chapter, noted with the Key Topic icon in the outer margin of the page. Table 17-3 lists these key topics and the page number on which each is found.

Key Topic

Table 17-3   Key Topics for Chapter 17

Key Topic Element	Description	Page Number
Paragraph	Infrastructure monitoring	384
Section	Log Aggregation	386
Section	Scanning	389
Section	Reporting	390
Section	Alert Response and Remediation/Validation	392
Figure 17-1	SCAP components	395
Section	NetFlow	399
Section	Vulnerability Scanners	403

Define Key Terms

Define the following key terms from this chapter and check your answers in the glossary:

> monitoring computing resources, monitoring systems, application monitoring, infrastructure monitoring, cybersecurity activity, log aggregation, alerting, scanning, reporting, archiving, alert response process, quarantining, alert tuning, cybersecurity tool, Security Content Automation Protocol (SCAP), benchmark, agent-based solution, agentless solution, security information and event management (SIEM) system, NetFlow, antivirus software, data loss prevention (DLP), Simple Network Management Protocol (SNMP) trap, vulnerability scanner

Review Questions

Answer the following review questions. Check your answers with the answer key in Appendix A.

1. What is the primary role of monitoring systems in cybersecurity?

2. In the context of cybersecurity, what purpose does log aggregation serve?

3. How does a report for senior management differ from a report for a technical team in the field of cybersecurity?

4. What is the mission of Security Content Automation Protocol (SCAP)?

5. What are the benefits and drawbacks of using agentless solutions for system monitoring?

This chapter covers the following topics related to Objective 4.5 (Given a scenario, modify enterprise capabilities to enhance security) of the CompTIA Security+ SY0-701 certification exam:

- Firewall

- IDS/IPS

- Web filter

- Operating system security

- Implementation of secure protocols

- DNS filtering

- Email security

- File integrity monitoring

- DLP

- Network access control (NAC)

- Endpoint detection and response (EDR)/extended detection and response (XDR)

- User behavior analytics

CHAPTER 18

Modifying Enterprise Capabilities to Enhance Security

This chapter starts with the basics of firewalls, rules, and access control lists and then moves on to more specialized topics, like web and DNS filtering. You'll learn about the role of ports and protocols and key email security standards, such as DMARC, DKIM, and SPF. This chapter also explores file integrity monitoring, network access control, and the cutting-edge area of endpoint security through EDR and XDR solutions. The chapter concludes with an overview of user behavior analytics, taking a comprehensive look at how technology and analytics are used to secure today's digital landscapes.

"Do I Know This Already?" Quiz

The "Do I Know This Already?" quiz enables you to assess whether you should read this entire chapter thoroughly or jump to the "Chapter Review Activities" section. If you are in doubt about your answers to these questions or your own assessment of your knowledge of the topics, read the entire chapter. Table 18-1 lists the major headings in this chapter and their corresponding "Do I Know This Already?" quiz questions. You can find the answers in Appendix A, "Answers to the 'Do I Know This Already?' Quizzes and Review Questions."

Table 18-1 "Do I Know This Already?" Section-to-Question Mapping

Foundation Topics Section	Questions
Firewall	1
IDS/IPS	2
Web Filter	3
Operating System Security	4
DNS Filtering	5
Email Security	6
File Integrity Monitoring	10

Foundation Topics Section	Questions
DLP	11
Network Access Control (NAC)	7
Endpoint Detection and Response (EDR)/Extended Detection and Response (XDR)	8
User Behavior Analytics	9
Implementation of Secure Protocols	12

CAUTION   The goal of self-assessment is to gauge your mastery of the topics in this chapter. If you do not know the answer to a question or are only partially sure of the answer, you should mark that question as wrong for purposes of self-assessment. Giving yourself credit for an answer you correctly guess skews your self-assessment results and might provide you with a false sense of security.

1. Which of the following tools is considered the most important element for network protection?

   a. Centralized servers

   b. Endpoint devices

   c. Vendor variety

   d. Firewall

2. What is the primary difference between an IDS and an IPS in terms of their operation?

   a. An IDS is proactive, whereas an IPS is reactive.

   b. An IDS is for monitoring, whereas an IPS is for blocking.

   c. An IDS is software based, whereas an IPS is hardware based.

   d. An IDS operates on an endpoint, whereas an IPS operates on a network.

3. In an agent-based web filtering approach, where is the software deployed?

   a. On a centralized server

   b. On the network router

   c. On individual user devices

   d. On external firewalls

4. What can administrators establish by using a Group Policy framework?

   a. DNS filtering rules

   b. Complexity of user passwords

   c. Intrusion detection systems

   d. Web filtering methods

5. What is the primary purpose of DNS filtering in a corporate environment?

   a. To increase Internet speed

   b. To monitor employee productivity

   c. To block access to malicious or inappropriate websites

   d. To provide VPN services for remote employees

6. What is the primary purpose of DMARC in email security?

   a. To encrypt email content

   b. To check the authenticity of the sending domain

   c. To prevent phishing attacks

   d. To act as a spam filter

7. Which technology is crucial for verifying that an email message has not been altered during transit and that it was sent from the actual domain it claims to be from?

   a. DMARC

   b. VPN

   c. Antivirus software

   d. Multifactor authentication

8. How does XDR differ from EDR in its focus?

   a. XDR focuses on endpoint devices.

   b. XDR focuses on cloud storage.

   c. XDR focuses on network traffic.

   d. XDR takes a holistic view across various channels and layers.

9. What technology does user behavior analytics (UBA) primarily use to track and assess user behavior on a network?

   a. Firewalls

   b. Machine learning algorithms

   c. Intrusion detection systems

   d. Web filters

10. What is the main function of file integrity monitoring in an IT environment?

   a. To improve the efficiency of data storage

   b. To alert administrators to unauthorized changes in files

   c. To enhance the speed of file access

   d. To provide backup solutions for data recovery

11. What is a key objective of deploying a data loss prevention (DLP) system in an organization?

   a. To facilitate easy transfer of data to the cloud

   b. To ensure that sensitive or critical information is not sent outside the corporate network

   c. To increase storage for sensitive data

   d. To permit the use of USB thumb drives for data transfer

12. When implementing secure protocols in a network environment, which of the following is *not* a key consideration to ensure the secure transmission of data?

   a. Selecting an appropriate encryption protocol

   b. Choosing the correct port for data transmission

   c. Deciding on a suitable transport method

   d. Determining the color scheme of the user interface

Foundation Topics

Firewall

A *firewall* is a network security device or software that monitors incoming and outgoing network traffic and decides whether to allow or block specific traffic based on a defined set of security rules. Its primary objective is to establish a barrier between a secure internal network and untrusted external networks, such as the Internet, to prevent unauthorized access and potential threats. The strategic deployment of firewalls extends beyond merely monitoring traffic and demands a sophisticated grasp of network structures coupled with a definitive security policy. A firewall's effectiveness is measured by its ability to filter traffic according to internal rules. The role of a security engineer is usually to help with the strategic placement of firewalls within the network topology—a decision that influences the capacity of the firewalls to protect without impeding network efficiency. This calls for a thoughtful design that incorporates multiple firewalls in a tiered arrangement, providing a multilayered defense system that encapsulates the concept of defense in depth. A defense-in-depth approach is an arrangement that enhances security by compartmentalizing the network into distinct zones and also ensures business continuity through redundant configurations, maintaining the integrity of security operations even in the face of system failures.

Firewalls must be agile and intelligent today, in the face of the ever-evolving array of cyber threats. Incorporating behavioral analytics into firewall management allows for a more adaptive approach to security, where firewalls can learn and adjust their rules based on observed network traffic patterns in order to identify and neutralize threats more effectively. The capability of firewalls to make context-aware security decisions further enhances this adaptive capability. By considering factors such as user identity, application types, and temporal patterns, firewalls can apply more granular security tailored to the unique demands of each network segment.

The management of firewall rules has evolved from static lists to dynamic sets that can self-adjust in real time in response to fluctuations in network traffic, emerging threats, and updated threat intelligence. This dynamic rule management is essential for maintaining a resilient defense that can swiftly respond to the complexities of modern network traffic and threat behaviors.

The integration of automation into firewall responses is a significant leap forward in network security. Automated processes enable firewalls to initiate immediate defensive actions, such as segmenting a compromised network zone or escalating alerts to security personnel. By embedding firewalls within a broader security strategy, an organization can ensure a proactive stance against threats, reducing the window of opportunity for attackers and minimizing the potential damage from breaches.

Rules

As with many other things in your life as a security engineer, firewall technology is a living component of the network and essential for protecting digital assets. The intelligent and strategic application of firewall technology forms the cornerstone of a robust network defense, empowering an organization to safeguard its data and systems against multifaceted threats.

Firewall *rules* exist to control the flow of data packets, ensuring that only legitimate traffic travels on an enterprise's network. But what happens when the routine traffic patterns change or when a network hosts a special event such as a webcast that attracts a global audience? This is where advanced firewall rule configurations come into play.

Consider a scenario where a company, Widgets Inc., with a primary public-facing IP address of 203.0.113.5, is preparing to launch a product through a webcast scheduled for 9 p.m. EST. The network administrators can configure time-bound rules to accommodate the anticipated spike in traffic.

A rule could be written as follows:

```
ALLOW TCP from ANY to 203.0.113.5 PORT 80 on 12/12/2023 from 8:30 PM
EST to 10:30 PM EST
```

This rule would temporarily permit incoming HTTP traffic to the company's web server, ensuring that potential customers from around the world have seamless access to the event.

As another example, let's say Widgets Inc. observes that its network is often targeted by a persistent attacker from a specific IP address range, 198.51.100.0/24. To strengthen its defenses, the organization could implement a rule that blocks all incoming connections from this range but allows a single trusted partner access to a specific service, such as FTP:

```
DENY ALL from 198.51.100.0/24 to ANY
ALLOW TCP from 198.51.100.10 to 203.0.113.5 PORT 21
```

As you can see, there is a need for reactive and anticipatory rules that adapt to both expected and unexpected network traffic patterns.

Optimizing these rules is equally important to prevent firewall rule bloat, which can slow down network performance and make rule management unwieldy. Rule optimization might include consolidating rules, where possible, and regularly reviewing and purging unnecessary or redundant rules. For example, if Widgets Inc. has several rules that allow traffic from different IP addresses in the same subnet to the same port on a server, they can be consolidated into a single rule:

```
ALLOW TCP from 198.51.100.0/24 to 203.0.113.5 PORT 22
```

Administrators can maintain an efficient and streamlined rule set by consolidating rules and making them as specific as necessary but as broad as possible. This practice improves the firewall's performance and enhances security by making the rules easier to review and audit—and it keeps you from running out the back door screaming.

Access Lists

An access list, also called an *access control list (ACL)*, is a fundamental feature of firewall technology, serving as a rule book that governs traffic flow through a network. ACLs can be configured to permit or deny traffic based on various criteria, including IP addresses, protocol types, port numbers, and even time of day, and they offer a granular level of control over network security.

An ACL is a sequence of ordered rules applied to data packets that are entering or leaving a network interface. Each packet is examined against the ACL rules until a match is found. If a packet satisfies the conditions of an allow rule, it is permitted through the firewall; if it matches a deny rule, it is blocked. An ACL is processed using a top-down approach, and as soon as a rule is matched, the processing stops. The order of rules is critical and should be carefully considered when configuring ACLs. Failure to configure ACLs in the correct order and consistently can cause big problems, and you can save yourself time by ensuring that all stakeholders are on board with the order early on.

Imagine that an organization, Acme Corp, wants to secure its internal network (192.168.10.0/24) from external threats but needs to ensure that its web server (192.168.10.5) remains accessible from the Internet.

Here's how an ACL might be configured on Acme Corp's firewall to achieve this:

Step 1.   Permit HTTP and HTTPS traffic to the web server:

```
ALLOW TCP from ANY to 192.168.10.5 PORT 80
ALLOW TCP from ANY to 192.168.10.5 PORT 443
```

This rule denies all other inbound traffic from external sources to any IP address within the internal network range.

Step 2.   Deny all other inbound traffic from the Internet:

```
DENY IP from ANY to 192.168.10.0/24
```

This rule denies all other inbound traffic from external sources to any IP address within the internal network range.

Step 3.   Permit internal traffic for intranet functionality:

```
ALLOW IP from 192.168.10.0/24 to 192.168.10.0/24
```

This rule allows unrestricted traffic within the internal network, enabling intranet activities and inter-departmental communications.

Step 4.   Deny all traffic by default (implicit deny):

```
DENY IP from ANY to ANY
```

This implicit deny rule is typically at the end of every ACL to ensure that any traffic not explicitly permitted is denied by default.

Based on these ACL configurations, Acme Corp's firewall will only permit external web traffic to the designated server and will block all other unsolicited inbound connections while allowing necessary internal traffic. It's a balance that maintains the accessibility of essential services and the network's security.

Ports/Protocols

NOTE   In a robust firewall system, managing ports and protocols serves as the center point for effective security measures. *Ports* are essentially virtual docks where network services can receive data. They range from well-known ports like HTTP on port 80 to ephemeral ports assigned dynamically. They are often targeted in various types of network attacks, making their management via firewalls critical.

A *protocol* is a set of rules and conventions that govern how data is transmitted and received over a network. These rules outline the syntax, semantics, and synchronization of communication, making it possible for devices on a network to understand each other and exchange data efficiently. Examples include TCP/IP for Internet communication and HTTP/HTTPS for web browsing. In the context of firewalls, protocols are essential because they dictate how specific types of traffic should be treated, enabling a firewall to make informed decisions on whether to allow or block incoming or outgoing packets based on their adherence to these established rules.

Now, let's look into the different technologies that work in tandem to provide nuanced control over ports and the associated protocols.

Packet filtering, both stateless and stateful, provides the first line of defense. Stateless packet filtering involves inspecting each packet in isolation, without considering any previous packets. This makes it less effective against complex attacks like IP spoofing. On the other hand, stateful packet inspection (SPI) retains a "state" memory to keep track of ongoing connections. This helps SPI distinguish between legitimate and malicious packets more effectively, making it more resilient to sophisticated attacks.

A Network Address Translation (NAT) gateway goes further by filtering traffic based on ports and IP addresses. Imagine that you have a web server inside your network that should be accessible from the outside. By using NAT, you can direct incoming HTTP traffic (typically port 80) to this server without exposing other services or ports to the external world. NAT can be configured to match incoming traffic—not just to the outbound IP address connection but also to specific ports, offering a granular level of control.

However, the buck doesn't stop here. An application-level gateway (ALG) applies security protocols to specific applications. Think of it as a discerning bouncer at a club who checks your ID and ensures that you adhere to the dress code. For example, an organization might permit SFTP (Secure File Transfer Protocol) traffic but block Telnet due to its inherent security risks. An ALG makes this possible by scrutinizing each packet to determine its application origin and taking action accordingly. While this layer of security is potent, it does require more computational resources, which could affect performance.

Circuit-level gateways work differently. They operate at the session layer and act as intermediaries between the transport and application layers of the OSI model. Once a trusted connection is established, circuit-level gateways allow data packets to flow freely between hosts without packet-level inspection. Although this saves on computational overhead, it may pose a risk if the established connection is later exploited for malicious activities.

The key is to balance stringent security measures with a network's operational needs, which starts with a deep understanding of how ports and protocols are managed by using firewalls.

Screened Subnet

The physical placement and configuration of firewalls can also significantly impact their effectiveness. For example, a back-to-back design places two firewalls surrounding a screened subnet or DMZ, adding an extra layer of security. A three-leg perimeter configuration as shown in Figure 18-1 is another option, providing distinct pathways for different types of traffic allowing for more granular control over ports and protocols.

A *screened subnet* is a specific network segment situated between an organization's internal network and an external network, usually the Internet. Figure 18-1 shows a screened subnet. Its primary function is to provide an additional layer of security by isolating sensitive systems from direct exposure to the external network. This third adapter manages traffic between the external network and the screened subnet, reinforcing the security posture and mitigating risks.

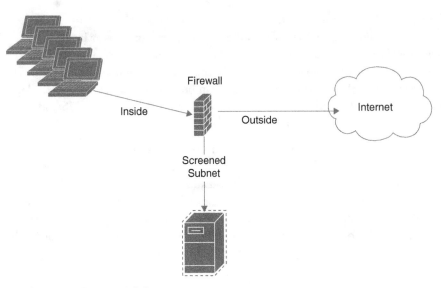

Figure 18-1   Screened Subnet

> **NOTE**   We discuss each of the tools and technologies separately in this chapter so that you understand how to work with each. But you should keep in mind that many of these technologies are consolidated into a single solution, a trend that will likely continue as we move forward.

IDS/IPS

In today's complex cybersecurity landscape, *intrusion detection systems (IDSs)* and *intrusion prevention systems (IPSs)* play vital roles in protecting network infrastructure. While both try to identify and mitigate malicious activities, IDSs and IPSs operate on distinct yet complementary paradigms. An IDS is tailored for monitoring and alerting on suspicious activities, whereas an IPS takes a more proactive stance, blocking and preventing known and potential threats.

This section focuses on the capabilities, trends, and challenges of IDS and IPS at the application layer—the layer that often serves as a critical line of defense against targeted attacks. Various methodologies have been developed for intrusion detection and prevention at this layer, ranging from signature-based techniques to heuristic or behavior-based approaches and anomaly detection.

Given the constant emergence of new attacks, particularly those aimed at exploiting vulnerabilities at the application layer, a nuanced understanding of these methodologies is indispensable. The goal of this section is to provide a comprehensive overview of the operational principles, strengths, and limitations of IDSs and IPSs in the context of application layer security.

Trends

Trends refer to the analysis of collected security data over time to identify patterns that could indicate the emergence of new threats or vulnerabilities. In IDSs/IPSs, this involves the examination of events and logs to track and anticipate the development of attack strategies, malware outbreaks, and the effectiveness of the current security measures.

IDSs and IPSs have evolved significantly in recent years to meet the challenges posed by increasingly sophisticated cyber threats. At one time, IDSs and IPSs were predominantly characterized by signature-based detection methods, which involved scanning incoming traffic for known patterns associated with malicious activity. However, as cyber adversaries became more inventive, the limitations of relying solely on signatures became evident. IDS and IPS technologies are now moving toward incorporating machine learning algorithms and behavioral analysis to dynamically adapt to new forms of cyber threats.

We have also seen a recent increase in IDS/IPS integration with cloud-based systems, which offers the benefits of scalability and centralized control. This increase reflects the broader shift toward cloud-native applications and the consequent need to secure them effectively. The cloud provides enhanced data analytics capabilities, providing more accurate threat detection and prevention.

Signatures

At the heart of any IDS/IPS lies a set of *signatures*, which are predefined patterns or rules that the system uses to identify possible threats. These signatures serve as a sort of DNA for identifying different types of cyberattacks. However, it's essential to understand that not all signatures are created equal.

In a basic form, a signature might consist of a string of bytes that identifies a known virus or malware. For example, a simple signature could be set up to detect attempts to exploit a known vulnerability in a web application. When a packet of data traveling through the network contains this particular string, the IDS issues an alert, and the IPS can block the packet altogether.

However, such fixed-pattern signatures have limitations. Cybercriminals often use techniques like polymorphic code to change the appearance of their malware while keeping its underlying functionality intact. This means that a signature that successfully identified a piece of malware yesterday might not recognize its slightly altered variant today.

To overcome these limitations, more sophisticated methods have been developed. Stateful signature-based detection, for instance, doesn't just look at individual packets but considers the sequence, or state, of a series of packets. Imagine someone trying to force entry into a building by trying many different keys; a stateful signature would not just flag the act of inserting a key but would alert based on repeated and rapid attempts.

As IDS and IPS technologies adapt to increasingly sophisticated attack vectors, their signatures must evolve. One solution to this is the adoption of heuristic or behavior-based signatures that evaluate actions in the context of what is typical or expected in a network. These can be highly effective but require careful tuning to minimize false positives.

An IPS serves a dual role in protecting the digital environment: It both identifies and neutralizes incoming threats. When you're setting up an IPS for the first time, it's common to configure it in what is known as "promiscuous," or passive, mode. This cautious start helps you evaluate how the system impacts your network's performance and stability. During this period, the IPS will identify potential security risks and notify administrators but won't actively block any traffic.

Once you're comfortable with the system's behavior and impact, transitioning to inline mode is the next logical step, empowering the IPS to participate in your security infrastructure actively. In this configuration, the IPS is positioned directly in the data path, and it makes real-time decisions about which network packets to allow and which to discard.

But it's crucial to understand that IPS technologies are not a monolith. They can be categorized into different types based on their deployment and capabilities:

- A network-based IPS focuses on protecting the network at large, scanning all the traffic that passes through a particular point in the network.

- A next-generation IPS (NGIPS) incorporates more advanced features like application awareness and integrated threat intelligence to provide a more robust security posture.

- A host-based IPS (HIPS) is installed directly on a user's computer to monitor and secure a specific device instead of a network.

Various methodologies and algorithms power IPS devices, including to the following:

- **Pattern matching and stateful pattern-matching recognition:** These are the backbone of traditional IPSs and involve scanning packets for known strings or sequences that indicate malicious activity.

- **Protocol analysis:** This involves examining data at the application layer to ensure that the network communications follow the expected protocols.

- **Heuristic-based analysis:** Algorithms judge the incoming data based on behavioral patterns or statistical benchmarks, allowing for more dynamic threat detection.

- **Anomaly-based analysis:** These algorithms monitor network behavior to establish a "normal" baseline and alert administrators to any significant deviations.

- **Global threat correlation capabilities:** Some advanced IPS solutions incorporate global threat intelligence to further enhance detection and prevention measures.

Key Topic

Web Filter

Now we are ready to dig into the nitty-gritty of web filtering. Picture this: You're a sysadmin at a large corporation, and you are tasked with ensuring that your network remains a sanctuary against the endless web threats lurking online. Well, web filtering is your Swiss Army knife for this mission. *Web filtering* is a mechanism that controls access to websites or specific web content based on predefined criteria, basically allowing you to be the bouncer for your corporate network club.

So, where do you start? You could go for an agent-based setup. In an *agent-based web filtering approach*, software is deployed directly onto individual user devices. This is like putting a little security guard on everyone's computer. This guard doesn't just work in the office but is always on duty, whether your employees are working in the office or clicking away at home. This approach makes it easier to manage a team that's frequently out of the office or that works remotely. But remember that it involves deploying software on someone's personal or work device, and you need to ensure that you've covered your legal and privacy bases and include your legal and HR folks in discussions about these actions.

But what if you're more of a controlling type, as most of us are with network security, and want to keep an eye on everything that goes through your network? A centralized proxy is your go-to. A *centralized proxy* is a server-based method of web filtering that functions as an intermediary between user devices and the Internet. This is essentially an intermediary that checks every request and decides whether it should go through. Imagine that you're the head of a major international airport, and your proxy is the TSA, which scrutinizes every passenger (or, in this case, data packet) to see if they should be allowed to board the flight (or enter your network). It's a robust solution, but it can slow things down if not optimized correctly—and we've all seen the lines when things slow down!

Now let's talk about universal resource locator (URL) scanning. You know how there are certain stores you'd advise people to avoid if they're looking for quality products? The web also has a lot of places you want your users to avoid for safety. *URL scanning* is a process that involve examining and categorizing web addresses to identify potentially harmful websites. URL scanning guides your network traffic away from potentially harmful websites. But the Internet constantly changes; new "bad stores" pop up, and old ones may get updated. Keeping your URL list updated is critical.

But let's be real, not everything in a "bad store" is actually bad. Enter content categorization. *Content categorization* is a more granular form of web filtering that involves examining individual elements within a website. Rather than blocking an entire website, you can use content categorization to allow or deny access to specific pages or types of content within a site. For example, a website might in general be a time waster, but it could have one great article on cybersecurity trends that your R&D team should read. Content categorization allows you to block access to the games and comics on the site while enabling access to that beneficial article.

To make all of what we've been discussing happen, you need to set up some block rules. Think of these rules as being similar to the house rules posted at a public pool: no running, no diving, and absolutely no bringing in hazardous material. *Block rules* are predefined criteria that administrators set to automatically prevent access to certain types of web content or specific websites. If a website violates your rules— maybe it's hosting malware or promoting phishing scams—it's out, no exceptions.

Don't forget about reputation. In much the way you'd trust a well-reviewed restaurant over a place cited for health code violations, you can use *reputation-based filtering* to block or allow websites based on their track record. It's not just about what the site looks like now but what it's done in the past, offering a more dynamic and, in many ways, safer way to filter content.

So, you're all set, right? Not so fast. There are still some hurdles to clear. Sometimes, a system gets it wrong, flagging harmless sites as harmful and vice versa. And beware of the tech-savvy rebels in your office. They might use a VPN to bypass your carefully constructed barriers. These challenges aren't insurmountable, though. Machine learning and real-time analytics are stepping up the game, making filters smarter and more adaptive than ever before.

Key Topic Operating System Security

Operating system security is a facet of cybersecurity that often serves as the first line of defense against unauthorized access and malicious attacks. *Operating system security* is the strengthening of the operating system—usually through configuration changes and software tools. Two prevalent methods used to enhance operating system security are the use of Group Policy and SELinux, each of which takes a unique system control approach.

Group Policy, which is particularly well known in Windows environments, is essentially a rule book for system administrators. A *Group Policy* framework allows administrators to establish detailed rules, or "policies," for how the operating system and various applications should behave. For example, an admin could set a policy that dictates the complexity of user passwords or that restricts access to certain system files.

Imagine that you're running an educational institution's IT infrastructure. You have a mix of faculty and students using computers for everything from academic research to social networking. Here's where Group Policy shines. With Group Policy, you can designate specific computer labs to run only educational software. For example, you could disable USB ports in computer labs to prevent data theft or the spread of malware, thereby limiting activities in this space. Consider this scenario: A student tries to plug in a USB drive to copy an exam paper illegally. The Group Policy settings would disallow this, rendering the USB ports inoperative. A message would appear saying, "An administrative policy restricts access to this port." In this manner, Group Policy acts as a digital handbook, listing what can and cannot be done and automatically enforcing these rules.

However, Group Policy is most effective within a domain environment, where a single server can push policies across multiple computers. Its limitation is that it is generally confined to Windows ecosystems, which creates challenges in heterogeneous environments.

SELinux, or Security-Enhanced Linux, is an open-source project initially developed by the U.S. National Security Agency (NSA). Unlike Group Policy, which is more about rule setting, SELinux is about role playing. SELinux employs mandatory access controls to restrict users and system processes to perform only authorized actions. For example, even if a web server is compromised, SELinux can prevent the attacker from accessing sensitive system files.

Let's consider SELinux in the context of a high-security research lab where sensitive projects are underway. The lab uses a custom Linux distribution fortified with SELinux policies. One of the lab members, Alice, has restricted access to only read and write data in a specific project folder. Now, suppose Alice's credentials are somehow compromised. An attacker gaining access to her account would be in for a surprise. SELinux's mandatory access controls would prevent the attacker from doing anything outside of what Alice can do—like trying to read confidential files in another project's folder. Even if the attacker tries to exploit a vulnerability in the system to escalate privileges, SELinux policies will serve as a final roadblock, containing the compromise within Alice's limited role. In essence, SELinux acts like a vigilant security guard, ensuring that everyone—both legitimate users and compromised accounts—acts strictly within their defined roles, adding an extra layer of security that's incredibly difficult to penetrate. Although powerful, SELinux is also notoriously complex; to use it effectively, you need to have a deep understanding of its various modules and policies. Also, while it is mainly designed for Linux distributions, its principles and methodologies can be applied to other Unix-like operating systems.

So, while Group Policy and SELinux offer robust solutions to system security, they do so in unique ways. Group Policy acts as a customizable rule book and is ideal for organizations running primarily on Windows. In contrast, SELinux offers a rigorous but complex set of security protocols that are better suited for Linux systems and those who need a high-security environment. Each has merits and challenges, and understanding both Group Policy and SELinux allows you to select the right tool for your particular needs.

Implementation of Secure Protocols

Implementing secure protocols is critical to network security, and it essentially involves creating encrypted pathways for data transmission. The *implementation of secure protocols* involves three key considerations: protocol selection, port selection, and transport method selection. Each component plays a crucial role in securing data exchange and mitigating the risk of unauthorized access or data leaks.

First, let's discuss protocol selection. *Protocol selection* refers to choosing the appropriate communication standard for data exchange in a network. This step is equivalent to choosing the cryptographic foundation for your network's communications. For instance, if you are running an e-commerce website, HTTPS (HTTP Secure) should be the standard protocol. It ensures that all data transferred between your server and a client is encrypted, providing a secure channel for sensitive activities like login or payment processing.

The next consideration is port selection. *Port selection* involves choosing specific entry and exit points, known as ports, in the network for data traffic. Ports are identified by numerical values and are mapped to particular services and protocols. Standard ports, like 80 for HTTP and 443 for HTTPS, are predefined for convenience, but nonstandard ports can also be used for added security.

Ports are like doorways through which data enters or exits a network. While standard ports such as 80 for HTTP and 443 for HTTPS are well known and commonly used, they can also be prime attack targets. Changing to nonstandard ports, especially for administrative interfaces or other sensitive areas, adds an extra layer of obscurity to your security measures, making it slightly more challenging for attackers to identify vulnerabilities.

Table 18-2 is by no means exhaustive, but it covers some of the most commonly encountered secure ports and protocols in various layers of the networking stack. Each protocol offers a unique set of advantages and trade-offs, making each one suited for specific tasks and environments.

Key Topic

Table 18-2 Sample Secure Ports and Protocols

Protocol	Port	Description	Common Uses
CIFS	445	Protocol for file sharing	Windows file sharing
DHCP	67/68 (UDP)	Dynamic Host Configuration Protocol	Automatic configuration of devices on IP networks
DNS	53	Domain Name System	Domain resolution
FTP	20/21	File Transfer Protocol	File transfer
FTP/S	990	Secure FTP	Secure file transfer
HTTP	80	Hypertext Transfer Protocol	Web traffic
HTTPS	443	Secure HTTP	Secure web traffic
IMAP2	143	Internet Message Access Protocol	Email retrieval
IMAP/S	993	Secure IMAP	Secure email retrieval
Kerberos	88	Authentication protocol	Network authentication
LDAP	389	Lightweight Directory Access Protocol	Directory services
LDAPS	636	LDAP over SSL/TLS	Secure directory services
MS SQL	1433	Microsoft SQL Server	Database management
NetBIOS	139	Network Basic Input/Output System	Windows networking
NTP	123	Network Time Protocol	Time synchronization
POP3	110	Post Office Protocol Version 3	Email retrieval
POP3/S	995	Secure POP3	Secure email retrieval
RADIUS	1812	Remote Authentication Dial-In User Service	Network authentication
RDP	3389	Remote Desktop Protocol	Remote administration

Protocol	Port	Description	Common Uses
SIP	5060	Session Initiation Protocol	VoIP and video conferencing
SMTP	25	Simple Mail Transfer Protocol	Email sending
SNMP Trap	162	SNMP trap	Network monitoring
SMTPS	465	Secure SMTP	Secure email sending
SNM	161	Simple Network Management Protocol	Network management
SSH/SFTP	22	SSH File Transfer Protocol/Secure Shell	Secure file transfer/shell
TACACS	49	Terminal Access Controller Access-Control System	Network device authentication
TELNET	23	Telnet protocol	Unsecured text communications

Finally, *transport method selection* pertains to how data packets are sent across a network. The selection and implementation of secure protocols for transporting data are fundamental when modifying enterprise capabilities to enhance security. Secure transport methods ensure that data remains confidential and unaltered during transmission. For web traffic, you should prioritize HTTPS over HTTP to encrypt the data between client and server and provide a secure channel even over unsecured networks.

Similarly, you should adopt TLS in place of SSL for secure communications. TLS is the more advanced and secure protocol, safeguarding data with robust encryption. Ensure that all services that previously relied on SSL, such as web servers and email clients, are updated to use TLS so that they are fortified against potential threats.

In scenarios requiring remote terminal access or command execution, SSH is the secure alternative to Telnet. Unlike Telnet, SSH provides encryption, securing remote sessions and data transfers from eavesdropping and on-path attacks.

For database connectivity, using secure SQL ports with encrypted connections is highly recommended. You can even change a SQL server's default port (port 1433) to a different port. Attackers seeking to take advantage of SQL data transfers will target this well-known port. This practice prevents the exposure of sensitive data to those who might intercept it on the network. Ensure that databases are only accessible over ports that support encrypted data transmission.

DNS Filtering

DNS filtering is the practice of blocking access to certain websites, web pages, or IP addresses. DNS filtering essentially serves as a traffic cop that allows or disallows data requests to domain names. It is crucial for preventing access to malicious or inappropriate sites. The real-world application of DNS filtering can be seen in corporate networks where, for instance, all employees' web traffic is routed through a DNS filter that blocks access to social media during work hours. However, this system isn't foolproof; savvy users can bypass DNS filters by using VPNs or other methods.

Email Security

In this age of digital communication, email remains one of the most commonly used methods of exchanging information. However, it is also one of the main vectors for cyberattacks such as phishing, spear phishing, and malware distribution. *Email security* refers to the collective measures used to secure the access and content of an email account or service. Several standards and technologies try to make email a more secure medium for communication, including Domain-Based Message Authentication, Reporting and Conformance (DMARC), DomainKeys Identified Mail (DKIM), Sender Policy Framework (SPF), and email gateways.

Domain-Based Message Authentication, Reporting and Conformance (DMARC) is critical in combating email-based attacks, especially those involving domain spoofing. Attackers often use a technique known as *spoofing* to make the "From" address in an email appear as though it's coming from a trusted source. DMARC provides a way for the email receiver to check that an email was actually sent from a particular domain and ensure that it wasn't altered during transit.

Here's how the DMARC process works:

Step 1. **SPF check:** The receiving mail server uses SPF to validate that the email is from an IP address listed in the DNS records of the sending domain. The email fails this check if the sending IP address is not listed in the SPF record.

Step 2. **DKIM check:** The receiving mail server also uses DKIM to check the digital signature in the email header against the public key published in the sender's DNS records. If the signature doesn't match, the email fails this check.

Step 3. **DMARC policy retrieval:** The receiving mail server retrieves the DMARC policy of the sending domain from its DNS records. This policy specifies what actions to take if the SPF or DKIM checks fail (for example, reject the email, mark it as spam, or let it pass through but report the failure).

Step 4.   **Policy enforcement:** Based on the DMARC policy, the receiving mail server decides whether to deliver the email to the recipient's inbox, send it to the spam folder, or reject it outright.

Step 5.   **Reporting:** DMARC allows the sender to specify an email address where reports about DMARC verification results can be sent. These reports help the sender understand who is sending email on their behalf, whether the emails are legitimate, and make adjustments as necessary.

The mechanism behind DMARC involves a combination of two established email authentication protocols: DKIM and SPF. When an email is sent from a domain that uses DMARC, it is first signed by the domain's mail server using DKIM, and the SPF record is checked to confirm that the email was sent from a server authorized by that domain. Upon receiving the email, the receiving mail server then performs its own checks against the DMARC policy of the sender's domain, which is published in DNS as a TXT record.

Allowing users to confirm who sent an email makes DMARC a valuable asset in preventing phishing attacks, in which an attacker might spoof a bank's email address to gather sensitive user information. DMARC also offers reporting capabilities that allow domain owners to gain visibility into how their email is used, making it easier to spot potential abuse. It's an open technology, and adopting it can significantly reduce the chances of your domain being used for nefarious purposes.

Before DMARC, there was ***DomainKeys Identified Mail (DKIM)***. This standard also tries to verify the authenticity of email messages by allowing the sender to sign parts of the email digitally. The recipient verifies the signature by checking the corresponding public key published in DNS TXT records. DKIM serves as a foundational layer for DMARC, enhancing email security by ensuring the integrity and origin of the message. Multiple RFCs have been developed for DKIM, such as RFC 6376 for signatures, RFC 5863 for deployment considerations, and RFC 5617 for Author Domain Signing Practices (ADSP).

Sender Policy Framework (SPF) is another crucial technology in the fight against email spoofing. SPF enables the email recipient to verify that the email was sent from a server authorized by the domain owner. This is accomplished by checking DNS records that list which servers can send emails on behalf of a specific domain. Organizations can enforce varying levels of strictness with SPF; some might choose to block all emails that fail SPF checks, while others may only mark them as suspicious. The challenge here lies in the ongoing maintenance of SPF records and encouraging widespread adoption, as the effectiveness of SPF is contingent on collective participation.

Last but not least, let's discuss email gateways. Email *gateways* are specialized servers that act as intermediaries between your email infrastructure and the outside world. They offer an additional layer of security by scanning incoming and outgoing emails for malware, spam, and other security threats. Commercial products like the Cisco Email Security Appliance (ESA) often include support for SPF, DKIM, and DMARC, integrating these standards into a comprehensive email security solution.

Implementing these email security mechanisms involves challenges. The accuracy of SPF records, for instance, requires continuous management. For DKIM, the complexity of cryptographic keys and DNS configurations could intimidate non-technical users. DMARC, while powerful, is most effective when used with SPF and DKIM. Email gateways, meanwhile, must be properly configured and regularly updated to adapt to emerging threats. Organizations may leverage automated tools to manage SPF and DKIM records and regularly audit their DMARC reports to overcome these challenges.

Key Topic File Integrity Monitoring

File integrity monitoring is a security process that involves checking files for changes or alterations. The system typically alerts administrators if files have been changed, tampered with, or otherwise manipulated. This is particularly useful for detecting unauthorized changes to system files or sensitive data. For example, a healthcare system might use file integrity monitoring to ensure that patient records have not been altered or accessed without proper authorization. One of the challenges here is dealing with the "noise" of false positives—changes that are authorized but flagged as suspicious.

Key Topic DLP

Data loss prevention (DLP) is an end-to-end goal to make sure that users do not send sensitive or critical information outside the corporate network. The term routinely describes software products that help a network administrator control the data that users can view or transfer. Intellectual property, corporate data, and customer data are some of the types of data with which you would use a DLP system or software to help protect against exfiltration. These systems, if configured correctly, can also alert you to an unauthorized person (attacker) attempting to transfer data that is classified as sensitive. After an incident, if it is determined that the DLP system not only missed the removal of sensitive documents but did not alert you, you will need to review the policies, restrictions, and alerts that are currently configured and review the attack account to determine what was removed and then document, reconfigure, and test. Your data is not only in your data center but also likely in one or more cloud services. Therefore, you must make sure your DLP system extends to your cloud assets and is enforced. All cloud systems should be considered base components of your data repositories. Because most DLP systems are centrally managed and contain central policies, a routine process should include reviewing and testing each rule. DLP policies can reach down into the endpoints to ensure that unauthorized USB thumb drives and other types of unapproved media are disallowed and alerted on. If your DLP solution has these or other capabilities, you should review each item and enforce where corporate policy allows.

> **TIP** For more information, consult NIST SP800-171 Rev. 2, "Protecting Controlled Unclassified Information in Nonfederal Systems and Organizations," at https://csrc.nist.gov/pubs/sp/800/171/r2/upd1/final.

Network Access Control (NAC)

Network access control (NAC) is a method for enforcing policy-driven security solutions at the network entry level. Before a device can connect to the network, NAC systems check whether that device complies with a set of predefined security rules, such as having updated antivirus software or specific system configurations. For instance, a university may use NAC to ensure that only devices with up-to-date anti-malware solutions can access the student database. A drawback of NAC solutions is that they can sometimes be circumvented, and they add an additional layer of complexity to network administration.

Endpoint Detection and Response (EDR)/Extended Detection and Response (XDR)

At its core, EDR focuses on endpoint-level security. An endpoint is any device that communicates back and forth with a network; this could be a desktop computer, a laptop, or a mobile device. EDR platforms continuously monitor these endpoints for signs of malicious activities. For example, let's say someone in the finance department opens an email attachment that turns out to be ransomware. The EDR system would detect unusual behavior—such as rapid encryption of files—and could either stop the process or alert the IT security team.

Endpoint detection and response (EDR) solutions are inward looking, focusing primarily on what's happening within the endpoints. EDRs analyze processes, file changes, and registry settings, among other internal indicators. However, this focus is both an asset and a limitation. While EDR solutions offer granular insight into the health and status of individual endpoints, they sometimes miss larger, orchestrated attacks that involve multiple network layers.

Enter XDR—the evolved, more sophisticated cousin of EDR. Whereas EDR zeros in on endpoint devices, *extended detection and response (XDR)* takes a holistic view of network security, correlating data across various channels and layers such as email, cloud, and network traffic. Imagine a scenario where a malicious email evades the spam filter and is opened by an employee, leading to a compromised endpoint. An XDR system would detect this and analyze abnormal network traffic and perhaps even changes in cloud storage files related to this breach.

The benefit of XDR is that it gives a broader, correlated view of network activity. By doing so, it can identify complex, multi-stage attacks that may be invisible to EDR solutions. However, the challenge with XDR is the level of complexity involved in its operation. Interpreting the interconnected data from multiple layers of a network requires a higher level of expertise, and the cost of implementing and maintaining XDR solutions is often significant.

In reality, a smaller organization focused on protecting a limited range of devices might find EDR adequate and more cost-effective. Larger enterprises with more complex infrastructures may opt for XDR for its comprehensive coverage and advanced threat detection capabilities.

Key Topic — User Behavior Analytics

User behavior analytics (UBA) is a field within cybersecurity that involves using machine learning algorithms to track, collect, and assess the behavior of users on a network to detect any unusual activity that could indicate a security threat. For example, if an employee usually accesses a specific set of files but suddenly downloads a massive amount of unrelated data, UBA systems can flag this as suspicious. Although effective, the challenge lies in fine-tuning these systems to avoid excessive false positives, which could otherwise flood administrators with alerts.

UBA is more than just setting up rules for acceptable behavior. Advanced UBA systems employ a variety of machine learning algorithms to establish baseline behaviors for each user, effectively learning what "normal" looks like in the context of an individual's job function and daily tasks. These algorithms analyze various variables, such as login times, the devices used, and the types of files accessed. But the algorithms don't stop at static rule sets; they continually adapt, incorporating new data to refine their understanding of normal behavior over time.

The applications of UBA are extensive and can cover internal and external security threats. Internally, UBA can be effective in detecting insider threats. For instance, if a disgruntled employee starts accessing sensitive company information they don't usually interact with, UBA tools would flag this as abnormal behavior deserving further scrutiny. Externally, UBA can help in scenarios where an outsider might have compromised an internal account. Even if the credentials are correct, the outsider's behavior while using those credentials will likely differ from the usual patterns, triggering alerts.

As advanced as UBA systems are, they are not without challenges. One of the significant hurdles is the issue of false positives. Especially during the initial stages, when the system is still learning, false alerts are likely. These can be anything from a night owl employee working late or someone accessing a different server for a legitimate, albeit uncommon, project. These false positives create unnecessary work for security teams and can also desensitize them to alerts, making it easier for actual threats to slip through.

In addition to the challenges posed by false positives, UBA requires constant fine-tuning and adjustment. As business operations evolve, what constitutes normal behavior may change, necessitating regular updates to the behavioral algorithms. Organizations must invest in training for their security teams to keep up with the latest user behavior analytics and machine learning trends for effective UBA implementation.

Finally, it's important to note that continuously monitoring employee behavior through UBA raises ethical and privacy concerns. Employers must balance the necessity for security with respect for employee privacy, which usually involves clear communication about what is being monitored and why.

Chapter Review Activities

Use the features in this section to study and review the topics in this chapter.

Review Key Topics

Review the most important topics in the chapter, noted with the Key Topic icon in the outer margin of the page. Table 18-3 lists these key topics and the page number on which each is found.

Table 18-3 Key Topics for Chapter 18

Key Topic Element	Description	Page Number
Section	Web Filter	421
Section	Operating System Security	423
Table 18-2	Sample Secure Ports and Protocols	425
Section	DNS Filtering	427
Section	Email Security	427
Section	File Integrity Monitor	429

Key Topic Element	Description	Page Number
Section	DLP	429
Section	Network Access Control (NAC)	430
Section	Endpoint Detection and Response (EDR)/ Extended Detection and Response (XDR)	430
Section	User Behavior Analytics	431

Define Key Terms

Define the following key terms from this chapter and check your answers in the glossary:

firewall, rule, access control list (ACL), port, protocol, screened subnet, intrusion detection system (IDS), intrusion prevention system (IPS), trend, signature, web filtering, agent-based web filtering approach, centralized proxy, URL scanning, content categorization, block rule, reputation-based filtering, operating system security, Group Policy, SELinux, implementation of secure protocols, protocol selection, port selection, transport method selection, DNS filtering, email security, Domain-Based Message Authentication Reporting and Conformance (DMARC), DomainKeys Identified Mail (DKIM), Sender Policy Framework (SPF), gateway, file integrity monitoring, data loss prevention (DLP), network access control (NAC), endpoint detection and response (EDR), extended detection and response (XDR), user behavior analytics (UBA)

Review Questions

Answer the following review questions. Check your answers with the answer key in Appendix A.

1. What would you use to keep confidential data from leaving the network?

2. If you want to filter web access based on predefined criteria, what mechanism would you employ?

3. What would you use to enforce policy-driven security measures at the point of network entry?

4. What system is designed to track, collect, and assess user behavior on a network for security threats?

5. What technology would you deploy if you wanted to focus on internal indicators in endpoint devices?

6. What solution would you consider for a more holistic view of network security, incorporating various channels like email and cloud storage?

This chapter covers the following topics related to Objective 4.6 (Given a scenario, implement and maintain identity and access management) of the CompTIA Security+ SY0-701 certification exam:

- Provisioning/de-provisioning user accounts
- Permission assignments and implications
- Identity proofing
- Federation
- Single sign-on (SSO)
- Interoperability
- Attestation
- Access controls
- Multifactor authentication
- Password concepts
- Privileged access management tools

CHAPTER 19

Implementing and Maintaining Identity and Access Management

This chapter explores the foundational elements of identity and access management, starting with single sign-on protocols like LDAP, OAuth, and SAML. It discusses the intricacies of permission assignments and the role of interoperability. The chapter also examines various multifactor authentication methods and advanced privileged access management tools, such as just-in-time permissions, password vaulting, and ephemeral credentials.

"Do I Know This Already?" Quiz

The "Do I Know This Already?" quiz enables you to assess whether you should read this entire chapter thoroughly or jump to the "Chapter Review Activities" section. If you are in doubt about your answers to these questions or your own assessment of your knowledge of the topics, read the entire chapter. Table 19-1 lists the major headings in this chapter and their corresponding "Do I Know This Already?" quiz questions. You can find the answers in Appendix A, "Answers to the 'Do I Know This Already?' Quizzes and Review Questions."

Table 19-1 "Do I Know This Already?" Section-to-Question Mapping

Foundation Topics Section	Questions
Provisioning/De-provisioning User Accounts	1
Permission Assignments and Implications	2
Identity Proofing	11
Federation	12
Single Sign-On (SSO)	3
Interoperability	7
Attestation	8
Access Controls	4

Foundation Topics Section	Questions
Multifactor Authentication	9, 10
Password Concepts	5
Privileged Access Management	6

CAUTION   The goal of self-assessment is to gauge your mastery of the topics in this chapter. If you do not know the answer to a question or are only partially sure of the answer, you should mark that question as wrong for purposes of self-assessment. Giving yourself credit for an answer you correctly guess skews your self-assessment results and might provide you with a false sense of security.

1. What is the primary purpose of de-provisioning in the context of identity and access management?

    a. Granting new permissions to users

    b. Assigning roles to new users

    c. Removing or disabling permissions and settings

    d. Implementing single sign-on (SSO)

2. What are implicit permissions in a digital environment?

    a. Permissions directly assigned by an administrator

    b. Permissions granted through SSO

    c. Permissions inherited through membership in a group or role

    d. Permissions set for files only

3. What is the primary benefit of single sign-on (SSO)?

    a. It increases the number of passwords a user has to remember.

    b. It reduces the number of authentication steps after the initial login.

    c. It enhances password complexity.

    d. It automatically assigns roles to users.

4. How does role-based access control (RBAC) differ from mandatory access control (MAC)?

    a. RBAC is controlled by the system, while MAC is controlled by the owner of a resource.

    b. RBAC is controlled by the owner, while MAC is controlled by the system.

    c. RBAC works with sets of permissions, while MAC works with individual label-based permissions.

    d. RBAC works with individual permissions, while MAC works with sets of permissions.

5. What is one reason for recommending longer passwords?

    a. Longer passwords are easier to remember.

    b. Longer passwords increase the chance of successful brute-force attacks.

    c. Longer passwords reduce the likelihood of successful brute-force attacks.

    d. Longer passwords are less secure.

6. What is the main goal of just-in-time (JIT) permissions in a privileged access management system?

    a. To maintain elevated permissions at all times

    b. To dynamically provision permissions for a limited period

    c. To increase the number of permissions

    d. To permanently assign roles to users

7. Why is interoperability particularly important in identity and access management (IAM) systems?

    a. To ensure faster data processing speeds

    b. To allow for varied information systems and applications to connect and exchange information seamlessly

    c. To reduce the overall cost of the IT infrastructure

    d. To increase storage capacity for user credentials

8. What is the primary purpose of attestation in the context of remote system authentication?

    a. To provide backup for system data

    b. To enable one system to provide reliable statements about its software to another system

    c. To facilitate anonymous web browsing

    d. To decrease the time taken for user authentication

9. Which of the following is the best example of a "something you know" factor in multifactor authentication?

   a. Fingerprint scan

   b. SMS message sent to a phone

   c. Passphrase or PIN code

   d. Smart card

10. In the context of MFA, what does a "something you have" factor refer to?

    a. The use of a user's physical characteristic for authentication

    b. A user's memory of personal information

    c. A personal ATM card for a user's checking account

    d. The time it takes for a user to log in

11. Which of these represents the best identity proofing option for a financial institution?

    a. Using only a username and a password for all transactions

    b. Employing a multilayer mechanism involving a password, two-factor authentication, and voice recognition for high-value transactions

    c. Relying solely on periodic reauthentication

    d. Implementing session timeouts without requiring reverification

12. What role does a federation serve in the authentication process?

    a. It provides backup storage for user data in case of system failure.

    b. It is a process by which one system authenticates a user and then communicates this verification to a second system.

    c. It is responsible for scanning and removing viruses from user emails.

    d. It is a tool for managing software updates across multiple devices.

Foundation Topics

Provisioning/De-provisioning User Accounts

In the identity and access management landscape, *provisioning* is essentially the process of setting up a user account with the necessary permissions and settings, thus granting the individual the ability to interact with various resources in a network. Conversely, *de-provisioning* is the practice of disabling or removing permissions and settings, and it typically occurs when an employee leaves the company or transitions to a different role. Well-managed provisioning (onboarding) and de-provisioning (offboarding) processes are crucial for ensuring that the right people have the proper levels of access at the right times. For example, when a new employee joins the sales department, a role-based provisioning system could automatically assign them access to CRM software but restrict their access to confidential financial databases. When that same salesperson leaves the company, de-provisioning the account should be as clear.

Permission Assignments and Implications

Permission assignment refers to the process of granting specific levels of access or types of activities to users, groups, or system processes in a digital environment. Permission assignments can be explicit, which means the administrator directly assigns permissions to a user or a group, or implicit, which means permissions are inherited through membership in a group or role. Permissions can be set for various resources, such as files, databases, and networks. They generally fall into categories like read, write, execute, and delete.

Windows file system permissions are primarily managed through access control lists (ACLs), which contain entries known as access control entries (ACEs) that define the permissible actions for users or groups. The fundamental permissions in Windows include read, write, execute, modify, and full control, each of which provides a different level of access to files and directories.

Permissions in Linux and macOS are more straightforward and include read, write, and execute permissions, which are defined for three categories of users: the file owner, the group, and others (the rest of the world). These permissions are often displayed and modified using the **chmod** command in a terminal, and understanding their numeric representation (for example, 755 for full owner access with read and execute access for groups and others) can help you quickly spot anomalies.

There are several types of permission assignments:

- **User-level permissions:** These are permissions set for individual users. For instance, a user might have permission to read and edit a specific document but not to delete it.

- **Group-level permissions:** These permissions are associated with a group of users. Anyone who is a member of the group inherits the group's permissions. These permissions are particularly useful in organizational settings where teams often require similar access levels.

- **Role-based permissions:** In more complex systems, permissions are often tied to the roles users perform rather than to individual users. For example, all users with the manager role might be permitted to approve budget expenditures.

- **Resource-based permissions:** These permissions are tied to specific resources and dictate who can perform what kind of operations on each resource. For example, a database table might be accessible for reading by one group and writing by another.

There are also some implications of permission assignments that you need to understand:

- **Security risks:** Incorrect permission assignments can lead to unauthorized access, data leaks, and other security threats. Overly permissive settings are particularly risky.

- **Usability concerns:** On the other hand, overly restrictive permissions can hinder productivity and workflow, as users might be unable to access the resources they need for their tasks.

- **Administrative overhead:** Managing permissions, especially in large or dynamic organizations, can be complex and time-consuming. Failing to promptly update permissions (for example, after an employee changes roles or leaves the organization) can have security and operational implications.

- **Audit and compliance:** Improper permission assignments can lead to non-compliance with regulatory standards, such as GDPR, HIPAA, or SOX, which can result in legal repercussions and fines.

- **Transitive risk:** In multi-tier systems, permissions might propagate in ways that are not immediately obvious, leading to unintentional granting of access at different layers of an application or system.

Understanding the mechanisms of permission assignments and the implications are essential for maintaining a secure, efficient, and compliant operational environment.

Effective permissions management often balances security and usability, necessitating periodic reviews and audits to ensure alignment with organizational policies and goals.

Identity Proofing

Identity proofing is the process through which an organization verifies a user's or system's identity. It's not just about making sure you are who you say you are but also ensuring that you are who you are supposed to be in the context of the system. This could involve multiple layers of verification, from something as simple as a password to something as complex as biometric data. In many systems, the proofing process goes beyond initial authentication and extends into ongoing verification, such as periodic re-authentication or session time-outs that require re-verification.

For instance, a financial institution might employ a multi-layer identity proofing mechanism that involves a password and username, a two-factor authentication process via a mobile device, and perhaps even a voice recognition system for transactions that exceed a certain monetary amount.

Federation

Federations are considered identity providers (IdPs). A *federation* is a process in which one system is responsible for authentication of a user, and that systems sends a message to a second system, announcing who the user is and verifying that the user was properly authenticated.

The most widely used federation mechanism today is Security Assertion Markup Language (SAML). SAML is an older open standard that allows IdPs to pass authorization credentials to service providers (SPs). OpenID Connect, which is a simple identity authentication protocol built on top of OAuth 2.0, is being used as a replacement for SAML. OAuth provides resource authorization and was created by Google, Twitter, and others to address SAML's lack of mobile platform capabilities.

Federation allows for single sign-on (SSO) without passwords. SSO is a technology that combines several different application logins into one. With SSO, a user must enter their login credentials (username and password) only one time on a single page and can then access all applications. In Figure 19-1, the federation server knows the username for a person in each application and presents that application with a token that says, "This person is domain\janesmith or janesmith@example.com." Because of the established trust between these interconnected systems, when the user accesses different applications, each one recognizes and accepts the token from the federation server, thus bypassing the need for repeated logins. A common example of this in action is the option to log in to various websites using your Facebook or

Gmail credentials. In this scenario, Facebook or Gmail acts as the identity provider. When you use these credentials, the website trusts the authentication already performed by Facebook or Gmail and grants access without requiring additional authentication steps. This process shows how federation, coupled with SSO, streamlines user access across different platforms and services.

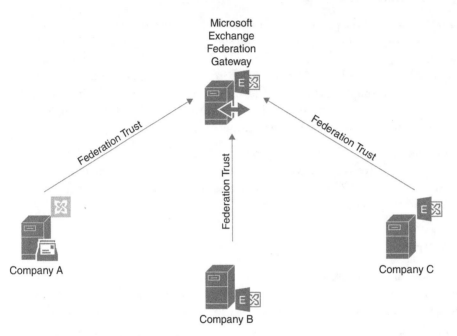

Figure 19-1   Federation Interactions

Attacking IdPs start by exploiting SSO. IdPs are considered trusted third parties, and when attackers are allowed to configure their own IdP and connect to unsuspecting targets, they might be able to compromise the security of all accounts on the SP for which they were configured. There are two known attack vectors: ID spoofing and key confusion. The real problem here is the trust assumptions of different components of the system. To prevent this type of attack from locking down systems, you should ensure that you are working only with trusted IdPs, enable consistent updating and patching of the systems you are responsible for to ensure that they have the latest libraries and binaries, and continuously review your logging and monitoring.

Attacking the federation—and we are not speaking about *Star Trek* here—usually starts with exploiting Active Directory, which we covered earlier. Another method is a golden SAML attack, which starts with a forged SAML token. It bypasses MFA requirements imposed by applications. Performing any number of the listed attacks would allow an attacker to impersonate an already authenticated user and, using preauthentication, would enable the attacker to proceed to company B and company C unopposed, with rights and privileges associated with that account on those systems and those granted by the federations.

Single Sign-On (SSO)

Single sign-on (SSO), as already discussed in this chapter, is a critical component of modern identity and access management systems that simplifies the user experience by enabling one set of credentials to provide access to multiple services or applications. In a networked environment with various services requiring distinct login credentials, the burden on the user and the security risks associated with password management can be considerable. SSO reduces the number of authentication steps a user must complete after initially logging in. This section explores various mechanisms commonly used to implement SSO, each of which has unique strengths, limitations, and use cases.

Lightweight Directory Access Protocol (LDAP)

Lightweight Directory Access Protocol (LDAP) is an application layer protocol that is used for accessing and modifying directory services data. It is part of the TCP/IP suite. Originally used in WAN connections, LDAP has developed over time into a protocol that is commonly used by services such as Microsoft Active Directory on Windows Server domain controllers. LDAP is the protocol that controls the directory service. This service organizes the users, computers, and other objects within Active Directory. Figure 19-2 shows an example of Active Directory. Note the highlighted list of users (known as *objects* in Active Directory) in the Users folder. Also observe other folders, which house other objects (such as the Computers folder, which holds Windows client computers).

> **NOTE**   Windows servers running Active Directory use parameters and variables for querying the names of objects—for example, CN=dprowse, where *CN* stands for common name and *dprowse* is the username. Taking it to the next level, consider DC=ServerName. *DC* stands for domain component, and *ServerName* is the variable and the name of the server. Microsoft is famous for using the name *fabrikam* as its test name, but, of course, you would use the name of your server. In the case of a server named fabrikam, an entire LDAP query might look something like this:
> ```
> <LDAP://DC=Fabrikam, DC=COM>
> ```

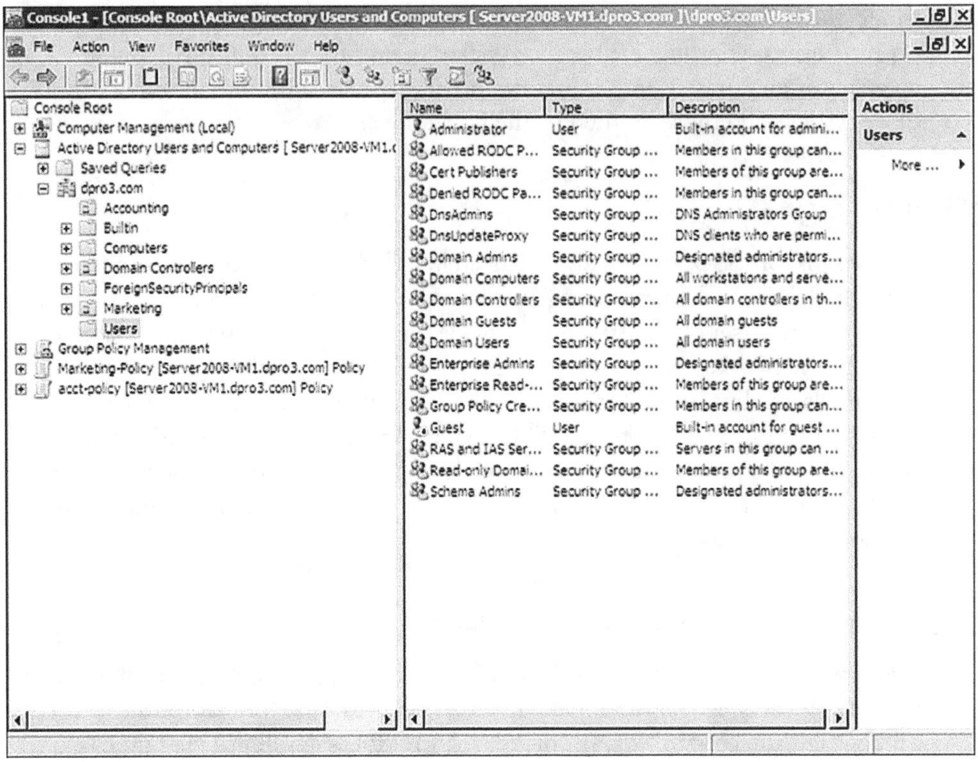

Figure 19-2 Active Directory Showing User Objects

OAuth

Open Authorization (OAuth) is a framework that provides authorization to a third-party entity (for example, a smartphone application) to access resources hosted on a resource server. In a classic client/server authorization framework, the third-party entity would receive the credentials from the resource owner (user) and then access the resource on the resource server.

The main issue OAuth resolves is providing the third-party entity authorization to access restricted resources without passing the client credentials to this third party. Instead of getting the user credentials, the entity requesting access receives an authorization token that includes authorization information, such as scope and duration, and that is used to request access to a resource hosted by the resource server. The OAuth schema is usually called *delegation of access*.

OAuth 2.0, defined in RFC 6749, includes four main roles:

- **Resource owner:** The party that owns the resource (for example, a user) and grants authorization to access some of its resources

- **Client:** The party that requires access to a specific resource

- **Resource server:** The party that hosts or stores the resource

- **Authorization server:** The party that provides an authorization token

In a basic OAuth exchange, as illustrated in Figure 19-3, the authorization involves six messages:

1. The client sends an authorization request to the resource owner or indirectly to the authorization server.

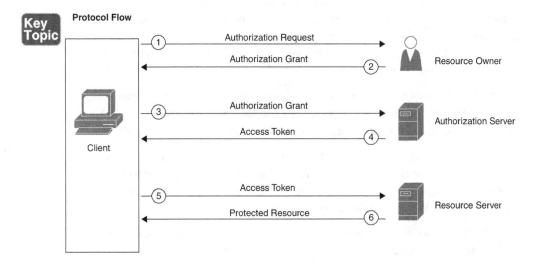

Figure 19-3 OAuth Exchange

2. The resource owner (or the authorization server on behalf of the resource owner) sends an authorization grant to the client.

3. The client sends the authorization grant to the authorization server as proof that authorization was granted.

4. The authorization server authenticates the client and sends an access token.

5. The client sends the access token to the resource server as proof of authentication and authorization to access the resources.

6. The resource server validates the access token and grants access.

For example, a user (the resource owner) may grant access to personal photos hosted at some online storage provider (the resource server) to an application on a mobile phone (the client) without directly providing credentials to the application but instead by directly authenticating with the authorization server (in this case, also the online storage provider) and authorizing the access.

Security Assertion Markup Language

Security Assertion Markup Language (SAML) is an open standard for exchanging authentication and authorization data between identity providers. SAML is used in many SSO implementations.

The OASIS SAML standard is currently the most commonly used standard for implementing federated identity processes. SAML is an XML-based framework that describes the use and exchange of SAML assertions in a secure way between business entities. The standard describes the syntax and rules to request, create, use, and exchange these assertions.

The SAML process involves a minimum of two entities: the *SAML assertion party* (or *SAML authority*), which is the entity that produces the assertion, and the *SAML relying party*, which is the entity that uses the assertion to make access decisions.

An assertion is the communication of security information about a subject (also called a principal) in the form of a statement. The basic building blocks of SAML are the SAML assertion, SAML protocol, SAML binding, and SAML profile (see Figure 19-4). SAML assertions can contain the following information:

- **Authentication statement:** Includes the result of the authentication and additional information, such as the authentication method, timestamps, and so on

- **Attribute statement:** Includes attributes about the principal

- **Authorization statement:** Includes information on what the principal is allowed to do

An example of an assertion is "User A, who has the email address usera@domain.com authenticated via username and password, is a platinum member, and is authorized for a 10% discount."

SAML defines the protocols used to transfer assertion messages. SAML bindings include information on how lower-level protocols (such as HTTP or SOAP) transport SAML protocol messages. SAML profiles are specific combinations of assertions, protocols, and bindings for specific use cases. Examples of profiles include Web Browser Single Sign-On, Identity Provider Discovery, and Enhanced Client and Proxy (ECP).

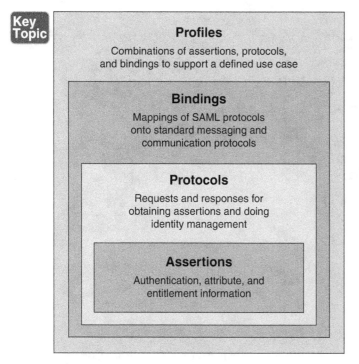

Figure 19-4   SAML Building Blocks

SAML also uses the concepts of identity providers (IdPs) and service providers (SPs). SAML can work in two different ways:

- **IdP-initiated mode:** In this mode, a user is already authenticated on the IdP and requests a service from the SP (for example, by clicking a link on the IdP's website). The IdP builds an assertion that is sent to the SP within the user request to the SP itself.

For example, a user who is authenticated on an airline website decides to book a rental car by clicking a link on the airline website. The airline identity and access management (IAM) system, which assumes the role of an IdP, sends assertion information about the user to the rental car IAM, which in turn authenticates the user and provides access rights based on the information in the assertion.

- **SP-initiated mode:** In this mode, a user initiates an access request to some resource on the SP. Because the federated identity is managed by a different IdP, the SP redirects the user to log in at the IdP. After the login, the IdP sends a SAML assertion back to the SP.

Figure 19-5 shows examples of IdP-initiated mode (on the left) and SP-initiated mode (on the right).

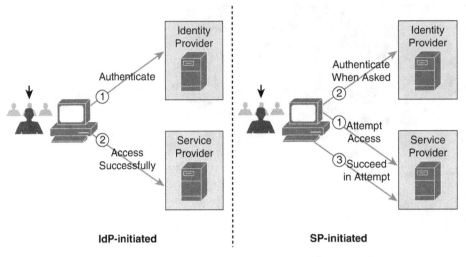

Figure 19-5   SAML IdP-Initiated Mode and SP-Initiated Mode

 # Interoperability

Interoperability refers to the ability of different information systems, devices, or applications to connect, work together, and exchange information in a coordinated manner, both internally and externally. In the context of identity and access management (IAM), interoperability is crucial for several reasons:

- **System integration:** IAM solutions must seamlessly integrate with various databases, applications, and authentication protocols. Lack of interoperability can create silos, complicating both access and auditing processes.

- **Business partnerships:** Organizations often collaborate with external partners, requiring secure yet accessible cross-boundary authentication and authorization mechanisms.

- **Future-proofing:** As new technologies and compliance requirements emerge, an interoperable IAM system can more easily adapt without necessitating an overhaul of existing security infrastructure.

Consider a multinational corporation that uses Microsoft Azure for its cloud-based services and also has a legacy on-premise Oracle database that contains sensitive financial data. The corporation also collaborates with various suppliers using various systems, from AWS to IBM Cloud.

In such a complex environment, an interoperable IAM system could be the backbone for unified access management. The IAM system would integrate the Microsoft Azure platform with the Oracle database through interoperability, providing a singular point of control. Simultaneously, it could accommodate the diverse systems used by external suppliers by using standard protocols such as SAML or OAuth. This unified approach not only simplifies management and increases security but also paves the way for smoother collaborations with external partners and easier adoption of future technologies.

Attestation

Attestation provides evidence or proof of something. The process of attestation allows one program to authenticate itself, and remote attestation is a means for one system to make reliable statements about the software it is running to another system. The remote party can then make authorization decisions based on that information.

> **NOTE** To find out more about attestation, see www.w3.org/TR/webauthn/.

Attestation statement formats are identified by a string, called an *attestation statement format identifier*, that is chosen by the author of the attestation statement format.

Attestation statement format identifiers should be registered with the registries for web authentication. Registration with the web authentication registries ensures standardization and prevents conflicts, which is critical for interoperability and trustworthiness in the attestation process. All registered attestation statement format identifiers are unique among themselves.

When the key pair is created, there is an option to request the attestation certificate. This optional information can be sent to the relying party as part of the registration process. The attestation is how authenticators prove to the relying party that the keys they generate originate from a genuine device with certified characteristics and establish a hardware root of trust.

The purpose of attestation is to cryptographically prove that a newly generated key pair came from a specific device. This process provides a root of trust for a newly generated key pair and enables you to identify the attributes of a device being used, how the private key is protected, and what kind of biometric or Trusted Platform Module (TPM) authentication system is being used.

A TPM quote operation is used to authoritatively verify the contents of a TPM chip's platform configuration registers (PCRs). During provisioning, a composite hash of a selected set of PCRs is computed. The TPM quote operation produces a composite hash that can be compared with the hash computed while provisioning.

Certain implementations of attestation are susceptible to replay, masquerading, tampering, and hardware attacks. A malicious attesting system can replay old values of measurements that correspond to a valid response before the attesting system became corrupted. In a masquerade attack, the attacker can send measurement lists and a TPM quote of another valid system to get the attacked system to trust it. To protect against these types of attacks, you should make sure you connect only to trusted third parties in which you have audit, logging, or certification of vulnerability tests performed regularly. You also should configure higher levels of logging on your own systems to catch abuse.

Key Topic # Access Controls

Access control models are methodologies by which admission to physical areas and, more importantly, computer systems is managed and organized. Access control, also known as an access policy, is extremely important when it comes to users accessing secure or confidential data. Some organizations also practice concepts such as separation of duties, job rotation, and least privilege. By using these best practices along with an access control model, you can develop a robust plan concerning how users access confidential data and secure areas of a building.

There are several models for access control, each of which has special characteristics that you should know for the Security+ SY0-701 exam.

Role-Based Access Control

Role-based access control (RBAC) is an access model that is controlled by the system and not by the owner of a resource. Although RBAC is controlled by the system, like mandatory access control (discussed later in this chapter), it is different from MAC in the way that permissions are configured. RBAC works with sets of permissions instead of individual permissions that are label based. A set of permissions constitutes a role. When users are assigned to roles, they can gain access to resources. A role might be the ability to complete a specific operation in an organization as opposed to the ability to access a single data file. For example, a person in a bank who wants to check a prospective client's credit score would be attempting to perform a transaction that is allowed only if that person holds the proper role. So roles are created for various job functions in an organization. Roles might have overlapping privileges and responsibilities. Also, some general operations can be completed by all the employees of an organization. Because there is overlap, an administrator can develop role hierarchies, which define roles that can contain other roles or that can have exclusive attributes.

Think about it. Have you ever noticed that an administrator or root user is extremely powerful—perhaps too powerful—while standard users are not powerful enough to respond to their own needs or fix their own problems? Some operating systems counter this issue by creating midlevel accounts such as auditors (in Microsoft) or operators (in Solaris), but for large organizations, this approach is not flexible enough. Currently, more levels of roles and special groups of users are implemented in newer operating systems. RBAC is used in database access as well and is becoming more common in the healthcare industry and government.

Rule-Based Access Control

Rule-based access control, also known as label-based access control, defines whether access should be granted or denied to objects by comparing the object label and the subject label. Rule-based access control is another model that can be considered a special case of attribute-based access control (ABAC). In reality, this is not a well-defined model, and it includes any access control model that implements some sort of rule that governs the access to a resource. Usually, rule-based access controls are used in the context of access list implementation to access network resources—for example, where the rule is to provide access only to certain IP addresses or only at certain hours of the day. In this case, the IP addresses are attributes of the subject and object, and the time of day is part of the environment attribute evaluation.

Mandatory Access Control

Mandatory access control (MAC) is an access control policy determined by a computer system, not by a user or the owner of a resource, as in DAC. Permissions are predefined in the MAC model, which has historically been used in highly classified government and military multilevel systems, although you will find lesser implementations of it in today's more common operating systems as well. The MAC model defines sensitivity labels that are assigned to *subjects* (users) and *objects* (files, folders, hardware devices, network connections, and so on). A subject's label dictates its security level, or level of trust. An object's label dictates what level of clearance is needed to access it, also known as a trust level (in a process known as *data labeling*). The access controls in a MAC system are based on the security classification of the data and "need-to-know" information—where a user can access only what the system considers absolutely necessary. Also, in the MAC model, data import and export are controlled. MAC is the strictest of the access control models.

An example of MAC can be seen in FreeBSD Version 5.0 and higher, where access control modules can allow for security policies that label subjects and objects. Policies are enforced by administrators or by the OS; this is what makes MAC mandatory and sets it apart from DAC. Another example is Security-Enhanced Linux (SELinux), which is a set of kernel modifications to Linux that supports DoD-style mandatory access controls, such as the requirement for a trusted computing base (TCB). Though often interpreted differently, a TCB can be described as the set of all hardware and software components that are critical to a system's security and all associated protection mechanisms. The mechanisms must meet a certain standard, and SELinux helps accomplish this by modifying the kernel of the Linux OS in a secure manner. Like DAC, MAC was also originally defined in The Orange Book, but it was defined as the Mandatory Security Policy—a policy that enforces access control based on a user's clearance and the confidentiality levels of the data.

> **NOTE**   Rule-based access control that uses labels is part of mandatory access control and should not be confused with role-based access control.

> **NOTE**   Other related access control models include Bell-LaPadula, Biba, and Clark-Wilson. Bell-LaPadula is a state machine model used for enforcing access control in government applications. It is a less common multilevel security derivative of mandatory access control. This model focuses on data confidentiality and controlled access to classified information. The Biba integrity model describes rules for the protection of data integrity. Clark-Wilson is another integrity model that provides a foundation for specifying and analyzing an integrity policy for a computing system.

Discretionary Access Control

Discretionary access control (DAC) is an access control policy that is generally determined by the owner. Objects such as files and printers can be created and accessed by the owner. Also, the owner decides which users are allowed to have access to the objects and what level of access they may have. The levels of access, or permissions, are stored in ACLs.

Originally, DAC was described in The Orange Book as the Discretionary Security Policy and was meant to enforce a consistent set of rules governing limited access to identified individuals.

> **NOTE**   The Orange Book, whose proper name is the Trusted Computer System Evaluation Criteria (TCSEC), was developed by the U.S. Department of Defense (DoD); however, The Orange Book is old (it's referred to in the 1990s movie *Hackers*), and the standard was superseded in 2005 by an international standard called the Common Criteria for Information Technology Security Evaluation (or simply Common Criteria). However, the DAC methodology lives on in many of today's personal computers and client/server networks.
>
> An entire set of security standards known as the "Rainbow Series" was published by the DoD in the 1980s and 1990s. Although The Orange Book is the centerpiece of the series (maybe not in the color spectrum, but as far as security content goes), there are other ones you might come into contact with, such as The Red Book, which is the Trusted Network Interpretation standard. Some of the standards have been superseded, but the Rainbow Series is the basis for many of today's security procedures.

An example of DAC would be a typical Windows computer with two users. User A can log on to the computer, create a folder, stock it with data, and then finally configure permissions so that only they can access the folder. User B can log on to the computer but cannot access User A's folder by default unless User A says it's okay and configures it as such. However, User B can create their own folder and lock down permissions in the same way. Let's say that there is a third user, User C, who wants both User A and User B to have limited access to a folder that they created. This is also possible; User C just needs to set specific permission levels, as shown in Figure 19-6. The first Properties window shows that User C (the owner) has full control permissions. This permission is normal because User C created the folder. In the second Properties window, you see that User C has given User A limited permissions.

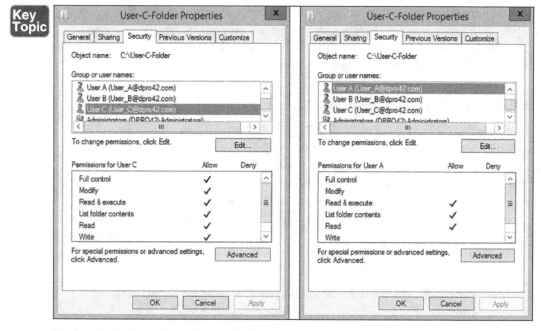

Figure 19-6 Discretionary Access in Windows

NOTE It's important to be aware of the standard naming conventions used in your organization. In Figure 19-6, the naming convention is *user@domainname*—for example, User_A@dpro42.com.

NOTE The owner of a resource controls the permissions to that resource. This is the core of the DAC model.

Windows networks/domains work in the same fashion. Access to an object is based on which user created the object and what permissions that user assigned to the object. In addition, in Windows networks, you can also group users together and assign permissions by way of roles. For more details, see the "Role-Based Access Control" section, earlier in this chapter.

In a way, DAC implemented in client/server networks is sort of a decentralized administration model. Even though you, as administrator, still have control over most or all resources (depending on company policy), the owners retain a certain amount of power over their own resources. But many companies take away the ability for users to configure permissions. They may create folders and save data to them, but the permissions list is often generated on a parent folder by someone else and is inherited by the subfolder.

There are two important points to remember about the DAC model. First, every object in the system has an owner, and the owner has control over its access policy. Second, access rights, or permissions, can be assigned by the owner to users to specifically control object access.

Attribute-Based Access Control (ABAC)

Attribute-based access control (ABAC) is an access model that is dynamic and context aware. Access rights are granted to users through the use of multiple policies that can combine various user, group, and resource attributes. This type of control makes use of IF-THEN statements based on the user and requested resource. For example, "*If* David is a system administrator, *then* allow full control access to the \\dataserver\adminfolder share." If an ABAC solution is implemented properly, it can be more flexible. As of this writing, many technologies—and organizations—are moving toward a more context-sensitive, context-aware mindset when it comes to authentication and access control.

Table 19-2 summarizes some of the attributes and identity terms that are used in account policies.

Key Topic

Table 19-2   Attributes and Identity Terms Used in Account Policies

Attribute/Term	Key Points
Network location	The location where users are connected to the network can be used to determine what access they have. For instance, a doctor connected to the guest network in the lobby should not have access to medical records. This is how the concept of geofencing works in identification and authorization.

Attribute/Term	Key Points
Geolocation	Geolocation involves determining the physical location of a user who is trying to authenticate. It is often used in the implementation of mobile device policies, where users are only allowed to access a network based on the location from which they are reaching the Internet.
Geotagging	Geotagging is the process of attaching location information in the metadata of files such as pictures taken by a smartphone. The implementation of a policy using geotagging would typically involve restricting the use of geotagging for sensitive locations or data.
Disablement/lockout	An account can be disabled or locked out based on specific attributes. For instance, if a user is known to be located in the United States but connects from China, this may be an indication that the user credentials have been compromised and should be temporarily disabled until the access can be verified.
Account audits	This is the process of auditing the permissions that are assigned to accounts on a system. Permissions are often added when needed but are never removed when not needed.
Impossible travel time/ risky login	This is a concept related to geolocation and geofencing in which a potential compromise is identified based on the fact that it would be impossible for a user to be in two places at once. For instance, if you authenticated at 3 p.m. EST from New York and then 10 minutes later tried to authenticate from Florida, this access would not be possible and would be an indicator of account compromise.

NOTE Another access control method is known as anonymous access control. This method uses attributes before access is granted to an object (for example, access to an FTP server). Authentication is usually not required.

Time-of-Day Restrictions

The concept of *time-of-day restrictions* operates on the principle that system access can be controlled based on the chronological context of a login attempt. This form of access control policy is particularly useful for enforcing security in an environment where user access should be confined to specific business or operational hours.

For example, consider an organization that operates predominantly during standard 8 a.m. to 6 p.m. business hours. Here, time-of-day restrictions would be configured to allow user authentications only between 8 a.m. and 6 p.m. Attempts to access the system outside these hours would be automatically denied. A time-of-day restriction reduces the window of opportunity for potential unauthorized access during off-hours and aligns user activity with expected work patterns, simplifying monitoring and anomaly detection.

This method can be applied with as much granularity as desired. For example, different time restrictions might apply to various user roles or departments. Administrative staff might have extended access times, while entry-level personnel might have more limited hours. In the case of systems with sensitive data, such as financial records or personal employee information, a time-of-day restriction acts as a supplementary control, adding a layer of security to protect against external threats and potential insider abuse.

Implementing time-of-day restrictions requires careful planning to ensure that legitimate access needs are met while maintaining the desired security posture. This often requires an analysis of user behavior patterns, business needs, and potential security risks.

Least Privilege

Least privilege means a user is given only the privileges needed to do their job and not one iota more. A basic example is the Guest account in a Windows computer. This account (when enabled) can surf the web and use other basic applications but cannot make any modifications to the computer system. However, least privilege as a principle goes much further. One of the ideas behind this principle is to run the user session with only the processes that are necessary, thus reducing the amount of CPU power needed. This will hopefully lead to better system stability and system security. Have you ever noticed that many crashed systems are due to users trying to do more than they really should be allowed to do—or more than the computer can handle?

The concept of least privilege tends to be absolute, although an absolute solution isn't quite possible in the real world. It is difficult to gauge exactly what the "least" number of privileges and processes would be. Therefore, as a security administrator, you should practice the implementation of *minimal* privilege, reducing what a user has access to as much as possible. Programmers also practice this principle when developing applications and operating systems, making sure that an app has only the least privilege necessary to accomplish what they need to do. This concept is also known as "the principle of least privilege."

Key Topic Multifactor Authentication (MFA)

Multifactor authentication (MFA) is the process of identifying a user by validating two or more claims presented by the user, each from a different category of factors. With MFA, also sometimes called two-factor authentication (2FA), a user is required to present more than one type of evidence in order to authenticate on a system. The major factors in MFA are based on a user's memory, possessions, and self. Take a moment to review each of these factors and reflect on how your personal traits apply to each of them:

- **Something you know:** A user ID, password, passphrase, PIN code, or secret code or the answer to a security question

- **Something you have:** A physical item like a smart card (CAC), RFID card, or token, certificate, email, SMS, or phone call

- **Something you are:** Biometrics such as your handprint, fingerprint, eyes or retina, facial recognition, or voiceprint

Implementations

MFA involves the use of various methods and technologies to strengthen security. These implementations go beyond the traditional username and password combo, adding layers of verification to reduce the risk of unauthorized access. Techniques range from biometric verification to hardware and software authentication tokens and specialized security keys. Each approach has unique advantages, drawbacks, and optimal use cases, all of which warrant careful consideration in the context of an organization's specific security requirements and operational needs.

Biometrics

Biometric identifiers are distinctive, measurable body measurements and calculations related to human characteristics. Biometrics are used for authentication and serve as a form of identification and access control. Many different aspects of human physiology, chemistry, or behavior can be used for biometric authentication, as detailed in the sections that follow. A common device used for biometrics is a fingerprint reader that uses mathematical representations of your fingerprint to authenticate you. Iris, retinal, or eye authentication requires you to look into a device that reads certain parts of your eye, and facial recognition involves scanning your face and identifying certain points of it. Another form of biometrics is voice recognition, as in the old movie *Sneakers* ("My voice is my passport. Verify me."), where your voiceprint is compared to a similar mathematical or audio analysis format to authenticate you. As with many other authentication methods, biometric systems have been successfully attacked over the years. Error rates allow attackers to come up with creative new tactics to bypass these methods.

Hard and Soft Authentication Keys

A token key can be a hardware or software device that regularly changes the code displayed or provides a new key code each time it is pressed and is based on a certain algorithm. One of the most common types is the RSA token key (see Figure 19-7).

Figure 19-7   RSA Token Key

Token-based authentication is a security technique in which a hardware security token provides a code to the user that expires after 60 seconds. The user must enter the code within the allotted time or must start over. Most of the older-style token keys relied on a vulnerable algorithm that was defeated, and so they have become obsolete. Universal 2nd Factors (U2F) is a relatively new method that uses an authentication standard called Fast Identity Online (FIDO).

Newer versions of hardware authenticator solutions support FIDO2, which replaces weak password-based authentication. One of the most common tokens used today is the YubiKey strong two-factor authentication USB token key. Some newer token-based systems are activated by a fingerprint.

NOTE   To find out more about YubiKey and strong two-factor authentication devices, see www.yubico.com/products/.

There are a few challenges with hardware tokens. They are expensive, easy to lose, and vulnerable to theft and breach of codes; they also require constant administration and maintenance.

Security Keys

Standard passwords are static codes that you change based on predetermined policies. Static codes are among the weakest and most insecure methods of authentication. They should be used only as a backup mechanism and are never considered secure because they are available in some physical form, whether on paper or stored digitally. *Security keys* are hardware devices that provide a robust alternative to traditional password-based security, offering a tangible second factor in 2FA or MFA scenarios. Unlike static passwords or codes, which can be compromised through various means like phishing, guessing, or brute-force attacks, security keys are physical tokens that must be present in order for access to be granted. They work on the principle of cryptographic proof, providing digital signatures that are unique to different login sessions.

When users attempt to access a protected system, they are prompted to insert their security key into a USB port or connect it via near-field communication (NFC) or Bluetooth. The security key then communicates with the service, confirming the user's identity using a cryptographic signature that cannot be reused, replayed, or intercepted, thus making unauthorized access exceedingly tricky.

Factors

In MFA, *factors* refer to the distinct categories of credentials used to verify a user's identity in the MFA process. These credentials are grouped based on the type of evidence they provide about the user's identity. The four widely recognized factors, which we discuss thoroughly in this section, are something you know (knowledge), something you have (possession), something you are (inherence), and somewhere you are (location). Each factor contributes to a more robust and layered security approach, ensuring that the additional verification steps prevent unauthorized access even if one factor is compromised.

Something You Know

Authenticating with a user ID and a password is considered single-factor authentication because it is a single-factor method. MFA factors are really authentication factors; an *authentication factor* is a category of credential that is used for identification purposes and identity verification. For MFA, each additional factor is intended to increase assurance that a person or system involved in a request or communication is who or what they are stated to be. ***Something you know*** is considered a knowledge factor; in the context of security, it's something the user possesses, such as a personal identification number (PIN), a username, a password, or an answer to a secret question. You have likely been asked to set up four or five questions to access your bank account, and when logging in, you are prompted to answer one of them.

Something You Have

Something you have is typically a physical object in your possession, such as a smart card, security token, USB token, your ATM card, or a key. Figure 19-8 illustrates MFA using something you are, something you know, and something you have and shows where they intersect to create two- and three-factor authentication.

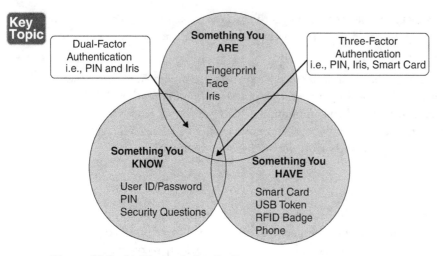

Figure 19-8   Multifactor Authentication

For example, say that a user goes to the bank, enters their automated teller machine (ATM) card into the machine, and is prompted for a PIN. After they enter the PIN correctly, they have full access to their account to withdraw money (only a certain dollar amount). This is an example of two-factor authentication, requiring both something the user has (a physical key—in this case, the ATM card) and something the user knows (their PIN). If this same person goes into the bank and wants to withdraw more than the ATM allows, they must provide a withdrawal slip, an ID the teller can use to verify the user is who they say they are, and an account number, or they must insert their ATM card in the indoor terminal, which prompts them to enter their PIN. This scenario is still considered two-factor authentication because it is all part of the same method; the teller is not making a machine-scan verification match of the person's face.

Something You Are

Something you are is an attribute such as a physical characteristic, something you can do (such as your signature, the way you type, mistakes you make, and patterns you tend to use), or the way you walk. It can also be where you're located or can be verified through a third party who vouches that they know you are who you claim to be. Here's a review of the "something you are" MFA attributes:

- **Something you can do:** Accurately reproducing a signature, writing technique, or typing technique

- **Something you exhibit:** Personality trait or behavior

- **Someone you know:** Authentication by chain of trust

- **Somewhere you are:** Geolocation, IP address, or where you're located

Somewhere You Are

The factor *somewhere you are* in MFA refers to the user's geographic location as a means of verification. This factor relies on the user's physical presence at a particular—often predefined—location to grant access to systems or services. It uses location-based technologies such as GPS, IP address recognition, or proximity to certain secure Wi-Fi networks to determine whether the access request originates from an authorized location. By incorporating this factor, an organization can enforce location-based access controls, adding a layer of security that helps prevent unauthorized access from locations outside trusted environments. This can be particularly effective in scenarios where access needs to be restricted to a corporate office, a secure room, or other controlled spaces.

Password Concepts

Password concepts encompass the guidelines and practices that ensure the creation of strong, secure passwords for protecting user authentication and access. A password often serves as the first line of defense in protecting sensitive information and access controls. As elementary as it may seem, the crafting and management of passwords can either significantly bolster or undermine your security posture.

This section delves into best practices for password management, covering an array of aspects, from complexity to expiration. These guidelines reflect traditional wisdom and the latest recommendations from authoritative bodies like NIST. By understanding and applying these principles, cybersecurity professionals can strike an effective balance between robust security and user-friendly access.

Password Best Practices

A *password* is a combination of characters (such as letters, numbers, and special characters) that should be kept secret, and it is the most common implementation of authentication by knowledge. *Password best practices* are recommended strategies and tactics for creating and managing passwords that enhance security. Password authentication is usually considered one of the weakest authentication methods, yet it's one of the most used due to its easy implementation.

The weakness of password authentication is mainly due to human factors rather than technological issues. Here's a list of some typical issues that lead to increased risk when using passwords as the sole authentication method:

- Users tend to use the same password across multiple systems and accounts.
- Users tend to write down passwords (for example, on sticky notes).
- Users tend to use simple passwords (for example, their child's name or 12345).
- Users tend to use the default system password given at system installation.

One of the most important steps in password management is creating a standard to define secure password requirements. This standard needs to be applied across an organization and for all systems. An organization should take into consideration the following requirements when building policies, processes, and standards around password creation:

Key Topic

- **Password length:** *Password length* refers to the number of characters in a password. Length is critical to a password's security. Longer passwords are inherently more secure than shorter ones, reducing the likelihood of a successful brute-force or dictionary attacks. While 8 characters has long been the standard minimum length, many experts now recommend at least 12 to 16 characters for enhanced security. Windows OS limits password lengths to 14 characters. macOS systems recommend using at least 15 characters, and Linux systems do not have a published limit. Increasing the length of a password creates a more significant number of potential combinations, making it increasingly difficult for attackers to crack it. It's a balancing act, however; excessively long passwords can be complicated for users to remember, increasing the chances that they will write them down or store them insecurely. In line with recent NIST guidelines, systems should allow for passwords up to a certain length, such as 64 characters. Still, they may mandate a minimum length to ensure a baseline level of security. Figure 19-9 shows an example of where you would audit and configure the password lengths, age, and other details of a password in Windows.

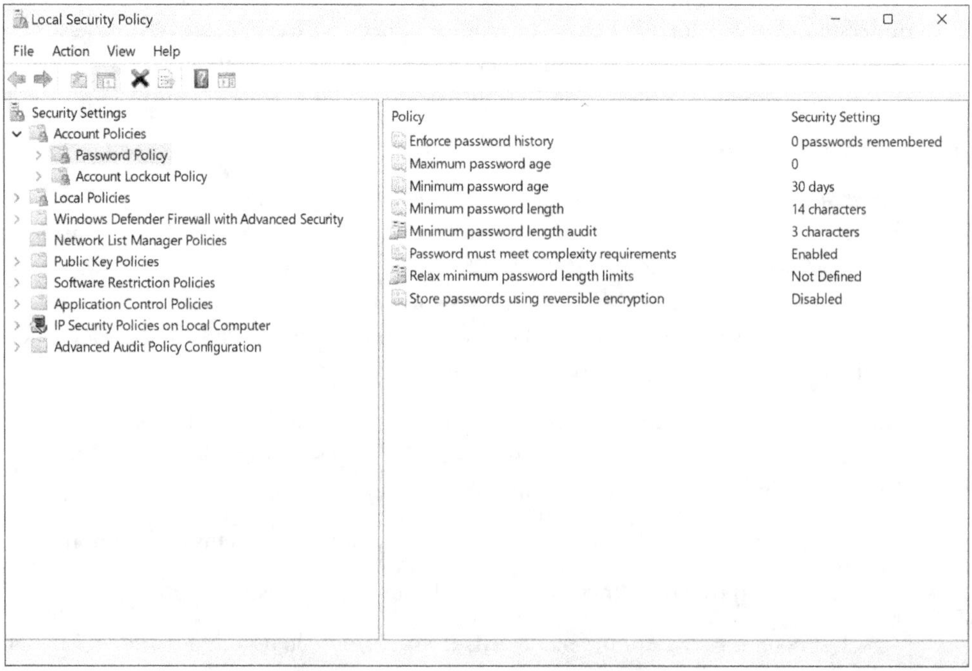

Figure 19-9 Windows Local Security Policy

- **Password complexity:** *Password complexity* involves the inclusion of various characters, such as uppercase and lowercase letters, numbers, and symbols, in a password to increase its unpredictability. Establishing a policy about password strength is very important to reduce the risk of users setting up weak passwords, which are easier to compromise via brute-force and other attacks. Complexity requirements—such as asking users to use a combination of characters, numbers, and symbols—contribute to increasing the strength of a password. Due to continued research on password use, NIST has recently updated its password guidelines. The following are some of the recent updates NIST has made to its password requirements in NIST SP 800-63b:

  - Users no longer have to use special characters.

  - Users should be able to use all characters.

  - Copying and pasting passwords is acceptable.

  - Password policies should not require employees to change passwords on a regular basis.

  - Password fields should allow for up to at least 64 additional characters on top of the required 8.

- **Password reuse:** *Password reuse*—the practice of using the same password across multiple accounts or systems—is discouraged due to the increased risk of widespread access if the password is compromised. Reusing the same password or part of it also increases the risk of password compromise. It is common practice to change just the last digit of a password or to use only two passwords repeatedly and swap them when required. Policy related to reusability should ensure that passwords are not reused within a given amount of time.

- **Password expiration:** *Password expiration* is a set period after which a password must be changed to a new one to reduce the chance of breach over time. Traditionally, setting an expiration date on passwords has been considered good practice. The logic is that, even if a password is compromised, the damage can be limited by automatically forcing users to update their passwords regularly. However, this approach has been reevaluated, as frequent password changes can lead to user frustration and poor security habits, like incremental changes to existing passwords. The most recent CIS and NIST guidelines recommend against mandatory periodic password resets unless there is evidence of compromise. Security professionals need to weigh the pros and cons of password expiration policies, considering both security and user experience.

- **Password age:** *Password age* is the amount of time a password has been in use, with older passwords generally considered at higher risk of exposure and therefore more in need of regular updating. The age of a password (or better, the maximum age of a password) is an important attribute. Changing a password frequently used to be considered a best practice. However, the longer a password is used, the higher the risk of password compromise. The password requirement policy should dictate the maximum age of a password. Recent CIS guidelines recommend changing passwords yearly. The full CIS Password Policy guideline can be found here: https://www.cisecurity.org/insights/white-papers/cis-password-policy-guide.

The policies around the creation of passwords should also specify whether a password is to be created by the user or is automatically generated by the system. A hybrid approach uses both methods, combining a user-chosen password with a system-generated one. Table 19-3 summarizes the pros and cons of each of these methods.

Table 19-3   Password-Generation Methods

Method	Description	Pros	Cons
User-generated password	Users generate passwords themselves.	Simple to remember.	Usually leads to an easily guessable password. Users may reuse the same password on multiple systems.
System-generated password	Passwords are generated by the system.	Strong passwords. Compliant with security policy.	These passwords are difficult to remember. Users tend to write down the passwords, defeating the purpose.
One-time password and token	Passwords are generated by an external entity (such as hardware or software) that is synchronized with internal resources. The device is usually protected by a user-generated password.	Users do not need to remember a difficult password.	More complicated infrastructure. It makes use of hardware or software to generate the token, which increases maintenance and deployment costs.

Password Managers

Password management is more than just a sidebar to the larger cybersecurity narrative; it's a full-fledged suite of practices and technologies designed to bolster the security fabric of an organization's authentication system. *Password managers* serve as digital vaults for securely storing and managing mountains of passwords. These software solutions store passwords and help generate strong, unique passwords for different accounts, thereby limiting the risk associated with password reuse. For instance, if you have an account with a social media platform and an online banking service, the password manager would ensure that both have distinct, hard-to-crack passwords. All you'd need to remember is a single password to unlock the password manager.

For example, in the Windows environment, Credential Manager is a built-in tool that stores credentials like usernames and passwords, allowing users to easily and securely retrieve them when needed. This functionality is integrated into the operating system, providing a seamless user experience.

In Apple's ecosystem, the macOS Keychain Access application performs a similar role, creating a secure environment where users can save their passwords, which are then encrypted and stored on the device. The Keychain syncs across devices via iCloud, ensuring that passwords are readily available on all of the user's Apple devices.

Beyond these built-in options, numerous third-party password managers offer advanced features such as cross-platform compatibility, secure sharing of credentials, and enhanced security protocols. Remember to consider the security risks of having all your passwords in one system and ensure that the protections applied to getting into the third-party service are robust. These third-party services often provide additional layers of protection, like two-factor authentication, and they can be tailored to meet an individual's or organization's specific security needs.

Passwordless

In a *passwordless authentication* system, the user's identity is verified through biometric data, hardware tokens, or even behavioral attributes, eliminating the need to remember and enter a password. A passwordless authentication approach can be convenient and secure, as it removes the human element, which is often the weakest link in the security chain. Imagine logging into your work system using a combination of a hardware token and your fingerprint; not only is this easier than remembering a complex password, but it also offers a dual layer of verification that would be difficult for intruders to spoof.

Privileged Access Management Tools

Key Topic

Privileged access management (PAM) is a system used to centrally manage access to privileged accounts. It is primarily based on the concept of least privilege. Typically, a privileged access management system is used to securely store the elevated credentials used by an organization and broker the use of those credentials based on criteria set by a PAM administrator. Many different PAM solutions, with varying features and functions, are available today.

Just-in-Time Permissions

Among the PAM approaches is the concept of *just-in-time (JIT) permissions*. JIT permissions focus on the dynamic provisioning of access permissions, typically for a limited period that specifically aligns with the time frame during which the permissions are required. Unlike traditional systems, where, for instance, a system administrator might have continual elevated access, JIT permissions are allocated as needed and for only as long as necessary. This strategy considerably minimizes the attack surface by reducing the time that high-level permissions are active. If an account is compromised, the chance that it has elevated permissions at a particular moment is significantly lower. Thus, JIT permissions aim to alleviate the risks associated with "standing privileges," where permissions are always on.

Password Vaulting

As a complement to JIT passwords, password vaulting serves as another indispensable tool. Remembering multiple complex passwords for different accounts is a Herculean task, often leading users to resort to insecure practices like password reuse. *Password vaulting* addresses this issue by providing a centralized, encrypted repository for storing various credentials. Access to this vault is safeguarded by a password, and additional MFA methods can further fortify security. The credentials in the vault are encrypted, rendering them useless if an attacker is able to gain access to the database. This centralized and secure storage system encourages the use of unique and complex passwords for each service, enhancing overall security hygiene.

Ephemeral Credentials

A secure and efficient solution for temporary access is to use *ephemeral credentials*, which are transient credentials that are automatically generated for a specific session or task. Unlike standing or even JIT permissions, these credentials are made invalid almost immediately after the job they were created for is complete. Automating the issuance and revocation process removes the risk of human error in leaving credentials active longer than necessary. Ephemeral credentials serve as another layer in a robust privileged access management strategy and are especially effective for short-term tasks and roles that don't require permanently elevated access.

Chapter Review Activities

Use the features in this section to study and review the topics in this chapter.

Review Key Topics

Review the most important topics in the chapter, noted with the Key Topic icon in the outer margin of the page. Table 19-4 lists these key topics and the page number on which each is found.

Table 19-4   Key Topics for Chapter 19

Key Topic Element	Description	Page Number
Section	Provisioning/De-provisioning User Accounts	439
Section	Permission Assignments and Implications	439
Section	Federation	441
Section	Single Sign-On (SSO)	443
Figure 19-3	OAuth Exchange	445
Figure 19-4	SAML Building Blocks	447
Section	Interoperability	448
Section	Attestation	449
Section	Access Controls	450
Figure 19-6	Discretionary Access in Windows	453
Table 19-2	Attributes and Identity Terms Used in Account Policies	454
Section	Multifactor Authentication (MFA)	456
Figure 19-8	Multifactor Authentication	460
List	Password settings	462
Table 19-3	Password-Generation Methods	464
Section	Privileged Access Management Tools	465

Define Key Terms

Define the following key terms from this chapter and check your answers in the glossary:

provisioning, de-provisioning, permission assignment, identity proofing, federation, single sign-on (SSO), Lightweight Directory Access Protocol (LDAP), Open Authorization (OAuth), Security Assertion Markup Language (SAML), interoperability, attestation, access control model, role-based access control (RBAC), rule-based access control, mandatory access control (MAC), discretionary access control (DAC), attribute-based access control (ABAC), time-of-day restriction, least privilege, multifactor authentication (MFA), biometric identifier, factor, something you know, something you have, something you are, somewhere you are, password concepts, password, password best practices, password length, password complexity, password reuse, password expiration, password age, password manager, passwordless authentication, privileged access management (PAM), just-in-time (JIT) permissions, password vaulting, ephemeral credentials

Review Questions

Answer the following review questions. Check your answers with the answer key in Appendix A.

1. What is the outcome when a user is de-provisioned in an identity and access management system?

2. How are explicit permissions typically assigned in a digital environment?

3. What does single sign-on (SSO) primarily alleviate in a networked environment?

4. Which access model uses sets of permissions to constitute a role?

5. What aspect of password security does length mainly affect?

6. How do just-in-time (JIT) permissions aim to minimize security risks?

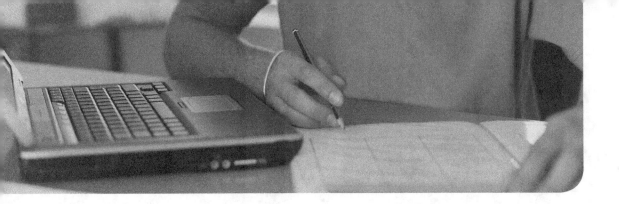

This chapter covers the following topics related to Objective 4.7
(Explain the importance of automation and orchestration related to secure
operations) of the CompTIA Security+ SY0-701 certification exam:

- Use cases of automation and scripting

- Benefits

- Other considerations

Understanding the Importance of Automation and Orchestration Related to Secure Operations

The chapter explores automation in cybersecurity, focusing on the continuous integration and continuous testing (CI/CT) pipelines that streamline code analysis, the build process, and deployment. It discusses the dual-edged nature of automation, outlining its benefits—such as efficiency and early vulnerability detection—while cautioning against challenges such as system complexity and false positives. The chapter also underscores the importance of continuous monitoring tools and the need for ongoing training and support in automated systems.

"Do I Know This Already?" Quiz

The "Do I Know This Already?" quiz enables you to assess whether you should read this entire chapter thoroughly or jump to the "Chapter Review Activities" section. If you are in doubt about your answers to these questions or your own assessment of your knowledge of the topics, read the entire chapter. Table 20-1 lists the major headings in this chapter and their corresponding "Do I Know This Already?" quiz questions. You can find the answers in Appendix A, "Answers to the 'Do I Know This Already?' Quizzes and Review Questions."

Table 20-1 "Do I Know This Already?" Section-to-Question Mapping

Foundation Topics Section	Questions
Use Cases of Automation and Scripting	1–5
Benefits	6, 7
Other Considerations	8–10

CAUTION   The goal of self-assessment is to gauge your mastery of the topics in this chapter. If you do not know the answer to a question or are only partially sure of the answer, you should mark that question as wrong for purposes of self-assessment. Giving yourself credit for an answer you correctly guess skews your self-assessment results and might provide you with a false sense of security.

1. What triggers the CI/CT pipeline in the code commitment process?
    a. A developer logs in to GitHub.
    b. A developer commits code changes to a version control system.
    c. New code is pushed to the production environment.
    d. Static analysis is performed.

2. What is the purpose of the static analysis stage in a CI/CT pipeline?
    a. Compiling the code
    b. Scanning the code for vulnerabilities like SQL injection
    c. Deploying the code to a production environment
    d. Running a suite of automated tests

3. What is one benefit of including automated tests in the CI/CT process?
    a. Reduced cost
    b. Increased complexity
    c. Early detection of vulnerabilities
    d. The need for manual intervention

4. What challenge may arise from using automated testing in a CI/CT pipeline?
    a. Reduced security
    b. Early detection of vulnerabilities
    c. False positives
    d. Time inefficiency

5. What role do APIs play in cybersecurity automation?
    a. Increasing complexity
    b. Facilitating communication between different software entities
    c. Reducing security
    d. Replacing static analysis tools

6. Which benefit directly affects employee retention in an organization using automation?

   a. Early detection of vulnerabilities

   b. Improved job satisfaction due to the removal of tedious tasks

   c. Reduced complexity

   d. Scalability

7. What does the term baseline refer to in the context of cybersecurity automation?

   a. A minimum level of code quality

   b. Predefined security settings and configurations

   c. The starting point for cost analysis

   d. A standard for personnel training

8. How does automation affect resource constraints in cybersecurity?

   a. Increases resource constraints

   b. Acts as a workforce multiplier

   c. Does not affect resource constraints

   d. Increases long-term cost

9. What is a downside of hastily implementing an automated system?

   a. Increased job satisfaction

   b. Early detection of vulnerabilities

   c. Technical debt

   d. Cost-effectiveness

10. What is an essential component of ongoing supportability in cybersecurity automation?

    a. Increasing complexity

    b. Ignoring software updates

    c. Personnel training

    d. Reducing redundancy

Foundation Topics

Use Cases of Automation and Scripting

When discussing secure operations in cybersecurity, we must recognize the transformative role that automation and scripting play. These technologies function as silent workhorses behind the scenes, executing repetitive tasks, ensuring policy compliance, and even responding to real-time security incidents. To gain an understanding of this topic, we will explore various use cases, ranging from user provisioning to integrations with application programming interfaces (APIs).

User Provisioning

User provisioning can be a major pain point when done manually. It involves setting up a user account with appropriate permissions and roles in the system. Instead of manually entering details for each new employee or role change, however, you can use automation tools that are integrated with human resources (HR) software to provision accounts automatically. Automating the process between HR and user account creation ensures that the right people have the right access at the right time. The other side of this coin is deprovisioning, which kicks in when an employee leaves the company or changes roles, and you need to remove or alter their permissions to maintain a secure environment. Automating user provisioning often reveals privilege creep or dormant accounts that could be removed.

Figure 20-1 shows what a manual process might look like for basic account setup of a new employee. First, HR would need to manually notify IT that a user is authorized for basic account setup. IT would then manually open a ticket to any administrators of specific services needed. If the new user is an accountant, the IT help desk might need to open several tickets to address the many accounting role–specific tools the new user requires. You can already see the many opportunities to inject user error in the process. A keystroke error could easily give someone overly permissive access to sensitive software systems.

Automation can remove some of the complexity and human error elements of user provisioning. Figure 20-2 shows how an organization might define basic role-based access and automate the scripting to direct IT ticketing systems to generate user provisioning processes. (For more on role-based access control, refer to Chapter 19, "Implementing and Maintaining Identity and Access Management.") In an automated use case, once HR gives permission to authorize a user to have an account, a large portion of the process can be automated.

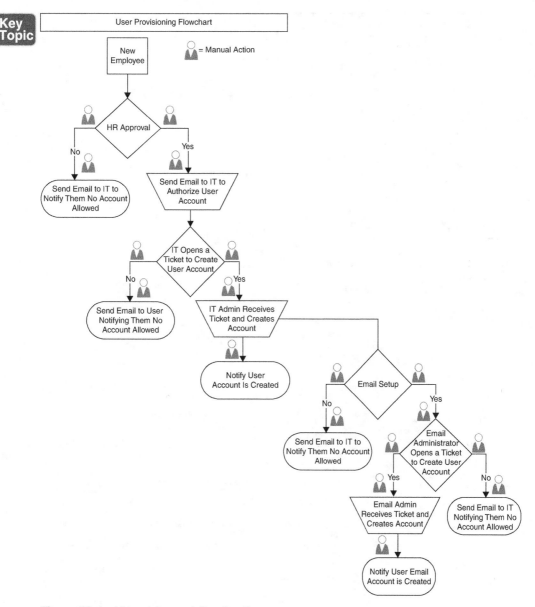

Figure 20-1 Manual Account Creation Process

NOTE A word of caution related to automated user provisioning: Avoid automation with administrator, or root level, access accounts. Elevated privileges that can expose sensitive data should be handled with care and attention.

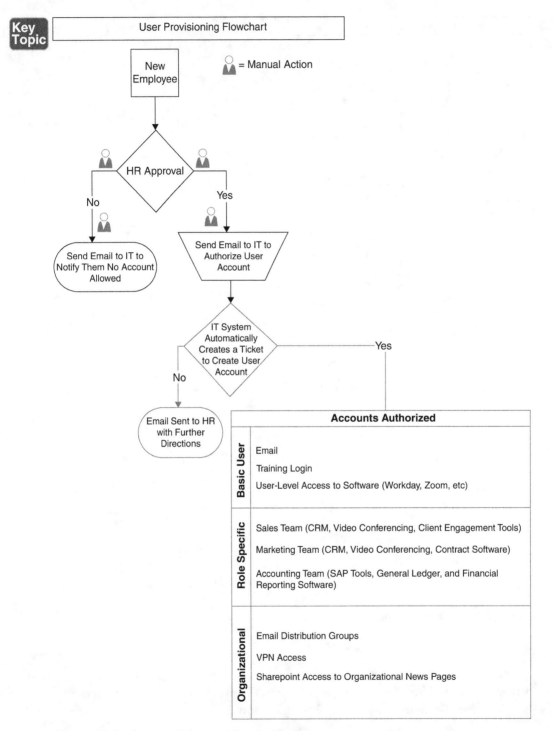

Figure 20-2   Automated Account Creation Process

Resource Provisioning

Resource provisioning refers to the automated setup, modification, or removal of digital assets such as virtual machines, databases, or storage units. Let's say you're an admin in a company that is experiencing rapid growth. Rather than individually configuring each new server or database, automation tools can spin up new resources in line with predefined policies. It's like setting up a production line for digital resources, ensuring uniformity and compliance while saving time. Automating resource provisioning can also help remove the human error involved in setting up new servers and systems.

Guard Rails

Guard rails are automated safety measures or rules set up within a system to restrict or control activities that could be harmful or that might be noncompliant with security policies. Guard rails act as internal checkpoints or barriers that guide user behavior and system interactions toward more secure and compliant outcomes. Suppose you work in a healthcare institution, where the privacy of patient records is critical. In such an environment, a guard rail might be set up to prevent the unauthorized transfer of sensitive patient data to external drives or cloud storage services that are not compliant with healthcare regulations such as HIPAA.

Security Groups

A *security group* is a collection of users that are categorized based on security policies, which can be automatically updated or modified to grant or restrict access to particular system resources. Instead of configuring firewall rules for each new server or application, you can use security group automation to apply predefined security group templates based on the role or function of a resource, which helps in maintaining a consistent security posture.

Ticket Creation and Escalation

Automation also simplifies the ticket creation and escalation process in incident response scenarios. An automated *ticket creation system* can detect an irregularity, such as an unauthorized login attempt, and create a ticket or an incident report in a system used for tracking issues, problems, or activities that require attention or action. If the irregularity *escalates*—say, multiple failed login attempts are detected—the ticket is automatically forwarded to a higher level of expertise or authority within the organization for further action.

Let's talk about turning services and access on and off. Automation allows admins to control permissions by *enabling or disabling services and access*, usually based on specific conditions or events, such as time of day or security incidents. For instance, an automated system can disable FTP access to a server outside regular business hours, reducing the window of opportunity for a potential cyberattack. As with so many other automation processes, you must ensure that the business agrees on who needs access in the off hours to prevent incorrectly cutting off user access.

Continuous Integration and Testing

Continuous integration and testing, or continuous integration and continuous testing (CI/CT), involves regular, automated integration of code changes, contributed by multiple developers, into a single repository, followed by an immediate series of rigorous automated tests to ensure code quality and security. It often utilizes automated tests to flag bugs, security vulnerabilities, and other issues. This operational strategy institutionalizes security measures, incorporating them as foundational elements in the development lifecycle.

The core philosophy behind CI/CT is to introduce incremental changes that are tested continuously, allowing for quicker detection and remediation of potential issues. The sooner a security flaw is identified, the faster and more efficiently it can be rectified, minimizing its impact and the overall risk to the organization.

Key processes of CI/CT include the following:

- **Code commitment:** Developers commit code changes to a version control system (for example, GitHub, GitLab). This triggers the CI/CT pipeline automatically.

- **Static analysis:** Static analysis tools scan the committed code for vulnerabilities such as SQL injection (SQLi) or buffer overflow. This pretest adds a layer of security before any dynamic testing occurs.

- **Automated build process:** The committed code is compiled, and an executable is built. Any errors in this process are flagged immediately, ensuring that the codebase remains stable.

- **Automated testing:** This phase includes running a suite of automated tests, which may include unit tests, integration tests, and security tests. Tools like OWASP ZAP or Selenium might be used to automate security checks.

- **Deployment:** If the code passes all tests, it is ready for deployment in a staging or production environment.

Continuous monitoring tools are employed to monitor application behavior and log activities. Any abnormal behavior is flagged, triggering alerts that allow for immediate action.

The following are some of the benefits of leveraging a CI/CT process:

- **Early detection:** Incorporating security checks into the CI/CT pipeline makes it possible to identify vulnerabilities early.

- **Consistency:** Automated tests are performed consistently across all code, reducing the risk of human error.

- **Time efficiency:** Automation allows development and security teams to focus on more complex tasks by reducing the manual workload.

- **Compliance:** Automated checks can be designed to ensure that code meets specific regulatory and compliance standards, reducing the risk of legal repercussions.

However, no process is free of challenges, and there are a few challenges with the CI/CT pipeline that you need to take into consideration:

- **Complexity:** The CI/CT pipeline can be complex to set up and maintain, requiring specialized skills.

- **Resource requirements:** The computing resources needed to run automated tests continually can significantly affect the cost.

- **False positives:** Automated testing is not foolproof and may generate false positives that need to be manually reviewed, which could consume time and resources.

While CI/CT involves some challenges, the long-term benefits of reduced risk and improved security posture are substantial enough to make the effort worthwhile.

Integrations and Application Programming Interfaces (APIs)

Integrations and application programming interfaces (APIs) refer to the automated linking of different computing services and software applications to work as a coherent system, often with APIs that allow different software entities to communicate with each other. By linking various security tools and platforms, automation can provide a unified view of an organization's security posture. For example, a security information and event management (SIEM) system could be integrated with an incident response platform to allow for automated data sharing and action triggers between the two.

While automation and scripting bring in a lot of efficiencies and enhanced security, they also introduce challenges, including system complexity, the potential for automation errors, and the need for ongoing maintenance. The pros often outweigh the cons, however, especially when automation is carefully planned and executed. With security, we never just "set it and forget it."

Benefits

As we continue to explore the numerous advantages of automation and scripting in cybersecurity, it is important to acknowledge that the benefits extend far beyond simplifying administrative tasks. Automation opens up a host of positive outcomes in an organization, affecting everything from the speed and efficiency of operations to the job satisfaction of the security team. This section explores the benefits of integrating automation into your security operations, touching on key aspects such as efficiency, standardization, scalability, and even the human factor of employee satisfaction. From freeing up time for complex problem solving to standardizing configurations for a more robust security posture, automation offers an array of advantages that make it essential in today's rapidly evolving cybersecurity environment.

Efficiency/Time Saving

Efficiency and time saving refer to the accelerated execution of tasks and processes, freeing human resources for more complex, strategic work. Consider the tedious task of log analysis. Without automation, security analysts might have to comb through logs manually to identify anomalies. However, with automation, logs can be analyzed in real time, and alerts can be sent when suspicious activities are identified. The time saved can be reinvested in tasks that require human ingenuity, such as strategic planning or complex problem solving.

Enforcing Baselines

Enforcing baselines refers to consistently applying predefined security settings and configurations across an organization's computing environment. For instance, you might require all Windows workstations in a finance department to meet a certain security standard required by the Sarbanes-Oxley Act. Automation can help in using Group Policy and other management frameworks.

Implementing an automated update management system using Windows Server Update Services (WSUS) is a strategic move for maintaining the security and compliance of workstation software in any department, particularly in finance, where data sensitivity is critical to the company. Leveraging WSUS for effective patch management and compliance assurance across Windows workstations in a finance department would involve the following facets:

- **Initial configuration:** You set up a WSUS server to manage updates across all Windows workstations within the finance department.

- **Group policy:** Using GPO, you configure the workstations to automatically connect to the WSUS server for updates.

- **Baseline definition:** You define a baseline requiring all workstations to install the latest security patches for Windows and Microsoft Office.

- **Automated checks and reports:** The WSUS server automatically checks for compliance. Any noncompliant workstations are listed in a daily report and might even be quarantined, depending on the organization's policy.

- **Automated remediation:** WSUS can either automatically push the required patches to noncompliant systems or flag them for manual review. This is also a good time to confirm whether you have any internal service-level agreement (SLA) requirements to review patch alerts for compliance systems.

Automation helps you ensure that all workstations meet a consistent security baseline, reducing the likelihood of vulnerabilities due to outdated software. However, remember that you need to periodically confirm that these updates are happening correctly.

Standard Infrastructure Configurations

Standard infrastructure configurations refers to the uniformity of system setups, meaning all systems are configured in a specific, predefined way to maintain security and efficiency. Let's say your organization uses Docker containers. Docker is a set of platform as a service (PaaS) products that use operating system–level virtualization to deliver software in software packages called containers. Automation can ensure that every new container deployed matches a standard, secure configuration, reducing the likelihood of a security vulnerability being introduced due to misconfiguration.

Scaling in a Secure Manner

Scaling in a secure manner refers to the ability to expand an organization's digital infrastructure while maintaining or enhancing its security posture. Imagine that your online retail business experiences a surge in traffic during the holiday season. Automation can scale up your resources to meet demand and ensure that each new server meets all security protocols, and it can even conduct automatic security audits on each server.

Employee Retention

Employee retention is an often-overlooked benefit of automation. It refers to the improved job satisfaction and retention rates achieved by removing tedious manual tasks from employees' job roles. Automation can free up an IT security team to engage in more meaningful, rewarding work, which can be a significant factor in retaining skilled employees in a competitive job market.

Reaction Time

Improving reaction time refers to responding quickly to security incidents or other operational events. For example, automated systems can detect a data breach within milliseconds and immediately lock down affected systems far faster than any human could. The reaction time can be crucial in minimizing damage in the event of a cyberattack.

Workforce Multiplier

Resource constraints are a major challenge in cybersecurity. Most organizations tend to work under tight budgets and in a dynamic threat environment. One of the benefits of automation is that it can act as a workforce multiplier. *Workforce multiplier* refers to enhancing a team's productivity by automating routine tasks. For instance, a small cybersecurity team of 5 people might be able to monitor and secure an organization that traditionally required a group of 20. The increase in efficiency is possible because automation takes care of repetitive tasks, allowing the small team to focus on higher-level, strategic activities.

Key Topic Other Considerations

For a balanced perspective, it's crucial to understand that while automation and scripting bring numerous benefits to cybersecurity, they also introduce several challenges and considerations that professionals should be aware of. This section explores some of these often-overlooked aspects, such as complexity, cost, and the potential for a single point of failure. We'll dive into these factors not as deterrents but as critical elements that must be managed for an automation strategy to be successful. If you go into implementing an automated solution with the goal of understanding the pros and cons, then you are better equipped to handle any challenges that arise.

Complexity

Complexity is an inherent characteristic of automated systems, which often require specialized design, implementation, and maintenance skills. A robust automated system may require integration between multiple tools and platforms, each with its own rules and requirements. You will likely need to include other departments when calibrating your solution, which means you will need to educate stakeholders on the pros and cons. As you add more layers to the automated process, the complexity increases, and you need skilled professionals to manage it. Updating and maintaining intricate workflows can become challenging as the systems evolve, particularly in large and dynamic environments.

Cost

Cost focuses on the financial expenditure involved with implementing, maintaining, and updating automated systems. Implementing automation tools and platforms often requires an initial investment in software, hardware, and human resources for setup and maintenance. Although these costs are usually offset by long-term benefits such as efficiency and reduced staffing, it's important to conduct a thorough cost/benefit analysis to ensure that the investment aligns with your organization's goals and budget.

When examining cost as a consideration related to automation, it's crucial to approach it through the lens of not just initial expenses but long-term investment and returns. For instance, let's say a chief information security officer (CISO) is considering implementing an automated security information and event management (SIEM) system that costs $40,000 up front, with an ongoing annual fee of $10,000 for updates and support. The CISO would need to assess the up-front and recurring costs and potential savings. If the automated SIEM system could reduce the time spent on log analysis by 30%, the CISO could quantify this time savings in monetary terms. If previously two full-time analysts were needed for this task, and each has an annual salary of $80,000, a 30% time savings would equate to $48,000 in salary costs per year ($160,000 in total salary for two analysts × 30% = $48,000). This cost/benefit analysis could demonstrate that the SIEM system could pay for itself within the first year, making it a cost-effective solution in the long run.

Single Point of Failure

Another consideration with automation is the potential for a single point of failure. A *single point of failure* is a component or an aspect of a system that, if it fails, will stop the entire system from functioning. An automated system, when not designed with redundancy and fail-safes, could become a bottleneck or single point of failure in your operations. If an automated system that controls multiple functions fails, the impact could be much more significant than the impact of a failure in a system with manual checks and balances. Building resiliency into automated processes is critical to prevent large-scale disruptions. However, you might find that redundancy isn't possible with older systems due to a lack of system availability. If you can't purchase a redundant server or software version because the manufacturer no longer makes them, then you have a real problem on your hands, which brings us to the issue of technical debt.

Technical Debt

Technical debt refers to the long-term cost of outdated systems, shortcuts, and temporary fixes that are sometimes implemented to roll out automated solutions quickly. While short-term time savers might offer a fast way to get automation up and running, they often result in additional time and resources being spent to fix or optimize these solutions later. It is essential to plan automation carefully, considering long-term maintainability over short-term gains.

You might be pressured into hastily implementing an automated patch management system to cope with a sudden increase in cyber threats. To roll it out quickly, the team might opt to skip several best practices, such as thoroughly testing each patch in a staging environment before deployment or passing the patch through the automation process described earlier. While this expediency allows the organization to improve its security posture quickly, the lack of adequate testing could result in compatibility issues, causing disruptions and system outages. The technical debt accrued by not following best practices would eventually require "repayment" in the form of resources spent troubleshooting and rectifying these issues. The initial time saved may be lost, and there may be additional costs related to emergency fixes as well as damage to the organization's reputation. Weighing the long-term implications of shortcuts and expedited solutions when implementing automation is essential, and you would do well to keep track of when you make these compromises.

Ongoing Supportability

Ongoing supportability is not just a checkbox on a list. *Ongoing supportability* is needed for the effective, long-term operation of automated systems. Automated systems can quickly become obsolete or vulnerable if not properly maintained.

Ongoing supportability involves several areas that require your focused attention: software updates, hardware compatibility, and personnel training, to name a few. When automated systems are not regularly updated to address new security vulnerabilities, they can weaken the organization's security posture. Similarly, as your hardware ecosystem grows or changes—perhaps due to mergers, acquisitions, or organic growth—the automated systems must remain compatible with the new components.

Personnel training is another key aspect. Technology staff should be trained to operate automated systems effectively and to troubleshoot and update them as needed. Investing in continual employee training ensures that your team is equipped to adapt to new software features or shifts in security protocols.

Table 20-2 lists some of the ways training can be beneficial for specific use cases. Ongoing personnel training is required to manage cybersecurity systems effectively, and this requirement extends beyond cybersecurity teams. Each element is crucial in fortifying an organization's cyber resilience, from initial onboarding to specialized training programs and real-world simulations for everyone at the company. This structured approach ensures that staff understand the automated systems they operate and can adapt to new software features or shifts in security protocols.

Key Topic

Table 20-2   Beneficial Training for Specific Use Cases

Aspect	Description	Examples
Initial onboarding	Introduction to the organization's cybersecurity infrastructure	Basic orientation, SOPs
Specialized training	Focused workshops and certification programs to gain specific expertise	SIEM workshop, IDS configurations, CISSP, CEH
Continuous training	Periodic courses and internal knowledge-sharing sessions for skill reinforcement	Refresher courses, lunch-and-learns
Real-world simulation	Scenario-based training exercises to simulate crisis situations	Crisis simulation, cyber drills, IDS alerts
Postmortem reviews	Analyzing cybersecurity events to fine-tune both automated systems and human responses	Incident retrospectives
Performance metrics	Quantitative assessments to evaluate skill levels and identify areas for improvement	KPI assessments

For instance, say that your organization relies heavily on an automated intrusion detection system (IDS). New types of cyberattacks emerge all the time. If the IDS is not updated to recognize these new attack vectors, it could potentially miss a critical intrusion, jeopardizing the entire organization. Regularly scheduled updates, system checks, and employee training sessions can go a long way toward preventing these events from happening due to human oversight.

Chapter Review Activities

Use the features in this section to study and review the topics in this chapter.

Review Key Topics

Review the most important topics in the chapter, noted with the Key Topic icon in the outer margin of the page. Table 20-3 lists these key topics and the page number on which each is found.

Table 20-3   Key Topics for Chapter 20

Key Topic Element	Description	Page Number
Section	Use Cases of Automation and Scripting	474
Figure 20-1	Manual Account Creation Process	475
Figure 20-2	Automated Account Creation Process	476
Section	Continuous Integration and Testing	478
List	Key processes of CI/CT	478
Section	Benefits	480
Section	Enforcing Baselines	480
Section	Other Considerations	482
Table 20-2	Beneficial Training for Specific Use Cases	485

Define Key Terms

Define the following key terms from this chapter and check your answers in the glossary:

user provisioning, resource provisioning, guard rails, security group, ticket creation system, escalate, enabling or disabling services and access, continuous integration and testing, integrations and application programming interfaces (APIs), efficiency and time saving, enforcing baselines, standard infrastructure configurations, scaling in a secure manner, employee retention, improving reaction time, workforce multiplier, complexity, cost, single point of failure, technical debt, ongoing supportability

Review Questions

Answer the following review questions. Check your answers with the answer key in Appendix A.

1. What pipeline approach is commonly used for streamlining code analysis, the build process, and deployment in the context of cybersecurity automation?

2. What are some of the key benefits of automation in cybersecurity?

3. What are the challenges associated with implementing automation in cybersecurity?

4. What role does continuous monitoring play in cybersecurity automation?

5. Why are ongoing training and support needed with automated cybersecurity systems?

6. Describe the dual-edged nature of automation in cybersecurity.

This chapter covers the following topics related to Objective 4.8 (Explain appropriate incident response activities) of the CompTIA Security+ SY0-701 certification exam:

- Process
- Training
- Testing
- Root cause analysis
- Threat hunting
- Digital forensics

CHAPTER 21

Understanding Appropriate Incident Response Activities

This chapter provides a comprehensive guide to incident response and digital forensics, covering each phase, from preparation to recovery. It emphasizes the importance of a well-structured process, including specialized techniques like root cause analysis and threat hunting. The chapter also delves into training and various testing methods, such as tabletop exercises and simulations, to ensure team preparedness. It also explores the legal and procedural aspects of digital forensics, including chain of custody, acquisition, and e-discovery. This chapter, which focuses on practical examples, is an invaluable resource for fortifying an organization's cybersecurity posture.

"Do I Know This Already?" Quiz

The "Do I Know This Already?" quiz enables you to assess whether you should read this entire chapter thoroughly or jump to the "Chapter Review Activities" section. If you are in doubt about your answers to these questions or your own assessment of your knowledge of the topics, read the entire chapter. Table 21-1 lists the major headings in this chapter and their corresponding "Do I Know This Already?" quiz questions. You can find the answers in Appendix A, "Answers to the 'Do I Know This Already?' Quizzes and Review Questions."

Table 21-1 "Do I Know This Already?" Section-to-Question Mapping

Foundation Topics Section	Questions
Process	1, 7
Training	2
Testing	3, 8
Root Cause Analysis	4
Threat Hunting	5
Digital Forensics	6, 9, 10

CAUTION   The goal of self-assessment is to gauge your mastery of the topics in this chapter. If you do not know the answer to a question or are only partially sure of the answer, you should mark that question as wrong for purposes of self-assessment. Giving yourself credit for an answer you correctly guess skews your self-assessment results and might provide you with a false sense of security.

1. Which of the following best describes the role of the owner in an incident response plan?

    a. Responsible for technical tasks only

    b. Responsible for communication with executive leadership only

    c. Responsible for coordinating communications, assigning tasks, and ensuring efficient execution of the plan

    d. Responsible for legal disclosures

2. What is the primary focus of role-based training in incident response?

    a. Technical aspects only

    b. Procedural and communication protocols

    c. Legal disclosures

    d. Media relations

3. Which of the following is not a component of effective simulation exercises in incident response?

    a. Environment

    b. External injects

    c. Media coverage

    d. Metrics

4. What is the primary benefit of conducting a thorough root cause analysis?

    a. Media attention

    b. Compliance with industry regulations

    c. Preventing the recurrence of similar incidents

    d. Legal protection

5. What is the main advantage of threat hunting in cybersecurity?

    a. Legal compliance

    b. Media relations

    c. Early detection and minimization of potential damage

    d. Resource allocation

6. Which of the following is not a specialized activity in digital forensics?

    a. Legal hold

    b. Chain of custody

    c. Media relations

    d. E-discovery

7. What constitutes the final goal of the recovery phase in an incident response process?

    a. Identifying the attacker's methodology

    b. Resuming normal business operations without remnants of the incident

    c. Calculating the total downtime caused by the incident

    d. Strengthening the network to prevent future attacks

8. In simulation exercises for incident response, what role do external injects play?

    a. They offer a metric for the team's performance evaluation.

    b. They serve as spontaneous variables to challenge the team's response capabilities.

    c. They simulate network downtime for testing infrastructure resilience.

    d. They provide a set of predetermined outcomes for the exercise.

9. In the evidence acquisition phase after an incident, which of these are prioritized according to the order of volatility?

    a. Disk images

    b. Network logs

    c. CPU cache and registers

    d. Changes to system configurations

10. What is the initial step in preserving digital evidence once it has been identified?

   a. Severing the Internet connection of the affected device

   b. Creating a bit-by-bit image of the device's storage

   c. Documenting the evidence in a chain of custody form

   d. Sealing the device in an antistatic bag

Foundation Topics

Process

The incident response process is made up of seven key elements that can be developed as an organization's security posture matures. Building an incident response plan involves some important considerations. First and foremost, backing from senior management is paramount. Occasionally, people use the terms *incident response process and incident response plan* interchangeably. It's important to note that the process is a roadmap to developing a specific plan for each organization; each incident response plan is as unique as the organization.

Building an incident response plan should not be a box-checking exercise or a process that's handed off to inexperienced employees. If senior management does not support this process, there is a risk that it will be filed away, and it will be incomplete and useless when needed. Senior leadership should outline critical processes, systems, and resources that are important to business continuity. Plan development involves defining the key stakeholders and obtaining contact details for key individuals and teams inside and outside business hours; this information needs to be included in the plan.

Figure 21-1 shows the NIST incident response lifecycle. The incident response process is a business process that enables you to remain in business. The list that follows describes the four phases in more detail.

> **NOTE**   For more details on NIST incident handling, see https://nvlpubs.nist.gov/nistpubs/SpecialPublications/NIST.SP.800-61r2.pdf.

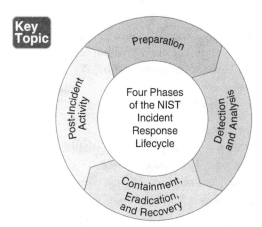

Figure 21-1   The Four Phases of the NIST Incident Response Lifecycle

1. **Preparation:** The quality of the response to an incident largely depends on incident response preparedness. In this phase, all components needed to effectively respond to an incident are identified, acquired, or created.

2. **Detection and analysis:** This phase primarily focuses on detection and discovery of indicators of compromise (IOCs). Having an incident reporting policy and procedure in place is critical to training.

3. **Containment, eradication, and recovery:** After stopping the problem from getting worse or spreading, you limit the damage and then regain control of the network and systems. Then recovery starts with restoration of systems to normal operations.

4. **Post-incident activity:** This phase focuses on lessons learned to improve the incident response capability and prevent this type of incident from happening again.

Preparation

Bridging the gap between theory and application, the preparation phase marks the critical juncture where strategic planning meets tactical readiness. This is where the incident response process transitions from an overarching strategy—a set of guiding principles backed by executive leadership—into a tangible and actionable plan. *Preparation* is the cornerstone of an effective incident response strategy, serving as a blueprint for how the organization will handle and recover from security incidents. The first step is to designate an owner for the incident response plan. This individual is responsible for coordinating communications, assigning tasks, and ensuring that the plan is executed efficiently. The owner's role is pivotal in bridging the technical and nontechnical aspects of incident response, ensuring that tasks assigned to security teams are precise and that updates to executive leadership are clear and devoid of jargon.

However, preparation goes beyond having a plan and an owner; it's about building a resilient framework tailored to various incidents. Technological preparations are crucial. For example, your security information and event management (SIEM) system should be configured to log and alert on suspicious activities effectively. Regular software updates and patches are also essential for mitigating vulnerabilities that could be exploited.

Human elements are equally important. Comprehensive training programs should be in place to educate all employees, not just the security teams, about their roles during an incident. This training should cover identifying phishing attempts, the procedures for reporting suspicious activities, and the importance of robust password hygiene.

Your preparation should also include the development of playbooks that offer specific guidance for different types of incidents, such as malware, insider threats, unauthorized access, ransomware, and phishing. These playbooks should be tested regularly through tabletop exercises to identify any gaps or areas for improvement.

A well-thought-out business continuity plan (BCP) and disaster recovery plan (DRP) should be part of your preparation. These plans outline the steps for ensuring that critical business functions continue during an incident and detail how to recover afterward.

Incorporating a risk matrix, as shown in Table 21-2, into your preparation phase can help you prioritize incidents based on their likelihood and impact. This data-driven approach guides the SOC in resource allocation and refines the specificity of your playbooks. The matrix also serves as a valuable tool during tabletop exercises, allowing teams to simulate responses to various risk scenarios.

> **TIP** A risk matrix displays the probability or likelihood versus the consequences of risk. Table 21-2 provides a sample matrix.

Key Topic

Table 21-2 Risk Matrix

Likelihood	Consequences				
	Not Significant	Minor	Moderate	Major	Severe
Very likely	Medium	High	High	Very high	Very high
Likely	Medium	High	High	Very high	Very high
Possible	Low	Medium	High	High	Very high
Unlikely	Low	Low	Medium	Medium	High
Rare	Low	Low	Low	Low	Medium

Detection

The *detection* phase is crucial for identifying signs of a security incident in its early stages. Unlike using the old notion of "patient zero," modern detection methods employ a combination of automated monitoring tools and human expertise to spot anomalies or suspicious activities. The detection phase is the initial stage, where signs of a security incident are identified. This involves using automated systems and human expertise to recognize unusual activities or anomalies, such as unexpected data transfers or multiple failed login attempts. The goal is to find a single compromised device and spot patterns that could indicate a more significant security issue. For example, unusual network traffic, multiple failed login attempts, or unexpected data transfers could all be signs of a security incident.

Analysis

Once an incident is detected, the analysis phase kicks in to dissect the nature and extent of the threat. In the *analysis* phase, the focus is on understanding the nature and scope of the detected security incident. Investigators collect and examine indicators of compromise (IoCs) to gain insights into an incident. For example, if malware is involved, the analysis would include studying the network traffic it produces, the specific IP addresses or domains it connects to, and any new files or processes it creates. This detailed examination helps to both quantify the extent of the incident and identify other systems that may also be compromised. It is also important to scrutinize new running processes, memory or disk storage changes, and registry key alterations. This comprehensive analysis serves two purposes: It helps in understanding the scope of the incident and aids in identifying other potentially compromised systems in the network.

Containment

Once the scope of an incident has been successfully identified, the containment process can begin. *Containment* involves isolating the compromised devices in the network from the rest of the network to stop the spread of the incident. Short-term containment may be used to isolate a device that is being targeted by attack traffic. Long-term containment may be necessary when a deep-dive analysis is required, which can be time-consuming. This process may involve taking a forensic image of the device and conducting detailed forensic analysis; the analysis may generate further IoCs and identification of the source, and it might need to be revisited.

Eradication

Many organizations don't understand the risks associated with improper eradication and how to actually fix a malware infection or breached system. Once an incident is successfully contained, the eradication of the threat can begin. This process varies depending on what devices have been compromised and what caused the compromise. *Eradication* involves the removal of the root cause of the incident, including malicious code or unauthorized access, to eliminate the threat. If possible, you should perform a complete wipe/reimage of the affected system. This step, of course, requires you to have good backups in place and the ability to establish the initial date/time of infection, rolling back to just before that. Besides reimaging systems, you should make sure you use the latest patches on all devices, disarm malware, disable compromised accounts, and change passwords. These are just a few examples of what may be required in the eradication phase for an incident.

Regardless of how you choose to eradicate an infection, you need to have a plan for immediate increased monitoring of any affected systems for some period of time after the eradication process, usually 30 days or longer. This plan is important to make sure the steps you took to fix the issue were effective and that you have no lingering malware, rootkits, backdoors, or additional compromised accounts. Reviewing event logs from both affected hosts and Active Directory logs for account usage should be a daily task.

Recovery

Recovery is the restoration and validation of system functionality for business operations to resume, ensuring that no traces of the incident remain. The incident response team brings affected production systems back online carefully to ensure that another incident doesn't take place. Important decisions at the recovery stage include determining the time and date from which to restore operations, how to test and verify that affected systems are back to normal, and how long to monitor the systems to ensure that activity is back to normal. The goal of the recovery phase of an incident is to restore normal service to the business. If clean backups are available, they can be used to restore service. Alternatively, any compromised device needs to be rebuilt to ensure a clean recovery. Additional monitoring of affected devices may need to be implemented.

Lessons Learned

The lessons learned phase should be performed no later than two weeks from the end of the incident. A post-incident review meeting is held to ensure that information is fresh on the team's mind. The main goals of the *lessons learned* phase are to update documentation that could not be prepared during the response process and investigate the incident further to identify its full scope, how it was contained and eradicated, and what was done to recover the attacked systems. After the threat has been fully remediated, the next step is to figure out how to prevent the issue from occurring again. The post-incident review is the platform used to discuss what went well during the incident and what processes and procedures can be improved. At this stage, the incident response plan is refined based on the outcome of the post-incident review, and procedures and playbooks are amended to reflect any agreed changes.

Key Topic

Training

In incident response activities, *training* is critical for equipping your team with the skills and knowledge they need to manage and mitigate security incidents effectively. The focus here is more than just technical aspects such as how to contain a malware outbreak or conduct forensic analysis. It's also about understanding the procedural and communication protocols that must be followed during an incident to ensure a coordinated and effective response.

Training for incident response often starts with role-based exercises. For example, system administrators may undergo training on properly isolating compromised systems without affecting business operations, while the legal team might be trained on the nuances of disclosure requirements. These role-based trainings are usually followed by integrated exercises that bring together multiple departments to simulate the cross-functional nature of incident response. A great place to introduce a multi-department approach to training is in your incident response plan (IRP). Your IRP can include roles and response actions that become the basis for a cross-departmental training plan.

One effective training method is to conduct simulated incident response exercises, such as tabletop scenarios or more advanced cyber range simulations. These exercises provide a safe environment to mimic real-world attacks, allowing the team to practice its response in a controlled setting. Going through the motions is not enough; it's important to understand why each step is crucial. For instance, failing to properly document actions taken during an incident could have legal ramifications, while delays in communication could exacerbate the impact of the incident.

The training value in incident response positively impacts several areas across the company. First, it prepares your team for the inevitable. Cyber incidents are not a matter of if but when; a well-trained team can mean the difference between a minor disruption and a major catastrophe. Second, training helps to identify gaps in your incident response plan. Every plan is flawed, and these exercises often reveal shortcomings that can be addressed before an actual incident occurs. Third, training fosters a culture of continuous improvement. After each training session or simulated exercise, lessons learned are integrated into the incident response plan, making the plan more robust and effective.

Incident response training is not a checkbox to be ticked off but an ongoing commitment. It's an investment in your team's capabilities and, by extension, in the resilience and security of your organization.

Testing

This section looks at the nitty-gritty details of testing as part of incident response activities. *Testing*, in the context of incident response, refers to the rigorous and systematic examination of an organization's incident response procedures, plans, and capabilities. It involves putting these components through various scenarios and simulations to ensure that they work as intended in the event of a cybersecurity incident. While we've previously discussed the importance of exercises like tabletops and simulations, we'll explore these methods in greater detail in this section, focusing on the distinctions that make them invaluable tools for any cybersecurity team. We will also explore what an actual tabletop exercise might look like for a team.

The Anatomy of a Tabletop Exercise

A *tabletop exercise* is a structured way of evaluating an IRP against hypothetical but realistic scenarios.

Here's a breakdown of the key elements that constitute a successful tabletop exercise:

- **Scenario design:** This is the hypothetical situation that the team will respond to. It should mirror real-world threats pertinent to your organization or industry. Your organization will only gain value from working through a scenario that has something to do with its business or industry. For example, if you're in the financial sector, a scenario might involve a spear-phishing attack aimed at the finance department.

- **Role assignment:** In a tabletop exercise, each participant is assigned a role that corresponds to their real-world responsibilities during an incident. Role assignments ensure role clarity and help participants internalize their duties, making the exercise more than just a theoretical discussion. A tabletop exercise allows you to practice in the same way you would actually respond.

- **Time constraints:** Real incidents don't happen in a vacuum; they unfold under time pressure. Introducing a timer in a tabletop exercise simulates this urgency, requiring the team to make quick yet informed decisions. You can use a digital clock on the wall or digital timers on all participants' computers.

- **Decision points:** Decision points are specific moments at which the exercise is paused to evaluate the actions taken to that point. They provide opportunities to scrutinize the effectiveness of the response and chances for real-time learning and strategy adjustment.

- **Documentation:** Document. Document. Document. Documentation involves keeping a detailed exercise record and capturing every action, decision, and discussion point. This documentation serves as an audit trail and a resource for refining your IRP. You might be forced to wait weeks to share the results of the tabletop exercise, and the detailed accuracy of your notes will determine the success level of your IRP.

The Intricacies of Simulation Exercises

Simulation exercises add a layer of realism by mimicking the technical environment and introducing real-time challenges. Here's how to make your simulation exercises as effective as possible:

- **Environment:** Every scenario occurs in a simulated environment, which refers to a sandboxed or isolated replica of your network. It provides a realistic backdrop, enhancing the effectiveness of the exercise. You might only be able to replicate some of your environment; however, you should try to get as accurate as possible to ensure that the folks participating in the simulation feel that the experience is authentic.

■ **External injects:** These are unexpected elements introduced during the simulation to test the team's adaptability. You might think of them as the "shock and awe" of your simulation. For example, a simulated power outage could occur halfway through resolving a malware attack.

■ **Metrics:** Key performance indicators (KPIs) are metrics used to evaluate the effectiveness of a response. Metrics could range from the time taken to identify the threat to the resources utilized during the response. You will need to work with the key stakeholders of the event to agree on what metrics matter to the team.

■ **Debriefing:** This is a post-exercise discussion where the team members review their performance, identify gaps, and discuss improvements. You might hear this referred to as "hotwash" or "after action review (AAR)." No matter what the event is called, the goal is the same: Review what happened.

Mock Example of a Tabletop Exercise

Let's take a look at what a tabletop exercise might look like:

■ **Scenario:** A ransomware attack has encrypted critical customer data.

■ **Roles:**

   ■ Incident commander: Jane

   ■ IT specialist: Mark

   ■ Legal advisor: Sarah

   ■ Communications lead: Emily

■ **Time Constraint:** 2 hours to resolve the incident.

■ **Exercise Flow:**

   1. **Initial Briefing:** Jane informs the team about the ransomware attack and assigns roles or reviews role assignments from the incident response plan (IRP).

   2. **First Decision Point:** Mark suggests isolating the affected servers to stop the spread of the malware. The team agrees, and Mark begins isolating the servers.

3. **Second Decision Point:** Sarah advises on the legal implications of the data loss and suggests notifying affected customers. Emily drafts a communication plan based on the facts received from Mark. Emily also captures a chain of events timeline log to share with company legal counsel for cyber insurance.

4. **Final Decision Point:** The incident team begins formulating final actions once the malware is contained and the team is confident no further damage from this malware incident is possible. The team discusses long-term solutions, including enhanced firewall settings and employee training.

5. **Documentation Review and Debrief:** All actions and decisions are recorded for future analysis. The logs Emily captured are reviewed with the team to ensure that all the facts are included.

By dissecting the elements of tabletop and simulation exercises and understanding their nuances, you can create a more resilient and effective incident response strategy customized to your team. You will find that practical scenarios are worth the investment to prevent confusion during an actual incident event.

Key Topic Root Cause Analysis

Root cause analysis is a critical investigative technique that delves deep into identifying the underlying reasons behind a security incident. When you identify the root cause, you're not just putting a band-aid on a symptom; you're preventing the recurrence of similar incidents. Root cause analysis is crucial for effective resource allocation, as understanding the root cause allows you to focus your efforts and resources on areas that will yield the most significant impact. Conducting thorough root cause analyses is often required to comply with various industry regulations, and failure to do so could result in penalties.

The process of root cause analysis starts with meticulous data collection, which involves gathering all relevant logs, user activities, and system changes that occurred around the time of the incident. Once the data is collected, a timeline analysis is performed to understand the sequence of events. A timeline analysis often provides invaluable insights into the root cause. Hypotheses are then developed and tested against the collected data. Once a hypothesis is confirmed, you've successfully identified the root cause and can proceed to develop a remediation plan to prevent future incidents. For instance, if you experience a data breach and find that an outdated software component was exploited, the root cause is the vulnerability and the lack of a regular update and patching mechanism.

Now that you understand the importance of a root cause analysis, you may wonder where to start. One technique you might use is the 5 Whys technique, which is an invaluable tool in the root cause analysis process, thanks to its simplicity and effectiveness. Originating from Lean manufacturing, this method involves asking "Why?" five times in succession to drill down into the cause-and-effect layers of a problem. The aim is to move beyond symptoms and arrive at the underlying root cause. For example, if a security breach occurs, the first "Why?" might reveal that an unauthorized user gained access to the system. The second "Why?" could show that the user exploited a vulnerability in the software. Continuing this line of questioning can lead to insights such as outdated security patches or a lack of regular audits. By the time you reach the fifth "Why?" you're likely to have identified a fundamental issue that, if addressed, can prevent the recurrence of the immediate problem and potentially other related issues. This technique is handy for organizations looking to cultivate a culture of continuous improvement in their incident response activities.

 ## Threat Hunting

Threat hunting is a proactive cybersecurity approach that involves searching through networks and data sets to detect and isolate advanced threats that often evade traditional reactive security measures. The value of threat hunting lies in its ability to detect threats early and minimize potential damage. It also enhances adaptability, allowing your security measures to quickly adjust to new types of attacks. Threat hunting also contributes to the skill development of your cybersecurity team, making them more adept at identifying what to look for in future investigations.

To conduct effective threat hunting, you first need to define clear objectives. Knowing what you're looking for could range from signs of lateral movement within your network to unusual admin activities or even attempts at data exfiltration. Once objectives are set, data is aggregated from various sources, including logs, network traffic, and endpoints. The data is then analyzed using various tools and techniques, ranging from statistical models to machine learning algorithms or human intuition. When a potential threat is identified, it's isolated in a controlled environment for further study. The insights gained from this process feed back into improving future threat-hunting endeavors and updating existing security measures. For example, suppose you notice an unusual data transfer pattern from a specific endpoint in your organization and find a piece of malware that was missed by your antivirus software. In this case, you've successfully hunted a threat that could have led to data exfiltration.

Digital Forensics

Digital forensics is a multidisciplinary approach to uncovering, analyzing, and pre-serving electronic evidence in investigations or legal proceedings. It encompasses a range of specialized activities, each with its own set of procedures, best practices, and legal considerations. This section delves into the specifics of legal hold, chain of custody, acquisition, reporting, preservation, and e-discovery, each of which is a cornerstone of a robust digital forensics strategy.

Legal Hold

Legal hold is the process of preserving electronically stored information that could be relevant to a legal matter or an investigation. It's not just about hitting the "save" button; it involves taking a formal action that prevents the alteration or deletion of specific data. For example, if an employee is suspected of leaking sensitive information, a legal hold would be placed on their email and chat records to ensure that no one, not even the IT department, can tamper with that potential evidence until the investigation is complete.

Chain of Custody

For evidence to be credible in court, you must follow strict rules. Following the proper chain of custody consistently and methodically has been challenging due to the dynamic nature of digital evidence. Cyberattacks and cybercrimes are evolving, and the invincible nature of these attacks makes it difficult to gather evidence. Investigators are required to adapt to changing crime scenes and the digital media that has been used to commit these crimes. It has become imperative for standard procedures to be coherent and to ensure harmony between the legal parties involved.

NOTE   The *chain of custody* provides a clear record of the path that evidence takes from acquisition to disposal. It is often required in court proceedings to prove that evidence hasn't been tampered with.

Acquisition

Acquisition in digital forensics refers to systematic collection of digital evidence from various sources to ensure its integrity for analysis and potential legal proceedings. Digital data acquisition is not merely a data dump; it's a meticulous operation that adheres to specific protocols and guidelines, such as RFC 3227, to maintain the authenticity and reliability of the evidence.

Imagine that your organization has just experienced a ransomware attack. Here's how you might go about acquiring evidence:

- **Order of volatility:** Start by capturing the contents of the CPU cache and registers, as this data is highly volatile. By following the guidelines provided in RFC 3227, you can ensure that you're adhering to industry standards, which adds credibility to your evidence collection process.

- **RAM:** Use specialized tools to capture the contents of RAM; for example, Volatility and Rekall follow industry standards and provide reliable results. Look for encryption keys or IP addresses that could point to the attacker's location.

- **Disk:** Using a forensic disk controller, create a bit-by-bit image of the affected hard drives. This type of image is crucial because it captures even the "slack space," or unused portions of the disk, which could contain remnants of valuable data.

- **Network logs:** Use network forensic analysis tools (NFATs) such as Wireshark or tcpdump to capture network traffic and logs. Focus on unusual outbound connections that could indicate data exfiltration.

- **Artifacts:** Look for unfamiliar files or changes in system settings. For example, unexpected changes in registry keys or unauthorized user accounts could be indicators of compromise.

Understanding each facet of the acquisition process is not just a procedural necessity; it's a cornerstone for building a resilient cybersecurity infrastructure. Here's why each component holds significant value:

- **Maintaining evidence integrity:** The sequence in which you collect data, especially volatile data, can make or break the credibility of your evidence. If the data is compromised, it becomes less reliable for forensic analysis and may even be inadmissible in legal proceedings.

- **Comprehensive analysis:** Each component, from RAM to disk to network logs, provides a different piece of the puzzle. Missing out on any of these could mean overlooking critical information that could help identify vulnerabilities or trace back to an attacker.

- **Resource optimization:** Knowing what to acquire helps focus your resources where they are most needed, which is especially crucial in large organizations where resources are often limited. For instance, if an attack vector is identified early in the RAM or disk, you can allocate more resources to those areas for more in-depth analysis.

- **Legal compliance and standards adherence:** Following a structured acquisition process ensures that you comply with legal requirements and industry standards. This safeguards the organization from legal repercussions and sets a high standard for cybersecurity measures.

- **Enhanced preparedness for future incidents:** A well-executed acquisition process is a blueprint for future incident responses. It helps identify what worked and what didn't, allowing for iterative improvements in your cybersecurity protocols.

- **Building stakeholder confidence:** Meticulous adherence to the acquisition process sends a message to stakeholders—management, customers, or regulatory bodies—that your organization is committed to maintaining the highest cybersecurity standards.

- **Facilitating interdepartmental collaboration:** A structured acquisition process often involves multiple departments, from IT to legal to compliance. The IT department handles the technical aspects, the legal department ensures compliance with laws, and the compliance department ensures adherence to industry standards. This collaboration fosters shared responsibility, which is invaluable in maintaining an organizationwide cybersecurity ethos.

By understanding the value and implications of each component in the acquisition process, you're not just collecting data but laying the foundation for a robust, compliant, and efficient cybersecurity framework that can adapt and improve over time. Your acquisition process can also be the deciding component with reliable evidence in any resulting litigation.

Reporting

Reporting is the documentation of all activities and findings throughout the forensic process. It serves as a record for internal review and can be a critical piece of evidence in court. A well-structured report includes a timeline of events, tools used, evidence found, and the steps taken during the investigation. Imagine a scenario where unauthorized access is detected on a company server. The forensic report would detail how the intrusion was discovered, what data was accessed, and the measures taken to prevent future breaches. This report would then be used to update security protocols and may be presented in court if legal action is taken against the perpetrator.

Preservation

Preservation involves safeguarding evidence from the moment it is identified until the end of its lifecycle. This involves creating a secure environment where the data can be stored, often in a tamper-evident manner. For instance, after identifying malware on a company laptop, a forensic analyst would isolate the device and make a bit-by-bit copy of the hard drive. This copy would then be stored in a secure, climate-controlled facility to maintain its integrity for future analysis or legal proceedings.

E-Discovery

E-discovery, or electronic discovery, involves identifying, collecting, and producing electronically stored information in response to a legal request. Unlike a general search, e-discovery is often subject to specific rules and protocols. For example, when a company requests specific emails from the other party during a corporate lawsuit, e-discovery professionals use specialized software to search, identify, and collect these emails, and they ensure that the emails are relevant and not privileged before handing them over.

Chapter Review Activities

Use the features in this section to study and review the topics in this chapter.

Review Key Topics

Review the most important topics in the chapter, noted with the Key Topic icon in the outer margin of the page. Table 21-3 lists these key topics and the page number on which each is found.

Table 21-3   Key Topics for Chapter 21

Key Topic Element	Description	Page Number
Figure 21-1	The Four Phases of the NIST Incident Response Lifecycle	493
Table 21-2	Risk Matrix	495
Section	Training	497
List	Tabletop exercise steps	499
Section	Root Cause Analysis	501
Section	Threat Hunting	502
List	Acquiring evidence	503

Define Key Terms

Define the following key terms from this chapter and check your answers in the glossary:

preparation, detection, analysis, containment, eradication, recovery, lessons learned, training, testing, tabletop exercise, simulation, root cause analysis, threat hunting, digital forensics, legal hold, chain of custody, acquisition, reporting, preservation, e-discovery

Review Questions

Answer the following review questions. Check your answers with the answer key in Appendix A.

1. Who is typically responsible for bridging the technical and nontechnical aspects of an incident response plan?

2. What is the main objective of role-based training in incident response?

3. Name an element that could be introduced during a simulation exercise to test a team's adaptability.

4. Why is root cause analysis considered crucial for effective resource allocation?

5. What is one key benefit of proactive threat hunting in cybersecurity?

6. What is the primary focus of digital forensics in the context of cybersecurity?

This chapter covers the following topics related to Objective 4.9 (Given a scenario, use data sources to support an investigation) of the CompTIA Security+ SY0-701 certification exam:

- Log data
- Data sources

CHAPTER 22

Using Data Sources to Support an Investigation

This chapter explores the various types of data sources that can be leveraged to support a cybersecurity investigation. It outlines the importance and utility of different kinds of log data, such as firewall logs, application logs, endpoint logs, and more. The chapter also explores other critical data sources, such as vulnerability scans, automated reports, dashboards, and packet captures. Each of these elements plays a vital role in painting a comprehensive picture during an investigation, aiding in everything from identifying vulnerabilities to tracking unauthorized access.

"Do I Know This Already?" Quiz

The "Do I Know This Already?" quiz enables you to assess whether you should read this entire chapter thoroughly or jump to the "Chapter Review Activities" section. If you are in doubt about your answers to these questions or your own assessment of your knowledge of the topics, read the entire chapter. Table 22-1 lists the major headings in this chapter and their corresponding "Do I Know This Already?" quiz questions. You can find the answers in Appendix A, "Answers to the 'Do I Know This Already?' Quizzes and Review Questions."

Table 22-1 "Do I Know This Already?" Section-to-Question Mapping

Foundation Topics Section	Questions
Log Data	1–3
Data Sources	4–7

CAUTION The goal of self-assessment is to gauge your mastery of the topics in this chapter. If you do not know the answer to a question or are only partially sure of the answer, you should mark that question as wrong for purposes of self-assessment. Giving yourself credit for an answer you correctly guess skews your self-assessment results and might provide you with a false sense of security.

1. What is the primary purpose of log data in cybersecurity?
   a. To provide a user interface
   b. To serve as a chronological record for troubleshooting and security monitoring
   c. To speed up network performance
   d. To serve as a backup for data

2. What type of information can you expect to find in endpoint logs?
   a. Network topology
   b. Activities on individual devices connected to the network
   c. SQL queries
   d. Business analytics

3. What do IPS/IDS logs specialize in?
   a. Identifying software updates
   b. Identifying potentially harmful activities within the network
   c. Monitoring employee productivity
   d. Managing cloud storage

4. What is the role of data sources in cybersecurity?
   a. To provide entertainment
   b. To collect, analyze, and present information supporting an investigation
   c. To serve as a backup solution
   d. To improve user experience

5. What is the primary focus of vulnerability scans?
   a. To identify weak points in the network
   b. To improve website SEO
   c. To manage employee payroll
   d. To facilitate video conferencing

6. What triggers the generation of automated reports?
   a. User requests
   b. Scheduled times or specific events

    c. Power outages

    d. Software updates

7. What tool is commonly used for packet captures?

    a. Microsoft Excel

    b. Adobe Photoshop

    c. Wireshark

    d. Google Analytics

Foundation Topics

Log Data

Log data refers to the systematically recorded information generated by software applications, operating systems, or hardware devices. This data captures various events, transactions, or activities within a system or network, serving as a chronological record that can be analyzed for troubleshooting, security monitoring, and compliance purposes. Log data is often crucial for investigations, as it can provide an immutable trail of system and user activities, helping to identify what happened, when it happened, and who was involved. The log data you collect from your systems and devices might seem pretty mundane; however, these logs could contain the precise evidence needed to investigate and successfully prosecute a crime. For log data to stand up in court as admissible evidence, you must put into place and operate with chain of custody in mind and take special precautions in collecting, handling, and storing the data. Many regulations, such as PCI DSS, HIPAA, and SOX, require the use of logs and log management. When set up properly and with due care, logs can provide an immutable fingerprint of system and user activity. In many cases, the logs tell a story about what really happened in an incident. They can tell what systems were involved, how the systems and people behaved, what information was accessed, who accessed it, and precisely when these activities took place. Due to the substantial volumes of log data generated in modern network environments, storage practices have evolved beyond traditional methods. While optical media like DVD-R was once standard, it is now an outdated approach due to its limited capacity and durability. Modern standards favor the use of high-capacity hard drives and cloud-based storage solutions. These methods offer enhanced scalability and resilience, which are crucial for handling extensive log records. Furthermore, cloud storage provides the benefits of remote accessibility and the potential for integration with advanced analytical tools.

Syslog is a standardized protocol used by various devices and systems to send event notification messages across an IP network to a syslog server. This protocol plays a critical role in the management and security of networks by enabling the centralized collection and storage of log data. These logs are essential for many operational tasks, including auditing, monitoring, troubleshooting, and analyzing to maintain system health and security.

Figure 22-1 illustrates syslog messages transmitted from network devices and servers to a centralized logging system. For instance, it shows how a mail server, specifically running postfix/smpd—indicative of a Linux host—has rejected a connection attempt because the host's identity information was unattainable. This is a practical example of how syslog can provide insights into network activities. Several visual syslog servers are available at no cost, with SolarWinds offering one such option.

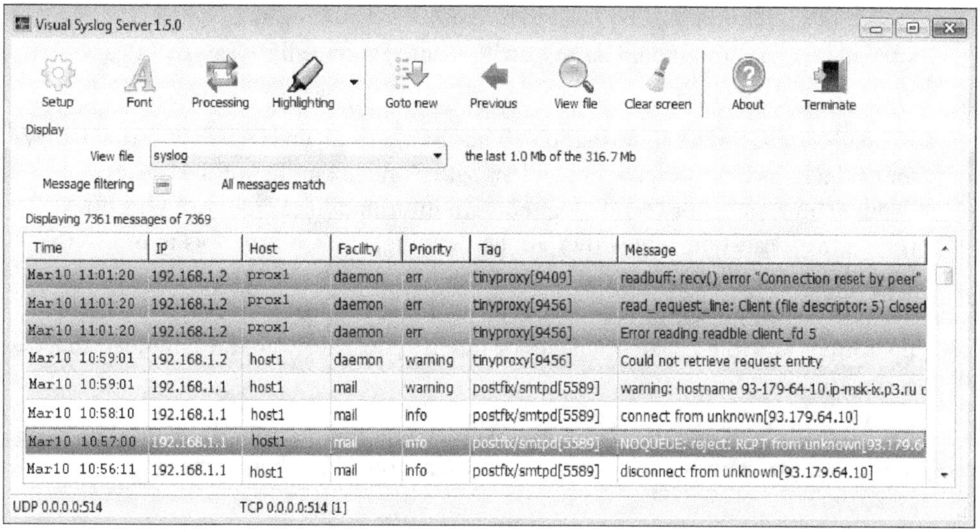

Figure 22-1   Visual Syslog Messages

Firewall Logs

Firewall logs are essential for monitoring the traffic allowed or denied through a network's firewall. These logs can reveal unauthorized attempts to access the network and help in understanding the traffic patterns that are typical for the organization. For example, a firewall log might show that an IP address from a foreign country attempted to connect to your server multiple times within a short period, which could be a sign of a potential attack.

Here's an example of part of a firewall log:

```
2023-09-23 14:32:10 ALLOW TCP 192.168.1.2 8.8.8.8 443 80
2023-09-23 14:32:11 DENY TCP 203.0.113.42 192.168.1.2 22 6000
```

The first entry in this example indicates that a device within the network (192.168.1.2) was allowed to connect to an external server (8.8.8.8) over HTTPS (port 443). The second entry shows that an external IP address (203.0.113.42) attempted to connect to an internal device on SSH port 22 and was denied. If port 22 is not supposed to be publicly accessible, this entry serves as an alert for a possible security issue that requires immediate action, such as blocking the suspicious IP address.

Application Logs

Application logs contain records of services, events, and systems within an application, providing near end-to-end visibility. The processes for implementing, managing, and reporting application logging need to be configured and reviewed before, during, and after an incident. You should parse, partition, and analyze all logs and data generated by an application.

Logged critical process information about user, system, and web application behavior can help incident responders build a better understanding of the breadth and depth of an attack. Application logs contain information related to applications run on the local system, how they are performing, and any attempts to utilize the applications. Depending on the level of logging, the logs can help in determining whether users exposed an unknown flaw in application programming or whether they attempted to escalate privileges or modify data they were not intended to have access to.

Figure 22-2 shows the interface of the Windows Event Viewer, a tool used to view logs about program, security, and system events on a Windows system.

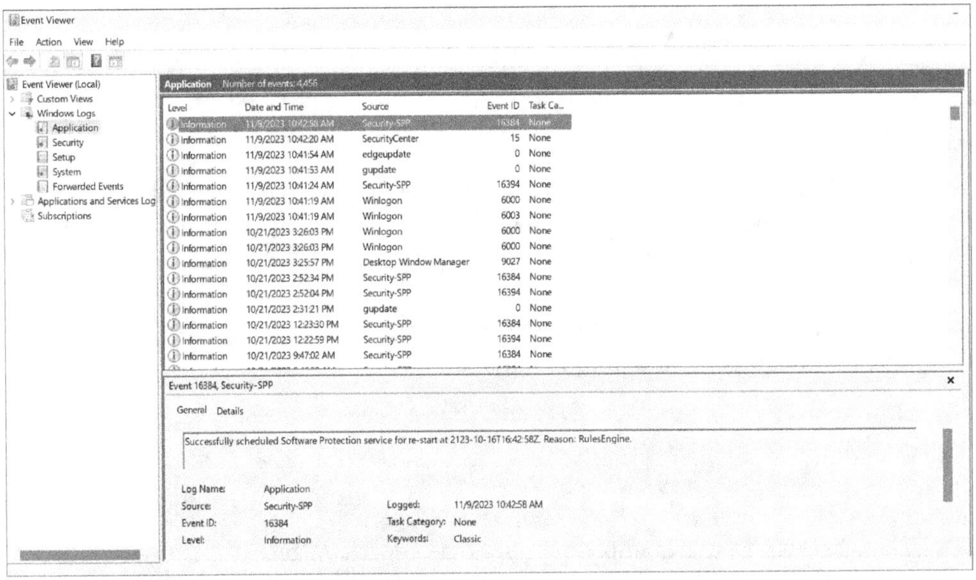

Figure 22-2   Windows Application Log Viewer

In the left sidebar, you see several categories under Windows Logs, indicating the different types of logs that can be reviewed, including Application, Security, Setup, System, and Forwarded Events. Each of these sections holds logs related to a specific area of the Windows operating system.

The main pane displays a list of individual events under the Application category. Each entry shows the level of the event (for example, Information), the date and time when the event was logged, the source (that is, the program or component that logged the event), the event ID (which is a unique identifier for each type of event), and the task category (which can sometimes provide more details about the event).

At the bottom of the screen is a detailed view for a selected event; for example, in Figure 22-2, it's for Event ID 16384 from the Security-SPP source. The description provides specific information about the event—in this case, "Successfully scheduled Software Protection service for restart at 2123-10-16T16:42:58Z. Reason: Rules-Engine." This description gives you insight into what occurred (in this case, that a service was scheduled to restart at a given time).

Endpoint Logs

Endpoint logs provide detailed information about activities on individual devices, such as computers and smartphones, that are connected to a network. These logs can help you identify suspicious or unauthorized behavior, such as the installation of unauthorized software or attempts to access restricted files. For instance, an endpoint log might reveal that a user attempted to install software that's not on the approved list, triggering a security alert.

Here's an example of part of an endpoint log:

```
2023-09-23 14:35:00 User "JohnDoe" initiated "New_Outbound_
Connection" to IP "203.0.113.42" on Port "8080"
2023-09-23 14:36:00 User "JohnDoe" executed "Unknown_
Application.exe"
```

The first entry in this example indicates that a user named JohnDoe initiated an outbound connection to an external IP address on port 8080. The second entry shows that the same user executed an application that was not recognized by the system's security software. Such entries can be invaluable for tracing unauthorized or suspicious activities. For instance, if Unknown_Application.exe is not a sanctioned application, this could be a sign of malware or unauthorized software installation that needs to be investigated further.

OS-Specific Security Logs

Operating system (OS)–specific security logs are all about the capabilities of the specific system you are trying to obtain logs from. Each system that has logs also refers to specific system messages that contain log records for the operating system events. Many of them show how system processes and drivers were loaded, errors that occurred during loading, and any failures that have occurred. In Windows, there are a few areas to obtain logs. For example, you can use the Event Viewer to collect .evt and .evtx files from other Windows-based machines. You can even sort by event ID and perform filtering and exporting. The Windows Admin Center can provide events from Event Viewer as well and allows you to export them.

On Linux hosts, log files are mostly contained in the /var/log directory. You should make it a regular process to collect these logs and store them as you would with other devices. Application, system, and security logs should be stored off-host when possible. Monitoring system logs provides proactive monitoring and helps you build a complete picture when an incident occurs; it helps you determine which systems were accessed and when, what files were accessed, which applications were installed, and whether the integrity of the system was compromised and how.

Figure 22-3 shows the Windows Event Viewer, where you can clearly see the event ID, level of logging, and type of message. Here, four types of messages are displayed: Warning, Critical, Information, and Error. Information messages are typically from the operating system to let you know that it performed some action like allowing a process to start. Errors are generated when processes fail to start. Critical messages indicate some serious failure, such as a system not shutting down properly. Warning messages are normal; Windows handles all of these events and recovers without any user intervention.

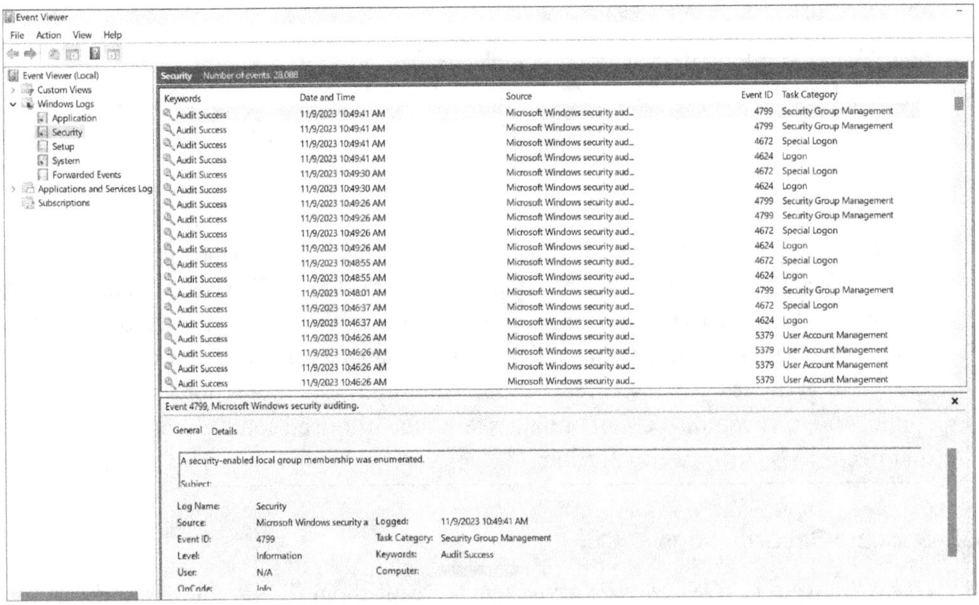

Figure 22-3 Windows Security Log Viewer

Figure 22-3 also shows a view of the Security section of the Windows Event Viewer interface, which is pivotal for security monitoring and incident response activities. The panel in this example is populated with security events and indicates Audit Success for each of them, which signifies the successful execution of monitored activities, such as user authentications or policy access checks. These logs are crucial for identifying patterns pointing to security threats or verifying compliance with security policies.

Each entry details the timestamped date and time when the event was recorded, the source of the event, which typically references the security component of Windows, the unique event ID for the particular security event, and the task Category, which includes subcategories such as Logon, Special Logon, and User Account Management.

Highlighted at the bottom is an event with the ID 4799, which details that security-enabled local group membership was enumerated. This action is typically performed to review group policies or access rights, which could be routine or part of a security audit. The timestamp and the fact that it's an audit success suggest that the action was expected and permitted.

This portion of the Event Viewer serves as an essential audit trail, capturing each security-related event, enabling system administrators to maintain oversight over security-relevant operations, and ensuring that any anomalous activities can be detected and investigated promptly.

The system log records error messages, warnings, and other information generated from the Windows operating system. It provides a wealth of information on what is going on with the system. System log records can also help you determine if, when, or where a user attempted to log in and failed, what user ID was used, and what IP address it came from.

IPS/IDS Logs

Key Topic

Intrusion prevention system (IPS) and intrusion detection system (IDS) logs are specialized records that identify potentially harmful activities within a network. These logs are generated by an IPS or IDS solutions, such as Snort or Suricata, and can alert you to various attacks, such as SQL injections or cross-site scripting. Let's review what a potential IPS/IDS log entry would look like and break down the information.

Here's an example of part of an IPS/IDS log:

```
2023-09-23 13:45:32 ALERT SQL Injection detected from
192.168.1.4
2023-09-23 13:46:10 ALERT Brute-force attempt from 203.0.113.7
```

The first entry in this example indicates that an SQL injection attack originating from the IP address 192.168.1.4 was detected. This serious alert warrants immediate investigation, as SQL injections can lead to unauthorized access to sensitive data.

The second entry shows a brute-force login attempt from the IP address 203.0.113.7. This is another red flag that could indicate an attacker is trying to gain unauthorized access, and it should be promptly addressed to prevent a potential breach.

Network Logs

Network logs capture data traffic that traverses the network infrastructure. These logs, which can be generated by network monitoring tools like Wireshark or Solar-Winds, provide insights into bandwidth usage, connection times, and the types of protocols being used. Let's take a look at a network log example.

Here's an example of part of a network log:

```
2023-09-23 14:20:15 INFO TCP Connection from 192.168.1.2 to
8.8.4.4
2023-09-23 14:21:00 WARNING Large data transfer to 203.0.113.8
```

The first entry in this example documents a standard TCP connection from an internal IP address, 192.168.1.2, to an external IP address, 8.8.4.4, which is often used for DNS resolution. This is generally considered normal traffic and may not require immediate attention. However, the second entry warns about a large data transfer to an external IP address, 203.0.113.8. This could be a sign of data exfiltration and should be investigated immediately to ensure that sensitive information is not leaked.

Metadata

Metadata is created from every activity you perform, whether it's on a personal computer or online, including every email, web search, and social or public application and interaction. *Metadata* is data that provides information about other data. There are many distinct types of metadata. On its own, it may have little or no relevance to an investigation. However, when metadata is used with other types of data and sources, the result can help you conduct an investigation.

Metadata security involves practice and policies designed to protect an organization from security risks posed by unauthorized access to the organization's metadata. Even metadata from Microsoft Word documents contains the names of authors and modifiers, dates of creation, and changes and file sizes. Metadata poses a risk of disclosure of private information, usually unknowingly, because metadata is hidden from plain view, and users may be unaware of it. It's likely that those outside your company shouldn't have access to this information.

There are several types of metadata you should be aware of. The first is descriptive metadata, which refers to elements like titles, dates, and keywords. For instance, when you download a video file, it contains metadata describing what the video is about as well as the name and date. With books, descriptive metadata includes book titles, author names, dates, pages, and key data locations.

Another form of metadata, structural metadata, provides information concerning a specific object or resource. Structural metadata records information on how a particular object or resource might be sorted. For example, with digital media (film on DVD, for example), each section has a certain film running time length.

Preservation metadata provides information that strengthens the entire process of making a digital file (object). This includes vital details required for a system to communicate or interact with a specific file and upholds the integrity of a digital file or object. Preservation Metadata: Implementation Strategies (PREMIS) mode is a preservation metadata standard for common factors such as actions taken on a digital file or the rights attached to it.

Use metadata is data that is sorted each time a user accesses and uses a specific piece of digital data. Use metadata is gathered in a clear and direct attempt to make potentially helpful predictions about a user's future behavior. This type of metadata can be used to understand fluctuations in data that have no pattern when there is really a pattern beneath the data.

There are even more types of metadata, including provenance metadata. This type of metadata is most relevant when something changes or is duplicated frequently, such as in the digital realm, where there are frequent changes. Administrative metadata informs users what types of instructions, rules, and restrictions are placed on a file. This information helps administrators limit access to files based on user qualifications.

Cell phones hold a ton of metadata. For example, the pictures you take provide GPS coordinates, the date and time the photo was taken, the language, the camera type, the flash setting, and more. From the coordinates of an image you post to Instagram, to metadata from emails, and public and private social media applications you use, to airline tickets and rental car details, your phone is a treasure trove of information.

Figure 22-4 shows metadata that can be accessed for a Microsoft Word file. By right-clicking the file and looking at the properties under Details, you can see the title, authors, subject, tags, and comments. Notice the Remove Properties and Personal Information link at the bottom; by clicking it, you can remove certain personal information.

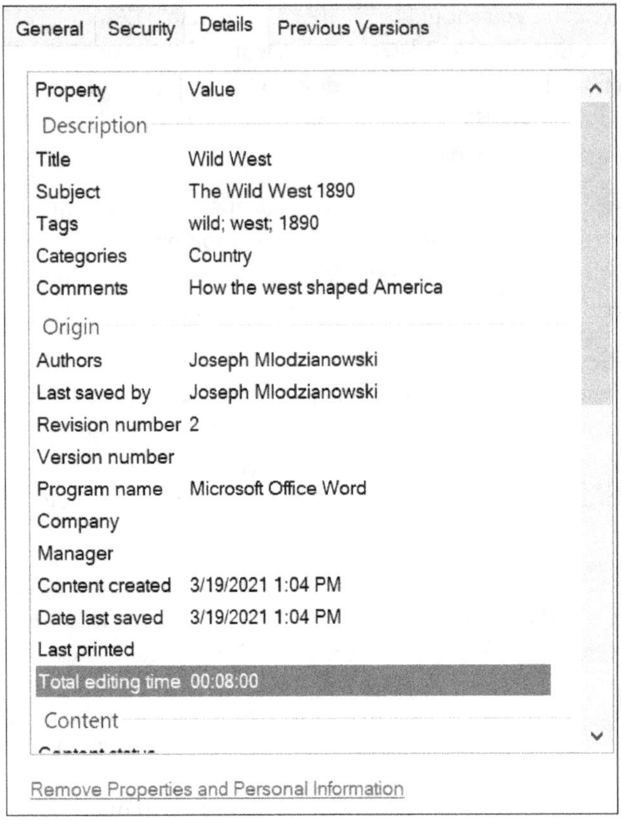

Figure 22-4   Metadata in a Microsoft Word File

Figure 22-5 shows an email header's metadata about an email message received from Hulu at hulumail.com. As you can see, this message provides email addresses for the server (Google server), how the email was handed off, and the path it took to get to my Gmail account (gmail email mx.google.com) server. So, grab some popcorn and look through the email headers to see what else you can find of interest.

NOTE   Metadata has proven to be very useful in regard to investigations, and practically everything digital contains metadata, including files, images, and email.

```
Delivered-To: josephml[REDACTED]
Received: by 2002:a0c:a909:0:0:0:0:0 with SMTP id y9csp66730qva;
        Sun, 21 Mar 2021 16:12:06 -0700 (PDT)
X-Google-Smtp-Source:
ABdhPJxQ8HrpkBG40Po3QMrmVkpiKtDAesu0AZC06KHsK5JvVpDeR3qr2ax581ruQifYBPjadTF8
X-Received: by 2002:a17:90b:2304:: with SMTP id mt4mr10546161pjb.179.1616368325904;
        Sun, 21 Mar 2021 16:12:05 -0700 (PDT)
Received-SPF: pass (google.com: domain of bounce-48_html-
587195878-4459521-1064447-76@bounce.hulumail.com designates 13.111.102.14 as permitted
sender) client-ip=13.111.102.14;
Authentication-Results: mx.google.com;
        dkim=pass header.i=@hulumail.com header.s=200608 header.b=JLJ9f2Oh;
        spf=pass (google.com: domain of bounce-48_html-
587195878-4459521-1064447-76@bounce.hulumail.com designates 13.111.102.14 as permitted
sender) smtp.mailfrom=bounce-48_HTML-587195878-4459521-1064447-76@bounce.hulumail.com;
        dmarc=pass (p=NONE sp=NONE dis=NONE) header.from=hulumail.com
DKIM-Signature: v=1; a=rsa-sha256; c=relaxed/relaxed; s=200608; d=hulumail.com;
h=From:To:Subject:Date:List-Unsubscribe:MIME-Version:Reply-To:List-ID: X-CSA-
Complaints:Message-ID:Content-Type; i=hulu@hulumail.com;
Received: by mta17.hulumail.com id hav9ca2fmd4p for <Josephm[REDACTED];
Sun, 21 Mar 2021 23:10:39 +0000 (envelope-from <bounce-48_HTML-
587195878-4459521-1064447-76@bounce.hulumail.com>)
From: Hulu <hulu@hulumail.com>
To: <Josephm[REDACTED]>
Subject: Grab Some Popcorn Joseph, New Movies Are Here 🍿
Date: Sun, 21 Mar 2021 17:10:39 -0600
List-Unsubscribe: <mailto:leave-fd7f10781a3c402029-fe15117872650d787d1378-
fe911074706d017f74-fe9515707360007972-ff921376@leave.hulumail.com>
MIME-Version: 1.0
Reply-To: Hulu <reply-fe911074706d017f74-48_HTML-587195878-1064447-76@hulumail.com>
List-ID: <1064447.xt.local>
X-CSA-Complaints: csa-complaints@eco.de
X-SFMC-Stack: 4
x-job: 1064447_4459521
Message-ID: <381a48a8-f826-4495-9ae5-40bc48256e48@las1s04mta1105.xt.local>
Feedback-ID: 1064447:4459521:13.111.102.14:sfmktgcld
Content-Type: multipart/alternative; boundary="kUCLh1WEWTlc=_?:"

--kUCLh1WEWTlc=_?:
Content-Type: text/plain; charset="utf-8"
Content-Transfer-Encoding: 8bit


Hulu



[{
"@context": "https://schema.org/",
"@type": "Organization",
"name": "Hulu",
```

Figure 22-5 Full Headers from a Gmail Email

Data Sources

Data sources are the various tools and methods used to collect, analyze, and present information that supports an investigation. These sources can range from vulnerability scans that identify weak points in a network to dashboards that provide real-time analytics. Understanding how to leverage these data sources effectively is crucial in a comprehensive approach to cybersecurity.

Vulnerability Scans

If there were no vulnerabilities in a network or computer system, there would be nothing to exploit, and the network attack surface would be greatly reduced. However, software vulnerabilities always exist and will continue to exist because applications are developed by people, and people make mistakes, all of which can allow attackers to compromise networks. *Vulnerability scans* are systematic examinations of networks, systems, or applications to identify and evaluate security weaknesses or flaws that attackers could exploit. These scans utilize specialized software tools to probe systems for known vulnerabilities, such as unpatched software, insecure configurations, and unprotected systems; they provide insights into potential security gaps that require remediation to strengthen the overall security posture. Running regular vulnerability scans is just the first step in your defensive posture. A network scan should include any devices that has an IP address—each workstation, laptop, printer, IoT device, router, switch, hub, IDS/IPS, server, wireless network, and firewall—and all the software running on each device. You should run both authenticated and unauthenticated scans because each type of scan provides insight into vulnerabilities found in services running on the network, open ports on devices that could allow malicious apps to run or communicate on them, and configurations or issues that affect security.

Vulnerability scan reports should be saved for at least 24 months, and certain regulations and industries require longer retention times. Some systems enable you to save these reports and compare them from month to month to get a better picture of your cybersecurity posture and improvements. Historical vulnerability scans can also provide significant insights after an incident. By comparing previous scans with the most recent ones, you can also look for variances in devices and systems that may have been changed. A change can be anything from additional TCP/UDP ports being shown as open to the detection of unauthorized software, scheduled events, or unrecognized outbound communications. When you find problems, you should make reimaging these devices a top priority.

Figure 22-6 shows basic vulnerability scan results from my internal network, 1.1.100.0/24, showing two certificate issues as medium-level threats. Vulnerability reports are perfect for engaging several departments in your organization, getting them involved and responsible for the overall posture.

Automated Reports

Automated reports serve as your eyes and ears within a network, offering a synthesized view of various security metrics and events. These reports are often generated by security information and event management (SIEM) systems such as Splunk or IBM QRadar. They can be configured to run on a daily or weekly schedule or can be triggered by specific events. Imagine receiving an automated report highlighting 15 failed login attempts from a single IP address within a 10-minute window. This could be a red flag indicating a brute-force attack attempt. Another report might alert you to three large data transfers to an external IP address within a short time frame, raising suspicions of potential data exfiltration. Automated reports like these enable you to spot irregularities and take corrective action swiftly, thereby minimizing the risk and impact of security incidents.

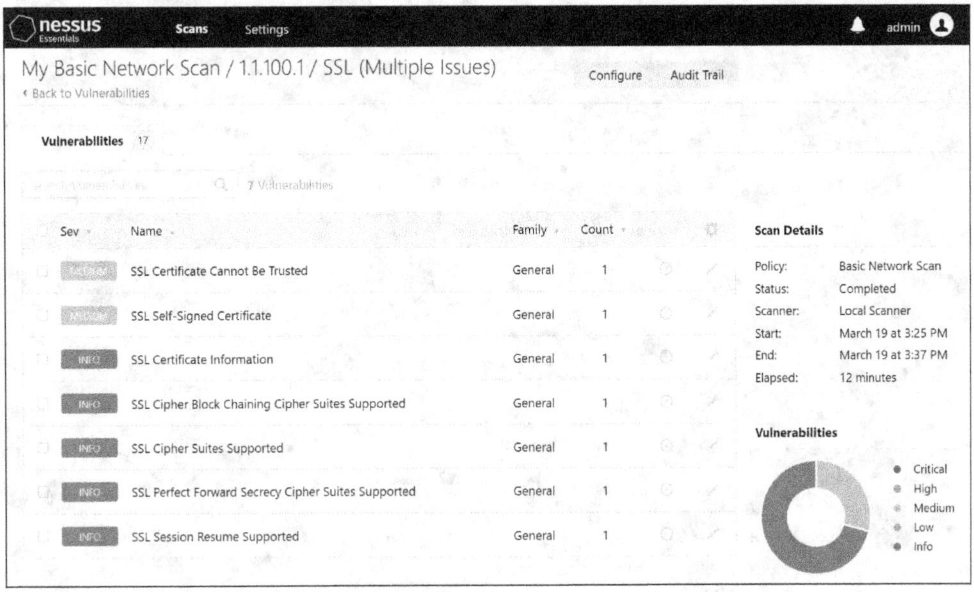

Figure 22-6   Vulnerability Scan Report

Dashboards

A *dashboard* is a user interface that organizes and presents information in an easy-to-read format, often using graphs, charts, and gauges. This centralized display aggregates data from multiple sources, providing a real-time overview of an organization's network and security status, allowing for prompt responses to threats and efficient monitoring of system health and performance. Dashboards are pivotal in managing the complex flow of information in cybersecurity operations. SIEM software works by collecting logs and event data generated by an organization's applications, security devices, and host systems and bringing it together into a single centralized platform, allowing companies to identify threats in real time. A SIEM system gathers data from antivirus events, firewall logs, and other locations and sorts this data into categories. When the SIEM system identifies a threat through network security monitoring, it generates an alert and defines a threat level based on predetermined rules.

The SIEM dashboard in Figure 22-7 provides a quick reference to the top threats that require security analyst attention. The section Alarms by Day Past 30 Days enables the analyst to trend network performance on threats. Top Classification shows types of active attacks in the last nine hours. Top Host (Origin) shows who is attacking and from where, as well as hosts impacted by attacks.

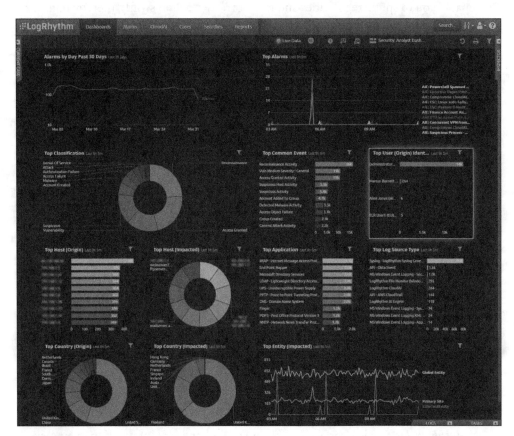

Figure 22-7   SIEM Dashboard

TIP   SIEM systems normalize and aggregate collected data. Log aggregation is the process by which SIEM systems combine similar events to reduce event volume.

NOTE   A SIEM dashboard contains multiple views that allow you to visualize and monitor patterns and trends. The intent of a SIEM dashboard is to give you a single pane of glass to view your network's or system's status and condition.

Packet Captures

Packet captures offer a granular view of network activity. Tools like Wireshark are commonly used to capture detailed data packets transmitted over a network. Say that you're reviewing a Wireshark capture, and you see a series of packets like this:

```
No. Time        Source          Destination   Protocol  Info
1   0.000000   192.168.1.2     8.8.4.4        TCP       80 > 443
[SYN] Seq=0 Win=5840 Len=0 MSS=1460
2   0.000200   8.8.4.4         192.168.1.2    TCP       443 > 80
[SYN, ACK] Seq=0 Ack=1 Win=5792 Len=0 MSS=1460
3   0.000400   192.168.1.2     8.8.4.4        TCP       80 > 443
[ACK] Seq=1 Ack=1 Win=5840 Len=0
4   0.001000   192.168.1.3     203.0.113.8    UDP       Source port:
5060   Destination port: 5060
```

The first three packets in this example show a typical TCP handshake between the source IP address 192.168.1.2 and the destination IP address 8.8.4.4. This is generally considered normal traffic. However, the fourth packet shows UDP traffic from the source IP address 192.168.1.3 to the external IP address 203.0.113.8. This UDP traffic could be especially interesting, as UDP is often used for streaming and might also indicate data exfiltration. Understanding the nuances of packet capture, as in this Wireshark example, can help you detect anomalies or malicious activities that might otherwise go unnoticed.

Chapter Review Activities

Use the features in this section to study and review the topics in this chapter.

Review Key Topics

Review the most important topics in the chapter, noted with the Key Topic icon in the outer margin of the page. Table 22-2 lists these key topics and the page number on which each is found.

Table 22-2   Key Topics for Chapter 22

Key Topic Element	Description	Page Number
Figure 22-2	Windows Application Log Viewer	514
Figure 22-3	Windows Security Log Viewer	516
Section	IPS/IDS Logs	517
Paragraph	Data sources	521
Paragraph	Packet capture example	525

Define Key Terms

Define the following key terms from this chapter and check your answers in the glossary:

log data, firewall log, application log, endpoint log, operating system (OS)–specific security log, intrusion prevention system (IPS) and intrusion detection system (IDS) logs, network log, metadata, data source, vulnerability scan, automated report, dashboard, packet capture

Review Questions

Answer the following review questions. Check your answers with the answer key in Appendix A.

1. What is necessary to have log data stand up in court as admissible evidence?

2. How do endpoint logs contribute to identifying unauthorized behavior?

3. What types of attacks might IPS/IDS logs alert you to?

4. How do vulnerability scans contribute to a network's defensive posture?

5. What kind of events could trigger an automated report in a SIEM system?

6. What is the utility of packet captures in understanding network activity?

This chapter covers the following topics related to Objective 5.1 (Summarize elements of effective security governance) of the CompTIA Security+ SY0-701 certification exam:

- Guidelines
- Policies
- Standards
- Procedures
- External considerations
- Monitoring and revision
- Types of governance structures
- Roles and responsibilities for systems and data

CHAPTER 23

Summarizing Elements of Effective Security Governance

This chapter provides a comprehensive overview of effective security governance, starting with the foundational elements of guidelines and policies. It delves into specialized policies such as business continuity and disaster recovery policies and outlines the importance of policies covering password and access control. The chapter also discusses procedural aspects, including change management and onboarding/offboarding, and explores the influence of external factors like regulatory and legal considerations. It concludes by examining various governance structures and the roles and responsibilities associated with systems and data.

"Do I Know This Already?" Quiz

The "Do I Know This Already?" quiz enables you to assess whether you should read this entire chapter thoroughly or jump to the "Chapter Review Activities" section. If you are in doubt about your answers to these questions or your own assessment of your knowledge of the topics, read the entire chapter. Table 23-1 lists the major headings in this chapter and their corresponding "Do I Know This Already?" quiz questions. You can find the answers in Appendix A, "Answers to the 'Do I Know This Already?' Quizzes and Review Questions."

Table 23-1 "Do I Know This Already?" Section-to-Question Mapping

Foundation Topics Section	Questions
Guidelines	1
Policies	2
Standards	3
Procedures	4
External Considerations	5
Monitoring and Revision	6
Types of Governance Structures	7
Roles and Responsibilities for Systems and Data	8

CAUTION   The goal of self-assessment is to gauge your mastery of the topics in this chapter. If you do not know the answer to a question or are only partially sure of the answer, you should mark that question as wrong for purposes of self-assessment. Giving yourself credit for an answer you correctly guess skews your self-assessment results and might provide you with a false sense of security.

1. What is the primary purpose of guidelines in an organization's security governance?

   a. To mandate specific actions

   b. To provide general recommendations

   c. To implement policies

   d. To define access controls

2. Which of the following best describes a policy in the context of IT and cybersecurity?

   a. A step-by-step instruction

   b. A general recommendation

   c. A formal, high-level statement

   d. A specific standard

3. What is the main focus of access control standards?

   a. To provide general recommendations

   b. To define who gets to access what

   c. To implement policies

   d. To monitor and revise security measures

4. What are procedures designed to do?

   a. Provide general recommendations

   b. Monitor and revise security measures

   c. Implement policies and standards

   d. Define who gets to access what

5. What do external considerations influence?

   a. Internal policies only

   b. Security governance

   c. Access control standards

   d. Procedures

6. What is a key component of monitoring and revision in security governance?

   a. Regularly reviewing logs and conducting audits

   b. Implementing new policies

   c. Providing general recommendations

   d. Defining who gets to access what

7. What is a characteristic of a centralized governance structure?

   a. Slower decision-making processes

   b. Multiple points of failure

   c. Decision-making authority at the top levels

   d. Tailored to unique departmental needs

8. Which of the following responsibilities of a processor pertains to ensuring the safeguarding of data through technical means?

   a. Data handling

   b. Security implementation

   c. Data accuracy

   d. Compliance

Foundation Topics

Guidelines

As you navigate the world of cybersecurity, understanding governance is crucial. Governance is the glue that holds all your security practices together, ensuring that they align with the organization's objectives. In this section, we'll kick things off by diving into guidelines.

Guidelines are general recommendations that aim to steer organizational behavior and decision making. They're more relaxed than policies or standards but provide helpful directional advice. For instance, guidelines can offer suggestions on best practices for secure coding, handling of sensitive data, or responses to common security incidents. Let's take a look at a few examples of guidelines so you can see how they are different from policies.

Consider these examples of guidelines:

Key Topic

- "Employees are strongly encouraged to lock their computers when stepping away from their desks. This simple action can deter unauthorized access."

- "It's highly recommended to enable two-factor authentication (2FA) for all corporate accounts. While not mandatory, 2FA adds an extra layer of security that can significantly reduce the risk of account compromise."

- "When developing software, consider implementing secure coding practices from the outset. Although this guideline is not enforced, adhering to it can minimize vulnerabilities in the final product."

Guidelines offer flexibility, allowing employees and departments some leeway in implementing security measures. You can see this in the use of phrases like "strongly recommended" and "highly recommended" instead of "you must." Guidelines are handy for hard-and-fast rules that need to be more practical. You can think of guidelines as your organization's best practices "wish list" that helps shape its proactive security culture.

Policies

A *policy* in the context of IT and cybersecurity is a formal, high-level statement or plan that outlines an organization's general beliefs, goals, objectives, and acceptable procedures for a specified subject area. Policies are essential for setting the organizational approach to various issues and are usually mandated by management or regulatory bodies.

Most organizations have policies governing various aspects in the business, including employee behavior and emergency procedures. The breadth and scope of policies can vary significantly. For instance, a small company might have a simple code of ethics, while a larger organization might certify to a particular standard, like ISO 9001:2015, which involves a rigorous process to show compliance with a comprehensive set of quality standards.

As someone involved in IT, your primary interest lies in policies securing the infrastructure and its users. In your role, you may collaborate with procedural documentation specialists, technical documentation specialists, and even external consultants. It's crucial to familiarize yourself with as many relevant policies and procedures as possible, particularly those focusing on security. However, it's essential to remember that while policies provide the framework, implementing and maintaining security must take precedence.

Now let's explore some common types of policies that focus on the security aspect of a business.

Acceptable Use

An *acceptable use policy (AUP)* defines the rules that restrict how a computer, network, or other system may be used. It states what users are and are not allowed to do when it comes to the technology infrastructure of an organization. Employees must often sign an AUP before they begin working on any systems. This policy protects the organization and also defines for employees exactly what they should and should not be working on. If a director asks a particular employee to repair a particular system that was outside the AUP parameters, the employee would know to refuse. If employees are found to be working on a system that is outside the scope of their work, and they signed an AUP, this is grounds for termination. As part of an AUP, employees enter into an agreement acknowledging they understand that the unauthorized sharing of data is prohibited. Also, employees should understand that they are not to take any information or equipment home without express permission from the various parties listed in the policy. Such a policy can sometimes be in conflict with a bring-your-own-device (BYOD) policy, where users are permitted to bring their own devices to work and use them for work purposes. Therefore, strong policies for data ownership need to be developed, identifying what portion of the data on a mobile device is owned by the organization and what portion is owned by the employee. Any organizational data on a mobile device should be backed up.

Information Security Policies

Information security policies are the backbone of an organization's cybersecurity posture. *Information security policies* outline the guidelines and procedures for protecting the organization's data and technology assets. They cover a range of topics, from data classification and encryption to network security protocols. For example, an information security policy might specify that all sensitive data must be encrypted in transit and at rest. These policies are often reviewed and updated regularly to adapt to emerging threats and compliance requirements.

Table 23-2 lists common information security policies you might encounter in a midsized company. As you look through the list, remember that these policies need to be updated constantly, and version control must be applied to ensure that users access the most recent copy of each policy.

Key Topic

Table 23-2   Examples of Information Security Policies

Policy Name	Description	Example Requirement
Data classification policy	Defines how data is categorized based on sensitivity.	All sensitive customer data must be labeled "Confidential" and encrypted.
Access control policy	Specifies who can access what resources and under what conditions.	Two-factor authentication is required for accessing any financial systems.
Network security policy	Outlines the configurations and security measures for network devices and infrastructure.	Firewalls must be configured to block all incoming traffic that is not explicitly required for business.
Endpoint security policy	Sets the security standards for individual devices like computers, smartphones, and tablets.	All endpoints must have updated antivirus software installed.
Encryption policy	Details the methods and protocols for encrypting data at rest, in transit, and during processing.	AES-256 encryption must be used for all data at rest.
Incident response policy	Describes the steps to take when a security incident occurs.	Incidents must be reported to the security team within 30 minutes of discovery.
Remote work policy	Sets the rules for employees who work outside the office.	VPNs must be used when accessing company resources remotely.
Password policy	Specifies the requirements for creating, managing, and storing passwords.	Passwords must be at least 12 characters long and include a mix of letters, numbers, and symbols.
Software update policy	Governs how software updates and patches are managed.	Critical security patches must be applied within 48 hours of release.
Compliance policy	Ensures that the organization meets all legal and regulatory requirements.	Regular audits must be conducted to ensure compliance with GDPR.

Business Continuity

A *business continuity policy* serves as a blueprint for maintaining essential operations in the face of unexpected disruptions. This type of policy is comprehensive, covering a range of scenarios from natural disasters to cyberattacks, and aims to minimize downtime and financial loss while ensuring the safety of personnel.

For example, a company's business continuity policy might specify that all critical data must be backed up daily to an on-site server and a geographically distant cloud storage service. This dual backup strategy ensures that if one backup fails or becomes inaccessible, the other can be used to restore operations. The policy could also mandate identification and prioritization of business-critical functions and associated technologies. This helps the organization focus its recovery efforts where needed, ensuring that the most crucial operations are restored first.

Another key element might be establishing an alternate work location with the infrastructure necessary to support the company's critical functions. Employees should be trained on transitioning to this location, and regular drills might be conducted to test the feasibility and efficiency of moving operations.

A business continuity policy might include a communication plan that details how employees will be notified of an incident and how to communicate with stakeholders during a crisis. This could involve a cascade calling system, where key personnel are informed first, and they then notify their respective teams, ensuring rapid dissemination of critical information.

The business continuity policy should also outline the roles and responsibilities during an incident, such as who is authorized to declare a disaster, who should be contacted for different types of incidents, and who is responsible for executing various components of the plan.

Disaster Recovery

A *disaster recovery policy* is a subset of a business continuity policy that focuses specifically on restoring IT infrastructure and operations after a crisis. A disaster recovery policy details the procedures for data recovery, system restoration, and other technical steps necessary to resume normal operations. For example, a disaster recovery policy might specify the use of off-site data storage and define the roles and responsibilities of the disaster recovery team.

Incident Response

An *incident response policy* outlines the procedures to follow when a cybersecurity incident occurs. This type of policy specifies who should be notified, how the incident should be contained, and the steps for eradicating the threat. For instance, an incident response policy might require immediate isolation of affected systems and timely notification of the organization's legal and public relations teams.

Software Development Lifecycle (SDLC)

A *software development lifecycle (SDLC) policy* governs the entire software development process, from inception to decommissioning. This type of policy is crucial for ensuring that software is developed in a manner that incorporates security and quality at every phase. Such a policy typically includes guidelines for requirements gathering, design, coding, testing, deployment, maintenance, and eventual software retirement.

For example, an SDLC policy at a midsized company might stipulate that all new software projects must undergo security risk assessment during the requirements-gathering phase to ensure that potential vulnerabilities are identified early, allowing for proactive mitigation strategies.

Another common requirement could be code reviews. An SDLC policy might mandate that all code be peer reviewed for security vulnerabilities before the testing phase. This adds an extra layer of scrutiny and helps catch issues that automated testing tools might miss. The policy could specify that all software must pass a suite of security tests before being deployed into the production environment. These tests could include penetration testing, vulnerability scanning, and compliance checks against industry standards such as the OWASP Top 10.

Finally, an SDLC policy might require that any third-party libraries or components used in the software be vetted for security vulnerabilities and comply with the company's licensing policies.

Change Management

A *change management policy* guides how changes to IT systems and processes are proposed, reviewed, and implemented. Such a policy aims to minimize disruptions and reduce the risks associated with changes. For instance, a change management policy might require formal approval from a review board and post-implementation monitoring to ensure no adverse effects on system stability or security.

Standards

In IT and cybersecurity, *standards* are established requirements or rules that describe the specific methods and practices to be followed. They are more detailed than policies and serve as the technical and operational how-to's for implementing the high-level guidelines outlined in policies. Standards ensure that everyone in an organization is on the same page regarding security measures, creating a more secure and efficient environment. This section delves into some key standards that are commonly implemented in midsized to large organizations.

Password Standards

Password standards are the cornerstone of an organization's access control strategy, setting forth the rules for creating, managing, and storing passwords. Password standards are essential for an effective access control strategy, ensuring that password creation, management, and protection are handled in such a way as to prevent unauthorized access. National Institute of Standards and Technology (NIST) SP 800-63B offers guidelines on digital identity and is useful when establishing baseline password standards.

According to NIST SP 800-63B, password standards might include the following:

- **Minimum length:** Passwords must be at least 12 characters long to resist attacks.

- **Complexity:** Passwords should include a mix of uppercase and lowercase letters, numbers, and special characters, providing sufficient complexity to resist attacks.

- **Expiration:** Passwords must be changed at regular intervals, though NIST SP 800-63B advises against arbitrary periodic changes unless there is a user request or evidence of a breach.

- **History:** To avoid the reuse of potentially compromised credentials, users should not reuse their last 10 passwords.

- **Lockout policy:** Following a series of unsuccessful login attempts, accounts should be temporarily locked to prevent brute-force attacks.

- **Two-factor authentication (2FA):** A second verification method should be used along with the password for enhanced security.

NIST SP 800-63B also includes these additional guidelines:

- **Salting:** When passwords are stored using cryptographic hashes, a unique salt should be added to each password to prevent attackers from using precomputed tables (rainbow tables) to crack the hashes.

- **Memorized secret verifiers:** Passwords should be hashed with a salt that is a 32-bit or longer random value. Remember that using memory-hard functions is recommended to mitigate the risk posed by attackers testing multiple passwords in parallel.

- **Secure storage:** A secure password manager for storing and managing passwords is recommended to reduce the risk of insecure practices like writing down passwords.

- **Service account passwords:** Special accounts, such as service accounts, may have unique requirements, such as less frequent rotation, and so these accounts should be monitored more stringently for anomalies and indicators of compromise.

Access Control Standards

Access control standards are pivotal in defining who gets to access what within an organization's network and systems. These standards lay the groundwork for ensuring that only authorized individuals can access specific resources to maintain data confidentiality, integrity, and availability.

Access control standards typically cover various types of access control mechanisms, including the following:

- **Role-based access control (RBAC):** With RBAC, access permissions are based on organizational roles. For example, a human resources manager might access personnel records but not financial data.

- **Discretionary access control (DAC):** With DAC, the owner of data or a resource has the discretion to grant access. This is common in shared folder scenarios where users can decide who else can view or edit the files.

- **Mandatory access control (MAC):** With MAC, access is granted based on predefined policies that classify information and the clearance levels of users. This is often used in government or military settings.

- **Attribute-based access control (ABAC):** With ABAC, access is granted based on a combination of attributes, such as the user's role, the data's classification, and current environmental conditions like time of day or location.

Access control standards should also specify the requesting, approving, and auditing access procedures. For instance, any request for elevated access might require managerial approval and a valid business justification. Once granted, this access should be reviewed periodically to ensure that it's still necessary for the user's job function.

Access control standards often include guidelines for logging and monitoring access. This could involve generating audit trails for all successful and unsuccessful access attempts, which can be reviewed regularly to detect unauthorized or suspicious activities.

Physical Security Standards

Physical security standards are designed to protect the tangible assets of an organization, including buildings, hardware, and personnel. These standards are crucial because even the most robust cybersecurity measures can be rendered ineffective if physical access to critical infrastructure is compromised.

Physical security standards generally cover the following areas:

- **Facility access:** Guidelines should specify who can enter the premises and specific areas. This often involves using access cards, biometric scans, or staffed security desks to control entry points.

- **Visitor management:** An organization should specify procedures for admitting and tracking visitors, perhaps by requiring them to sign in and be escorted by an employee. Visitors may also be given temporary badges with limited access permissions.

- **Surveillance:** Cameras, motion detectors, and other surveillance equipment may be used to monitor and record activity. The standards should specify where these devices are placed and how the footage is stored and reviewed.

- **Equipment security:** Measures should be implemented to secure servers, workstations, and other hardware against theft or tampering. This could involve locking devices to desks or storing them in secure rooms with restricted access.

- **Environmental controls:** An organization may implement systems like fire suppression, climate control, and alarms for unauthorized entry or hazardous conditions. Such controls are essential for protecting hardware and data from environmental risks.

- **Emergency response:** An organization may implement guidelines for responding to various emergencies, such as fires, floods, or active shooter situations. These guidelines may include evacuation plans and communication protocols.

Physical security standards should also outline the responsibilities of employees in maintaining physical security. For example, employees might be required to display their badges at all times and report any suspicious activity or security incidents immediately.

Encryption Standards

Encryption standards are guidelines that dictate how data should be encrypted and decrypted within an organization. These standards are vital for ensuring the confidentiality and integrity of sensitive information both in transit and at rest. Organizations can safeguard against unauthorized access and data breaches by adhering to established encryption standards, reinforcing their overall security posture.

Encryption standards typically cover the following key areas:

- **Data classification:** Encryption standards may identify the types of data that require encryption. For example, personally identifiable information (PII), financial records, and proprietary research may all be classified as requiring high-level encryption.

- **Encryption algorithms:** Encryption standards may specify which encryption algorithms are approved for use. Algorithms like AES (Advanced Encryption Standard) and RSA are commonly recommended due to their proven security and efficiency.

- **Key management:** Encryption standards may include guidelines for generating, distributing, storing, and retiring encryption keys. This includes using hardware security modules (HSMs) or key management services to manage cryptographic keys securely.

- **Data in transit:** Encryption standards may address encrypting data as it moves across networks. This often involves using protocols like HTTPS for web traffic and TLS (Transport Layer Security) for email and other types of communication.

- **Data at rest:** Encryption standards may include requirements for encrypting data stored on various media types, such as hard drives, databases, and cloud storage. Disk encryption solutions like BitLocker or FileVault may be recommended for this purpose.

- **End-user guidelines:** Encryption standards may include instructions for employees on how to handle encrypted data. This could include guidelines on sharing encrypted files, using encrypted messaging apps, or storing sensitive information on encrypted USB drives.

- **Compliance and auditing:** Encryption standards may include procedures for regularly reviewing and auditing the organization's encryption practices to ensure that they meet internal and external standards, such as GDPR or HIPAA.

Procedures

Procedures are specific, detailed instructions designed to implement policies and standards in an organization. They serve as a roadmap for day-to-day operations, ensuring that all activities align with the organization's security objectives. Procedures are often written in a step-by-step format and may include flowcharts or diagrams for clarity. Now let's delve into some common types of procedures that are crucial in the realm of IT security.

Change Management

Change management is a structured approach to transitioning individuals, teams, and organizations from a current state to a desired future state. In the IT landscape, change management procedures are particularly crucial because they help mitigate risks associated with altering system configurations, updating software, or implementing new technologies. Change management procedures are designed to ensure that changes are introduced, controlled, and coordinated.

The change management procedure often starts with a formal proposal for an alteration called a change request. A change request usually includes details like the change, why it's necessary, who will be responsible for it, and what resources will be required. Once the change request is submitted, it goes through an approval process involving key stakeholders, such as IT managers, security officers, and sometimes even legal advisors. Changes made outside a structured change management process can potentially violate compliance regulations and expose the company to risks.

After approval, the change moves into the planning phase. A detailed plan outlines the steps to implement the change, complete with timelines and responsibilities. Risk assessments are also conducted to understand the potential impact of the change on the organization's security posture.

The next phase is testing, at which point the change is implemented in a controlled, non-production environment. This helps identify issues or conflicts, allowing for adjustments before the change is rolled out organizationwide.

Once testing is successful, the change is implemented in the production environment. This is often done in stages, starting with less critical systems and gradually moving to more critical ones. Each stage is closely monitored to ensure that the change has the intended effect and does not cause disruptions or security vulnerabilities.

Finally, a post-implementation review is conducted to evaluate the success of the change and identify lessons learned. This review helps in refining future change management procedures. For more information on change management, take a look back at Chapter 3, "Understanding Change Management's Security Impact," which covers change management in detail.

Onboarding and Offboarding

Onboarding is the process of adding a new employee to an organization and to its identity and access management system. This process incorporates user training, formal meetings, lectures, and human resources employee handbooks and videos. Depending on the organization, it may also include background checks and social media analysis. It can also be implemented when a person changes roles within an organization. Onboarding is a socialization technique that is used to ultimately provide better job performance and higher job satisfaction. Onboarding is associated with federated identity management. It is also sometimes connected to an employee's *role* in the company and therefore to RBAC.

NOTE Many organizations use social media analysis to research a potential employee or volunteer. The procedure to do this includes investigating the person's online presence on Facebook, Instagram, LinkedIn, and other social media platforms.

Offboarding, which is the converse of onboarding, involves procedurally removing an employee from a federated identity management system, restricting their rights and permissions, and possibly debriefing the person or conducting an exit interview. This step is taken when a person changes roles within an organization or departs the organization altogether.

Many organizations commonly work with business partners, but no business relationship lasts forever, and new ones are often developed. Onboarding and offboarding also can apply to business partners. The main concern is access to data. Extranets are commonly used technologies with business partners. These technologies allow an organization to carefully select which data the business partner has access to. As relationships with business partners are severed, a systematic audit of all shared data should be made, including the various types of connectivity, permissions, policies, and even physical access to data.

Playbooks

A *playbook* in the context of IT and cybersecurity is a detailed procedural guide that provides a standardized approach for responding to various types of incidents, events, or processes. Playbooks guide IT professionals and security teams, outlining the steps that should be taken to handle specific scenarios effectively. The objective is to ensure a quick, coordinated, and effective response, minimizing impact and reducing recovery time.

A typical playbook begins with an incident identification section, which outlines the indicators, or triggers, that signify a particular event has occurred. An indicator, or trigger, could range from multiple failed login attempts suggesting a brute-force attack to unusual data transfers indicating potential data exfiltration.

After the incident identification section, a playbook typically has an initial assessment section. Here, the severity of the incident is gauged, and initial containment strategies are considered. Initial assessment often involves quickly gathering facts, such as what systems are affected, who needs to be involved, and what the potential impact could be.

Next, a playbook is likely to outline the response strategy. This is the core of the playbook, detailing the step-by-step procedures for containing and mitigating an incident. It may include technical steps, such as isolating affected systems or blocking malicious IP addresses, and communication steps, like notifying affected stakeholders or escalating to a higher level of management.

A playbook might also include a recovery and restoration section that guides the team through restoring systems to their normal state. This could involve patching vulnerabilities, restoring from backups, or implementing new security measures to prevent future incidents.

Finally, a playbook often includes a lessons learned section that facilitates a post-incident review. This part of the playbook helps teams evaluate the effectiveness of their response, identify gaps in their procedures, and update the playbook for future incidents.

External Considerations

External considerations are factors outside an organization that influence its security governance. These considerations often dictate the minimum requirements for compliance and can range from legal obligations to industry-specific guidelines. Understanding these external elements is crucial for an organization to ensure that its security measures are effective and compliant with external standards and laws.

Regulatory

Regulatory considerations are paramount for organizations that operate in sectors governed by specific laws and regulations. *Regulatory rules* dictate how an organization must handle various data types, conduct transactions, and even interact with consumers. For example, healthcare organizations in the United States are bound by the Health Insurance Portability and Accountability Act (HIPAA). This act mandates strict controls over patient information, requiring encryption, access controls, and regular audits. Failure to comply with these regulations can result in severe financial penalties, loss of license, and even criminal charges in extreme cases. Organizations must comprehensively understand the regulatory landscape in which they operate. This often involves regular training for staff, periodic internal and external audits, and implementation of specialized compliance software to monitor adherence to these regulations.

Legal

Legal considerations are broader than regulatory rules and can encompass a variety of obligations and potential liabilities. Legal considerations can range from contractual agreements with business partners that specify security requirements to laws regarding consumer data protection. For instance, if an organization stores customer data, it may be subject to data breach notification laws that require it to inform affected parties and regulatory bodies in the event of a data breach. In addition, organizations must be aware of intellectual property laws, which can dictate how proprietary information is stored, shared, and used. Failure to adhere to these legal considerations can result in lawsuits, financial penalties, and reputational damage. To navigate this complex legal landscape, organizations often consult with legal experts who specialize in cybersecurity law, conduct regular legal audits, and establish protocols for legal compliance.

Industry

Industry-specific considerations are guidelines, best practices, or requirements that are widely accepted in a particular sector but that may not be legally mandated. They can include industry standards, frameworks, or certifications that organizations choose to adopt to gain a competitive edge, enhance their reputation, or meet customer expectations. For example, a software development company might adhere to the secure software development lifecycle (SSDLC) framework to ensure that security is integrated throughout development. Similarly, financial institutions often follow the Payment Card Industry Data Security Standard (PCI DSS) to secure and strengthen payment card transaction systems.

Adhering to industry-specific considerations is often a strategic move that can offer various benefits, such as increased customer trust and easier compliance with future regulations. However, it also requires a commitment to continuous improvement and often involves regular audits, employee training, and updates to security protocols. Organizations usually keep an eye on industry trends through membership in industry associations, participation in industry-specific forums, and use of publications and reports that offer insights into emerging best practices and technologies.

Local/Regional

Local/regional considerations are the specific rules, regulations, or cultural norms that apply to a particular geographic area. They can range from local data protection laws to regional industry standards. For example, a healthcare provider in the United States must comply with HIPAA. A similar institution in Europe would need to adhere to the General Data Protection Regulation (GDPR). Understanding these localized requirements is crucial for organizations operating in multiple jurisdictions or considering expansion. Failure to comply can result in fines, legal action, and reputational damage.

National

National considerations encompass laws, regulations, and standards that are applicable across a country. They often include data protection laws, cybersecurity regulations, and industry-specific guidelines. For instance, the Federal Information Security Management Act (FISMA) sets comprehensive guidelines to protect government information, operations, and assets in the United States. Organizations operating nationally must be well versed in these overarching rules to ensure full compliance and prevent legal complications.

Global

Global considerations involve international laws, treaties, and standards that have wide-reaching implications for organizations operating in multiple countries. They can include international standards like ISO 27001 for information security management or global regulations like GDPR, which has extraterritorial reach. An organization with a global footprint must navigate a complex web of international laws and standards, often requiring specialized legal and compliance teams. The challenge here is to harmonize the various rules from different jurisdictions into a cohesive governance strategy. This usually involves a multidisciplinary approach, incorporating legal, compliance, and IT teams to ensure that the organization's security posture aligns with international requirements.

Monitoring and Revision

Monitoring and revision are integral components of effective security governance. These processes ensure that your guidelines, policies, standards, and procedures remain current, effective, and aligned with the evolving threat landscape. Continuous monitoring involves regularly reviewing logs, conducting audits, and analyzing performance metrics to assess the effectiveness of your security controls. Security information and event management (SIEM) systems often facilitate this, aggregating and analyzing data from various sources to provide a comprehensive view of an organization's security posture.

Revision involves updating and modifying these governance elements based on the insights gained from monitoring. For example, if an audit reveals that a particular access control standard is not being adhered to, a revision may be necessary to clarify or strengthen that standard. Revisions can be triggered by changes in external considerations, such as new or updated regulations, technological advancements, or shifts in organizational strategy.

The key to successful monitoring and revision is a well-defined process that includes regular intervals for review, criteria for what constitutes a need for revision, and a clear workflow for implementing changes. A well-defined process ensures that your security governance framework remains agile, allowing for quick adaptation to new challenges or opportunities.

Types of Governance Structures

In security governance, the chosen structure can significantly impact how effectively an organization responds to security challenges. Different types of governance structures offer various advantages and limitations, and understanding them can help you tailor your approach to your organization's specific needs. This section examines some common governance structures that are often employed to oversee and manage security initiatives.

Boards

The board is often the highest echelon of governance within an organization, usually comprising C-level executives, such as the CEO, CIO, and CISO, along with other senior leaders and sometimes external advisors or stakeholders. The board's role in security governance is multifaceted and carries significant weight.

First, a *board* is responsible for setting the strategic direction of the organization's security posture. It evaluates and approves the overarching security policies and ensures that they align with the broader business objectives. This strategic alignment is crucial for justifying the resources allocated to security initiatives, including budgets and personnel.

Second, a board often serves as the final approval authority for significant security initiatives and expenditures. For example, if an organization is considering implementing a new type of security technology, such as a next-generation firewall, its board would typically need to approve this implementation, especially if it involves a substantial financial investment.

Third, a board is responsible for risk management at the highest level. It reviews risk assessments and ensures that the organization's risk tolerance is clearly defined and adhered to. It might also be involved in crisis management, providing guidance and making critical decisions during significant security incidents.

Finally, a board has a fiduciary duty to stakeholders, including shareholders and employees, to ensure that the organization is taking adequate steps to protect its assets and data. This responsibility often extends to ensuring compliance with various regulatory frameworks, such as GDPR, HIPAA, or PCI DSS, which can carry severe penalties for non-compliance.

Committees

A *committee* functions as a specialized governance body in an organization, focusing on particular aspects of security or operational needs. Unlike a board, which operates at a strategic level, a committee is likely to delve into the tactical and operational aspects of governance. A committee is usually composed of subject matter experts, department heads, and sometimes external consultants who bring specialized skills.

One of the primary roles of a committee is to provide detailed oversight of a specific security initiative or program. For example, a data protection committee might be responsible for ensuring that all of the organization's data handling and storage practices align with GDPR requirements. This committee would work closely with the legal and IT departments to review current practices, recommend improvements, and oversee the implementation of any changes.

Another key function of a committee is to act as an advisory body to the board or senior management. It would conduct in-depth analyses of specific issues, such as emerging threats or regulatory changes, and present its findings and recommendations for action. This specialized focus allows the board to make well-informed decisions based on expert insights.

A committee also plays a role in monitoring and auditing. For instance, a security audit committee might regularly review the effectiveness of the organization's security controls and procedures. It would identify gaps or weaknesses and recommend corrective actions to ensure that the organization's security posture remains robust.

In addition, a committee may be responsible for stakeholder communication. Whether updating employees on new security protocols or liaising with external auditors, a committee can ensure that all relevant parties are informed and engaged.

Government Entities

Government entities play a unique role in governance structures, particularly national security, public safety, and regulatory compliance. Unlike boards and committees in private organizations, government entities operate under a legal mandate to protect the public interest. They are often responsible for setting and enforcing standards and regulations that private organizations must follow.

For instance, in the United States, the Federal Trade Commission (FTC) is responsible for protecting consumers, and it sets guidelines and regulations that organizations must adhere to when collecting and storing consumer data. Similarly, the National Institute of Standards and Technology (NIST) provides a framework for improving critical infrastructure cybersecurity, which many organizations adopt as a best practice.

Government entities also serve as authoritative bodies for dispute resolution and legal enforcement. If an organization is found to violate data protection laws, for example, a government entity would be responsible for investigating the issue and imposing penalties, if necessary. This adds an extra layer of accountability for organizations, ensuring that they maintain rigorous security protocols.

Government entities often collaborate with private organizations to address broader security concerns. For example, the Cybersecurity and Infrastructure Security Agency (CISA) in the United States works closely with the private sector to defend against cyber threats to critical national infrastructure. Such partnerships allow for a more coordinated and effective response to evolving security challenges.

In some cases, government entities become the subject of governance structures, especially when their actions or policies have significant implications for privacy and security. Oversight committees, which are often made up of elected officials, may be established to review these entities' activities and ensure that they align with legal requirements and public expectations.

Centralized/Decentralized

Understanding the difference between centralized and decentralized governance structures is crucial for implementing effective security measures. Each approach has a unique set of advantages and challenges, and the choice between the two often depends on an organization's specific needs and scale.

Centralized Governance

In a *centralized governance structure*, decision-making authority is concentrated at the top levels of the organization. This often leads to quicker decision-making processes, as fewer individuals are involved. For example, in a centralized IT governance model, a single department might be responsible for all IT-related decisions, including security protocols, data management, and compliance. This can result in a uniform implementation of policies and standards, as there is a single control point.

However, the centralized model can also have drawbacks. It may not be as responsive to the unique needs of different departments or business units. In addition, a centralized system can create a single point of failure; an error on the part of the central authority can have widespread implications.

Decentralized Governance

A *decentralized governance structure* distributes decision-making authority across different parts of the organization. This approach allows for more localized control, benefiting organizations that have diverse needs or that are spread across multiple geographic locations. For instance, a multinational corporation might allow its regional offices to set their security protocols in accordance with local laws and regulations.

The decentralized model fosters innovation and adaptability, as individual units can tailor their approaches. However, this can also lead to inconsistencies in how policies and procedures are applied, potentially creating gaps in the organization's security posture.

Organizations sometimes opt for a hybrid approach, combining centralized and decentralized governance elements. For example, an organization might centralize certain functions like compliance and risk management while allowing individual business units to control their operational procedures.

Roles and Responsibilities for Systems and Data

Defining roles and responsibilities for systems and data is paramount in IT security governance. This clarity ensures that everyone knows who is accountable for what, reducing ambiguities and potential security risks. It also helps establish a chain of command and a framework for decision making, especially when incidents occur. This section delves into the key roles in governance systems and data: owners, controllers, processors, and custodians/stewards.

Owners

In the governance structure, the owner role is pivotal and carries significant weight. The *owner* is typically a senior executive or department head who is responsible for a specific system or data set in the organization. Their role is not merely titular; it comes with crucial responsibilities that directly impact the organization's security posture.

These are the key responsibilities of owners:

- **Asset classification:** Owners are responsible for classifying an asset—such as a system or a data set—based on its importance to the organization. This classification helps determine the level of security controls that need to be applied.

- **Policy formulation:** Owners play a key role in formulating and approving policies that govern the use and security of an asset. This could range from access controls to encryption standards.

- **Risk assessment:** Owners are often involved in risk assessments, identifying potential vulnerabilities and threats to the asset. They must then approve the appropriate risk mitigation strategies.

- **Compliance oversight:** Ensuring that an asset complies with internal policies and external regulations falls under an owner's purview. They must liaise with legal and compliance teams to ensure that the asset meets all regulatory requirements.

- **Budget allocation:** Security measures often require financial resources. An owner usually approves security controls, software, and personnel training budgets.

- **Incident response:** If a security incident affects an asset, the owner is the ultimate decision-making authority. While they may not be involved in the immediate response, they are responsible for approving the course of action.

Consider a healthcare organization that maintains a patient database. The owner of this database could be the chief information officer (CIO), who would be responsible for classifying the database as a high-priority asset, given the sensitive nature of the data. They would work with the IT and legal departments to ensure that the database complies with healthcare regulations like HIPAA. The CIO would also approve the budget for implementing strong encryption methods to protect the data and would be the ultimate authority in decision making if a data breach were to occur. Owners set the tone for how seriously an organization takes data and system security, and so their role in the governance structure is indispensable.

Controllers

The role of a controller in an organization's governance structure is particularly significant when it comes to data management and protection. Unlike owners, who have overarching responsibility for systems or data, *controllers* are specifically tasked with determining why and how to process personal data. This role is often highlighted in contexts where data protection regulations like the GDPR are applicable.

These are the key responsibilities of controllers:

- **Data processing objectives:** A controller defines the objectives for collecting and processing data. They decide what data is needed, how it will be used, and who can access it.

- **Legal compliance:** One of a controller's primary duties is to ensure that all data processing activities comply with relevant laws and regulations. This includes obtaining necessary permissions and providing disclosures.

- **Data quality:** A controller ensures the accuracy and quality of data. This often involves setting up validation checks and periodic reviews.

- **Security measures:** While they may not implement security controls directly, a controller is responsible for ensuring that adequate security measures are in place to protect the data. This could involve specifying encryption methods or access controls.

- **Data subject rights:** A controller must facilitate the rights of data subjects, such as the right to access, correct, or delete their data. They are often the point of contact for data subjects who wish to exercise their rights.

- **Accountability and recordkeeping:** A controller is required to maintain records of data processing activities and must be able to demonstrate compliance with data protection laws.

In a financial institution, a controller could be the data protection officer (DPO). The DPO would determine how customer data is used for credit assessments and ensure that this use complies with financial regulations and data protection laws. They would also be responsible for ensuring that customers can easily access and correct their data and would oversee the implementation of security measures like two-factor authentication for customer accounts.

A controller is integral to an organization's data governance and compliance efforts. Their decisions directly impact how data is handled, who has access to it, and how secure it is, making them a key player in the governance ecosystem.

Processors

In the context of data governance, the term *processor* refers to any individual, department, or third-party service that processes data on behalf of the controller. Whereas the controller sets the "why" and "how" of data processing, the processor is responsible for carrying out the actual processing activities in accordance with the controller's directives.

These are the key responsibilities of a processor:

- **Data handling:** A processor is responsible for the handling of data, including collection, storage, retrieval, and deletion. They must follow the guidelines and procedures set forth by the controller.

- **Security implementation:** Whereas the controller may specify what security measures should be in place, the processor is often responsible for implementing those measures. This could include encrypting data at rest or in transit, setting firewalls, or configuring access controls.

- **Data accuracy:** A processor must ensure that the data they handle is accurate and up-to-date. This could involve running validation checks or updating records when new information becomes available.

- **Compliance:** A processor must comply with the legal and regulatory requirements governing the data they are handling. This includes adhering to data retention policies and facilitating audits.

- **Reporting and documentation:** A processor often must provide reports or documentation to the controller, in compliance with the set guidelines and legal requirements.

- **Incident response:** In the event of a data breach or another security incident, the processor is usually responsible for immediate remediation actions and must report the incident to the controller as quickly as possible.

Consider a healthcare organization that uses a third-party billing service to handle patient invoices. In this scenario, the healthcare organization acts as the controller, setting policies on how patient data should be used and protected. The third-party billing service, the processor, would securely handle and store patient financial data, generate invoices, and ensure that all activities comply with healthcare regulations like HIPAA.

Custodians/Stewards

Custodians, often called data stewards, play a vital role in managing and safeguarding data. Unlike owners or controllers, who have a more strategic role, *custodians (or stewards)* are usually responsible for the technical aspects of data storage, maintenance, and security. They are the individuals or teams directly involved in data handling, ensuring that it remains secure, accessible, and usable.

One of the primary responsibilities of a custodian is to implement and maintain the security measures outlined in the organization's policies. This could involve working with firewalls, managing encryption keys, or configuring access controls. The custodian is also responsible for regular data backups and ensuring that data can be recovered during a system failure or another catastrophic event.

Another key aspect of the custodian's role is data quality assurance. They are often tasked with running regular checks to ensure that the data is accurate, consistent, and up-to-date. This could involve anything from removing duplicate entries to updating outdated information. In some cases, custodians may also be responsible for tagging or classifying data, making it easier to manage and retrieve.

Custodians also play a role in compliance. They are typically responsible for ensuring that data is stored and managed in accordance with relevant laws and regulations. This could involve retaining records for a specific period or storing data in a particular format. Custodians may also be involved in audits, providing the necessary documentation and evidence to demonstrate compliance.

For example, in a financial institution, a custodian might ensure that customer data is securely stored and that all transactions are encrypted. They would also be responsible for running regular security audits, ensuring compliance with financial regulations, and providing data for internal reports or external audits. In this role, the custodian acts as the guardian of the data, ensuring that it is managed in accordance with both internal policies and external regulations.

Chapter Review Activities

Use the features in this section to study and review the topics in this chapter.

Review Key Topics

Review the most important topics in the chapter, noted with the Key Topic icon in the outer margin of the page. Table 23-3 lists these key topics and the page number on which each is found.

Table 23-3   Key Topics for Chapter 23

Key Topic Element	Description	Page Number
List	Examples of guidelines	532
Table 23-2	Examples of Information Security Policies	534
List	Comprehensive password standards	537
List	Access control standards	538
Section	Procedures	541
Section	Monitoring and Revision	545
Section	Centralized/Decentralized	548
List	Key responsibilities of owners	549

Define Key Terms

Define the following key terms from this chapter and check your answers in the glossary:

guideline, policy, acceptable use policy (AUP), information security policy, business continuity policy, disaster recovery policy, incident response policy, software development lifecycle (SDLC) policy, standards, password standards, access control standards, physical security standards, encryption standards, procedures, change management, onboarding, offboarding, playbook, external considerations, regulatory rules, board, committee, centralized governance structure, decentralized governance structure, owner, controller, custodian (or steward)

Review Questions

Answer the following review questions. Check your answers with the answer key in Appendix A.

1. How do guidelines differ from policies in an organization's security governance?

2. What is the role of a policy in the context of IT and cybersecurity?

3. What is the primary focus of access control standards in an organization?

4. What is the purpose of procedures in implementing an organization's security governance?

5. How do external considerations impact an organization's security governance?

6. What are the key activities involved in the monitoring and revision process with security governance?

This chapter covers the following topics related to Objective 5.2 (Explain elements of the risk management process) of the CompTIA Security+ SY0-701 certification exam:

- Risk identification
- Risk assessment
- Risk analysis
- Risk register
- Risk tolerance
- Risk appetite
- Risk management strategies
- Risk reporting
- Business impact analysis

CHAPTER 24

Understanding Elements of the Risk Management Process

This chapter explores risk management, covering the initial steps of risk identification and assessment, including various approaches, such as ad hoc and continuous methods. It delves into risk analysis metrics such as single loss expectancy (SLE) and annualized loss expectancy (ALE) and discusses the importance of probability and impact. The chapter outlines the roles of risk registers, organizational risk tolerance, and appetite. It concludes with an overview of risk management strategies and business impact analysis metrics such as recovery time objective (RTO) and recovery point objective (RPO), emphasizing the importance of resilience and preparedness in organizational risk planning.

"Do I Know This Already?" Quiz

The "Do I Know This Already?" quiz enables you to assess whether you should read this entire chapter thoroughly or jump to the "Chapter Review Activities" section. If you are in doubt about your answers to these questions or your own assessment of your knowledge of the topics, read the entire chapter. Table 24-1 lists the major headings in this chapter and their corresponding "Do I Know This Already?" quiz questions. You can find the answers in Appendix A, "Answers to the 'Do I Know This Already?' Quizzes and Review Questions."

Table 24-1 "Do I Know This Already?" Section-to-Question Mapping

Foundation Topics Section	Questions
Risk Identification	1
Risk Assessment	2
Risk Analysis	3
Risk Register	4

Foundation Topics Section	Questions
Risk Tolerance	5
Risk Appetite	6
Risk Management Strategies	7
Risk Reporting	8
Business Impact Analysis	9–10

CAUTION   The goal of self-assessment is to gauge your mastery of the topics in this chapter. If you do not know the answer to a question or are only partially sure of the answer, you should mark that question as wrong for purposes of self-assessment. Giving yourself credit for an answer you correctly guess skews your self-assessment results and might provide you with a false sense of security.

1. What is the primary goal of the risk identification phase in risk management?

   a. To manage risks

   b. To create a comprehensive list of risks

   c. To evaluate the impact of risks

   d. To assign risk owners

2. Which type of risk assessment is conducted in response to an immediate need, such as a sudden security breach?

   a. Recurring risk assessment

   b. Ad hoc risk assessment

   c. Continuous risk assessment

   d. One-time risk assessment

3. In risk analysis, what does the term *probability* quantify?

   a. The potential consequences of a risk

   b. The likelihood of a specific risk occurring

   c. The individual responsible for a risk

   d. The level of risk an organization is willing to accept

4. What does *impact* refer to in the context of risk analysis?

    a. The likelihood of a risk occurring

    b. The potential consequences or effects on an organization

    c. The individual or department responsible for a risk

    d. The level of risk an organization is willing to accept

5. Who is responsible for managing a particular risk in an organization?

    a. Risk reporter

    b. Risk assessor

    c. Risk owner

    d. Risk analyst

6. What does *risk appetite* indicate?

    a. The level of risk an organization is willing to accept

    b. The individual responsible for a risk

    c. The likelihood of a risk occurring

    d. The potential consequences of a risk

7. Which risk management strategy would an organization be using if it purchased cybersecurity insurance for a group of servers in a data center?

    a. Avoid

    b. Mitigate

    c. Transfer

    d. Accept

8. What is the primary purpose of risk reporting in IT and cybersecurity?

    a. To provide a snapshot of the organization's risk landscape

    b. To assign risk owners

    c. To evaluate the impact of risks

    d. To manage risks

9. What is the primary purpose of calculating mean time to repair (MTTR) in a disaster recovery plan (DRP)?

   a. To determine the cost-effectiveness of spare parts stockpiles

   b. To understand the operational impact of repair times and guide decision making for redundancy

   c. To predict when a system failure might occur

   d. To calculate the number of failures per billion hours of operation

10. How is mean time between failures (MTBF) used in designing a robust disaster recovery plan (DRP)?

    a. In determining the average repair time for failed devices or systems

    b. In predicting the cost and time needed for regular system maintenance

    c. In anticipating the frequency of potential failures and planning for system resilience

    d. In calculating the total downtime experienced during an outage

Foundation Topics

Risk Identification

Risk identification is the initial phase in the risk management process, during which an organization pinpoints the potential threats and vulnerabilities that could adversely affect its assets, operations, or objectives. This phase is crucial because an organization can't manage risks it hasn't identified. The goal of risk identification is to create a comprehensive list of risks based on various categories, such as operational, financial, strategic, and compliance-related risks.

Let's take a look at what you might discover during the risk identification phase:

- **Cybersecurity threats:** During the risk identification phase, you might identify potential cybersecurity threats like phishing attacks, ransomware, or unauthorized access. For instance, you might recognize that your organization is vulnerable to phishing attacks due to inadequate employee training.

- **Natural disasters:** Your organization might face risks related to natural disasters such as floods, earthquakes, or hurricanes, especially if it is located in a region that is prone to such events. For example, a data center located in a flood-prone area would identify flooding as a significant risk.

- **Regulatory risks:** Failing to comply with industry regulations or laws could result in fines or legal action, so it is important to identify any regulatory risks your organization faces. A healthcare provider, for instance, would identify the risk of not complying with health information privacy laws.

- **Supply chain risks:** Your organization might identify vulnerabilities in the supply chain, such as a single point of failure or dependency on a particular supplier for critical components. A manufacturing company might identify that it relies too heavily on a single supplier for key raw materials, making it vulnerable to supply chain disruptions.

- **Human errors:** Your organization might identify risks it faces related to mistakes made by employees or contractors that could lead to data breaches or operational disruptions. For example, your organization might identify that its current data backup procedures are complex and prone to human error.

When risks are identified early in the process, an organization can assess the likelihood and impact of each risk. Risk identification sets the stage for effective risk mitigation strategies and informed decision making.

Risk Assessment

Risk assessment is the analytical engine of the risk management process. *Risk assessment* is the process of evaluating identified risks to gauge their potential impact and likelihood and to inform the organization's risk management strategies. Risk assessment is not a one-size-fits-all process; it can be tailored to fit an organization's needs and circumstances.

The following sections look at a few ways to approach risk assessment.

Ad Hoc

An *ad hoc risk assessment* is situation specific and often reactive. It is conducted in response to an immediate need, such as a sudden security breach or a newly discovered vulnerability. For example, if a company experiences an unexpected data leak, an ad hoc risk assessment would be conducted to evaluate the severity of the breach and the steps needed to contain it. This type of assessment is not pre-scheduled and is generally initiated to address urgent or unforeseen issues.

Recurring

Recurring risk assessments are systematic and occur at predetermined intervals, such as quarterly, biannually, or annually. They are part of the organization's structured risk management program. For instance, a financial institution might conduct recurring risk assessments to evaluate compliance with banking regulations. These assessments are beneficial for tracking long-term risk trends and ensuring that previous risk mitigation strategies are still effective. You can also gather more consistent data by using the same framework or a similar one for every recurring assessment. Consistent data typically results in more reliable key performance indicators (KPIs).

One-time

A *one-time risk assessment* is conducted for a specific event or condition and is not intended to be repeated. For example, before launching a new product, a company might conduct a one-time risk assessment to evaluate potential market risks, compliance issues, or cybersecurity vulnerabilities. This type of assessment is highly focused and aims to provide a snapshot of the risks associated with a particular initiative or change.

Continuous

Continuous risk assessment is an ongoing process that involves constantly monitoring and evaluating the risk landscape. This approach captures real-time risk changes, enabling more proactive and dynamic risk management. For instance, a healthcare provider using electronic health records (EHRs) might employ continuous risk assessment to monitor for unauthorized access or data anomalies. This allows the organization to quickly respond to new risks as they emerge.

Each approach has advantages and limitations that can be combined to create a more robust risk assessment framework. Organizations can better tailor their risk assessment processes to their needs, enhancing their overall risk management efforts. Do not be afraid to mix and match approaches. Consistency is the key to assessments.

Risk Analysis

Risk analysis is the next logical step after risk assessment, diving deeper into the specifics of each identified risk. *Risk analysis* involves quantifying or qualifying the potential impact and likelihood of risks, providing a more granular view that informs risk treatment strategies. This section explores the various methods and metrics used in risk analysis.

Just as we discussed earlier, when you assess risks, they are often recognized threats, but risk assessment can also take into account new types of threats that might occur. When risk has been assessed, it can be mitigated up until the point at which the organization will accept any residual risk. Generally, risk assessments follow a particular order, such as these steps:

Step 1.   Identify the organization's assets.

Step 2.   Identify vulnerabilities.

Step 3.   Identify threats and threat likelihood.

Step 4.   Identify potential monetary impact.

The fourth step, also known as impact assessment, involves determining the potential monetary costs related to a threat.

An excellent tool to use during a risk assessment is a risk register, also known as a risk log, which helps track issues and address problems as they occur. After the initial risk assessment, you, as security administrator, will continue to use and refer to the risk register. (We will discuss risk registers in greater detail later in this chapter.) A risk register can be a great tool for just about any organization but can especially be of value to certain types of organizations, such as manufacturers, that use a supply chain. Such an organization would want to implement a specialized type of risk management called supply chain risk management (SCRM). The organization would collaborate with suppliers and distributors to analyze and reduce risk. One approach that an organization can take to identifying risks and controls is the application of a risk control assessment, which can be completed by a third party or by an internal team. The internal team can complete a risk control self-assessment

(RCSA). This process is often used by financial institutions that are subject to regulatory compliance. A great approach to visually representing the results of a risk assessment is the use of a risk matrix/heat map, as shown in Figure 24-1.

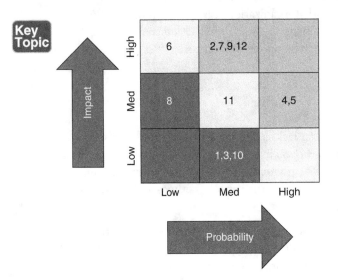

Figure 24-1   Risk Matrix/Heat Map

Table 24-2 summarizes common terms associated with risk analysis.

Table 24-2   Common Risk Analysis Terms

Term	Description
Risk appetite	The types and amounts of risk, on a broad level, an organization is willing to accept in its pursuit of value.
Inherent risk	The level of risk an organization would experience if the correct mitigation were not in place.
Residual risk	The risk left over after a detailed security plan and disaster recovery plan have been implemented.
Control risk	The risk that a control that is in place may not detect risk or may fail to protect the environment.
Risk awareness	The ability of an organization to identify risks before they become threats. Risk awareness refers to the overall preparedness of an organization to mitigate risk.
Risk mitigation	According to NIST, is the process of "prioritizing, evaluating, and implementing the appropriate risk-reducing controls/countermeasures recommended from the risk management process."

The two most common risk assessment methods are qualitative and quantitative.

Qualitative Risk Assessment

Qualitative risk assessment is an assessment in which numeric values are assigned based on the probability that a risk will occur and the impact it might have on the system or network. Unlike its counterpart, quantitative risk assessment, it does not assign monetary values to assets or possible losses. It is the easier, quicker, and cheaper way to assess risk but cannot assign asset value or give a total for possible monetary loss.

With qualitative risk assessment, ranges can be assigned, such as 1 to 10 or 1 to 100. The higher the number, the higher the probability of risk, or the greater the impact on the system. As a basic example, a computer without antivirus software that is connected to the Internet will most likely have a high probability of risk; it will also most likely have a great impact on the system. You could assign the number 99 out of 100 as the probability of risk. You are not sure exactly when it will happen but are 99% sure that it will happen at some point. Next, you could assign the number 90 out of 100 as the impact of the risk. This number implies a heavy impact, such as the system crashing or being rendered unusable at some point. There is a 10% chance that the system will remain usable, but it is unlikely. Finally, you multiply the two numbers together to find the qualitative risk: $99 \times 90 = 8910$. That's 8910 out of a possible 10,000, which is a high level of risk. The way to mitigate risk in this example would be to install antivirus software and verify that it is configured to auto-update. By assigning these types of qualitative values to various risks, you can make comparisons between one risk and another and get a better idea of what needs to be mitigated and what doesn't.

The main issue with this type of risk assessment is that it is difficult to place an exact value on many types of risks. The type of qualitative system varies from organization to organization—and even from person to person; it is a common source of debate as well. This makes qualitative risk assessments more descriptive than truly measurable. However, by relying on group surveys, company history, and personal experience, you can get a basic idea of the risk involved.

Quantitative Risk Assessment

Quantitative risk assessment measures risk by using numbers such as exact monetary values. It attempts to give an expected yearly loss in dollars for any given risk. It also defines asset values to servers, routers, and other network equipment.

Three values are used when making quantitative risk calculations:

- *Single loss expectancy (SLE)* is the loss of value in dollars based on a single incident.

- *Annualized rate of occurrence (ARO)* is the number of times per year that the specific incident occurs.

■ *Annualized loss expectancy (ALE)* is the total loss in dollars per year due to a specific incident. The incident might happen once or more than once; either way, this number is the total loss in dollars for that particular type of incident. It is computed using the following calculation:

SLE × ARO = ALE

For example, suppose you want to find out how much an e-commerce web server's downtime will cost your company per year. You need some information such as the average web server downtime in minutes and the number of times server downtime occurs per year. You would need to know the average sale amount in dollars and how many sales are made per minute on this e-commerce web server. This information can be deduced by using accounting reports and with further security analysis of the web server, as discussed later in this chapter. For now, let's just say that over the past year, the web server failed seven times. The average downtime with each failure was 45 minutes. That equals a total of 315 minutes of downtime per year, which is close to 99.9% uptime. (The more years you can measure, the better the estimate will be.) Now let's say that this web server processes an average of 10 orders per minute, with average revenue of $35 per order. This means that $350 of revenue comes in per minute. As mentioned earlier, a single downtime event averages 45 minutes, corresponding to a $15,750 loss per occurrence. Therefore, the SLE is $15,750. Ouch! Some salespeople are going to be unhappy with your 99.9% uptime! But you're not done. You can calculate the ALE by multiplying the SLE ($15,750) by the ARO. Because the web server failed seven times last year, SLE × ARO would be $15,750 × 7, which equals $110,250 (the ALE). This example is shown in Table 24-3.

Key Topic

Table 24-3   Quantitative Risk Assessment Example

SLE	ARO	ALE
$15,750	7	$110,250
Revenue lost due to each web server failure	Total web server failures over the past year	Total loss due to web server failure per year

Apparently, you need to increase the uptime of the e-commerce web server! Many organizations demand 99.99% or even 99.999% uptime; 99.999% uptime means that the server will have only 5 minutes of downtime over the entire course of the year. Of course, to accomplish this, you first need to scrutinize the server to determine precisely why it fails so often. What exactly are the vulnerabilities of the web server? Which ones have been exploited? Which threats exploited those vulnerabilities? By exploring the server's logs, configurations, and policies and by using security tools, you can discern exactly why this happens so often. However, this analysis should be done carefully because the server is involved in a lot of the business for the company.

It isn't possible to assign a specific ALE to an incident that will happen in the future, so new technologies should be monitored carefully. Any failures should be documented thoroughly. For example, you might maintain a spreadsheet that contains the various technologies your organization uses; their failure history; their SLE, ARO, and ALE; and mitigation techniques that you have employed and when they were implemented.

Table 24-4 compares the different aspects of quantitative risk assessment and qualitative risk assessment.

Table 24-4   Risk Assessment Types

Risk Assessment Type	Description	Key Points
Qualitative risk assessment	Assigns numeric values to the probability of risks and the impacts they can have on the system or network.	Numbers are arbitrary. For example, they might be 1–10 or 1–100.
Quantitative risk assessment	Measures risk by using exact monetary values. It attempts to give an expected yearly loss in dollars for any given risk.	Values are specific monetary amounts. ALE is calculated as follows: $SLE \times ARO = ALE$ MTBF can be used for additional data.

NOTE   Most organizations in the medical, pharmaceutical, and banking industries use quantitative risk assessments; they need to have specific monetary numbers in order to measure risk. Many banking institutions go a step further, adhering to the recommendations in the Basel I, II, and III accords, which describe how much capital a bank should put aside to deal with financial and operational risks if they occur.

Probability

Understanding the concept of probability is crucial for practical risk analysis and management. *Probability* quantifies the likelihood of a specific risk occurring and is often expressed as a percentage. It is a foundational metric that informs various other aspects of risk analysis, such as SLE and ALE.

This section looks at how you can leverage the concept of probability in real-world scenarios.

Data-Driven Decision Making

Probability enables you to make data-driven decisions. By analyzing historical data, you can calculate the probability of specific risks occurring. For example, if your organization has experienced five phishing attacks in the past year, you could use data on these attacks to estimate the probability of future attacks. This data-driven approach enables you to allocate resources more effectively.

Risk Prioritization

Knowing the probability of various risks helps in prioritizing them. Risks with higher probabilities may require immediate attention and resource allocation compared to those with lower probabilities. For instance, if the probability of a data breach is 40% and a hardware failure is 10%, you would likely prioritize implementing stronger cybersecurity measures over implementing hardware redundancy.

Financial Planning

Probability is often used in calculating the potential financial impact of risks, aiding in budget allocation for risk mitigation strategies. For example, if the probability of a server failure is 20% and the potential loss is $10,000, you can factor this into your financial planning for backup solutions or insurance.

Scenario Analysis

Probability can be used in scenario analysis to model different outcomes based on varying probabilities. For example, based on various probability percentages, you could model a cybersecurity incident's best-case, average-case, and worst-case scenarios. This exercise might provide valuable insights into how prepared your organization is for different levels of risk.

Communication and Reporting

A well-calculated probability metric can be a powerful tool in communicating risks to stakeholders. It provides a quantifiable measure that can be easily understood and acted upon. For example, telling your board there's a 70% chance of a significant cybersecurity incident in the next quarter is more impactful than simply saying the risk is high.

Continuous Monitoring and Adjustment

Probability is not static; it changes as new data becomes available or the organization's environment changes. Continuous monitoring lets you update the probability metrics, ensuring that your risk management strategies align with the current risk landscape.

Likelihood

The term *likelihood* in risk analysis is often used interchangeably with probability, but subtle differences do exist that you should be aware of. Whereas probability is a numeric quantification, likelihood is usually a qualitative descriptor of the chance of a particular event occurring. It's expressed in terms such as "highly likely," "likely," "unlikely," and "highly unlikely." Understanding the nuances of likelihood can significantly enhance your risk management strategies.

Let's look at how to apply the concept of likelihood in real-world scenarios.

Risk Categorization

Likelihood can be used to categorize risks into different levels, making it easier to communicate the urgency or severity of a risk to non-technical stakeholders. For example, describing a potential data breach as "highly likely" can quickly convey the need for immediate action, even to those who may not understand the numerical probability.

Decision-Making Frameworks

Using likelihood as a qualitative measure can simplify complex decision-making processes. For instance, you might use a risk matrix in which one axis represents the impact of a risk and the other represents its likelihood (refer to Figure 24-1). Risks that are high impact and highly likely would be prioritized for immediate action.

Resource Allocation

Understanding the likelihood of various risks can guide you in allocating resources more effectively. For example, risks deemed "highly likely" might warrant more immediate investment in preventive measures, whereas those considered "unlikely" might be placed lower on the priority list.

Sensitivity Analysis

Likelihood can be used in sensitivity analysis to understand how sensitive specific risk outcomes are to variable changes. For example, if a slight shift in market conditions makes a financial loss "likely" instead of "unlikely," that's a sign that the organization should prepare more rigorously for that risk.

Stakeholder Communication

As with probability, the concept of likelihood can be a powerful tool in stakeholder communication. It's often easier for people to grasp and act upon qualitative descriptors like "likely" or "unlikely" than numerical probabilities. This can be particularly useful in high-stakes meetings where decisions need to be made quickly.

Exposure Factor

Exposure factor (EF) is a crucial metric in risk analysis that quantifies the percentage of loss a particular asset would experience if a specific threat were to materialize. It's expressed as a percentage and is a foundational element in calculating SLE, the monetary loss expected from a single event. Understanding and accurately determining the exposure factor can significantly enhance your risk management strategies.

Before you can determine the exposure factor, you need to clearly understand the value of the asset you're assessing. It could be a physical asset, such as a server, or an intangible one, such as proprietary software. Knowing the asset's value helps you calculate the potential loss accurately, making EF a more reliable metric.

Imagine that AlphaTech is a company that provides cloud storage services to its customers. Its primary data center is an asset that generates an average of $500,000 in revenue per month. AlphaTech identifies a risk: a potential distributed denial of service (DDoS) attack that could incapacitate the company's servers. Through risk analysis, AlphaTech estimates that if such an attack occurs, there's a likelihood that the company will lose access to 40% of its data center capacity, affecting their revenue streams due to service disruption. In this case, the EF is 40%—the percentage of the asset's value that could be lost if the threat materializes.

To find the SLE for AlphaTech in the event of a DDoS attack, you use this formula:

$$SLE = Asset\ value \times EF$$

If the asset value (monthly revenue) is $500,000, and EF is 40%, you calculate SLE as follows:

$$SLE = \$500,000 \times 0.40 = \$200,000$$

For AlphaTech, the SLE in the event of a DDoS attack that reduces its data center capacity by 40% would be $200,000. This figure represents the expected monetary loss for a single occurrence of this specific threat. Understanding and calculating the SLE helps AlphaTech and similar companies effectively prepare and prioritize their risk management and mitigation strategies.

Exposure factor also plays a critical role in business impact analysis (BIA). We will discuss BIA in a moment. For now, by understanding the EF for various assets and scenarios, you can better predict the potential impact on business operations and continuity. For example, if the EF for a critical server failing is 80%, immediate action is required to mitigate this risk.

Once you've determined the EF, you can prioritize risk mitigation strategies more effectively. For example, an asset with a high EF would require robust protective measures, such as redundant systems or frequent backups, to minimize potential loss.

Understanding the exposure factor can also guide financial planning, particularly in setting aside reserves for potential losses or investing in preventive measures. For example, if the EF for a data breach involving customer data is 60%, you might invest in advanced encryption methods to protect that data. Your CFO and other executives will appreciate receiving a quantifiable number for risks rather than a more traditional qualitative assessment.

Impact

Impact, in the context of risk analysis, refers to the potential consequences or effects on an organization if a specific threat materializes. It's a critical metric that helps quantify the severity of a risk and is often expressed in financial terms but can also include non-monetary consequences like reputational damage or loss of customer trust. Understanding the concept of impact can significantly enhance your risk management strategies.

One of the most straightforward ways to measure impact is in monetary terms. Impact could be the cost of data loss, system downtime, or legal fees. Accurately calculating the financial impact of a risk event helps in budget allocation for risk mitigation. However, the impact of a risk event can extend beyond immediate financial loss to long-term reputational damage. For instance, a data breach could lead to a loss of customer trust, which may not have direct financial implications but could severely affect future revenue.

Some risks can significantly impact your organization's capability to operate. For example, a cyberattack that takes down an e-commerce website could result in lost sales and operational disruptions that have cascading effects on suppliers, logistics, and human resources. The impact of failing to meet compliance requirements can be severe, including hefty fines and legal penalties. In some cases, non-compliance could even result in the suspension of business operations. Therefore, understanding the potential regulatory impact is crucial for risk assessment.

As with other risk metrics, the potential impact of risks is not static. It can change due to various factors, such as market conditions, technological advancements, or regulation changes. You might even see a change in risk metrics due to a shift in cultural interpretation of a threat. Continuous monitoring and periodic reassessment are crucial for keeping your impact assessments current.

Risk Register

A *risk register* is a centralized repository that records identified risks, their charac-teristics, and their management plans. It is a critical risk management tool that pro-vides a structured way to track and evaluate risks over time. Let's delve into the key components of risk registers and how they can be leveraged in real-world scenarios.

Key Risk Indicators (KRIs)

Key risk indicators (KRIs) are metrics that measure the potential impact and likeli-hood of identified risks. KRIs are essential for monitoring risk levels and triggering alerts when risks reach certain thresholds. They can be quantitative, such as financial loss, and qualitative, such as reputational damage. KRIs can be set up in a security information and event management (SIEM) system to trigger alerts for unusual activities, such as multiple failed login attempts, which could indicate a potential security breach.

Risk Owners

The *risk owner* is the individual or department responsible for managing a particu-lar risk. Risk owners are accountable for implementing risk mitigation strategies and monitoring the risk over time. In an organization, the IT department may own cybersecurity risks, while the legal department may own compliance risks. Clearly defining risk owners ensures that there's accountability and that risks are actively managed.

Risk Threshold

The *risk threshold* is the level of risk that an organization is willing to accept. Exceeding this level triggers a response, such as escalation to higher management or initiating a predefined risk mitigation strategy. Setting a risk threshold helps in auto-mating the risk response process. For instance, if a financial risk crosses a specific dollar amount, it could automatically trigger a review process or activate a contin-gency plan.

You can systematically track and manage risks by maintaining a good risk register, which helps ensure that you're not caught off guard when risks materialize. Table 24-5 shows an example of what a risk register might look like in an organization. A risk register like this one allows for better resource allocation, as you can quickly identify risks that require immediate attention and that are within acceptable limits. Taking a proactive approach to risk management can save your organization time, money, and, potentially, its reputation.

Key Topic

Table 24-5   Risk Register Example

Risk ID	Description	Key Risk Indicator	Risk Owner	Risk Threshold	Current Status	Mitigation Plan
1	Data breach	Financial loss	IT Dept	$10,000	Under Threshold	Implement 2FA
2	Non-compliance	Legal penalties	Legal Dept	2 incidents	Over Threshold	Review compliance policy
3	Supply chain disruption	Operational delay	Ops Dept	5 days	Under Threshold	Diversify suppliers
4	Reputational damage	Customer churn	Marketing	10%	Under Threshold	Crisis communication plan

Let's review each section in the risk register example in Table 24-5:

- **Risk ID:** The risk ID is a unique identifier for each risk that makes it easier to track and manage risks. It's usually a numeric or alphanumeric code. Assigning a unique ID to each risk ensures that no ambiguity exists when discussing or monitoring it. This is particularly useful in larger organizations where multiple departments may be involved in risk management.

- **Description:** The description provides a brief but clear explanation of the risk, outlining what it is and why it's a concern. A well-articulated description ensures that everyone in the organization understands the nature of the risk, which is crucial for effective management and mitigation.

- **Key risk indicator (KRI):** As previously discussed, KRIs are metrics that measure the potential impact and likelihood of identified risks. KRIs are essential for ongoing monitoring. They provide quantifiable or qualifiable measures that, when reached or exceeded, trigger an action or alert.

- **Risk owner:** The risk owner is the individual or department responsible for managing the risk. Assigning a risk owner ensures accountability and ensures that the risk is actively managed. The owner is responsible for implementing mitigation strategies and monitoring the risk over time.

- **Risk threshold:** The risk threshold is the level of risk that an organization is willing to accept before action is required. Setting a risk threshold helps automate the risk response process. If a risk crosses this threshold, it triggers a predefined action or escalation, ensuring timely intervention.

- **Current status:** The current status indicates whether the risk is above or below the defined threshold. It provides a real-time snapshot of the risk, allowing for an immediate understanding of whether the risk is currently a concern that needs to be addressed.

■ **Mitigation plan:** The mitigation plan outlines the steps that will be taken to reduce the risk or its impact. This is the action plan that the risk owner will execute to manage the risk. This must be clearly defined so that everyone is clear about what steps must be taken.

Risk Tolerance

Risk tolerance is the specific amount of risk that an organization is willing to accept as it pursues its business objectives. Risk tolerance is a guiding metric for decision making, particularly in IT and cybersecurity. Risk tolerance is often quantified through various metrics such as financial loss thresholds, downtime allowances, or acceptable levels of data exposure.

Risk tolerance plays a pivotal role in shaping an organization's cybersecurity posture. For example, a financial institution with a low risk tolerance may invest heavily in multilayered security solutions, including advanced firewalls, intrusion detection systems, and regular third-party security audits. The goal is to minimize the potential for data breaches or financial loss resulting in reputational damage, even if it means a higher up-front investment in security measures.

On the other hand, a tech startup with a high risk tolerance might prioritize speed and innovation over stringent security protocols. The "move fast and break things" mindset is common in the startup world. A tech startup might opt for rapid development cycles and quicker deployments, accepting the associated risks as a trade-off for potential market advantage. In this scenario, the IT department might employ a more agile approach to security, using real-time monitoring tools to manage risks as they arise rather than investing in extensive preemptive measures.

Risk Appetite

Risk appetite is the level of risk an organization is willing to accept to pursue its objectives. It's a broader concept than risk tolerance and is often categorized into three types: expansionary, conservative, and neutral. Each category has distinct characteristics that influence an organization's approach to risk, particularly in the IT and cybersecurity domains.

Expansionary

An *expansionary risk appetite* means the organization is willing to accept higher levels of risk to capitalize on growth opportunities. In the IT sphere, this often translates to early adoption of emerging technologies or methodologies. These early adoptions typically promise significant competitive advantages, even if they haven't been fully vetted for security risks. For instance, a company with an expansionary risk appetite might be among the first to implement blockchain technology for secure transactions. It would accept the associated uncertainties and vulnerabilities as a calculated risk for potential market leadership.

Conservative

A *conservative risk appetite* indicates a preference for lower levels of risk, with a focus on stability and sustainable growth. Organizations with this mindset often opt for tried-and-true technologies and are likely to invest in enhancing existing security measures. For example, a healthcare provider with a conservative risk appetite might prioritize HIPAA compliance and patient data security over adopting the latest medical software that has yet to be proven. The IT department in such an organization would likely focus on robust encryption methods, multifactor authentication, and regular security audits to minimize risks.

Neutral

Organizations with a *neutral risk appetite* take a balanced approach. They are willing to accept some level of risk but not at the expense of stability. In the IT context, this could mean opting for a hybrid approach to technology adoption. For instance, the IT department might implement a hybrid cloud solution, leveraging the scalability and flexibility of public cloud services while maintaining sensitive data on a more secure private cloud. This balanced approach allows the organization to benefit from technological advancements without exposing itself to undue risk.

Risk Management Strategies

This section looks into the details of risk management strategies. *Risk management strategies* are systematic approaches to managing and mitigating risks in an organization or in a project. They involve identifying potential risks, assessing their impact and likelihood, and implementing measures to transfer, avoid, mitigate, or accept those risks, based on the organization's risk tolerance and appetite. These strategies typically seek to minimize the negative impacts of risks on organizational objectives while maximizing opportunities. Organizations usually employ one of the following general strategies when managing a particular risk:

Key Topic

- Transfer the risk to another organization or to a third party.
- Avoid the risk.
- Mitigate the risk.
- Accept some or all of the consequences of a risk.

Risk Transfer

It is possible to transfer *some* risk to a third party. An example of **risk transference** (also known as risk sharing) would be an organization purchasing cybersecurity insurance for a group of servers in a data center. With risk transference , an organization still takes on the risk of losing data in the event of equipment failure, theft, and disaster but transfers the risk of losing money to a third party.

Risk Acceptance

Most organizations are willing to accept a certain amount of risk, a practice known as **risk acceptance**. Within this framework are two specific scenarios to consider: risk exemption and risk exception. **Risk exemption** refers to a situation where a known vulnerability is intentionally left unaddressed, often due to its low impact or the high cost of mitigation. This is a calculated decision that is usually documented and approved by senior management. On the other hand, **risk exception** occurs when a vulnerability is discovered but cannot be immediately addressed due to constraints such as IT budgeting or resource availability. In such cases, a temporary workaround may be implemented until resources for a more permanent solution become available. Both exemption and exception are strategic choices influenced by factors like IT budgeting and resource management. These decisions are made carefully, weighing the potential impact of a vulnerability against the cost and feasibility of mitigation solutions.

Risk Avoidance

Some organizations opt to avoid risk. **Risk avoidance** usually entails not carrying out a proposed plan because the risk factor is too great. An example of risk avoidance would be a high-profile organization deciding not to implement a new and controversial website based on its belief that too many attackers would attempt to exploit it.

Risk Mitigation

The most common goal of risk management is to exercise **risk mitigation**, which involves putting in place enough protections to lower the overall risk to a level that is acceptable to the organization. It is impossible to eliminate all risk, but it should be mitigated as much as possible within reason. Usually, budgeting and IT resources dictate the level of risk mitigation and what kinds of deterrents can be put in place. For example, installing antivirus/firewall software on every client computer is common; most companies do this. However, installing a high-end, hardware-based firewall at every computer is not common; although this method would probably make for a secure network, the amount of money and administration needed to implement that solution would make it unacceptable.

After risk transference, risk avoidance, and risk mitigation techniques have been implemented, an organization is left with a certain amount of residual risk—the risk that is left over after a detailed security plan and disaster recovery plan have been implemented. There is always risk because a company cannot possibly foresee every future event, and it cannot secure against every single threat. Senior management as a collective whole is ultimately responsible for deciding how much residual risk there will be in a company's infrastructure and how much risk there will be to the company's data. Often, no one person is in charge of this level, but it will be decided on as a group.

There are many different types of risks to computers and computer networks. Of course, before you can decide what to do about particular risks, you need to assess what those risks are.

Risk Reporting

In IT and cybersecurity, *risk reporting* involves the systematic documentation and dissemination of risk assessments, risk analysis findings, and risk management strategies to relevant stakeholders. These stakeholders could range from C-level executives to department heads and external regulatory bodies. The reports often include key metrics, such as KRIs, to provide a snapshot of the organization's risk landscape.

For example, if you're an IT manager overseeing a network upgrade, your risk report might include data on potential security vulnerabilities introduced by the new network components. Depending on the severity and impact of the identified risks, this report would be shared with the CISO (chief information security officer) and potentially even the board of directors. The report would outline the identified risks, the steps to mitigate them, and any residual risks that need to be accepted or further addressed.

The format of a risk report can vary, but it often includes an executive summary, detailed findings, recommendations, and an action plan. Some organizations use specialized risk management software to automate risk report creation, while others may use a more manual approach involving spreadsheets and presentations.

You should be prepared to develop a risk report and know how to do it effectively so you are ready when you are asked to produce one. Developing a good risk report ensures that risks are understood and managed and that the organization's risk posture is aligned with its risk tolerance and appetite. Mastering the art of risk reporting is a valuable skill for anyone involved in risk management. Figure 24-2 shows an example of a risk report for the network upgrade we just discussed. See if you can identify the sources of the KRIs or how you might go about assessing the risks in this report.

Sample Risk Report

Executive Summary
This report aims to identify, assess, and propose mitigation strategies for the risks associated with the upcoming network upgrade project. The primary focus is on potential security vulnerabilities the new network components could introduce.

Key Risk Indicators (KRIs)
- Number of identified vulnerabilities: 3
- Potential financial impact: $200,000
- Risk Severity: High

Detailed Findings
1. **Risk: Unauthorized Access**
   - Likelihood: High
   - Impact: Severe
   - Mitigation: Implement multi-factor authentication
   - Residual Risk: Moderate
2. **Risk: Data Leakage**
   - Likelihood: Moderate
   - Impact: High
   - Mitigation: Data encryption and regular audits
   - Residual Risk: Low
3. **Risk: Network Downtime**
   - Likelihood: Low
   - Impact: Moderate
   - Mitigation: Redundant systems and backup power supply
   - Residual Risk: Low

Recommendations
1. Prioritize the implementation of multi-factor authentication to reduce the risk of unauthorized access.
2. Conduct regular security audits to ensure data integrity.
3. Establish a contingency plan for potential network downtime.

Action Plan
- Implement multi-factor authentication by Q2.
- Schedule the first security audit for Q3.
- Complete contingency planning by the end of Q2.

Figure 24-2   Sample Risk Report

Business Impact Analysis

A *business impact analysis (BIA)* is a process used to determine the potential impacts that may result from the interruption of time-sensitive or critical business processes. This section starts by covering recovery time objectives and recovery point objectives, and it then describes mean time to repair and mean time between failures. From there, it covers functional recovery plans, single points of failure, and disaster recovery plans. It concludes with a look at mission-essential functions, identification of critical systems, and site risk assessment.

Recovery Time Objective (RTO)

The *recovery time objective (RTO)* is the time by which a business process must be restored after a disruption to avoid unacceptable consequences. Basically, it's the maximum allowable downtime for a specific operation, system, or application. For example, if an e-commerce website goes down, the RTO might be as short as a few minutes, given the direct impact the outage would have on sales and customer experience. RTOs inform decisions like how much to invest in redundant systems or when to opt for cloud-based disaster recovery solutions that can be spun up quickly.

Recovery Point Objective (RPO)

The *recovery point objective (RPO)* is the maximum amount of data, as measured by time, that can be lost due to a disruption. It answers the question, "How much data can we afford to lose?" For instance, if you're running a financial transaction system, the RPO might be close to zero, as even a small amount of data loss could be catastrophic. Knowing the RPO helps an IT team determine the frequency of backups. If the RPO is low, more frequent backups are necessary, and a more robust backup solution might be required.

Mean Time to Repair (MTTR)

Mean time to repair (MTTR) refers to the average time required to repair a failed device or system and restore it to an operational state. MTTR is a critical factor in maintenance and disaster recovery processes; it impacts the total downtime experienced during an outage.

When considering a disaster recovery plan (DRP), MTTR is a key performance indicator. It helps an organization understand the operational impact of repair times and guides the decision-making process for employing redundancy or keeping spare parts. For systems that are not time sensitive, maintaining a stockpile of spare parts can be a cost-effective alternative to redundancy. However, if network and system uptime is crucial, finding cost-effective redundancy solutions is imperative.

NOTE   In the upcoming server room scenario, look for an indication that some equipment lacks redundancy, such as single-instance servers. In such cases, understanding MTTR is essential to develop contingency plans.

For equipment that an organization cannot afford to have down, it is vital to either implement redundant systems or ensure rapid repair capabilities to maintain service continuity.

Mean Time Between Failures (MTBF)

Mean time between failures (MTBF) is a reliability metric that quantifies the expected average time between failures for a system or component. It is important to understand how often a product is likely to fail during operation. For instance, an MTBF of 1 million hours suggests that, on average, a failure can be expected once every 1 million hours of operation. This statistic is derived from historical data collected from various customers who use the product.

Another metric similar to MTBF is failure in time (FIT), which denotes the number of failures per billion hours of operation. MTBF, along with FIT, plays a vital role in formulating a robust disaster recovery plan (DRP), as it helps anticipate the frequency of potential failures.

In environments with proper planning, MTBF is used to design systems that can withstand most failures. This is achieved through redundancy measures such as multiple power sources and data backups, which ensure that single points of failure are minimized. In the following server room example, redundancy is demonstrated through dual domain controllers and web servers that provide failover redundancy to maintain operations without downtime in the event of a component failure.

When an environment is planned properly, it can withstand most failures barring total disaster by using the following redundancy precautions:

- Redundant power in the form of power supplies, UPSs, and backup generators

- Redundant data, servers, ISPs, and sites

An important concept here is single point of failure. A single point of failure is an element, an object, or a part of a system that, if it fails, causes the whole system to fail. By implementing redundancy, you can bypass just about any single point of failure.

There are two methods to combat single points of failure. The first is to use redundancy. If employed properly, redundancy keeps a system running, with no downtime. However, this solution can be pricy, and we all know there is only so much IT budget to go around. The alternative is to make sure you have plenty of spare parts lying around. This is a good method if your network and systems are not time critical. Installing spare parts often requires you to shut down the server or a portion of a network. If this risk is not acceptable to an organization, you'll have to find the cheapest redundant solutions available. Research is key, but don't be fooled by hype: Sometimes the simplest-sounding solutions are the best.

Say that your server room has the following powered equipment:

- Nine servers
- Two Microsoft domain controllers (DCs)
- One DNS server
- Two file servers
- One database server
- Two web servers (which second as FTP servers)
- One mail server
- Five 48-port switches
- One master switch
- Three routers
- Two CSU/DSUs
- One PBX
- Two client workstations (for remote server access without having to work directly at the server) within the server room

It appears that there is already some redundancy in place in this server room. For example, there are two DCs. One of them has a copy of Active Directory and acts as a secondary DC if the first one fails. There are also two web servers, and if the primary one fails, the other web server is ready to take over. (This type of redundancy, known as *failover redundancy*, has a secondary system that is inactive until the first one fails.) In this scenario, two client workstations are used to remotely control the servers; if one fails, the other one is available.

The rest of the servers and other pieces of equipment in this scenario are one-offs—single instances in need of something to prevent failure. There are a lot of them, and you need to implement a lot of redundancy. Taking a detailed approach to preparing for problems that can arise in a system makes for a good IT contingency plan. Try to envision the various redundancy methods that could be used with each of the items listed previously for this server room example.

Chapter Review Activities

Use the features in this section to study and review the topics in this chapter.

Review Key Topics

Review the most important topics in the chapter, noted with the Key Topic icon in the outer margin of the page. Table 24-6 lists these key topics and the page number on which each is found.

Table 24-6   Key Topics for Chapter 24

Key Topic Element	Description	Page Number
Section	Risk Identification	561
Section	Risk Assessment	562
Figure 24-1	Risk Matrix/Heat Map	564
Table 24-2	Common Risk Analysis Terms	564
Table 24-3	Quantitative Risk Assessment Example	566
Table 24-4	Risk Assessment Types	567
Table 24-5	Risk Register Example	573
List	Managing a particular risk	575
Section	Risk Reporting	577
Figure 24-2	Sample Risk Report	578

Define Key Terms

Define the following key terms from this chapter, and check your answers in the glossary:

risk identification, risk assessment, ad hoc risk assessment, recurring risk assessment, one-time risk assessment, continuous risk assessment, risk analysis, qualitative risk assessment, quantitative risk assessment, single loss expectancy (SLE), annualized rate of occurrence (ARO), annualized loss expectancy (ALE), probability, likelihood, exposure factor (EF), impact, risk register, key risk indicators (KRIs), risk owner, risk threshold, risk tolerance, risk appetite, expansionary risk appetite, conservative risk appetite, neutral risk appetite, risk management strategy, risk transference, risk acceptance, risk exemption, risk exception, risk avoidance, risk mitigation, risk reporting, business impact analysis (BIA), recovery time objective (RTO), recovery point objective (RPO), mean time to repair (MTTR), mean time between failures (MTBF)

Review Questions

Answer the following review questions. Check your answers with the answer key in Appendix A.

1. What is the main difference between risk identification and risk assessment in the risk management process?

2. Describe a situation in which an ad hoc risk assessment would be appropriate.

3. How does probability differ from impact in the context of risk analysis?

4. Who is typically responsible for implementing risk mitigation strategies in an organization?

5. What are the three types of risk appetite, and how do they differ in their approach to risk?

6. What key metrics are often included in risk reporting to provide a snapshot of an organization's risk landscape?

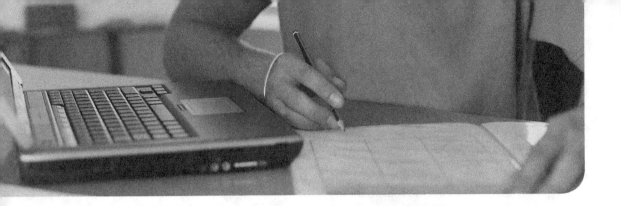

This chapter covers the following topics related to Objective 5.3 (Explain the processes associated with third-party risk assessment and management) of the CompTIA Security+ SY0-701 certification exam:

- Vendor assessment
- Vendor selection
- Agreement types
- Vendor monitoring
- Questionnaires
- Rules of engagement

Understanding the Processes Associated with Third-Party Risk Assessment and Management

This chapter is a comprehensive guide to third-party risk management, focusing on vendor assessment, selection, and ongoing monitoring. It emphasizes the importance of well-defined service-level agreements (SLAs) and covers various assessment methods, such as penetration testing and the right-to-audit clause. The chapter also delves into internal audits and independent assessments, providing a balanced view of a vendor's risk profile. The chapter highlights supply chain analysis as a critical element and also discusses the vendor selection process, including due diligence and conflict of interest. Various agreement types, including master service agreements (MSAs), are explored in detail. The chapter concludes with practical insights into vendor monitoring, use of questionnaires, and the importance of clear rules of engagement, all enriched with real-world examples and cautionary notes.

NOTE   Use of the terms *master* and *slave* is ONLY in association with the official terminology used in industry specifications and standards and in no way diminishes Pearson's commitment to promoting diversity, equity, and inclusion and challenging, countering, and/or combating bias and stereotyping in the global population of the learners we serve.

"Do I Know This Already?" Quiz

The "Do I Know This Already?" quiz enables you to assess whether you should read this entire chapter thoroughly or jump to the "Chapter Review Activities" section. If you are in doubt about your answers to these questions or your own assessment of your knowledge of the topics, read the entire chapter. Table 25-1 lists the major headings in this chapter and their corresponding "Do I Know This Already?" quiz questions. You can find the answers in Appendix A, "Answers to the 'Do I Know This Already?' Quizzes and Review Questions."

Table 25-1   "Do I Know This Already?" Section-to-Question Mapping

Foundation Topics Section	Questions
Vendor Assessment	1
Vendor Selection	2
Agreement Types	3, 4
Vendor Monitoring	5
Questionnaires	6
Rules of Engagement	7

CAUTION   The goal of self-assessment is to gauge your mastery of the topics in this chapter. If you do not know the answer to a question or are only partially sure of the answer, you should mark that question as wrong for purposes of self-assessment. Giving yourself credit for an answer you correctly guess skews your self-assessment results and might provide you with a false sense of security.

1. What is the primary purpose of a service-level agreement (SLA) in vendor assessment?

    a. To define the vendor's marketing strategies

    b. To outline the level of service expected from a service provider

    c. To establish a confidential relationship between parties

    d. To specify the profits each partner will get

2. What is a key aspect of due diligence in the vendor selection process?

    a. Determining the vendor's marketing reach

    b. Evaluating the vendor's cybersecurity measures and protocols

    c. Establishing the rules of engagement

    d. Setting up the disaster recovery drills

3. What does a memorandum of understanding (MOU) primarily outline?

    a. The level of service expected from a service provider

    b. Mutual roles and responsibilities in a project or partnership

    c. The terms and conditions of a partnership between two business entities

    d. The work activities, deliverables, and timeline a vendor must execute

4. What is the primary function of a master service agreement (MSA)?

   a. To define the level of service expected from a service provider

   b. To outline mutual roles and responsibilities in a project or partnership

   c. To agree to most of the terms that will govern future transactions or future agreements

   d. To establish a confidential relationship between parties

5. What is a critical aspect of vendor monitoring in a healthcare organization using a third-party service for storing patient records?

   a. Real-time data access tracking

   b. Marketing strategies

   c. Vendor's financial stability

   d. Vendor's marketing reach

6. What is the primary purpose of questionnaires in vendor selection and monitoring?

   a. To establish a confidential relationship between parties

   b. To extract nuanced information about a vendor's operational resilience and data handling practices

   c. To define the level of service expected from a service provider

   d. To agree to most of the terms that will govern future transactions or future agreements

7. What do the rules of engagement primarily dictate?

   a. The level of service expected from a service provider

   b. How various activities and interactions will be conducted between an organization and a vendor

   c. A vendor's cybersecurity measures and protocols

   d. The terms and conditions of a partnership between two business entities

Foundation Topics

Vendor Assessment

Before we begin this discussion of third-party risk management, we need to mention that the following information is *not* intended as legal advice. Before signing any contracts, an organization should strongly consider consulting with an attorney.

Organizations typically have in-depth policies concerning vendors. Issues often occur due to the level of agreement between an organization and a vendor not being clearly defined. A proper service-level agreement (SLA) that an organization examines carefully before signing can be helpful. A basic service contract is usually not enough; a service contract with an SLA will have a section within it that formally and clearly defines exactly what a vendor is responsible for and what the organization is responsible for. It might also define performance expectations and what the vendor will do if a failure of service occurs, time frames for repair, backup plans, and so on. To benefit the organization, these points are usually legally binding and not informal. Consequently, it benefits an organization to scrutinize an SLA before signing it, and the organization's attorney should be involved in this process.

For instance, a company might use an ISP for its Internet connection. The customer will want to know what kind of fault-tolerant methods are on hand at the ISP and what kind of uptime to expect, which should be monitored by a network administrator. The SLA might have some sort of guarantee of measurable service that can be clearly defined—perhaps a minimum level of service and a target level of service. Before a company signs an SLA such as this, it is recommended that an attorney, the IT director, and other organizational management review the document carefully and make sure that it covers all the points required by the organization.

On a separate note, a business partners agreement (BPA) is a type of contract that can establish the profits each partner will get, what responsibilities each partner will have, and exit strategies for partners. This often applies to supply chain and business partners.

NOTE   You will also see *BPA* stand for blanket purchase agreement (BPA) in an SLA that requires products and services over and over again. This type of agreement, which is similar to a blanket order, is common in government contracts, but some organizations use them also.

One issue to address is to ensure that there is some type of ending for the contract length. Some less-than-reputable cloud service providers design open-ended BPAs. Try to avoid them. We will explore this concept deeper a little later in this chapter.

Penetration Testing

Penetration testing, often called *pen testing*, is the process of running simulated cyberattacks against a system to check for vulnerabilities. The process is essential for understanding how well a vendor's system can safeguard against attacks. It's not just about finding vulnerabilities; it's about understanding the depth of those vulnerabilities and how they could be exploited.

There are different types of penetration tests, each with a focus that we have reviewed in greater depth earlier in this book. As a quick refresher, an unknown environment test mimics an external cyberattack and starts with no prior knowledge of the system. In contrast, a known environment test is more comprehensive and is conducted with full knowledge of the system. The choice between these types depends on what you aim to learn from the test. A partially known environment test is a mix of the other two types and is generally customized to the client's desires.

You might see pen tests in nearly any security position. An organization might hire a third-party cybersecurity firm to conduct penetration testing on a prospective vendor's systems. This could be particularly important for sectors like finance or healthcare, where data breaches could severely affect reputations. The test results would then be analyzed to determine if the vendor meets the organization's cybersecurity standards.

Right-to-Audit Clause

A *right-to-audit clause* is a contractual provision that grants one party the right to perform audits on another party to ensure compliance with specified criteria. This clause maintains transparency and accountability between an organization and a vendor.

The audit scope can vary and should be explicitly defined in the contract. It may include financial audits, compliance audits, or security audits. However, there are limitations. For example, the clause may specify that audits can only be conducted during regular business hours and with reasonable notice to avoid disrupting the vendor's operations.

In practice, a right-to-audit clause might be invoked if there are suspicions of non-compliance or after a security incident involving the vendor occurs. For instance, if a healthcare provider works with a third-party billing service, the right-to-audit clause could be used to ensure that the vendor complies with healthcare regulations like HIPAA. The clause provides a legal pathway to verify that the vendor maintains the agreed-upon standards, safeguarding the organization's data and reputation.

One important thing to remember is that most cloud vendors do not allow their systems to be audited. Of course, there are several reasons for this, including the incredible logistics that would be involved with 20,000+ customers all wanting ad hoc audits. Companies attempt to include right-to-audit clauses in their contracts with varying levels of success.

Evidence of Internal Audits

Evidence of internal audits refers to the documentation and findings from audits conducted within a vendor's organization. These audits are self-initiated and aim to assess the effectiveness of the internal control environment, including compliance with legal requirements and internal policies. Access to a vendor's internal audit evidence is essential for gaining insights into the vendor's operational integrity and risk management effectiveness.

The evidence may include audit reports, corrective action plans, and compliance certificates. Internal audits may be financial audits, security audits, or operational audits. Each type of audit serves a different purpose. For example, a financial audit focuses on the accuracy of financial statements, while a security audit evaluates the robustness of cybersecurity measures.

In practice, you might see a financial institution request evidence of internal audits from a cloud service provider before entering into a contract. This evidence would be scrutinized to ensure that the vendor has robust data protection measures and complies with regulations such as GDPR or CCPA. The internal audits act as a self-check mechanism for the vendor, and their evidence serves as a confidence-building measure for the client organization.

Independent Assessments

An *independent assessment* is an evaluation conducted by a third-party organization that is not directly involved in a vendor's business operations. Such an assessment provides an unbiased view of the vendor's compliance and risk management status. These assessments are often more trusted than internal audits because impartial experts conduct them.

Common types of independent assessments include SOC 2 reports, ISO certifications, NIST CSF cybersecurity risk assessments, and third-party penetration tests. Such an assessment is usually conducted based on industry standards and best practices and provides a benchmark for evaluating the vendor's capabilities.

For instance, a healthcare organization looking to contract with a software provider might require an independent assessment to verify that the vendor's product meets HIPAA compliance standards. The assessment would be conducted by a third-party organization specializing in healthcare compliance, ensuring an unbiased evaluation.

Evidence of internal audits and independent assessments offer complementary perspectives on a vendor's risk profile. While internal audits provide a view from within the organization, independent assessments offer external validation of the vendor's compliance and security posture.

Supply Chain Analysis

Supply chain analysis is the process of thoroughly evaluating every element and process in a vendor's supply chain, from raw material sourcing to product delivery. This analysis is crucial for understanding the potential risks introduced by third-party suppliers, subcontractors, and other entities that the vendor relies on. A weak link in the supply chain can expose an organization to various risks, including operational disruptions, quality issues, and security vulnerabilities.

A thorough supply chain analysis often includes evaluation of supplier credentials, manufacturing processes, logistical arrangements, and even geopolitical factors that might affect supply chain stability. Frameworks like the NIST Cybersecurity Framework or the ISO 28000 series on supply chain security can serve as guidelines for conducting such an analysis.

The risks identified could be multifaceted, ranging from the financial instability of a supplier to lax cybersecurity measures in a subcontractor's systems. These risks are categorized into operational risks, compliance risks, and cybersecurity risks, among others.

An organization in the healthcare sector might use supply chain analysis to evaluate a medical device vendor. This would involve scrutinizing the suppliers of hardware components, the software development practices, and the logistics companies responsible for device delivery. The analysis would identify potential risks that could compromise patient safety, data security, or compliance with healthcare regulations.

Various tools and techniques can be used for supply chain analysis, including the supplier audits discussed earlier, SWOT analysis, and advanced methods like data analytics and machine learning algorithms that can be used to predict potential future risks based on historical data.

Vendor Selection

Vendor selection is a critical process that involves evaluating and choosing a third-party service or product provider that best aligns with an organization's needs, goals, and risk tolerance. This process is not just about cost-effectiveness; it also includes factors like quality, reliability, and security. This section examines two key aspects of vendor selection: due diligence and conflict of interest.

Key
Topic **Due Diligence**

Due diligence refers to the comprehensive appraisal of a vendor's business practices, financial stability, reputation, and compliance with relevant laws and regulations. It's an essential step in vendor selection to ensure that the organization partners with a reliable and competent third party. Cybersecurity professionals are occasionally brought in during a due diligence review to ensure that the organization follows industry best practices.

The due diligence process often includes, but is not limited to, the following activities:

- **Financial audits:** Review of the vendor's financial statements to assess stability

- **Legal checks:** Verification of compliance with industry-specific laws and regulations

- **Security assessments:** Evaluation of the vendor's cybersecurity measures and protocols

For instance, if you're selecting a cloud service provider, due diligence involves scrutinizing the provider's data center locations and compliance certifications, as well as the results of third-party security audits. The goal is to ensure that the vendor meets your organization's data sovereignty and security requirements.

Conflict of Interest

A *conflict of interest* arises when a vendor has competing professional or personal interests that could interfere with their ability to act in the best interests of your organization. Identifying and managing conflicts of interest is crucial for maintaining the integrity of the vendor selection process.

Conflicts of interest can manifest in various ways, such as:

- **Financial conflicts:** These conflicts occur when a decision maker in an organization has a financial stake in the vendor company.

- **Relational conflicts:** These conflicts occur when personal relationships could influence vendor selection.

- **Competitive conflicts:** These conflicts occur when a vendor may also be a competitor in some aspects of the business.

Let's suppose for a moment that a key decision maker in your organization is a close relative of a vendor's CEO. This relationship could bias the vendor selection process and must be disclosed and managed to ensure a fair evaluation.

Agreement Types

In third-party risk assessment and management, the types of agreements you enter into can significantly impact the level of risk your organization assumes. Agreements are the legal backbone of any vendor relationship, outlining both parties' responsibilities, expectations, and boundaries. The parties start out as friends and high-fiving before the work begins, but in the end, the contract may decide who remains happy. Understanding the nuances of different agreement types is crucial for ensuring that an organization is adequately protected and that the vendor relationship is clearly defined. This section covers various types of agreements, including service-level agreements (SLAs), memorandums of agreement (MOAs), and memorandums of understanding (MOUs), among others. It also looks at master service agreements (MSAs), which are overarching contracts that govern multiple individual agreements or projects.

Table 25-2 outlines key agreement types you might encounter as a security professional. You should always read agreements carefully, and you should read them several times. It is important to understand key information related to the service you are providing to or receiving from another entity.

Key Topic

Table 25-2   Key Agreement Types

Agreement Type	Definition	Example
Service-level agreement (SLA)	A contract that defines the level of service expected from a service provider	In a cloud computing SLA, metrics like uptime and latency are specified.
Memorandum of agreement (MOA)	A written document that specifies a cooperative, but generally non-legally binding, relationship between two parties	Two companies engage in a joint marketing campaign and outline responsibilities.
Memorandum of understanding (MOU)	A less formal agreement that outlines mutual roles and responsibilities in a project or partnership	A cybersecurity firm and a nonprofit collaborate on a community awareness program.
Master service agreement (MSA)	A contract reached between parties in which the parties agree to most of the terms that will govern future transactions or future agreements	A software development company and a client agree on the general terms that will govern all future projects.
Work order (WO)/ statement of work (SOW)	A formal document that describes the work activities, deliverables, and timeline involved when a vendor performs specified work for a client	A WO/SOW is issued for a specific IT project, detailing the scope and expected deliverables.

Agreement Type	Definition	Example
Non-disclosure agreement (NDA)	A legally binding contract that establishes a confidential relationship between parties	An NDA is signed before a new employee is given access to sensitive company information.
Business partners agreement (BPA)	An agreement that outlines the terms and conditions of a partnership between two business entities	Two tech companies form a partnership to co-develop a new software product and outline their roles in a BPA.

Vendor Monitoring

Vendor monitoring is a critical, ongoing activity that is the backbone of effective third-party risk management. *Vendor monitoring* is a process that goes beyond merely checking compliance boxes; it's about actively ensuring that vendors meet or exceed the performance, security, and reliability standards outlined in contractual agreements. The scope of vendor monitoring can be extensive, covering areas like quality of service, data protection, and even ethical considerations like labor practices.

Consider a healthcare organization that uses a third-party service for storing patient records in a real-world scenario. In this context, vendor monitoring would involve real-time data access tracking, regular audits to ensure HIPAA compliance, and performance metrics to measure uptime and speed. Automated tools can be employed to provide alerts for any unauthorized data access or downtime that violates the SLA. Periodic reviews would be conducted to reassess the vendor's capabilities in light of evolving regulations and threats.

Questionnaires

Questionnaires serve as a foundational element in both the vendor selection process and ongoing vendor monitoring. These are not mere fill-out forms but strategic tools to extract nuanced information. A well-crafted questionnaire can reveal insights into a vendor's operational resilience, data handling practices, and corporate culture, indicating reliability and integrity.

For example, in the financial sector, a questionnaire could include questions that probe the vendor's practices around data encryption, multifactor authentication, and incident response. The answers can provide illumination, but the real value often lies in the follow-up. If a vendor indicates that they have an incident response plan, the next step is to ask for evidence, such as records of response drills or third-party audit reports. This depth of inquiry can provide a multidimensional view of the vendor's capabilities and preparedness, far beyond what surface-level metrics can offer.

NOTE   A word of caution on questionnaires: Many vendors get consumed by the volume of questionnaires they must fill out to satisfy internal and independent auditors. Keep an eye on how much time your team spends completing these questionnaires.

Key Topic Rules of Engagement

The term *rules of engagement* refers to the agreed-upon guidelines that dictate how various activities and interactions will be conducted between an organization and a vendor. This includes everything from the escalation procedures for resolving issues to the protocols for changing services or products provided. For example, the rules of engagement would outline the steps for reporting a security vulnerability discovered in software provided by the vendor, the expected response time from the vendor, and the process for remediation. Having clear rules of engagement ensures that both parties know exactly what to do in different scenarios, reducing ambiguity and potential conflicts. This is particularly important in high-stakes areas like cybersecurity, where a delayed or improper response can have severe consequences.

You should include walkthroughs of several scenarios that require your security team to use published rules of engagement with a vendor during disaster recovery drills. It is a good idea to include your vendors in tabletops and exercise the rules of engagement before you need them in an actual incident.

Chapter Review Activities

Use the features in this section to study and review the topics in this chapter.

Review Key Topics

Review the most important topics in the chapter, noted with the Key Topic icon in the outer margin of the page. Table 25-3 lists these key topics and the page number on which each is found.

Table 25-3   Key Topics for Chapter 25

Key Topic Element	Description	Page Number
Section	Vendor Assessment	588
Section	Due Diligence	592
Table 25-2	Key Agreement Types	593
Section	Vendor Monitoring	594
Section	Questionnaires	594
Section	Rules of Engagement	595

Define Key Terms

Define the following key terms from this chapter and check your answers in the glossary:

penetration testing, right-to-audit clause, evidence of internal audits, independent assessment, supply chain analysis, vendor selection, due diligence, conflict of interest, service-level agreement (SLA), memorandum of agreement (MOA), memorandum of understanding (MOU), master service agreement (MSA), work order (WO)/statement of work (SOW), non-disclosure agreement (NDA), business partners agreement (BPA), vendor monitoring, questionnaire, rules of engagement

Review Questions

Answer the following review questions. Check your answers with the answer key in Appendix A.

1. What is the role of an SLA in defining the relationship between an organization and its vendor?

2. What activities are commonly included in the due diligence process during vendor selection?

3. What is the difference between a memorandum of agreement (MOA) and a memorandum of understanding (MOU)?

4. How does a master service agreement (MSA) govern future transactions between parties?

5. What are some key aspects that should be monitored in a healthcare organization that uses a third-party service for storing patient records?

6. What kind of information can a well-crafted questionnaire reveal about a vendor?

This chapter covers the following topics related to Objective 5.4 (Summarize elements of effective security compliance) of the CompTIA Security+ SY0-701 certification exam:

- Compliance reporting
- Consequences of non-compliance
- Compliance monitoring
- Privacy

CHAPTER 26

Summarizing Elements of Effective Security Compliance

This chapter provides a comprehensive guide to understanding the intricacies of security compliance in an organization. It kicks off with an exploration of compliance reporting, emphasizing that internal and external audits serve as more than just records, providing actionable insights for fortifying security controls. The chapter then focuses on the repercussions of failing to comply and details the financial, operational, and reputational costs involved. It also outlines the essentials of compliance monitoring, from the proactive steps involved in due diligence to the formalities of attestation and acknowledgment. Automation's role in streamlining these processes is also discussed. The chapter concludes with a deep dive into privacy, examining the legal frameworks that govern data protection at various jurisdictional levels, the responsibilities of data controllers and processors, and emerging principles such as the right to be forgotten.

"Do I Know This Already?" Quiz

The "Do I Know This Already?" quiz enables you to assess whether you should read this entire chapter thoroughly or jump to the "Chapter Review Activities" section. If you are in doubt about your answers to these questions or your own assessment of your knowledge of the topics, read the entire chapter. Table 26-1 lists the major headings in this chapter and their corresponding "Do I Know This Already?" quiz questions. You can find the answers in Appendix A, "Answers to the 'Do I Know This Already?' Quizzes and Review Questions."

Table 26-1 "Do I Know This Already?" Section-to-Question Mapping

Foundation Topics Section	Questions
Compliance Reporting	1
Consequences of Non-compliance	2
Compliance Monitoring	3, 8, 9
Privacy	4–7, 10

> **CAUTION**   The goal of self-assessment is to gauge your mastery of the topics in this chapter. If you do not know the answer to a question or are only partially sure of the answer, you should mark that question as wrong for purposes of self-assessment. Giving yourself credit for an answer you correctly guess skews your self-assessment results and might provide you with a false sense of security.

1. What is the primary purpose of internal compliance reporting?

    a. To create records for external audits

    b. To assess the effectiveness of controls such as firewalls

    c. To allocate resources for staff parties

    d. To prepare for annual board meetings

2. What could sanctions in cybersecurity mean for a healthcare provider?

    a. Increased funding from the government

    b. Restricted ability to transmit patient records electronically

    c. Mandatory staff retraining in customer service

    d. Expansion of healthcare services

3. What does due diligence involve in the context of cybersecurity?

    a. Gathering information to understand potential risks

    b. Allocating resources for marketing

    c. Preparing for external audits

    d. Focusing solely on data encryption methods

4. What is the primary focus of privacy in the context of cybersecurity?

    a. Safeguarding data against unauthorized access

    b. Expanding the organization's market reach

    c. Looking at employee benefits

    d. Streamlining internal processes

5. What do legal implications in the context of privacy primarily refer to?

    a. Ethical considerations

    b. Obligations and potential penalties related to data

    c. Marketing strategies

    d. Employee training programs

6. Who is responsible for determining the purposes and means of processing personal data?

   a. Controller

   b. Processor

   c. Both the controller and the processor

   d. Neither the controller nor the processor

7. What is the first task for a security analyst when a data subject exercises their right to be forgotten?

   a. Notify the media.

   b. Locate and erase the specified data from all systems.

   c. Conduct an external audit.

   d. Update the organization's privacy policy.

8. Which of the following best describes the purpose of an attestation in cybersecurity?

   a. To provide a formal declaration that an organization's security controls meet required standards

   b. To automatically monitor and respond to security incidents

   c. To catalog and map data stored in an organization's systems

   d. To set policies dictating how long data should be stored

9. What role does automation play in compliance monitoring?

   a. It formally declares that security controls meet specific standards.

   b. It uses software tools to perform tasks like vulnerability scanning and compliance checking.

   c. It involves cataloging different types of data stored within an organization.

   d. It sets the duration for which different types of data should be stored.

10. What is the purpose of a data inventory in an organization?

    a. To confirm that an organization's security controls meet specific standards

    b. To automate the process of monitoring network traffic and detecting vulnerabilities

    c. To identify where different types of data are stored within the organization's systems

    d. To define the duration for which different types of data should be stored

Foundation Topics

Compliance Reporting

Compliance reporting is more than a routine task; it's a structured process that serves dual functions. It offers internal stakeholders actionable insights by systematically documenting metrics like the number of thwarted unauthorized access attempts or the percentage of employees completing mandatory security training. On the other hand, it fulfills external obligations by creating detailed documents that adhere to industry-specific regulations and standards, often within strict time frames, to avoid penalties.

These are some examples of compliance reports you may encounter:

- **FCPA compliance:** This report reviews due diligence programs or internal accounting controls and typically assesses the effectiveness of measures taken to prevent corrupt practices and ensure adherence to the Foreign Corrupt Practices Act.

- **PCI DSS compliance:** This report, which summarizes the documentation and testing of security controls, is essential for businesses handling credit card transactions. This report demonstrates adherence to the Payment Card Industry Data Security Standard by detailing how customer payment information is protected.

- **HIPAA or GDPR compliance:** A HIPAA compliance report involves measures for safeguarding patient health information, and a GDPR compliance report includes protocols for protecting personal data and privacy rights within the European Union.

Cloud-based solution compliance reporting takes on additional complexity. Enterprises are required to continuously ensure that cloud-based authorization meets regulatory requirements. This involves providing proof that sensitive data stored or processed in the cloud is adequately secured against unauthorized access or breaches. The dynamic nature of cloud environments necessitates ongoing monitoring and validation of access controls and data security measures.

Some enterprises, especially those handling highly sensitive data or operating under stringent regulatory frameworks, may host everything in-house. This decision is often driven by the desire to maintain tighter control over data and infrastructure, simplifying compliance with specific regulations. However, this approach also involves weighing the trade-offs between the benefits of cloud computing, such as scalability and cost-efficiency, against the need for direct control over compliance-related aspects.

Internal Reporting

Internal compliance reporting is a cornerstone of an organization's security integrity. *Internal compliance reporting* involves systematic documentation that is often facilitated through internal audits conducted by an in-house team. Such an audit assesses the effectiveness of various controls, such as firewalls and data access policies. The findings from these internal reports are not mere records; they are actionable data. For instance, if an audit reveals outdated data encryption protocols, the organization can immediately allocate resources to update these protocols or initiate staff retraining.

External Reporting

External compliance reporting furthers an organization's accountability by focusing on adherence to external standards and regulations. These reports are usually formatted according to specific guidelines and are submitted to regulatory bodies, third-party auditors, or industry-specific organizations. For example, a company involved in credit card transactions may need to submit a PCI DSS compliance report to financial institutions. The stakes are high in external reporting; inaccuracies can lead to fines, increased scrutiny, or even legal action. For instance, a financial institution that incorrectly reports its capital ratios could face severe repercussions.

Key Topic Consequences of Non-compliance

Understanding the consequences of non-compliance is not just a regulatory necessity but a cornerstone for effective cybersecurity management. Cybersecurity leaders are often called upon to identify cybersecurity causes and explain the impacts of non-compliance. Each type of consequence—fines, sanctions, reputational damage, loss of license, or contractual effects—has a unique set of cybersecurity implications that can significantly affect an organization's operations and long-term viability. Let's review a few common consequences and how they relate to cybersecurity.

Fines

Fines are monetary penalties and often the most immediate and tangible consequence of non-compliance. In cybersecurity, fines can be levied for various reasons, such as for data breaches, unauthorized data access, or failure to report incidents in a timely manner. For instance, under GDPR, fines can reach €20 million (about $21 million) or 4% of a company's annual global turnover, whichever is higher. A fine is a financial burden and a red flag indicating systemic failures in cybersecurity measures. When a fine is issued, the organization may need to completely overhaul its cybersecurity infrastructure, including updating its firewall configurations, data encryption methods, and employee training programs.

Sanctions

Sanctions can include restrictions or limitations imposed on an organization. In cybersecurity, sanctions could mean restricted access to sensitive data or networks until compliance is achieved. For example, a healthcare provider found to be non-compliant with HIPAA may face sanctions that limit its ability to transmit patient records electronically. The organization may need to conduct a comprehensive review of its cybersecurity protocols, implement more robust data encryption methods, put in place more stringent access controls, and regularly conduct cybersecurity audits to lift the sanctions.

Reputational Damage

Reputational damage refers to negative impact on an organization's public image and credibility due to non-compliance with regulations or standards and often manifests after an incident like a data breach. The damage to an organization's reputation due to non-compliance can have long-lasting impacts on its business operations. For example, when a data breach occurs, customers and partners may lose faith in the organization's ability to safeguard data. How often do you think less of a company after you hear that it has suffered a data breach? This loss of trust can lead to a decline in customer engagement, reduced revenue, and even the withdrawal of investors. Organizations often have to invest heavily in cybersecurity measures to rebuild their reputation. They may start public relations (PR) campaigns that transparently discuss the steps they're taking to prevent future breaches, including implementing advanced threat detection systems or conducting regular third-party security audits.

Loss of License

Losing a license to operate is one of the most severe consequences an organization can face, and in many cases, it can occur due to lapses in cybersecurity. An organization in a regulated industry that loses its license is prohibited from legally operating. For example, a financial institution that fails multiple cybersecurity audits could lose its operating license, which would effectively shut down the business. Organizations must comply with industry-specific cybersecurity regulations to prevent such catastrophic outcomes. They can maintain compliance by continuously monitoring and improving their cybersecurity posture, including conducting regular penetration testing and security certifications.

Contractual Impacts

Contractual impact refers to adverse effects on existing agreements and future business relationships due to an organization's failure to comply with legal, regulatory, or agreed-upon standards. Non-compliance can lead to severe important repercussions, including contract termination and legal disputes. In cybersecurity, failing to meet the security standards outlined in a service-level agreement (SLA) could result in contract termination. You can imagine that losing a contract would be devastating after you spend a lot of time answering third-party vendor questionnaires, navigating contracts, and finally settling on a vendor. All of these extra actions and renegotiations lead to immediate loss of revenue and necessitate a comprehensive review and upgrade of cybersecurity measures to win lost contracts or secure new ones. This could involve enhancing intrusion detection systems, implementing more rigorous data backup protocols, and renegotiating contracts to include more robust cybersecurity clauses.

Compliance Monitoring

Compliance monitoring is not a one-time event but an ongoing process of ensuring an organization's adherence to regulatory guidelines and internal policies, particularly cybersecurity. Compliance monitoring involves a range of activities, from due diligence and care to attestation and acknowledgment, as well as both internal and external monitoring mechanisms. Automation plays a crucial role in streamlining these processes, as discussed several times in earlier chapters. Each component has specific implications for cybersecurity, affecting everything from data protection protocols to incident response strategies. Let's look at some of the tools you can have in your security toolbox for compliance monitoring.

Key Topic
Due Diligence/Care

The terms *due diligence* and *due care* are often used interchangeably in compliance monitoring, but they have nuanced differences that are crucial in cybersecurity. *Due diligence* is the proactive process of gathering information and taking steps to understand all the potential risks and liabilities before making decisions. It involves a comprehensive review of all systems, processes, and policies to identify vulnerabilities and assess the effectiveness of current security measures. For example, due diligence could involve a detailed analysis of a software vendor's security protocols before a contract is formed with them. This might include examining their encryption methods, data storage practices, and incident response plans.

On the other hand, *due care* is the ongoing practice of maintaining a system or process that has already been established. Due care includes the actions taken to apply the information gathered during the due diligence phase. It means continually updating security protocols, conducting regular audits, and ensuring that all staff are trained in security best practices. For instance, if due diligence reveals that an organization's susceptibility to phishing attacks is higher than an industry average, due care would involve implementing anti-phishing training for employees and deploying email filtering software.

Failure to exercise due diligence and due care can have severe regulatory implications. For instance, under GDPR, organizations are required to conduct risk assessments (due diligence) and implement appropriate security measures (due care) to protect personal data. As discussed earlier in this chapter, non-compliance could result in fines and legal repercussions.

Various tools and techniques can assist you in exercising due diligence and due care in your environment. These tools range from risk assessment frameworks like NIST's Cybersecurity Framework to automated compliance management platforms for tracking and documenting due diligence and due care activities.

Let's look at some ways an organization would exercise due diligence and due care using the NIST Cybersecurity Framework:

- **Due diligence:** An IT manager at a healthcare organization uses the framework to assess the organization's current cybersecurity posture. They perform a gap analysis against the framework's five core functions: Identify, Protect, Detect, Respond, and Recover. This process helps identify areas where the organization lacks cybersecurity measures, such as insufficient employee training on secure data handling or outdated malware protection software.

- **Due care:** Based on the NIST Cybersecurity Framework analysis findings, the organization implemented several improvements. For instance, it updated its cybersecurity policies, introduced regular employee training on data security, and upgraded its intrusion detection systems. In these ways, the organization has demonstrated ongoing due care in maintaining and enhancing its cybersecurity defenses.

NOTE   NIST Cybersecurity Framework 2.0 is still in draft. NIST 2.0 introduces the category Governance in addition to the original five categories Identify, Protect, Detect, Respond, and Recover.

And here are some ways an organization would exercise due diligence and due care using automated compliance management platforms:

- **Due diligence:** A financial services firm employs an automated compliance management platform to continuously monitor compliance with regulations like Sarbanes-Oxley (SOX) and GDPR. The platform automatically gathers data from various systems, performs compliance checks, and flags any areas of non-compliance, such as unencrypted customer data or lack of proper access controls.

- **Due care:** In response to the compliance alerts, the firm takes corrective actions. It implements more robust encryption protocols for customer data and revises its access control policies. The automated platform documents these actions, showing a record of proactive measures taken over time to maintain compliance, reflecting due care in organization operations.

These examples demonstrate how organizations can apply NIST's Cybersecurity Framework and automated compliance management platforms in practical ways. By following these guidelines and leveraging these tools, organizations can effectively navigate the complexities of cybersecurity risk management and regulatory compliance.

Attestation and Acknowledgment

Attestation is a formal declaration or confirmation that specific criteria, processes, or systems meet the required security standards. Attestation often involves a third-party auditor assessing an organization's security controls and providing a formal report. Typically, an attestation report is a SOC 2 (Service Organization Control 2) Type II attestation that confirms the effectiveness of these controls over a period of time. A cloud service provider may undergo a third-party audit to attest that its data centers meet specific security standards. This attestation serves as a form of assurance to clients that their data is being handled securely.

NOTE A SOC 2 report is a key document that evaluates an organization's information systems relevant to security, availability, processing integrity, confidentiality, or privacy. Developed by the American Institute of CPAs (AICPA), SOC 2 reports are crucial for service providers handling customer data, particularly in cloud computing and SaaS environments. To learn more about SOC 2 reports and how they integrate into a risk management program, visit https://www.aicpa-cima.com/resources/landing/system-and-organization-controls-soc-suite-of-services.

Acknowledgment is the act of formally accepting or recognizing specific conditions, often documented through signatures or formal agreements. We often see acknowledgments in the form of compliance certificates or signed agreements that an organization will adhere to certain security protocols or standards. For instance, an employee may acknowledge that they have read and understood the company's cybersecurity policy by signing a document. You should always stress to users that acknowledging training is a legally binding activity! This acknowledgment is a formal record that the employee is aware of the policy and, by implication, will comply with it.

Internal and External

Internal compliance monitoring refers to activities and mechanisms in an organization that ensure adherence to laws, regulations, and policies. Internal compliance monitoring often involves internal audits, routine checks, and self-assessments. Internal monitoring can include regular vulnerability scans, penetration tests, and reviews of access controls in the organization's network. For example, an organization might have an internal compliance team responsible for regularly auditing the security configurations of its servers. This team would use specialized software to scan for vulnerabilities and manually review system logs to detect unauthorized activities.

Internal compliance monitoring is often managed by specialized teams within an organization, such as the information security team or the compliance department. These teams are responsible for developing and implementing the compliance monitoring plan, which outlines the specific activities, timelines, and responsibilities for internal monitoring.

External compliance monitoring, on the other hand, involves third-party entities that evaluate an organization's adherence to laws, regulations, and standards. This can include regulatory audits, third-party security assessments, and certifications from industry bodies. For instance, a healthcare provider might be subject to an external audit to ensure compliance with HIPAA regulations. This audit would be conducted by a third-party organization specializing in healthcare compliance. Oftentimes, you will only have access to an external audit once the results are formally published.

Various tools and technologies can be used for internal and external compliance monitoring. Internal tools you might use during an internal compliance check include security information and event management (SIEM) systems. External audits tend to leverage specialized auditing software for in-depth assessments. If you have an external audit where the auditing agency is leveraging their software, remember to scan and verify their software is compliant on your network.

Automation

Automation in compliance monitoring refers to using software tools and technologies to automatically perform tasks that would otherwise require manual effort. Automation can continuously monitor network traffic, detect vulnerabilities, and even respond to certain security incidents without human intervention. Just as with compliance checking, you have a lot of options when looking to automate this process. Security information and event management (SIEM) systems can automatically collect and analyze logs from different sources to identify suspicious activities. Automated vulnerability scanners can continuously scan an organization's network to identify security weaknesses, even during off hours or weekends. Configuration management tools can ensure that system settings comply with security policies, which can also provide metrics on any systems that are out of compliance.

Automation is most effective when integrated with manual processes. For instance, while an automated system might detect a potential security incident, a human analyst may be needed to interpret the results and decide on the appropriate course of action. As with any other automated alert, there may be a lot of false positives, and you will want to be the last line of decision making before potentially changing system configurations.

You also need to confirm what regulations your organization is required to follow. Some regulations may require specific types of automated monitoring. For example, the Payment Card Industry Data Security Standard (PCI DSS) mandates the use of automated tools to monitor access to cardholder data. You can work with your legal department to stay informed about all regulations the organization must adhere to and keep IT systems aligned with those requirements.

Key Topic — Privacy

Privacy is an ethical obligation and a legal mandate that organizations must adhere to. As data becomes increasingly valuable, safeguarding it against unauthorized access and ensuring its proper use have become critical components of compliance. This section explores legal frameworks that govern cybersecurity privacy at various jurisdictional levels and the roles and responsibilities of those who handle data. It explores how privacy impacts data subjects—the individuals to whom data pertains—and the distinctions between data controllers and processors. This section also discusses the concept of data ownership, the importance of maintaining a data inventory, and the emerging principle of the right to be forgotten.

Legal Implications

Legal implications in the context of privacy refer to the obligations, liabilities, and potential penalties that organizations face in relation to the collection, storage, and processing of personal data. These implications are shaped by myriad laws and regulations that vary depending on the jurisdiction, the type of data, and how the data is used. Understanding the legal landscape is essential for organizations to comply with all relevant laws and mitigate the risks associated with data breaches or misuse.

This section introduces the complex legal frameworks that govern privacy at local, national, and global levels. Remember that you can only control what you are aware of and understand.

At the local or regional level, privacy laws can be quite specific, often tailored to a particular area's unique needs and cultural norms. For instance, in the United States, different states have privacy laws that impose specific business requirements. California has the California Consumer Privacy Act (CCPA), which focuses on consumer rights such as the right to access and correct personal information. New York has the Stop Hacks and Improve Electronic Data Security Act (SHIELD Act), which requires businesses to implement reasonable security measures to protect private information. Nevada has an online privacy law that requires websites to post a privacy notice.

In addition, there are similar regional legal approaches to protecting privacy outside the United States. In the European Union (EU), the General Data Protection Regulation (GDPR) applies to all member states and also allows for some regional variations. GDPR laws often focus on consumer rights, such as the right to access and correct personal information, and may require businesses to implement specific security measures to protect this data.

National privacy laws serve as the foundational framework for data protection within a country, often superseding or complementing local and regional laws. National privacy laws tend to be comprehensive and usually encompass various sectors, data types, and data processing activities. For example, in the United States, the Federal Trade Commission (FTC) enforces federal consumer protection laws covering privacy policies and data security. The Children's Online Privacy Protection Act (COPPA) is a U.S. federal law that specifically targets collecting personal information from minors.

If your organization has employees or clients in other countries, you will likely encounter other national privacy laws. In Canada, for example, the Personal Information Protection and Electronic Documents Act (PIPEDA) governs how businesses handle personal information in the course of their commercial activities. As another example, Australia's Privacy Act includes 13 Australian Privacy Principles (APPs) that outline how personal information is to be handled, used, and stored.

National laws often have specific enforcement mechanisms, including regulatory agencies overseeing compliance. For instance, the Information Commissioner's Office (ICO) in the United Kingdom is responsible for enforcing the Data Protection Act. Such enforcement agencies have the authority to issue fines, conduct audits, and even bring legal action against non-compliant organizations.

As mentioned earlier, if your organization has a global presence, your security approaches must match that need. Global privacy laws are increasingly important in a world where data flows across borders. Global privacy law frameworks are designed to harmonize data protection regulations across countries, making it easier for organizations to operate internationally. The GDPR is a prime example, affecting not just EU member states but also any organization worldwide that processes the data of EU citizens. Its reach is extraterritorial, meaning non-compliance could result in fines even for an organization that has no physical presence in the European Union, such as a U.S.-based company.

Another example is the Asia-Pacific Economic Cooperation (APEC) Privacy Framework, which aims to promote information privacy, foster confidence in electronic commerce, and facilitate cross-border information flow among the 21 APEC member economies. Organizations that operate in multiple APEC countries can benefit from having a common set of privacy principles.

Global privacy frameworks often require organizations to appoint data protection officers (DPOs) or similar roles responsible for ensuring compliance across various jurisdictions. They may also mandate data protection impact assessments (DPIAs) for high-risk data processing activities to ensure that organizations proactively evaluate and mitigate risks to data subjects. You can help maintain global compliance by building relationships with your organization's DPOs and DPIAs and including them in regular cybersecurity meetings.

Data Subject

A cornerstone for effective data protection strategies is understanding that a *data subject* is an individual whose personal data is being processed. This understanding shapes several aspects of a security analyst's responsibilities.

As an analyst, you are likely to need to conduct a risk assessment to identify potential vulnerabilities that could compromise a data subject's information. Knowing who a data subject is helps you categorize data based on sensitivity and determine what level of protection is required. Once you understand a data subject's role and the nature of the data they are associated with, you can effectively assign an accurate data classification. For example, customer data may require different security controls than employee data. The classification guides you in implementing appropriate encryption methods, access controls, and monitoring mechanisms.

Controller vs. Processor

Two roles are often defined in data protection frameworks, particularly the GDPR:

- **Controller:** The *controller* is the entity that determines the purposes and means of processing personal data. Essentially, the controller decides why and how personal data will be processed.

- **Processor:** The *processor* is the entity that processes personal data on behalf of the controller. While they don't decide on the why and how, they are responsible for carrying out the controller's instructions.

The controller is generally responsible for ensuring that the data is adequately protected and that the processor complies with relevant security measures. On the other hand, the processor must adhere to the security requirements set forth by the controller, such as encryption standards or access controls.

Ownership

Ownership in the context of data refers to who has the legal rights and control over data. Understanding data ownership is crucial for setting up appropriate access controls, encryption, and auditing mechanisms. Knowing who owns data helps you determine who should have what level of access. For instance, in a corporate setting, you may want to ensure that HR-owned data is accessible only by HR personnel and select executives.

Data owners may have specific requirements for how their data should be encrypted. You need to consult with a data owner to understand these requirements and implement them accordingly. In addition, data owners often have to approve who can audit their data, in accordance with organizational rules on data ownership. In such a case, you would coordinate with them to ensure that only authorized personnel are conducting audits and that audit trails are maintained for compliance.

Data Inventory and Retention

Data inventory and retention are two interconnected aspects you must manage to ensure an organization's cybersecurity posture and compliance with legal requirements.

Data inventory is a catalog or map that identifies where different data types are stored within an organization's systems. This inventory is not a one-time task; it's an ongoing process that you will frequently conduct, especially when new data assets are added or existing ones are modified. A data map is critical for conducting risk assessments and planning data protection strategies.

Data retention refers to policies that dictate how long specific data types should be stored. Understanding these policies is crucial for a security analyst, as it informs the setup of automated data deletion or archiving mechanisms. For instance, if an organization's policy states that customer data should be deleted after two years of inactivity, this rule would be programmed into the data management system to execute automatically.

The need for compliance with legal and regulatory requirements often shapes data retention policies. Security analysts often ensure that these policies are well documented and strictly followed. Failure to adhere to these policies could lead to legal repercussions for an organization. You should be prepared to play a vital role in aligning data retention policies with compliance requirements and mitigating risks and potential liabilities.

Right to Be Forgotten

The *right to be forgotten*, also known as *data erasure*, is a legal provision that allows individuals to request the deletion of their personal data. A security analyst plays a pivotal role in ensuring that these requests are executed accurately and in compliance with relevant regulations. When a data subject exercises this right, the first task for the security analyst is to locate and completely erase the specified data from all systems, including backups. This is a meticulous process that requires a deep understanding of where data resides within an organization's infrastructure.

Following the deletion, the security analyst must then run verification checks to confirm that the data has been entirely removed from all storage systems, leaving no residual traces. This verification process is crucial for the data subject's peace of mind and the organization's legal standing.

Finally, documentation is a key component of this process. The security analyst is responsible for maintaining a detailed record of the deletion process, from the initial request to the final verification. This documentation indicates that the organization has complied with the data subject's request and relevant legal requirements, safeguarding the organization from potential legal repercussions. As with practically everything in cybersecurity, it's important to document, document, document.

Chapter Review Activities

Use the features in this section to study and review the topics in this chapter.

Review Key Topics

Review the most important topics in the chapter, noted with the Key Topic icon in the outer margin of the page. Table 26-2 lists these key topics and the page number on which each is found.

Table 26-2   Key Topics for Chapter 26

Key Topic Element	Description	Page Number
Section	Compliance Reporting	602
Section	Consequences of Non-compliance	603
Section	Due Diligence/Care	605
Section	Privacy	609

Define Key Terms

Define the following key terms from this chapter and check your answers in the glossary:

compliance reporting, internal compliance reporting, external compliance reporting, fine, sanction, reputational damage, losing a license, contractual impact, due diligence, due care, attestation, acknowledgment, internal compliance monitoring, external compliance monitoring, automation, legal implications, national privacy laws, data subject, controller, processor, ownership, data inventory, data retention, right to be forgotten

Review Questions

Answer the following review questions. Check your answers with the answer key in Appendix A.

1. What is the role of internal audits in internal compliance reporting?

2. How might sanctions affect a healthcare provider's ability to operate?

3. Describe the difference between due diligence and due care in the context of cybersecurity.

4. What are the key components of privacy in cybersecurity?

5. What responsibilities does a controller have in data protection frameworks?

6. What steps are involved for a security analyst when a data subject exercises their right to be forgotten?

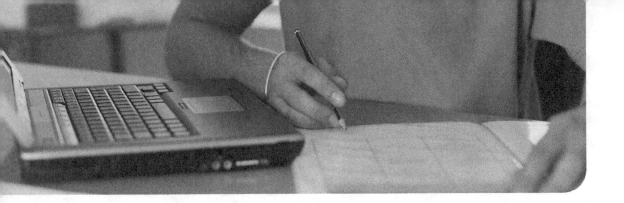

This chapter covers the following topics related to Objective 5.5 (Explain types and purposes of audits and assessments) of the CompTIA Security+ SY0-701 certification exam:

- Attestation
- Internal
- External
- Penetration testing

CHAPTER 27

Understanding Types and Purposes of Audits and Assessments

This chapter looks at audits and assessments in cybersecurity, starting with the foundational role of attestation. It breaks down internal and external audits, detailing the importance of compliance checks and third-party evaluations. The chapter also covers the spectrum of penetration testing, from physical to integrated approaches, including a look at different testing environments and reconnaissance techniques.

"Do I Know This Already?" Quiz

The "Do I Know This Already?" quiz enables you to assess whether you should read this entire chapter thoroughly or jump to the "Chapter Review Activities" section. If you are in doubt about your answers to these questions or your own assessment of your knowledge of the topics, read the entire chapter. Table 27-1 lists the major headings in this chapter and their corresponding "Do I Know This Already?" quiz questions. You can find the answers in Appendix A, "Answers to the 'Do I Know This Already?' Quizzes and Review Questions."

Table 27-1 "Do I Know This Already?" Section-to-Question Mapping

Foundation Topics Section	Questions
Attestation	1
Internal	2
External	3
Penetration Testing	4–7

CAUTION   The goal of self-assessment is to gauge your mastery of the topics in this chapter. If you do not know the answer to a question or are only partially sure of the answer, you should mark that question as wrong for purposes of self-assessment. Giving yourself credit for an answer you correctly guess skews your self-assessment results and might provide you with a false sense of security.

1. What is the primary purpose of attestation in cybersecurity audits and assessments?

    a. To add a bureaucratic step

    b. To affirm or certify the validity of a process, system, or data

    c. To identify vulnerabilities

    d. To simulate cyberattacks

2. Who is primarily responsible for overseeing the internal audit process within an organization?

    a. Senior management

    b. Audit committee

    c. External auditors

    d. Security analysts

3. What distinguishes an independent third-party audit from other types of external audits?

    a. It is conducted by an organization that has a vested interest in the outcome.

    b. It is conducted by an in-house team.

    c. It is conducted by an organization that does not have a vested interest in the outcome.

    d. It is conducted by the audit committee.

4. What is the main objective of offensive penetration testing?

    a. To detect and respond to an attack

    b. To discover and exploit vulnerabilities

    c. To evaluate the organization's defensive measures

    d. To gather information without touching the target system

5. What is another term for integrated penetration testing?

   a. Red teaming

   b. Unknown environment testing

   c. Purple teaming

   d. Blue teaming

6. In unknown environment penetration testing, what is the primary challenge?

   a. Identifying vulnerabilities through internal probing

   b. Identifying vulnerabilities through external probing

   c. Gathering information without touching the target system

   d. Simulating cyberattacks

7. What is the focus of passive reconnaissance?

   a. Actively interacting with the target system

   b. Gathering information without touching the target system

   c. Exploiting vulnerabilities

   d. Evaluating the organization's defensive measures

Foundation Topics

Attestation

Attestation is a foundational concept in audits and assessments, especially within cybersecurity. At its core, *attestation* is the formal act of affirming or certifying the validity of a process, system, or set of data. It is not merely a bureaucratic step; it's a critical component that adds a layer of trust and integrity to an organization's cybersecurity posture.

In cybersecurity, attestation often takes the form of a signed statement or digital certificate confirming that specific security controls are in place and functioning as intended. For example, a system administrator may attest that all servers are running the latest security patches, or a security officer may attest that a newly implemented firewall meets all organizational and regulatory requirements.

The process of attestation usually involves several key steps:

Key Topic

Step 1.   **Evaluation:** Before someone can attest to the validity of a system or process, the system or process must be thoroughly evaluated. This could involve reviewing logs, running tests, or conducting internal audits.

Step 2.   **Documentation:** All findings from the evaluation phase should be meticulously documented. This documentation supports the attestation and may be reviewed during future audits.

Step 3.   **Approval:** A senior-level executive or a designated authority within the organization must review and approve the attestation. This adds an extra layer of scrutiny and accountability.

Step 4.   **Issuance:** Once approved, the attestation is formally issued—possibly as a digital certificate, a signed document, or an entry in a compliance database.

Step 5.   **Review and update:** Cybersecurity is a dynamic environment, and as such, attestations may need to be reviewed and updated regularly to reflect changes in the security landscape or organizational policies.

Attestation is not a one-size-fits-all process; it can be tailored to fit various organizational needs and compliance requirements. For instance, in a healthcare setting, attestation might focus on compliance with HIPAA regulations, and a financial institution might require attestations related to the Payment Card Industry Data Security Standard (PCI DSS).

Internal

Internal audits and assessments are evaluations conducted within an organization to scrutinize its various operations, including cybersecurity measures. Unlike external audits, which third-party organizations often perform, internal audits are carried out by an in-house team. The primary aim is to identify strengths and weaknesses in the organization's systems, processes, and controls. An internal team always takes the mindset that it's better to find a problem yourself before someone external finds it for you.

The term *compliance* in the context of internal audits refers to adherence to laws, regulations, and organizational policies. A compliance audit is a comprehensive review to ensure that an organization follows external laws and regulations and internal policies and procedures. For example, an internal compliance audit might assess whether an organization's IT department handles data storage in alignment with GDPR regulations or whether employee access controls meet the company's security policy criteria.

These are the key steps in a compliance audit:

Step 1.   **Scope definition:** This step involves determining what laws, regulations, and policies are applicable. You should always ensure that there are no ambiguities with the scope definition; otherwise, the data gathering and results could be unhelpful.

Step 2.   **Data gathering:** This step involves collecting evidence, such as logs, configurations, and employee interviews.

Step 3.   **Analysis:** This step involves evaluating the gathered data against the defined scope.

Step 4.   **Reporting:** This step involves documenting findings, including any non-compliance, and recommending corrective actions.

The *audit committee* is a dedicated group responsible for overseeing the audit process. This committee usually consists of a mix of senior management and subject matter experts. Their role is to ensure that audits are conducted effectively, transparently, and in line with organizational objectives. The audit committee reviews audit plans, evaluates findings, and often has the final say in implementing recommended changes. As you will see later in this chapter, the audit committee must have broad authority to hold others accountable for closing findings that appear in vulnerability scans or other audits that each respective department is responsible for.

Responsibilities of the audit committee often include the following:

■ **Audit planning:** Approving the scope and methodology of upcoming audits

- **Review:** Periodically reviewing audit reports and findings

- **Oversight:** Ensuring that corrective actions are implemented

- **Accountability:** Holding relevant departments or individuals accountable for lapses in compliance or security

A *self-assessment* is an internal review conducted by the staff directly responsible for the assessed area rather than by a separate internal audit team. These assessments are generally less formal than full-scale audits but are invaluable for continuous improvement. For example, a network administrator might conduct a self-assessment to ensure that all firewalls are correctly configured. Self-assessments are as thorough and professional as you make them. Generally, you might plan for at least two formal internal audits per year, with an informal audit performed quarterly.

Key elements of self-assessments include the following:

- **Identification:** It is important to recognize what areas or processes need to be evaluated. Use the same level of rigor in identifying areas as you do for defining the scope with an internal audit.

- **Checklist creation:** You need to develop a list of criteria to assess against.

- **Evaluation:** You should conduct the assessment based on the checklist.

- **Action plan:** You should create a plan to address any identified gaps identified in the self-assessment.

External

External audits and assessments are evaluations of an organization's operations, including its cybersecurity measures, conducted by entities from outside the organization. You might see these audits done by management consulting firms or boutique companies that specialize in external audits. An external audit offers an unbiased perspective on the effectiveness of internal controls, policies, and procedures. Let's delve into the various types of external audits: regulatory audits, examinations, assessments, and independent third-party audits.

A *regulatory audit* is a type of external audit mandated by law or industry standards, such as HIPAA in healthcare or PCI DSS in payment card processing. The primary purpose of such an audit is to ensure that an organization fully complies with established laws or regulations. The audit process begins with defining the scope, which is determined by the specific regulations that are applicable to the organization. Data gathering follows, with evidence like system configurations, logs, and employee interviews collected. The data-gathering phase can take the longest and may have the largest impact on internal systems and employees. The gathered data is then analyzed to evaluate compliance with the regulations. Finally, a report is generated, documenting findings and recommending corrective actions if noncompliance is detected. Regulatory audits are important for avoiding legal repercussions and maintaining customer trust.

An examination is a type of external audit that is more focused than a regulatory audit. *Examinations* are often conducted to verify an organization's specific claims or compliance assertions. For example, an examination might be performed to validate that an organization's data encryption methods are as robust as claimed. The audit committee, which oversees internal and external audits, would review the examination plan, periodically check the findings, and ensure that corrective actions are implemented based on the recommendations. Examinations are particularly useful for validating the effectiveness of specific security controls or processes.

An *assessment* is a type of external audit that aims to evaluate the effectiveness of an organization's overall security posture. Assessments are more flexible than regulatory audits with predefined scopes based on laws. An assessment starts by identifying key areas or processes that need to be evaluated, such as network security or data protection. A checklist of criteria is then developed, and the assessment is conducted against this checklist. An action plan addresses any identified weaknesses that are found. You might see an assessment follow a similar format to a regulatory audit in that you define a scope, do data gathering, and then produce results. The audit committee holds relevant departments accountable for implementing these actions. An assessment is valuable for obtaining a holistic view of an organization's security strengths and weaknesses.

An *independent third-party audit* is a type of external audit conducted by an organization that does not have a vested interest in the audit outcome. These audits are often the most rigorous and are considered highly reliable. Similarly to a regulatory audit, an independent third-party audit is typically done by a management consulting firm or boutique firms that specializes in audits. The audit committee also plays a crucial role here, approving the audit plan, reviewing the findings, and overseeing the implementation of recommended changes. Independent third-party audits are often sought after for their unbiased nature, providing a comprehensive and impartial evaluation of an organization's cybersecurity measures.

Penetration Testing

Penetration testing is a critical diagnostic tool for assessing the robustness of an organization's cybersecurity measures. By simulating cyberattacks in a controlled environment, penetration testing enables an organization to proactively identify vulnerabilities, determine the effectiveness of its defensive mechanisms, and meet compliance requirements. This section explores the various facets of penetration testing, from the physical aspects that safeguard hardware to the offensive and defensive strategies that protect data and network integrity. It also explores how the scope and knowledge level of the testing environment—whether known, partially known, or unknown—can impact the depth and breadth of the assessment. Finally, this section examines the initial steps of gathering intelligence about the target system, known as reconnaissance, and the methods employed therein.

Figure 27-1 shows an overview of the penetration testing lifecycle, with each circle representing a stage in the penetration testing process.

Key Topic

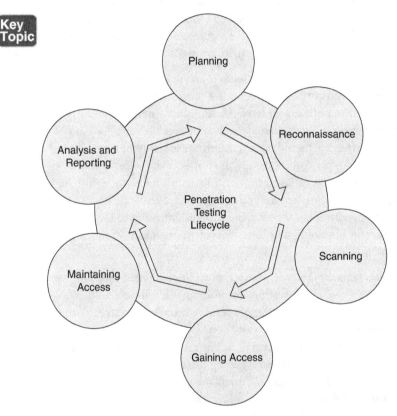

Figure 27-1   Penetration Testing Lifecycle

Here's a description of the steps in the lifecycle:

Key Topic

Step 1.   **Planning:** This initial phase involves defining the scope and goals of the penetration test, including the systems to be tested and the testing methods to be used. This stage sets the ground rules and objectives and also involves gathering intelligence to understand how the target operates and its potential weaknesses.

Step 2.   **Reconnaissance:** Also known as the intelligence-gathering phase, this step involves collecting as much information as possible about the target system to find ways to infiltrate it. This can be done through public information gathering, social engineering, network mapping, and more.

Step 3.   **Scanning:** This phase involves using technical tools to scan the target's systems to understand how they respond to intrusion attempts. Scanning can be for live systems, open ports, running services, and system architectures. Automated tools are typically used in this phase to gather detailed information like application and operating system versions.

Step 4.   **Gaining access:** This stage involves using the information obtained from reconnaissance and scanning to exploit system, network, or application vulnerabilities. The goal is to enter the system and potentially increase the access privileges to an administrator level, allowing further exploration and exploitation.

Step 5.   **Maintaining access:** Once access is gained, the next step is to ensure that this access can be maintained to understand the level of persistence that an actual attacker could achieve. This might involve creating backdoors into the system or other methods to stay connected to the system.

Step 6.   **Analysis and reporting:** The final phase involves analyzing the data collected during the penetration test to identify and understand the security lapses and detailing the findings in a report. The report documents the findings, the exploitation processes, the sensitive data accessed, and the amount of time the tester could remain in the system undetected. The report should also provide recommendations for addressing each vulnerability.

Physical penetration testing is a specialized form of assessment that targets the actual devices in an organization's security posture. It involves evaluating the effectiveness of physical barriers and controls, such as door locks, access cards, and surveillance systems. The focus is preventing unauthorized individuals from gaining physical access to critical assets like servers, network hardware, and sensitive documentation. You might encounter this type of testing when assessing the security of data centers, office buildings, or any facility that houses critical infrastructure. The aim is to uncover vulnerabilities like easily bypassed locks or inadequately monitored entrances that a would-be attacker could easily bypass.

Offensive penetration testing, also known as red teaming, is an aggressive approach to identifying security vulnerabilities by simulating cyberattacks. This form of testing is designed to mimic the tactics, techniques, and procedures (TTPs) that real-world attackers would use to compromise a system. It goes beyond merely identifying vulnerabilities to actively exploiting them, providing a realistic assessment of what an actual cyberattack could achieve. You'll likely see this type of testing carried out by individuals who have a deep understanding of attack vectors and exploitation techniques, such as penetration testers or security analysts. The objective is to discover and exploit vulnerabilities like insecure code, misconfigured servers, or weak authentication mechanisms before malicious actors can exploit them. Taking a proactive approach allows an organization to prioritize remediation efforts based on the severity and exploitability of the discovered vulnerabilities.

Defensive penetration testing, commonly called blue teaming, focuses on an organization's ability to detect, contain, and mitigate security incidents. Unlike offensive testing, which actively seeks to exploit vulnerabilities, defensive testing evaluates the robustness of monitoring tools, incident response protocols, and alerting mechanisms. You may encounter this type of testing in roles focused on incident response, security monitoring, or threat hunting. The aim is to scrutinize how well the organization's security operations center (SOC) or incident response team can identify and manage a simulated attack. This involves real-time analysis of network traffic, system logs, and alerts to ensure that intrusions can be promptly detected and adequately addressed.

Integrated penetration testing is a holistic approach that fuses the proactive elements of offensive testing with the reactive components of defensive testing. You will sometimes hear this approach called purple teaming. This dual-pronged strategy provides a 360-degree view of an organization's security landscape. The red team works the offense, the blue team works the defense, and together they form the purple team. You'll often see this type of testing in more mature security environments where the focus is on identifying vulnerabilities and refining incident response procedures. The objective is to uncover weaknesses and evaluate the organization's ability to detect, respond to, and recover from simulated cyberattacks. By integrating offensive and defensive methodologies, organizations can better understand their security posture, allowing for a balanced and well-rounded security strategy.

In *known environment penetration testing*, or white box testing, the testers are armed with comprehensive information about the system's architecture, including network diagrams, source code, and credentials. This level of access enables a deep dive into the system to identify vulnerabilities that may not be apparent in a less informed scenario. This type of testing is usually carried out by people who are involved in secure code review or architectural analysis. While it allows for a meticulous and exhaustive evaluation, it may not fully mimic the conditions of a real-world attack where the attacker lacks such detailed information. A known-environment test can also be cheaper for the organization since the pen test team will not waste time trying to crack passwords or encryption on the network. The test team can move past the initial reconnaissance and test internal systems.

In *partially known environment penetration testing*, or gray box testing, the penetration testers operate with a subset of the system's information. They might know some server names, have limited credentials, or be aware of some architectural details, but they don't have the complete picture. This type of test is more aligned with real-world scenarios where an attacker might have gleaned some insider information through social engineering or initial reconnaissance but lacks a complete understanding of the system. This type of test requires testers to think like an attacker and also consider defensive measures, taking a balanced view of the system's security posture.

In *unknown environment penetration testing*, also known as black box testing, penetration testers are in the dark, with no prior knowledge of the system's architecture, network diagrams, or any other insider information. This scenario simulates the conditions an external attacker faces when trying to infiltrate a system. This type of testing requires testers to assess the organization's external-facing assets, like web applications or network perimeters. The primary challenge here is identifying vulnerabilities through external probing, as this is an actual test of an organization's first line of defense. It is important to have a clear scope of work and signed agreements on what should be tested.

Table 27-2 helps you better understand the various types of penetration tests, based on the level of knowledge about the environment, the level of realism, common techniques used, and the risk of detection for each type. You can use this table as a quick reference to grasp the nuances and applicability of each testing type.

Key Topic

Table 27-2   Overview of Penetration Test Types

Type of Penetration Test	Level of Knowledge	Realism	Common Techniques	Risk of Detection
Known environment	Full knowledge	Low	Detailed scanning, source code analysis	Low
Partially known environment	Limited knowledge	Moderate	Basic scanning, limited inside information	Moderate
Unknown environment	No prior knowledge	High	Blind scanning, social engineering	High

Reconnaissance is the foundational phase of any penetration testing exercise. *Reconnaissance* is the stage where testers collect preliminary data or intelligence on the target system to better plan their attack strategies.

In *passive reconnaissance*, the tester adopts a low-profile approach, gathering information without touching the target system. This could involve tasks like DNS enumeration, public record searches, or social engineering tactics like pretexting or phishing. Suppose you're in a role that requires threat intelligence gathering. In that case, you'll often use passive reconnaissance to collect data to help identify potential vulnerabilities or areas of interest without alerting the target.

Active reconnaissance is more direct and involves interacting with the target system. It could include port scanning, such as by using nmap, sending specially crafted packets to the target, or running vulnerability scans. While this method can provide more granular details about the system's vulnerabilities, it's also more likely to be "noisy" and set off alarm bells in intrusion detection systems. If you're in a role that involves active probing of systems, you'll need to be skilled in techniques that evade detection while still gathering the necessary data. You can also study active reconnaissance techniques in a defensive SOC role to better identify when an attack or reconnaissance is happening on your systems.

Chapter Review Activities

Use the features in this section to study and review the topics in this chapter.

Review Key Topics

Review the most important topics in the chapter, noted with the Key Topic icon in the outer margin of the page. Table 27-3 lists these key topics and the page number on which each is found.

Key Topic

Table 27-3   Key Topics for Chapter 27

Key Topic Element	Description	Page Number
List	Process of attestation	620
Paragraph	Internal audit	621
List	Compliance audit steps	621
List	Self-assessment key elements	622
Paragraph	Regulatory audit	622
Paragraph	Penetration testing	623
Figure 27-1	Penetration Testing Lifecycle	624
List	Penetration testing lifecycle	624
Table 27-2	Overview of Penetration Test Types	627

Define Key Terms

Define the following key terms from this chapter and check your answers in the glossary:

> attestation, internal audit, compliance, audit committee, self-assessment, external audit, regulatory audit, examination, assessment, independent third-party audit, physical penetration testing, offensive penetration testing, defensive penetration testing, integrated penetration testing, known environment penetration testing, partially known environment penetration testing, unknown environment penetration testing, reconnaissance, passive reconnaissance, active reconnaissance

Review Questions

Answer the following review questions. Check your answers with the answer key in Appendix A.

1. What is the key role of the audit committee in an internal audit?

2. How does an independent third-party audit differ from a regulatory audit?

3. What is the primary focus of offensive penetration testing, and how does it differ from defensive penetration testing?

4. Describe the main challenge in an unknown environment penetration test.

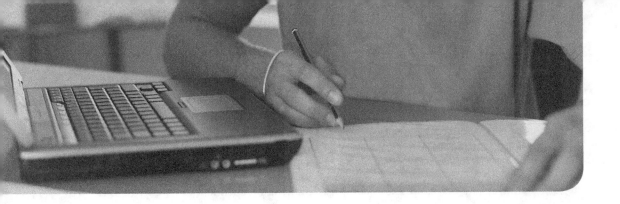

This chapter covers the following topics related to Objective 5.6 (Given a scenario, implement security awareness practices) of the CompTIA Security+ SY0-701 certification exam:

- Phishing

- Anomalous behavior recognition

- User guidance and training

- Reporting and monitoring

- Development

- Execution

CHAPTER 28

Implementing Security Awareness Practices

This chapter delves into security awareness practices, offering a comprehensive guide to implementing effective measures. It covers everything from recognizing phishing attempts and anomalous behaviors to user training on various security aspects like password management and operational security. The chapter also addresses the unique challenges that hybrid and remote work environments pose. Special attention is given to reporting and monitoring mechanisms and the development and execution of security programs.

"Do I Know This Already?" Quiz

The "Do I Know This Already?" quiz enables you to assess whether you should read this entire chapter thoroughly or jump to the "Chapter Review Activities" section. If you are in doubt about your answers to these questions or your own assessment of your knowledge of the topics, read the entire chapter. Table 28-1 lists the major headings in this chapter and their corresponding "Do I Know This Already?" quiz questions. You can find the answers in Appendix A, "Answers to the 'Do I Know This Already?' Quizzes and Review Questions."

Table 28-1 "Do I Know This Already?" Section-to-Question Mapping

Foundation Topics Section	Questions
Phishing	1
Anomalous Behavior Recognition	2
User Guidance and Training	3
Reporting and Monitoring	4
Development	5
Execution	6

CAUTION   The goal of self-assessment is to gauge your mastery of the topics in this chapter. If you do not know the answer to a question or are only partially sure of the answer, you should mark that question as wrong for purposes of self-assessment. Giving yourself credit for an answer you correctly guess skews your self-assessment results and might provide you with a false sense of security.

1. What is the primary objective of phishing campaigns?

    a. To compromise as many accounts as possible

    b. To educate users

    c. To test an organization's security measures

    d. To update an organization's security policies

2. Why is it important to be able to recognize unexpected behavior in an organization's security posture?

    a. To improve employee performance

    b. For early detection of potential security threats

    c. To update security policies

    d. To reduce operational costs

3. What is the primary purpose of policy and handbooks in user guidance and training?

    a. To provide entertainment

    b. To introduce new employees to the team

    c. To outline the company's history

    d. To govern how employees interact with digital assets

4. What is the focus of recurring reporting in reporting and monitoring?

    a. Assessing the effectiveness of marketing strategies

    b. Assessing the effectiveness of an organization's security measures

    c. Evaluating employee performance

    d. Updating an organization's financial records

5. What is the main focus during the development phase of a security awareness program?

   a. Rolling out training modules

   b. Implementing monitoring tools

   c. Identifying key objectives and defining scope

   d. Launching simulated attacks

6. What is the primary activity during the execution phase of a security awareness program?

   a. Creating a detailed project plan

   b. Identifying key stakeholders

   c. Implementing the security awareness program

   d. Defining measurable goals

Foundation Topics

Phishing

Phishing is a form of social engineering attack aimed at tricking individuals into divulging sensitive information, such as login credentials or financial details. It often takes the form of deceptive emails, messages, or websites that appear legitimate but that are designed to deceive the recipient. Understanding the intricacies of phishing is crucial for both individual users and organizations in order to maintain a secure environment.

A phishing *campaign* is an organized effort by an attacker or attackers to distribute phishing messages to a large number of targets. Phishing campaigns can vary in complexity and scale, from simple email blasts to highly targeted spear-phishing attacks aimed at specific individuals within an organization. The objective is to compromise as many accounts or systems as possible. Campaigns often employ a variety of tactics, such as impersonating trusted entities or using urgent language, to manipulate a recipient into taking a specific action, like clicking a link or downloading an attachment.

Recognizing a phishing attempt is the first line of defense in preventing a successful attack. There are several indicators to look out for:

- **Mismatched URLs:** The hyperlink text may say one thing, but hovering over it reveals a different URL.

- **Poor grammar and spelling:** Official communications are usually well written. Look out for errors in the text.

- **Requests for sensitive information:** Legitimate organizations will never ask for sensitive information via email.

- **Unsolicited attachments:** Be wary of unexpected attachments, as they may contain malware.

- **Too good to be true:** Offers that seem too good to be true usually are.

Once a suspicious message is reported, immediate action is required to contain the threat and prevent further damage. Here are the steps to follow when responding to a reported suspicious message:

Step 1.   **Isolate the threat:** If possible, quarantine the email message to prevent further interaction with other employees.

Step 2.   **Analyze the content:** Examine the message for any phishing indicators and verify its authenticity.

Step 3.   **Notify IT security:** Report the incident to the IT security team for further analysis and action.

Step 4.   **Make users aware:** Inform the reporting user and, if necessary, the entire organization about the incident to raise awareness and prevent further clicks.

Step 5.   **Update security measures:** Based on the findings, update security protocols, filters, and training to guard against similar future attacks.

Anomalous Behavior Recognition

Anomalous behavior recognition is a critical aspect of cybersecurity that focuses on identifying actions or patterns that deviate from established norms or expected behavior within a network or system. Such deviation from regular activity could indicate a security threat, such as unauthorized access or data exfiltration. Recognizing anomalous behavior is vital for preemptive threat detection and timely incident response. Let's delve into the different types of anomalous behaviors you might encounter.

Risky behaviors are actions that may not be intentionally harmful but that can expose an organization to vulnerabilities or threats. Table 28-2 provides a detailed breakdown of various types of risky behaviors, how they are identified, and their potential impacts on an organization.

Table 28-2   Types of Risky Behavior

Type of Risky Behavior	Identification Method	Potential Impact	Recommended Action
Use of unauthorized software	Monitoring software installation logs or using application allow lists to flag unauthorized installations.	Introduces unknown vulnerabilities and potential for malware infection.	Uninstall unauthorized software and educate users on the risks involved.
Weak password practices	Conducting regular password audits to identify weak or commonly used passwords.	Makes it easier for attackers to gain unauthorized access.	Enforce strong password policies and possibly initiate forced password changes.
Disabling security protocols	Monitoring system logs for changes to security settings, such as firewall or antivirus status.	Exposes the system to a wide range of potential attacks.	Re-enable security protocols and educate users on the importance of these measures.

Type of Risky Behavior	Identification Method	Potential Impact	Recommended Action
Sharing sensitive data	Using data loss prevention (DLP) tools to monitor data transfers.	Risk of data leakage or unauthorized access to sensitive information.	Block the data transfer and educate users on proper data handling procedures.
Using unsecured networks	Using network monitoring tools to identify connections to unsecured or public Wi-Fi networks.	Potential for on-path attacks or data interception.	Disconnect from the unsecured network and educate users on the risks of using such networks.

Unexpected behavior refers to actions or patterns of activity that deviate from established norms or baseline behaviors. These anomalies can be indicative of security incidents or vulnerabilities. Recognizing unexpected behavior is crucial for early detection of potential security threats. Table 28-3 provides a detailed breakdown of various types of unexpected behaviors, how they are identified, and their potential impacts on an organization.

Key Topic

Table 28-3   Types of Unexpected Behavior

Type of Unexpected Behavior	Identification Method	Potential Impact	Recommended Action
Unusual login times	User behavior analytics tools	Risk of compromised account	Investigate login activity; possibly reset credentials
High data transfer rates	Network monitoring tools	Risk of data exfiltration or leakage	Limit data transfer; investigate user activity
Multiple failed login attempts	SIEM systems or event logs	Possible brute-force attack attempt	Lock account temporarily; investigate source
Access to sensitive areas	Access control logs	Possible compromised account or insider threat	Revoke access; investigate user activities
Running unknown scripts or applications	Endpoint detection and response solutions	Risk of malware infection or system compromise	Terminate script/application; conduct security scan

Unintentional behavior refers to actions users take that inadvertently put the organization's cybersecurity at risk. Unlike risky or unexpected behavior, which may be deliberate or indicative of malicious intent, unintentional behavior usually stems from a lack of awareness or understanding of security best practices. Review the various types of unintentional behavior in Table 28-4.

Table 28-4   Types of Unintentional Behavior

Type of Unintentional Behavior	Identification Method	Potential Impact	Recommended Action
Sharing passwords	User interviews, audits	Compromised account security	Educate users on secure password practices; reset passwords
Using unsecured networks	Network monitoring tools	Data interception	Educate users on VPN usage; monitor for suspicious activity
Downloading unverified software	Endpoint security software	Malware infection	Remove software; run malware scan; educate users
Clicking on suspicious links	Email filtering software	Phishing attacks	Educate users on recognizing phishing attempts; scan system for malware
Failing to update software	Patch management systems	Exploitation of known vulnerabilities	Educate users on the importance of updates; apply necessary patches

Identification and mitigation of unintentional behavior often start with regularly scheduled user interviews and audits, which can help pinpoint users who may be unaware of security best practices. Automated monitoring tools complement these efforts by flagging unusual or risky behavior that might actually be unintentional. Once such behavior is identified, education is the most effective mitigation strategy. Education can take various forms, including workshops, online courses, or informational handouts. You might even consider hosting a brown-bag lunch or impromptu training for your organization to educate others on what types of behaviors put the organization at risk. Alongside educational initiatives, it's crucial to have clear and enforceable company policies that outline the repercussions of unintentional risky behavior.

User Guidance and Training

User guidance and training empowers employees to participate in organizational security actively. This section delves into various elements of user guidance, from policy documents to real-world training scenarios, each designed to equip staff with the knowledge and skills they need to protect themselves and their organization. Let's explore these topics in detail.

Policies and handbooks outline the rules, guidelines, and procedures that govern how employees interact with the organization's digital assets. These documents are often tailored to specific roles within the organization but generally aim to be comprehensive in scope. Here are some examples of what they might look like:

- **Information security policy:** This document outlines the organization's approach to managing and securing information. It may cover data classification, acceptable use, and incident response procedures.

- **Acceptable use policy (AUP):** This document focuses on acceptable behavior when using company-owned resources, such as computers, networks, and email systems. It may include clauses on software downloads, Internet usage, and data storage.

- **Incident response handbook:** This is a step-by-step guide for employees responding to various security incidents, from a lost company badge to a full-scale data breach.

- **Remote work policy:** Now that remote work has become common, this type of policy has become a necessity. Such a document outlines the security protocols for employees working outside the office, covering topics like VPN usage, device security, and data access permissions.

- **Employee onboarding handbook:** This policy, which is often the first policy document a new hire interacts with, can cover a broad range of topics including the company's cybersecurity policies and procedures.

> **NOTE**   One word of caution: Bring human resources (HR) into the room whenever you draft a policy or handbook. HR can ensure that you are not accidentally infringing on rights and can provide a unique perspective on how others outside of IT might interpret a policy.

Situational awareness in cybersecurity refers to the ability to identify, process, and comprehend what is happening in the digital environment. Situational awareness involves understanding the threats that could affect an organization and how to respond to them. For instance, employees should be trained to recognize a sudden surge in failed login attempts as a potential brute-force attack and know the procedures for reporting it. As another example, a security professional should know that if an attack on a system not used in their organization is happening, they do not need to use vital resources to respond.

Insider threats are security risks that come from within an organization. They could be employees, contractors, or anyone else with inside information concerning the organization's security practices, data, and computer systems. Training should focus on recognizing signs of potential insider threats, such as unusual data transfers or unauthorized access to sensitive areas, as well as reporting mechanisms. You can also leverage DLP and SIEM systems to look for indicators of compromise (IoC) that can alert you to insider threats.

Another program you might consider is setting up an insider threat program. This type of program aims to identify, prevent, and mitigate risks from individuals within an organization who have access to sensitive information. It involves a multidepartmental approach, incorporating HR, Legal, IT, and Security departments to develop comprehensive policies based on risk assessments. Employees are educated through training sessions and real-world simulations, and monitoring tools and user and entity behavior analytics (UEBA) are employed to detect suspicious activities. A detailed incident response plan and clear reporting mechanisms are also essential components of such a program. Regular audits ensure the program's effectiveness and legal compliance, and adjustments should be made as needed. The ultimate goal is not just to prevent malicious activities but to foster a culture of security awareness and responsibility across the organization.

Password management is a cornerstone of organizational security, and it's not just about creating a strong password. *Password management* involves implementing and following proper strong password procedures that ensure the ongoing integrity and robustness of an organization's security posture. Training should emphasize the critical nature of using strong, unique passwords for different services and applications. A strong password typically combines uppercase and lowercase letters, numbers, and special characters. Using unique passwords for different sites ensures that other passwords remain secure if one of them is compromised. Employees should be aware of the risks of reusing passwords across multiple platforms. If one account is compromised, it could lead to a domino effect, putting other accounts and sensitive data at risk.

Multifactor authentication adds an extra layer of security and should be a standard procedure in password management. Training should cover MFA, its importance, and step-by-step guidance on enabling it for various services. Proper procedures also involve regular audits to ensure that employees comply with the organization's password policies. These audits can identify weak or reused passwords and ensure that MFA is enabled where required.

Social engineering is a manipulative technique that exploits human psychology to gain unauthorized access to systems, data, or physical locations. Training should cover the theoretical aspects of social engineering and include real-world examples and simulations to help employees recognize various social engineering tactics, such as phishing emails, pretexting, and smishing (SMS phishing), and it equips them with the knowledge to respond appropriately.

To give you a sense of what a social engineering attack via smishing might look like, consider the following fictitious dialogue between an attacker and an employee:

> **Attacker (via SMS):** "Hi, [Employee's Name], this is [Manager's Name] from IT. We're doing an emergency system check today. Can you please confirm your login credentials to expedite the process?"

> **Employee (via SMS):** "Hi, I wasn't aware of an emergency system check. Shouldn't this be done through official channels?"

> **Attacker (via SMS):** "We usually would, but time is of the essence. We need to act fast to prevent a system failure. Your immediate cooperation is crucial."

> **Employee (via SMS):** "I understand the urgency, but I can't share my login credentials via text. I'll call the IT department directly to verify."

This employee has demonstrated proper awareness and response to a potential smishing attack by refusing to share sensitive information via text and opting to verify the request through official channels.

Operational security (OpSec) involves processes and decisions to protect sensitive information from unauthorized access. Training in this area should cover best practices for maintaining OpSec, especially in diverse work environments, from traditional office settings to remote workspaces.

A clean desk policy is one of the most straightforward yet effective policies that can be implemented to improve operational security. Such a policy mandates that all employees clear their desks at the end of each workday, storing all sensitive documents securely. Computer screens should also be locked when unattended, even for short periods, to prevent unauthorized access. A clean desk policy is particularly beneficial in open office settings where visitors, contractors, and other employees could easily access sensitive information that is left unattended.

The transition to *hybrid and remote work environments* has brought about several new security challenges that organizations must address. Hybrid work is a work model that supports both in-office and remote office working locations. A remote work model supports working on-the-go or in a less formal small-office/home-office (SOHO) setting. Challenges in hybrid and remote work environments range from securing home networks to the risks associated with using public Wi-Fi for work-related tasks. Training should be comprehensive, covering these new challenges in detail to equip employees with the knowledge and tools they need to maintain a secure work environment, regardless of location.

One of the first challenges in a remote work setting is ensuring that the home network is as secure as the corporate network. Employees should be trained to set strong passwords for their Wi-Fi networks, enable firewalls, and keep all devices updated with the latest security patches.

Virtual private networks (VPNs) are another crucial element in remote work security. A VPN encrypts the Internet connection, making it more difficult for attackers to intercept data. Employees should be trained to set up and use a VPN while working remotely to ensure a secure connection to the organization's network.

Using public Wi-Fi for work-related tasks is fraught with risks, including the potential for data interception and unauthorized access. Employees should be educated about these risks and trained to avoid using public Wi-Fi for work. If using public Wi-Fi is unavoidable, an organizational policy should require use of a VPN to secure the connection.

Key Topic · Reporting and Monitoring

Reporting and monitoring processes enable organizations to keep track of security incidents, assess the effectiveness of current security measures, and make data-driven decisions for future strategies. This section delves into the unique characteristics and importance of two types of reporting and monitoring: initial and recurring.

Initial reporting is the first line of defense when a security incident occurs or a vulnerability is discovered. *Initial reporting* is the immediate actions taken to document and communicate the details of an incident to the relevant parties. For example, if an employee receives a phishing email, the initial report would include the sender's details, the content of the email, and any links or attachments the email contained. This initial report is then escalated to the cybersecurity team for further analysis and action.

Monitoring at this stage involves real-time tracking of system logs, network traffic, and other relevant data to identify any unusual or unauthorized activities. Initial monitoring aims to contain the incident and prevent further damage by quickly identifying the source and nature of the threat.

Whereas initial reporting and monitoring are reactive measures, recurring reporting and monitoring are proactive. *Recurring reporting* involves periodic reviews and audits to assess the effectiveness of an organization's security measures. Reports may be generated weekly, monthly, or quarterly and usually include metrics like the number of detected incidents, response times, and resolution rates.

Recurring monitoring is an ongoing process that involves continuously scanning the organization's networks and systems for vulnerabilities and threats. You must plan your team's time to ensure that recurring reporting is factored into your labor plans. Monitoring could include regular scans of firewall logs, intrusion detection systems, and application activity. The objective is to identify vulnerabilities before they can be exploited to allow for timely remediation.

Development

The development phase lays the groundwork for a successful security awareness program. *Development* involves identifying the key objectives, defining the scope, and setting measurable goals. For instance, the development phase could include creating a detailed project plan that outlines the timeline, resources, and budget required to implement the security awareness program. This is also the stage at which you identify the key stakeholders, such as senior management, IT teams, and end users, and define their roles and responsibilities in the program.

During the development phase, you create or curate the training materials, design the simulations, and set up the reporting and monitoring mechanisms. Developing content at this phase could involve creating training modules on phishing awareness, setting up a simulated phishing campaign, or implementing a new incident reporting tool. The key is to ensure that the program is comprehensive, covering all aspects of cybersecurity relevant to your organization, and is tailored to your workforce's specific needs and risks.

 ## Execution

Execution is where the rubber meets the road. All the planning, development, and strategizing culminate in implementing the security awareness program during this phase. Execution involves rolling out the training modules, initiating monitoring tools, and launching simulated attacks or exercises. For example, you might start with an organizationwide email announcing the new security awareness initiative and then hold the first training session on recognizing phishing attempts.

During the execution phase, monitoring the program's effectiveness in real time is crucial. This could involve tracking metrics like user engagement with the training materials, the number of incidents reported, and the success rate of simulated attacks. Any gaps or shortcomings identified should be immediately addressed, and the program should be fine-tuned as needed.

Like the development phase, the execution phase is not a one-time event but an ongoing process. Cyber threats are continually evolving, and so should your security awareness program. Regular updates, new training modules, and periodic reviews are essential to ensure that the program remains practical and relevant.

Chapter Review Activities

Use the features in this section to study and review the topics in this chapter.

Review Key Topics

Review the most important topics in the chapter, noted with the Key Topic icon in the outer margin of the page. Table 28-5 lists these key topics and the page number on which each is found.

Table 28-5 Key Topics for Chapter 28

Key Topic Element	Description	Page Number
Section	Phishing	634
Paragraph	Anomalous behavior recognition	635
Table 28-2	Types of Risky Behavior	635
Table 28-3	Types of Unexpected Behavior	636
Table 28-4	Types of Unintentional Behavior	637
Section	User Guidance and Training	638
List	Examples of policies/handbooks	638
Section	Reporting and Monitoring	641
Section	Execution	642

Define Key Terms

Define the following key terms from this chapter and check your answers in the glossary:

campaign, anomalous behavior recognition, risky behavior, unexpected behavior, unintentional behavior, policies and handbooks, situational awareness, insider threat, password management, social engineering, operational security (OpSec), hybrid and remote work environments, initial reporting, recurring reporting, development, execution

Review Questions

Answer the following review questions. Check your answers with the answer key in Appendix A.

1. What tactics are commonly used in phishing campaigns to manipulate recipients?

2. Why is it crucial to recognize unexpected behavior in an organization's security framework?

3. What is the primary role of policies and handbooks in an organization's user guidance and training?

4. What are some key activities that take place during the execution phase of a security awareness program?

CHAPTER 29

Final Preparation

The first 28 chapters of this book cover the technologies, protocols, design concepts, and considerations you need to understand in order to pass the CompTIA Security+ SY0-701 certification exam. However, most people need more preparation than simply reading the first 28 chapters of this book. This chapter, along with the book's Introduction, suggest hands-on activities and a study plan that will help you complete your preparation for the exam.

Hands-on Activities

The CompTIA Security+ SY0-701 certification exam is not a hands-on exam. However, one of the best ways to learn about cybersecurity vulnerabilities, threats, and techniques is to perform some hands-on exercises. You can practice using basic tools like Wireshark, tshark, tcpdump, and nmap. Good places to start are with Kali Linux (https://kali.org) to become familiar with some of the most common open-source attack tools and Security Onion (https://securityonion.net) to become familiar with tools related to incident response.

TIP Although building your own test lab is beyond the scope of this book, you might want to check out https://h4cker.org/lab. It will guide you through building your own lab and using many of these tools. You can also use the web-based hands-on environment Try Hack Me (https://tryhackme.com). The most effective way to learn the skills necessary to pass the exam is to build your own lab, break it, and fix it.

Suggested Plan for Final Review and Study

This section lists a suggested study plan from the point at which you finish reading this book through Chapter 28 until you take the CompTIA Security+ SY0-701 certification exam. You can ignore this four-step plan, use it as is, or modify it to better meet your needs:

Step 1. **Review key topics:** You can use the table at the end of each chapter that lists the key topics in each chapter or just flip the pages looking for key topics.

Step 2. **Review testable content:** CompTIA maintains a list of testable content known as the CompTIA Security+ SY0-701 certification exam blueprint. Review it and make sure you are familiar with every item that is listed. You can download a copy from https://www.comptia.org/certifications.

Step 3. **Study the "Review Questions" sections:** Go through the review questions at the end of each chapter to identify areas in which you need more study.

Step 4. **Use the Pearson Test Prep software to practice:** The Pearson Test Prep practice test software provides a bank of unique exam-realistic questions that is available only with this book.

The Introduction of this book provides detailed instructions for how to access the Pearson Test Prep practice test software. This database of questions was created specifically for this book and is available to you either online or as an offline Windows application. As covered in the Introduction, you can choose to take the exams in one of three modes: Study mode, Practice Exam mode, or Flash Card mode.

Summary

The tools and suggestions listed in this chapter have been designed with one goal in mind: to help you develop the skills required to pass the CompTIA Security+ SY0-701 certification exam and gain the skills needed to start your cybersecurity operations career. This book has been developed from the beginning both to present you with a collection of facts and to help you learn how to apply those facts. Regardless of your experience level before reading this book, it is our hope that the broad range of preparation tools and the structure of the book will help you pass the exam with ease. We wish you success on your exam and hope that our paths cross again as you continue to grow in your cybersecurity career.

Answers to the "Do I Know This Already?" Quizzes and Review Questions

Chapter 1

Do I Know This Already? Quiz

1. b. Managerial controls involve decisions and the management of risk, focusing on procedures, legal and regulatory policies, and vulnerability management/scanning.

2. b. Technical controls are executed by computer systems, including mechanisms such as firewalls, access control, and cryptography.

3. d. Physical controls involve securing physical access to an organization's building and equipment and implementing physical access security methods.

4. c. Managerial controls encompass business and organizational processes and procedures, which include user awareness and training.

5. c. Managerial controls encompass business and organizational processes and procedures, such as security awareness training and formal change-management procedures.

6. d. Preventive controls are employed before an event occurs and are designed to prevent incidents. They enforce security policy and are meant to prevent incidents from happening, and they typically include measures such as intrusion prevention systems (IPSs), access lists, and passwords.

7. a. Deterrent controls are designed to discourage potential attackers. The presence of these controls can deter threat actors from executing offensive assaults on the environment. Typical deterrent controls include door locks, lighting, and visible cameras.

8. b. Detective controls aim at monitoring and detecting unauthorized behavior and hazards. These controls alert of failures in other controls and can identify unwanted events during or after they have occurred.

9. c. Corrective controls are used after an event has occurred. They limit the extent of damage, help the company recover from the damage quickly, and provide measures to lessen harmful effects or restore the system being impacted.

10. b. Directive controls, also known as instructive controls, are strategies established to guide the operation and use of systems within an organization. They serve to instruct or direct individuals toward secure behavior through standards, procedures, policy guidelines, and security awareness training programs.

Review Questions

1. Managerial

2. Operational

3. Technical

4. Preventive

5. Deterrent

6. Detective

7. Corrective

8. Compensating

9. Physical

10. Physical

Chapter 2

Do I Know This Already? Quiz

1. c. The confidentiality component of the CIA triad is designed to protect information from unauthorized access and disclosure, keeping it confidential and accessible to authorized users only.

2. c. Non-repudiation in cybersecurity provides assurance that someone cannot deny the validity of a transaction or communication, preventing individuals from denying their actions.

3. c. In the AAA (authentication, authorization, and accounting) framework, authentication involves verifying the identity of a user, usually through the input of valid credentials like a username and password.

4. b. In the CIA (confidentiality, integrity, and availability) triad, availability ensures that systems and data are accessible and usable when needed by authorized users, safeguarding against interruptions in access.

5. a. The primary goal of conducting a cybersecurity gap analysis is to compare the organization's existing security measures against an ideal state or industry standards to identify areas of improvement and vulnerability.

6. b. In the Zero Trust model, adaptive identity involves identifying users or systems based on context, such as behavior, location, or devices used, and contributes to the principle of never trusting and always verifying.

7. c. In the Zero Trust security framework, the data plane is responsible for enforcing policies determined by the control plane and executing the security measures defined.

8. c. An access control vestibule in a facility protection plan creates a buffer zone at the facility's entrance and provides an additional layer of access control, ensuring that only authorized individuals gain entry.

9. d. Infrared sensors are most effective for detecting movement due to changes in heat levels, as they can identify the thermal energy produced by an object.

10. b. A honeytoken's primary function in a cybersecurity system is to act as a decoy or trap, serving as an early warning system for unauthorized access or system breaches by alerting when interacted with.

Review Questions

1. Non-repudiation ensures that someone cannot deny the validity of a transaction, thereby maintaining data integrity and accountability.

2. Authentication ensures the legitimacy of people by verifying their identities before granting access to a system, thus preventing unauthorized access.

3. Authenticating systems increases security by ensuring that only trusted and verified systems can interact, reducing the risk of malicious attacks or data breaches.

4. A gap analysis identifies the differences between an organization's current cybersecurity practices and the desired or ideal state, highlighting areas of improvement.

5. The Zero Trust model enhances security by assuming that no user or system is trustworthy by default, thereby necessitating continuous verification and minimizing the risk of breaches.

6. In a Zero Trust security framework, the control plane is responsible for making intelligent decisions based on policies; it defines the security protocols.

7. The data plane in the Zero Trust model enforces the policies determined by the control plane, ensuring that only authorized traffic is allowed.

8. Adaptive identity in a Zero Trust architecture is a dynamic method of identifying and authenticating users or systems based on context, such as behavior, location, or device.

9. An access control vestibule enhances physical security by creating a buffer zone at an entrance and providing an additional layer of access control.

10. In the context of intrusion detection, a honeypot is a trap set to detect or deflect attempts at unauthorized use of information systems. A honeynet is a network set up with intentional vulnerabilities to divert attackers from the actual network. A honeytoken, on the other hand, is a piece of data that serves as bait for intruders; its access or use signals an alert that unauthorized activities are occurring.

Chapter 3

Do I Know This Already? Quiz

1. a. An ineffective approval process could lead to changes being implemented without thorough vetting, which could inadvertently lead to the introduction of new system vulnerabilities.

2. c. In this context, the owners are the individuals or teams responsible for specific assets, such as databases or applications, and hence they are accountable for their security.

3. d. In this context, stakeholders are individuals or groups that have a vested interest in the organization's security posture. This could include a wide range of entities, from system users and IT staff to management and customers.

4. c. The approval process is a crucial business procedure that dictates how changes impacting security are approved and who holds the authority to make such decisions.

5. b. The allow list, or whitelist, is a list of approved inputs a user or machine can perform on a system. It specifies permitted values and rejects everything else.

6. c. Restricted activities are specific actions or operations in a computer or network system that are limited or prohibited to uphold cybersecurity standards. They are typically defined by allow and deny lists.

7. b. Understanding all technical implications of any new or existing system ensures that functionality and security can be maintained for that system. It involves knowing the potential consequences or effects of technology-related decisions or events.

8. b. Good documentation provides detailed information about a system or process, ensuring a clear understanding of system operations. This makes it easier to train new staff and troubleshoot issues. System documentation is typically the starting point when trying to ascertain any software or system dependencies.

9. c. Updating a diagram is the process of editing the current diagram of a system or network and inserting any changes that have occurred since the diagram was initially created. It ensures that everyone has an accurate and up-to-date picture of the system, which can significantly enhance troubleshooting and system upgrades.

10. a. A version control system records changes to a file or set of files over time to make it possible to recall specific versions later. This system allows you to track modifications, pinpoint when and by whom those changes were made, and, if necessary, revert to an earlier version. Effective version control is essential for managing changes, troubleshooting issues in a collaborative environment, and communicating updates to policies and procedures throughout an organization.

Review Questions

1. The primary purpose of patch management in an organization's security operations is to maintain up-to-date systems, fix vulnerabilities, and enhance system security.

2. Business processes in security operations coordinate tasks and procedures to accomplish specific organizational goals or deliver products or services. Each process, such as approval mechanisms or ownership protocols, can shape an organization's security posture.

3. The approval process dictates how changes impacting security are approved and who has the authority to make such decisions. It helps ensure that all necessary precautions are taken into consideration and that planned changes will not introduce new vulnerabilities.

4. In terms of security operations, ownership of assets ensures that each asset is consistently maintained, protected, and updated according to security requirements. The owners define the security requirements of the assets, manage their risk profile, and address any vulnerabilities.

5. Technical implications in cybersecurity refer to the potential consequences or effects of technology-related decisions or events, such as alterations to network infrastructure or modifications to security protocols.

6. An allow list, or whitelist, is a list of approved inputs a user or machine can perform on a system. It defines permitted values and rejects everything else, and thus it plays a crucial role in system security.

7. The downside of relying solely on a block list, or deny list, for input validation is that such a list is hard to implement and maintain and easy for an attacker to bypass, as it is impossible to anticipate all possible inputs and attack vectors.

8. Restricted activities in cybersecurity are specific actions or operations within a computer or network system that are limited or prohibited in order to uphold cybersecurity standards.

9. Documentation provides information about a system or process. It ensures a clear understanding of system operations, making it easier to train new staff and troubleshoot issues.

10. Version control in IT and cybersecurity domains is essential as it records changes to a file or set of files over time so that you can recall specific versions later. It allows an organization to track modifications, pinpoint when and by whom changes were made, and, if necessary, revert to an earlier version.

Chapter 4

Do I Know This Already? Quiz

1. c. The main function of public key infrastructure (PKI) is to bind public keys with corresponding user identities. This is typically done through certificates issued by a certificate authority (CA).

2. a. Asymmetric encryption uses a pair of keys (public and private) for communication, thereby enhancing security. A message encrypted with a public key can only be decrypted with the corresponding private key and vice versa.

3. b. Full-disk encryption involves applying encryption to an entire hard drive, including data, files, the operating system, and software programs.

4. d. A cipher suite in Transport Layer Security (TLS) typically includes a combination of key exchange algorithm, bulk encryption algorithm, message authentication code (MAC) algorithm, and potentially signatures and an authentication algorithm.

5. a. The main difference between a stream cipher and a block cipher lies in the way they encrypt data. A stream cipher encrypts plaintext digits one at a time, whereas a block cipher encrypts large blocks of digits at once.

6. d. A digital signature serves to verify the authenticity of digital messages and ensure that they were not altered in transit.

7. c. The feature of a blockchain that makes it difficult to cheat or change the system is the duplication and distribution of the digital ledger of transactions across the entire network of computer systems on a blockchain.

8. c. Distinguished Encoding Rules (DER) is used for X.509 certificates. It has restrictive rules for length, character strings, and how elements are sorted.

9. c. P12/PFX is a binary format based on PKCS#12 that is used to store a server certificate, intermediate certificates, and a private key in one encryptable file.

10. b. If a certificate file uses the .der extension, the certificate file is in binary form.

11. a. Hardware Security Modules (HSMs) are specialized physical devices designed to manage digital keys and handle critical cryptographic processes, including encryption and decryption. They provide a secure environment for these operations, protecting sensitive keys from unauthorized access and tampering.

12. b. Obfuscation in data security is the process of altering or disguising data to make it less easily understood or interpreted.

13. c. Hashing is a technique used to create a unique, fixed-length value (hash) from data, such as a file or password. It is primarily used for authentication purposes, to verify data integrity, and to ensure that the data has not been altered.

14. a. Salting involves adding random data to a password before hashing it. This practice is used to enhance password security by introducing variability.

15. b. Key stretching is a technique used to enhance the security of weaker keys, typically passwords or passphrases. It does this by applying an algorithm that requires significantly more computational resources to test each potential key during a brute-force attack.

16. b. The open public ledger in blockchain transactions acts as a transparent and immutable record, verifying the authenticity of accounts involved in the transactions and ensuring the availability of funds.

Review Questions

1. Public key infrastructure (PKI) contributes to an organization's security operations by establishing a hierarchical framework for the secure exchange of information. It uses asymmetric cryptography to create key pairs, binding public keys to identities through certificates issued by a trusted certificate authority (CA).

2. PKI ensures the secure exchange of digital certificates by creating asymmetric key pairs and distributing the public key, binding it with user identities through a certificate authority.

3. Disk encryption converts data into unreadable code to secure it. Full-disk encryption applies to an entire hard drive, partition-level encryption secures specific disk segments, and file-level encryption protects individual files.

4. Hashing ensures the authenticity of a file or data by mapping it to a fixed-length value, which changes entirely if even a single bit of the data is altered. Salting adds an additional value to the end of the password during hashing to change the hash value produced, enhancing security.

5. Padding divides a message into fixed-size data blocks to align with the specific block size accepted by the hashing algorithm. This contributes to the

avalanche effect as a change in one bit anywhere in the message will change the entire hash value.

6. Digital signatures verify the authenticity of digital messages or documents by using asymmetric cryptography, providing assurance that a message was created by a known sender and wasn't altered in transit. The key properties required are that the signature's authenticity can be verified using the corresponding public key, and generating a valid signature without knowing the private key should be computationally infeasible.

7. A blockchain differs from a typical database by storing data in blocks that are chained together in chronological order. The most common data stored on a blockchain is a ledger for transactions.

8. The open public ledger verifies the authenticity of accounts in a blockchain transaction, preventing sales if insufficient funds are available. It eliminates the need for a central authority as the ledger is stored on personal devices of individuals and businesses using the blockchain, with all members having access to the ledger.

9. A certificate authority (CA) issues certificates to users, verifying their identities to secure communications. To obtain a digital identity certificate, a user's computer initiates a certificate signing request (CSR), presenting proof of the user's identity and a public key that is matched to the CA's private key for certificate issuance.

10. The concept of the root of trust in PKI refers to the foundational element that is inherently trusted in a security architecture. Unlike the web of trust model, which decentralizes trust, the root of trust is a centralized point that provides a secure baseline for cryptographic operations and key management.

Chapter 5

Do I Know This Already? Quiz

1. a. Unskilled attackers, often referred to as *script kiddies*, are typically juveniles. They tend to use simple techniques, utilizing code written by others that is freely available online. They have limited resources and usually aim to enhance their reputation in the hacking world.

2. b. An advanced persistent threat (APT), often tied to a nation-state actor, is an entity with the highest level of resources, including open-source and covert sources of intelligence. The high resource availability and motivation make APTs some of the most dangerous foes.

3. b. Shadow IT refers to the practice of using IT systems, software, and services without the explicit approval of the corporate IT department.

4. b. Hacktivists are typically protesting against something they disagree with, such as a political stance, a religious belief, or a human rights issue.

5. a. Hacktivists are generally motivated by their disagreement with certain political, religious, or human rights issues.

6. c. Nation-state actors typically have significant resources and funding at their disposal, allowing them to perform sophisticated cyberattacks. These resources can include advanced hacking tools, highly skilled personnel, and substantial funding to support their operations.

7. c. The main intent of criminals in the context of cyber threats is to make money. This can involve various activities such as stealing sensitive data for sale or ransom, conducting fraud, or disrupting services for ransom.

8. c. Active intrusion typically begins with an adversary targeting a victim and using various capabilities to launch an attack.

9. b. The unauthorized transfer of data from a computer is known as data exfiltration. It is one of the common motivations for hackers to infiltrate systems and networks.

10. d. Hackers can be driven by deeply held political ideologies or philosophical concepts. These individuals often believe their actions are justifiable or necessary, based on their beliefs.

Review Questions

1. The term commonly used to describe an unskilled attacker who uses code written by others that is freely available on the Internet is *script kiddie*. Even though their methods are simple, these unskilled attackers can inflict significant damage on insecure systems.

2. A hacktivist is usually far more competent than an unskilled attacker. Whereas an unskilled attacker uses others' code without much technical understanding, a hacktivist typically has more knowledge and skills, and their activities can range from hacking for social change to promoting political agendas or even full-blown cyberterrorism.

3. An advanced persistent threat (APT) typically has the highest level of resources, including open-source intelligence (OSINT) and covert sources of intelligence. The extreme motivation, along with these resources, makes APTs some of the most dangerous foes. Often, APTs are tied to nation-state actors and are involved in activities such as stealing intellectual property, causing disruption, and compromising critical infrastructure.

4. Shadow IT refers to the use of IT systems, network devices, software, applications, and services without the approval of the corporate IT

department. This can pose significant risks to an organization as employees may unknowingly introduce vulnerabilities that may be exploited by threat actors. For instance, unpatched servers or unmonitored applications can easily be compromised, potentially leading to data breaches.

5. Hacktivists are typically motivated by the desire to protest against something they do not agree with, such as political or religious beliefs or human rights issues. Their actions often include disruption techniques, denial-of-service (DoS) attacks, or website defacement. On the other hand, cybercriminals are typically motivated by financial gain.

6. An internal threat actor might be motivated by money offered by an external actor for stealing information or causing disruption. The internal actor could be a disgruntled employee who leaves a backdoor to later access confidential information or to trigger a denial-of-service condition on critical systems and applications.

7. Resources and funding play significant roles in the level of sophistication and capability of cyberattacks. For example, nation-state actors with access to substantial resources and funding can launch more advanced and sophisticated attacks than can unskilled attackers, hacktivists, or disgruntled employees, who generally have limited resources and funding.

8. Active intrusions are scenarios where an adversary targets a victim and uses various capabilities along with some form of infrastructure to launch an attack against the victim. These capabilities can be various forms of tools, techniques, and procedures, and the infrastructure serves as the link between the adversary and the victim.

9. In the context of cybersecurity threats, data exfiltration refers to the unauthorized transfer of data from a computer. This can often be a significant motivation for hackers and cyberattackers, particularly those interested in obtaining sensitive or valuable information.

10. Philosophical/political beliefs are deeply held views related to political ideologies or philosophical concepts. A threat actor motivated by such beliefs might engage in cyber activities to promote their beliefs, challenge opposing viewpoints, or disrupt entities that contradict their ideologies.

Chapter 6

Do I Know This Already? Quiz

1. c. Smishing, which is a combination of "SMS" and "phishing," is a type of attack that involves using SMS messages to trick recipients into actions like downloading malicious software or providing personal information.

2. c. With SMS challenge/response, a question is sent to the user's phone via SMS, asking if the authorization attempt is approved. If the user texts back "Yes," authentication is completed, and if the user texts back "No," authentication fails. It is a less-secure form of strong authentication that is vulnerable to on-path attacks.

3. b. Attackers can embed destructive code within an image to spread malware. When the image is opened, the hidden code may be executed, leading to system compromise.

4. b. Client-based security requires that software (an agent) be installed on the client device itself to actively monitor and protect against malicious activities. It can provide more granular control and customization but may be more resource intensive.

5. b. Unsupported systems and applications are software tools or platforms that do not receive regular updates, security patches, or technical support, often because they have reached their official end-of-life (EOL). Without updates, these systems become prime targets for cybercriminals and pose significant security risks.

6. b. WEP (Wired Equivalent Privacy) is considered outdated and susceptible to exploitation due to its weak encryption and vulnerabilities.

7. c. War-dialing involves scanning a list of telephone numbers and dialing them in search of computer systems and fax machines, filtering out numbers associated with voice lines.

8. b. Continuous monitoring and vendor risk management, including regular security assessments and contractual obligations, help in identifying and addressing security gaps in vendors.

9. c. Vishing, or voice phishing, refers to phishing attacks accomplished by telephone conversations that are often used to steal sensitive information.

10. c. Typosquatting leverages human error when typing a URL. An attacker registers a domain that is a common typo of a legitimate site to host malware or impersonate the real website. Victims who type in the wrong URL are subject to this attack.

Review Questions

1. Image-based threats involve the malicious manipulation of digital images to hide malware or other harmful actions. Safeguards such as updated antivirus/anti-malware software and cautious downloading from untrusted sources can help mitigate this risk.

2. Client-based security involves installing software on client devices. It provides granular control but can be resource intensive. Agentless security involves

centrally monitoring and enforcing policies. It offers a lighter footprint and easier management.

3. Organizations can mitigate risks of unsupported systems by upgrading to supported software versions or implementing specific security controls and regularly reviewing support status.

4. Wireless networks can be susceptible to unauthorized access and eavesdropping if they are improperly configured or if they lack robust encryption protocols. Implementing robust encryption like WPA3 and educating users about safe network usage can mitigate these risks.

5. Wired networks can be vulnerable if proper segmentation and access controls are not implemented. Implementing network segmentation, access controls, and continuous monitoring are techniques for mitigating these risks.

6. Bluetooth networks can be exploited if devices are set to "discoverable" mode or if known vulnerabilities are not patched. Ensuring that devices are not in "discoverable" mode and keeping systems updated can minimize risks.

7. MSPs manage IT services for other companies and can introduce risks if they are not properly secured. Ensuring that MSPs follow stringent security protocols and undergo regular assessment can mitigate this risk.

8. Vendors with inadequate cybersecurity measures can become a weak link in the supply chain. Regular security assessments, contractual obligations, and continuous monitoring can mitigate these risks.

9. Vishing is phone or voice phishing, in which attackers might impersonate legitimate institutions to steal sensitive information. Being cautious about unsolicited phone requests for personal information and verifying caller identity can protect against vishing.

10. Typosquatting is a type of attack that leverages human error when typing URLs. An attacker registers a misspelled domain to impersonate a real website and possibly host malware. Users should be cautious and double-check URLs to avoid falling victim to typosquatting.

Chapter 7

Do I Know This Already? Quiz

1. c. Memory injection involves introducing malicious code into a system's memory. This makes detection challenging because the code runs within a legitimate process.

2. b. Implementing stack protection is a security mechanism specifically designed to prevent buffer overflow.

3. b. Applying the least-privilege principle helps mitigate OS-based vulnerabilities by restricting unnecessary access rights.

4. d. Implementing a content security policy (CSP) and proper input validation are common strategies for mitigating both SQL injection and XSS vulnerabilities.

5. b. The three main types of XSS vulnerabilities are stored XSS, reflected XSS, and DOM-based XSS.

6. c. An end-of-life (EOL) hardware vulnerability occurs when a product no longer receives support and security updates from the manufacturer, leaving it susceptible to exploitation.

7. c. Resource reuse in virtualization involves sharing physical resources, and a vulnerability in this case might allow one virtual machine to access data remnants from another.

8. c. A public cloud is a type of service in which a provider offers applications and storage space to the general public over the Internet. Examples include free, web-based email services and pay-as-you-go business-class services such as Google Cloud Platform, Microsoft Azure, and Amazon Web Services (AWS).

9. c. Patch management, where the provider offers regular updates and patches for known issues, is essential for maintaining the security of software products in the context of supply chain vulnerabilities.

10. c. Side loading refers to the practice of installing applications on a mobile device from sources outside the official app store. Side-loaded applications may contain malicious code or bypass security controls.

Review Questions

1. The application layer is susceptible to vulnerabilities like memory injection, where malicious code is introduced into a system's memory, and buffer overflow, which occurs when data exceeds a buffer's capacity. These vulnerabilities can be mitigated through careful coding practices, thorough testing, mechanisms like stack protection, and continuous monitoring.

2. Race conditions occur when a system's behavior depends on the timing of events, leading to unpredictable results or security flaws. Preventing these vulnerabilities requires careful synchronization and control to ensure proper order and safe access to shared resources.

3. Operating system–based vulnerabilities may arise from improper configurations, outdated components, or design flaws. They can be mitigated by adhering to patch management, applying the least-privilege principle, and implementing robust monitoring and logging systems.

4. SQLi vulnerabilities allow attackers to manipulate queries, while XSS allows the injection of malicious scripts into web pages. Mitigation includes proper input validation, parameterized queries, least-privilege access for databases, and implementation of a content security policy (CSP) to prevent unauthorized script execution.

5. Side loading refers to installing applications on a mobile device from sources outside the official app store. This practice can introduce vulnerabilities because side-loaded applications can contain malicious code or may bypass security controls. Restricting side loading through device policies and educating users about the risks associated with unofficial app sources can mitigate this threat.

6. Firmware vulnerabilities can allow unauthorized control over hardware functions, and EOL hardware lacks essential updates. Mitigation includes regular updates to firmware, validation of signatures, hardware-based security features, and proactive replacement or upgrading of EOL hardware.

7. Virtualization vulnerabilities such as VM escape can lead to unauthorized host system access, and resource reuse may allow data leakage between virtual environments. Mitigation involves proper virtual environment configuration, regular updates, secure data-clearing techniques, proper resource isolation, and monitoring for suspicious behavior in the virtual environment.

8. Public clouds, like AWS or Google Cloud, are susceptible to data breaches due to their open nature. They are often targeted for DDoS attacks and may suffer from insecure APIs. Private clouds offer more control and security but are not immune to insider threats that could expose sensitive data. Community clouds cater to specific groups and suffer from the same vulnerabilities as public and private clouds but may be targeted based on the communities they serve.

9. Interconnected risks in the supply chain can lead to vulnerabilities at various stages, from manufacturing to delivery. Regular assessments, audits, and secure sourcing from trusted suppliers can mitigate these risks. Clear contracts and alignment with security practices are also essential.

10. Side loading can introduce vulnerabilities as it allows the installation of applications from unofficial sources. Jailbreaking removes manufacturer restrictions, potentially exposing a device to threats. Organizations can mitigate these vulnerabilities by restricting side loading, employing security measures to detect/prevent jailbreaking, and educating users about risks.

Chapter 8

Do I Know This Already? Quiz

1. b. Ransomware is a specific type of malicious software that locks or encrypts files on a victim's computer and then demands a ransom, typically in cryptocurrency, to unlock or decrypt the files.

2. c. Phishing and spear-phishing attacks are common methods cybercriminals use to deliver ransomware. These deceptive tactics lure victims into clicking on malicious links or opening infected attachments that install ransomware on their systems.

3. b. Physical attacks focus on tangible components like hardware, data storage mediums, and physical locations. They can result in visible damage to hardware, unauthorized physical access, or tampering with physical connections.

4. a. An amplified DDoS attack takes advantage of network protocols that send larger responses to small requests, thereby flooding the victim with substantial traffic. A reflected DDoS attack, on the other hand, uses the victim's IP address as the source, directing responses from various servers to the victim, resulting in unwanted traffic. Both types of attacks lead to denial-of-service conditions, but they use different mechanisms.

5. c. Buffer overflow attacks exploit flaws in an application's memory handling, allowing for the execution of arbitrary code or causing the application to crash.

6. a. A downgrade attack forces the rollback of a strong algorithm to an older, weaker one and may be combined with an on-path attack.

7. c. Password spraying attempts to compromise a system by using a large number of usernames with commonly used passwords, avoiding the rapid lockouts associated with brute-force attacks.

8. b. An account lockout might suggest a brute-force attempt to access an account and would necessitate further investigation to determine the cause.

9. d. Detecting multiple simultaneous sessions from a single user account may indicate unauthorized access or sharing of credentials, requiring analysis to determine the nature of the activity.

Review Questions

1. Malware includes malicious software such as viruses, worms, and Trojan horses. A virus attaches itself to legitimate files and spreads when those files are executed. A worm is a standalone program that replicates itself to spread to other computers without human interaction. A Trojan horse appears to be legitimate software but contains malicious code. Each of these operates differently, but they all can cause harm to computer systems.

2. Amplified and reflected DDoS attacks are two specialized types of DDoS attacks that flood a system with unwanted traffic. An amplified attack utilizes network protocols that respond with more data than received, overwhelming the victim's system. A reflected attack forges the victim's IP address as the source, causing servers to send responses to the victim, leading to a flood of traffic. Both amplified and reflected DDoS attacks aim to render the target system unresponsive, but they use different mechanisms.

3. Ransomware is a type of malware that restricts access to files or systems, demanding payment for restoration of access. Common infection methods include phishing and spear-phishing. Examples include WannaCry and NotPetya. Ransomware often uses encryption, making the files inaccessible without a decryption key, which is typically provided upon payment (cryptoviral extortion).

4. Defending against brute-force attacks requires various strategies and considerations. Offline brute-force attacks target hashed files, whereas online attempts involve repeated direct login attempts. Measures include using strong password hashing, incorporating salts into password hashes, employing account lockout policies, requiring CAPTCHA challenges, and continuously monitoring for unauthorized access.

5. Physical attacks target tangible components of information systems, causing potential visible damage or unauthorized access. Measures to deter these attacks include secure facilities, surveillance, and regular monitoring of physical access. Implementing these measures can protect hardware, data storage mediums, and physical locations from tampering or unauthorized access.

6. A buffer overflow attack works by writing more data to a buffer (temporary data storage area) than the buffer can handle. This overflow can overwrite adjacent memory locations, causing unexpected behavior such as crashes, data corruption, or the execution of arbitrary code by attackers. Its potential consequences include unauthorized system access and control, application malfunction, and data loss. To prevent buffer overflow attacks, organizations can use programming languages and compilers that manage memory safely, implement runtime protections, and perform regular code reviews to detect potential vulnerabilities.

7. A replay attack involves the unauthorized capture and retransmission of valid authentication data, such as tokens or credentials. By reusing valid data, an attacker can gain unauthorized access to a system or perform fraudulent transactions. Organizations can mitigate the risks of replay attacks by implementing time-based restrictions on authentication data, using encryption, and employing single-use or expiring authentication tokens. These strategies make it difficult for attackers to reuse intercepted authentication data effectively.

8. Blocked content refers to security measures that prevent access to malicious or unauthorized websites, files, or emails. It serves as an indicator of potential malicious activity or risk exposure. An increase in blocked content might signify an active threat or a higher-risk environment. Security professionals might respond to such an increase by further investigating the nature of the blocked content, analyzing traffic patterns, and possibly tightening security controls. Understanding the source and nature of the blocked content can guide appropriate response measures, whether that means adjusting existing security settings or launching a more comprehensive threat assessment.

Chapter 9

Do I Know This Already? Quiz

1. b. The goal of segmentation is to isolate groups of hosts and enhance security by limiting access to sensitive information.

2. b. ACLs allow administrators to define rules to grant or deny permissions to specific IP addresses, protocols, or ports, controlling network access.

3. b. In healthcare, patching is vital to protect patient confidentiality by fixing vulnerabilities in systems handling personal health information.

4. c. In manufacturing, downtime for patching can affect production schedules, making this a specific challenge in the patching process.

5. c. The principle of least privilege minimizes the potential damage from accidental mishaps or intentional malicious activities by limiting access permissions.

6. b. Encryption transforms data into a coded form, making it unreadable without the correct decryption key, thus protecting it from unauthorized access.

7. c. A host-based intrusion prevention system (HIPS) provides real-time protection by monitoring the behavior of the host system and blocking or alerting administrators to potential attacks.

8. b. The primary benefit of implementing a centrally managed application allow list is the granular control it offers over the applications allowed to run on a system or network.

9. b. Isolating a compromised endpoint is crucial in preventing the spread of malware or other malicious activities to other parts of the network.

10. c. The main objective of encryption is to protect the confidentiality and integrity of data by converting it into a coded form that can be read only with the correct decryption key or algorithm.

11. b. Monitoring in cybersecurity is focused on the continuous observation and analysis of system activities to identify and respond to potential security incidents.

12. a. Configuration enforcement is crucial for maintaining the security and compliance of IT systems. By standardizing and consistently applying system settings and policies, organizations can ensure that all network elements adhere to security best practices and policies, reducing vulnerabilities and maintaining a secure IT environment.

13. c. Decommissioning in IT lifecycle management refers to the process of systematically removing hardware, software, or subsystems from active service.

Review Questions

1. Network segmentation is the process of dividing a computer network into subnetworks or segments. This improves performance by reducing network congestion and latency, and it enhances security by isolating groups of hosts together. If a breach occurs in one segment, the impact can be confined, preventing compromised systems from accessing the entire network.

2. An access control list (ACL) defines rules that control traffic into and out of a network, granting or denying permissions to specific IP addresses, protocols, or ports. In a multi-department enterprise, ACLs can be configured to ensure that only authorized personnel within specific departments can access sensitive data, such as financial information. This is a way to maintain confidentiality and integrity across the organization.

3. Patching refers to updating or fixing systems by applying updates or patches. Fixing known vulnerabilities enhances security. Different industries approach patching differently due to their unique requirements and challenges. For instance, the healthcare industry prioritizes protecting patient confidentiality, while the financial sector focuses on compliance with regulatory requirements, and the manufacturing industry is concerned about potential disruptions to production schedules.

4. The principle of least privilege dictates that individuals or systems should have only the minimal access needed to accomplish tasks. In a hospital setting, this might mean that nurses have access to patient medical records but not to financial information, while IT technicians might have rights to update software but not to access confidential HR records. Following this principle limits the risk of unauthorized access and potential damage.

5. Common hardening techniques include use of encryption and installation of endpoint protection, host-based firewalls, and host-based intrusion prevention systems. These techniques contribute to security by eliminating unnecessary functions, restricting access, employing protective tools, and setting stringent configurations, making it harder for potential intruders to exploit weaknesses. These practices can be applied to hardware and software to strengthen an organization's security posture.

6. Encryption is a critical hardening technique that transforms data into coded form, making it unreadable without the proper decryption key. It can be used to protect data stored on disks (full disk encryption) or specific files, folders, or data transmitted over networks. Encryption ensures that even if unauthorized access is gained, the data remains unintelligible without the proper keys, providing a robust layer of security.

Chapter 10

Do I Know This Already? Quiz

1. d. A responsibility matrix is an outline that divides responsibilities between a cloud service provider (CSP) and a customer, defining who is responsible for security, compliance, operations, and management in the cloud environment.

2. b. The primary benefits of utilizing a hybrid cloud architecture are flexibility, scalability, and diverse deployment options with consideration for data integration, network connectivity, security, compliance, and cost.

3. c. Software-defined networking (SDN) was originally created to decouple control from the forwarding functions in networking equipment. SDN was created to use software to centrally manage and "program" the hardware and virtual networking appliances to perform forwarding.

4. c. An air gap in network infrastructure refers to a computer system with no physical connection to other networks that reduces the likelihood of network attacks. An air-gapped system has no physical connection to other computers or networks, making it harder to attack through the network.

5. c. A container image, in the context of containerization, bundles a program and its dependencies into a single artifact and can be composed of a series of file system layers.

6. b. The primary purpose of virtualization in cloud and networking architectures is to create multiple simulated environments or dedicated resources from a single physical hardware system.

7. b. PLCs and RTUs, in the context of SCADA systems, are microcomputers that communicate with objects like turbines, machines, and gauges and that route information to SCADA software.

8. c. The inability to patch effectively across all architectures leads to vulnerabilities, data breaches, and system downtime.

9. b. Risk transference involves shifting specific risks to another party, such as through outsourcing or insurance, but does not remove accountability if a vulnerability is leveraged in that risk. It represents a calculated approach to managing uncertainty, allowing organizations to focus on core competencies and reduce liability while maintaining responsibility for the transferred risks.

Review Questions

1. The original purpose of SDN was to decouple control from the forwarding functions in networking equipment to allow centralized management and programming of the hardware and virtual networking appliances.

2. An air-gapped system contributes to network security by having no physical connection to other computers, networks, or unsecured systems, thus reducing the likelihood of network attacks.

3. A container image is composed of a program and its dependencies bundled into a single artifact under a root file system. These images are made up of file system layers, with each layer adding, removing, or modifying files from the preceding layer.

4. Virtualization enables efficient utilization of resources, flexibility in deploying applications, and improved scalability.

5. SCADA systems are crucial for industrial organizations because they help maintain efficiency, process data for smarter decisions, and communicate system issues to help mitigate downtime.

6. Designing architecture with patch management in mind is essential to enable seamless updates without disturbing existing functionalities, reducing risks of vulnerabilities, data breaches, and system downtime. Strategies may include building a system that can automatically test and validate patches across components, including embedded systems and cloud infrastructure, and implementing centralized patch management strategies and robust testing protocols.

Chapter 11

Do I Know This Already? Quiz

1. c. Strategic device placement enhances security by optimizing the positioning of hardware devices to minimize exposure to potential threats and maximize efficiency and accessibility.

2. b. In a fail-closed configuration, the entire system shuts down or becomes inaccessible when a component fails. This type of configuration can be used to protect sensitive information or operations.

3. b. Understanding device attributes like active and passive monitoring helps in selecting and configuring devices that meet the specific security, performance, and reliability needs of a network.

4. a. In an active/passive configuration, the passive device takes over and becomes active when the primary active device goes offline. This ensures continuity in the operation.

5. b. A jump server serves as a gateway to access other devices within a network, often providing a secure means of remote access to internal systems.

6. a. 802.1X and EAP are frameworks that are used within port security to control access to a network and secure authentication, respectively.

7. b. UTM is associated with NGFWs as it integrates multiple security features into one enterprise-level solution, providing comprehensive protection against various threats.

8. b. A VPN allows devices on different networks to securely connect as if they were on the same private network, providing secure communication over public or untrusted networks.

9. b. Effective controls are vital in managing risks because they allow for the systematic assessment and mitigation of risks, ensuring that they are reduced to acceptable levels.

Review Questions

1. Device placement can determine how well a network is protected against unauthorized access and potential threats. For instance, placing a firewall close to a network's perimeter can prevent unauthorized access, enhancing security.

2. A fail-open system continues to operate even if a part fails, whereas a fail-closed system shuts down if a part fails. The choice of which to implement depends on the system's function and the need to protect sensitive information. For example, a DNS server might be set to fail open, while a firewall might be set to fail closed.

3. Device attributes define how a device operates within a network. Inline configurations interact directly with network traffic, while tap/monitor configurations passively observe. These choices influence the device's ability to manage or monitor traffic.

4. Active/active means both devices are simultaneously active, while in active/passive, one is a standby device. Active/active allows for load balancing and failover, whereas active/passive ensures continuity if the active device fails.

5. These network appliances each play specific roles, from facilitating remote access (jump servers) to balancing network load (load balancers) and

preventing or detecting intrusions (IPSs/IDSs). They all contribute to the security and efficiency of a network.

6. Port security with 802.1X and EAP ensures that only authenticated devices can access the network, thus preventing unauthorized access and potential security breaches.

7. UTM is an out-of-the box solution that integrates various security features, such as firewall, antivirus/anti-malware, and intrusion prevention into a single system. An NGFW is an enterprise-level solution often used to implement UTM, which provides a more efficient and streamlined security solution for a larger organization.

8. A VPN encapsulates and encrypts data to securely transmit it over public or untrusted networks. This ensures privacy and integrity by protecting the data from unauthorized access or modification.

9. Selecting effective controls involves identifying potential risks, assessing their impact, and choosing appropriate controls that align with the organization's goals, risk tolerance, and specific scenarios. This process helps ensure a balanced approach to risk management.

Chapter 12

Do I Know This Already? Quiz

1. b. Regulated data is subject to laws and regulations, often because of its sensitive nature.

2. c. Source code would be classified as confidential or proprietary information in a commercial setting.

3. c. Data at rest is data stored in databases, file systems, or storage media.

4. d. Transport Layer Security (TLS) is the primary method for securing data that is moving from one location to another.

5. b. Data in use refers to data being accessed, processed, or manipulated.

6. b. GDPR regulates how European citizens' data must be stored.

7. c. Masking is the process of replacing specific data in a database with fictitious but structurally similar data.

8. b. Segmentation involves dividing a network into various segments to isolate data or resources.

9. c. Permission restrictions specify who can do what within a system or a network. You can, for example, restrict access to certain personnel within a company to view the files.

10. b. Geotagging involves embedding geographic identification information, such as latitude and longitude coordinates, into various digital media, such as photographs, websites, or SMS messages.

Review Questions

1. Regulated data is subject to laws and regulations, often due to its sensitivity. Intellectual property refers to creative works, inventions, and designs protected by legal rights like patents, copyrights, or trademarks.

2. The first step is to classify assets or data based on the potential damage that could result from a breach to the confidentiality, integrity, or availability of that asset or data.

3. Data in transit refers to data moving from one location to another, such as across networks, while data at rest refers to data that is stored and not actively moving.

4. The GDPR mandates that companies store European citizens' data within EU borders unless an equivalent level of protection is guaranteed elsewhere.

5. Security concerns include the inadvertent revelation of the location of high-profile executives or other key organizational members, making them targets for attacks.

6. Hashing a password is the process of converting the password into a fixed-length string of characters, protecting the original password from direct exposure.

7. The primary purpose of data masking is to replace specific data with fictitious but structurally similar data.

8. Tokenization involves replacing sensitive information with a placeholder or "decoy" value, called a token, to reduce the risk in the event of a data breach.

9. The main objective of segmentation is to isolate data or resources, limiting cross-segment data access and reducing the risk of internal breaches.

10. With RBAC, permissions are assigned to roles, whereas with ABAC, access is granted based on additional attributes like location, time, and type of device.

Chapter 13

Do I Know This Already? Quiz

1. c. The primary benefit of using a multi-cloud system is to reduce dependency on a single cloud service provider, mitigating risks such as downtime and security issues.

2. c. COOP addresses emergencies from an all-hazards approach, so it is applicable to a broad range of circumstances.

3. b. Technology capacity planning focuses on the computational power, software, and hardware needed to meet future organizational demands.

4. a. Tabletop exercises are used to validate and improve an organization's incident response plan (IRP).

5. a. A hot site is a near duplicate of the original site and can be up and running within minutes. A company uses a hot site if would face financial ruin if its primary site became inaccessible for even a short period.

6. b. A warm site offers a good amount of configuration yet remains less expensive than a hot site. It might need to have backups of data restored and may require some setup before it can be used.

7. b. The primary benefit of an onsite backup strategy is fast access to backups for quick recovery.

8. c. A UPS provides near-instantaneous protection from input power interruptions by supplying energy stored in batteries or supercapacitors.

9. a. The primary difference is that load balancing distributes incoming network or application traffic across multiple servers to enhance system availability, whereas clustering connects multiple servers to function as a single system, contributing to recovery by allowing for seamless failover.

10. b. The primary reason for implementing platform diversity is to reduce systemic risks resulting from having a single point of failure. By diversifying platforms, an organization increases its resilience and enhances its ability to recover from security incidents and technical failures.

Review Questions

1. High availability is a key component of continuity of operations planning (COOP) that is related to ensuring that critical systems are always accessible and minimize downtime. High availability architecture generally includes redundant hardware, software, and communication paths to eliminate single points of failure.

2. Capacity planning is the practice of foreseeing and preparing for future computational and storage needs. It is crucial for an organization's long-term strategy as it ensures that resources like CPU, memory, storage, and network bandwidth are adequately allocated and scalable to meet future demands.

3. Testing the effectiveness of an incident response plan involves conducting various exercises, such as tabletop exercises, simulated attacks, and full-scale exercises. This process is critical for identifying gaps, refining procedures, and ensuring that team members know their roles, thereby enhancing the organization's preparedness for actual incidents.

4. Parallel processing involves running tasks concurrently on both the primary and secondary systems to ensure that the backup system will produce the same output as the primary system under similar conditions. This contributes to system resilience by ensuring that the failover system is both operational and reliable.

5. Table 13-2 outlines different elements of backup strategies, including onsite backups, offsite backups, backup frequency, encryption, snapshots, recovery, replication, and journaling. Each of these elements has unique benefits and drawbacks related to speed of recovery, vulnerability to disasters, or resource consumption. By using a composite of multiple methods, an organization can tailor its backup strategy to its specific needs and risk profile.

Chapter 14

Do I Know This Already? Quiz

1. c. The primary goal of application security is to prevent data or code within an app from being stolen or intercepted.

2. b. The primary purpose of conducting an inventory when capturing a baseline configuration is to list all hardware and software components in use in the organization.

3. c. The secure cookie attribute is set by the application server in an HTTP response.

4. a. Geofencing is an advanced technique for hardening mobile devices.

5. b. The main goal of a site survey is to plan and optimize a Wi-Fi network.

6. b. Storage segmentation is crucial for a successful BYOD implementation to ensure clear separation between organizational and personal information, applications, and other content on the device.

7. b. A key feature of WPA3-Personal is the optional use of 192-bit AES encryption. It allows for a more secure wireless connection compared to WPA2, offering users the flexibility to opt for stronger encryption methods when setting up their wireless network.

8. c. Sandboxing helps prevent unauthorized or malicious code from affecting the system.

9. b. One of the primary roles of monitoring in cybersecurity is continuous surveillance of systems.

10. c. Upon detecting fraudulent activities, the monitoring system in a financial institution could be programmed to temporarily freeze the account.

Review Questions

1. A router that prevents anyone from viewing a computer's IP address from the Internet provides hardware application security.

2. Common web security vulnerabilities that improper input validation can lead to include cross-site scripting (XSS) and SQL injection.

3. Secure session cookies can be exploited in an attack known as session hijacking or cookie hijacking.

4. SAST tools give developers real-time feedback while they code.

5. The six steps involved in effectively running a static code analysis are finalize the tool, create the scanning infrastructure and deploy the tool, customize the tool, prioritize and onboard applications, analyze scan results, and provide governance and training.

6. Before a developer can sign their work, they need to generate a public/private key pair and receive a code signing certificate from a trustworthy certificate authority (CA).

7. When sandboxing is used, the email attachment is sent to a sandbox environment, where it is automatically opened and executed to check for malicious behavior.

8. Besides detecting current issues, monitoring also creates an audit trail that can be used for future analysis, regulatory compliance, and legal proceedings.

Chapter 15

Do I Know This Already? Quiz

1. c. Vendor assessment aims to assess the credibility and security measures of vendors, ensuring that they comply with industry standards and legal requirements.

2. b. TPRM emphasizes that risk assessment is not a one-time activity and requires continuous monitoring of a third party's security measures.

3. b. The assignment/accounting process establishes lines of responsibility and accountability for each asset within an organization.

4. b. Monitoring and asset tracking provide continuous visibility into the status, location, and condition of all assets, aiding decisions related to security, budgeting, and operations.

5. c. Sanitization aims to remove data from storage devices so that it cannot be recovered.

6. a. Data retention involves securely storing specific types of information for a mandated period, according to either company policy or legal requirements.

Review Questions

1. Leaders from the supply department, the engineering department for software engineering procurements, and any leaders who can offer insights into details of the asset under review should be involved in the procurement process.

2. TPRM involves evaluating and managing the risks associated with outsourcing services or buying products from third-party vendors. It includes performing due diligence on a third party's security policies, track record, and compliance with industry standards. Continuous monitoring of the third party's security measures is essential.

3. The assignment and accounting process is crucial for maintaining a secure and organized environment and establishes lines of responsibility and accountability. Two main aspects are ownership, which designates the responsible individual or department, and classification, which informs the level of security and oversight each asset will require.

4. The subprocesses in the disposal and decommissioning phase include sanitization, which is removing data from a storage device; destruction, which is physical disassembly or obliteration of hardware assets; certification, which refers to the documentation and validation that the decommissioning process has been executed per company policy and applicable laws; and data retention, which involves keeping certain types of information for a specified period.

Chapter 16

Do I Know This Already? Quiz

1. b. Static analysis focuses on examining source code, bytecode, or binaries before an application is run.

2. a. Dynamic analysis involves examining an application while it is operational.

3. b. A responsible disclosure program aims to provide a framework for the ethical reporting of vulnerabilities.

4. b. A false positive inaccurately flags an activity as a threat, which can be distracting and misleading for a security team.

5. c. CVSS provides a robust mechanism for evaluating the severity of vulnerabilities.

6. b. Vulnerability classification involves sorting vulnerabilities based on criteria such as risk level or component affected.

7. b. Patching often presents challenges related to scheduling and system downtime.

8. a. Analysts should be familiar with the specific incidents and conditions that a cyber insurance policy covers.

9. b. Unlike automated scans, audits involve detailed manual reviews, often by third parties or internal teams.

10. a. Different audiences, such as technical teams or management, have different requirements and focuses when it comes to reporting.

Review Questions

1. Static analysis focuses on examining an application's source code, bytecode, or binaries before the application is executed. This preemptive measure allows for the identification of issues like hardcoded passwords or insecure cryptographic storage techniques that might be difficult to spot during runtime.

2. A false positive in cybersecurity refers to a situation in which an activity is incorrectly flagged as a threat. False positives are false alarms that can act as a smokescreen that distracts security teams from real issues and potentially hides actual vulnerabilities.

3. The main goal of a responsible disclosure program is to provide a structured framework that encourages the ethical reporting of security vulnerabilities. Such a program typically outlines procedures for external researchers to securely report vulnerabilities they've discovered and often provides a secure reporting mechanism like encrypted email or a dedicated online portal.

4. CVSS stands for Common Vulnerability Scoring System. Its primary function is to provide a standardized mechanism for assessing the severity and nature of software vulnerabilities. By quantifying these attributes, it aids security professionals and organizations in making informed decisions about risk mitigation.

5. One challenge often associated with patching is that it may require system downtime, disrupting regular business operations. Compatibility issues can also arise, and a patch meant to fix one vulnerability might inadvertently break other functionalities.

6. When crafting a cybersecurity report, it's crucial to consider the type of audience. Different audiences like technical teams or senior management have distinct sets of key performance indicators (KPIs) and concerns. For example, while an IT manager might want detailed information on attack vectors, the company executives are likely to be more interested in the overall risk posture and potential business impact.

Chapter 17

Do I Know This Already? Quiz

1. d. Monitoring systems generate real-time reports and issue alerts based on conditions like CPU overuse or unauthorized login attempts, ensuring that systems are running optimally.

2. c. Security information and event management (SIEM) systems help sift through the noise in the large volumes of aggregated logs and identify anomalies that could indicate security threats.

3. b. Reporting translates the often technical language of cybersecurity into formats that stakeholders can understand and act on.

4. c. Hypertext Markup Language (HTML) is not listed as part of the current SCAP specifications.

5. c. Agent-based solutions often provide more in-depth data and control than do agentless solutions.

6. a, b, c. DLP software classifies regulated, confidential, and business-critical data and identifies violations of organizational policies.

Review Questions

1. The primary role of monitoring systems is to ensure that systems are running optimally, are free of vulnerabilities, and are not participating in any unauthorized activities.

2. The purpose of log aggregation is to collect data from multiple sources into a centralized location for various security analyses.

3. A report for senior management is likely to include high-level information about potential business impact and strategic recommendations for risk mitigation, and a report for a technical team will delve into the intricacies of detected vulnerabilities and recommended courses of action.

4. The mission of Security Content Automation Protocol (SCAP) is to maintain system security by ensuring that security configuration best practices are implemented, verifying the presence of patches, and maintaining complete visibility of the security posture of systems and the organization at all times.

5. The benefits of using agentless solutions include simplicity and reduced system load, but these solutions may lack the depth of monitoring or control provided by agent-based solutions.

Chapter 18

Do I Know This Already? Quiz

1. c. DNS filtering is primarily used to block access to malicious or inappropriate websites, acting as a "traffic cop" by allowing or disallowing data requests to certain domain names, ensuring network security, and adhering to corporate policies

2. b. An intrusion detection system (IDS) focuses primarily on monitoring and alerting on suspicious activities in a network, whereas an intrusion prevention system (IPS) goes a step further by actively blocking and preventing both known and potential threats.

3. c. In an agent-based web filtering approach, the software is directly deployed onto individual user devices. This allows for more granular control and is especially beneficial for teams that are frequently out of the office or that work remotely.

4. b. By using a Group Policy framework, administrators can establish rules, or policies, that control various aspects of the operating system and applications. For example, they could set policies governing the complexity of user passwords to enhance overall security.

5. c. Domain Name System (DNS) filtering acts as a "traffic cop," permitting or blocking data requests to specific domain names based on predefined criteria.

6. b. Domain-Based Message Authentication Reporting and Conformance (DMARC) ensures the authenticity of the sending domain in an email. It also verifies that the email content has not been altered during transit, reducing the risk of spoofing attacks.

7. a. DMARC is crucial for verifying that an email message was indeed sent from the domain it claims to be from and that the contents have not been altered during transit, thus combatting email-based spoofing attacks.

8. d. Extended detection and response (XDR) expands on the capabilities of endpoint detection and response (EDR) by taking a holistic view of network security. It correlates data across multiple channels and layers, such as email, cloud storage, and network traffic, providing a more comprehensive security overview.

9. b. User behavior analytics (UBA) predominantly utilizes machine learning algorithms to continuously track, collect, and assess user behavior in a network. This helps in identifying any unusual activity that could be indicative of a security threat.

10. b. The main function of file integrity monitoring is to alert administrators about unauthorized changes in files, which helps in detecting potential security breaches or data manipulation.

11. b. The key objective of a DLP system is to ensure that sensitive or critical information does not leave the corporate network unauthorized, thus protecting against data exfiltration.

12. d. Implementing secure protocols for network security involves choosing an appropriate encryption protocol, selecting the correct port, and deciding on a suitable transport method. The color scheme of the user interface is irrelevant to these technical considerations and does not impact the security of data transmission.

Review Questions

1. Data loss prevention (DLP) devices are used to prevent confidential data from leaving a network.

2. Web filtering is the mechanism used to control access to websites based on predefined criteria.

3. Network access control (NAC) is used to enforce policy-driven security solutions at the network entry level.

4. User behavior analytics (UBA) is designed to track, collect, and assess the behavior of users on a network to detect any unusual activity indicating a security threat.

5. Endpoint detection and response (EDR) focuses on what's happening within the endpoints, analyzing processes, file changes, and registry settings.

6. Extended detection and response (XDR) provides a holistic view of network security by correlating data across various channels and layers, like email, cloud, and network traffic.

Chapter 19

Do I Know This Already? Quiz

1. c. Removing or disabling permissions and settings is the primary purpose of de-provisioning.

2. c. Implicit permissions are permissions inherited through membership in a group or role.

3. b. SSO simplifies the user experience by reducing the number of authentication steps a user must complete after initially logging in.

4. c. RBAC works with sets of permissions based on a role in the company, whereas MAC works with individual label-based permissions.

5. c. Longer passwords are inherently more secure than shorter ones, reducing the likelihood of successful brute-force or dictionary attacks.

6. b. JIT permissions are dynamically provisioned access permissions that are typically granted for a limited period and align specifically with the time frame during which the permissions are required.

7. b. Interoperability is particularly important in IAM systems to allow varied information systems and applications to connect and exchange information seamlessly. It facilitates system integration, enables secure business partnerships, and allows for flexibility in adapting to new technologies and compliance requirements.

8. b. The primary purpose of attestation in remote system authentication is to enable one system to provide reliable statements about its software to another system. The other system can use these statements in making authorization decisions.

9. c. A "something you know" factor in multifactor authentication is knowledge-based evidence such as a passphrase or PIN code.

10. c. In MFA, a "something you have" factor is an object in the user's possession, such as a security token or smart card, that is used for verification.

11. b. Employing a multilayer mechanism involving a password, two-factor authentication, and voice recognition for high-value transactions is the best selection for sensitive transactions commonly found at a financial institution.

12. b. Federation is a process by which one system authenticates a user and then communicates this verification to a second system.

Review Questions

1. De-provisioning results in the disabling or removal of a user's permissions and settings, such as when the individual leaves the company or changes roles. This process ensures that users do not retain unnecessary access, reducing potential security risks.

2. Explicit permissions are assigned when an administrator directly specifies the types or levels of access for a user or a group. This is in contrast to implicit permissions, which users or groups might inherit based on their membership in a group or role.

3. SSO primarily reduces the burden on users by cutting down the number of authentication steps required after initial login. This streamlining reduces the

security risks associated with password management by minimizing the number of credentials a user needs to manage.

4. Role-based access control (RBAC) involves using sets of permissions that collectively define a role. Unlike mandatory access control (MAC), which is label based, RBAC is structured to allow for more flexibility in how permissions are configured.

5. Password length mainly contributes to resistance to brute-force or dictionary attacks. A longer password increases the number of possible combinations, making it more challenging for attackers to crack the password.

6. JIT permissions reduce security risks by dynamically provisioning access for only a limited time that generally corresponds to the specific time frame when the permissions are required. This approach reduces the attack surface by limiting the time during which elevated permissions are active and lowering the chances of misuse if an account is compromised.

Chapter 20

Do I Know This Already? Quiz

1. b. The CI/CT pipeline is triggered when developers commit code changes to a version control system such as GitHub or GitLab.

2. b. Static analysis in the CI/CT pipeline is for scanning committed code for vulnerabilities.

3. c. One of the benefits of automated tests in the CI/CT process is early detection of vulnerabilities.

4. c. Automated testing in CI/CT pipelines can generate false positives that need to be reviewed manually.

5. b. APIs are used to facilitate communication between different software entities to work as a coherent system.

6. b. Removing tedious tasks from employees' roles improves job satisfaction and thus affects employee retention.

7. b. In the context of cybersecurity automation, a baseline is a set of predefined security settings and configurations.

8. b. Automation acts as a workforce multiplier by taking care of repetitive tasks, thereby enhancing a team's productivity.

9. c. Hasty implementation of automated systems may result in technical debt due to shortcuts or temporary fixes.

10. c. Personnel training is a key aspect of ongoing supportability, ensuring that the team is equipped to adapt to new features or shifts in protocols.

Review Questions

1. The continuous integration/continuous testing (CI/CT) approach allows for the seamless integration and testing of code changes, enhancing both the efficiency and the security posture of software development processes.

2. Automation can drastically reduce the time required to perform security tasks, enable early detection of security vulnerabilities through constant monitoring, and streamline the entire security infrastructure.

3. The deployment of automation can introduce complexities, as systems have to be configured and maintained properly. False positives can also occur, requiring human judgment for validation. Overreliance on automated systems can sometimes lead to overlooking nuances that a human expert might catch.

4. Continuous monitoring tools help keep an eye on a system's security posture and detect anomalies in real time. These tools are crucial for quick response to emerging threats and vulnerabilities, allowing for rapid mitigation strategies.

5. Ongoing training and support are required to keep personnel up-to-date. Automated systems are ever evolving and constantly become more complex, and human operators need continuous training and support to effectively manage these systems and adapt to changes.

6. Both benefits and challenges come with automation. While automation offers substantial advantages such as efficiency and early vulnerability detection, it also presents challenges, such as increased system complexity and the potential for false positives, which need to be carefully managed.

Chapter 21

Do I Know This Already? Quiz

1. c. The owner is responsible for coordinating communications, assigning tasks, and ensuring efficient execution of the incident response plan. The owner bridges the technical and nontechnical aspects of incident response.

2. b. Role-based training equips team members with the skills and knowledge they need for a coordinated and effective response.

3. c. Effective simulation exercises focus on the environment, external injects, and metrics to evaluate the effectiveness of the response.

4. c. Root cause analysis allows you to focus your efforts and resources on areas that will yield the most significant impact and prevent recurrence.

5. c. Threat hunting allows for the early detection of threats and enhances adaptability.

6. c. Digital forensics encompasses legal hold, chain of custody, acquisition, reporting, preservation, and e-discovery.

7. b. The final goal of the recovery phase in an incident response process is to resume normal business operations without remnants of the incident, ensuring that systems are fully functional and secure.

8. b. External injects play the role of spontaneous variables in simulation exercises for incident response, challenging the team's response capabilities by introducing unexpected elements to the scenario.

9. c. According to the order of volatility, the CPU cache and registers are prioritized during the evidence acquisition phase after an incident, as this data is highly volatile and needs to be captured first to ensure its preservation.

10. b. The initial step in preserving digital evidence once it has been identified is to create a bit-by-bit image of the device's storage to capture an exact replica of the data for future analysis.

Review Questions

1. The owner of the incident response plan is typically responsible for bridging the technical and nontechnical aspects. This individual coordinates communications, assigns tasks, and ensures that the plan is executed efficiently, making sure that the technical and executive teams are on the same page.

2. The main objective of role-based training in incident response is to equip team members with the skills and knowledge they need to manage and mitigate security incidents effectively. This includes understanding both the technical aspects, such as how to contain a malware outbreak, and the procedural and communication protocols that must be followed during an incident.

3. An element like a simulated power outage could be introduced during a simulation exercise to test the team's adaptability. These unexpected elements, known as external injects, challenge the team to adapt to unforeseen circumstances while managing the incident.

4. Root cause analysis is crucial for effective resource allocation because it involves identifying the underlying reasons behind a security incident. By understanding the root causes, an organization can focus its efforts and resources on areas that will yield the most significant impact, thereby preventing the recurrence of similar incidents.

5. One key benefit of proactive threat hunting is its ability to detect threats early and minimize potential damage. Unlike traditional reactive security measures, threat hunting allows your security measures to adjust quickly to new types of attacks, enhancing the overall security posture.

6. The primary focus of digital forensics in the context of cybersecurity is to uncover, analyze, and preserve electronic evidence for investigations or legal proceedings. It is a multidisciplinary approach that includes specialized activities like legal hold, chain of custody, acquisition, reporting, preservation, and e-discovery.

Chapter 22

Do I Know This Already? Quiz

1. b. Log data serves as a systematic and chronological record that can be analyzed for troubleshooting, security monitoring, and compliance purposes.

2. b. Endpoint logs provide detailed information about activities on individual devices, such as computers and smartphones, that are connected to a network.

3. b. IPS/IDS logs are specialized records that identify potentially harmful activities within a network.

4   b. Data sources are tools and methods used to collect, analyze, and present information that supports an investigation.

5   a. Vulnerability scans focus on identifying weak points in a network and all the software running on devices within it.

6   b. Automated reports can be configured to run on a daily or weekly schedule or can be triggered by specific events, such as multiple failed login attempts.

7. c. Wireshark is commonly used for packet captures to offer a granular view of network activity.

Review Questions

1. For log data to be admissible in court, it must be collected, handled, and stored with a chain of custody in mind. This ensures the integrity of the data and confirms that it provides an immutable fingerprint of system and user activity. This is crucial for investigations and legal proceedings, as it can help identify what happened, when it happened, and who was involved.

2. Endpoint logs provide detailed information about activities on individual devices connected to the network, such as computers and smartphones. They can reveal suspicious or unauthorized behavior such as the installation of unauthorized software or attempts to access restricted files. This information is invaluable for identifying security risks and taking appropriate action.

3. IPS/IDS logs are specialized records that identify potentially harmful activities within a network. These logs can alert you to various types of attacks, such as SQL injections or cross-site scripting, allowing you to take immediate action to mitigate threats.

4. Vulnerability scans identify weak points in a network, including each device that has an IP address and the software running on it. By running both authenticated and unauthenticated scans, you gain insight into vulnerabilities in services, open ports, and configurations that affect security. This is the first step in establishing a strong defensive posture for a network.

5. Automated reports in a SIEM system like Splunk or IBM QRadar can be triggered by specific events such as multiple failed login attempts from a single IP address or large data transfers to an external IP address. These reports enable you to spot irregularities and take corrective action swiftly.

6. Packet captures offer a granular view of network activity. Tools like Wireshark are commonly used to capture detailed data packets transmitted over a network. Packet captures can help you understand the types of data being transmitted, identify potential security risks, and troubleshoot network issues.

Chapter 23

Do I Know This Already? Quiz

1. b. Guidelines aim to steer organizational behavior and decision making through general recommendations.

2. c. A policy is a formal, high-level statement that sets the organizational approach to various issues.

3. b. Access control standards are pivotal in defining who gets to access specific resources within an organization.

4. c. Procedures are specific, detailed instructions designed to implement the policies and standards in an organization.

5. b. External considerations influence an organization's security governance, dictating minimum requirements for compliance.

6. a. Monitoring and revision involve regularly reviewing logs, conducting audits, and analyzing performance metrics.

7. c. In a centralized governance structure, decision-making authority is concentrated at the top levels of the organization.

8. b. The processor is responsible for the implementation of security measures specified by the controller, which may include encrypting data, setting firewalls, or configuring access controls.

Review Questions

1. Guidelines provide general recommendations to steer organizational behavior and decision making. Unlike policies, they are not mandates but

offer directional advice. For instance, guidelines can suggest best practices for secure coding or handling sensitive data.

2. A policy is a formal, high-level statement that outlines an organization's general beliefs, goals, objectives, and acceptable procedures for a specific area. It sets the organizational approach to various issues and may be mandated by management or a regulatory body.

3. Access control standards are pivotal in defining who gets to access what within an organization's network and systems. They lay the groundwork for ensuring that only authorized individuals can access specific resources, thereby maintaining data confidentiality, integrity, and availability.

4. Procedures are specific, detailed instructions that are designed to implement the policies and standards in an organization. They guide day-to-day operations and ensure that all activities align with the organization's security objectives. They often include step-by-step formats, flowcharts, or diagrams for clarity.

5. External considerations are factors outside of an organization that influence its security governance. They can range from legal obligations to industry-specific guidelines and often dictate the minimum requirements for compliance.

6. Monitoring and revision are integral to effective security governance. They involve regularly reviewing logs, conducting audits, and analyzing performance metrics to assess the effectiveness of security controls. Security information and event management (SIEM) systems often facilitate this by aggregating and analyzing data from various sources.

Chapter 24

Do I Know This Already? Quiz

1. b. The primary goal of risk identification is to create a comprehensive list of risks based on various categories.

2. b. An ad hoc risk assessment is conducted in response to an immediate need, such as a sudden security breach.

3. b. Probability quantifies the likelihood of a specific risk occurring and is often expressed as a percentage.

4. b. Impact refers to the potential consequences or effects on an organization if a specific threat materializes.

5. c. The risk owner is the individual or department responsible for managing a particular risk.

6. a. Risk appetite indicates the level of risk an organization is willing to accept to pursue its objectives.

7. c. Risk transference involves transferring risk to another organization or a third party, such as by purchasing cybersecurity insurance.

8. a. Risk reporting provides a snapshot of an organization's risk landscape.

9. b. The primary purpose of calculating MTTR in a DRP is to understand the operational impact of repair times and guide decision making for redundancy.

10. c. Mean time between failures (MTBF) is a reliability metric that is used in disaster recovery planning to anticipate the frequency of potential failures of a system or component.

Review Questions

1. The main difference between risk identification and risk assessment is their focus. Risk identification aims to create a comprehensive list of potential threats and vulnerabilities, whereas risk assessment evaluates identified risks to gauge their potential impact and likelihood. Risk identification is the initial phase, and risk assessment serves as the analytical engine that informs risk management strategies.

2. An ad hoc risk assessment would be appropriate when there's an immediate need, such as a sudden security breach or a newly discovered vulnerability. For example, if a company experiences an unexpected data leak, an ad hoc risk assessment can be conducted to evaluate the severity of the breach and the steps needed to contain it.

3. Probability and impact are both crucial metrics in risk analysis but serve different purposes. Probability quantifies the likelihood of a specific risk occurring and is often expressed as a percentage. Impact, on the other hand, refers to the potential consequences or effects on an organization if a specific threat materializes. Impact helps quantify the severity of a risk and can be expressed in financial terms or can include non-monetary consequences like reputational damage.

4. The risk owner is typically responsible for implementing risk mitigation strategies in an organization. This individual or department is accountable for monitoring the risk over time and ensuring that mitigation strategies are effectively implemented.

5. The three types of risk appetite are expansionary, conservative, and neutral. Expansionary risk appetite involves taking on higher levels of risk for growth opportunities. Conservative risk appetite focuses on lower levels of risk and steady, sustainable growth. Neutral risk appetite is open to some level of risk but in a balanced manner.

6. Key risk indicators (KRIs) are often included in risk reporting to provide a snapshot of an organization's risk landscape. These indicators help stakeholders, ranging from C-level executives to department heads, understand the current state of risk in an organization.

Chapter 25

Do I Know This Already? Quiz

1. b. An SLA formally and clearly defines what a vendor is responsible for and what the organization is responsible for.

2. b. Due diligence involves evaluating a vendor's business practices, including its cybersecurity measures.

3. b. An MOU outlines mutual roles and responsibilities but is generally less formal than other types of agreements.

4. c. An MSA is an overarching contract that governs multiple individual agreements or projects.

5. a. Vendor monitoring in a healthcare context would involve real-time data access tracking and regular audits to ensure HIPAA compliance.

6. b. Questionnaires serve as strategic tools to extract nuanced information about a vendor.

7. b. Rules of engagement dictate the agreed-upon guidelines for activities and interactions between an organization and a vendor.

Review Questions

1. A service-level agreement (SLA) formally and clearly defines the responsibilities and expectations of both a vendor and an organization. It sets the performance expectations and outlines what the vendor will do if a failure of service occurs. It's a legally binding document that should be scrutinized before it is signed.

2. The due diligence process during vendor selection commonly includes activities like financial audits to assess the vendor's stability, legal checks to verify compliance with industry-specific laws, and security assessments to evaluate the vendor's cybersecurity measures and protocols.

3. A memorandum of agreement (MOA) is a written document that specifies a cooperative but generally non-legally binding relationship between two parties. It often outlines responsibilities in detail. A memorandum of understanding (MOU), on the other hand, is less formal and outlines mutual roles and responsibilities in a project or partnership without being legally binding.

4. A master service agreement (MSA) serves as an overarching contract that governs the terms for future transactions or agreements between parties. It sets the general terms that will apply to multiple individual agreements or projects, providing a framework for future interactions.

5. In a healthcare organization that uses a third-party service for storing patient records, key aspects to monitor include real-time data access tracking, regular audits for HIPAA compliance, and performance metrics like uptime and speed. Automated tools can be used for alerts on unauthorized data access or downtime that violates the SLA.

6. A well-crafted questionnaire can reveal nuanced information about a vendor's operational resilience, data handling practices, and corporate culture. It can provide insights into the vendor's compliance with legal requirements and preparedness for various scenarios, offering a multidimensional view of the vendor's capabilities.

Chapter 26

Do I Know This Already? Quiz

1. b. Internal compliance reporting involves systematic documentation to assess the effectiveness of various controls, such as firewalls.

2. b. Sanctions could mean restricted access to sensitive data or networks, such as limiting a healthcare provider's ability to transmit patient records electronically.

3. a. Due diligence is the proactive process of gathering information to understand all potential risks and liabilities before making decisions.

4. a. Privacy focuses on safeguarding data against unauthorized access and ensuring its proper use.

5. b. Legal implications refer to the obligations, liabilities, and potential penalties that organizations face in relation to data.

6. a. The controller determines the purposes and means of processing personal data.

7. b. When a data subject exercises their right to be forgotten, the first task for a security analyst is to locate and completely erase the specified data from all systems, including backups.

8. a. Attestation in cybersecurity refers to a formal declaration or confirmation, often involving a third-party auditor, that specific criteria, processes, or systems meet required security standards.

9. b. Automation in compliance monitoring refers to the use of software tools and technologies to automatically perform tasks that would otherwise require manual effort.

10. c. Data inventory involves creating a catalog or map that identifies where different data types are stored within an organization's systems.

Review Questions

1. The role of internal audits in internal compliance reporting is to systematically document and assess the effectiveness of various controls in the organization, such as firewalls and data access policies. These audits generate actionable data that can be used to improve security measures, such as updating outdated encryption protocols.

2. Sanctions could severely limit a healthcare provider's ability to operate by restricting access to sensitive data or networks. For example, if a healthcare provider is found to be non-compliant with HIPAA, they may face sanctions that limit their ability to transmit patient records electronically. A comprehensive review of cybersecurity protocols would be required to lift the sanctions.

3. Due diligence is the proactive process of gathering information to understand all potential risks and liabilities before making decisions. It involves a comprehensive review of systems, processes, and policies. Due care, on the other hand, is the ongoing responsibility to maintain and update security measures based on the information gathered as part of due diligence.

4. The key components of privacy in cybersecurity include safeguarding data against unauthorized access and ensuring its proper use. This involves understanding legal frameworks at various jurisdictional levels and the roles and responsibilities of data handlers such as controllers and processors.

5. In data protection frameworks, particularly under the GDPR, the controller is responsible for determining the purposes and means of processing personal data. They decide why and how the data will be processed and are generally responsible for ensuring that the data is adequately protected.

6. When a data subject exercises their right to be forgotten, the first task for the security analyst is to locate and completely erase the specified data from all systems, including backups. Following the deletion, verification checks are run to ensure complete removal, and the entire process is documented for compliance purposes.

Chapter 27

Do I Know This Already? Quiz

1. b. Attestation is the formal act of affirming or certifying the validity of a process, system, or set of data, and it adds a layer of trust and integrity to an organization's cybersecurity posture.

2. b. The audit committee is responsible for overseeing the audit process, ensuring that audits are conducted effectively, transparently, and in line with organizational objectives.

3. c. An independent third-party audit is conducted by an organization that does not have a vested interest in the audit outcome. Such audits are highly reliable and unbiased.

4. b. The main objective of offensive penetration testing is to discover and actively exploit vulnerabilities. This type of testing provides a realistic assessment of what an actual cyberattack could achieve.

5. c. Integrated penetration testing is sometimes referred to as purple teaming because it combines elements of both offensive (red teaming) and defensive testing (blue teaming).

6. b. In unknown environment penetration testing, the primary challenge is identifying vulnerabilities through external probing, making it a true test of an organization's first line of defense.

7. b. Passive reconnaissance focuses on gathering information without directly interacting with the target system and is often used for threat intelligence gathering.

Review Questions

1. The audit committee is responsible for overseeing the entire audit process in an organization, including approving audit plans, evaluating the findings, and having the final say in implementing recommended changes. The committee usually consists of a mix of senior management and subject matter experts who ensure that audits are conducted effectively, transparently, and in line with organizational objectives.

2. An independent third-party audit is conducted by an organization that does not have a vested interest in the audit outcome, making it highly reliable and unbiased. On the other hand, a regulatory audit is typically mandated by law or industry regulations and may not necessarily be conducted by an impartial entity. Both types of audits are external, but an independent third-party audit is often sought after for its unbiased nature.

3. The goal of offensive penetration testing is to actively discover and exploit vulnerabilities in a system by simulating cyberattacks. This proactive approach is designed to mimic the tactics, techniques, and procedures that real-world attackers would use. Defensive penetration testing, in contrast, focuses on evaluating how well an organization's security measures can detect and respond to an attack. It involves monitoring system logs, intrusion detection systems, and other security mechanisms during the testing process.

4. In unknown environment penetration testing, also known as black box testing, the penetration testers have no prior knowledge of the system. This scenario closely mimics the conditions an external attacker would face. The primary challenge here is identifying vulnerabilities through external probing as this is a true test of an organization's first line of defense.

Chapter 28

Do I Know This Already? Quiz

1. a. A phishing campaign aims to compromise as many accounts or systems as possible by distributing deceptive messages to a large number of targets.

2. b. Recognizing unexpected behavior is crucial for the early detection of potential security incidents or vulnerabilities.

3. d. Policy and handbooks provide the rules, guidelines, and procedures that govern how employees interact with the organization's digital assets.

4. b. Recurring reporting involves periodic reviews and audits to assess the effectiveness of an organization's security measures, including metrics like the number of detected incidents and response times.

5. c. The development phase involves identifying the key objectives of, defining the scope of, and setting measurable goals for the security awareness program.

6. c. The execution phase involves rolling out the training modules, initiating the monitoring tools, and launching simulated attacks or exercises.

Review Questions

1. Phishing campaigns often employ tactics such as impersonating trusted entities or using urgent language to manipulate a recipient into taking a specific action, like clicking a link or downloading an attachment. These tactics aim to deceive the recipient and compromise as many accounts or systems as possible.

2. Recognizing unexpected behavior is crucial for the early detection of potential security threats. These anomalies can be indicative of security incidents or vulnerabilities. Early detection enables an organization to take timely action to mitigate risks and prevent further damage.

3. The primary role of policies and handbooks in an organization's user guidance and training is to provide the rules, guidelines, and procedures that govern how employees interact with the organization's digital assets. These documents serve as a foundational framework for ensuring that employees adhere to best practices in cybersecurity.

4. During the execution phase of a security awareness program, key activities include rolling out the training modules, initiating the monitoring tools, and launching simulated attacks or exercises. During this phase, all the planning, development, and strategizing culminate in the implementation of the program.

Index

W

REGISTER YOUR PRODUCT at PearsonITcertification.com/register

Access Additional Benefits and SAVE 35% on Your Next Purchase

- Download available product updates.

- Access bonus material when applicable.

- Receive exclusive offers on new editions and related products.
  (Just check the box to hear from us when setting up your account.)

- Get a coupon for 35% for your next purchase, valid for 30 days. Your code will
  be available in your PITC cart. (You will also find it in the Manage Codes
  section of your account page.)

Registration benefits vary by product. Benefits will be listed on your account page
under Registered Products.

PearsonITcertification.com–Learning Solutions for Self-Paced Study, Enterprise, and the Classroom
Pearson is the official publisher of Cisco Press, IBM Press, VMware Press, Microsoft Press,
and is a Platinum CompTIA Publishing Partner–CompTIA's highest partnership accreditation.
At **PearsonITcertification.com** you can

- Shop our books, eBooks, software, and video training.
- Take advantage of our special offers and promotions (pearsonitcertifcation.com/promotions).
- Sign up for special offers and content newsletters (pearsonitcertifcation.com/newsletters).
- Read free articles, exam profiles, and blogs by information technology experts.
- Access thousands of free chapters and video lessons.

Connect with PITC – Visit PearsonITcertifcation.com/community
Learn about PITC community events and programs.

PEARSON IT CERTIFICATION

Addison-Wesley • Cisco Press • IBM Press • Microsoft Press • Pearson IT Certification • Prentice Hall • Que • Sams • VMware Press

ALWAYS LEARNING   PEARSON

To receive your 10% off
Exam Voucher, register
your product at:

www.pearsonitcertification.com/register

and follow the instructions.